Edwin H. Maynard
11/22/74

TWO CENTURIES OF METHODIST CONCERN: BONDAGE, FREEDOM AND EDUCATION OF BLACK PEOPLE

JAMES P. BRAWLEY

VANTAGE PRESS

New York   Washington   Hollywood

FIRST EDITION

Copyright © 1974 by The Board Of Education (for the
Council of Presidents of Black Colleges) United Methodist
Church

Published by Vantage Press, Inc.

516 West 34 Street, New York, New York 10001

Manufactured in the United States of America

Standard Book No. 533-00649-X

PREFACE

The Methodist Episcopal Church came into existence in America at a time of revolution and reform. It has, from its inception, been identified with and involved in reform movements. It has been rooted in the social order and its active identification with the problems of society has been in a large measure the source of its strength and spiritual life.

Slavery and its aftermath were aspects of a major problem continually growing in magnitude, with which the Methodist Church was concerned from its beginning. The very nature of the Christian tradition, the very nature of the Methodist doctrine, and the very nature of the church itself in the social order, all gave the Methodist Episcopal Church concern for this major human problem of national and international scope. There was a continuing concern and involvement for a century before the Emancipation. This involvement on a wider scale and in greater depth impelled the Methodist Episcopal Church to action before and after Emancipation. This concern activated a ministry in depth, beginning in the late 18th Century, involving evangelism, moral reform, and education.

The establishment of schools for Negroes immediately following the Civil War was not the point of beginning of the Methodist Episcopal Church in its ministry to Negroes. At the time of its organization in 1784 it immediately came to grips with a major social problem rooted historically in colonialism. Slavery as a human problem was entirely inconsonant with the doctrine of John Wesley and his associates. They never yielded their principles regarding slavery, never quieted their voices against it, and never relinquished their efforts to destroy it as a social evil in American life. The record reveals constant efforts on the part of the Methodist Episcopal Church to deal with the human problems of slavery as an institution from 1784 to 1860. This does not mean that there was complete unanimity in either thinking or action regarding this problem. There was division between the North and the South, and also in the North and in the South as well; but the major division was between the North and the South, which resulted in the separation in 1844.

The Church did not withdraw from the scene during the tragic war years 1860 to 1865. After Emancipation it continued its ministry, but on a larger scale, with the aim of giving a more inclusive service in greater depth, administering to the total problems created by a long period of slavery and its aftermath, and by the newly freed slaves, ushered helplessly into a new society and a desperate situation.

The post-emancipation ministry to the Freedmen had several phases of emphasis: (1) evangelism; (2) moral rehabilitation from the ravages of slavery, the building of character; (3) a new appraisal and appreciation of self in terms of a person of value; (4) rehabilitation and a new cohesiveness of the black family; (5) citizenship and political efficiency; (6) economic development; and (7) education.

There was need for self-discovery as Freedmen in a new society and self-appraisal as persons with large human potential, rather than chattel property or "inferior" beings in a society of so-called superiors. The Freedmen had to be rehabilitated from the annihilating ravages of personality by slavery, and to create self-confidence and group consciousness. They had to overcome conditioning experiences and stigma of a caste classification, designation as chattel property, and the label of inferiority without ability to learn complex lessons, consigned to a "place" in society as only "hewers of wood and drawers of water."

During the first thirty years following Emancipation many denominations established schools for the Freedmen which grew into some of the best small colleges of the nation. It is probable that no denomination did so much for the education of the Freedmen and subsequent generations of Negro youth as the Methodist Episcopal Church. The continuous effort to support good schools and colleges for Negro youth over a period of more than one hundred years has been a tremendous contribution to the adjustments made by the Negro, the leadership developed, and the remarkable progress made in the American society, continuously under most adverse circumstances.

It was clearly realized by the leaders of the Methodist Episcopal Church who provided education for the Freedmen that they were not dealing with just a group in isolated classrooms, learning to read and write, but they were working with a group of people with large human capacity and potential, limited by great disadvantages and thrown into an unfavorable, and often hostile, society to begin a new way of life and to "prove themselves." Thus, the schools established were begun in a not-too-friendly social order by which they would be affected, and of which the schools and the Freedmen had to be a part.

The movement by the Methodist Episcopal Church in the field of education for Negro youth and the social structure and climate in which both the church and the schools have operated are described here to point up the tremendous work done over the period of a century, and the magnificent achievements wrought. But, the task is far from being finished.

After the passing of a hundred years, marked by extraordinary progress and accomplishments, it must still be said that the problems of human relations and racism loom before us today in greater magnitude and complexity. A century of Methodist concern, investment of thousands of dedicated lives, and expenditure of much money have merely made clearer the issues and opened the vista of greater opportunity, so men of vision, goodwill, and hope may see and pursue with more determination what clearly lies ahead as duty and responsibility in better education for black people and in better human relations.

The second century begins with the invaluable asset of greater recognition of the potential of black people and the indispensability of their involvement in and by the Church in bringing to fulfillment the spiritual mission of the Church and the realization of better race relations in our American society. The challenge is compelling and the demand is inescapable.

J.P.B.

ACKNOWLEDGMENTS

The Author, with much appreciation, acknowledges his indebtedness to many people whose help contributed so largely to the production of this volume. The Council of Presidents of the Black Colleges of the United Methodist Church authorized the writing of this document and sponsored financially its publication. The cooperation of the Presidents individually in supplying materials and in reading the manuscript contributed much to the production of this work.

Special acknowledgment and thanks are due Bishop James S. Thomas for his critical reading of the manuscript and for his many helpful suggestions; also, for his writing the introduction.

Documents and reports of the Freedmen's Aid Society made available by the office of the Associate Secretary, Dr. D. W. Wynn, were invaluable sources of primary data. Through Mrs. J. N. Rodeheaver materials relating to the Woman's Home Missionary Society were supplied, for which grateful acknowledgment is made.

Special acknowledgments and thanks are due Librarian Wilson N. Flemister for extensive use of the archives of the Interdenominational Theological Center Library.

The Author is indebted to the many publishers and authors who graciously gave permission to quote from their publications, acknowledgment having been appropriately made and credit duly given.

Without the competent clerical assistance of Miss Barbara Harkins, Mesdames Helen Bronson, Marian McDonald, and Mary E. James, producing this manuscript would have been much more difficult.

Finally, grateful acknowledgment is made for the help given by my wife, Mrs. Georgia W. Brawley, who gave encouragement over the long period the research and writing were in progress, and read the manuscript page by page for corrections and improved English usage.

James P. Brawley

FOREWORD

(History of the Negro Colleges Related to the
United Methodist Church)

The Methodist Episcopal Church has historically held Christian education as one of its primary missional emphases. From the time of its organization in America in 1784, it has agonized with the problem of race, institutionalized slavery, and discrimination. TWO CENTURIES OF METHODIST CONCERN: BONDAGE, FREEDOM AND EDUCATION OF BLACK PEOPLE brings these two concerns together in clear perspective and relates how the Methodist Episcopal Church has struggled to deal with the basic conflict and the consequent issues. One significant result of this concern was the establishment of schools for freedom after the close of the Civil War. The Methodist Episcopal Church was among the institutions that established Aid Societies to promote this objective, operating from the position that the freedmen's greatest need was education to enable them to read the Bible, and that it was the obligation of the Church to elevate and Christianize them. The Freedmen's Aid Society became the Church's primary instrumentality for achieving these purposes during the postwar years.

It is safe to state that no other confessional body has grappled with the underlying issues to the same degree as has the Methodist Church, and no author before Dr. James P. Brawley has attempted to chronicle the role of the Methodist Church in the education of Negro youth so comprehensively. This task has been accomplished with accuracy, care, and sensitivity. This work makes a significant historical contribution in placing in one volume data which trace the origin and growth of the schools founded by the Methodist Episcopal Church, and in pointing up the contribution which these institutions have made and continue to make in service to the Church and society-at-large.

It is important that such a work be published at a time when much that is at the heart of higher education is under attack; when all of higher education is experiencing serious financial exigencies; when the involvement of the Church in higher education is seriously questioned; and the justification for the continued existence of the predominantly black church-related college is challenged. It reaffirms that education abides as warranting a high priority in the hierarchy of the Church's missional emphases, and that the strengthening of a group of institutions with a special and unique heritage continues to be valid. It establishes that the United Methodist Church is wise to invest in their future.

As a historic document, "TWO CENTURIES OF METHODIST CONCERN:. . ." is incomparable, and for the serious scholar, it will be an invaluable resource. Herein is set the frame of reference in which the United Methodist Church, having undergone substantial restructuring for new mission, may address itself to the new challenge of strengthening the predominantly black institutions so that they may achieve their full potential as agencies for the creation of a new order in society.

The Presidents' Council, composed of the Presidents of the current institutions treated in "TWO CENTURIES OF METHODIST CONCERN:. . ." is pleased to sponsor the publication of this volume, and acknowledges with appreciation the cooperation and financial assistance given by the Continuing Corporation of the Woman's Home Missionary Society of the Methodist Episcopal Church.

Isaac H. Miller, Jr.
President
The Council of Presidents

INTRODUCTION

It is one of the peculiar ironies of American history that so little careful research has been done on the colleges for black youth. The reasons for this situation are peculiar in the sense that the historian Kenneth Stampp could write about slavery as "the peculiar institution." Deep in the minds of too many white Americans, there seems to be the firm conviction that all black colleges are inferior, that they are so simple they can be known by surface analyses, and that they must "prove themselves" before they are worthy of unconditional financial grants. One has only to consider the persistence of the questions concerning the worth of these colleges to document this fact. Over and over again, black educators are faced with the revealing question: how do you justify the black college?

Obviously, there are many ways to meet this strange twist of the American mind. One is a dignified attempt to restrain oneself when, as late as 1967, two outstanding scholars made a hasty study of all black colleges and then made the profound announcement that they are an educational wasteland. Another way is to correct these opinions — as the black college presidents have done for 118 years — to strive for excellence in teaching against seemingly insuperable odds. Still another is to point to the alumni of these colleges whose records in graduate and professional schools have been worthy of much more research than they have received.

Dr. James P. Brawley has chosen what is certainly the most endurable way of answering those who continue to question the lasting contribution of the black college. By careful research, he has illuminated the history and socio-economic conditions that have shaped the life of the twelve black colleges of the United Methodist Church. Out of a rich treasure of his forty years in higher education, he has written about facts, interpretations, movements and personalities. Reflecting upon his quarter of a century as an outstanding college president, he has been true, both to the keen insights of an outstanding administration and the balanced judgments of the scholars.

The significance of this book is found in at least three specific and important landmarks in history. In the first place, Dr. Brawley illuminates the beginnings of these institutions and thereby makes an outstanding contribution to history. Few Americans know the elementary facts that: many of the early black colleges grew out of the finest expression of missionary zeal; several of the land-grant colleges for black people grew out of colleges started earlier by the church; these colleges were served by some of the most outstanding leaders of their time; the church support for these colleges, while often sacrificial, has never been enough to put them on a sound financial footing; the alumni of these colleges have made records in academic and community life that validate the teaching and quality of relationships of the black college.

In the second place, this book gives keen insight into the personalities who made these colleges centers of remarkably good, even great, teaching. While American higher education has moved a great distance from Mark Hopkins and his student on a log, it has never found an adequate substitute for a great teacher who cares enough for the student to give him the best possible opportunity to learn and, at the same time, the best possible atmosphere in which to attain a sense of dignity.

Finally, Dr. Brawley has given us a book which reveals, both with candor and with appreciation, the dilemma which America would face without colleges like these. No perceptive person who has analyzed the search for black identity and dignity during the last ten years could minimize America's need for centers of education in which the highest academic training is combined with humanistic sensitivity and Christian perspective. The question is not so much "How do you justify the black college?" but "When will America and the church face up to the debt they owe to institutions whose contributions to the society have far out-distanced investments made in them?"

This is a book which should be read by a wide spectrum of the American population. It is not simply a book about black people; it is a book about a segment of history, about a church, about higher education. And it is my prediction that it will be a constant source of light and hope for many years to come.

James S. Thomas

CONTENTS

Part I

*Colonialism, Black Bondage, and
The Methodist Episcopal Church*

Part II

The Methodist Episcopal Church and the Freedmen's Aid Society, 1866-1916

Part III

Founding and Development of Institutions, 1866-1916

Part IV

Historical Account of Individual Institutions

Part V

*Financial Support; Personalities; A Century
of Service; Status*

Part VI

*The Church and The Historically Negro College
In A New Era of Change*

PART I.

COLONIALISM, BLACK BONDAGE, AND THE METHODIST EPISCOPAL CHURCH

CHAPTER 1

BEFORE THE COMING OF METHODISM

Newcomers to America in Search of Freedom,
    Liberty and Wealth

Several motives drove the early American settlers from England to a new land across the Atlantic. Some came in search of liberty and freedom from the domination of the English Crown. Some came in search of religious freedom. Some wanted a new form of government, where citizenship could be determined by the rule of the people. The early settlers were motivated by more than a desire for liberty and freedom. The new world held before them a promise of wealth and a dream of riches.

As they set themselves about to form colonies, the high level of education and the dominance of the clergy enabled the settlers in New England to build a high moral and spiritual foundation, resisting the aristocracy and royalty of the home land and leaning more in the direction of a theocratic government.[1] The ideals of the Puritans and Quakers furnished the dynamics for church, school, and government.

For the South the motivation was more in the field of commerce and economics. The Southern colonies, beginning with Virginia, were closely linked with the commercial companies of England. Economic exploration and exploitation were the dominating motives. Thus arose the large plantations and the slave trade. While the religious and moral motives were dominant in New England this section did not escape the commercial motivation of the South.

The First One Hundred and Seventy-Five Years

From the beginning of the American colonies in 1607 to the Declaration of Independence in 1776 the colonial development and expansion were influenced by changing thought of the whole Western world. In Europe there was emergence from serfdom and feudalism; there was rebellion against the domination of the royalty and the tyranny of kings. The upheaval of the Western world started a sensitive reaction to the intolerance of the

19

Established Church. Thus, the hope of the New World in America was for a new civilization and a haven of escape from oppression.

The colonies settled by merchants and capitalists seeking opportunities for wealth and power in the New World were established during the long struggle in England between the middle class and the Crown. The struggle between the royalty and the middle class extended through a succession of rulers climaxing in the English Revolution of 1688 and the famous English Bill of Rights in 1689.

The New Englanders preserved the spirit of liberty and reform which characterized the dissenting group in England. In New England, the humanitarian movement found fertile soil and gave birth to some of the champions of human justice who gave themselves to the fight and struggle for human freedom in America.

The antithesis of the New England group may be found in those who formed the colonies of the South. These represented the social, political, commercial, and religious spirit of the Crown and Church of England, in whom was absent, for the most part, that liberal and humanitarian spirit which characterized the Puritans and the Quakers.

There were two political characterizations of the Southern colonies, namely, economic and aristocratic. The political power of the Old South (1607-1860) was concentrated in the hands of slaveholders. Political power was determined in the main by ownership of property, ownership of slaves, and social prestige, which prestige automatically attended ownership of land and slaves. Slavery was a selfish economic advantage to the slaveholder and it gave the planter political power and prestige, which increased in aristocracy in proportion to the number of slaves held.

The Origin, and the Development of
American Slavery to 1776

The Dutch vessel that landed on the shore of Virginia in August, 1619, bringing twenty slaves began the African slave trade in colonial America. This was the beginning of a gruesome institution that was to transport millions of men, women, and children to the American shores and shackle them body, mind, and soul into human bondage. This was the beginning of the great American tragedy, the race problem that has extended across the long period of three centuries.

The process of the slave trade linked the South and New England in commerce and involved both the Southern and

Northern colonies in the slave trade in Africa. It was commercial exploitation that built up the slave trade and the slave population during the Colonial period. Charles and Mary Beard point out that "Under the pressure of profit-makers the Southern colonists, always clamoring for cheap labor, were in time abundantly supplied with African bondsmen and even in the North, slavery spread as widely as economic conditions would permit. After tentative beginnings, the Negro population grew by leaps and bounds; on the eve of the Revolution it was more than half a million."[2]

Several factors tended to deepen the roots and strengthen the system in colonialism. First, slavery was a well-established practice in England and elsewhere in Europe. It was not abolished in England until 1833.

Second, while the Puritans in New England were the bearers of the spirit of liberty and freedom, there was no widespread conviction against slavery, and consequently no strong effort during the colonial period to prohibit it. It should be said, however, that the seed of opposition to slavery resided in the high moral idealism and religious depth of the Puritans, and later sprang up to give force to the anti-slavery movement.

A third factor that deepened the roots of slavery in the colonial period was its economic success. The increase of production and the expansion of frontiers provided the economic wealth which made possible the realization of the dream of the New World.

A fourth factor that strengthened the colonial institution of slavery was the political advantages to the Southern colonies. Political power and social prestige were based on the size of the plantation and the number of slaves owned.

It was not until the latter part of the Colonial period that slavery became a moral and religious issue. When it became a moral and religious issue, the conflict with the economic and political interest was inevitable.

The slave trade during the Colonial period provided an investment in labor and human life that laid the economic foundation upon which the nation was built, and the institution of slavery engulfed America in a shame which can never be completely blotted out and a debt which can never be fully paid. These factors contributed to the complexity of the slavery problem and the conflict within and without the Church.

The Methodist Episcopal Church
    and Slavery Conflict

There was no organized Methodist Church in America during

21

the Colonial period. Organized Methodism had its inception only a few years after the colonies became an independent nation. It came at a propitious time. Methodist societies had formed the framework of Methodist activities.

From the middle of the 18th Century to the end of the American Revolution, an increasing number of anti-slavery voices were heard in the colonies, joined by voices in England for the abolition of slavery there and here. A chorus of voices was heard coming from such men as Denis Diderot and Jean Jacques Rousseau of France; John Locke and John Woolman of England; and Thomas Jefferson, George Washington, and others in America, who not only protested slavery but in a broader context defended the "rights of man," which rights stemmed from the "natural" man, such rights being inherent in all men.[3]

In the midst of the growing power of social revolution the stage was set for early Methodists to become a part of the movement and to raise their voices in protest against human injustices, slavery being not the least of these.

With strong revolutionary orientation in England and the Colonies, such stalwart Methodist leaders as Francis Asbury, Thomas Coke, and John Wesley himself, and others, later were to become the Fathers of the Methodist Episcopal Church in America. They protested slavery and gave impetus to social reform in the newly organized Methodist Church and in the new nation.

The Declaration of Independence: Its Impact Upon Slavery,
    Social Philosophy, and the Church

The Pilgrim Fathers landed at Plymouth in 1619 having left England to inhabit a new land of freedom. A new world of freedom emerged from the dependent colonies into a new nation beginning in 1776.

Indeed they did "bring forth upon this continent a new nation, conceived in liberty and dedicated to the proposition that all men are created equal." This philosophy gave rise to the Revolutionary War with the mother country, and set in action a chain of problems — philosophical, social, political, and religious — that have reverberated across two centuries of American life.

The Declaration of Independence, written by Thomas Jefferson and adopted in 1776, was a liberating document inherent in which was all that the new American nation envisioned for more than two centuries to come; for, indeed, this was the foundation of American Democracy.

The philosophy of natural rights was a common possession of English thinkers of the 17th century. Thomas Jefferson, framer of

22

the Declaration of Independence, accepted the philosophical concept of the "self-evident truths that all men are created equal and that all are endowed with certain unalienable rights." The philosophy of equality as set forth in the Declaration of Independence was born of necessity.

The whole question of equality in the American colonies comes to focus against a background of practices, customs, philosophies, traditions, powers, and oppressions in Europe. The American colonies were struggling for independence and found a powerful ally in this philosophy employed in the European Revolution which culminated in 1688.

In the South the prevailing political and social influence of the planters, the landed aristocracy, is sufficient evidence of the fact that equality in this section was far from being a fact. It was impossible for equality to exist in the South where the social structure of the region was based upon aristocracy, social classes, and slavery, which are the exact antithesis of equality.

Neither before nor after the Declaration of Independence did a large representation of the American people believe in equality. Immediately after the Declaration of Independence in 1776 the situation began to be embarrassing. It was evident everywhere that equality did not exist. It was recognized that in order for equality to exist the whole economic, political, and social structure involving slavery would have to be drastically changed. Equality could not exist where political control was concentrated in the hands of a landed aristocracy and owners of slaves, and where social prestige was a possession of the few in an aristocracy based on wealth and political power.

The conclusion of the arguments regarding equality as stated in the Declaration of Independence depended upon the position taken regarding the institution of slavery, and regarding the status and rights of the Negro as a human being, as a free man, and as a citizen. Here is where the North and South parted ways on the issue of slavery and the right of all human beings to freedom and equality.

The Declaration of Independence and the
Methodist Position on Slavery

The thinking and attitude of the early Methodists regarding the Declaration of Independence as it involved the liberty and freedom of slaves is reflected in the first rule and declaration of the Methodist Episcopal Church which follows:

We view as contrary to the golden law of God, on which

23

hang all the law and the prophets, and other unalienable rights of mankind, as well as every principle of the revolution, to hold in the deepest abasement. . .so many souls that are capable of the image of God. We, therefore, think it our most bounden duty to take immediately some effectual method to extirpate this abomination from among us.[4]

The principles set forth in the Declaration of Independence and the position and humane spirit of early American Methodism on slavery were entirely congruous.

The Methodist Episcopal Church Organized in a
Period of Ferment Generated by the
Declaration of Independence
and the Slavery Conflicts

The Methodist Episcopal Church, organized in 1784, took form at a time when the spirit of revolution was sweeping over the Western world, including the American colonies. The battle against slavery was still being waged in England. The Declaration of Independence and the American Revolution came as a result of unrest and demand for relief from the pressures of England upon the American colonies. There was also a felt need for reform within the American colonies. T. V. Smith points out that:

. . . .The American Revolution, while primarily a revolt against the English governmental irritation. . . .was at the same time a vigorous protest, and in many cases, quite deliberately so, against American inequalities that in kind, if not in degree, matched perfectly those of European growth, and the philosophy of equality is but a corollary of a larger ideal-system that had already been found to be a useful instrument of destruction against all sorts of inequalities and oppressions. [5]

The Declaration of Independence and the American Revolution dealt with issues of universal concern in which the new Methodist Episcopal Church in America had to be involved, particularly the issue of slavery and the discrepancy between slavery and the principles of the Declaration of Independence. Involved also was the conflict between slavery and the basic moral and religious philosophy of John Wesley himself and his associates.

24

REFERENCES AND NOTES

1. Merriam, Charles Edward, *A History of American Political Theories*, p. 15.
2. Beard, Charles A. and Mary R., *The Rise of American Civilization*, New York: The MacMillan Company, 1930, p. 107.
3. Cameron, Richard, *Methodism and Society in Historical Perspective*, p. 95.
4. Cameron, *op. cit.*, p. 99.
5. Smith, T. V., *The American Philosophy of Equality*, p. 35.

CHAPTER 2

THE NEW NATION, METHODISM, SLAVERY AND ABOLITIONISM

The Young Nation and the Widening and Deepening Currents of the Slavery Evil

The Declaration of Independence, when written, had no reference or application to the American slave. Inasmuch as the Negro slave was only chattel property no thought was given to him as a person and it was not anticipated in the Southern colonies that he would be freed and become a citizen, although for a brief time it looked as if the new nation might begin with the slave trade outlawed and slavery on its way out. The word slave did not appear in the Constitution but the new nation wrote human bondage into its very foundation.[1]

The Declaration of Independence created much ambivalence North and South, particularly in the North, regarding slavery. The conflict between the lofty principles of the Declaration of Independence and the actual practice continued to grow. During the period of about four and a half decades 1789-1833, the lines between the antagonist and the protagonist were tightly drawn, and the opposing positions were made clear and emphatic. The northern section of the country, which had never been a strong slave-holding section, began to assess the institution on the basis of moral principles. This new assessment, no doubt, stemmed from the latent Puritan idealism; the principles of the Declaration of Independence; and the swelling currents of social and political reform, the effects of which were felt throughout the Western world as well as in America.

Every Northern state had abolished slavery before the closing of the foreign trade in 1808 by Federal law. No Southern state had taken such action. By 1808 slavery was on the wane everywhere above the Delaware River — and the moral objection to the institution was deepening.[2]

As the slavery conflict sharpened, the opposing camps identified themselves for and against the slavery issue. It was inevitable that the issue would divide the country into sections,

North and South.

At the beginning of the 19th Century seven of the original thirteen colonies were free. The slave-holding states of the original colonies were Delaware, Georgia, Maryland, North Carolina, South Carolina, and Virginia. Vermont was added to the free states and Kentucky and Tennessee made the number of slave states equal to the free states. Ohio, Indiana and Illinois were admitted to the Union as free states, while Louisiana, Mississippi, and Alabama came in as slave states.[3]

The division of the several states into two sections set the stage for the battle between the anti-slavery group and the pro-slavery group during the three decades leading to the war beginning in 1860.

It should be said at this point that the anti-slavery and pro-slavery groups were not divided entirely by geographical sections. It was to the credit of a large number of liberal Southerners that they joined the anti-slavery group and migrated from the South to fight against slavery.[4]

The Methodist Episcopal Church and Slavery

In the early beginnings of Methodism while it was just a number of related societies, the Quakers (Society of Friends) exerted strong influence upon Methodist thinking and action. The writings of the American Quaker Anthony Benezet greatly influenced Wesley's thinking in the writing of his *Thoughts Upon Slavery*.[5]

Asbury came to America in 1771 to help strengthen the Methodist Societies. He was one of the minority who wanted to see emancipation become a fact. He, probably more than any other man, was responsible for the Methodist movement in America against slavery.

Asbury preached to Negro, as well as white, congregations and was deeply impressed by the response of the Negroes to his preaching. He "encouraged the Methodists to mold Wesleyan background, moral enthusiasm, revolutionary ideals, and Quaker examples into a mild, but aspiring disapproval of slavery."[6]

The concern of the early Methodists regarding slavery is expressed in the Conference Minutes of 1780 as follows:

Does the Conference acknowledge that slavery is contrary to the laws of God, man, and nature, and hurtful to society; contrary to the dictates of conscience and pure religion, and doing that which we would not that others should do to us or ours? Do we pass our disapprobation on all our friends who keep slaves and advise their freedom? Yes.[7]

At the same Conference the following rule was adopted: "Ought not this Conference to require those traveling preachers who hold slaves to give promise to set them free? Yes."[8]

This rule was confirmed by the Annual Conference, but considerable time was required to make it completely effective; in fact, it added to the threat of a serious division among the Societies.

The Conference of 1780 went further to approve a statement which provided for religious instruction to the slaves and the continuous exertion of pressure for eventual emancipation.[9]

Despite the threatening division within the small Methodist membership in America Asbury held them together and the Virginia Conference in 1783 passed a resolution on slavery similar to the one passed earlier by the Baltimore Conference.[10]

Cameron points out the difficulty of the problem faced by Asbury and the liberal Methodists when it is noted that the center of gravity of Methodism was in the South. Of the native-born Americans among the ninety-eight men who were admitted to Conference during the eleven years from 1774 to 1784 inclusive, all were from the South. "There were nearly fifteen thousand members in the Methodist Societies in 1784; of these, only about twenty-five hundred lived north of Maryland."[11]

Through the skillful leadership of Asbury, the basic work was done and the foundation laid for a stronger anti-slavery position when the Methodist Episcopal Church was organized in 1784. His efforts were reinforced by Thomas Coke, an uncompromising opponent to slavery, who was sent to America by John Wesley to help organize the Methodist Church.

John Wesley's Opposing Position

It is reasonable to believe that John Wesley, more than any other single man, molded the outlook and activities of the early Methodists in America. Wesley was a perfectionist. He believed in holy perfection. Perfection was the watchword of Christian living. Wesley, however, did not see perfection as a static ideal, but as a creative transformation of life and a continuous process of growth in love and good works.[12] Being a social reformer, Wesley saw perfection being achieved through involvement in society.

Wesley had a conviction that Negro slavery was one of the greatest evils that a Christian should fight. In 1743 he wrote into the General Rule the prohibition of "the buying or selling of the bodies and souls of men, women, and children, with an intention

29

to enslave them."[13] In 1774, after reading Anthony Benezet's anti-slavery pamphlet, Wesley wrote his *Thoughts Upon Slavery* in which he reviled "the enslavement of the noble by barbarous and inferior white men."[14]

The rational and moral bases of Wesley's opposition to slavery may be noted in the following lines from his *Thoughts Upon Slavery*:

> But, waiving for the present all other considerations, I strike at the root of this complicated villainy. I absolutely deny all slave-holding to be consistent with any degree of natural justice, mercy, and truth. No circumstances can make it necessary for a man to burst in sunder all the ties of humanity. It can never be necessary for a rational being to sink himself below a brute. A man can be under no necessity of degrading himself into a wolf. . . .
>
> Have you, has any man living, a right to use another as a slave? It cannot be, even setting Revelation aside. Liberty is the right of every human creature as soon as he breathes the vital air, and no human being can deprive him of that right which he derives from the law of nature.[15]

While Wesley advanced no plan to abolish slavery, he created for early Methodism a strong anti-slavery sentiment and emphasized the moral urgency to work for the effectiveness of that sentiment for the abolition of slavery. Throughout his whole ministry of more than a half century Wesley was unalterably opposed to slavery.

> The last letter he ever wrote, and one of the noblest, was the famous one supposed to have been addressed to William Wilberforce, four days before his death February 25, 1791, in which he laid his hands in blessing, as it were, on the man who was to lead the fight to a successful conclusion. It contained these words: ". . .Go on, in the name of God and in the power of his might, till even American slavery (the vilest that ever saw the sun) shall vanish away before it."[16]

Signs of Retreat

Early in the 19th century there were signs of a retreat on the slavery issue by the Methodist Church. At the General Conference in New York City in 1844 Dr. John P. Durbin said:

> The history of the Church shows this point indisputably,

30

that the highest ground that has ever been held upon the subject of slavery was taken at the very organization of the Church, and the concessions have been made by the Church continually from that time to this in view of the necessities of the South. Even the language of the question about slavery was mitigated. It had been, "What regulation shall be made for the extirpation of the crying evil of African slavery?" In 1804 it was changed to, "What shall be done for the extirpation of the evil of slavery?" In 1808 all that relates to slave-holding among private members was stricken out, and no rule on the subject has existed since.[17]

Matlack points out that the rules against traveling preachers holding slaves, on slave-holders being official members, on buying and selling slaves, and on gradual emancipation of all slaves were utterly cancelled for four states in the South, embracing one-fifth of the Church members.[18]

The framing and administering of the Discipline to please slave-holding Methodists came very near to extirpating the spirit of liberty. Bishop Asbury was in his declining years and much less active because of age; and Bishop Coke had returned to England. "The inspiration of their joint zeal in the anti-slavery struggle was not at work in the Conference as formerly,"[19] and their leadership was sorely missed.

The Methodist Episcopal Church and Abolitionism

During the period 1789 to 1833 anti-slavery sentiment developed in the North, after slave trade had been legally abolished. The Quakers were largely the source of the developing sentiment and they gave leadership in the early stages of this development as well as later when the movement was well on the way. Rigid church rules were set up by the Quakers and they disowned some of their members who refused to free their slaves. Other churches, such as the Methodist and Baptist, dismissed their members for slave-holding. The Quakers, however, were most consistent in holding to the idealism of the period.

The first abolition society was founded in Pennsylvania in 1774.[20] Societies rose in most of the middle-Atlantic colonies such as Rhode Island, Connecticut, New Jersey, Delaware, Maryland, and as far south as Virginia.[21] In New York where the Abolition Society was organized in 1785 such outstanding personalities as John Jay and Alexander Hamilton served as the first and second presidents, respectively.[22]

Between 1830 and 1860 the slavery controversy increased in

31

magnitude and reached its climax, beginning the Civil War.

Several events contributed to the thirty years of intense struggle over slavery. The Revolution in France in July, 1830, had its influence. In 1831 the South Hampton Massacre in Virginia occurred. In the same year the Boston *Liberator* was founded, edited by William Lloyd Garrison. The controversy reached its height during this thirty-year period. The doctrine of the antagonist and the protagonist of slavery was clearly stated, and strong arguments against and for slavery were debated. Slavery from the point of view of religion was debated and questions discussed as to whether slavery was in conflict with the principles of Christianity. Arguments were propounded as to whether slavery was in conflict with the basic principles on which the nation was founded.[23]

The anti-slavery movement took on a number of forms, expressed itself in various types of organizations, and was advanced under several types of leadership. James G. Birney and Theodore D. Weld were identified with the student movement for abolition at Lane Seminary, Cincinnati, Ohio. The student abolition movement brought about serious conflict with the faculty and trustees of Lane Seminary, most of whom were blinded by race prejudice or favored the colonization movement.

The most radical type of abolition movement was led by William Lloyd Garrison, the most eminent leader of the extreme abolitionists. This group demanded unconditional abolition of slavery without compromise. They based their arguments on the principles of the Declaration of Independence and adhered firmly to the belief that all men are created equal and are endowed with inalienable rights which are independent of government and cannot justly be taken away.

The extreme abolitionist group stirred Methodism, North and South, giving rise to conflict within the Northern Conferences, and between the Methodists of the North and the Methodists of the South. Articles, pamphlets, and books were written to strengthen the anti-slavery fight. Among these were *The Liberator*, edited by William Lloyd Garrison; *Uncle Tom's Cabin*, written by Harriet Beecher Stowe; *My Bondage and My Freedom*, by Frederick Douglass; and *Thoughts Upon Slavery*, by John Wesley.

The strongest defender of slavery in the South was John C. Calhoun from South Carolina, the most illustrious political figure in the period of the old South. He was ably supported by A. T. Bledsoe, who wrote *An Essay on Liberty and Slavery;* W.G. Simms, who wrote *Institutes of Slavery;* and F. R. Dew, who wrote *Review of the Debates in the Virginia Legislature.* These Southern defenders of slavery shaped, in a large measure, the thinking and action in the Southern Region.

Abraham Lincoln is recognized by many as the most effective abolitionist of the period. He adhered firmly to the principle expressed in the Declaration that all men are created equal. He saw this as the foundation principle of all free government. In agreement with the Declaration of Independence, Lincoln saw all men equal in the possession of the unalienable rights expressed in the Declaration of Independence which are life, liberty and the pursuit of happiness.

In his opposition to slavery, Lincoln declared that "no man is good enough to govern another man without that other's consent." Abraham Lincoln was the abolitionist and political master who put an end to slavery by signing the Emancipation Proclamation which became effective January 1, 1863.

It should be pointed out that not all of the anti-slavery sentiment was in the North. There were many white people of the South who were opposed to slavery on the basis of their own idealism as well as the principles of the Declaration of Independence.

Methodists and the Abolition Movement

Asbury, Wesley, Coke, Garrettson, and other early Methodist leaders created a rich heritage regarding Methodism's stance on slavery and passed this heritage on to leaders in the abolition movement. Early Methodism had been stirred by the Great Awakening and later by the sweep of the Evangelical Movement. Thus, they put into their opposition to slavery the fervor of evangelicalism.[30]

Principal abolition leaders in the early stages of the movement were LeRoy Sunderland, George Storrs, and Orange Scott. Sunderland was one of the first converts to the abolition movement by William Lloyd Garrison. Storrs and Scott also came under the influence of Garrison. All three of these men were Methodist ministers; Sunderland, a minister at Andover, Massachusetts; Storrs, a minister in New Hampshire, and Scott, a minister who worked closely with Sunderland and Storrs. These men took the leadership in organizing societies for the abolition of slavery and gave leadership, frequently unwanted, in Conferences of Methodism. Despite the powerful influence of William Lloyd Garrison upon the Methodist abolitionists the relationship between them was not harmonious. In *The Liberator*, Garrison made frequent attacks upon the Methodists which attacks were reciprocated.[31]

Orange Scott became one of Garrison's most outspoken critics. He joined the persuasive Southern abolitionist, James G. Birney, along with Louis and Arthur Tappan, New York philanthropists, in favoring the use of political pressure to achieve abolition. Birney believed that abolitionists should be asked to vote for men who would most likely support the abolition cause. Garrison repudiated this approach. Scott, LeRoy Sunderland, George Storrs, *et al*, led the New England Methodists against Garrison's "folly."[32] The conflict resulted in a victory for the Garrisonians who took over the American Anti-Slavery Society in 1840. Scott, Sunderland, and Storrs withdrew from the American Anti-Slavery Society, joining Birney and the New York Abolitionists in organizing the American and Foreign Anti-Slavery Society.[33]

Not only was there conflict between the Methodist abolitionists and the Garrisonian abolitionists, but there was also conflict between the Methodist abolitionists and other Methodists.

A "New England Anti-slavery Society" was organized in 1832, which recommended a national movement. The American Anti-slavery Society, consequently, was organized at Philadelphia in 1833 by a convention of sixty-three abolitionists from eleven states of the Union.[34]

During 1835 the society expended $30,000; issued one million publications; employed fourteen lecturing agents, who organized more than five hundred auxiliary societies.[35]

The Methodist Episcopal Church opposed the society and its activities. Annual Conference after Annual Conference in the North passed resolutions declaring its opposition to the immediate freeing of the slaves as waged by the abolitionists, and went further to bring to trial Methodist ministers who identified themselves with the abolitionists, or promoted abolitionist views. Such action was taken by the Ohio Conference in 1835; the Baltimore Annual Conference in 1836; the New York Annual Conference in 1836; the Philadelphia Annual Conference in 1838, with strong protest against Rev. O. Scott and Rev. G. Storrs, who were promoting the modern abolitionism within the bounds of the Conference; action was taken against the movement by the Pittsburgh Conference in 1838; and by the Michigan Conference in the same year.[36]

The abolition movement outside of the Methodist Church grew in intensity and subjected the abolition activities within the Methodist Church to severe criticism. The first Methodist Anti-Slavery Society was organized in 1834 and its activities revitalized the abolition movement within the Church. There were at least two groups of Methodists who were opposed to the Methodist Anti-Slavery Society and the abolition movement in general. One of the groups was giving support to the Colonization Society and thought that this was the best method of dealing with the question of slavery. The second group opposed to the Methodist Anti-Slavery Society was the group that favored slavery and wanted to maintain the institution without interference. The second opposition group can be understood when it is recalled that the center of gravity of Methodism as pointed out above was in the South.

A final word on Methodist abolitionism is quoted from Donald G. Matthews:

> Methodist abolitionism began under the aegis of men converted by William Lloyd Garrison and the lecturers of the American Anti-Slavery Society. Appealing to the Wesleyan anti-slavery heritage, evangelists such as Orange Scott, LeRoy Sunderland, and George Storrs converted hundreds and, through these hundreds, thousands of Americans to abolitionism. Although the Methodist Episcopal Church never became "abolitionized," it did provide an excellent institutional framework within which to direct an anti-slavery revival.[37]

The Great Methodist Schism of 1844

From 1784 on, there were sharp conflicts and differences of social views among the adherents of the Methodist Episcopal Church regarding Negro slavery. As pointed out in a previous discussion, it was in 1784 that the Discipline of the Methodist Episcopal Church stipulated a rule providing for and requiring all preachers in the Church to dispose of their slaves permanently, and prohibiting the "buying or selling the bodies and souls of men, women, and children, with an intention to enslave them." After sixty years of struggle, the issue of slavery reached a dramatic and tragic climax when the church separated in 1844 into two groups; the Northern group retaining the name "Methodist Episcopal Church," and the Southern group taking the name "Methodist Episcopal Church, South," the Southern Church having set up its organization in 1845. The incident leading to the crisis resulting in separation centered around Bishop James O. Andrew. The story goes:

> Between 1840 and 1844 he became involved in slavery through the bequest of a Negro girl (Kitty) to him from a lady in Georgia, to be held until she was old enough to be sent to

Liberia. The girl refused to go to Liberia and the laws of Georgia prevented the Bishop's freeing her. Bishop Andrew came into possession of a Negro boy who was bequeathed to his wife by her mother. The boy refused to go North to gain his freedom when this was suggested. The law preventing the boy's freedom, the Bishop "became an unwilling slaveholder."[38]

Information spread among the Methodists of the North during the quadrennium, 1840-1844, and Bishop Andrew's case came before the General Conference in 1844.

On June 1, 1844, by vote of 110 to 68 the General Conference adopted the Finley resolution which required Bishop Andrew to desist from officiating as a Bishop until he had freed himself from the institution of slavery.[39]

This action led to the Great Schism of 1844, which resulted in the separation into the second and third main bodies of Methodism, the Methodist Protestant group having withdrawn in 1828. These three bodies existed as separate branches of Methodism until they re-united in 1939.

The Methodist Episcopal Church and Slavery, 1844-1865

Just as the separation in 1844 created two major branches of Methodism it also created two groups of slaves associated with the two branches of Methodism, respectively. The Methodist Episcopal Church, which was the Northern branch, had taken action outlawing the holding of slaves by any members associated with this branch of Methodism. Associated with the Methodist Episcopal Church, South were Negro slaves who had been associated with the Methodist Church in the slave-holding states prior to 1844. The Methodist Episcopal Church, South, continued its efforts to provide some religious instruction for the slaves related to that branch of Methodism. It is estimated that by 1860 over 180,000 Negro children were under instruction.[40]

The Negro membership of the Methodist Episcopal Church, South, was segregated, the same pattern which had always existed. The religious instruction that was given the slaves was limited and directed in a large measure toward an accommodation to slavery. By the beginning of the war in 1860 the total number of Negroes associated with the Methodist Episcopal Church, South, is estimated to have been over 200,000.[41]

The Methodist Episcopal Church continued its interest in the slaves after 1844. Because of the hostilities between the two major

36

branches of Methodism it was difficult for the Methodist Episcopal Church to carry on this work among the slaves. They were suspected of creating dissatisfaction among slaves and promoting uprisings against slavery. Some work with the Negro churches was permitted by the slave owners, but with close supervision.

After 1844 the separate Negro churches of the Northern branch were included in the white Conferences. These churches, however, were maintained on a separate basis. There were repeated requests by Negroes for the organization of Conferences to include their churches related to the Methodist Episcopal Church. This matter came before the General Conference of 1848 and request was denied.[42] It was thought best not to organize the Negro work into Conferences at that time. This decision, however, did not indicate any diminishing of the interest of the Methodist Episcopal Church in its Negro membership. It was not until after the war that the Methodist Episcopal Church in 1865 began to establish Annual Conferences that included Negro membership in the South. These, however, were mixed racially and were evidence of the continued interest of the Methodist Episcopal Church in the Negro members.

REFERENCES AND NOTES

1. Brown, Ina Corinne, *The Story of the American Negro*, p. 41f.
2. Beard, Charles and Mary R., *The Rise of American Civilization, I*, p. 651.
3. *Ibid.*
4. Dumond, Dwight Lowell, *Anti-Slavery Origins of Civil War in The United States, pp. 6f.*
5. Matthews, Donald G., *Slavery and Methodism*, pp. 7f.
6. *Ibid.*
7. Minutes, Methodist Annual Conference, 1780, p. 12.
8. *Ibid.*
9. *Ibid.*
10. Matthews, *op, cit.*, p. 9
11. Cameron, Richard M., *Methodism and Society in Historical Perspective, I.*, p. 96f.
12. Cameron, *op. cit.*, p. 34.
13. See Wesley's *Journal.*
14. Wesley, John, *Thoughts Upon Slavery*, 1774.
15. Wesley, *Thoughts Upon Slavery*, quoted by Matlack, pp. 40f.
16. Quoted by Cameron, *op. cit.*, p. 53.
17. Matlack, pp. 68f.
18. *Ibid.*, p. 69.
19. Matlack, *op. cit.*, p. 73.
20. Beard, *op. cit.*, p. 73.
21. U. S. Commission on Civil Rights, *Freedom of the Free* (1963), p. 12.
22. *Ibid.*
23. Dumond, *op. cit.*, p. 71.
24. Dumond, *op. cit.*, pp. 30-31.
25. Merriam, Charles E., *American Political Theories*, p. 216.
26. Simkins, Francis Butler, *A History of The South*, pp. 106f.
27. Merriam, *op. cit.*, p. 239.
28. Merriam, *op. cit.*, p. 228.
29. *Ibid.*
30. Cameron, Richard M., *Methodism and Society in Historical Perspective*, pp. 25, 31.
31. See *William Lloyd Garrison and His Times*, by Oliver Johnson, pp. 75ff; p. 158.
32. Matthews, Donald G., *Slavery and Methodism*, p. 17.
33. See *Anti-Slavery Reporter*, June, 1840, p. 3.
34. Matlack, *op. cit.*, p. 80.
35. *Ibid.*, p. 82.
36. See Matlack, *op. cit.*, pp. 82ff and pp. 109-118.

37. Matthews, *op. cit.*, p. 285.
38. Garber, Paul N., *The Methodists are One People*, p. 46.
39. *Ibid.*, p. 49f.
40. McTyeire, Holland N., *A History of Methodism*, p. 386
41. Garber, Paul N., *The Methodists are One People*, p. 41.
42. Barclay, Wade Crawford, — *History of Methodist Missions in the United States, 1845-1939, Vol. III*, p. 302.

CHAPTER 3

THE NEGRO'S HOPE FOR FREEDOM,
HIS EMANCIPATION, AND HIS NEW WORLD

The Negro and His Hope for Freedom

For two and a half centuries Negroes in America groaned under the heavy burden of slavery. The lot of the Negro slave was not so good as that of the early indentured servants who could look forward to the end of seven years and the gaining of freedom. For the Negro slave, the future was as dark as a hundred midnights and life was only an endless path of blighted longings. Yet, the longings continued to well up in a hopeless heart that would not despair of hope.

Human beings, though not so regarded with potentials as other human beings and having the spark of divinity, were bought and sold for the price of chattel property. Slavery raised its horned head as the most villainous of all villainies. It proved the accuracy of this description by the sufferings of millions of helpless slaves — with lashed and bleeding backs, horrified by sickness and untimely, but oft welcomed death; afflicted with endless pathos of frustrations and fears; and discouraged by the deprivation of freedom, joys and happiness, the birthrights of every person.

To escape the unbearableness of slavery, some courageously faced the danger of flight by way of the Underground Railroad. A few expressed their belligerence by insurrections. Some bought their own freedom. Others were fortunate enough to be manumitted by kindly disposed masters. One thing common among all was a passionate desire to be delivered from the torment of bondage.

Despite the conditions of the long blighting years of discouragement, longings continued to well up in the hearts of the slaves and the star of hope continued to shine. In lines of poetic verse and in plaintive melodies of music they expressed their longings and hopes in such spirituals as "Oh, By and By, I'm Gonna Lay Down This Heavy Load," or, "There's a Better Day A'coming, Hallelujah."

The endless hope of the Negro slave is well-described in the words of W. E. B. DuBois:

41

Away back in the days of bondage they thought to see in one divine event the end of all doubt and disappointment; few men ever worshipped freedom with half such unquestioning faith as did the American Negro for two centuries. To him, so far as he thought and dreamed, slavery was indeed the sum of all villainies, the cause of all sorrows, the root of all prejudice; emancipation was the key to a promised land of sweeter beauty than ever stretched before the eyes of wearied Israelites. In song and exhortation swelled one refrain — Liberty; in his tears and curses the God he implored had freedom in his right hand. At last it came — suddenly, fearfully, like a dream.[1]

The long night ended and the dawn of day came in the Emancipation Proclamation January 1, 1863.

The Civil War and Emancipation

The agitation against slavery in the late years of the Colonial period, the early abolition of slavery in the Northern states, the cessation of the African slave trade in 1808 by Act of Congress, the ineffective results of the Colonization Movement, and a growing recognition outside of the South of the moral implications of slavery, all combined to give force to efforts to destroy the institution of American slavery.

It was inevitable that the division between the North and the South would lead to the Civil War which was begun with the firing on Fort Sumter April 12, 1861, and ended with the surrender of General Lee at Appomattox April 9, 1865. The Emancipation Proclamation had been issued by President Lincoln January 1, 1863, in the midst of the civil strife. It required, however, over two more years of battle to bring the freedom proclaimed in the Emancipation Proclamation. Further, it required three significant amendments to the Constitution (the 13th, 14th and 15th Amendments) to make freedom and citizenship a reality.

Slavery issue as an institution and abolition were deep concerns of President Lincoln. There is abundant evidence to show that he hated slavery and wanted to see it abolished. "If Weld and Birney were abolitionists, Lincoln was one; and if they had a plan, he had a better one,"[2] says D. L. Dumond. He further states that Lincoln thought, "It was a moral and political evil which menaced the rights of free men, was contrary to the principles enunciated in the Declaration of Independence and a violation of eternal principles of right."[3]

Lincoln had a conviction that not only should the Negro be free from slavery, but he should be free to develop also the talents

42

he might possess and should enjoy the fruits of his own labor.

A final insight into Lincoln's conviction on slavery is found in the following words:

> Fondly do we hope, fervently do we pray, that this scourge of war may speedily pass away. Yet, if God wills that it continue until all the wealth piled by the bondsmen's two hundred years of unrequited toil shall be sunk, and until every drop drawn with the lash shall be paid by another drawn with the sword, as was said two hundred years ago, still must it be said that the judgments of the Lord are true and righteous altogether.[4]

The Emancipation Proclamation of 1863 joined all of these issues, which were resolved only after several years of bloody civil strife and decades of sectional conflicts after the smoke of battle had cleared away.

The Freedmen in a New and Frightening World
of Freedom

The war ended and 4,000,000 slaves were freed. The long years of work of the abolitionists came to fruition. Freedom came as a just reward for two and one-half centuries of servitude, and military service by the bondsmen themselves in the Union Army during the Civil War.

The coming of freedom was a time for shouting and jubilation, weeping and exultation. The far away day had dawned in disbelief. The hope that had continued generation after generation, for more than two centuries, was suddenly realized. The day of rejoicing had come. The newly-freed bondsmen sang a new song, "Free at Last, Free at Last; I Thank God Almighty, I'm Free at Last." And again they sang, "Shout, O children! Shout, you are free! For God has bought your liberty!" As the days of great jubilation waned the rejoicing continued in a quieter vein. The reality of freedom began to dawn upon the Freedmen and reflection upon their new state brought realization of a terrible responsibility in the frightening new world into which they had entered. There was a transition from slaves to Freedmen; from chattel property to human beings; from serfdom to citizenship; from an "inferior" person to a man striving for dignity and recognition.

For the first time in their lives, they could travel; they could see; they could talk to friends and sit at sundown and in moonlight, listening and imparting wonder-tales. They could

43

hunt in the swamps, and fish in the rivers. And, above all, they could stand up and assert themselves. They need not fear the patrol; they need not even cringe before a white face, and touch their hats.[5]

Here was a new group of free people in a new American scene, poor economically and bereft of learning. DuBois aptly states the situation in these words: "To be a poor man is hard, but to be a poor race in a land of dollars is the very bottom of hardship."[6] He further states, regarding the newly-freed Negro: "He felt the weight of his ignorance — not simply of letters, but of life, of business, of the humanities, the accumulated sloth and shirking and awkwardness of decades and centuries shackled his hands and feet."[7]

The Coming of a New World

Freedom became more frightening in the new world when the Freedmen experienced scorn and glaring depreciation and disparagement. They soon discovered that they were in a new world where they would have to fight hard for dignity, work, citizenship, education, money, and property. They had to work hard to escape the continued status of a servant and to create a culture all their own. Amid discouragements they had to struggle against the powers of an established order that would forever keep them bound to the earthly traditions and customs of the past. Here and there a kindly hand of a former master was extended in friendship. There was the help and influence of those who had helped to abolish slavery and gain freedom for the Negro. The responsibility, however, rested upon the Negro himself to overcome the barriers he faced and begin the march of a new century of progress and development.

The need for help was evident in the fact that four million newly freed Negroes were without economic foundation. In fact, their economic plight was pitiful. They had been freed to go their way without homes, land, or any substantial means of support. The conditions were generally below the standards of a high code of moral living. This was due to the moral ravages of slavery through the destruction of family life, the encouragement of promiscuous breeding to increase the slave population and, not the least of all, by the advantage taken of Negro women by white males. The Freedmen were untrained in the bare rudiments of cultural life. Knowledge of business procedures was lacking. What training they had was almost exclusively for plantation labor and, in a large measure, this was looked upon with disdain because this

44

was all that they had done for centuries and slavery degraded labor. There were exceptions to all these conditions, but in the main they applied to the general population of the Freedmen.

In the wilderness of helplessness, the Freedmen needed help. It was a need to which the Methodists of the North and other denominations responded. In the words of the Fifth Report of the Freedmen's Aid Society:

Four millions of people, ignorant, and degraded by long-continued oppression and wrong, had just been emancipated, and had passed from the condition of chattelism and vassalage into manhood and freedom. But they carried with them in their transition the sad effects of their former state. True, the chains which bound their hands and fettered their limbs were broken; but ignorance, vice, and oppression had forged fetters for the soul that the Act of Emancipation could not sunder. A dash of the pen made them free, but it could not make them intelligent and moral. This crowning act of our martyred President, in all its sublimity, must be supplemented by long-continued sublime action, that the work of redemption so auspiciously commenced may be carried forward by educating and elevating the race, eliminating as far as possible the fearful wrongs and vices of the past, as the surest pledge to the highest elevation and the purest manhood.

We rejoice at the noble specimen of Christian character occasionally exhibited by slaves; but these were exceptions, illustrations of what the grace of God could do in spite of slavery, rather than its legitimate fruits; fruitage of religious instruction on the part of Christian people, in opposition to the laws of chattelism, forbidding all efforts to instruct and elevate its victims.[8]

The destructive war had been fought for the most part on Southern soil. Cities were destroyed, homes and schools burned, and looting generally took place. Charleston, Columbia, Atlanta, Chattanooga, and Vicksburg were among the cities most severely damaged. The economy of the South reflected the ruins and losses of the whole region. Plantation production was reduced to a minimum. Poverty lurked over much of the region. Embittered millions of white people and four million newly-freed slaves constituted a new Southern region with new problems and conditions that made living together in the community difficult, to say the least. The Freedmen and a majority of the white population suffered the same plight.

The Climate of the South

When the Civil War came to an end and the South and its whole economy had to be rebuilt, the plantation economy — based on slave labor — had to be changed, which change lessened for a time the productivity of the agricultural system. The plantation system was modified from free labor of the slave to cheap labor by Negro tenants and sharecroppers.

The climate of the South was not favorable to the Freedmen, nor was it conducive to good race relationships and economic development. The hostile climate stemmed from two main sources: (1) The very nature of conditions and attitudes resulting from two and a half centuries of human exploitation in slavery, the defeat in war and the abrupt disruption and mutation of a system which had been the foundation of the antebellum way of life in the South; and (2) The antagonistic approach, in many instances, to the South by the North in post-war adjustments. The climate had been greatly influenced by the Northern Group who came into the region following the close of the Civil War. Cameron observes that:

> It was unfortunate that Northern Methodism came to a full realization of her power at just the juncture when a mood of vindictiveness was settling over the North. The Methodist Episcopal Church's thrust into the South was undeniably productive of some good in the evangelization and, especially, the education of the freedmen, but its dealings with the Methodist Episcopal Church, South, and their property savored too much of ecclesiastical imperialism, and at the expense of a conquered foe, to produce anything but resentment among the white brethren in the South.[9]

The Methodists were joined by other denominational groups from the North whose dealings with the Southern people were no less offensive.

> The Methodists were a uniquely powerful sect. The Episcopalians and the Presbyterians in the South and the Congregationalists in New England could count among their members a majority of the upper-class industrial, agricultural, and professional groups. The yet chaotic Baptist expansion, until recently concentrated in the frontier, was most effective still among the least secure and less well-educated citizenry. The ably led Methodist Episcopal Church was the most dynamic, the fastest growing, and, excepting the minuscule Quakers and the

46

sectionally limited Unitarians and Congregationalists, the most dedicated to social reform of the nation's organized churches. . . .When the Methodist bishops and preachers spoke, politicians listened no less attentively than did their congregations.[10]

The effect of Northern groups on the attitudes of the South extended far beyond mere church relations. The economic, political, and social life of the people was affected as much as the church life.

The people of the South had become embittered by the war and their defeat. The economic changes severely affecting the region created poverty with many attendant problems. Because of their defeat in the war, the freedom granted the slaves, and military occupations by the Federal Government a feeling of distrust was created and there was fear of the Freedmen lest they and the Northern group would form a coalition to inflict reprisals upon the South.

The attitude developed during the long period of slavery continued, and all of the antebellum arguments were kept alive. These arguments had to do with the claim of the inferiority of the Negro and the belief that he had a definite "place" in society and that he should never rise above the low status of inferiority and serfdom. It was believed, consequently, that the Negro should forever be a "hewer of wood and a drawer of water," and that his chief function was to labor for the advancement of the white race and white civilization. There were, therefore, no qualms in exploiting the labors of the Negro.

There was widespread illiteracy among the Freedmen which is easily understood because very little instruction, while they were in slavery, was permitted. There was also a high percentage of illiteracy among the white people. The 1850 Census showed 8.27 percent of the adult white population of the slave states were illiterate as compared with 3.36 percent in the non-slave holding states. Simkins points out that "there was a negative attitude on the part of white people toward public school education. Many common people in the South were unwilling to take advantage of such schools as the states provided. Those who could afford it sent their children to private schools. There was not a great deal of interest in the public schools and great numbers of the illiterate or semi-illiterate people were proud of their ignorance of 'book-learning.' "[11] There were few public schools for white children and no public schools for Negro children. It was thought that to keep the Negro illiterate would help to keep him "in his place."

Beginning the Struggle for Identification as a Human Being, as a Man, and as a Citizen

With the shackles of slavery thrown off, the Freedmen began to make the transition into a theoretically free world and to establish themselves as men among men and as citizens in a free society. The marks of slavery were clearly branded upon them and every effort of chicanery and deception was employed to prolong the slave status and impose upon the Freedmen the continuation of the caste system. Aware of their new status, the Freedmen sought the true feeling of freedom and independence. It was necessary to fight against increasing resentment toward their freedom and the established ideas, arguments and practices regarding the inferiority of the Negro. Uncritical acceptance of the theory of biological inequality and racial inferiority was the greatest cause for the prevailing race prejudice and intolerance among the intellectual and cultural classes of the society.[1][2]

It was important to develop a sense of independence and group consciousness. They could not be a significant part of the white culture so they had to develop a culture of their own. This meant the development of a community within a community, dependent, in a large measure, upon the larger community, but separated in fact in most of the essential aspects of the larger community. The Freedmen had to relate themselves to the extent that they could, to the larger community and at the same time develop their own community where they could be themselves and be free of domination. There was a strong desire to develop Negro leadership and this leadership had to be developed within the confines of the Negro community. It was much like pulling themselves up by their own bootstraps without having boots. It was difficult, but this was the only way to achievement and self-realization. The importance of lifting themselves, individually and in masses, was clearly seen for the good of all and in order to compel respect of the white people of the larger community.

The struggle for racial identification led to political adventures, some of which were successful, others complete failures. Nevertheless, important lessons were learned. It was necessary for the economic status of the group to be improved and business enterprises to be established. This involved buying of land and establishment of homes. It was recognized that property ownership was the key to citizenship, security, and progress.

In the process of the achievement of identity, numerous community organizations engaged their interest and activity on a large scale. The church was the most important organization where leadership found expression. Fraternal orders were established which again gave opportunity for leadership. There was a passion for education, believing that education was the magic key to all success and an escape from the menial labors with which the black man had been identified for centuries. Therefore, schools, including day schools, night schools, industrial schools, Sunday Schools, and colleges, became important institutions of the community where young and old endeavored to learn. In these endeavors were hopes, privations, and sacrifices on the part of individuals and whole families.

The Freedmen experienced much opposition in their endeavors to achieve identity. In order to survive the opposition and to achieve their objectives, they had to find ways of accommodation that made possible their survival and the establishment of good will in the larger community, as they pursued their goals.

The Federal Government Gives a Helping Hand

After Emancipation the whole nation in general, and the South in particular, faced the problem of maintaining freedom of a group that was unable to do much for itself and unable to hold back the forces that attempted to return Negroes to slavery and continue the old system and old way of life of the antebellum South. Recognizing the need for aid and its own responsibility, the Federal Government through an act of Congress, March 3, 1865, established a Bureau in the War Department for the care of refugees and Freedmen. Major General Oliver O. Howard was appointed Commissioner of the new Bureau on May 12, 1865. The need of aid from such a Bureau was urgent because of the conditions of the Freedmen and also, as DuBois points out, there were "three things that the conquered South fought with bitter determination: (1) any Federal interference with labor, (2) arms in the hands of Negroes, (3) votes for Negroes,"[3] and a fourth might be added, education of the Freedmen.

DuBois further states that "the Freedmen's Bureau was the most extraordinary and far-reaching institution of social uplift that America has ever attempted. It had to do not simply with emancipated slaves and poor whites, but also with the property of Southern planters. It was a government guardianship for the relief and guidance of white and black labor from a feudal agrarianism to modern farming and industry."[4]

Five years after the Bureau was established, through a special Congressional Committee, General Howard reported expenditures of $12,965,395.40; he had exercised oversight and care for the freedmen and refugees in seventeen states and the District of Columbia, a territory of 350,000 square miles, and had cooperated

49

with benevolent societies, aiding in the education of hundreds of thousands of pupils, and in the relief of vast numbers of destitute and homeless persons of all ages and both sexes.[15]

REFERENCES AND NOTES

1. DuBois, W. E. B., *The Souls of Black Folk.*, p. 18.
2. Dumond, Dwight Lowell, *Anti-Slavery Origins of the Civil War.*, p. 107.
3. *Ibid.*
4. Richardson, James D., ed., *Messages and Papers of the Presidents*, (10 Volumes, Washington, D. C., 1896-99) VI., p. 276.
5. DuBois, W. E. B., *Black Reconstruction in America 1860-1880*, p. 122.
6. DuBois, *The Souls of Black Folk*, p. 20.
7. *Ibid.*
8. Fifth Annual Report of the Freedmen's Aid Society, pp. 4f.
9. Cameron, Richard M., *Methodism and Society in Historical Perspective*, pp. 194f.
10. Carter, Hodding, *The Angry Scar, The Story of Reconstruction*, (Garden City, New York: Doubleday and Company, 1959), p. 81.
11. Simkins, Francis B., *A History of the South*, pp. 172f.
12. Simkins, *Ibid.*
13. DuBois, *Black Reconstruction In America 1860-1880*, p. 223.
14. *Ibid.*, p. 219.
15. *Ibid.*, p. 229.

PART II.

THE METHODIST EPISCOPAL CHURCH
AND THE FREEDMEN'S AID SOCIETY, 1866 — 1916

CHAPTER 4.

THE FREEDMEN'S AID SOCIETY

Educational Interests Prior to 1866

As far back as the Colonial Period some efforts were exerted toward the education of Negroes, prompted by a religious motive. The purpose of this education was to prepare Negroes for church membership and to enable them to read the Bible. Some who promoted education for Negroes had another motive also. There was a question as to whether or not a church member could be held in slavery. After this question had been resolved by legal enactment, there was no further conflict relating to the education of the slaves and free Negroes, although definite restrictions were imposed by slaveholders.

Beginning with the Methodist societies organized prior to 1784 there had been and continued to be a dominant Methodist interest in the American problem relating to the Negro. The Methodists' part in the abolition movement led to the major divisions of the Church, North and South, in 1844. It continued its identification with the movement into the Civil War.

In 1860 the Methodist Episcopal Church itself had more than 300 workers in the Southern field. Between 1844 and 1860 the Methodist Episcopal Church expended $1,500,000 upon Negro missions.

The efforts of the Methodist Episcopal Church were not limited to the South.

A Committee was appointed in 1853 by the Cincinnati Conference of the Methodist Episcopal Church to inquire into and report what best could be done to promote the interests of the people of color. It recommended the opening of a school, and in 1856 was founded Wilberforce University, of which Richard S. Rust was the third President; he conducted its affairs with skill and zeal from 1858 to 1863, when it was sold to the African Methodist Episcopal Church for ten thousand dollars.[1]

After the war ended, the Methodist Episcopal Church was on the scene in the South. It had recommended in 1864 the

55

establishment of the National Freedmen's Bureau which Congress approved in 1865.

Work with Commissions

Prior to the establishment of the Freedmen's Bureau by the Federal Government a number of denominations had been at work ministering to the needs of the Freedmen. In fact, the work began before the close of the war. The Methodist Episcopal Church became a part of this movement by various denominations to minister to Freedmen in many different ways.

The General Conference of 1864 took cognizance of the humane work in behalf of the Freedmen of the United States as prosecuted by the leading Freedmen's aid commissions — undenominational societies, organized to unite in a common work the friends of the Freedmen throughout the country, without reference to their religious opinions. . . .The Commissions were, therefore, approved by the General Conference as engaged in a work of benevolence of special interest, and commended to our people everywhere so worthy of their sympathy and support.[2]

A number of commissions established in the East and West which developed into a National Commission administered to the needs of the Freedmen. Several denominations participated in the work of the commissions giving substantial support. Principally among these denominations were the Congregationalists, the Baptists, the Presbyterians, and the Methodist Episcopal Church. After several years of such support to the non-denominational commissions various churches began to pull away from the national commission and to establish societies within the respective denominations.

Freedmen's Aid Society Established

Like other major denominations the Methodist Episcopal Church withdrew its support from the Commission, deeming it wise to set up its own society within the Methodist Church. The need, the scope of work, and their missionary zeal impelled the Methodists to expand their work with the Freedmen through the establishment of the Freedmen's Aid Society of the Methodist Episcopal Church.

When the Methodist Episcopal Church was considering withdrawal from the commissions and establishing a society of its own, the following appraisal of the work of the commissions was given:

It should be known what the commissions, as now organized, are accomplishing. Those in the West have planted schools in the more important points in the Mississippi Valley, maintaining in these schools, during the past year, an average, at least, of one hundred teachers, mostly Christian men and women, opened Sunday schools, relieved the poor, cared for the orphan.

It should also be stated that, after efforts extending through the past two and a half years, the several undenominational societies have been united in a National Commission, having its branches in the East and West, a movement that may possibly benefit the work in various ways.[3]

Organization and Incorporation

On August 7, 1866, a group of ministers and laymen met, pursuant to call, at the Trinity Methodist Episcopal Church in Cincinnati, Ohio. The following excerpts are taken from the Minutes.

> Trinity Methodist Episcopal
> Church, Cincinnati, Ohio
> August 7, 1866

In pursuance with a call, a Convention of ministers and laymen met this day, at 2 o'clock P.M., in Trinity Methodist Episcopal Church, Cincinnati, Ohio, to confer in regard to the work of relief and education required in behalf of the Freedmen.

The following persons were present, viz., Bishop D. W. Clark, Revs. Adam Poe, J. M. Reid, R. S. Rust, J. M. Walden, J. R. Stillwell, and Mr. J. P. Larkin, of Cincinnati, Ohio; Rev. Luke Hitchcock and Hon. Grant Goodrich, of Chicago, Ill.; Rev. B. P. Crary, of St. Louis, Mo.; and Rev. Robert Allyn, of Lebanon, Ill.

Bishop T. A. Morris could not attend the meeting but gave his strong endorsement in a letter in response to the call. Dr. F. C. Holiday could not attend the meeting, but gave thorough endorsement to organizing a society by and within the

57

Methodist Episcopal Church.

Bishop D. W. Clark was chosen Chairman, and Rev. J. M. Walden, Secretary.[4]

By request of the meeting Rev. J. M. Walden submitted a statement as follows (Excerpts from the statement):

Since the organization of the Western and Northwestern Freedmen's Aid Commissions, the membership of the Methodist Episcopal Church have been aiding these Societies in Prosecuting their work in behalf of the Freedmen. We have met to consider whether the times and work require the organization of a society to be controlled entirely by members of our own Church.

* * *

The following considerations, among others, have suggested such a movement to those who have given attention to the question:

1. The organization of denominational societies by other branches of the Christian Church. The Freedmen's Aid Commissions, though not national, were at first the representatives of nearly all the leading denominations in the Freedmen's relief work. In their Boards of officers these denominations were represented, and contributions for the support of the work were received alike from all; but most of the denominations have organized societies within themselves, or made special arrangements — viz.: The United Presbyterians, Brethren, Friends, Old School Presbyterians, Baptists, Congregationalists, and Protestant Episcopal Churches — leaving the New School Presbyterian and Methodist Episcopal Churches the only denominations of any size which have continued their cooperation, without diversion with the Commissions.

2. These denominational societies are cooperating with and strengthening the missionary efforts of their respective churches, by sustaining schools at those points where their missionaries are laboring; hence the question comes up whether the contributions of Methodists might not, and ought not to be made to aid our mission-work in the same way among Freedmen.

3. A large percent of the home collections come from the Methodist Churches and people. During the past year about $100,000 in cash has been collected in the West. . . .I think I am safe in saying that not less than fifty percent of the whole amount has come from the membership of the Methodist Episcopal Church. . . .

4. The funds thus contributed are expended by unde-nominational societies. While other denominations have

organized their own societies, or selected their special denominational agencies, they are as largely represented among the officers and directors of the Commissions as before they made these sectarian movements. . . .

These are the leading facts which have led to the call of this convention, and forced upon us the question: shall we organize a Methodist Freedmen's Aid Society, or shall we still cooperate with existing Commissions?

* * *

I may briefly mention some of the possible results of the new movement within the pale of our own Church, at least such as have occurred to my mind:

1. The schools organized would be supplied with Methodist teachers, and might be under the local supervision of our Missionaries, thereby securing to them a religious character congenial to the habits and feelings of the colored people.

2. It would give our missionary work greater favor with the Freedmen. . . .

3. It would further strengthen our missionary work by furnishing Sunday School teachers, and increase the efficiency of the Sunday schools by making them a part of the Church Movement.

4. At a moderate estimate it should secure fifty thousand dollars, to be applied to these schools in connection with our Missionary-work. . . .

5. At many points the Freedmen might aid in supporting schools.

6. Under the new Freedmen's Bureau bill the Government is to provide every society with schoolhouses for all the teachers they can support.

7. A Methodist Freedmen's Aid Society would give our Church a more direct, and hence a greater, interest in the education of the Freedmen, and consequently increase the zeal of the mission-work in their behalf.

8. If there should arise a necessity for ecclesiastical legislation in regard to this work, the experience acquired within the time intervening between this and the next session of the General Conference would be of great service in shaping such legislation.[5]

There were other speeches or addresses, and extended discussion on the question of organizing a Methodist Freedmen's Aid Society. Letters favoring the Organization were sent by some who could not be present. Among those speaking were:

Dr. Rust, Rev. Dr. Poe, Rev. J. R. Stillwell, Chaplain J. R.

Locke, Rev. J. C. Gibson, Rev. Dr. Crary, Dr. Allyn, Dr. Hitchcock, and Bishop Clark.[6]

At the conclusion of the speeches the following resolution was approved unanimously:

> *Resolved.* That the time has come for the organization of a Society for the relief and education of the Freedmen and people of color in general, to cooperate with the Missionary and Church Extension Society of the Methodist Episcopal Church.[7]

After unanimous action adopting the resolution to organize the Freedmen's Aid Society of the Methodist Episcopal Church a committee was appointed consisting of Dr. Walden, Judge Goodrich, Dr. Crary, Dr. Hitchcock, and Dr. Rust to draw up a plan of organization and to prepare a draft of a constitution. At this same convention on March 8th the committee made its report.[8]

The Constitution of the Freedmen's Aid Society was approved by the Convention. Thus the persons named in the report including the Bishops of the Church constitute the founders of the Freedmen's Aid Society of the Methodist Episcopal Church.

After the adoption of the Constitution by the Convention, the first officers of the Society were elected.[9]

President — Rev. Bishop Davis W. Clark, D. D.
Vice Presidents — Major-General Clinton B. Fisk,*
    Hon, Grant Goodrich, Rev. I. W. Wiley, D. D.
Treasurer — Rev. Adam Poe, D. D.
Corresponding Secretary — Rev. J. M. Walden, D. D.
General Field Superintendent — Rev. R. S. Rust, D. D.
Recording Secretary — Rev. J. Morrison Reid, D. D.

Bishop Clark served as President of the Society until his death in 1871.

Incorporation

The work of the Freedmen's Aid Society was carried forward for several years before the incorporation of the Society. On November 1, 1870, the articles of the incorporation were drawn up.[10]

---

*For whom Fisk University was named

60

First Appeal by the Bishops of the Church

Immediately following the perfection of the organization of the Freedmen's Aid Society the Bishops of the Church sent to the pastors and members of the Methodist Episcopal Church the first appeal for the support of the work of the Society. This appeal follows:

To the Pastors and Members of the Methodist Episcopal Church:

Dear Brethren — The emancipation of four million of slaves has opened at our very door a wide field calling alike for mission and educational work. It has developed upon the Church a fearful responsibility. Religion and education alone can make freedom a blessing to them. The school must be planted by the side of the Church; the teacher must go along with the missionary. In no other way can our work reach its highest success among the Freedmen of the South. They claim this culture as immortal beings, at our hands. Without it their true position as members of the society can never be attained. It is needful, that they may sustain proper domestic relations among themselves, and that their children may be saved from the blighting effects entailed by the system of slavery. It is indispensable to the highest and most permanent success of our mission work among them. And then, too, a consideration of vital importance to the Christian world, is the fact that from among themselves the ministers are to be raised up who shall conserve, carry forward, and make permanent the work of Christianizing and educating the race.

The time may come when the States in the South will make some provision for the education of the colored children now growing up in utter ignorance in their midst. But thus far they have made none, nor perhaps can it soon be expected of them. Christian philanthropy must supply this lack. While other Churches, North and South, are entering this broad field, we have our own work and our own duty to perform. We can not turn away from the appeal that comes home to our consciences and hearts. Nor can we delay. *The emergency is upon us, and we must begin to work now.*

As a suitable channel through which the benefactions of our Church to this object may best reach their design, the Freedmen's Aid Society of the Methodist Episcopal Church has been organized. It is designed to cooperate with our missionary work in the South, and, in fact, a supplement to that work.

61

There are openings for hundreds of teachers at this moment. Hundreds of teachers are ready to go. The means to send them are only wanting.

In view of the great emergency of the case, and the certainty that the benefactions of our people can better reach their end through our own channels than any other, we command to you the Freedmen's Aid Society of the Methodist Episcopal Church. And especially would we urge upon all pastors and congregations, in view of the present great and pressing wants, to make for the object a collection as soon as practicable.

We also recommend that the Churches in the East contribute with special reference to the establishment of schools in the Southern States bordering upon the Atlantic, and that the Churches in the West direct their efforts especially to the States lying south of them in the great Mississippi Valley. We further recommend to the Executive Committee of the Freedmen's Aid Society, to distribute the schools established by them in the South, so as to cover the whole territory of the South as far as practicable, so that the fruits of this blessed work may be most widely diffused.

Done by order of the Board of Bishops, at New York City, November 8, 1866.

D. W. Clark, Sec'y of the Board.[1][1]

The Freedmen's Aid Society Seeks Recognition

In an effort to strengthen the Southern work, in 1868 the General Conference (of the Methodist Episcopal Church) took two important actions. The first was with reference to the conferences established in the South and the second was with reference to the Freedmen's Aid Society.

The 1868 General Conference repealed the action of 1864 which, in determining that the conferences formed in the Southern states should be 'Missionary Conferences,' restricted their rights and privileges, and declared the Alabama, Delaware, Georgia, Holston, Mississippi, South Carolina, Tennessee, Texas, Virginia and North Carolina, and Washington conferences to be Annual Conferences vested with all the rights, privileges, and immunities usual to Annual Conferences.[1][2]

Regarding the Freedmen's Aid Society the 1868 General Conference gave the Society its sanction and commended it to the General Church for support. The Conference, however, did not give recognition to the society as a General Conference organization, thinking that the Society would not be needed for any great length of time. The Freedmen's Aid Society was commended to the Annual Conferences and urged to place it on their list for annual collections.[13]

The 1872 General Conference "placed the Freedmen's Aid Society among the benevolent associations of the Church and made it the duty of each pastor to present the claims of this enterprise to its people and to take a collection in its behalf."[14] To the 1872 General Conference a memorial was presented by the Board of Directors of the Freedmen's Aid Society "asking that this Society might be received into full connection, placed under the Jurisdiction of the General Conference, and welcomed to all the advantages the Church can afford." A number of reasons were given, supporting the request for this action by the General Conference. The memorial was referred to the Committee on Freedmen and its report to the General Conference was adopted: "*Resolved.* 'That the prayer of the memorialists for the official recognition of the Freedmen's Aid Society be granted, and that said society be and hereby is, recognized as a regular constituted society of the Methodist Episcopal Church.' "[15]

Historical Interest in the Problem

Methodist interests in freeing and elevating the Negro in America began with Francis Asbury in the early 1770's. The Civil War and Emancipation removed the shackles of slavery from the hands and feet of the Negroes but it remained for the Church to give relief and provide education to free their minds and spirits. The attitude and feeling of a deep sense of responsibility on the part of the Methodist Episcopal Church may be noted in the words of Bishop Gilbert Haven:

What then is the service to which the Master calls us? This, and this only: to abolish from the national action and the arising from color or origin; all thought and feeling that such distinctions are divinely intended to separate members of the same human family, who are and must ever be one in blood and in destiny, in sin and in salvation, in Adam and in Christ. . . .The medical and the legal bodies have admitted them (the Negroes) as equals; not so the clerical. . . .The Church in America gives itself earnestly to the support of this heaven-hated sin. . . .She separates God's ministries of the least tinged with this complexion into conferences by themselves.[16]

63

The following statement from an address by Bishop Thomson further amplifies the attitude of the Methodist leaders:

After all it may be said, "These are negroes — an inferior race." Should this be granted, would it justify us in ignoring their claims upon our sympathy and assistance? *We* are inferior to angels, but do they feel no interest in our welfare, or sympathy in our sorrows? Were they dwelling on earth would they be justified in oppressing us? What father would allow a child of superior powers to crush a crippled brother? But *is* the negro inferior? Take the testimony of Reverdy Johnson, who said to a deputation of the Freedmen's Aid Union of England: "As well might we say that a black horse does not belong to the class of horses, as to indulge in any such idea." The same gentleman says, "The blacks are as capable of learning as the whites."[1] [7]

REFERENCES AND NOTES

1. Buckley, James M., *A History of Methodism in the United States*, p. 297.
Note: Wilberforce University, located at Xenia, Ohio, has been for more than a century the most widely known institution of the African Methodist Episcopal Church and has rendered excellent service.
2. Annual Report of the Freedmen's Aid Society, 1868, p. 3.
3. Report of the Freedmen's Aid Society of the Methodist Episcopal Church, August 7, 1866, p. 5 (Organization Convention).
4. Report of the Freedmen's Aid Society, 1866-1875, p. 3.
5. *Ibid.*, pp. 5-9.
6. *Ibid.*, p. 9f.
7. *Ibid.*, p. 10.
8. See Appendix, Exhibit; Constitution of the Freedmen's Aid Society of the Methodist Episcopal Church.
9. Reports of the Freedmen's Aid Society of the Methodist Episcopal Church, 1866-75, p. 14.
10. Freedmen's Aid Society Report, 1888, pp. 5-6.
11. Freedmen's Aid Society Report, 1866, p. 1.
12. Barclay, *History of American Missions*, Vol. 3, p. 313.
13. *The Doctrines and Discipline of the Methodist Episcopal Church*, 1868, p. 330 (The General Conference Journal, 1868, p. 332).
14. Sixth Annual Report, Freedmen's Aid Society of the Methodist Episcopal Church, 1873, p. 5.
15. Sixth Annual Report, Freedmen's Aid Society, 1873, pp. 36f.
16. *Methodist Quarterly Review*, 47 (1865), pp. 286 and 272; and Cameron, *op. cit.*, p. 201.
17. Freedmen's Aid Society Report (Third), 1869, pp. 18f.

CHAPTER 5

EXPANSION OF THE ORGANIZATION AND WORK
OF THE FREEDMEN'S AID SOCIETY

Efforts to Change the Name and Management

The Freedmen's Aid Society, prior to the General Conference of 1868, was in name and work Methodistic, but had no official approval of the Church. In 1868 the General Conference accorded to it the recognition of a Methodist Society, but kept it on probation for four years. In 1872 the Society was adopted by the General Conference and given a place among the connectional societies of the church.[1] It is interesting to note that the organization of the Freedmen's Aid Society antedated the Board of Education by two years, the latter being organized in 1868 and incorporated in 1869.

For several decades the work of the church in the field of education for Negro youth was carried on under the name and guidance of the Freedmen's Aid Society. Several attempts were made to change the name of the society and to expand its work. Despite much pressure, the General Conference, guided by the leaders and managers of the Freedmen's Aid Society, refrained from changing the name and adhered firmly to the original purpose of providing education for Negro youth. When the name was changed and the work expanded to provide education for white youth in the South, the church did not lose sight of the original purpose of the Freedmen's Aid Society.

The first request for a change in name and organization of the Freedmen's Aid Society was to the 1876 General Conference. R.W. Hammett from Arkansas presented the following resolution to the Conference:

Whereas, The Freedmen's Aid Society cannot meet all that is demanded by the claims of education without destroying its efficiency, therefore it is respectfully requested of the General Conference to organize a society known as the Education Aid Society of the Methodist Episcopal Church, yet so as not to retard the efficiency of the Freedmen's Aid Society.[2]

This resolution was referred to the Committee on education.

Another delegate from Arkansas presented a similar resolution to the Conference.

The resolutions referred to the Committee on Education were not approved. The committee made the following report to the General Conference which was approved by the Conference:

In view of the work which must be done for our church by the Freedmen's Aid Society in promoting Christian Education among the colored people of the South, your committee beg leave to submit the following recommendations for adoption:

1. That the Freedmen's Aid Society retain substantially its present organization.

2. In view of the importance and extent of its work, that a very large increase of its annual income should be contributed by the Church.

3. That the Board of Managers of this Society are hereby instructed to apportion the amount annually determined to be asked for among the several Annual Conferences.

4. That, in the management of the funds committed to its trust and work accomplished, the Freedmen's Aid Society is worthy of the fullest confidence and heartiest support of the Church.

5. That we commend the collections for this Society to the preachers and people, assuring them that no more worthy charity calls for their aid, and that no field of christian effort promises better returns for money and labor expended than this work among the freedmen of the South.[3]

Several resolutions were presented to the General Conference asking for a merging of the Freedmen's Aid Society with the Missionary Society, most of which were referred to the Committee on Freedmen and were rejected.[4]

Efforts were continued to change the name and organization of the Freedmen's Aid Society. These efforts failed when the General Conference of 1880 took action approving the report of the Committee on Freedmen's Aid and Southern work.[5]

There were some in the 1880 General Conference who thought that all educational work of the church should be under one board. Recommendations were made that the work of the Freedmen's Aid Society be placed under the Board of Education. After much debate, the General Conference approved the following report and resolution of the Committee on Freedmen's Aid and Southern Work:

Your Committee has had under consideration a paper asking for the consolidation of the Freedmen's Aid Society with the Board of Education, and would recommend the passage of the following resolution:

RESOLVED, That inasmuch as the Freedmen's Aid Society has a specific field, we do not consider it advisable to unite it with the Board of Education.[6]

To the 1880 General Conference M. J. Talbot presented a resolution which was referred to the Committee on Freedmen requesting that the Freedmen's Aid work in the South be placed "in the charge of the Educational, Church Extension, and Missionary Societies."[7]

Report of Freedmen's Aid Society:

The question of transferring the work undertaken by the Freedmen's Aid Society to the Missionary or Church Extension Society was thoroughly discussed by a large and intelligent committee, and the conclusion was reached, with scarcely a dissenting voice, that the greatest advantage to all the interests concerned could be secured by retaining the present distinct organizations of the Church Benevolences, and by vigorously prosecuting the specific work undertaken by each.[8]

Report of Committee on Freedmen's Aid Society and Southern Work:

In view of the work that must be done by this Society in promoting the cause of Christian education in the South, your committee reports the following resolutions for adoption:

RESOLVED 1. That the Freedmen's Aid Society retain its present organization.

RESOLVED 2. That in view of the importance and extent of the work, the contributions to this Society should be largely increased.

RESOLVED 3. That our pastors, in presenting the claims of this society to the church, should remind our people that a portion of the appropriations of this Society will be made for the education of the white population connected with our Church in the Southern states, but not to the embarrassment of the work among our people of color.[9]

As the work of the Freedmen's Aid Society expanded and extended to white people as well as colored, new problems arose. The climate being what it was in the South, the rise of the problem of race in connection with the schools was inevitable.

In the early years of the work of the Freedmen's Aid Society the policy was established that there should be no segregated institutions, neither in schools nor churches. Facing the stern reality of the problem after beginning the educational work with the white people in the South the managers of the Freedmen's Aid and Southern Education Society pursued a course of expediency.

Regarding mixed schools and support of education of white people of the Church in the South, the General Conference of 1884 approved the following resolutions:

RESOLVED 1. That we must sincerely rejoice in the progress made in the work of education among our colored people in the South, and pledge ourselves to stand by and assist them in the further prosecution of this work to the extent of our ability, and, so far as possible, to the extent of their need in this direction.

RESOLVED 2. That we heartily sympathize with our white membership in the South in their efforts to provide adequate educational facilities among themselves, and assure them of such cooperation and assistance as we may be able to render.

RESOLVED 3. That the question of separate or mixed schools we consider one of expediency, which is to be left to the choice and administration of those on the ground and more immediately concerned; PROVIDED, there shall be no interference with the rights set forth in this preamble and these resolutions.

RESOLVED 4. That the entire educational work in the Southern States should be under the direction of one society.

RESOLVED 5. That in view of the great success of the Freedmen's Aid Society during the past four years in carrying forward the educational work in the South, this Society ought to have the full charge of this work in that section.

RESOLVED 6. That the pastors, in presenting the claims of this Society, in making appeals for funds, should state plainly that the work is among both races, and that all contributors should be allowed, when they may desire to do so, to designate where theirs should go.[10]

C. O. Fisher presented the following, signed by T. A. Fortson and twenty-eight others, which was referred to the Committee on Freedmen's Aid:

Whereas, There is now an effort to change the name of the Freedmen's Aid Society of the Methodist Episcopal Church; and

Whereas, we believe that said Society should remain a monument to the colored people for whom it was organized, and that its name is a stimulus in taking collections for it; and

Whereas, we believe that a change of the name of Freedmen's Aid Society is a step that will finally lead to the destruction of said Society; therefore,

RESOLVED, That the name of the Freedmen's Aid Society remain as it now is.[11]

O. E. McIntire presented the following, which was referred to the Committee on Freedmen's Aid Work in the South:

Whereas, The Freedmen's Aid Society was designed by its founders to aid the colored; and

Whereas, There is great objection on the part of the colored people to the change of the name as proposed by the Board of Managers of said Society, therefore,

RESOLVED 1. That the name 'Freedmen's Aid Society' be continued and the Society be especially instructed to raise funds and expend them in aiding colored schools only.

RESOLVED 2. That the white educational work in the Society be hereby transferred to the Board of Education, and that the Charter of said Society be so enlarged as to give that Society power to organize, raise funds, and aid white schools in the South.[12]

Through the educational work begun among Southern white people of the Church in 1880, a number of institutions had been established by 1888. With this development under the direction of the Society, the name "Freedmen's Aid Society" was thought no longer to be appropriate. Resolutions for and against the change were presented to the General Conference of 1888, some of which follow:

Hugh Boyd presented the following which was referred to the Committee on Freedmen's Aid work in the South:

RESOLVED 1. That the name of the Freedmen's Aid Society be changed to the Southern Educational Society and

71

that thirty percent of all funds collected be applied to white schools already in existence.

RESOLVED 2. That no school be established in our white conferences in the South without a majority of the Annual Conferences in which such school is to be erected consenting.[13]

Change of Name

The General Conference of 1888 officially changed the name of the Freedmen's Aid Society* when it adopted the report of its Committee on Freedmen's Aid:

Report of Committee on Freedmen's Aid, etc.
Report No. 1:
RESOLVED 1. That it is the sense of this Committee that in order to secure greater efficiency in the administration of the work of this Society it is expedient to substitute the name Freedmen's Aid and Southern Education Society of the Methodist Episcopal Church, for the present name: Freedmen's Aid Society of the Methodist Episcopal Church.

The work of the Freedmen's Aid and Southern Education Society shall be the establishment and maintenance of institutions of learning in the Southern states among freedmen and others who have special claim upon the people of America for help in the work of Christian education. In presenting the claims of this cause the preacher in charge shall state plainly that the educational work of this Society is among both colored and white people.[14]

Action having been taken by the General Conference changing the name, the Society was legally established under the new name "Freedmen's Aid and Southern Education Society," by the Court of Common Pleas of Hamilton County, State of Ohio, July 27, 1888.[15]

In the General Conference of 1892 there was continued effort to change the name of the Society. The following recommendations presented to the General Conference state some of the reasons for the continued interest in the changing of name:

Recommendations

1. The Name — "It is obvious that the term 'Freedmen' is no longer applicable to any portion of those for whose benefit the work of the Society is prosecuted. During the earlier years the

*See Appendix A.

72

Society extended material aid to the needy and homeless freed people, in addition to its school work; but that form of beneficence has been discontinued, and properly so. Its present mission is educational, and its recognized field comprises the Southern states; hence, we suggest the question of dropping the term 'Freedmen's Aid' — thereby leaving the name 'The Southern Educational Society of the Methodist Episcopal Church' which correctly designates its work.[16]

No action was taken by the General Conference of 1892 effecting the change of the name of the Freedmen's Aid and Southern Education Society.

The discussion of the name of the Society was continued in the 1896 General Conference. Several resolutions were presented requesting that the name be changed again. The Committee on the Freedmen's Aid and Southern Education Society made the following report:

> Your Committee, to whom certain papers touching a change of name for the Society were referred, begs leave to report:
> 1. There are two such papers — one from the Delaware Conference asking that the name be changed to the Southern Education Society, another from the Upper Mississippi Conference asking that no change be made.
> 2. Your Committee, in view of all the facts in the case, the success of the society under its present name, the advantage of retaining that part of the name which keeps distinctly before the Church the people of African descent, and the desirability of preventing the confusion of this with any other society—believe that the name should remain unchanged.[17]

The *Journal* shows that "on motion by D. H. Moore the above report Number 1 by the Committee on Freedmen's Aid and Southern Education Society was adopted."[18]

Indicating the work of the society had expanded in the location of schools, the following report was made:

> Your Committee begs leave to report as follows:
> Location of our schools — In the location of our schools throughout the South the Society has wisely sought to establish institutions of collegiate grade in great centers of Negro population, and where two or more Annual Conferences can be united in their support. Ten institutions of higher grade are located in as many states, extending from Maryland to Texas. The twelve of academic grade are so located as to be feeders to those central institutions, the courses of study so arranged that

73

students can pass from various classes in different departments into classes of a similar grade in the higher schools.

In the work of the Society among the white people of the South the same wise policy has been carried out.

The purpose has been to establish three institutions of collegiate grade among the whites, namely, at Fort Worth, Texas; Little Rock, Arkansas, and Chattanooga and Athens, Tennessee.[19]

Summarization of Actions Taken Re: Freedmen's
Aid and Southern Education Society

In 1872 it was given a place among the connectional agencies of the Church; in 1880, the work was extended to the white people of the South; in 1888, the name was modified by the insertion of the phrase 'Southern Education'; in 1892, two Corresponding Secretaries were elected instead of one, the work of the Society was more clearly defined, and a General Committee provided for, organized in the same manner as those of the Missionary and Church Extension Societies. In each of these successive stages in the development of the Society, the General Conference recognized and fully endorsed what had previously been accomplished, and used its best judgment in providing for the constantly-increasing responsibilities incident to the development of a great educational movement.[20]

On Consolidation of Benevolent Societies

In the interest of economy and effectiveness of services extensive effort was made to combine several of the benevolent organizations of the church.

It was proposed that the home department of the Missionary Society, the Board of Church Extension, and the Freedmen's Aid and Southern Education Society be consolidated. In view of the fact that such a consolidation involved legal questions concerning bequests, annuities, tenure of property, and the change of charters under laws and special enactments of several states, it was thought that hasty legislation by the General Conference (1900) would be unwise. The following action was taken:

BE IT RESOLVED 1. That we do not consider it either advisable or practicable that any consolidation should take place at present.

2. That a commission shall be appointed by the Bishops, which shall consist of three Bishops, six laymen, and six

ministers, which commission shall consider the question of the consolidation of the benevolent societies of the Church, and shall make a plan for consolidation, if it shall be found practicable, and publish such a plan in the Church papers at least one year before the meeting of the next General Conference, and report to the next General Conference.[21]

Commission Report

Plan for Consolidation of the Benevolent
Societies of the Church

The several benevolent societies of the Church shall be consolidated into three, under the following corporate names:

1. The Board of Foreign Missions of the Methodist Episcopal Church.
2. The Board of Home Missions and Church Extension of the Methodist Episcopal Church.
3. The Board of Education of the Methodist Episcopal Church, or the Board of Education, Freedmen's Aid, and Sunday Schools of the Methodist Episcopal Church (as the General Conference may determine). . . .
4. The Freedmen's Aid and Southern Education Society of the Methodist Episcopal Church is hereby directed to obtain from the State of Ohio an amended act of incorporation under the corporate name of 'The Board of Education of the Methodist Episcopal Church,' or, 'The Board of Education, Freedmen's Aid and Sunday Schools of the Methodist Episcopal Church,' but preserving the identity of the existing corporation. And it shall have all the rights and privileges and shall assume all the duties of the Board of Education Incorporated under the laws of the State of New York, and the Sunday School Union, Incorporated under the laws of the State of New York, and the Tract Society Incorporated under the laws of the State of New York. The Office of this Board of Education, etc., shall be in the city of Cincinnati.[22]

The Freedmen's Aid and Southern Education Society of the Methodist Episcopal Church is hereby directed to obtain from the State of Ohio an amended act of incorporation under the corporate name of "The Board of Education of the Methodist Episcopal Church" or "The Board of Education, Freedmen's Aid and Sunday Schools of the Methodist Episcopal Church," but

75

preserving the identity of the existing corporation. And it shall have all the rights and privileges and shall assume all the duties of the Board of Education, Incorporated under the laws of the State of New York, and the Sunday School Union, incorporated under the laws of the State of New York. The office of this Board of Education, etc., shall be in the City of Cincinnati.[23]

To the Board of Education, etc., shall be committed all the work now under the care of the present Board of Education, the Freedmen's Aid and Southern Education Society, and the Sunday School Union and Tract Society.[24]

General Conference Action, 1880 to 1908

The General Conference of 1880 expressed its judgment that white school work was authorized by the charter and that it ought to be maintained as far as practicable without limiting the paramount work of the Society, so that for thirty years it furnished educational aid to schools for each of the races. In 1888 the name was changed to "The Freedmen's Aid and Southern Education Society"[25] to indicate more clearly the field and to express more fully the genius of its work. The General Conference of 1904 provided for the consolidation and readjustment of the work of the Benevolent Boards of the Church. When this consolidation was effected, the Freedmen's Aid Society was merged with the Board of Education and the Sunday School and Tract Society into "The Board of Education, Freedmen's Aid and Sunday Schools." The General Conference of 1908 redistributed the work of this Board to three organizations, putting the white schools of the South under the care of the Board of Education, creating a new Board to which were assigned the Sunday School interests, and restored to the Freedmen's Aid Society its original name and work, namely, "The establishment and maintenance of institutions for Christian education among the colored people of the Southern states and elsewhere." This action took out of the control of the Society twenty-two schools (for white people).

Change of Charter

In 1888 the Charter was changed to The Freedmen's Aid and Southern Education Society, and for twenty years the Society carried on educational work for both races in the South. In 1906, by General Conference action in 1904, the Society was merged with the Board of Education and the Sunday School Union, into the Board of Education, Freedmen's Aid and Sunday Schools, and

76

for two years its work continued in that connection. The General Conference of 1908 at Baltimore re-organized this combination creating The Board of Sunday Schools, The Board of Education, and The Freedmen's Aid Society out of the combined Societies. The white work in the South was put in charge of the Board of Education, and the Freedmen's Aid Society restored to its original name and work, having in charge at the time of the separation eight years ago 22 schools, with 505 teachers and 7,661 students, and a property valuation including real estate, buildings, and equipment of $1,452,698.[26]

The educational work for Negroes of the Methodist Episcopal Church continued under the name of The Freedmen's Aid Society until May, 1920.

Establishment of Department of Educational Institutions
    for Negroes

At the 1920 General Conference there was a great deal of sentiment in favor of changing the name of the Freedmen's Aid Society to a more appropriate name inasmuch as more than a half century had passed since emancipation and freedom. The following recommendations were presented to the General Conference and approval given, the resolution having been adopted May 24, 1920.

In accordance with this General Conference action, the name and charter of this Board were changed from the Freedmen's Aid Society of the Methodist Episcopal Church, to The Board of Education for Negroes, of the Methodist Episcopal Church, incorporated under the laws of the State of Ohio.[27]

The Board of Education for Negroes remained a corporation, but was a part of the General Board of Education of the Methodist Episcopal Church. By legislation of the General Conference of 1924, the Board of Education for Negroes became a department of Education for Negroes within the General Board of Education.[27]

In 1928 by action of both the General Conference and the Board of Education, interests of Negro education were made more fully integrated with those of all the educational institutions of the Church. The Department of Education for Negroes remained unchanged through the remaining years of the Methodist Episcopal Church down to unification, 1939. After unification in 1939 and reorganization of benevolent agencies of the church, the

Department of Educational Institutions for Negroes continued as a part of the General Board of Education of the Church and remains so to the present, known as the Department of Educational Institutions for Negroes, Division of Higher Education.

Of much significance after unification of the three branches of Methodism in 1939 and the reorganization in 1940 was the election of a Negro Associate Secretary to the Staff of the Board of Education to represent primarily the interest of higher education for Negro youth in The Methodist Church. Dr. Matthew Simpson Davage, a layman and an outstanding educator in the Church for several decades, was elected to this new position of Associate Secretary and held the position with distinction and exceptional service to the Church at large from 1940 to the time of his retirement in 1952. Dr. Davage was succeeded in this position by the Reverend Dr. James S. Thomas, who gave able leadership in this work until he was elected to the Episcopacy in 1964. Dr. Daniel W. Wynn succeeded Dr. Thomas as Associate Secretary and is the present incumbent.

78

LUKE HITCHCOCK, D. D.   ADAM POE, D. D.   J. M. REID, D. D.   B. F. CRARY, D. D.
J. M. WALDEN, D. D., Sec'y.   BISHOP CLARK, Pres't.   R. S. RUST, D. D.
ROB'T ALLYN, D. D.   JUDGE GOODRICH.   T. M. EDDY, D. D.   J. F. LARKIN, Esq.

Founders of Freedmen's Aid Society of the Methodist Episcopal Church, 1866.

Bishop Davis W. Clark, First President of the Freedmen's Aid Society.

Left, Bishop John M. Walden, First Corresponding Secretary of the Freedmen's Aid Society. Right, Dr. Richard S. Rust, First Field Agent of the Freedmen's Aid Society.

First Officers of the Woman's Home Missionary Society, Founded 1880. Left, Mrs. Lucy Webb Hayes. Right, Mrs. Elizabeth L. Rust.

William H. Grogman, First Negro Teacher Employed by the Freedmen's Aid Society.

John Wesley Gilbert, Graduate of Paine College and First Negro Teacher Employed at Paine.

Aerial View of Bennett College Campus. Exclusive of Upper Left Portion.

John O. Gross Science Hall, Bethune-Cookman College.

Richard V. Moore Gymnasium, Bethune-Cookman College.

High Rise Dormitory for Men, Claflin College.

H. V. Manning Library, Claflin College.

E. O. Thayer Hall, Clark College.

H. W. Warren-Gilbert Haven Hall, Clark College.

Aerial View of Dilllard University Campus.

Agard-Lovinggood Administration Building, Huston-Tillotson College.

Library, Huston-Tillotson College.

Gilbert-Lamberth Chapel and Music Hall, Paine College.

George Williams Walker Science Building, Paine College.

M. L. Harris Library and Fine Arts Center, Philander Smith College.

Commencement Scene, Philander Smith College.

Aerial View of Rust College Campus.

Willis Jefferson King Administration Building, Wiley College.

Aaron Baker Science Building, Wiley College.

Gammon Hall Interdenominational Theological Center.

Wallace Hall—Men's Dormitory, Kenwood Refectory—Dining Hall, Crary Hall —Girl's Dormitory, Morristown College.

Hulda M. Lyttle Hall—Nurses' Residence, Meharry Medical College.

Group of Buildings, Meharry Medical College.

REFERENCES AND NOTES

1. Sixth Annual Report, Freedmen's Aid Society, 1873, p. 5.
2. General Conference Journal, 1876, p. 135.
3. General Conference Journal, 1876, p. 310.
4. General Conference Journal, 1876, p. 311.
5. General Conference Journal, 1880, p. 293.
6. General Conference Journal, 1880, p. 295.
7. General Conference Journal, 1880, p. 243.
8. *Ibid.*, p. 621.
9. General Conference Journal, 1880, p. 345 (cf. Freedmen's Aid Society Report).
10. General Conference Journal, 1884, p. 366.
11. General Conference Journal, 1884, p. 232.
12. *Ibid.*, pp. 194f.
13. General Conference Journal, 1888, p. 202.
14. General Conference Journal, 1888, p. 451.
15. See attached Exhibit, p. 12a.
16. General Conference Journal, 1892, p. 702.
17. General Conference Journal, 1892, p. 409.
18. General Conference Journal, 1892, p. 178.
19. General Conference Journal, 1896, pp. 409-410.
20. General Conference Journal, 1896, p. 212.
21. General Conference Journal, 1900, pp. 463, 464.
22. General Conference Journal, 1904, pp. 530-532.
23. General Conference Journal, 1904, pp. 666-667.
24. General Conference Journal, 1904, p. 531.
25. Freedmen's Aid Society Report, July 1888, p. 6. (Decree changing name).
26. General Conference Journal, 1920, pp. 639f.
27. *The Christian Educator*, May, 1924, p. 1.

CHAPTER 6

THE FREEDMEN'S AID SOCIETY, THE FIRST
FIFTY YEARS — 1866-1916

Dedication and Opposition

The Freedmen's Aid Society established itself firmly in the Southern region early after its organization, rendered effective service, and performed a yeoman task during the first half century of its existence. There has never been a group in the Church that went to its task with more zeal, enthusiasm, dedication and determination than the early leaders of the Freedmen's Aid Society. They approached the work and persevered with complete abandon, and with a willingness to suffer ostracism, to vie with incredible difficulties, and to sacrifice all but the joy of dedicated service.

The corresponding secretaries of the Freedmen's Aid Society, the missionaries who went into the South in connection with the Missionary and Church Extension Society, the early presidents and principals of the schools, and the early teachers faced stern and abusive opposition. They had to confine their social life for the most part to the schools where they worked and to the constituency for whom they labored. They were ostracized in the communities and were not welcomed even to the established Methodist churches of the South. Consequently, they identified themselves with the churches established by the Church Extension Society of the Methodist Episcopal Church and with the Conferences which were then mixed, and also with the Negro churches. It was difficult for the workers to extend themselves into the larger community and get the support which would have made progress much more rapid. But in the face of opposition and difficulties these devotees to this task persevered and accomplished a magnificent work.

The Negro Problem

The leaders in the Freedmen's Aid Society always linked the work of the schools and the church to the "Negro problem." The Negro problem was the central difficulty in the Southern region

81

during this period and because of its historic background and growing intensity, it became recognized as the American problem. In almost every report of the corresponding secretaries the "Negro problem" is discussed along with the work accomplished in the schools.

Despite these difficulties, the work was extended and rapid progress was made. At the end of the first decade of the work of the Freedmen's Aid Society, a report was given to the General Conference of 1876. This report states, in part:

> Our Society is also a factor in the social and civil problems of the South. It is demonstrating that the freedmen may become good scholars and accomplished teachers, thereby preparing the way for the introduction of a public free-school system. It encourages them to fit themselves for positions of responsibility, where their moral worth as well as mental requirements, must be recognized. It sustains a large corps of Christian teachers, whose efficiency as instructors is only equalled by their zeal in true missionary work — men and women whose unselfish devotion is a constant interpretation of the Christian love of those who give to this cause — men and women whose very presence is an inspiration to those who are struggling up from an entailed degradation.[1]

Concerns of Freedmen's Aid Society Leaders

With reference to the extent of the work of the schools and the nature of the accomplishments the report to the General Conference in 1876 states further that:

> The influence of the Society is felt all over the South. Fifty thousand have been taught in its day, and a larger number in its Sunday Schools. Hundreds of preachers now laboring among this people and thousands of teachers engaged in instructing the children have been taught in institutions established and sustained by this Society, which has provided in the South a school property worth more than two hundred thousand dollars.[2]

It becomes clear that the Freedmen's Aid Society during the first half century was dealing with certain basic problems, the solution of which was essential to the development and progress of the Negro people. First and foremost as indicated above was the race problem. The Freedmen's Aid Society was also deeply concerned with the religious life of the students and the

82

motivation of these young people for service to their people in America and in Africa. There was no less interest in and emphasis upon the cultural development of the students in the schools which might have its outreach into the community. Because of the deprived cultural background of the newly freed people it was important to lay stress upon cultural development; not so much a vain type of cultural development, but fundamental culture that would give these people in themselves a desire to acquire the highest type of dignity as persons and as a group.

The education emphasized throughout the first fifty years had as one of its chief aims to strengthen the Negro group economically. This was one reason why so much emphasis was placed upon manual arts and industrial education. It was thought that the best way for the Negro to gain independence was through productive labor and the development of economic strength.

The missionaries and the educators in connection with the Freedmen's Aid Society were not alone in this philosophy regarding the development of the Negro group. The Negroes themselves had ambitions to acquire these developments. These were the longings of their souls and they committed themselves to the attainments of these objectives with hope and sacrificial efforts.

Schools Established

The schools developed rapidly and over a wide geographical area during the first decade of the Freedmen's Aid Society.

This Society has been operating since November 1, 1866, a period of seventeen months, and in view of the embarrassments with which it has had to contend, it has accomplished a noble work — one that cannot fail to encourage the hearts of all interested in the oppressed race.[3]

Within the first seventeen months of the operation of the Freedmen's Aid Society in the South fifty-nine schools were established as follows:[4]

Tennessee	17
Georgia	11
Alabama	4
Kentucky	3
Louisiana	9
Mississippi	1
Arkansas	1

Virginia	3
S. Carolina	8
N. Carolina	2
	59

After it became evident that the church could not supply the South with elementary and secondary schools, and that it was not expedient to try to do so even if it could, the Society then began to withdraw from the elementary field and to concentrate on academies, preparatory schools, and colleges. They reduced the number and attempted to improve the quality.

By 1900 all of the institutions listed below had been established by the Freedmen's Aid Society, and some support given. While the Society discontinued the practice of establishing separate and independent elementary schools, there were elementary schools attached to all of the institutions listed below. Some of the academies and normal schools were discontinued or combined with other institutions by 1916. The elementary grades were attached to all of the academies and colleges well into the 1920's and 1930's.

Following are lists of institutions for Negroes founded and supported by the Freedmen's Aid Society within its first fifty years of history:[5]

Colleges

1. Bennett College, Greensboro, North Carolina
2. Central Tennessee College, Nashville, Tennesee (Later Walden University)
3. Claflin University, Orangeburg, South Carolina
4. Clark College, Atlanta, Georgia
5. Samuel Huston College, Austin, Texas
6. Morristown College, Morristown, Tennessee
7. Morgan College, Baltimore, Maryland
8. New Orleans University, New Orleans, Louisiana
9. Shaw University, Holly Springs, Mississippi (Later Rust College)
10. Philander Smith College, Little Rock, Arkansas
11. George R. Smith College, Sedalia, Missouri
12. Wiley University, Marshall, Texas

Academies

1. Alexandria Academy, Alexandria, Louisiana
2. Baldwin Seminary, Baldwin, Louisiana

84

3. Centenary Biblical Institute, Baltimore, Maryland (Later Morgan College)
4. Central Alabama Academy, Huntsville, Alabama
5. Cookman Institute, Jacksonville, Florida
6. Delaware Academy, Princess Anne, Maryland
7. Gilbert Academy, Baldwin, Louisiana
8. Haven Academy, Waynesboro, Georgia
9. Key West Academy, Key West, Florida
10. LaGrange Academy, LaGrange, Georgia
11. Meridian Academy, Meridian, Mississippi
12. Normal School, Rome, Georgia
13. Richmond Normal School, Richmond, Virginia
14. Rust Biblical and Normal Institute, Huntsville, Alabama (Later Central Alabama College)
15. Texas Training School, Austin, Texas (Later Samuel Huston College)
16. Union Normal School, New Orleans, Louisiana
17. Virginia Collegiate and Industrial Institute, Lynchburg, Virginia
18. West Tennessee Academy, Mason, Tennessee
19. Orphan Home, Baldwin, Louisiana
20. LaTeche Seminary, Baldwin, Louisiana

Theological School
1. Gammon Theological Seminary, Atlanta, Georgia
Medical School
1. Meharry Medical School, Nashville, Tennessee

During this same period, 1866-1916, the institutions established in the South for whites were as follows: colleges and/or universities, 3; academies, 19.[6]

Types of Schools Established

As has already been pointed out, the early schools established had to be of necessity elementary schools. Within the first two years of the work of the Freedmen's Aid Society in the south, 59 elementary schools were established. By 1868 there were three normal schools and institutes. Some of the elementary schools developed into academic and preparatory schools within a few years and later into colleges. The same is true of the normal institutes. After 1872 less emphasis was placed upon the establishment of elementary schools and more emphasis upon the development of schools already established to higher levels of work. By 1884 there were seven institutions of collegiate rank, four theological schools, one medical school and several academies and preparatory schools. By 1900, 34 years after the founding of the first school in the gun-factory at Nashville, Tennessee, there were twenty institutions operating as academies and preparatory schools, eleven colleges with curricula leading to the Bachelor of Arts or Bachelor of Science degree, one Junior College, one theological school and one medical school. By this time the several theological departments related to the colleges had been transferred to Gammon Theological Seminary in Atlanta, Georgia, which was established in 1883, and became separately chartered in 1888.

The report of the Freedmen's Aid Society, November, 1912, shows nine academies and preparatory schools, eleven four-year colleges, one theological school and two medical schools.[7] The elementary schools supported by the Freedmen's Aid Society were located on the same campuses as the academies and colleges, the emphasis being upon developing the institutions upward and strengthening the college work. By the end of the first fifty years, 1916, there were still nine academies and preparatory schools being supported by the Society, eleven four-year colleges, one junior college, one theological school, and two medical schools. The end of the first half century extended into the period when increasing emphasis was being placed upon standardization. Therefore it was necessary for the Freedmen's Aid Society to continue to reduce the work of the lower level schools and to concentrate upon improving the four-year college.

The Enrollments

The enrollments in the elementary schools were understandably large. Here is where the educational efforts were concentrated during the first few years of the work of the Freedmen's Aid Society. During the period 1866 through 1868 the report shows that over 7,000 students were enrolled at the elementary school level.[8] The report of the Freedmen's Aid Society in 1885 shows the distribution of enrollments as follows: the academic and preparatory schools, 530; college enrollments, 120; enrollment in the normal schools, 1,610; in the theological school, 310; and in the medical school, 60; intermediate, 980; and primary, 653; total of 4,263.[9]

By 1900 there were 7,054 students enrolled in the academies and preparatory schools of the Society. There were 246 enrolled at the college level, 233 in the theological school and 354 in the medical schools.[10] By 1916 the number of students enrolled in the academy and preparatory schools had dropped to 1,756 and the college enrollment had gone up to 3,250. In this year there were only 79 theological students while the number of medical school students had climbed to 590.[11]

In the early years of the work of the Freedmen's Aid Society teachers were scarce. The only supply had to come from the North. The 1868 report shows a total of 80 teachers employed in all of the schools;[12] in 1884 there were 105 teachers;[13] in 1900 there were 416 teachers reported;[14] by 1912, the number had decreased to 366[15] and in 1916 the total was 351.[16] The drop in teachers in 1912-1916 might be attributed to two factors: one is the fact that the work at the elementary school level was being diminished and eliminated and the enrollments became more sparse as movement was made from the lower to the higher levels. The second factor is that during the period 1912-1916 World War I was in progress and this, plus the economic depression, affected the number of students in school and the number of prepared teachers available for employment.

Total Plant Value

When the work of the Freedmen's Aid Society began in 1866 it owned no property and almost in every case the school founded had a humble beginning in an old building that had been used for other purposes or in the basement of a church. Beginning with no grounds or buildings the Society by 1884 had purchased land and erected buildings with a total value of $366,000.[16a] By 1900, sixteen years later, the plant value had increased to $1,407,700[17] and to a $1,409,965 increase in 1912.[18] By 1916, the plant value of the schools owned by the Freedmen's Aid Society amounted to $1,886,200.[19] In addition, equipment and furniture amounted to $121,550. The total value of plant and equipment was $2,007,750.[20]

Total Endowment

The Freedmen's Aid Society held no endowments for its schools until 1884. The report shows for this year $63,000.[21] By 1912 there was a total endowment of $565,249.31.[22] Of this amount Gammon Theological Seminary held $462,764.62.[23] By 1916 the endowment of Gammon Theological Seminary had increased to $505,524.85.[24] The Freedmen's Aid Society held endowment for several other schools totaling $174,640.35,[25] making a grand total of $680,165.20 in endowment for the institutions for Negro youth of the Freedmen's Aid Society.

REFERENCES AND NOTES

1. Journal of the General Conference, 1876, p. 617.
2. Journal of the General Conference, 1876, p. 623f.
3. Report, Freedmen's Aid Society, 1868, p. 7.
4. Report, Freedmen's Aid Society, 1868, p. 10.
5. Various Freedmen's Aid Society Reports.
6. Freedmen's Aid and Southern Education Report, December-January, 1899-1900, p. 48f.
7. Report, Freedmen's Aid Society, November, 1912, p. 9.
8. Freedmen's Aid Society Report, 1868, p. 10.
9. Freedmen's Aid Society Report, 1885, p. 5.
10. General Conference Journal, 1900, p. 756.
11. General Conference Journal, 1916, p. 1419.
12. Freedmen's Aid Society Report, 1868, p. 15.
13. Freedmen's Aid Society Report, 1884, p. 605.
14. General Conference Journal, 1900, p. 754.
15. General Conference Journal, 1912, p. 1278.
16. General Conference Journal, 1916, p. 1419.
16a. General Conference Journal, 1884, pp. 620ff.
17. General Conference Journal, 1900, pp. 754f.
18. *The Christian Educator*, November, 1912, p. 9; also General Conference Journal, 1916, p. 1419.
19. *The Christian Educator*, May, 1916, p. 22; General Conference Journal 1916, p. 1419.
20. *Ibid.*
21. General Conference Journal, 1884, pp 620ff.
22. General Conference Journal, 1912, pp 1273ff.
23. General Conference Journal, 1912, p. 1273.
24. General Conference Journal, 1916.
25. *Ibid.*, p. 1409.

PART III.

FOUNDING AND DEVELOPMENT OF INSTITUTIONS, 1866-1916

CHAPTER 7

PROBLEMS, POLICIES, OBJECTIVES, AND PHILOSOPHY

The Problem Re-emphasized

The problem in 1866 was one that was two and one-half centuries old — the race problem. The Civil War and Emancipation shifted the problem to a different battleground and made possible other approaches. The problem was not merely historical and current. Its magnitude and depth projected it far into the future. Another 100 years have passed. Much progress has been made, but the problem of human relations and injustices still haunt, beset, and perplex the Church and nation.

The problem in 1866 which beset the leaders of the Methodist Episcopal Church, which were barriers and handicaps to the Freedmen and to those who worked with them through the Freedmen's Aid Society, may be expressed as follows:

1. The Freedmen were *Negroes* and constituted a caste in the American society. Being Negroes unfortunately carried degrading connotations.

2. They had been slaves and were victims of all sorts of psychological, sociological and degrading effects of slavery.

3. The Freedmen were thought, particularly by the South, to be inferior. This stigma had been borne for centuries and had been drilled into the mind and very being of the former slaves.

4. They were illiterate. Not having much of an opportunity for learning to read and write, approximately 90 percent of the Freedmen were illiterate.

5. They were thought to be incapable of learning and becoming educated.

6. The Freedmen were destitute economically — they were homeless, jobless, and helpless.

7. In a large measure the Freedmen were disintegrated. Their families had been separated and their homes broken. Family and home rehabilitation was imperative before the work of elevation and education could become effective.

8. They were for the most part common laborers, not having

91

had a chance to prepare for any occupation other than menial labor.

9. They were not considered citizens. Their citizenship had to be established by constitutional amendments (13th, 14th and 15th Amendments) and incessant efforts for decades following.

10. They had no rights that were thought should be respected by the white South.

11. The climate of the region both local, and regional, was not conducive to the development of the Freedmen economically, politically, socially, and educationally. They were ignorant of the new ways of life inherent in freedom. Their problems had to be approached and assistance given through the Church.

The Freedmen had a passionate desire for recognition; for the achievement of manhood, citizenship, and education; and to rise above their conditions. The work of the Church with the Freedmen was carried on with strong missionary zeal as a continuation of the interest it had had in the slaves and the abolition of slavery. Had it not been for the interest of the Methodist Episcopal Church in slavery during the period of almost a century prior to Emancipation, there might not have been the sustained labors and sacrifices by this Church for the uplift and education of the Freedmen. The leaders in this movement had a thorough grasp and a profound understanding of the problems of the Freedmen and the kind of ministry needed. In an early report to the General Conference it was stated that:

The grave problem in regard to this people, which has long baffled both statesmen and Christians, is being wrought out in our own day. While the Government is investing the neglected and despised bondsmen with freedom, the way opens for Christian benevolence to throw around them those elevating influences of civilization by which they may be prepared for the higher achievements of man. The way opens for the Church of Christ to carry to them the Gospel which, instead of countenancing their servitude, sanctions their liberty and recognizes their manhood.[1]

Policies Relating to Church and Schools

In the period immediately preceding Emancipation and for several decades afterwards, the Methodist Episcopal Church struggled with policies within the Church relating to people of

92

color. In the light of the social status of the Freedmen and the existing Southern opinion, with historic roots, regarding them as a race, it was imperative that every effort be made to establish policies with reference to both church and schools that would enhance the human dignity of the Freedmen and accord them all recognition as men. In this connection the establishment of several Negro annual conferences had much debate. Several General Conferences had voted against the establishment of separate annual conferences for colored people. Memorials from Negroes had been presented to the General Conference as early as 1848 for separate Negro conferences. The 1864 General Conference on recommendation of a special committee authorized the organization of one or more Negro mission conferences.[2] The Delaware Conference was organized as the first Negro Annual Conference of the Methodist Episcopal Church.[3] The same General Conference (1864) authorized the Bishops, when in their judgment they deemed it expedient, within the next four years, to organize a conference or conferences within the Southern states and territories.[4]

After the close of the Civil War reconstruction of Methodism among Negroes in the South by the Methodist Episcopal Church and providing education for the Freedmen went hand in hand. Policies adopted applied to conferences and schools alike. The General Conference of 1860 received memorials asking for the extension of powers of the conferences (Mission) of Colored Local Preachers. Such extension of powers would have given conferences of Colored Local Preachers the status of an Annual Conference. The General Conference did not grant the extended powers requested, but appointed a special committee on the state of the work among people of color. The appointment of the Special Committee was supported by the address of the Bishops in 1864 which declared in part:

> The Provision adopted by the General Conference in 1856, though an advance on former legislation, is not, we believe, sufficient to meet the necessities of the colored people. The time has now come, in our judgment, when the General Conference should carefully consider what measures can be adopted to give increased efficiency to our church among them.[5]

On recommendation of the Special Committee the General Conference authorized the organization of one or more Negro Mission Conferences "where the exigencies of the work may demand it" with the provision that white ministers might be transferred to them "when it may be practicable and deemed necessary."[6]

In 1864 the General Conference also authorized the Bishops, 'when in their judgment they deemed it expedient, within the next four years, to organize a Conference or Conferences in the Southern States and in the Territories.'[7]

In their address at the 1868 General Conference the Bishops reported that 'under the specific authority' given them four years before, nine Conferences had been organized in that part 'of our Southern territory' not previously included in Annual Conferences. . . .The majority of the preachers were freedmen, many of whom as slaves had been licensed Local Preachers. The total number of Traveling Preachers in 1871, according to a computation made by L. C. Matlack, was 630, of whom 250 were white and 370 were Negroes. Lay members in the same year numbered approximately 135,000, of whom 47,000 were white and 83,000 were of African descent.[8]

The 1868 General Conference repealed the action of 1864 which, in determining that the Conferences formed in the southern states should be 'Mission Conferences': restricted their rights and privileges and declared the Alabama, Delaware, Georgia, Holston, Mississippi, South Carolina, Tennessee, Texas, Virginia and North Carolina, and Washington Conferences to be Annual Conferences 'vested with all the rights, privileges and immunities usual to Annual Conferences.' In anticipation of this action these Conferences had elected provisional delegates — twenty-five in number — who on presentation of their credentials were admitted to membership in General Conferences. Thus for the first time in the history of the Church Negroes were seated as General Conference delegates.[9]

It was the policy of the Methodist Episcopal Church to maintain mixed conferences all over the Church wherever there were Negro members and churches. This policy extended into the Southern States and the establishment of Annual Conferences after the Civil War. A large number of Negroes thought that separate Annual Conferences would give them a better chance to administer the conferences and develop the kind of leadership desired. A trend was developing for Negroes to seek independence and separateness in churches and other organizations. There was a division of opinion on this question among both Negro and white groups. Dr. J. C. Hartzell said:

It is not a question of social equality among the races. That

94

is a question no legislation can touch, either in State or Church. It is not a question of compelling the races to sit in the same Church. That is a matter which must largely, if not altogether, be left to the people themselves. It is not a question of the organization of districts in the annual conferences. . . .What, then, is the question? It is this: Shall all our ministers in the same territory in the South meet together once a year in conference, colored and white, just as we meet on this floor, and together transact the business of the Church, and receive their appointments from its Bishop? But, it is said, if we allow the people to organize Churches, and sometimes even districts, separately, why not so organize conferences? Why, sir, the difference is distinct and broad. In the one case you submit for the time being to the wishes of the localities, even though prejudice may rule, but in the other you commit the Church by legislation to a separation based upon race distinction. . . .To my mind we stand at a pivotal point, in the history of the Church. Let us do right, and our children will commend us. Separate on the color line, and we stab our friends in the South, and bring upon us the contempt of our enemies.[10]

Under the authority given the Bishops by the General Conference to organize separate conferences, this development took place rapidly. The separate conferences were mixed racially and did not all become exclusively Negro conferences for several quadrennia.

Both in the organization of conferences and the establishment of schools and colleges in the South the policy of the Methodist Episcopal Church was retained to have all institutions open to all. The General Conference of 1884 expressed itself on this matter and recorded the following discussion and action in its Minutes:

Inasmuch as there has been a great deal of discussion, both in the religious and secular press, of caste in the Methodist Episcopal Church; and inasmuch as caste is a curse to any nation, and more especially to a religious denomination, and inasmuch as we believe that caste prejudice is a sin, and is born of ignorance and hate; that it narrows the mind, imbitters the heart, and harms the American citizens both as men and as Christians; therefore, be it

Resolved, That it is the sense of this General Conference that no trustees of church, school, colleges, or universities, nor any pastor, principal, president, or any other person in authority of church or school property, belonging to or under the control of the Methodist Episcopal Church, should exclude any person or persons from their churches, schools, colleges, or universities, of good moral character, on account of race, color, or previous condition of servitude.[11]

The same General Conference (1884) heard a similar resolution declaring its policy on race:

Resolved, That this General Conference declares the policy of the Methodist Episcopal Church to be, that no member of any society within the Church shall be excluded from public worship in any and every edifice of the denomination, and no student shall be excluded from instruction in any and every school under the supervision of the Church, because of race, color, or previous condition of servitude.[12]

This resolution was adopted.[13]

Although the General Conference took two separate actions affirming the policy of the Church on the matter of race and color, it also approved a resolution in the report of the Freedmen's Aid Society which left the matter of mixed schools to "the choice and administration of those on the ground and more immediately concerned."[14] This was probably the first indication of a weakening by the Northern workers in the South and an inclination to substitute expediency for strong policy adopted by the General Conference.

The leaders and representatives of the Methodist Episcopal Church working in the South faced real and difficult problems. Although they did not yield their convictions, it was necessary to view the possibilities of their accomplishments in a practical manner. In the climate and amidst difficulties they had to proceed in a manner that guaranteed the maximum successful achievements. Cameron says that "some of the hopes entertained by the Northerners were visionary, and some of their methods were questionable, but there is no doubt that they were carried forward to sacrificial and beneficial work by a genuine sense of mission."[15]

Apart from the fact that Southern Methodists regarded the Northern occupation of the section as schismatic, they deemed the actions and affiliations of the representatives of the Methodist Episcopal Church their sufficient grounds for excluding them from all fellowship with themselves. As a result the missionaries were socially ostracized by their co-religionists in a fashion that caused much sectional bitterness. Aggrieved at his presence and seeing in him only the politician and the

96

incendiary, the Southerner sought to avoid contact with the missionary whenever possible.[16]

Concerns of the Freedmen's Aid Society Movement

There were specific concerns which motivated the workers. (1) They were concerned in the early stages of their work with the conditions and welfare of the Freedmen. These conditions have been pointed out above. (2) There was concern and a deep desire to give the status of equality as a man and as a citizen to all Freedmen. (3) In order to achieve status the Freedmen had to develop economic strength. A part of the concern of the Freedmen's Aid Society was to help the Freedmen achieve this economic strength. (4) There was concern for political involvement and development of citizenship. (5) As a framework for achieving the objectives of its work, the Freedmen's Aid Society worked for the establishment of Annual Conferences to facilitate the programs and activities. (6) The major concern of the Freedmen's Aid Society was to establish schools and colleges, to complement the Annual Conferences of the Church, and to provide leadership for the Church, and the larger community of the Freedmen.

The Freedmen's Aid Society and the Missionary and Church Extension Societies of the Methodist Episcopal Church joined hands and combined their efforts at many points in their work for the Freedmen in the South. This was in the plan from the inception of the Freedmen's Aid Society. "Missionaries and teachers unitedly cultivate this vast field, and harvest sheaves for the garner of the Lord."[17]

The purpose of the missionary work of the Methodist Episcopal Church in the South developed inviting openings for schools among Freedmen and demonstrated that such schools are essential to its highest usefulness among that people.[18] The missionaries acknowledged their indebtedness to the teachers for valuable assistance and gave assurance that they find their most efficient aid in gaining access to the hearts of the people. The educational work was seen as being closely related to missions, aiming at the culture of the heart as well as the intellect.[19]

Our policy has been to sustain schools in places selected by our missionaries, so that teachers and ministers might cooperate in elevating and saving the people. The teachers cooperate with the missionaries in preaching the Gospel, holding meetings, sustaining Sunday-schools, and in every good work calculated to educate the people, and save their souls.[20]

General Educational Objectives. The general objectives of the Freedmen's Aid Society were (1) to provide elementary education through the common schools established and supervised by the Society. (2) To provide Christian education which was emphasized in the common schools of the Society and extended through the whole system of education to the highest level of academic preparation. Biblical study was the main source of training in this area. (3) It was the general aim of the Freedmen's Aid Society to provide for the literary and cultural attainment of the students. (4) Special emphasis was placed upon professional attainment in the areas of theological training and teacher training. Later the objectives included training in medicine and law. (5) Preparatory education was provided as a background and foundation for collegiate work. (6) Industrial training was listed among the objectives early in the development of the educational program.

Because of the high percentage of illiteracy and the absence of public schools the Freedmen's Aid Society conceived its first task to be to help the Freedmen become literate and to master the fundamental tools of education. The Society therefore established elementary schools at the beginning and taught the basic elements of reading, writing, and arithmetic. Everywhere the educational program was initiated there was need to begin with these fundamentals of learning.

Philosophy. The leaders in the Freedmen's Aid work had great faith in the possibilities of reform through the schools they established, and they had great faith in the capacities of the learners. In the Report of 1869 of the Society it is stated:

> Only give them an opportunity and they will furnish a demonstration of their ability to range the more elevated fields of thought as well as of the humbler walks of science. Time and the facilities for culture will vindicate the capacities of this race, and intellect will soar above the distinctions of color, and assert its claim to an equality of privilege and attainment.[21]

It was thought by the Freedmen's Aid Society that its work in education among the Freedmen should prepare them for living and for making a living. The first emphasis was upon the Christian aspects of life and upon church life. It was thought that education should give motivation for service. Therefore the Christian religion was the broad and solid foundation upon which all education was to be built.

The civic and community life was important. In the schools the

98

Freedmen were taught the function and importance of government and believed that good citizenship was the result of knowledge and a clear understanding of government, and participation in all forms of government from the local level to the national level.

Preparation for the improvement of the economic life was an essential part of the philosophy of the leaders of the Freedmen's Aid Society. Consequently, provisions were made for educational training that would lead to proficiency in skilled labor. Industrial education and manual training assumed an important position in the system of education established. After several decades of growth most of the schools established, carried industrial departments, some of which provided an extensive and elaborate program of industrial training and mechanics.

The development of the cultural life of the Freedmen, particularly those that attended these schools, was most important. In establishing the various levels of education the beginning was made with the elementary school and finally reached the college and university. The provisions for the development of the cultural life through education were in the areas of liberal arts, classical education, philosophy, and the fine arts. Within an almost incredibly short time the students were studying the higher elements of English, literary criticism, higher mathematics, Latin, Greek, philosophy, and other cultural branches.

The philosophy of the Freedmen's Aid Society provided professional preparation in theology, teacher training, medicine, dentistry, and law. Many of the early schools established developed into colleges and universities with courses for preparation in these professional areas.

Many of the "colleges" and "universities" were not really educational institutions of these levels at the beginning, but they represented the hope that the Freedmen's Aid Society had for these schools as colleges and universities. This hope in numerous cases was translated into good institutions that became worthy of being called colleges and universities.

The schools from the elementary level to the university level reflected the philosophy of the leaders of the Freedmen's Aid Society and reflected also their great faith in the capacities and abilities of Negro students to master any and all of the branches of learning and to fulfill the needs for educational endeavors and accomplishments in society.

Emphasis upon Life Work

Throughout the first half century of the work of the Freedmen's Aid Society, great emphasis from the elementary school level through the college was upon preparation for a life's work. Making a life was emphasized with as much importance as making a living. Students were taught the sacredness of life and the importance of the use of one's life as being as sacred as life itself. The philosophy underlying this emphasis was made explicit that life's fulfillment comes in the use made of one's life.

With the emphasis on the sacredness of life the service motive became paramount and usefulness and service to community and to the church were real goals. The evangelistic mood of the time and the missionary zeal of the northern workers in these schools as well as the missionary emphasis in the northern church stimulated a missionary zeal in the students. The one purpose which was basic in the education sought was service to the oppressed group of which the students were a part and service as missionaries in Africa. It was out of this kind of climate and emphasis that the motto for one of the colleges came, namely, "Culture for Service."

As a part of the curriculum religious instruction was strongly emphasized. This was a part of the philosophy of education of the period and this emphasis extended to all the institutions founded and controlled by the several denominations.

There was always a consciousness on the part of the leaders of the Freedmen's Aid Society, and the Presidents and teachers in these schools that the intellectual and moral and religious elevation of the students was not only a good philosophy but a relevant development in the life of the students as a part of the spiritual dimension of his education.

REFERENCES AND NOTES

1. Freedmen's Aid and Southern Education Society, 1868-77, p. 7; cf. *General Conference Journal,* 1864, p. 441.
2. *General Conference Journal,* 1864, pp. 486f.
3. Barclay, W. C., *History of Methodist Missions,* III, 304.
4. *Ibid.*
5. *General Conference Journal,* 1864, Appendix, p. 279.
6. Barclay, *op cit.,* p. 303.
7. *Ibid.,* p. 304.
8. *Ibid.,* p. 309.
9. Barclay, *op. cit.,* p. 303.
10. Quoted from Barclay, p. 316. Original Source: *Christian Advocate,* LI (1876), 23 (June 3), 182.
11. *Journal of the General Conference,* 1884, p. 128.
12. *Ibid.,* p. 334.
13. *Ibid.,* 1884, p. 280.
14. *Ibid.,* 1884, p. 366 (Resolution 3).
15. Cameron, Richard M., *Methodism and Society in Historical Perspective,* p. 200.
16. Farish, Hunter D., *The Circuit Rider Dismounts, A Social History of Southern Methodism, 1865-1900,* p. 158.
17. Report of the Freedmen's Aid Society, 1868, p. 11.
18. Report of the Freedmen's Aid Society, 1866-75, Organization Convention, p. 13.
19. *Ibid.*
20. Fourth Annual Report, Freedmen's Aid and Southern Education Society, 1871, p. 5.
21. Third Annual Report of the Freedmen's Aid Society, 1869, p. 4.

CHAPTER 8

THE ESTABLISHMENT AND DESCRIPTION OF SCHOOLS

First Schools, Places and Numbers

The Methodist Episcopal Church after 1866 accelerated its efforts to provide schools for the Freedmen. By 1869 the Freedmen's Aid Society had established a total of 59 elementary schools for the Freedmen. They were distributed as follows:

Tennessee, 7; Georgia, 20; Alabama, 5; Kentucky, 2; Mississippi, 8; North Carolina, 1; South Carolina, 9; Virginia, 3.[1]

The purpose of the Freedmen's Aid Society was to provide elementary schools as a beginning for the education of the Freedmen. It was thought that within a short time the state would provide common schools for Negro children as a part of the state school system and that the Freedmen's Aid Society would cease establishing common schools and would withdraw support leaving the elementary education to the state. It was the plan that as the Church withdrew from elementary education it would concentrate upon theological education, teacher training, and collegiate work.

A large number of elementary schools were established for the Freedmen, because there were few, if any, public schools for Negro children. In fact, there were few public schools for white children. The public school system in the South was slow in its development after 1865 for several reasons. First, the South was not committed to free public schools for all of the children. This was a development to come later. In the second place, the South was poor, suffering from the economic reversal as a result of the Civil War. It was not until early in the 20th century that the beginning of a good public school system was developed in the southern states.

The Freedmen's Aid Society had thought from the beginning that free public education would early be provided by the states. This did not occur, but the Church felt it was not its responsibility to continue to establish schools on the elementary level. Consequently, the Church began to withdraw from the elementary school except at certain institutions which developed into academies and preparatory schools and later into colleges. The

Sixth Annual Report of the Freedmen's Aid Society, 1873, comments on its work as follows:

> The Society has aided in the introduction of the New England System of education into the South. We first planted the free-school there; then the normal school and the college, and the university; for wherever the first goes, the others, sooner or later, are sure to follow.[2]

The New England system which was established applied not only to elementary schools but also to all levels including the college. In line with the plan and philosophy of the Freedmen's Aid Society the early schools laid the foundation for more advanced work. While the elementary work continued in connection with the upper levels at many of the institutions emphasis was placed upon work above the elementary level.

Types of Schools and Programs Developed

In view of the encouraging results achieved the leaders of the Freedmen's Aid Society ventured to expand the schools upward. It was stated in the Sixth Annual Report that:

> This Society (in connection with similar associations) has demonstrated to the South, that the freedmen possess good intellectual abilities, and are capable of becoming good scholars. Recognizing the brotherhood of mankind, and knowing that intellect does not depend upon the color of the skin nor the curl of the hair, we never doubted the negro's ability to acquire knowledge and to distinguish himself by scholarly attainments.[3]

There were two main needs which demanded education beyond the elementary level. One was the training of teachers and the other the training of ministers.

Normal Schools

The development of Normal Schools for the training of Negro teachers was in line with the general trend of the time in teacher training. Normal schools were being established in many areas of the United States, particularly in the Northern section. The establishment of Normal Schools for the training of teachers gained impetus from the philosophy of Pestalozzi whose thinking in the areas of education of children and the training of teachers revolutionized teacher training in Europe and in the United States.

104

E. P. Cubberley states that:

> Pestalozzi possessed a deep and abiding faith, new at the time, in the power of education as a means of regenerating society. . . .Not only the intellectual qualities of perception, judgment, and reasoning need exercise, but the moral powers as well.[4]

The Pestalozzian approach stimulated much interest because it greatly expanded the concept of learning and the method of teaching. He emphasized learning through sense perception. This was a departure from rote memory and mere repetition of words, to emphasis upon ideas about things. Pestalozzi's idea of involving the exercise of moral powers in the process of education was closely related to the purposes and aims of education as seen by leaders of the Freedmen's Aid Society.

Another phase of the importance of the Normal School may be seen in the following excerpt from the Third Annual Report of the Freedmen's Aid Society:

> Especial attention has been given to the establishment of schools for the training of teachers, believing that we could exert in no other way a more extensive and enduring influence. Whoever furnishes the education of a people controls the current of thought, and molds future generations; and Methodism owes it to herself, to humanity, and to God, to take an active part in the reconstruction of the South upon the broad principles of religious freedom. . . .We must select the most promising pupils, place them in the Normal School, and prepare them as rapidly as possible for guides and educators. Hundreds are now employed in teaching with success, who were educated in these schools; and if they shall be liberally sustained, the time is not far distant when they will be able to supply the surrounding country with well-qualified Christian teachers. . . .Religion must be inwrought into the very fabric of the soul, and not merely impressed upon the surface, and this must be done in the process of their education, and not postponed until the work is completed.[5]

Description of the Normal School Program

The Normal Schools established by the Freedmen's Aid Society, as well as the Normal Schools generally, followed several levels of preparation. Most of the early normal schools were equivalent to the four-year high schools. At the beginning the normal course consisted of two years above the common school grades. The course was for the most part advanced training in the elementary and common school subjects. As the normal course developed it became a four-year course.

The four-year normal course paralleled the preparatory course, but the four-year normal course was quite different in subject matter in the last two years. While the preparatory course was designed to prepare students for collegiate work, the normal course led to a certificate for teaching.

In the process of development of the teacher training program the course was extended first to one year above high school and became known as the higher normal course. As requirements for certification were raised the normal course became a two-year college course paralleling the first two years of college course that led to a degree. Often the degree Bachelor of Pedagogy was awarded at the end of the two-year college normal course.

The normal course at institutions under the Freedmen's Aid Society, as well as other normal schools, was the chief agency for the preparation of teachers until the end of the first four decades of the 20th century. Many of the early normal schools founded by the state grew into four-year teachers colleges. The normal schools at the Freedmen's Aid colleges consisting of two years on the college level coincided with the state schools for the preparation of teachers. This pattern of teacher training evolved into an emphasis upon requirements for a bachelor's degree for those expecting to teach, and their being certified in particular subject matter or major field of concentration.

Theological Schools

At the very beginning of the work of the Freedmen's Aid Society in establishing schools, much emphasis was placed upon theological training. The conferences of the Methodist Episcopal Church in the South had evolved into separate Negro conferences with increasing churches and membership. The need was for ministers to pastor the churches of these conferences, and to give religious leadership to the Negro people.

At all of the colleges founded before 1875 there was a theological department, placing great emphasis upon training ministers:

Central Tennessee College—a theological department
Claflin University—Baker Theological Seminary
Clark University—Clark Theological Seminary (later Gammon Theological Seminary)

106

Morgan College—Centenary Biblical Institute
New Orleans University—Thomson Biblical Institute
Shaw University—theological classes.

The Fifth Annual Report of the Freedmen's Aid Society comments on the need for teachers and ministers:

> The great want of our work in the South, at the present time, is educated teachers and ministers. Our primary schools prepared the way for graded and normal schools, and these will furnish students for the theological seminary and college. . . .We must provide a few Biblical schools, where these young men can be properly trained and prepared for the ministry. The candidates for our Conference must have specific and thorough preparation for their work. The interests at stake are too momentous to be intrusted to illiterate and inexperienced youth. The age in which we live, the field we cultivate, the character of the opposition which we encounter, the consequences involved, demand cultivated intellects, pure hearts, and holy enthusiasm. Endow our seminaries, where we may furnish such young men, and the South, blighted by oppression, and scarred by the thunderbolts of war, shall bud and blossom as the rose.[6]

The Fifth Annual Report also describes the preparation the minister should receive in a theological seminary:

> Their ministers should be good English scholars, familiar with the elementary branches, able to communicate their thoughts in an intelligible manner; and, though their style may be destitute of rhetorical beauty, it must be characterized by accurate expression and convincing power. The fields of science and literature, if possible, should be investigated. The natural sciences should be studied; for these shed light upon the sacred page. With the principles of intellectual and moral science they should be familiar; for these affect every fiber of the warp and woof of human life. No study should be neglected, if opportunity affords, that sheds light upon the Bible. . . .The Bible is the minister's textbook, and whatever else he may be ignorant of, he must study and understand this.[6]

In 1882 a substantial grant was made to Clark Theological Seminary by the Reverend Elijah Gammon to strengthen the ministerial training program. In 1888 this became a separate theological seminary on an adjoining campus to Clark University taking the name of Gammon Theological Seminary.[7] As this seminary grew it became the one center of training of Negro ministers for the Methodist Episcopal Church and other denominations. With the development of Gammon Theological Seminary, the seminaries at the other Methodist institutions for Negroes were discontinued and Gammon became the mecca for the training of Methodist ministers.[8]

Academies and Preparatory Schools

The academy movement in American education represented a type of school suggested by Benjamin Franklin in 1749 when he wrote his *Proposals Relating to the Education of Youth in Pennsylvania.* The academy was flourishing at the time the Freedmen's Aid Society was establishing schools for the Freedmen in the South. This type of school was used rather extensively by the Freedmen's Aid Society, a number of such schools having been established for Negro youth during the first two decades of the work of the Society.

The academy was a combination of the New England Latin grammar school and the English school. "In a sense the curriculum of the academy was an effort to combine the values and content of the Latin schools and the English schools into one institution."[9] Efforts were made to retain some of the classical emphasis of the Latin Grammar School and at the same time democratize the education, making it more practical for the general population seeking an education. The academy was for the most part a private school with boarding facilities. Its popularity was due in a large measure to the fact that the public high school had not come into existence.

The Freedmen's Aid Society continued its emphasis upon the academy for the purpose of providing secondary education. Most of the academies established were separate from the colleges and did not go beyond the four years of high schools. The academies established for Negro youth apart from the colleges between 1868 and 1889 were:

1. Haven Academy, Waynesville, Ga.		1868
2. Central Alabama Academy, Huntsville, Alabama		1870*
3. LaGrange Academy, LaGrange, Ga.		1870
4. Cookman Academy, Jacksonville, Fla.		1872
5. Gilbert Academy, Winsted, La.		1875

*Evolved from Rust Institute, founded in 1866.

6. Samuel Huston College, Austin, Texas	1878**
7. Meridian Academy, Meridian, Miss.	1879
8. Morristown Academy, Morristown, Tennessee	1881
9. Delaware Academy, Princess Anne, Md.	1888
10. LaHarpe Academy, New Orleans, La.	1888
11. Alexandria Academy, Alexandria, La.	1889
12. West Tennessee Academy, Mason, Tenn.	——[10]

In connection with the colleges the Academy emerged into the preparatory school. The preparatory school was designed specifically to prepare students for collegiate work. For several decades after 1900 the preparatory school was continued in connection with the four-year college. It afforded a basis for the selection of top ranking students for college work. So thorough was the work in the preparatory schools that those students who finished this work and entered college usually completed the college course for the Bachelor's degree. The mortality was very low.

The preparatory courses were three years in length until about 1900. Between 1900 and 1910 the preparatory curriculum became a four-year course in all of the Freedmen's Aid Society schools.

Institutions for White Students

A number of such institutions were established for white youth and were supported by the Freedmen's Aid and Southern Education Society as follows:

Ellijay Academy, Ellijay, Ga.	1874
Kingsley Academy, Bloomingdale, Tenn.	1877
Powell's Valley Academy, Well Spring, Tenn.	1878
Mt. Zion Academy, Mt. Zion, Ga.	1880
Leicester Academy, Leicester, N. C.	1881
Baldwin Academy, Baldwin, La.	1882
Mallalieu Academy, Kinsey, Ala.	1884
Parrottsville Academy, Parrottsville, Tenn.	1886
Fairview Academy, Trapp Hill, N. C.	1887
Graham Academy, Marshalberg, N. C.	1887
Woodland Academy, Cumberland, Miss.	1887
Demorest Academy, Demorest, Ga.	1890
Bloomington College, Bloomington, Tenn.	——

**Founded 1876 as Andrews Normal School at Dallas, Texas.

Holston Academy, New Market, Tenn.   —

McLemoresville Academy, McLemoresville,
  Tenn.   —

Murphy College, Svierville, Tenn.   —

Roanoke Academy, Roanoke, Va.   —

Summertown Academy, Summertown, Tenn.   —11

With the rise of the public common school the Freedmen's Aid Society discontinued the establishment of elementary schools. The elementary schools already established either merged into academies and preparatory schools or were discontinued. Because of the poor quality of public high schools for Negro youth, or the complete absence of high schools for Negroes which was more frequently the case, the preparatory schools connected with the Freedmen's Aid Society colleges were continued through the late 1920's and early 1930's.

Reasons for the discontinuation of the academies and preparatory schools by the Freedmen's Aid Society:

1. Classical training gave way to more practical emphasis.
2. Provision of Public Elementary Schools.
3. Rise of the Public High Schools.
4. Failure of academies and preparatory schools generally to meet the needs of democratized education.
5. Reduction of the number of schools to be supported by the Freedmen's Aid Society.
6. Influence of accreditation agencies.
7. In an effort to become accredited the colleges had to disassociate the preparatory schools from the college.
8. Increased financial burden required elimination of lower level schools.
9. The church and the colleges could no longer do the educational work of the state. So long as the colleges carried the academies and preparatory schools, just so long did they delay the assumption of responsibility by the states for secondary education.

The College

The four-year colleges established by the Freedmen's Aid Society were adapted to the social and intellectual climate of the time. Higher education in the South generally was offered in private institutions. This was particularly true of higher education for Negro youth. The private schools invariably were those founded by the Church. During the first 50 years of the existence of the colleges for Negroes, they were strictly under the auspicies of the Church.

More than two decades of the 20th century passed before there was much interest in providing public higher education for Negroes in the South. Until the late 1930's the highest percentage by far of Negro students in colleges was in private colleges. This was due in a large measure to the fact that the early public institutions of higher education for Negroes, when they finally came into existence, emphasized for the most part agriculture and trades and provided some training for teachers. The Negro clientele was more interested in the type of education provided in private institutions by the Church.

Early in the history of the colleges for Negro youth in the South, and until well into the 20th century, the general purposes of the colleges were to provide training for teachers and ministers, and to give moral and religious training to all students. Training of missionaries for leadership and missionary work in Africa was an important objective. The purpose in the large was to give enlightenment to the Negro race through the students who attended college. The program and instruction were influenced by the John Locke philosophy of formal discipline. Mental discipline and the development of the mind, logical thinking and rationality were thought to be most desirable outcomes of the curriculum. To achieve this kind of development much stress was placed upon classical learning, the liberal arts, derived from the Aristotelian *Seven Liberal Arts.* Therefore Latin, Greek and classical literature, and mathematics occupied high priority in the curriculum.

A number of four-year colleges emerged from the academies and preparatory schools rather rapidly. By 1896 two four-year colleges and universities had emerged from academies under the Freedmen's Aid Society of the Methodist Episcopal Church. Two more of the academies developed into four-year colleges about 1900.

College Enrollments

The enrollments at the college and university level were small. This was due to several reasons: one, there were not many students in high school. There were no public high schools for Negro youth. The number available for college was small.

A second reason was that most of the students at the secondary school level either took the normal course in preparation for teaching or an industrial course in preparation for more immediate employment.

A third reason was due to the fact that the preparatory course

111

leading to college and the college course itself were most rigorous, consisting of Latin, Greek, mathematics and science in the curriculum on the preparatory level and through the four years of college.

A fourth reason for the small number of college students was the fact that the college course was long and expensive. Most Negro students seeking an education had neither the time nor money to spend so many years in college.

The College Curriculum—Leading to a Bachelor of Arts Degree and a Bachelor of Science Degree

The four-year college in many instances evolved from the four-year academy and preparatory school. The preparatory course was a preparation for college, and a diploma or certificate from the preparatory school was usually a sufficient criterion for admission to college. The four-year college course led either to the Bachelor of Arts degree or the Bachelor of Science Degree. The course leading to the Bachelor of Arts degree was known as a classical course and the scientific course led to the Bachelor of Science degree.

Exhibit A on page 113 shows the classical course leading to the Bachelor of Arts degree and Exhibit B on page 114 shows the scientific course leading to the Bachelor of Science degree. As a rule a student pursuing one of these degrees took all of the courses in the curriculum to qualify for graduation. There were only a few, if any, electives.

The University

Several of the colleges carried the name of university early in their history. When the term university was first applied, the hope was that at some time in the near future, the institution would be a university. The growth was much more rapid than one would expect, and the institutions did become universities, such as Claflin University, Clark University, New Orleans University, Shaw University, Walden University, and others.

Exhibit A

Four-Year Classical Course
(Bachelor of Arts)
(Freshman)[1] [2]

Fall	Winter	Spring
Livy	Latin Literature	Tacitus
Solid Geometry	Algebra	Algebra
General History	General History	General History
Greek	Political Economy	Greek
	Greek	Reviews

(Sophomore)

Fall	Winter	Spring
Horace	Horace	Cicero's Essays
Greek	Greek	Greek
Chemistry	Chemistry	Chemistry
Trigonometry	Trigonometry	Surveying
	Sociology	Reviews

(Junior)

Fall	Winter	Spring
Latin	Latin	Latin
Geology	Geology	General Biology
Greek	Greek	Greek
Analytics	Analytics	Mechanics

(Senior)

Fall	Winter	Spring
History of Civilization	Astronomy	Astronomy
Ethics	Psychology	Theism
Evidences of Christianity	Logic	History of
Commercial Law or	Human Body	Philosophy
Economics		Thesis

113

Exhibit B

Four-Year Scientific Course
(Bachelor of Science)
(Freshman)[13]

Fall	Winter	Spring
Livy	Latin Literature	Tacitus
Solid Geometry	Advanced Algebra	Advanced Algebra
General History	General History	General History
Zoology	Zoology	Reviews
	Political Economy	

(Sophomore)

Fall	Winter	Spring
Horace	Horace	Cicero's Essays
Trigonometry	Trigonometry	Surveying
Chemistry	Chemistry	Chemistry
Physics	Physics	Physics
	Sociology	Reviews

(Junior)

Fall	Winter	Spring
Analytics	Analytics	Mechanics
Geology	Geology	Geology
Electricity	Quantitative Analysis	Quantitative Analysis

(Senior)

Fall	Winter	Spring
Calculus	Astronomy	Astronomy
Ethics	Psychology	Theism
Evidences of Christianity	Logic	History of Philosophy
Commercial Law or Economics	Human Body	Thesis

The study of the Bible as a daily textbook is required.[14]

There were several processes by which these institutions became universities. The first was by the extension of the four-year college course and offering post-graduate work in the several areas of the four-year college program. An advanced degree was awarded upon completion of the graduate work.

The post-graduate studies at Walden University will illustrate this phase of university work:

Post-Graduate Studies. Students wishing to pursue a higher course of study for other degrees will have the opportunity to take such courses as they choose, with the approval of the faculty, under the following regulations:

1. A standing committee shall be appointed by the Faculty, to be known as the Committee on Graduate Studies, which shall have power to formulate regulations for all graduate work, and conduct examinations of all candidates for higher degrees. The regulations adopted by the committee shall be presented to the Faculty for approval.

2. The degree of Master of Arts, Master of Science, Doctor of Philosophy, and Doctor of Science may be conferred on the grounds of advanced scholarship and independent work in certain special lines. The conditions upon which these degrees will be given are as follows:

(1) The candidate for Master's degree must be a graduate of Walden University, or of some institution whose degrees are accepted by this College as equivalent to its own, or he must give satisfactory proof that he possesses an equivalent preparation for graduate studies. He must become enrolled with the Committee on Graduate Studies, and comply with its requirements. He must spend one year in resident work, or at least two years *in absentia,* in the pursuit of such courses of study as may be selected by him and prescribed by the committee. He must pass satisfactory examinations on the studies pursued, present a creditable thesis, and pay the required fees.

(2) The candidates for a Doctor's degree must be a baccalaureate graduate of Walden University or of another institution of similar grade. He must become enrolled with the Committee on Graduate Studies, and comply with its regulations. He must spend at least three scholastic years, or their equivalent, in independent research. One of these must be spent at this institution, but, if found impracticable to spend a year in resident work, the candidate may study four years *in absentia.* He must pass satisfactory examinations on the studies pursued, present a thesis showing independent research, and pay

115

the required fees.[15]

The programs and requirements were essentially the same for all of the universities, where post graduate work was offered.

A second manner in which the colleges became universities was by adding schools and departments as follows: (1) Universities had extensive normal departments for the preparation of teachers and advanced work was often pursued beyond the requirements for the Bachelor of Pedagogy Degree. (2) Schools of Fine Arts—art, music, etc. (3) Industrial departments were very elaborate. These were not considered academic altogether but they carried important implications for the educational program and they helped to achieve some of the main purposes of education. The industrial departments and schools of the universities provided technical training. (4) Agricultural departments were important phases of the university program at several of the institutions. (5) Professional schools constituted certain phases of the university: (a) theological schools; (b) medical schools; (c) schools of law; (d) pharmaceutical schools.

The Charters and Policies

The charters for the four-year colleges were secured during the period between 1866 and 1900, most of them having been secured during the Reconstruction Period which ended in 1877. The charters secured during this period were broad and liberal. They reflected the policies of the Freedmen's Aid Society and the Methodist Episcopal Church. Although they were granted by the respective states they were in line with the reforms and liberal thinking of the Reconstruction Period, particularly as reflected in certain Civil Rights Acts (*e.g.*, 1875). The charter granted Clark College shown in Appendix is typical of the charters granted the Negro colleges of the Freedmen's Aid Society.

Industrial Education

Emphasis upon industrial education became widespread in the schools of the South shortly after the Civil War. The academy had tended to democratize education forming a bridge that shifted from the classical emphasis in the Latin grammar school to a more practical education in the Academy.

The economic situation of the South demanded practical training to rehabilitate the economy. After 1875 the demand for manual, industrial and commercial education was met in the

116

secondary schools. From this time on through the first two decades of the 20th century manual training and industrial education were popularized as means of meeting the practical needs of a high percentage of those attending school.

In line with these general trends, the schools under the auspices of the Freedmen's Aid Society of the Methodist Episcopal Church developed programs in manual training and industrial education which grew to large proportions in many of the schools, particularly the academies and to some extent in the first two years at the college level. The 21st Annual Report of the Freedmen's Aid Society, 1888, lists the following industrial schools or departments:[16]

Claflin College of Agriculture and Mechanics Institute, Orangeburg, S.C.	15	305
John F. Slater School of Industry, Nashville, Tennessee	5	62
Schools of Industry, New Orleans University	3	102
Schools of Industry, Rust University, Holly Springs, Mississippi	4	35
Schools of Industry, Centenary Biblical Institute, Baltimore, Maryland	2	30
Manual Training-School, Philander Smith College, Little Rock, Arkansas	4	64
Industrial School, Bennett Seminary	3	13
Schools of Industry, Wiley University, Marshall, Texas	4	55
Schools of Industry in Cookman Institute, Jacksonville, Florida	2	18
Schools of Industry, Gilbert Seminary, Baldwin, Louisiana	4	70
Classes in Huntsville Normal Institute, Huntsville, Alabama	2	48
Schools in Clark University, Atlanta, Georgia	11	62

These twelve schools or departments are indicative of the place which industrial education had in the thinking of the leaders of the Freedmen's Aid Society.

In the 22nd Annual Report of the Freedmen's Aid Society, 1889, the following comments are made by Dr. J. C. Hartzell with reference to industrial training:

117

In harmony with the most advanced thought of the age among scientific educators, both secular and religious, we are seeking to educate the hand, as well as the head and heart. Industrial training is to some extent given in all our schools. Largely by donations year by year from the John F. Slater Fund, through its agent, Dr. A. G. Haygood, we are enabled, in connection with several of the larger institutions, to have industrial schools which for efficiency and success are very creditable. . . .

The importance of this department of our teaching can scarcely be overestimated. It is the one feature of our work that is universally commended, North and South. Students do better literary work who spend two or three hours in the shop each day, and the object lesson as to the dignity of labor is invaluable.[17]

It may be noted that the industrial training was emphasized not merely from the practical point of view but as a part of the basic philosophy of education.

Manual training or industrial education was not merely a concern of individual schools in the local community but a concern of the whole church. This concern continued over several decades. In 1908 a report was made to the General Conference of the Methodist Episcopal Church on the importance and development of the work in industrial education at the several institutions under the supervision of the Freedmen's Aid Society. The following excerpts come from that report to the General Conference.

Industrial Education. Manual training is becoming more and more one of the most important features of the work of our schools in the South. Industrial education was begun in 1866 when our schools were first organized, and has been enlarged from time to time until now we have 3,167 students taking systematic studies in twenty-four different lines of industrial pursuits.

While some form of industrial education is taught in all the schools under our supervision and care, the main strength of our industrial work is centered at six strategic points, in the midst of the Black Belt, at the very doors of the people who need it most. These centers are Claflin University, Orangeburg, S. C., Morristown Industrial and Normal Institute at Morristown, Tenn., Clark University at Atlanta, Ga., Gilbert Industrial College at Baldwin, La., Wiley University at Marshall, Tex., and Rust University at Holly Springs, Miss. . . .

The Board has appropriated from the general fund during

118

this quadrennium for industrial instruction proper $35,400, and $35,000 has been put into industrial buildings and equipment. During the year just closed, 2,959 students were instructed in 24 trades and industries.[18]

Industrial education for Negro youth extended far beyond the interest of the Methodist Episcopal Church. It was a general concern that included industrial education for Negroes as a part of the general development in education all over the country. The United States Department of the Interior expressed its interest in industrial education for Negro youth as late as 1916. The following excerpts from the 1916 Report of the Department of the Interior, Bureau of Education, indicate the concern and thinking of this Department:

> The real meaning of industrial education has been largely misunderstood by the colored people and many of their friends. It is not strange that a race only recently freed from slavery, industrial and otherwise, should question industrial education, especially when it saw the people of the white race bending every nerve to give their sons and daughters "book learning." Fortunately, the white people both of the South and of the North are now realizing the importance of industrial education for their children, with the result that the industrial facilities for white pupils are increasing so rapidly as to surpass by far those for colored pupils. Nine states have already established state systems of industrial education, and a number of other states have provided funds for vocational schools, while practically every modern city school system recognizes industrial training as one of its primary aims.
> ...The underlying principle of these schools is the adaptation of educational activities, whether industrial or literary, to the needs of the pupil and the community.[19]

While industrial education was advocated as an important phase of education for Negro youth it was also a basic part of the philosophy of education for the country as a whole. The industrial education in the United States was a forerunner to development of the present technical and engineering schools and the agricultural experiment colleges. The emphasis on industrial education in the Freedmen's Aid Schools and in education generally stemmed in large measure from the influence of the American Industrial Revolution which began about 1850. This emphasis was amplified by the influence of the first and second Morrill Congressional Acts, 1862 and 1890, respectively.

In the late 19th century a sharp conflict developed between advocates of industrial education for Negroes and advocates of liberal arts and classical education. This conflict reached its height in the controversy between Booker T. Washington, the founder of Tuskegee Institute and the advocate of industrial education, and W. E. B. DuBois, the advocate of liberal and classical education.

Booker T. Washington built Tuskegee Institute and became a distinguished and internationally known educator on the basis of the philosophy of training the hand as well as training the mind. He preached a doctrine of the dignity of labor saying: "No race can prosper till it learns that there is as much dignity in tilling a field as in writing a poem."[20]

W. E. B. DuBois attacked Washington's emphasis on manual training or industrial education to the apparent neglect of higher education. He stated that:

> Mr. Washington's programme naturally takes an economic cast, becoming a gospel of work and money to such an extent as apparently almost completely to overshadow the higher aims of life. . . .Mr. Washington's programme practically accepts the alleged inferiority of the Negro races.[21]

DuBois' claim was for the liberal and classical education; the training and discipline of the mind; the creation of ideas and the development of the higher qualities of the individual.

Although the DuBois-Washington controversy was long and divisive, a close analysis of the basic philosophies of the two men would indicate that their points of view were not incompatible. The thinking of both DuBois and Washington had strong influence upon the program emphases of the private schools and colleges, including those under the auspices of the Freedmen's Aid Society.

120

REFERENCES AND NOTES

1. Third Annual Report, Freedmen's Aid Society, 1869, p. 6.
2. Sixth Annual Report of the Freedmen's Aid Society, 1873, p. 12.
3. *Ibid.*
4. Cubberley, Elwood P., *The History of Education*, pp. 542f.
5. Third Annual Report of the Freedmen's Aid Society, 1869, pp. 7-8.
6. Fifth Annual Report of the Freedmen's Aid Society, 1872, p. 7f.
7. Catalog, Clark University, 1882-1883, p. 15.
8. Report, Freedmen's Aid and Southern Education Society, July 1, 1889, p. 4. (Due action taken by the several Negro Annual Conferences.)
9. Butts, R. Freeman and Cremin, Lawrence A., *A History of Education in American Culture* (New York: Henry Holt and Company, 1953), pp. 126-127.
10. Report of the General Committee of the Freedmen's Aid and Southern Education Society, 1892, p. 18.
11. *Ibid.*
12. Exhibits A and B taken from the Thirty-Seventh Annual Catalogue of the Walden University (1902-1903), p. 12f.
13. *Ibid.*
14. *Ibid.*
15. Thirty-Seventh Annual Catalogue of Walden University (1902-1903), pp. 75f.
16. Twenty-First Annual Report of the Freedmen's Aid Society (1888); p. 13.
17. Twenty-Second Annual Report of the Freedmen's Aid Society (1889), pp. 14-15.
18. Journal of the General Conference, 1908, pp. 1272-1273.
19. Department of the Interior, Bureau of Education Bulletin, 1916, No. 38, Vol. I, pp. 81-82.
20. Washington, Booker T., *Up From Slavery* (Dodd, Mead, and Company, 1965), p. 140.
21. DuBois, W.E.B., *Souls of Black Folk* (Fawcett Publications, Inc., 1961), p. 48.

CHAPTER 9

A BRIEF HISTORICAL SKETCH OF THE WOMAN'S HOME
MISSIONARY SOCIETY, THE METHODIST EPISCOPAL
CHURCH IN RELATION TO THE FREEDMEN'S
AID SOCIETY

Origin and Organizations

From the inception of the Freedmen's Aid Society in 1866, the women of the Methodist Episcopal Church were interested in the work done in the South by this Society. A feeling developed among them that the women as a group should become involved in this or a similar enterprise.

Some of the women entertained hope of participating in the work of the Freedmen's Aid Society. At a meeting of women May 12, 1875, in Baltimore, a committee was appointed to petition the Freedmen's Aid Society, urging the election of women as members of its Board of Managers. This was not looked upon with favor, as the Act of Incorporation of the Freedmen's Aid Society stated that males only were eligible as members.[1]

"The services connected with the Ninth Anniversary of the Freedmen's Aid Society of the Methodist Episcopal Church were held in Pittsburgh, Penn., the 10th and 11th of December, 1876."[2] On Sunday morning several addresses were given at various churches including discourses by Bishop Bowman, Bishop Wiley, Dr. Rust, and others representing the Freedmen's Aid Society. Among the speakers were two women: Mrs. Willing and Mrs. Wheeler, at different churches.[3]

Monday afternoon a Woman's meeting was held at South Common Church. Mrs. Bishop Clark presided, and addressed the meeting upon the necessity of awakening a deeper interest among the women in behalf of the poor freed women in the South. Mrs. Dr. Rust assured the audience that a widespread influence had been awakened in behalf of this cause in the Church, and read extracts from numerous letters received from influential ladies, in which immediate action was urged, warm sympathy expressed and financial aid proferred. Mrs. Wheeler

123

delivered an address, setting forth the importance of this work, and the influence of Christian women in advancing the interests of Christ's cause. Mrs. Willing followed with a speech in which she portrayed the degraded condition of this people, and urged the duty of extending to them immediate relief. These speeches were intensely interesting, and awakened deep interest in the audience.[4]

The men of the Freedmen's Aid Society saw the need of the work contemplated by the women and gave them every encouragement. The Annual Report, 1878, of the Freedmen's Aid Society points out one weakness in the work of the schools of the Society, namely, the absence of the cooperating home influences. There was realization of the importance of improving the conditions of the homes of the freed people. This depended largely upon improving the women of the home. These reasons urged the uniting of the proposed plan of the Woman's Home Missionary work with the already established work of the Freedmen's Aid Society, and making it cooperative with the schools.[5]

There was a small group of women of the church who maintained that the women could and should organize and direct an independent society. Among these women were Mrs. F. S. Hoyt, Mrs. James Dale, and Mrs. John R. Whetstone of Cincinnati. Other strong supporters and leaders in the movement to serve freed women of the South were Mrs. Bishop Clark, Mrs. Dr. Rust, Mrs. Jennie F. Willing, Mrs. J. C. Hartzell, and others.

Mrs. Rust was fired by her first-hand experience when she toured the Annual Conferences in the South, with her husband, in January, 1877. In New Orleans they attended the Louisiana Annual Conference. The Minutes of the Louisiana Conference January 13, 1879 record the following expression by the Conference:

Whereas, the Board of Managers of the Freedmen's Aid Society of the Methodist Episcopal Church are maturing plans for Christian work among the freedwomen of the South:
Resolved 1, That we have heard of this movement with great pleasure. . .
Resolved 2, That we are pleased to see in our midst Mrs. Dr. Rust, a prominent representative of this movement, and hereby request her to address the Conference and explain the character of the work contemplated.[6]

Through Bishop Wiley, who presided over the Louisiana Annual Conference, and Dr. and Mrs. Rust, who were then residing in New

Orleans, the women's movement received great encouragement and support. Bishop Wiley, speaking in Cincinnati urged the promotion of a Society and created profound interest there and in other parts of the North.

Encouraged and financially aided by more contributions, Mrs. Hartzell established a mission school with three teachers. Each succeeding year the work grew. This program was so successful that it became a showcase for future planning.[7]

In making its report to the General Conference May 27, 1880, the Committee on Freedmen's Aid and our Southern work (Report No. II), stated in part:

The work inaugurated among the Freedwomen of the South has already borne precious fruit, and gives promise of adding much to the usefulness of this Society. The work contemplated is to send Christian women into the homes of the colored people and by good counsel aid in the work of establishing and maintaining Christian homes among them. Schools are to be organized for the girls and women in connection with our churches and the institutions of the Society.[8]

The action of the 1880 General Conference gave approval to the work among Negro women and girls by the women of the Church. This was a signal for them to go forward with the organization of the Society.

Soon after the close of the General Conference a call was issued to the ladies of Cincinnati and vicinity and on June 8, 1880, a meeting was held at Trinity Methodist Episcopal Church of that city at which it was decided to form a new organization to be known as the Woman's Home Missionary Society with a recommendation for special attention to the Southern Field.[9]

Its plan of organization makes provision for Conferences, a Board of Managers composed of representatives from the several Conference Societies, and an Executive Board of twenty-one ladies, to be elected by the General Board of Managers at its annual meeting. The Executive Board is composed of the officers and twelve Resident Managers as follows:

President, Mrs. Rutherford B. Hayes;

Vice Presidents: Mrs. Bishop Wiley, Mrs. Dr. F. S. Hoyt, Mrs. Bishop Clark, Mrs. Amos Shinkle and Mrs. Dr. Walden.

Corresponding Secretary, Mrs. R. S. Rust

Recording Secretary, Mrs. James Dale

Treasurer, Mrs. A. R. Clark

Resident Managers: Mrs. Dr. John Davis, Mrs. Dr. Nast, Mrs. John L. Whetstone, Mrs. Dr. Comegys, Mrs. Dr. H. B. Ridgaway, Mrs. W. F. Thorne, Mrs. Ada Wiley Jones, Mrs. John R. Wright, Mrs. A. Wessel, Mrs. E. House, Mrs. C. B. Bowman and Mrs. N. W. Harris[10]

It is significant to note that the first National President of the Woman's Home Missionary Society was Mrs. Rutherford B. Hayes, then the First Lady of the land. It was fortunate for the Society to have as its first President and leader a woman of such great stature, influence, and ability. Again, it was fortunate for the Society to have so many other prominent women to fill important offices and to exert great influences as leaders.

The First Annual Report of the Women's Home Missionary Society shows the officers of the Society as follows:

President

Mrs. Rutherford B. Hayes — Fremont, Ohio

Vice Presidents

Mrs. John David — Elm Street, Cincinnati
Mrs. F. S. Hoyt — York Street, Cincinnati
Mrs. Bishop Clark — Elm Street, Cincinnati
Mrs. Amos Shinkle — Covington, Ky.
Mrs. John M. Walden — Walnut Hills, Cincinnati

Recording Secretary

Mrs. James Dale — 434 Broadway, Cincinnati

Corresponding Secretary

Mrs. R. S. Rust — 339 W. Fourth St., Cincinnati

Treasurer

Mrs. A. R. Clark — 169 York St., Cincinnati

Resident Managers

Mrs. Bishop Wiley — Fairmount, Cincinnati
Mrs. Richard Dymond — Cincinnati

126

Mrs. John L. Whetstone	—Mt. Auburn, Cincinnati
Mrs. C. G. Comegys	— Cincinnati
Mrs. J. H. Bayliss	— Walnut Hills, Cincinnati
Mrs. W. F. Thorne	— Cincinnati
Mrs. Mary Haven Thirkield	— Cincinnati
Mrs. Charles Coffin	— Fairmount, Cincinnati
Mrs. A. Wessel	— Walnut Hills, Cincinnati
Mrs. E. House	— Mt. Auburn, Cincinnati
Mrs. W. M. Ampt	— Cincinnati
Mrs. John Simpkinson	— Walnut Hills, Cincinnati

The Woman's Home Missionary Society was now an established organization, ready to cooperate with the Freedmen's Aid Society and to supplement its work in many important aspects.

Fourteen years earlier, August, 1866, the Freedmen's Aid Society had been organized in the same city, Cincinnati, and in the same church, Trinity Methodist Episcopal Church. It was the interest of the women in the field of work in which the Freedmen's Aid Society was engaged that gave birth to the idea of a woman's organization.

Relation of Certain Women to the Men of the
Freedmen's Aid Society

It is worth noting here the relationship of certain women in the founding and early work of the Woman's Home Missionary Society to the men and early work of the Freedmen's Aid Society.

Mrs. Clark: Mrs. Clark was the wife of Bishop Davis W. Clark. Bishop Clark was one of the founders of the Freedmen's Aid Society; he was the first President of the Society, and until his death in 1871, he labored hard and long in establishing Annual Conferences in the Southern Region, and in the establishment of schools to train Negro preachers and teachers. Mrs. Clark was closely related to this work of her husband.

Mrs. Walden: Mrs. Walden was the wife of Dr. J. M. Walden, later Bishop Walden. Dr. Walden was one of the founders of the Freedmen's Aid Society and was its first Recording Secretary and its first Corresponding Secretary, which position he held until 1868, when he was elected a bishop in the Methodist Episcopal Church. Mrs. Walden was well acquainted with the work and field of the Freedmen's Aid Society through the labors and leadership of Bishop Walden.

Mrs. Rust: Mrs. Rust was the wife of Dr. Richard S. Rust, one of the founders of the Freedmen's Aid Society. When Dr. Walden became a Bishop in 1868, to succeed him Dr. Rust was elected

General Field Superintendent of the Freedmen's Aid Society. He traveled extensively over the Southern region visiting all of the Freedmen's Aid Society schools, purchasing property and helping them to become firmly established. Ofttimes Mrs. Rust traveled with Dr. Rust and gained first hand information regarding conditions, needs, and scope of the field of work. Her visit to New Orleans in January, 1877, and the contact with Dr. and Mrs. J. C. Hartzell illustrates the influence of the early contacts with the Freedmen's Aid Society work, on the developing idea of a woman's organization to work cooperatively in this field.

Mrs. Wiley: Mrs. Wiley was the wife of the Rev. I. W. Wiley, who was among the first ministers and laymen called to the organization convention at Cincinnati August, 1866, and at that meeting became one of the Vice Presidents of the Freedmen's Aid Society. Thus, the Rev. Wiley was identified with the Freedmen's Aid Society from its inception as a Vice President, a member of the Executive Committee and a member of the Board of Managers. On the death of Bishop Clark in 1871, the Rev. Wiley became the second President of the Freedmen's Aid Society, in 1872 became a bishop in the Church and presided over a number of annual conferences in which Freedmen's Aid Society schools were located; *e.g.,* the Louisiana Conference where New Orleans University was located; the Texas Conference, where Wiley College was located in Marshall which college was named for him.

Mrs. Wiley accompanied her husband on trips to these and other annual conferences and visited the colleges related to his annual conferences. She, therefore, had a profound interest in the total work and was able to relate effectively the work of the Woman's Home Missionary Society to that of the Freedmen's Aid Society.

Mrs. Hartzell: Mrs. Hartzell, the wife of the Rev. J. C. Hartzell, labored with her husband in the fertile field of the Louisiana Conference. Rev. Hartzell became a member of the Louisiana Conference in 1871, and from the beginning was a tower of strength in the building of the Louisiana Conference and the development of New Orleans University. In these fields of her husband's labors and leadership Mrs. Hartzell was challenged and inspired by the needs and opportunities for work with Negro women. Both Rev. Hartzell and Mrs. Hartzell fully identified themselves with the Freedmen's Aid Society and helped to open the door for the Woman's Home Missionary Society work in New Orleans and elsewhere.

Mrs. Thirkield: Mrs. Mary Haven Thirkield was the daughter of Bishop Gilbert Haven who for a number of years had been associated with the Freedmen's Aid Society, and she was the wife

128

of the Rev. Wilbur P. Thirkield who in 1883 became the first dean of the Clark University Theological Seminary. All her life she had been associated with the work of the Freedmen's Aid Society through her father and husband.

Mrs. Darnell: Mrs. Darnell was the wife of the Rev. S. B. Darnell, the first President of Cookman Institute, Jacksonville, Florida, a Freedmen's Aid Society school. He was President from 1872 to 1894. Mrs. Darnell was in the work of the Freedmen's Aid Society eight years before the organization of the Woman's home Missionary Society. The years of experience at Cookman Institute formed the basis of Mrs. Darnell's interest in the cooperative relations of the Freedmen's Aid Society and the Woman's Home Missionary Society.

Mrs. Dunton: In 1873 the Rev. L. M. Dunton and Mrs. Dunton went to Orangeburg, South Carolina, to become associated with Claflin University, a Freedmen's Aid Society school. For forty-nine years Rev. and Mrs. Dunton were associated with Claflin, thirty-eight of which Dr. Dunton was President. This long period of association with the Freedmen's Aid Society work qualified Mrs. Dunton for effective service in the cooperative service and relationship of the Freedmen's Aid Society and the Woman's Home Missionary Society.

Mrs. Richardson: The husband of Mrs. Richardson, the Rev. G. W. Richardson, was associated with the work at Dallas 1876 and Austin, Texas, which was the beginning of Samuel Huston College, a later institution of the Freedmen's Aid Society. This became a cooperative interest of the Freedmen's Aid Society and the Woman's Home Missionary Society.

It is clear, then, that a number of women associated with the founding, organization and development of the Woman's Home Missionary Society including those mentioned above and others, were closely associated with the Freedmen's Aid Society through their husbands or some other close relationship. In these associations and relationships the Freedmen's Aid Society and the Woman's Home Missionary Society sustained a wedlock in a tremendous work for six decades.

Homes and Schools of the Woman's Home Missionary
    Society Related to Colleges of the Freedmen's Aid Society

Mrs. Ruth Esther Meeker has produced a monumental volume*

*Mrs. Ruth Esther Meeker — *Six Decades of Service, 1880-1940.* A History of the Woman's Home Missionary Society of the Methodist Episcopal Church, 1969.

in which she gives a detailed and complete account of the homes and schools established by the Woman's Home Missionary Society, both those related to college campuses and others located elsewhere. In connection with the respective colleges, this writer has given a brief account of the work of the homes as a part of or a supplement to the programs of the colleges. Only a listing of the homes, with brief comments, is necessary at this point.

Chronological Listing

1881 — "Thayer Home in Atlanta, Georgia always wore a halo," says Mrs. Meeker. This was the first home established by the Woman's Home Missionary Society to provide home training and industrial education for Negro women and girls. The model home was the idea of the Rev. Edward O. Thayer who came to the presidency of Clark College in 1881 and in the same year built Fisk Cottage on the campus, named in honor of Mr. E. C. Fisk of Boston who gave $500 on the building of the cottage. The Woman's Home Missionary Society assumed responsibility for the home. In October 1883 Miss Flora Mitchell of Boston was placed in charge of the home and she remained as Superintendent almost four decades.

The Home was expanded through the fund-raising efforts of the Woman's Home Missionary Society and a new home was dedicated in June, 1888. The Rock River and New England Societies gave generously to the new home and requested that it be named in honor of President Thayer. Thus, from 1888 to 1941 this first Home, associated with Clark University (Clark College), Atlanta, Georgia was known as Thayer Home. In 1941 when Clark College was relocated to its present site, the previous emphasis upon a home for girls gave way to a more academic emphasis. The work in home economics became a major department, supported by the Woman's Home Missionary Society, later the Woman's Division of Christian Service. Thayer Hall on the present Clark College campus provides facilities for continuing the work begun in 1881, on a larger scale, and Thayer Hall perpetuates the memory of one of the college's great presidents.

1883 — Simpson Home, on the campus of Claflin University, opened November 12, 1883, with Miss Ella J. Betts as matron.[11] Mrs. Dunton, wife of the President, took the initiative in raising money for better facilities and a new cottage for a home. Mrs. R. W. P. Goff, President of the Philadelphia Conference society, subscribed $500. The conference society undertook the building of a home as a special project "and named it the Matthew Simpson Memorial Home in memory of Bishop Simpson."[12]

Simpson Home continued until 1902. New administrative policies brought about a change and Simpson Home became the Matthew Simpson School of Domestic Science.[13] Final disposition of the property was made in 1907.

1884 — E. L. Rust Home was opened October 1, 1884, on the campus of Rust University, (Rust College) then Shaw University, Holly Springs, Mississippi. In 1890 the name of the university was changed to Rust University in honor of Dr. Richard S. Rust, Corresponding Secretary of the Freedmen's Aid Society. The E. L. Rust Home was dedicated March 10, 1885, as the Elizabeth L. Rust Industrial Home, in honor of the wife of Dr. Richard S. Rust, and in recognition of the services of Mrs. Rust, Secretary of the Bureau for colored work in the South.

One of the distinctive features of the E. L. Rust Home in its early years was the spirit of sharing and its outreach into the community. The interest and concerns of the girls of the Home touched many poor, aged people and former slaves in Holly Springs, too feeble to work. Rooms were furnished in an old building on the school grounds for an "old Sisters' Home." This became a cooperative enterprise with the Woman's Home Missionary Society of the local church in the community.

Miss Sophia Johnston the first Superintendent of the Home served from 1884 to 1897. Succeeding the three superintendents that served from 1897 to 1903, Miss Ella Becker became Superintendent in 1903. Miss Rebecca Barbour became Assistant Superintendent in 1905. Miss Becker and Miss Barbour served as a team until their retirement in 1927. During this long period of their services E. L. Rust Home was most effective in its Christian influence upon the young women residents there and in training for home making, and church and community services.

After the destruction of the main building on the Rust College campus in 1940, E. L. Rust Home became E. L. Rust Hall, serving as the main dormitory for women on the college campus. Interest and support of the Woman's Home Missionary Society shifted to the work in home economics which became an academic department of the college. Miss Elfreda Myser, beginning in 1932, was the last Superintendent of E. L. Rust Home; she also served as Director of Religious Education for the college. This was a new area of academic service in which the Woman's Home Missionary Society participated.

1884 — Adeline Smith Home, the original home on the Philander Smith College campus, Little Rock, Arkansas, was dedicated February 25, 1884. This home "was the shadow of Mrs. Hilda Nasmyth, Superintendent from 1896 to 1930,"[14] succeeding Miss Elizabeth McIntosh who was Superintendent the

131

first eleven years.

A larger building to house twenty-four was dedicated March 7, 1888, Mrs. Philander Smith having contributed generously toward its erection. In 1900 the Home was enlarged to accommodate seventy-five girls. All of the girls in the Home attended Philander Smith College and the high school girls on the college campus took domestic science at Adeline Smith Home.

Changing conditions necessitated changes in plans and work of Adeline Smith Home. In 1930 the Society took over Webb Hall, the dormitory for college women and also the college dining hall and the work of Adeline Smith Home was transferred to Webb Hall. The services of Adeline Smith Hall, as it was known after 1930, came to a close in 1934 and the Woman's Home Missionary Society withdrew from Little Rock.

1886 — Kent Home on the Bennett Seminary Campus Greensboro, North Carolina, was opened November 1, 1886, and dedicated May 2, 1887.[15] Mrs. James Kent of Gloversville, New York, supplied a large portion of the money for the building, and the Home was named in memory of her late husband.[16] Fire destroyed the building December 17, 1909. A new and larger home was opened in 1911.[17] In 1921 the program was improved and expanded, the Home having a capacity of forty-three. The young women of Kent Home were among the best students at Bennett College. Kent Home was a forerunner of a larger and more significant enterprise on which the Woman's Home Missionary Society embarked in 1926 in cooperation with the Methodist Board of Education. Bennett College for Women became the fruitful result of this cooperative venture.

1889 — Peck Home, at New Orleans University, was established in 1889, as "a loving tribute from the Central New York Conference Society of the Woman's Home Missionary Society of the Methodist Episcopal Church to Bishop Jesse T. Peck and his wife."[18]

Fire totally destroyed the building in 1897. The lot which was some distance from the university campus was sold in 1899 for a considerable increase over the purchase price in 1887. A free lot was offered by the university on which to locate the Home. It was not, however, until 1912 that Peck Home was built with a capacity of forty at a cost of $27,000.00.[19] The School of Domestic Art and Science became the department of home economics for the university. In 1935 when New Orleans University merged with Straight College to form Dillard University the interest and support of the Woman's Home Missionary Society were continued in Gilbert Academy on the same grounds, until the academy was discontinued in 1949.

1891 — King Industrial Home at Wiley University, Marshall, Texas, was completed in the face of 1891. The Home was named in memory of Mrs. Jane King of Delaware, Ohio, who left a legacy of $2,300 to the work of the Woman's Home Missionary Society. The third floor of the Home was completed in 1899, giving a total capacity of sixty girls, and ranked as one of the largest homes in this work of the Society. Miss E. O. Elliott was superintendent for ten years, assisted by Miss Clara I. King of Fairfield, Iowa. A high standard of training and religious development during this period gave King Home an exceptionally high rating; so much so that "a King Home girl was a status symbol in Marshall."[20]

On January 9, 1919, King Home was completely destroyed by fire. A new building begun in the spring of 1920 was ready for occupancy that fall. The new King Home burned November 11, 1921. The Society decided not to rebuild. "The Board of Trustees deeded the property to the Board of Negro Education for expansion of Wiley."[21] The insurance on the building was later applied to the debt on Browning Home, Camden, South Carolina.

1892 — New Jersey Home at Morristown Seminary, Morristown, Tennessee, was completed in May 1892 and opened in October. The Home came as a result of the interests and efforts of the women of the New Jersey Conference Society, from which it took its name. This was one of the smaller homes operated by the Woman's Home Missionary Society, but gained distinction from the high caliber of girls it enrolled. "Three of the most widely known missionaries left an imprint here; Miss Anna Mosher, 1894-1903; Miss Louella Johnson, 1903-1913; Mrs. May G. Lawrence, 1915-1920."[22] As a result of a fire at Morristown Institute in January 1922 and the erection of a new building, which provided accommodations for all the girls, the New Jersey Conference Home closed in 1924.[23]

1904 — Eliza Dee Home, in Austin, Texas, was opened in October 1904. This Home was operated in cooperation with Samuel Huston College. It was named in memory of Mrs. Eliza M. Dee of Burlington, Iowa, whose bequest of $3,000.00 to the Woman's Home Missionary Society made possible the purchase of property in Austin. Miss Clara I. King was transferred from King Home in Marshall to become Superintendent of Eliza Dee Home, where she spent twenty-four fruitful years. A most beautiful building was erected in 1918 to accommodate fifty girls. In 1931 Eliza Dee Home became a freshman dormitory for the college. The work in home economics became an academic department of the college, supported by the Woman's Home Missionary Society.

1926 — Bennett College for Women. The work of the Woman's Home Missionary Society in cooperation with colleges founded by the Freedmen's Aid Society reached its climax in 1926. Bennett College, founded in 1873, until 1926 was a co-educational college. A bold and creative step was taken in changing the co-educational college to a Woman's College, to be operated primarily by the Woman's Home Missionary Society, but in cooperation with the Board of Education of the Methodist Episcopal Church. The wisdom of the cooperative venture has been strongly vindicated for almost a half century.

Other Homes and Schools Not Related to
  College Campuses

In addition to the homes established by the Woman's Home Missionary Society and operated on or near college campuses in cooperation with the Freedman's Aid Society, several other homes and schools were established and operated by the Woman's Home Missionary Society for the training or education of Negro children and youth.

Following is a brief account of the institutions, listed in chronological order:

1885 — Haven Home. Haven Industrial Home and School was founded in 1885 in Savannah, Georgia, and named for Bishop Gilbert Haven. After a long period of needed and fruitful service, and several relocations in the vicinity of Savannah, the doors of Haven School closed in June, 1932, and merged with Boylan School in Jacksonville, Florida.[24]

1886 — Boylan Home. In April, 1886, Miss Harriet E. Emerson opened the doors of Boylan Home in Jacksonville, Florida, and served as Superintendent eighteen years.[25] Cookman Institute, which was founded three years earlier by the Freedmen's Aid Society, and Boylan Home were in the same city, but were completely separate. With the merging of Haven School with Boylan in 1932, the name was changed to Boylan-Haven School. In 1933 it became a Junior-Senior High School. It is still in operation under the auspices of the Woman's Division of Christian Service, the United Methodist Church.

1886 — Speedwell Home. In 1886 mission property was deeded to the Woman's Home Missionary Society and the mission school was continued at Speedwell near Savannah. The first name given was the Mary Haven Home in memory of Bishop Gilbert Haven's mother who in early 1880, before the Woman's Home Missionary Society was organized, gave a five dollar gold piece to Mrs. R. S. Rust "for the work among freedwomen in the South." Since there was a Haven Home at Savannah, it was decided in 1907 to change the name of Mary Haven Home to Speedwell Industrial Home.[26]

In 1920 the Speedwell property was leased and finally sold to the Board of Education of Chatham County, Georgia, for public school purposes.[27]

1887 — Allen Home. Allen Home was opened October 30, 1887 at Asheville, North Carolina. The property, valued at $5,000.00 was given to the Woman's Home Missionary Society by the Reverend Lewis M. Pease, "on condition that a graded industrial school would be sustained there for Negro people."[28] The generosity of Mrs. Marriage Allen, an English woman visiting in Asheville, made possible the acquisition of additional land and the erection of a new building which was dedicated February 9, 1897. The building was named Allen Home in honor of Mrs. Allen, the donor. Allen Home has served historically as an accredited high school and an excellent boarding school for Negro girls.

1887 — Browning Home and Mather Academy. In 1884 Mrs. James Mather, Corresponding Secretary of the New England Conference Society, encouraged the Conference to obtain permission to establish a home for girls in Camden, South Carolina. Mrs. Mather donated an acre of land. Mrs. Fanny O. Browning of Montville, Connecticut, left a legacy of $2,000 which was used in completing and furnishing the home. In appreciation the Conference named the home for her. The school was opened in September, 1887. The Society purchased a twenty-seven acre plantation from Mrs. Mather for $2,000. In 1890 the National Society (Woman's Home Missionary Society) took over the work. Mrs. Mather and her sister, Miss Lucy Babcock, built a chapel with dormitory rooms overhead. The chapel was named the Babcock Chapel. With later gifts, Mrs. Mather requested that the school be named Mather Academy in honor of her husband. The Home and School then bore the name Browning Home and Mather Academy. May 14, 1901, Mrs. Mather died leaving one-half of her estate to the school. Browning Home and Mather Academy has served the community as an accredited school of academic quality, an excellent boarding school for girls, and a splendid cultural center for the Camden community.

1921 — Sager-Brown Home. This school, located at Baldwin, Louisiana, was opened September 21, 1921, with a rich heritage. About 1869 John M. Baldwin of Berea, Ohio, and W. L. Gilbert of Winsted, Connecticut, gave $20,000 and $50,000 respectively for school purposes in Baldwin, Louisiana, for Negro people. Several schools and an orphanage had been located there, the last being Gilbert Academy and Agriculture School. In 1918 Gilbert Academy was transferred to New Orleans and became the high school department of New Orleans University. The property at Baldwin was offered by the Board of Negro Education of the

Methodist Episcopal Church to the Woman's Home Missionary Society. A home was built carrying the name Sager-Brown in honor of two women of the Central New York Conference: Mrs. Addie G. Sager of Syracuse, and Mrs. C. W. M. Brown of Elmira. Since 1940 the Sager-Brown Home has been under the auspices of the Woman's Division of Christian Service.

1935 — Gilbert Academy. From 1918 to 1935 Gilbert Academy was the high school department of New Orleans University. When New Orleans University merged with Straight College in 1935 to form Dillard University, Gilbert Academy was taken over by the Woman's Home Missionary Society and remained on the old New Orleans University site as a private high school. It was a high school of distinction for fifteen years, and was discontinued in June, 1949.

While four of the six separate homes and schools accounted for above are still in operation, it should be pointed out that none of the homes established by the Woman's Home Missionary Society in connection with Freedmen's Aid Society colleges is now in existence. The homes became dormitories for the colleges and the work in home economics became academic departments of the colleges. In several instances where formerly there were homes, appropriations are made to the colleges by the Woman's Division of Christian Service to support the work in home economics or to provide furnishing and supplies for a woman's dormitory. Bennett College is an exception, where the college is primarily under the auspices and management of the Woman's Division of Christian Service of the United Methodist Church.

REFERENCES AND NOTES

1. Meeker, Ruth Esther, *Six Decades of Service*, 1880-1940. A History of the Woman's Home Missionary Society of the Methodist Episcopal Church, 1969, p. 5.
2. Freedmen's Aid Society Ninth Annual Report, 1877, p. 24.
3. *Ibid.*
4. *Ibid.*
5. Freedmen's Aid Society Annual Report, 1878, p. 16f.
6. Minutes, Louisiana Annual Conference, January 13, 1877.
7. Meeker, *op. cit.*, p. 6.
8. *Ibid.*, p. 7.
9. *Ibid.*
10. Freedmen's Aid Society Report, 1880, p. 16f; and, First Annual Report, Woman's Home Missionary Society, Methodist Episcopal Church, 1882, p. 3.
11. Meeker, *op. cit.*, p. 115.
12. *Ibid.*
13. *Ibid.*, p. 116.
14. *Ibid.*, p. 125.
15. *Ibid.*, p. 129.
16. *Ibid.*
17. *Ibid.*
18. *Ibid.*, p. 142.
19. *Ibid.*
20. *Ibid.*, p. 143.
21. *Ibid.*, p. 144.
22. *Ibid.*, p. 150.
23. *Ibid.*, p. 151.
24. *Ibid.*, p. 128.
25. *Ibid.*, p. 129.
26. *Ibid.*, p. 132.
27. *Ibid.*
28. *Ibid.*

CHAPTER 10

CHARACTERIZATION OF THE SECOND HALF
CENTURY — 1916-1966

In the first half century the schools of the Freedmen's Aid Society had substantial growth, both with regard to the number of schools established and the levels of work offered. It was such schools as these, founded and supported by several denominations, that had provided, by far, most of the education for Negroes.

At the beginning of the second half of the first century of work there were 10,000,000 Negroes in the United States, 9,000,000 of whom were in the South.[1]

Thomas Jesse Jones in 1916 pointed up the implications of the problems inherent in the situation for the South and the nation. He stated that, "No racial group in the United States offers so many problems of economic and social adjustment as the 10,000,000 Negroes. Though the churches and philanthropic societies seem to have much more interest in immigrants and Indians, the Negroes rival both these groups in total numbers and surpass them in the difficulty of the questions to be solved."[2] Jones indicated three elements in racial adjustment at that time; the North, the South, and the Negro; and pointed out several outstanding facts in the study of the educational phase of adjustment:

> First, the large place which the Negroes occupy in the life of the American people and especially of the South; second, the maintenance of a double system of public schools in the South where the per capita wealth is considerably below the general average of the country; and, third, the good work of Negro private schools maintained mainly by northern philanthropy.[3]

The Negro occupied a most important but unrecognized and unaccepted place in American life in 1916, the same as at present. The miserably poor public education provided for Negroes in a dual educational system in the South in 1916, before and after, tells a story of dark tragedy for black children. Relief from greater tragedy for Negroes and the South came with the philanthropic efforts to build a better public school system, in addition to the benevolent efforts of the church bodies.

A Period of Transition and of Efforts to Improve Negro Education 1916-1939

Transitional Influences

During the first decade, 1916-1926, a number of influences were at work, bringing about changes in schools and education for Negro youth. The progress of the first fifty years in the development of private Negro schools had set the tone and created a deep consciousness of need and desire for better schools. World War I had great impact on the thinking regarding education and the provisions that should be made. The Negro population became mobile as never before, hordes of Negroes moving from farms to the cities of the South, and even greater numbers migrating to northern and western cities. Lack of educational facilities in the South for Negro children was one of the principal causes of migration. Philanthropic agencies became interested in improving the educational facilities and opportunities for Negro children and moved in on a large scale of operation. Principally among these agencies were the Anna T. Jeanes Fund, the Phelps-Stokes Fund, the Rosenwald Fund, all providing assistance at the elementary and secondary school levels. The Slater Fund, providing funds and facilities for industrial education, had been operative in the field since 1882. The General Education Board provided millions of dollars for the advancement of Negro education at the college, university, and professional school levels.

Through the funds granted by the Rosenwald Fund hundreds of communities in the South were provided with school buildings for Negro children. It must be observed that Negroes themselves on a matching basis, gave more money for public school buildings for their children than either the Rosenwald Fund or the state.

As a result of the philanthropy of these agencies and interests, public education for Negro children in the dual educational system of the South was improved, and relieved the church boards, such as the Freedmen's Aid Society, of the necessity of providing elementary and secondary education for Negro children.

Other Direct Influences

In the process of transition and change other direct influences came to bear upon the Freedmen's Aid Society schools and other private schools for Negroes. In 1913 the Association of Colleges

140

for Negro Youth was organized at Knoxville, Tennessee.[4] The purpose of this Association was to establish and apply standards for Negro colleges and secondary schools, and to improve the quality of their work. The meetings of the Association from 1913 to 1916 considered a wide range of standards relating to entrance requirements, college degrees, specialization in and for professional work, uniformity of records, deficiencies of entering students, control of athletics, preparation of teachers for public schools, and many other topics and problems. Because of the World War (I) the Association of Colleges for Negro Youth became dormant for a whole decade. When it was revived in 1926, its attention was directed toward securing accreditation recognition by the Association of Colleges and Secondary Schools of the Southern States, which did not then give any consideration to the accreditation of "Negro schools." In the early 1930's the Southern Association began a "courtesy" rating of Negro colleges, listing them in one of three classes, A, B, and C.

State Departments of Education had their influence on the standardization of the Negro colleges. The colleges were constantly under the surveillance of State Departments of Education which granted certificates to teachers, and were often visited by state educational associations.

Influence of Studies, Surveys, and Reports

Frequent studies, surveys and reports were made for the improvement of all phases of the work of the schools and colleges. It was the widely accepted practice in the decades of the 1920's and 1930's to make surveys for the improvement of schools of all levels. The Negro schools did not escape the rigors of this practice.

The managers of the Freedmen's Aid Society were among the first to initiate studies of the schools of the Society for their improvement.

The General Conference of 1916 received the following report:

Your Committee on Freedmen's Aid recommends for your adoption the following:
The report of the Freedmen's Aid Society, referring to the inspection and classification of the schools of the Society, has been carefully reviewed. Your Committee approves the same and recommends that every effort be made by the Board of Managers to comply, where expedient, with the findings and recommendations of the special commissions, but in no case shall action be taken without consulting the Board of Local Trustees.[5]

141

This report and action by the General Conference represent a continuing interest and effort to improve the schools under the supervision of the Freedmen's Aid Society, later the Board of Education for Negroes.

The Thomas Jesse Jones Study and Report

In 1916 Thomas Jesse Jones under the supervision of the Bureau of Education, Department of the Interior, and in cooperation with the Phelps-Stokes Fund, made a monumental study of Negro education in the United States and made a far-reaching report that influenced the course and development of Negro institutions for decades. The report troubled the placid waters of many boards and administrators when it pointed out that:

> Though a large number of the schools for colored people are called 'colleges' and even 'universities,' there are very few institutions that have equipment for college work or pupils prepared to study college subjects. Most of the subjects taught are of the typical classical type.[6]

At the time of Jones' study and report the Freedmen's Aid Society of the Methodist Episcopal Church had under its supervision eighteen schools, not including professional schools, with a total of 5,059 students, of which 3,263 were enrolled on the elementary school level, 1,600 on the secondary school level, and 196 on the college level.[7] This college enrollment was the second largest of all the nineteen church bodies maintaining schools for Negroes, as reported by Jones.[8]

The following are some of the specific recommendations in the Jones report relating specifically to the schools of the Freedmen's Aid Society:[9]

1. That all work below the ninth grade be classed as grammar school and that such work be discontinued as soon as local conditions warrant.
2. That college and secondary work given in the same institution be kept distinct.
3. That teaching loads for instructors be reduced.
4. That class periods be not less than 45 minutes.
5. That more flexibility in courses of study be allowed.
6. That the training of the teachers be upgraded.
7. That science equipment be improved.
8. That libraries be improved, eliminating worthless books and

providing books of value.

9. Installation of a uniform system of records.

10. Improvement of administrative policies, clarifying and enlarging the powers of the presidents.

The Thomas Jesse Jones report had far-reaching effects in the improvement of the schools for Negroes as the responsible boards and administrators attempted to implement the recommendations.

Changes for Improvement, Prior to 1939

In 1920, by action of the General Conference, the Methodist Episcopal Church, the name of the Freedmen's Aid Society was changed to the Department of Education for Negroes, Board of Education. Although the emphasis in this change was upon a shift from the historical connotation of the previous name, the change also presaged significant changes to come later in the scope and nature of education to be provided by the Negro institutions related to the Board of Education. From quadrennium to quadrennium actions were taken and changes made to validate an increasingly high quality of educational work.

During the period 1920 to 1930, in the light of the improvements in public education, a number of the schools of elementary and secondary character, founded by the Freedmen's Aid Society were discontinued. By 1930 industrial work had been discontinued in all of the institutions under the Methodist Board. Preparatory schools in connection with the colleges began to disappear, and by the late 1930's all had been discontinued. Conversely, greater emphasis was placed upon work at the college level and the strengthening of college courses. The college enrollments were greatly increased. The curriculum, under the pressure of social, economic, and cultural changes, lost the classical emphasis and became more contemporary. The colleges sought recognition by state departments of education for certification of graduates, and sought accreditation by such agencies as the University Senate of the Methodist Episcopal Church, and the Regional Accrediting Agencies.

Arthur J. Klein of the United States Office of Education in his survey of Negro Colleges and Universities in 1928, lists eleven institutions under the supervision of the Methodist Board of Education, as follows:

1. Philander Smith College
2. Bethune-Cookman College
3. Clark University

143

4. New Orleans University
5. Rust College
6. Claflin University
7. Walden College
8. Morristown Normal and Industrial College
9. Samuel Huston College
10. Wiley College
11. Bennett College for Women

The Board was also making annual grants to Morgan College, independently controlled.[10] Klein found a considerable advancement in the administration of the Methodist colleges for Negroes from what it was in 1916. Boards of Trustees of three of the colleges, Clark, Bethune-Cookman, and Bennett had local authority in their administration, the Church Board from its northern headquarters exercising partial supervision. Local trustees, however, appeared to be without real power, as particularly all the business of the colleges was transacted directly between the presidents of the institutions and the central office in Chicago.[11]

It was noted by Klein that the General Conference had "authorized the Board of Education to turn over control of any of the schools under its jurisdiction to local boards of trustees whenever property becomes secure and expenses assured."

Four significant institutional changes occurred between 1920 and 1939.* In 1923, Cookman Institute at Jacksonville, Florida, was merged with Daytona Normal and Industrial Institute for Negro Girls to form Bethune-Cookman College at Daytona. In 1926 Bennett College was changed from a co-education institution to Bennett College for women under the joint control of the Woman's Home Missionary Society and the Board of Education, Methodist Episcopal Church. In 1935 New Orleans University and Straight University of New Orleans, Louisiana, consummated merger to form Dillard University at New Orleans, Louisiana. In 1937 Morgan College changed to a state college, becoming Morgan State College, at Baltimore, Maryland. These were major institutional changes, and without doubt, the most significant changes in the second half of the century up to that time.

Unification — 1939

Unification of the three branches of Methodism in 1939 closed an era. The Methodist Episcopal Church under whose auspices the

*For details see the individual institutional historical chapters below.

144

Negro institutions were founded, and sponsored for more than seven decades, reunited with the branch of Methodism that had separated almost a century before over the slavery issue. In the reunion the Methodist Episcopal Church became a part of The Methodist Church. In The Methodist Church, the colleges, historically serving Negro students came into new relationships, with opportunities for increased support and new outreaches in race relations.

Status, Problems and Developments, 1940-1966

The Negro colleges under the auspices of the Board of Education of the Methodist Church in 1940 entered a new period, having survived the period of the great economic depression, 1929 to 1941. During the period of the depression the financial survival was made possible by aid from outside philanthropy such as the General Education Board of New York, and within the Church, from "Saint Anonymous," who later was learned to be Mr. and Mrs. Henry Pfeiffer.

The transition was made from the depression into a period of war (World War II) with its attendant problems. The war brought problems of decreasing enrollments, the loss of men from the student bodies and the faculties. Student unrest and general instability characterized the climate of the campuses.

At the beginning of the period in 1941, the general church support of the Negro institutions had fallen almost to an irreducible minimum. The Methodist Church, formed through the reunion of the Methodist Episcopal Church, the Methodist Episcopal Church, South, and the Methodist Protestant Church, had the difficult problem of healing the wounds of the past, the Negro having been a thorn in the wounded flesh, and now a problem in the healing process of the new Methodism. New relationships, new understanding, and new support had to be discovered, for race as an issue was a disturbing threat to harmony in the new church.

"Race Relations Sunday" was inaugurated for two purposes; one, to help create better race relations through inter-racial understanding; and two, to raise funds for the Negro colleges. With a fair measure of success, the observance of Race Relations Sunday has been in practice since 1941.

Paine College in Augusta, Georgia, having been a missionary enterprise of the Methodist Episcopal Church, South, from its beginning in 1883, was in 1941, added to the list of Negro colleges under the auspices of the Board of Education of The Methodist Church.

145

Social Changes and the Years of the 50's

At the close of the war in 1945, the economy generally had a turn upward. The return of veterans, with provisions to continue their education, gave a big boost to the already increasing college enrollments and helped to strengthen college finances. The colleges, however, at once began to feel the effects of the pressure of social change. As far back as 1936, with the court decision in the Murray Case at the Law School of the University of Maryland, desegregation of all-white institutions at the level of higher education had its beginning. With a series of such court decisions, by the early 1950's it was clear that the new access of Negro students to all-white institutions in the southern and border states would have telling effects on all-Negro colleges. In 1953 twelve of the seventeen southern and border states and the District of Columbia maintaining segregated institutions of higher education had begun to admit Negro students to their graduate and professional schools, and seven state and municipal colleges were admitting Negro students to undergraduate level programs. By this time twenty-eight all-white private institutions, almost exclusively church related, had opened their doors to Negro students.

During the years of the 1950's, increasingly the question was raised with louder and louder voices, What is the fate of the Negro colleges? Is there need for Negro colleges? At this early stage of desegregation and with only a bit of tokenism in enrolling Negro students in predominantly white institutions, it was being said that Negro colleges were perpetuating segregation and should be abolished. The Negro college became an issue in the Methodist Church on the basis of perpetuating segregation and affected in no small measure fund raising on Race Relations Sunday for their support. A clear *raison d'être* had to be given for their continued support. This still is not a dead issue. The instability and insufficiency of support of the Black colleges of Methodism has never ceased to be a cause for great concern.

Accreditation and the best quality of education that could be provided, constantly engaged the attention of the Black colleges of Methodism. When the Southern Association of Colleges and Schools opened its doors in 1957 for the first time to Negro college membership, two of the Black colleges of the Methodist Board of Education gained membership. Another one had for a number of years held membership in the North Central Association of Colleges and Secondary Schools. By 1961 all but one held membership in the Southern Association of Colleges and

146

Schools and in the North Central Association. At present all of the Black colleges of the United Methodist Church are so accredited, with full membership.

Involvements of the Sixties

Beginning with 1940, each succeeding decade was fraught with an avalanche of changes, pressures, demands, and problems on the one hand, and on the other hand there came unprecedented governmental assistance for the acquisition of buildings and equipment.

The student revolution on the campus of the Black college, along with movement of students into the community and places of business challenged the age-long practices, customs and codes of discrimination and segregation. The Black student revolution was inevitable for several reasons; first, the time was right and the climate ready for recognition of all people as human beings with dignity and the right to freedom and relief from repression and the age-long indignities heaped upon people of color.

The universal Declaration of Human Rights in 1948 had created a world climate for rebellion against oppression, injustice, discrimination and humiliation of the darker peoples of the world. Students felt a world kinship in the desire for a new way of life. They, however, were more immediately stimulated by Civil Rights movements historically supported by their predecessors. And, still more immediately, they were themselves victims from day to day of gruesome humiliations too agonizing to bear.

Secondly, the courts had prepared the way in decisions bearing on segregation and gave encouragement to make the venture to change the hoary customs, though this was a daring and dangerous expedition.

In the third place, the generations of the sixties were heirs of a heritage of culture and courage, accumulated over a period of a century through education in schools that had for their purpose the freeing of the mind and spirit of black people. The revolution had to come, for it was inherent in the Declaration of Independence, it was inherent in democracy, it was inherent in the Universal Declaration of Human Rights, it was inherent in a free society, and it was inherent in black people seeking true dignity and freedom as human beings.

Once the revolution proved successful in the community, forces were redirected to the campus with pressure for freedom from rules and regulations, and pressures for changes in many aspects of education, in administration, and policies affecting student life and their participation in policy making. It is not disturbing that

147

the unrest and pressures are so much a part of the campus ferment. Whether these pressures, changes, and this ferment will be utilized and converted into a real process of education is a matter of no little importance.

The mid-sixty years brought resources from the Federal Government in grants and loans for buildings and equipment, in which the predominantly Negro colleges shared, that made possible greatly improved facilities for education. Because of the heavy debts imposed and the discontinuation of grants for equipment and projects, the colleges are left in precarious circumstances, and with the boon of government aid there is a concomitant bane.

New Problems of Competition

In recent years the Black colleges, particularly the private colleges, have felt the impact of competition as they have never felt it before. Heretofore, the competition of Black colleges was, for the most part, with other Black colleges. The competition has now been extended to all areas of operation and with all types of institutions, white and black, large and small, the financially affluent, and the financially poor.

Competition for Students

With the admission of Negro students to the formerly all-white institutions in the South, the competition for top-ranking Black students has become defeatingly keen. With prestige, affluence, and scholarship aid made available from large foundations for Black students to attend the predominantly white colleges and universities, the Black colleges find it difficult to meet the competition. If the Black colleges were given the same grants to offer scholarship aid to Black students, the competition would be fair. Under the current circumstances the competition is not only difficult, but unfair. The Black colleges will likely continue to get good students and will do an excellent job, but they find it difficult to get a fair share of the best Black students because of the type of competition they must meet.

Competition for Faculty

Many of the top Black teachers that were once available to Black institutions, to strengthen their faculties are being lured to the faculties of the larger predominantly white institutions, for larger salaries. Black teachers are being picked off from Black colleges by the more affluent white institutions for their faculties, for research, and for administrative positions. Obviously this places the Black college in a most difficult competitive position. This is a critical problem which can be solved only with larger and more adequate financial resources for Black colleges.

Competition for Finances

The Black colleges face competition among themselves and with white institutions for finances from the Federal Government, from foundations, from corporations, from alumni support where the alumni hold degrees also from white institutions; and within the church there is competition for the educational dollars.

Without question the survival of the Black colleges and the quality of their education will be determined by their ability to compete favorably in the areas mentioned above.

Summary of Institutional Changes In
  the Period 1916-1966

Between 1916 and 1966 a number of major changes were made affecting certain of the institutions founded by the Freedmen's Aid Society. The following notations summarize chronologically the various changes made.

1923 — Cookman Institute at Jacksonville, Florida, was merged with Daytona Normal and Industrial Institute for Negro Girls, to form Bethune-Cookman College, located at Daytona Beach, Florida.

1923 — Central Alabama College after a disastrous fire was permanently closed.

1924 — Virginia Collegiate and Industrial Institute was closed and its interests transferred to Morgan College.

1925 — George R. Smith, after a fire that destroyed the main building, was closed.

1926 — Bennett College, coeducational, in 1926 became Bennett College for Women.

1927 — Haven Institute and Conservatory of Music in Meridian, Mississippi, was closed.

1935 — Walden College in 1922 was reduced to a Junior College; in 1928 it became a four-year academy, and in 1935 was permanently closed.

1935 — New Orleans University merged with Straight College (Congregational) in New Orleans to form Dillard University.

1937 — Morgan College in this year was taken over by the State of Maryland and became Morgan State College. Morgan Christian

Center was established.

1940 — Paine College of Augusta, Georgia, supported by the Christian Methodist Episcopal Church and the former Methodist Episcopal Church, South, became one of the institutions under the auspices of the Board of Education of the Methodist Church.

1941 — Clark University became Clark College in 1940, and in 1941 was relocated to become one of the cooperating institutions of the Atlanta University Center on the West Side of Atlanta.

1952 — Samuel Huston College and Tillotson College (Congregational), Austin, Texas, were merged to form Huston-Tillotson College.

1958 — Gammon Theological Seminary was relocated to the West Side in Atlanta and became the pivotal unit in the new Interdenominational Theological Center.

At The End of The First Century

As the first century closed in 1966, twelve of the institutions founded by the Freedmen's Aid Society remained. Nine of these were four-year colleges, one junior college, one medical college, and one theological seminary. In the meantime, Paine College had been added to the list.

The status of the current group of Negro institutions will be set forth in a later chapter.

150

REFERENCES AND NOTES

1. Jones, Thomas Jesse — "Negro Education; A study of private and higher schools for colored people." Department of the Interior Bureau of Education Bulletin, 1916. No. 38, p. 4.

2. *Ibid*, p. 3.

3. *Ibid*

4. *Ibid*, p. 170.

5. Journal, General Conference, May 27, 1916, p. 659.

6. Jones, Thomas Jesse, *op. cit.* No. 39, Vol. II, p. 16.

7. *Ibid*, p. 127.

8. *Ibid*, (See table, p. 127) and p. 139.

9. *Ibid*.

10. Klein, Arthur J. — "Survey of Negro Colleges and Universities," Department of the Interior Bulletin, 1928. No. 7, p. 21.

11. *Ibid*.

12. *Ibid*.

PART IV.
HISTORICAL ACCOUNT OF
INDIVIDUAL INSTITUTIONS

CHAPTER 11

A BRIEF HISTORICAL ACCOUNT OF THE FOUNDING
AND DEVELOPMENT OF BENNETT COLLEGE

A. Institutions Extant

Bennett College had its humble beginning in 1873 in the unplastered basement of St. Matthew's Methodist Episcopal Church, with Mr. W. J. Parker in charge. In 1874 the Freedmen's Aid Society took over the school,[1] under the auspices of which it remained over a half century. In 1874 the Reverend Edward O. Thayer, a graduate of Wesleyan College, became the second Principal. In the first few years only local pupils were enrolled — the average attendance was seventy-five, ranging in age from fourteen to thirty-five.

There was an urgent need for land and a school building. The colored people of North Carolina were deeply interested and helped in raising funds for the school's development. Reverend Thayer reported that:

> A collection taken by the colored people of the Methodist Church at Greensboro amounted to *one hundred and five dollars.* This amount was made up of small contributions, the Sabbath-school children bringing their pennies, which, at the suggestion of their parents and pastor, they have been saving for this purpose. One little fellow, who had received a Sabbath-school prize of a dollar, brought it and placed it on the altar. This will convey to the reader an idea of the interest the people feel in the enterprise.[2]

Name

Mr. Lyman Bennett of Troy, New York, donated $10,000 for the school. In appreciation of its first large donor, the school was named Bennett Seminary in his honor. The North Carolina Conference of the Methodist Episcopal Church gave help in purchasing twenty acres of land. Within a year the first building, Bennett Hall, was erected and dedicated. From this time to 1883 this institution was known as Bennett Seminary, which then became Bennett College. The Seminary was located on the highest point of land near Greensboro, within one mile of the center and commanding a fine view of the whole region.

By 1879 the little school begun in the basement of a church in 1873, had grown into an institution with four departments, including college level courses. The Freedmen's Aid Society reported "we now have full normal, college, preparatory and theological courses, and our students pass examinations very creditably."[3] The rapid progress in the development of the advanced courses and the achievement of the students were facilitated by an unusual situation. It was reported that "the colored people of this section are, as a rule, better educated and in more prosperous circumstances than in most parts of the South."[4] It was encouraging for the Society to note that "among the young people there is a fine material for future statesmen, professional men of all kinds, and even *bishops.*"[5] Without question many professional men came out of that section and out of Bennett College. It should be noted that the two Black Bishops of The Methodist Episcopal Church, elected in 1920, came out of this section, namely Bishop Robert E. Jones, and Bishop M. W. Clair, Sr., the first two Black Bishops elected in The Methodist Episcopal Church, and Bishop Robert N. Brooks, elected in The Methodist Church, several quadrennia later, was a third one from this section.

The Reverend E. O. Thayer gave excellent leadership as the second Principal of Bennett Seminary, bringing the institution to a high point in its development. In 1881 President Thayer was transferred to the Presidency of Clark University in Atlanta. On his leaving the North Carolina Conference it was written in its Minutes:

> While we regretted to see Professor Thayer leave us after we had become so well acquainted with him and learned to love him for the great interest he took in the elevation of our race, yet we rejoice that we have at the head of the school one who in every respect is a worthy successor of our much-beloved Thayer.[6]

The "worthy successor" to President Thayer was the Reverend Wilbur F. Steele who remained in the Presidency eight years, resigning in 1889.[7]

Bennett Seminary continued its growth under the Principalship of Reverend Steele. The North Carolina Conference in October 1888 expressed its satisfaction as follows:

> Bennett Seminary, at Greensboro, is still in a healthful and prosperous condition, and is doing for our people in the State a most excellent work. Its courses of study are full, its work

thorough, and its corps of instructors is able and faithful as can be found in any similar institution in the South.[8]

The Report of the Freedmen's Aid and Southern Education Society in 1888 listed work being offered in four departments with enrollments as follows:

College	11
Normal	38
English Courses	84
Music	16

The total enrollment, without duplications, was given as 130 students.[9]

Woman's Home Missionary Society

In 1886 industrial work for young women was begun on the Bennett Campus under the auspices of the Woman's Home Missionary Society of the Methodist Episcopal Church. The North Carolina Conference resolved to express its thanks for the "magnificent Kent Home," established by the Woman's Home Missionary Society "at a cost of nearly $4,500.00."[10]

Rev. Charles N. Grandison, President

The year 1889 was significant for Bennett Seminary, for the Negro people, and for the Freedmen's Aid Society. The Reverend Charles N. Grandison was elected President of Bennett. He was the first Negro President of Bennett Seminary, and the first Black President of any of the institutions founded by the Freedmen's Aid Society. The North Carolina Conference took note of this appointment and the appointment of Bennett's first Black teacher:

We also note with unspeakable satisfaction the recognition by the Society of the talent of our own race as shown in the appointment of our brother, C. N. Grandison, to the Presidency, and John P. Morris to the professorship of Greek and Mathematics, in Bennett Seminary.
We have all confidence in the character and ability of Prof. Grandison and his faculty.[11]

In 1891 the collegiate division listed an enrollment of 222 students and a faculty of seven. The total value of the plant was estimated to be $30,000.[12]

157

The Reverend Grandison, in 1892, indicated a new dormitory as one of the chief needs, with students pouring in every day. He said also that industrial facilities were greatly needed, "to prepare for industry, thrift, economy, and wealth to meet the mooted Negro problem."[1][3]

President Grandison was a brilliant man and an eloquent speaker. Bennett made substantial progress under his short administrative leadership of only three years.

Professor Jordan D. Chavis Becomes President

Professor Jordan D. Chavis became President of Bennett College in the summer of 1892, succeeding the Rev. Charles N. Grandison. The North Carolina Conference in session October, 1892, acknowledged with satisfaction the work of the new President, Professor J. D. Chavis.[1][4]

Reverend Chavis was born near Greensboro, August 9, 1863. At the age of twelve, under great difficulties of poverty and lack of school facilities, he had acquired the rudiments of education.[1][5]

The following story gives an interesting incident in the early life of President Chavis, and tells how he first became interested in Bennett:

It was during this period that the Freedmen's Aid Society started its work of Christian Education in North Carolina. The Foundation of Bennett was laid near the roadside where the boy Chavis passed daily, seated on his ox-wagon loaded with wood. When his eyes first saw this great, new sight, he determined then to go to that college some day. Two poor white boys, who were on a similar team, laughed at young Chavis, and ridiculed his ambition. 'Who'd have a little ruff n----- like you in a place like dat?' He did enter, was converted to Christ, graduated from the course as then laid down. Later he graduated from Clark University in 1887 with the degree A.B. In 1889 he graduated from the full course of Gammon Theological Seminary. . . .On leaving the Seminary in '99 [sic] ['89] he was elected Superintendent of the Colored Schools of Winston, North Carolina. When he was called from that work to a professorship in Bennett College, the City School Board offered him double his former salary to remain. Feeling he owed so much to the work of the Freedmen's Aid Society, he took the position in Bennett College at a much smaller salary, and went North to take special studies for the work of his new position. In 1893 [sic] [1892] he was elected President of the College, which position he has held since, and added much to

158

the facilities of the work and the value and improvement of the property in that place. The five-story brick building for boy's dormitory, the pride of the North Carolina Conference, has been erected under the untiring labors of President Chavis.[16]

President Chavis gave exceptional leadership in expanding the plant and program of the college, and in increasing the enrollment. North Carolina Hall, a dormitory for male students was completed with pride at a cost of $14,163.78. "Male students, teachers, and professors, several graduates who were first-class carpenters, masons, and tinners, gave their services free of charge; otherwise, the building would have cost $20,000."[17] Toward the cost, $8,092.30 was raised by the people on the grounds; $6,071.48 was raised by the secretaries in charge. This was a signal demonstration of self-help and support. "Not one dollar was appropriated for this building by the Society. There was no debt."[18] Bennett College, the Society reported, "under the able and aggressive Presidency of Dr. Chavis, is crowded as never before."[19]

The Reverend Chavis gave Presidential leadership to Bennett College for a period of thirteen years, 1892 to 1905. This was the longest, and probably the most fruitful, period of Presidential Administration of the college up to that time.

Rev. Silas A. Peeler Becomes President

Beginning the school year September, 1905, the Reverend Silas A. Peeler assumed the presidency of Bennett College, succeeding Dr. J. D. Chavis.[20] The Reverend Peeler served as President eight years, 1905 to 1913. The new President was a graduate of Clark University, Atlanta, Georgia, and held the B.D. degree from Gammon Theological Seminary.

At the end of the school year 1903-1904 Bennett College had a faculty of fifteen teachers, an enrollment of 251 students and a total property value of $35,000.[21] The reports for the school years 1910-11 and 1911-12 show a faculty of eleven teachers, 237 students and a total property value of $36,000.[22]

President Peeler was unable to make desired progress because of a situation which the North Carolina Conference lamented in the Report of the Committee on Education at its 1912 session:

Dr. S. A. Peeler, with his faculty, is doing all that one can do,. . . .,under the circumstances to make the school a greater power for good than it has been in the past.

I would that there could be started here again within our ranks that old-time enthusiasm and zeal that used to characterize this conference for Bennett.[23]

159

Change of Administration

Succeeding the Reverend S. A. Peeler as President of Bennett College, in 1913, was Professor J. E. Wallace. The following report on Mr. Wallace gives some information regarding his qualifications as an educator:

> Professor J. E. Wallace, the new President of Bennett College, Greensboro, North Carolina, was born in Toronto, Canada, October 21, 1858. He finished the course in the public schools of Toronto and entered the college course at South Carolina University, Columbia, S. C., continuing in this college until the *Junior year*, when the institution was closed to colored students, after which he finished his A.B. degree course in Claflin University, Orangeburg, S. C. He served as Chief Clerk in the office of the United States District Attorney in South Carolina from 1881 to 1885, taught school in that state, and was principal of Howard High School, Columbia, S. C., from 1886 to 1900, after which he became Professor of English and Pedagogy at the State College for Colored in Orangeburg. Since 1903 he has been Professor of English at Claflin University and Dean of the Normal Department.

* * *

> Professor Wallace both by training and experience is well-equipped for the new duties that have come to him as President of Bennett College. It is a just recognition of his faithful service at Claflin University that he has been chosen to the Presidency of Bennett.[24]

The administration of President Wallace was short, only two years, ending in 1915. A long-needed residence for the President was erected while the Professor was President at a cost of $3,000.[25] Though no major school building was erected, the total property value advanced from $36,000 at the beginning of his administration to $44,500 in 1915.[26] The enrollment increased from 290 in 1913 to 368 in 1915.[27]

The Presidency of Dr. Frank Trigg

In 1915 the Reverend Frank Trigg succeeded President J. E. Wallace as head of Bennett College. His administration covered a period of eleven years ending in 1926.

The Reverend Trigg came to the Presidency of Bennett College from the Principalship of Virginia Collegiate Institute at

160

Lynchburg, Va. Bennett College was then at a low ebb and heavily in debt. During his administration the enrollment averaged around 300 students. The plant value increased from $44,500 in 1915 to $200,000 in 1924.[28]

A fire in January 1921 which destroyed Carolina Hall,[29] a boy's dormitory in which was located the auditorium and several classrooms,[30] made urgent the need for new buildings. The new buildings erected were a girl's dormitory, a refectory and classroom building, with provisions for the Science Department.[31] These three buildings were dedicated at Commencement time in May, 1924. The plant value in 1926 was $325,000.

President Trigg, though quiet and unobtrusive, was an unusual man. He was born in Virginia of slave parents. After the close of the war he remained on the farm. One day, still only a boy, gathering the harvest, he accidentally had an arm cut off below the elbow by a threshing machine. It seemed that his doom was sealed. His former Master and Mistress were good friends to the boy and his mother. His Mistress told him he was going to begin his education under her supervision. She gave him excellent training and a few years later his former Master shared with young Trigg his small means and helped him enter Hampton Institute. He graduated from Hampton in 1873 and began teaching.[32] He later entered the ministry.

> His success in Virginia attracted the attention of the Freedmen's Aid Society who asked him to head Bennett College. . . . President Trigg shouldered the responsibilities and directed not a little of his attention toward securing properly equipped teachers. Step-by-step he fought to bring the school back on its feet. The local school authorities realized that a new man had come into their providence and asked him to allow Bennett College to take over the local high school and make it the headquarters for the county.[33]

Not only was the physical plant expanded during the latter years of President Trigg's administration, but the academic program was greatly improved. Professor Isaac H. Miller, a graduate of Rust College, who had had wide and rich academic experience at several of the Freedmen's Aid Society institutions, notably director of the Normal Program at Clark University in Atlanta, and Principal of Cookman Institute, Jacksonville, Florida, came to Bennett College in 1923 to give direction to the academic program as Dean. Mr. Miller was a man of unusual capabilities in the field of education and was most methodical in his educational approaches. It should be noted that Professor Miller is the father of the incumbent President of Bennett College.

Having accomplished an excellent work, the Reverend Trigg retired from the Presidency of Bennett College in June, 1926, as plans were being developed to change the institution to a Woman's College.[34]

Kent Home

The work of the Woman's Home Missionary Society in the interest of Negro girls became associated with the educational work of the Freedmen's Aid Society at Greensboro, North Carolina, early in the history of Bennett College. This related program continued as a part of the basic education of girls at Bennett for a period of forty years.

In 1886 the Woman's Home Missionary Society of the Troy Conference in New York, having just been organized, became eager to establish a home in connection with Bennett Seminary to train girls in "womanly occupations."[35] An appeal was made for money. When the results of the appeal for the enterprise were insufficient — "when the last sugar bowl had been emptied" — Mrs. James Kent of Gloversville, New York, supplied the lack and the building was named Kent Hall in memory of her late husband.[36] Kent Home was opened November 1, 1886, dedicated May 2, 1887.[37] This work grew in importance and popularity, until space became inadequate to accommodate all the girls desiring to enter.

On December 17, 1909, fire completely destroyed Kent Hall.

A spacious new Kent Home was opened in 1911, including the Lucy A. Snider Library and space for the domestic science department. . . .In the improvement and expansion program carried out in 1921 the domestic science room was enlarged, equipment added, and the capacity of the home increased to forty-three. It was filled to capacity. Kent Home was now in its finest years and exerted an ever-widening influence.[38]

The cooperative enterprise carried on at Bennett by the Woman's Home Missionary Society and the Freedmen's Aid Society for a period of forty years developed into a much larger and more significant venture in the new Bennett College for Women in 1926.

An Expanded Concept and New Level
   of Operation

The Woman's Home Missionary Society had its beginning at a time when there was an emerging emphasis upon the new functions of women in domestic life, and her leadership role in the church and in society. In this general aura of developing importance and prestige the idea of education became a part of the missionary passion of the Woman's Home Missionary Society. In extending education to Negro women, which was a primary objective of the society, education was functionalized and adapted to the conception of primary needs. These needs were not conceived to be menial in nature. The training and educational emphases began at the level of the primary needs of the person, of the home, and of the community, and were applied at every level, aiming at functional preparation, and at the fullest development of the individual personality, and the highest type of womanhood. These were, and are, true functions of education.

In 1926, at the time the Woman's Home Missionary Society assumed a much larger responsibility for Bennett as an exclusively Woman's College, a new level of educational provision and involvement was reached. Out of the experiences and developments of the past and under the pressure of need to advance to new frontiers in education for Negro women, as well as for women generally, Bennett College for Women became the most exciting venture in education the society had thus far envisioned.

Bennett College for Women

The retirement of Dr. Frank Trigg in 1926 as President of Bennett College closed an era in the history of this institution. The college since its founding in 1873 had been co-educational and had rendered an excellent educational service in the North Carolina region and in the Methodist Church. The improvements made during the last four or five years prior to 1926 gave hope of a larger service. There was apparent need of a service in education that would go beyond that of the previous half century in kind and in quality.

Social ferment and changes made necessary a transition to new emphases and a wider range of preparation for functions and demands in a changing society. In 1926, less than a decade had passed since the close of World War I. The whole of American life,

163

and particularly Negro American life, was in transition, being influenced by the effects of the War. Mobilization, migration and urbanization were bringing changes in Negro life in the South and everywhere. Negro family life was being changed. Negro employment was changing. Political activities were increasing. Woman's suffrage and gainful employment pointed to further changes and new opportunities. The place and potency of women in American social life were gaining in importance. These social changes stimulated a ferment in education. Educational institutions sought standardization. They adopted programs of specialization and related these programs more specifically to employment opportunities. These trends characterized changes in educational institutions for Negro youth, and as the enrollments of women in the colleges increased, more attention was given to the specific types of education that would qualify them for careers, and social participation.

Prior to 1926, neither the Freedmen's Aid Society nor the Woman's Home Missionary Society of the Methodist Episcopal Church had operated an institution for Negro women separately and exclusively for women at the college level. Leaders in the Woman's Home Missionary Society said:

For some years the question of a first-class woman's college as a part of the system of schools for our Negro membership has been discussed. The Woman's Home Missionary Society had the establishment of such a school under consideration. The student body of Bennett College. . . .had nearly four girls to one boy. The location and the buildings seemed admirable for the establishment of a woman's college.[3][9]

So came the decision to change the historically co-educational Bennett College at Greensboro to a college for women only. This decision was the beginning of a new era in the history of Bennett College, and in cooperative relationship of the Board of Education for Negroes of the Methodist Episcopal Church, and the Woman's Home Missionary Society of the same denomination.

Setting Sail

Dr. Thomas F. Holgate of Northwestern University and a member of the Methodist Board of Education, and Mrs. W. H. C. Goode of the Woman's Home Missionary Society were two key figures in the beginning of Bennett College for Women. "By action of the Board of Education," said Dr. Holgate, "in February, 1926, Bennett College at Greensboro, North Carolina, formerly

164

co-educational, became a woman's college, under the patronage of the Board of Education and the Woman's Home Missionary Society, jointly."[40]

The Woman's Home Missionary Society took similar action, making this a co-operative enterprise. In the words of Mrs. Goode, "the working relationship was on a 50-50 financial basis with supervision vested in a Board of Trustees composed of equal representation from the Woman's Home Missionary Society and the Board of Education with a few members-at-large by both groups."[41]

The two cooperating Boards agreed to make appropriations of $10,000.00 each, annually, for current operation.[42] A systematic plan was immediately devised to secure funds for the college from outside sources.

David Dallas Jones, President

To give administrative leadership to the new Bennett College for Women, Mr. David Dallas Jones was elected President by the Board of Trustees. Mr. Jones, a native of Greensboro, North Carolina, was a Methodist of long standing and a younger brother of Bishop Robert E. Jones of the Methodist Episcopal Church. Mr. Jones brought to the presidency an excellent background of education and experience. He held the B.A. degree from Wesleyan University, Middletown, Connecticut, and in 1930 earned the M.A. degree from Columbia University.[43] He was a member of Phi Beta Kappa. From 1911 to 1914 Mr. Jones was a member of the International Committee of the Y.M.C.A., and from 1914 to 1923 he was Executive Secretary of the Pine Street Y.M.C.A., St. Louis, Missouri. He was a business man in Atlanta and a member of the Atlanta Inter-racial Commission when he was elected President of Bennett College.

Mr. Jones, and Bennett College also, were fortunate in his having a wife, Mrs. Susie Williams Jones, who complemented so well his qualities and efforts. Mrs. Jones held a B.A. degree from the University of Cincinnati. She was active in the Y.W.C.A. and on the National level of the church.

Mr. and Mrs. Jones made a great team in initiating and carrying forward the program of Bennett College. For thirty years Dr. and Mrs. Jones were the central and directing force of the college, and a strong influence upon the lives of thousands of young women whose good fortune it was to be students whom they touched.

In 1926 Bennett College for Women began with an academic program ranging from the seventh grade through the first year of college. By the end of 1931-32 all high school work had been discontinued, and the four-year college program engaged full attention. The college started in 1926 with ten students. Fourteen years later the student body numbered 356, drawn from twenty-seven states and the District of Columbia.[44]

The rapid growth and popularity of Bennett College was due in a large measure to the physical development and beauty of the campus. In a much larger measure, however, the rapid growth and increase in students must be attributed to the quality and personality of the leadership of the college, to the recruitment program, to the educational emphases, and the results of the whole educational endeavor, evident in the intellectual, cultural and personality development of the students. The late Mrs. Goode pointed out that the philosophy of the President and faculty "was summed up in the Bennett ideals: sense of responsibility, loyalty to one's self as well as others, freedom of activity in work and play, open-mindedness in all matters, and a purposefulness that engenders consecration to an ideal."[45]

Early in its new life, Bennett College became an unusual place of educational exploration and human development. "The dedicated Bennett faculty believed that everything touching the life of the student was educative. Therefore, the activities were chosen for value in student development. Religious education, health education, dramatics, and music contributed to the well-rounded program."[46]

Recognition

From the beginning in 1926, Bennett College endeavored to maintain high academic standards. In recognition of the achievement of this endeavor, the Southern Association of Colleges and Secondary Schools in 1932 placed Bennett on its accredited list as a four-year college. It was admitted to membership in the American Association of Collegiate Registrars, and in 1934 Bennett College was granted membership in the Association of American Colleges.[47] The Southern Association of Colleges and Secondary Schools in 1935 gave Bennett "A" rating.[48]

With the encouraging recognition continuing to be given, Bennett College moved forward to achieve more fully the goals and ideals which it had set. Some of these goals and ideals were expressed by Bishop Robert E. Jones when he delivered Bennett's first Founders Day Address. He said in part:

Bennett has made new ideals. What we are trying to work out here is an institution for women different from any other

166

institution of its kind. We are to show Negro consciousness, Negro culture, Negro self-denial. We are to bring out the best of the native ability of Negro life.[49]

Philanthropy and Other Support

Bennett College demonstrated early that it was on the way to becoming an unusual college with high standards and appealing goals. It was able to elicit favorable responses from philanthropists and foundations, and support from church conferences and other sources. In 1930 the General Education Board of New York City "made a conditional grant of $250,000 for endowment provided the administration could raise an equal sum for new buildings and equipment."[50] "Local citizens, various boards, agencies, and friends contributed to the campaign for matching gifts."[51]

Mr. and Mrs. Henry Pfeiffer of New York City made a grant of $247,000 for buildings.[52] Other foundations, boards, and agencies such as the Carnegie Corporation, the Phelps-Stokes Fund, the John F. Slater Fund, and the Julius Rosenwald Fund, over a period of years made substantial grants to Bennett College in support of its program. The Board of Education of the Methodist Church, the Woman's Home Missionary Society, later the Woman's Division of Christian Service, have supported Bennett since 1926 with regular appropriations, and substantial special appropriations and gifts for special purposes.

The North Carolina Conference, within the bounds of which Bennett College was located, gave sacrificial support to the college. At its October 1929 session a report was made on the "Bennett College Self-Denial Offering Fund." Also, "A resolution pleading for the continuance of our support to Bennett College, including the Self-Denial Offering of $2,500, was presented by R. G. Morris, and was enthusiastically received by the conference."[53] The resolution was passed.[54] At the next session of the North Carolina Conference a resolution was passed committing the conference "to raise, within a period of three years, $25,000.00 for the special endowment fund for Bennett College for Women."[55]

A bequest of $20,000 from the estate of Peter Clark, a former resident of Greensboro, represented the largest single gift to Bennett from a Negro.[56] By far, the Pfeiffer-Merner family has been Bennett's most generous benefactor, having given to the college well over a million dollars. In more recent years, during Dr. Player's Presidency, the Ford Foundation has given philanthropic support to Bennett College, having given in 1964 a grant of $1,000,000 for use as follows: "One-tenth of the face of the grant, plus the income on the existing year-end residue, to be used in each year during the period 1964-1974."[5][7]

Summary of Growth and Development of
Bennett College, 1926 to 1956

When Bennett started as a new college for women in 1926 the campus consisted of thirty acres, and several buildings, three of which were new.[5][8] In 1924 the buildings and grounds were valued at $200,000.[5][9] Between 1924 and May, 1926 three new buildings were added at a cost of $125,000,[6][0] making a total property value of approximately $325,000. In the course of the fourteen years from 1926 to 1940 the campus increased to forty-two acres, and the following six buildings were erected:[6][1]

1933 Thirkield Gymnasium
1934 Pfeiffer Hall — an upper-class dormitory
1934 Merner-Pfeiffer Heating Plant
1937 Henry Pfeiffer Science Hall
1938 Annie Merner Hall — a dormitory for sophomores
1939 Thomas F. Holgate Library

In 1940 construction had been started on two additional new buildings — Pfeiffer Memorial Chapel and the Carrie Barge Hall, a dormitory.

Assessment of Bennett College was made in 1940 by the Woman's Home Missionary Society as follows:

In its fourteen years of existence as a woman's college, under the leadership of President David D. Jones, Bennett has made unusual progress. Its work has attracted nation-wide attention. Its major support has come from the Board of Education and the Woman's Home Missionary Society of the former Methodist Episcopal Church, which latter organization has taken a very personal interest in all affairs pertaining to the welfare of the College. Bennett has also received large gifts for permanent improvement and maintenance from both Northern and Southern philanthropists, as well as from the General Education Board, the Carnegie Corporation, and the Julius Rosenwald Fund. Beginning with ten students and a few inadequate buildings, Bennett has grown until today its student body numbers 356, drawn from twenty-seven states and the District of Columbia. In June construction began on the Memorial Chapel, the gift of Mrs. Henry Pfeiffer of New York, and on Carrie Barge Hall, a dormitory, the gift of the Woman's Home Missionary Society.

* * *

Bennett has won for itself a definite and important place in the field of Negro education. Its graduates are successful homemakers, teachers, and social workers, librarians, and business women. Staffed by a faculty carefully selected and thoroughly devoted to the educational development of young people, it is generally acknowledged to be a living, growing, and progressive institution.[62]

Along with the development of the physical facilities, Bennett College made strides in building an able and well-selected faculty, which devoted itself to the work of creating new ideals and building a strong instructional program, relevant to the aims and objectives set forth.

From 1940 to 1956, Bennett College continued to make phenomenal progress in physical development, strength of faculty, development of academic and cultural programs, in enrollment and alumnae accomplishments. With the beautiful new Pfeiffer Chapel and Carrie Barge Hall completed in 1940, the religious program was greatly enhanced, and additional space for accommodation of dormitory students made possible a large increase in students. At the end of the thirty-year period of Dr. Jones' administration the physical plant consisted of forty-two acres of land, thirty-three buildings, and endowment amounting to $1,500,000.[63]

End of a Fruitful Administration

The death of Dr. David Dallas Jones, January 24, 1956, brought to an end a period of remarkable administrative leadership as the first President of Bennett College for Women. This was a golden period in the life of the college, which only dedication and hard work can provide. Many tributes were paid Dr. Jones at his funeral in Pfeiffer Memorial Chapel January 27, 1956. A later editorial tribute in the *Central Christian Advocate* summarized well the work and spirit of the late Dr. Jones at Bennett College for Women. In part the editorial said:

In the death of David Dallas Jones the church has lost one of its most forthright, persistent and successful ambassadors of Christian culture in higher education.

...One is amazed at the rapid growth of Bennett both in physical plant and student body, and its list of successful alumni [sic] is a most impressive one. But the most remarkable thing about it all is the spirit which Dr. Jones so largely set in

169

motion and so progressively kept alive. There were certain values which he kept before him and for which he increasingly worked.

...He was always certain of the direction he wanted to go, and was unyielding when he was convinced he was right. . . .

President Jones was a man who felt deeply about life. He was uncompromising in his convictions and bold in his opposition to injustice. Yet he was one of the first to extend a helping hand in the time of need. He believed that religion should be the core of higher education in the church-related college, and should express itself in the total range of college activities.[64]

Board of Control

A significant factor in progress of Bennett College for Women has been a strong board of control from the beginning to the present. In 1926 the first board of trustees was made up of an equal number of trustees from the Board of Education and the Woman's Home Missionary Society, and several others elected by the representatives of the two cooperating agencies. "In the late thirties, the sponsoring agencies transferred the property of this progressive institution to the Bennett College Board of Trustees,"[65] which became, for the most part, an independent board. It still, however, has stated representation from the two sponsoring agencies. At present nine members of the Bennett Board are elected by the Board of Education of the United Methodist Church, nine are elected by the Woman's Division of Christian Service of the United Methodist Church, and nine at large are elected by the board.[66]

Dr. Willa B. Player, President

On October 22, 1955, at a meeting of the Board of Trustees, President David D. Jones, because of his serious illness was made President Emeritus. At his request and to insure the continued progress of Bennett College, Dr. Willa B. Player was made President.[67]

Dr. Player, a native of Akron, Ohio, had joined the Bennett faculty in 1930.[68] She received the B.A. degree from Ohio Wesleyan University, and the M.A. degree from Oberlin University. She did additional graduate study at the University of Chicago, the University of Wisconsin, and a year of study at the University of Grenoble, Grenoble, France. Dr. Player earned her doctorate degree from Columbia University. In 1953 her alma mater, Ohio Wesleyan University, honored her with the degree Doctor of

170

Laws.[69] Her membership in scholarly societies and educational organizations makes a long list.

With her academic preparedness, her efficiency, and her dedication Dr. Player early became an important part of Bennett College and the college became a part of her. As a teacher of French, later director of admissions, and in other relationships to the college, Dr. Player became one of Dr. Jones' most valuable assets in establishing standards, and goals, and in carrying forward the academic program, and the process of selecting students. In 1952 she was made Vice President of Bennett, in charge of instruction.[70]

Becoming President in October, 1955, Dr. Player gave administrative leadership to Bennett College for a period of ten and a half years. During this period the enrollment was significantly increased, the faculty was strengthened, substantial development of the physical plant was made, and the endowment was increased. One of the most outstanding achievements of Bennett College during Dr. Player's Presidency was admission to membership in 1957 in the Southern Association of Colleges and Schools, being one of the first fifteen Negro four-year colleges to be admitted to membership. By the end of Dr. Player's administration the value of the buildings and grounds stood at $4,143,238; (book) value of the endowment was $1,887,808 (market value, $2,834,077), and the total assets were valued at approximately $9,000,000.[71]

Dr. Player rendered valuable service as a member of The Methodist Church. The high respect in which she was held as an educator was nationwide, evidenced numerous times, signally when she was invited to serve as a consultant on a state committee in preparation for the White House Conference on Education which met in Washington, D. C.

Dr. Player Resigns the Presidency

Dr. Player's Presidency of Bennett College for Women came to an end with her resignation, effective March 1, 1966, when she assumed the position of Director of the Division of College Support, in the U. S. Office of Education, Department of Health, Education, and Welfare. On leaving Bennett Dr. Player said: "My most noble dream for the school and its alumnae was that the best should be attained."[72]

When Dr. Player resigned, the Board of Trustees appointed an interim committee of the board to administer the affairs of the College until a new President was elected. Dr. Chauncey G. Winston, Dean of Instruction, was made Chairman of the

171

Committee and assumed the position of Acting President March 1, 1966.

Dr. Isaac H. Miller, Jr., President

On May 23, 1966 Dr. Isaac H. Miller, Jr., was elected by the Board of Trustees to the Presidency of Bennett College. He assumed office September 1, 1966.[73]

Dr. Miller came to the Presidency of Bennett College with superb academic training and a rich background of professional experience as a college and medical school teacher of biochemistry and as a research scientist in chemistry. He earned the B.S. degree from Livingstone College, the M.S. degree, and the Ph.D. degree in biochemistry from the University of Wisconsin. His membership in honor societies and his honors and awards are many. His writings for scientific journals are extensive. He was elected to the Presidency of Bennett College from the position of Associate Professor of Biochemistry at Meharry Medical College where he had been on the faculty since 1954.

With his fine family — wife, four sons and a daughter — and with his excellent educational background and keen insights into the problems and needs of present-day higher education, it can be anticipated with much assurance that Bennett College will move forward with steady progress under the able leadership of Dr. Miller.

REFERENCES AND NOTES

1. Freedmen's Aid Society Report, 1879, p. 37.
2. Report of the Freedmen's Aid Society, 1875, p. 37.
3. Freedmen's Aid Society Report, 1879, p. 39.
4. *Ibid.*
5. *Ibid.*
6. Minutes, North Carolina Conference, January 26-30, 1882, p. 20.
7. *Ibid.*
8. Journal, North Carolina Conference, October 25-29, 1888, p. 23.
9. Report, Freedmen's Aid and Southern Education Society, 1888, p. 37.
10. Journal, North Carolina Conference, October, 1886, p. 34.
11. Journal, North Carolina Conference, October, 24-28, 1889, p. 301.
12. Report, Freedmen's Aid Society and Southern Education Society, 1891, p. 18.
13. *Ibid.*
14. Journal, North Carolina Conference October 19-22, 1892, p. 32.
15. *The Christian Educator*, December, 1901 — January, 1902, p. 4.
16. *Ibid.*, pp. 4f.
17. *The Christian Educator*, December, 1900 — January, 1901, p. 27.
18. *Ibid.*
19. *The Christian Educator*, February 3, 1901, p. 45.
20. *The Christian Educator* Report, Freedmen's Aid and Southern Education Society, November, 1905, p. 16.
21. *Ibid.*, November, 1904, p. 31.
22. *The Christian Educator*, November, 1911, p. 17; and November, 1912, p. 22.
23. Journal, North Carolina Conference, October 2-7, 1912, p. 35.
24. *The Christian Educator*, November, 1911, p. 17; and November, 1912, p. 22.
25. *The Christian Educator*, November, 1915, p. 9.
26. *Ibid.*, p. 24.
27. *Ibid.*
28. *The Christian Educator*, November, 1924, p. 16.
29. *The Christian Educator*, February, 1922, p. 5.
30. *The Christian Educator*, May, 1924, p. 5.
31. *Ibid.*

32. *The Christian Educator*, August, 1926, p. 8.
33. *Ibid.*, p. 9.
34. *Ibid.*
35. Kent Home-Historical Notes of the Woman's Home Missionary Society, 1966.
36. *Ibid.*
37. *Ibid.*
38. *Ibid.*
39. *The Christian Educator*, May, 1928, p. 3.
40. Memorandum, Dr. Thomas F. Holgate, 1926.
41. Mrs. W. H. C. Goode, Unpublished Manuscript, 1940; and Mrs. Ruth Esther Meeker, *op. cit.*, p. 176.
42. Dr. Holgate, *Loc. cit.*
43. *Who's Who In America*, 1948-49.
44. Meeker, *op. cit.*, p. 177.
45. Goode, *Loc. cit.*
46. *Ibid.*
47. Meeker, *op. cit.*, p. 177.
48. Simmons, Virginia — Bennett History, p. 4.
49. *The Christian Educator*, February, 1931, p. 15.
50. Meeker, *op. cit.*, p. 177.
51. *Ibid.*
52. Simmons, Virginia, Manuscript, "Bennett History," June, 1939 (With appendix, Jan. 1958). Note: Miss Simmons (later Mrs. Nyabongo) is a graduate of Bennett College, and was a member of the faculty at the time her "Bennett History" was written, about 1939.
53. Journal, North Carolina Conference, October 23-27, 1929, p. 11.
54. *Ibid.*, p. 35.
55. Journal, North Carolina Conference, November 5-9, 1930, p. 38.
56. Simmons, *Loc. cit.*, p. 8.
57. Letter from President Isaac H. Miller, Jr., February 3, 1971.
58. *The Christian Educator*, May, 1926, p. 1.
59. *The Christian Educator*, November, 1924, p. 16.
60. *The Christian Educator*, February, 1926, p. 2.
61. Meeker, *op. cit.*, pp. 177f.
62. Fifty-Ninth Annual Report, Woman's Home Missionary Society, 1939-1940, p. 223.
63. *The Central Christian Advocate*, February 15, 1956.
64. *Ibid.*, p. 9.
65. Meeker, *op. cit.*, p. 178.
66. *American Universities and Colleges*, 10th Edition, 1968, p. 1088.

67. *The Methodist Woman*, January, 1956, p. 20.
68. *Ibid.*
69. *Ibid.*
70. *Ibid.*
71. Data from President's Office; and *American Universities and Colleges*, 10th Edition, 1968, p. 1088 (For June, 1967).
72. *The Central Christian Advocate*, April 1, 1966, p. 3.
73. Letter from Dr. Isaac H. Miller, February 3, 1971.

CHAPTER 12

A BRIEF HISTORICAL ACCOUNT OF
BETHUNE-COOKMAN COLLEGE

Bethune-Cookman College emerged in 1923 from a merger of two institutions. This historical account will be given in three sections: first, an historical statement on the founding and development of Cookman Institute in Jacksonville, Florida, where it existed for a half century; second, a statement will be given on the founding and existence of the Daytona Normal and Industrial Institute for Negro Girls, which had a life of separate existence for twenty years in Daytona Beach, Florida; and, third, an account will be given of the merging of these two institutions in 1923, and the subsequent development of Bethune-Cookman College.

I. Cookman Institute

Cookman Institute had its beginning as a successful night school in 1872 at Jacksonville, Florida. The Freedmen's Aid Society in the first year of the school contributed one hundred and fifty dollars toward its support.[1] It was through the interests and efforts of the Rev. W. B. Osborn and the Rev. Samuel B. Darnell that the school was begun.[2] It was announced that the school "will bear the honored name of the lamented Cookman, who took so deep an interest in the full redemption of this unfortunate people."[3]

The Florida Winter Home Association purchased four thousand acres of land on the Arlington River, adjoining the Home, and pledged ten percent of the net proceeds of the sale of lots for the permanent establishment of a school to be named after the Rev. Alfred Cookman.[4]

A Board of Trustees was established consisting of the following named persons: Bishop M. Simpson, D.D., His Excellency, Governor O. B. Hart, Rev. Daniel Curry, D.D., Wm. Matthews, C. L. Robinson, Rev. Adam White, Rev. D. P. Kidder, D.D., Geo. M'Cord, Rev. Wm. M'Donald, Rev. W. B. Osborn, Rev. S. B. Darnell, W. G. Colby, Rev. N. Webster, Rev. R. S. Rust, D.D., E. Remington, W. C. DePauw, Chas. W. Blew.[5]

177

To insure prompt and energetic action to found a school upon an enlarged and liberal basis, friends of education in the North expressed a willingness to give influence to and pledge funds for the support of this enterprise.[6]

The Rev. Samuel B. Darnell became the first President of Cookman Institute, which position he held until 1894.

From its inception the Cookman Institute was closely identified with the Florida Annual Conference. In fact, its life was rooted in the Conference. The Black people of the Methodist Episcopal Church in Florida were keenly aware of the need and value of education and always expressed appreciation for the opportunities for education made available through the Church, for almost the only education provided was through this Church School.

The Florida Annual Conference in session in 1878 heard and approved the following report from its Committee on Education:

> *Resolved*, That we are as much as ever convinced of the need of education among our people, as the foundation on which we hope to rise, and the method of our rising.
>
> *Resolved*, That we will encourage and urge the people we represent to avail themselves of the common schools of the State, and to make sacrifices, in order to secure the benefits of the school system to the rising generation.
>
> *Resolved*, That we learn with great pleasure of the success of our own Cookman Institute, under the direction of Rev. S. B. Darnell, at Jacksonville — founded and sustained by the Freedmen's Aid Society of our Church.
>
> *Resolved*, That we encourage our youth, and especially our young men, who contemplate entering upon the work of the ministry, to avail themselves of the rare and liberal benefits of Cookman Institute as an important and necessary preparation for the sacred calling.
>
> W. W. Hicks
J. G. Howard
C. C. Manigault
W. J. Salmond.[7]

According to the report of the Freedmen's Aid Society in 1879 there were in Florida a hundred thousand Negro people, unable to provide schools for their children. Many schools were closed for the want of teachers, or the disposition to afford these people the advantages of an education.[8]

Progress was being made in the development of Cookman Institute. The Freedmen's Aid Society reported, "we have

178

buildings worth five thousand dollars. These are built of brick with metal roofs, accommodating one hundred and fifty pupils. The dormitory erected last year will accommodate twenty-five boarders."[9]

The Florida Conference rejoiced in the progress of this, their school, and continued to resolve to acknowledge with gratitude the benevolent character of the Methodist Episcopal Church in sustaining in their midst the only school of high grade for the people of color in the State of Florida.

The Florida Conference in its 1882 Annual Session gave a bit of history of the development of Cookman Institute in the following excerpt from the Minutes:

Cookman Institute in Jacksonville is doing a noble work, with S. B. Darnell for its Principal, who, with his devoted wife, first started this Institution; first in Old Zion Church, then a small building, with tower pointing heavenward, saying to people of Florida and southern Georgia, 'come and receive the light we can give and the help you need to become teachers and preachers of the Truth as it is in Jesus.'[10]

These early years of development were difficult for Cookman Institute. The Freedmen's Aid Society's Report for 1882 reveals the financial problem of the school:

The Cookman Institute, at Jacksonville, Florida, has been embarrassed by a small debt incurred in the erection of its new school building, and a thousand dollars has been appropriated during the year towards its liquidation. Great credit is due Rev. S. B. Darnell for his successful efforts in raising funds for the erection of buildings and for filling the school with students, and in generously bearing so many burdens connected with the institute, the President of which he has been from its establishment.[11]

The financial problems of 1882 seem to have been mere "growing pains." The Committee on Education of the Florida Conference in 1883, gave a brighter report on the Institute, saying:

Your Committee would report with pleasure its present prosperous condition. It has been our pleasure to examine its buildings erected at a cost of $12,000. We find its dormitories well supplied with necessary furniture and neatly kept. Its chapel is commodious and well lighted and beautiful in its appointments. We have also had the privilege of seeing some of

179

its exercises, and are impressed with the faithfulness and genuineness with which the work is done.[1 2]

In this same vein the 1885 session of the Florida Annual Conference makes mention of the need for additional buildings and the possibility of a larger enrollment. The interest of the Florida Conference is indicated in the statement that of the $12,000 spent on buildings for Cookman Institute, the Conference had raised $10,000. The Freedmen's Aid Society contributed $2,000 and purchased the land. The value of the total property at that time was given at $18,000.[1 3]

By 1886 Cookman Institute had extended its curriculum three years above the common branches, to include classical studies; two classes in theology were also included.[1 4]

The place and value of Cookman Institute in the education of the Freedmen were fully realized by the Florida Conference, which the Conference clearly stated in its Minutes of 1889:

The educational system, poor and feeble as it is, has spread its network all over the South, but without the energies of the churches to supplement the state, the results would be quite abortive in much of this vast territory of our national domain. Especially is this true among the freedmen. Only in the more favored localities would their schools be of any consequence in diffusing the most rudimentary forms of an education. The millions of money spent and hundreds of teachers at work under the more powerful denominations are accomplishing good no mortal man can estimate.

Cookman Institute sustains to this State what other institutions do to other States, and no school in our commonwealth is doing for the people what it is for its patrons.[1 5]

To the Florida Conference in 1890 it was reported that the enrollment was at 350 students. The school was better organized, the grades more clearly defined, and "the classical department moving along in higher branches, conquering new fields of thought, and getting disciplined minds that will bring greater returns when put to work among the active forces of this civilization."[1 6] Industrial training had also been included for young men, supported by the John F. Slater Fund.

At this same Conference the report of the Committee on Education made reference to the performance of Cookman Institute students and graduates on county examinations. "The quality of work done in this school was clearly seen during the examination for teachers in our public schools in various counties, during last summer and fall. Our students brought great credit upon themselves and Cookman Institute — many averaging from 80 to 100 per cent."[17]

The Conference expressed its appreciation of and gratitude to Rev. S. B. Darnell and wife, "whose patient, earnest and untiring zeal under Divine Guidance have made possible our prosperous Cookman, which we behold with much admiration and love."[18]

The report of the Freedmen's Aid and Southern Education Society for 1890-1891 points up the growth and strength of Cookman Institution at that time. The value of land and buildings was estimated to be $30,000. There were four buildings — Main Hall, two dormitories, and a teachers' home. The enrollment in all departments was 431.

Rev. Darnell commented that, "The presence of choice teachers, such as we have been fortunate to obtain, gives character to the work and profit to the pupils."[19]

For twenty-two years, 1872 to 1894, Cookman Institute was under the administration of the Rev. Samuel B. Darnell as President. The institution experienced its greatest growth under his leadership. In 1894, because of ill health, Rev. Darnell resigned from the Presidency of Cookman, having rendered a remarkable service. As was said a year or two earlier with reference to Cookman Institute: "No village now in our commonwealth can there be found where some of the influence of our work cannot be traced."[20] And, so it was with the influence of the Rev. Samuel B. Darnell.

For three years after the resignation of Rev. Samuel Darnell the office of President was vacant at Cookman Institute. The vacancy of the office for this period was made necessary because of the retrenchment by the Freedmen's Aid and Southern Education Society, forgoing the expense of the President's salary in order to keep within the financial limits of receipts.[21] The school was in charge of Miss Lillie M. Whitney for 1894-1895, and during 1895-1896 there was a joint Principalship of Miss Lillie M. Whitney and Miss Carrie Fairchild.[22] Miss Fairchild had charge of the institute during the school year 1896-1897. In 1897, the Reverend S. W. Kemerer, a graduate of Hamline University and a member of the Minnesota Conference of the Methodist Episcopal Church was elected President of Cookman Institute.

In his district report to the Annual Conference in January, 1898, Rev. S. A. Huger, Presiding Elder of the Jacksonville District, stated that:

The past year for various causes has not been a very brilliant one for Cookman Institute when compared with former years. The strong competition of other schools around us, together with difficulties arising within its walls, detracted from it that strong influence which heretofore drew numbers of scholars from the fields and cities of our beautiful State.[23]

The Conference Committee on Education commented on Cookman Institute as follows:

Cookman Institute has for twenty years stood foremost among the institutions of our State, under the excellent management of Prof. Darnell, but changes and financial depressions have greatly retarded her progress, especially in the enrollment of students. We thank the ladies, Misses Whitney and Fairchild, for their labors and believe they did from their hearts what they could and as faithfully as they knew how. And, now, in the wisdom of the authorities, they have sent to us a man in whom we discern the Spirit of Christ and impresses us that he is made up of the right-material to succeed. Thus, the Committee takes the position to pledge the hearty support of the Conference in sending students and raising the full amounts apportioned to this Conference.[24]

The Christian Educator indicates that the Rev. S. W. Kemerer was in charge of Cookman Institute during the two years 1897-98 and 1898-99.[25] President Kemerer resigned the position as President to take post graduate studies. He was succeeded by Professor H. R. Bankerd,[26] who held the position only one year.

No President is listed for the year 1901-02, but *The Christian Educator* lists L. M. Whitney and R. S. W. Thomas as Principals in 1902.[27] Again no President is listed for 1903.

For a ten-year period, from the time of President Darnell's resignation to 1904, Cookman Institute suffered because of the absence of strong and continuous administrative leadership such as that given by the Rev. Darnell during the first twenty-two years of the life of the institution.

The next President gave good leadership for a period of five years. In 1904 Dr. James T. Docking was elected President of Cookman Institute.[28]

The Christian Educator reported:

Rev. Dr. J. T. Docking of the New England Conference has been elected to the Presidency of Cookman Institute. He comes to us after years of successful work in the pastorate, and after a thorough preparation in Boston University. He brings to his aid the assistance of his accomplished wife. The people have gladly received them, and he begins his work with the promise of unusual success.[29]

The school was making good progress under the administration of Dr. Docking, when he was removed in 1909 by his election to the Presidency of Rust College in Holly Springs, Mississippi.

Dr. Docking was succeeded at Cookman Institute by The Rev. G. Barts Stone,[30] the length of whose administration was exceeded only by that of Dr. Darnell. The Rev. Stone was from West Nanticoke, Pennsylvania, and came to the Presidency of Cookman Institute highly recommended by educators and influential men of the church. He was formerly a teacher at Grant University.

In 1911 President Stone reported two buildings constituting the plant, with $940.88 on hand to apply on a President's house. There were fourteen teachers and 422 students.[31]

The report for 1912 shows a property value of $32,062, a President's residence, $4,000, and an enrollment of 470 students.[32]

Thomas Jesse Jones in his Report on the Study of Negro Education, in 1916, gave the school a good rating. At that time the enrollment was 408, of which 359 were in the elementary grades and forty-nine were in courses at the secondary school level — 17 in the normal course, and 32 in the college preparatory course.[33]

In the Spring of 1919, after ten years at Cookman Institute, Rev. Stone returned to the pastorate in his own conference. "His industry and integrity, combined with a faithful Christian example, have been of inestimable value in training the minds of students who have come to Cookman during the past decade," said *The Christian Educator*.[34]

After the retirement of President Stone, Cookman Institute became affiliated with and put under the care of Clark University and its president at Atlanta, Georgia. It was intended that with this arrangement Cookman would benefit by the sympathy and inspiration of the larger institution, and the Cookman graduates were directed to Clark to complete their college training.[35]

To facilitate the affiliation of Cookman with Clark, President King selected Professor Isaac H. Miller, who had been in charge of the Normal Department at Clark since 1913, to be principal of Cookman.[36] The school had at this time an enrollment of 250 students in the elementary grades and high school. The curriculum included also the following special courses: Normal training,

183

music, domestic science, sewing, shoemaking, printing, business, and agriculture.[37]

Cookman Institute had a separate existence of fifty-one years, including the three or four years of its affiliation with Clark University. The first twenty-two years of its life, during the administration of its first President, the Rev. S. B. Darnell, were more prosperous and promising. After four or five years of temporary administration and the great Jacksonville fire of 1901 which destroyed the Institute, the school had a struggle to get back to the peak it had earlier attained. The Reverend G. B. Stone gave devoted leadership during the ten years of his administration. The fact that the Institute was placed under the supervision of Clark University in 1919 gave some evidence of its inability to become a strong college at any time in the immediate future. Mr. I. H. Miller was a strong man in the field of education and might have in time developed Cookman into the kind of institution it was first contemplated it should become. Because of the strong competition that developed there in Jacksonville, one of the schools being Boylan Home for Girls, operated by the Woman's Home Missionary Society of the Methodist Episcopal Church, and because of the inadequacy of operating finances, it was not difficult for the Board of Education for Negroes, formerly the Freedmen's Aid Society, to agree to merge Cookman Institute with the Daytona Normal and Industrial Institute for Negro Girls in Daytona Beach, Florida.

II. Daytona Normal and Industrial
   Institute for Negro Girls

Mrs. Mary McLeod Bethune was a most remarkable woman. She grew up in humble surroundings in rural South Carolina and toiled her way through cotton fields to Scotia Seminary, Concord, North Carolina. After graduation, with great ambition and a noble dream in her heart she went to Daytona, Florida, and there in 1904 with a great faith and one dollar and fifty cents she founded a school, an enterprise destined to give fame to its founder and to be an inestimable blessing to generation upon generation of Negro youth. The one dollar and a half was meager monetary capital, but the unlimited capital which Mrs. Bethune possessed was her faith, her enthusiasm, her ability, her dedication to service, and her willingness to work. The first frame building she erected was named "Faith Hall," from which an unbelievable institution has grown.

When Mrs. Bethune went to Daytona Beach with her limited financial capital but with great vision, she secured five dollars

184

which was paid as earnest money on a lot in Daytona.[38] She wisely decided to start the school at Daytona where large numbers of sympathetic and well-to-do northern people spent their winters. She interested many of these people in the establishment of the school, among whom were Mr. James N. Gamble of Cincinnati, Ohio, who for a long time was one of her most liberal supporters; Mrs. F. M. Chapman from Englewood, New Jersey; Mr. Harrison Rhodes, Mr. F. C. Walcott, Lieutenant-Colonel Theodore Roosevelt, Mrs. Willard D. Straight of New York City; and Mr. Smith G. Young of Lansing, Michigan.[39]

Out of the vision of what Mrs. Bethune wanted to do for her people in the field of education, the school was named "The Daytona Normal and Industrial Institute for Negro Girls."

Within ten to twelve years the school plant had developed to include fifteen acres in the city of Daytona, four frame buildings and several cottages, and movable equipment valued at $2,175.00. The total plant was valued at $30,575.00.[40]

Dr. Thomas Jesse Jones, in 1916, described the school as being "a well-managed school of elementary and secondary grades, with some provision for teacher training."[41] In addition, there was The McLeod Hospital and Training School for Nurses, with courses including: cooking, sewing, laundering, and minor courses in rug weaving, broom making, chair caning, some raffia work, and gardening and poultry raising.[42]

The Institute was chartered in 1920 in the State of Florida under the name "Daytona Normal and Industrial Institute for Negro Girls." The object of the corporation was stated as follows:

> The object of this corporation shall be to establish and maintain an institution for the moral, physical, spiritual, industrial and intellectual education ₁and advancement of negroes [sic]. That these purposes may be accomplished, the Trustees shall have the power to establish a hospital and any departments, schools or branches that they may deem advisable.[43]

Provision is made in the charter that the membership of the corporation shall consist of a Board of Trustees, composed of white persons and Negroes whose qualification of membership shall be fidelity to the object of the corporation; said Board of Trustees to be composed of not less than nine and not more than twenty-five persons.[44]

In addition to the Board of Trustees there shall be an Advisory Board of Five or more persons whose duties and manner of election shall be determined by the By-laws of the corporation.[45]

Provision was made that Mrs. Mary McLeod Bethune should be a life member of both the corporation or Board of Trustees, and of the Advisory Board.[46]

Mrs. Bethune, the founder of the Daytona Normal and Industrial Institute for Negro Girls was its President the entire period of its separate existence, and subsequently, she was President of the merged institutions from 1923 to 1942.

Merger of Cookman Institute and Daytona Normal
and Industrial Institute for Negro Girls

Early in 1923 talks were begun regarding the merging of Cookman Institute and Daytona Normal and Industrial Institute for Negro Girls. In a letter[47] dated February 13, 1923, from Dr. I. Garland Penn, Corresponding Secretary, Board of Education for Negroes, M. E. Church, to Dr. P. J. Maveety who held a similar position, Dr. Penn apprises Dr. Maveety of his visit to Daytona Institute, Daytona, Florida, on February 5th, indicating that he "found one of the best and most statesmanlike projects I have yet seen for our people." Describing the plant Dr. Penn said:

It is a plant with something like five buildings — two of them being new brick buildings representing an expenditure of not less than $125,000. One of these is used for the administration and classroom building, with a large and commodious chapel which will seat upward of 800 people. The other, a dormitory, has just been erected and will be dedicated on March 5th. This will house 150 girls. . . .the other buildings are of wood, but neatly kept. . . .[48]

"This institution," said Dr. Penn,

is certainly a monument to Mrs. Bethune. . . .Principal and who is so loyally supported by her board of white and colored trustees, among who [sic] are such men as Mr. James M. Gamble, Chairman of the Board, and other representative men and women of wealth who are tourists and have their summer [winter] homes at Daytona and Daytona Beach.

Mrs. Bethune welcomed Dr. Penn, as she "had long desired to confer with some of the leaders of her race as to what was the wise thing to do in the further development of the institution so as to insure its permanency." Dr. Penn conferred with Mrs. Bethune and several other key members of her Board of Trustees, whom Mrs. Bethune called together for an informal meeting. The

186

conversational discussion of matters relating to a possible merger was so agreeable that on the next day, February 6th, Dr. Penn wrote Mrs. Bethune, in an informal way, "soliciting information as to the possibilities of such a merger, and if the same would be agreeable to you and your Board of Trustees." As a basis for agreement or decision, the following considerations were stated by Dr. Penn:

1. Merge the two institutions, sell the Cookman Institute property in Jacksonville and transfer funds and all equipment to the merged institution in Daytona Beach.
2. The merged institution would be coeducational; funds from the sale of the Cookman property to provide a dormitory for men.
3. Mrs. Bethune would be president of the merged institution, to give leadership in this new venture. The faculty of the Daytona Normal and Industrial Institute would remain intact.
4. The merged institution would become an institution of the Methodist Episcopal Church. The Board of Trustees and the Advisory Board would remain; added members to come from the Methodist Church.
5. Available "an annual appropriation by our Board for the maintenance of the institution, and such other appropriations as might be necessary for repairs from time to time, just as is done for other institutions operated by our Board."

Following Dr. Penn's letter of February 6, 1923, to Mrs. Bethune, there was held in Daytona March 6th a joint meeting of a committee from the Board of Education for Negroes, Methodist Church and a committee from the Board of Trustees of the Daytona Normal and Industrial Institute. Pursuant to the joint meeting of the two committees, a document of thirteen points for consideration dated March 9, 1923, was drawn up by the Trustees of Daytona Normal and Industrial Institute and was presented to the Managers of the Board of Education for Negroes, Methodist Episcopal Church. This document was signed by the following members of the Board:

> James N. Gamble, President
> D. H. Rutter, Secretary
> Mrs. C. H. Ranslow
> Smith G. Young, Chairman, Finance Committee
> Mary McLeod Bethune

On April 17, 1923, the document mentioned above was reviewed by the Board of Managers of the Board of Education for Negroes and was revised in the presence of and approved by Mr. James N. Gamble, President of the Board of Trustees of the Daytona Normal and Industrial Institution; Mrs. Mary McLeod Bethune, Principal of the Institute; Dr. C. F. Goss, member of the Board of Trustees.[4][9]

Item Eight of the document was among the most important, if not the most basic of the thirteen items of the document agreed upon. Because of its importance, item eight follows:

Eight: The Board of Trustees, as now constituted, of the Daytona Normal and Industrial Institute, in view of the transferring and conveying to the Board of Education for Negroes, of the Methodist Episcopal Church, the fee simple title to the property now owned by the Daytona Normal and Industrial Institute, expect and understand that the Board of Education for Negroes, of the Methodist Episcopal Church, are to appropriate within one year from this date, for the use of the Daytona Normal and Industrial Institute, the sum of One Hundred Thousand Dollars ($100,000.00) (which includes any returns that may be realized from the sale of the Cookman Institute property), and to pay it in cash as required for construction of buildings and for equipment during the year from April 1, 1924, to April 1, 1925. It also is expected and understood that the Board of Education for Negroes will recommend that, within and during the time from April 1, 1925, to September 1, 1926, or as soon thereafter as the funds made available by the Church for its schools for Negroes will permit, the Board appropriate and pay over for the use of the Daytona Normal and Industrial Institute another one hundred thousand dollars ($100,000.00) in cash as required for the construction of buildings and for equipment.

It is expected and understood that, during the year from April 1, 1924, to April 1, 1925, the Board is to appropriate and pay over, as required during the school year for maintenance and development of the Daytona Normal and Industrial Institute, a minimum of Twenty Thousand Dollars ($20,000.00) in cash (which includes the current expense appropriation now regularly made to Cookman Institute); that, thereafter, the Board of Education for Negroes will pay annually for the maintenance of the Institute such sums as may become necessary to continue the work in its present high quality, and to provide for development commensurate with the importance of the Institute in the growing system of schools fostered by the Board of Education for Negroes; that, provided this contemplated merger becomes effective, the Board will, during the year and prior to April 1, 1924, appropriate and pay over during the school year the sum of Twenty Thousand Dollars ($20,000.00) in cash as required for maintenance and development, provided such appropriation and payment can legally be made by the Board.

The merger appeared to be a certainty at this time. In a letter to Dr. I. Garland Penn April 24, 1923, Mrs. Bethune expressed her complete satisfaction regarding the pending consummation of the plan.

On June 21, 1923, Dr. I. Garland Penn wrote Messrs. J. H. Blodgett, C. C. Manigault and others, Jacksonville, Florida, saying:

Your petition of recent date forwarded to our Executive Committee through your representative, Hon. J. H. Blodgett was graciously received at a meeting of the Committee June 20, 1923. The petition concerning the merger of Cookman Institute and the Daytona Normal and Industrial Institute was read and your representative Mr. Blodgett was given opportunity to comment thereon. Following the presentation by Mr. Blodgett a statement was made by Bishop Richardson, the Resident Bishop of the Atlanta Area, who is a member of our Board, and one of the Secretaries of this Society. After all statements had been made, on motion the office was requested to reply to your communication, which is as follows:

'The merger of the Cookman Institute and Daytona Normal and Industrial Institute has been practically concluded, by action of the Board of Managers called for that purpose and cannot be reversed by the Committee.'

Dr. Penn, in his letter of June 21st to Mr. Blodgett, further stated that:

With all the parties concerned having been consulted at a special meeting of the Board of Managers with the Committee from the Trustees of the Daytona Institute, the tentative agreements were gone over and further approved. Since that time, all matters have been put into the hands of the attorneys representing the two Boards, to perfect the merger, and the advice of Educational authorities at New York has been sought and their approval given, so that in the procedure which covers from February to June, there was ample time to make any

189

objections before the matters had reached final decision. We have received the second approval of the Advisory Board of Cookman Institute, dated as late as June 13th, 1923, in which the following sentence is used:

'NOW THEREFORE, Be it resolved that this Board now in its lawful session do hereby consent to, ratify and approve the proposed merger of the said schools as now being negotiated, and that the Board at Cincinnati, Ohio, be informed of the willingness and desire on the part of this Board to assist, consent to and approve all the acts and deeds done and to be done by said Board at Cincinnati for the perfection of this proposed merger in and for the high purposes and good which dominate the mind of the Board in bringing about this proposed merger of these two schools. . . .'[50]

The merger of Cookman Institute with Daytona Normal and Industrial School was not accomplished without opposition. Many of the Methodists and people in and around Jacksonville strenuously opposed the merger, because this meant the removal of Cookman Institute from Jacksonville and consequently an apparent loss of their institution. Many favored the merging of all the Methodist interests there in the city, namely, Cookman Institute, Boylan Home, and Brewster Hospital; the latter two institutions being under the management of the Woman's Home Missionary Society.

Merger Consummated

The merger of Cookman Institute and Daytona Normal and Industrial Institute was consummated April 17, 1923, under the name "The Daytona Normal and Industrial Institute." In effecting the merger, the name of Mrs. Bethune's school was used without change; all of the property title of the former Daytona Normal and Industrial Institute was transferred without debt and in fee simple to the Board of Education for Negroes, the Methodist Episcopal Church; the school was to be co-educational; the Board of Education for Negroes was to have and name a majority of the members of the Board of Trustees of the new institution; the charter was to be changed, making provision for these new amendments; in addition to the academic work being done at that time, the new institution was to become a junior college as soon as possible; Mrs. Bethune, by agreement, was to remain President of the new institution the rest of her natural life, so long as competent; and Mrs. Bethune was to be a life member of the Board of Trustees, and of the Advisory Board. The financial support to be given the new Daytona Normal and Industrial Institute as agreed upon has been stated above.

The first session of the newly merged institutions began in September, 1923.

The property of Cookman Institute at Jacksonville was sold to the public school authorities of the City of Jacksonville for the sum of $45,000.[51] The money from the sale of this property was transmitted to the Daytona-Cookman Collegiate Institute, to apply on a men's dormitory then in process of erection.[52]

III. Bethune-Cookman College

In a letter from Mrs. Bethune, dated December 20, 1923, to Dr. Penn, Mrs. Bethune stated that "there is still a great unrest among the Alumni Association of Cookman Institute. They are begging that the school be called Bethune-Cookman College. I think to do this would heal the sore places and the whole of Florida would be more harmonious."

On January 15, 1924, the Rev. D. H. Rutter, Pastor of the Community Methodist Episcopal Church at Daytona, and also a member of the Board of Trustees of Daytona Normal Institute, wrote Dr. Penn, saying: "We believe it would be a wise policy to name this institution 'The Bethune-Cookman Institute, or College.'" The official name of this institution became Daytona-Cookman Collegiate Institute, which title it carried until March, 1929.

An amended charter was issued, dated March 13, 1929, in which several significant changes were made in the old charter which was amended at the time of the merger in 1923. The first important amendment in 1929 was the change of the name from "Daytona-Cookman Collegiate Institute" to "Bethune-Cookman College."

A second important amendment gave the Board of Trustees the authority to fill vacancies on the Board on nomination by the trustees, "subject to approval by the Board of Education of the Methodist Episcopal Church." The amended charter did not provide for "a majority of the members of the Board of Trustees to be members of the Methodist Episcopal Church." It did provide, however, that the Florida and South Florida Conferences and the Saint Johns River Conference of the Methodist Episcopal Church, "shall always have one member on said Board of Trustees."

The early years after the merger of the two institutions were years of adjustment — adaptation to the new co-educational arrangement, acquiring physical facilities, development of program

191

and staff, and sustaining a new relationship to the Methodist Episcopal Church at large, and more specifically to the supporting conferences.

The elementary and high school work was retained for some years, but the college moved in the direction of a program above the high school level. Emphasis was placed upon teacher training through the Normal Department, which was two years above high school. The Junior College work grew less rapidly than the Normal Department, but as the Junior College became accredited in the early 1930's, the work in this area took on new life and growth.

Some of the problems faced by this institution may be noted in the following excerpts from a report in 1928:

> The effect of bank failures, of the burst of the Boom Bubble, of financial slumps and hurricane storms, has been keenly felt in this institution. Yet, Bethune-Cookman has opened her doors this Fall with an enrollment far in advance of that the same time last year when economic conditions were not quite so bad as they are at the present time. . .
>
> . . .Our outlook as to the real work of the school is brighter than ever before. . . .The college department at Bethune-Cookman is larger than ever before. . . .Bethune-Cookman's goal for herself seems much nearer in this her twenty-fifth year of service. . . .[53]

Despite the financial difficulties of the State of Florida and the entire nation in the 1930's Bethune-Cookman continued to move forward. The progress of the college is reflected in the following statement from *The Christian Educator:*

> Bethune-Cookman is undergoing a phenomenal growth. Four years ago the two classes of the Junior College Department registered eleven students. All others were enrolled in the high school. This term, seventy-five have been classified above the high school. Meantime, all classes have been eliminated below the ninth grade.
>
> . . .The Board of Education through its movement, 'Better Schools for Negroes,' is just beginning a splendid financial campaign for $365,000 to secure new buildings and endowment. Negroes of Florida were asked to raise $50,000. They subscribed $60,000, over by $10,000.[54]

Bethune-Cookman College remained a two-year Junior College until 1943, and carried also a parallel two-year teacher-training course. The college had "A" rating by the Southern Association of

Colleges and Secondary Schools. It remained under the administrative direction of Mrs. Bethune until her retirement in 1942.

In the course of three to four decades Bethune-Cookman College probably had more wealthy people visit its campus than any other institution of its kind in the southern region. Spending the winters at Daytona, Daytona Beach, and other nearby Florida winter resorts, these wealthy people came to the campus as visitors daily and especially on Sunday afternoons. They were attracted to the campus by the magnetic personality of a remarkable woman, Mrs. Mary McLeod Bethune. They were interested in the incredible story of the life of Mrs. Bethune, which she could tell so movingly. They were interested in the school which grew from a beginning of a dream, one dollar and a half, and a great faith. They were interested in what was being done for black boys and girls. They were thrilled every Sunday afternoon by the programs of great music superbly rendered. So, Bethune-Cookman became more than an academic community of students and teachers, it became the crossroads of culture and human relations, sustained by the glow of the personality of an admirable woman, Mrs. Bethune, the President.

From the time the little school was begun in "Faith Hall" in 1904, through the merger of the two institutions that became Bethune-Cookman College, up to her retirement in 1942, Mrs. Bethune was the life and spirit of this institution. The true story of Bethune-Cookman College cannot be told without telling in some detail the life, ambition, and achievements of its founder and for almost four decades its President and moving spirit.

Born and reared in the cotton fields of South Carolina in 1875 she was one of seventeen children.[55] Mary McLeod was eleven years old before the first school was established in her rural community by the Presbyterian Board Missions.[56] She attended Scotia College in Concord, North Carolina, from 1888 to 1895, and Moody Bible Institute in Chicago from 1895 to 1897.[57] After several years of teaching experience in South Carolina; Haines Institute, Augusta, Georgia; and Palatka, Florida, Mrs. Bethune founded her school in 1904 at Daytona, Florida.

Not only was Mrs. Bethune known as an outstanding leader in the field of education but also she stood out brilliantly in a number of other fields. She was founder and first President of the Southern Federation of Colored Women, covering four states.[58] She was President of the National Association of Colored Women's Clubs, 1924-28, and founder of the National Headquarters for the National Association of Colored Women in Washington, D. C.,

1926.[59] She was a recipient of the Spingarn Medal Award in 1935. In the race relations struggle carried on over many years by outstanding Black leaders, Mary McLeod Bethune was known as "The First Lady of the Struggle."[60]

When the New Deal, under President F. D. Roosevelt, brought a number of bright young Negro men and other leaders into government service, "Mrs. Bethune. . .unofficially presided over the 'Black Cabinet.' "[61] She was a member, earlier, of the White House Conference on Child Health and Welfare and made a distinct contribution.[62] "Dr. Ida M. Tarbell, noted writer, nominated Mrs. Bethune as one of the fifty living American women who stand foremost as contributors to the welfare of the country in business, arts, professions, social service and other callings."[63] Mrs. Bethune was the only Negro woman on the list.

Mrs. Bethune was received in England by Lady Astor, by the Lord Mayor of London and his wife, and by the Lord Provost of Glasgow and the Lady of Glasgow.[64]

During almost the entire period of President Roosevelt's administration and for several years afterward, Mrs. Bethune was associated with some phase of government programs. Her involvement in government programs took her away from the Bethune-Cookman campus often and for long periods. Although the college had a strong dean in Dr. James A. Bond, the college administration was weakened considerably by the long periods of absence of the President. Numerous administrative problems began to arise, the most serious of which was financial, and the college suffered to such an extent that Mrs. Bethune had to make a decision as to whether she would continue her services to the Federal Government or return to Bethune-Cookman College. She decided to return to Bethune-Cookman to help resolve some of the critical problems, and in the meantime to begin search for her successor as President.

In 1937 it was suggested that Bethune-Cookman College become affiliated with Clark University in Atlanta. It was thought that since Bethune-Cookman was doing only two years of academic work at the college level, a relationship with Clark University might be helpful in providing a four-year program for Bethune-Cookman. A program to this end, with courses and credits, was worked out, but the relationship never became extensive. It was the hope of Mrs. Bethune and Dean Bond that the last two years might soon be added to make Bethune-Cookman a four-year college.

In 1942 Mrs. Bethune retired, after thirty-eight years of leadership to the Daytona Normal and Industrial Institute for Negro Girls, later Bethune-Cookman College. During those thirty-eight years she became known as an outstanding educator. She was recognized as a leader in interracial affairs, being a prominent member of the first Inter-racial Commission. She was an outstanding leader of women's organizations. She was a most valuable aid to the government programs sponsored by President Franklin D. Roosevelt. Mrs. Bethune was one of the most influential personalities in America, her influence stemming from her common sense and good judgment, from her incisiveness and social sensitivity; from her great poise and her ability to command great audiences through her powerful platform eloquence. Bethune-Cookman College reflected the spirit of this great woman who was an inspiration to the young and old. And, so it was until she passed away in 1955.

James A. Colston, President

In late 1942 Professor James A. Colston* was elected President of Bethune-Cookman College to succeed Dr. Mary McLeod Bethune. He came to the presidency holding the Bachelor of Science degree from Morehouse College, Atlanta, Georgia, and the Master of Arts degree from Atlanta University. His immediately previous position was Principal of Ballard School, Macon, Georgia, under the auspices of the American Missionary Association, having previously taught in Atlanta, and having served as Principal of Rigby Junior High School, Ormond, Florida. He had also been director of the Extension Division of the Hampton Institute Summer School, Jacksonville, Florida.[65] At a young age Mr. Colston had proved to be a leader in education.

Bethune-Cookman was still listed as a Junior College when Mr. Colston became President and remained so listed during the period of his administration.
In 1947 Mr. Colston resigned the post at Bethune-Cookman College after a tenure of five years.

Richard V. Moore Becomes President.

Mr. Colston was succeeded in the Presidency of Bethune-Cookman College by Mr. Richard V. Moore, the present incumbent. Mr. Moore, a native of Quincy, Florida, took the Bachelor of Arts degree from Knoxville College, Knoxville, Tennessee, and the Master of Arts degree from Atlanta University.

*Mr. Colston is listed for the first time as President of Bethune-Cookman College in the *Christian Education Magazine*, March-April, 1943, p. 17.

"For a number of years he served as Principal of Booker T. Washington High School, Pensacola, Florida. He resigned this position in 1946 to become State Supervisor of Negro Secondary Schools of Florida, working directly from the State Department of Education, Tallahassee, Florida.

"President Moore brings to Bethune-Cookman a broad background in the fields of education and human relations," said *The Christian Education Magazine.*[66]

President Moore knew Mrs. Bethune and was well acquainted with the institution when he became President. Mrs. Bethune lived on the campus during several years of President Moore's early administration, until her death. Through his knowledge of and sensitivity to the history and philosophy of the college, and through natural ability President Moore immediately grasped the spirit of Bethune-Cookman College and began to move it forward.

It was announced early in 1948 that Bethune-Cookman, as a senior college, had been awarded "A" classification by the Southern Association of Colleges and Secondary Schools.[67] It had held the same rating as a Junior College.

On receiving "A" rating as a four-year senior college, Bethune-Cookman moved ahead to achieve more fully its purposes.

Mrs. Eloise Troutman Thompson, writing in the *Christian Education Magazine*, stated that "The program of the college is designed to translate in a concrete and tangible manner the purpose of the college into a way of life. To achieve this objective, the college," she said, "has formulated the following divisions: (1) Division of Humanities, (2) Division of Natural Sciences and Mathematics, (3) Division of Social Studies, (4) Division of Education and Psychology, (5) Division of Home Economics, and (6) the Division of Trades."[68]

The curriculum was designed with emphasis upon the training of the Head, Heart, and Hand; and with further emphasis upon the motto of the college: "Our Whole School for Christian Service."[69]

When the merger was consummated in 1923 to form Bethune-Cookman College the total value of the two plants was $312,000. The value of the physical plant June 30, 1969, was $5,056,264.00.[70] There were less than 200 students in the high school department and the college classes in 1923-1924, the first year of the merger. The enrollment for 1968-1969 was 1,232. Though the amount is much too small, the college can rely upon an endowment of $1,372,545.00.[71]

Under the able administrative leadership of President Moore, Bethune-Cookman College experienced its greatest growth during the decade of the sixties. He has made a magnificent contribution

196

over a period of twenty-five years, to the building of a great institution, and the achievement of the dreams and high ideals of education which both Mrs. Bethune, the founder, and he envisaged over many decades.

Within the next few years Dr. Moore will retire from the Presidency of Bethune-Cookman College. He will transmit to his successor and coming generations a great heritage, rich in ideals of Christian higher education, churchmanship, dedication, and service to mankind.

REFERENCES AND NOTES

1. Sixth Annual Report, Freedmen's Aid Society, 1873, p. 34.
2. *Ibid.*
3. *Ibid.*
4. *Ibid.*
5. *Ibid.*
6. *Ibid.*
7. Minutes, Florida Annual Conference, January 9-15, 1878, p. 11.
8. Twelfth Annual Report, Freedmen's Aid Society, 1879, pp. 39f.
9. *Ibid.*
10. Minutes, Florida Annual Conference, January 5-9, 1882, p. 16.
11. Freedmen's Aid Society, Fifteenth Annual Report, 1882, p. 7.
12. Minutes, Florida Annual Conference, January 3-8, 1883, p. 23.
13. Minutes, Florida Annual Conference, 1885, p. 22.
14. Minutes, Florida Annual Conference, January 21-25, 1886, p. 18.
15. Minutes, Florida Annual Conference, January 22-27, 1889, p. 16.
16. Minutes, Florida Annual Conference, January 22-27, 1890, p. 26.
17. *Ibid.*, p. 28.
18. *Ibid.*
19. Report, Freedmen's Aid and Southern Education Society, 1890-98, p. 219.
20. Minutes, Florida Annual Conference, January 20-25, 1892, p. 20.
21. *The Christian Educator*, April-May, 1896, p. 75.
22. *Ibid.*
23. Minutes, Florida Annual Conference, January 13-17, 1898, p. 30.
24. *Ibid.*
25. *The Christian Educator*, December-January, 1898-99, p. 38.
26. *Ibid.*, p. 49.
27. *The Christian Educator*, November, 1902, p. 19.
28. *The Christian Educator*, November, 1904, p. 20.
29. *Ibid.*, p. 19.
30. *The Christian Educator*, November, 1909, p. 10.
31. *The Christian Educator*, November, 1911, p. 21.
32. *The Christian Educator*, November, 1912, p. 26.
33. Jones, Thomas Jesse, *Negro Education*. U.S. Bulletin, 1916, No. 39, Vol. II, p. 166.

34. *The Christian Educator*, May, 1919, p. 8.
35. *The Christian Educator*, May, 1920, p. 3.
36. Stowell, Jay S., *Methodist Adventures in Negro Education*, p. 80.
37. *Ibid.*
38. *The Christian Educator*, May, 1924, p. 11.
39. *Ibid.*, May, 1923, p. 1.
40. *Ibid.*, May, 1923.
41. Jones, Thomas Jesse, *Negro Education — A Study of the Private and Higher Schools for Colored People in the U. S.*, Vol. II, 1916, p. 178.
42. *Ibid.*
43. *Ibid.*
44. The Original Charter, p. 1.
45. *Ibid.*
46. *Ibid.*, p. 2.
47. *Ibid.*
48. See Letter in Archives file, Interdenominational Theological Center Library.
49. *Ibid.*
50. Revised Document Board of Trustees, Daytona Normal and Industrial Institute, and Board of Managers, Board of Education for Negroes, April 17, 1923.
51. Letter dated June 21, 1923, from Dr. I. Garland Penn to Messrs. J. H. Blodgett, C. C. Manigault, *et al.* Archives, Interdenominational Theological Center Library.
52. Letter, September 25, 1924, from the Board of Managers to Rev. George C. Douglass, Treasurer of the Board of Education, for Negroes, Cookman Correspondence, Archives, I. T. C. Library.
53. *Ibid.*
54. *The Christian Educator*, November, 1928, p. 5.
55. *Ibid.*, November, 1931, p. 8.
56. Randolph, Richard, *The Negro Vanguard*, p. 123.
57. *Ibid.*, p. 129.
58. *Who's Who in Colored America*, 1941-1944.
59. *Ibid.*
60. *Ibid.*
61. Randolph, *op. cit.*, p. 243.
62. *Ibid.*, p. 255.
63. *The Christian Educator*, February, 1931, p. 216.
64. *Ibid.*
65. *The Christian Educator*, August, 1927, p. 5.
66. *Christian Education Magazine*, September-October, 1943, p. 22.
67. *Ibid.*, September-October, 1947, p. 32.
68. *Ibid.*, March-April, 1948, p. 32.

69. *Ibid.*, January-February, 1949, p. 9.
70. *Ibid.*
71. Letter from President Richard V. Moore, June 11, 1970.

CHAPTER 13

A BRIEF HISTORICAL SKETCH OF CLAFLIN
UNIVERSITY, NOW CLAFLIN COLLEGE

Claflin University, like many of the Freedmen's Aid Society Schools, had a humble beginning and a unique development. Its origin and early years were motivated by the need for trained ministers and teachers, and a need to lift the cultural level of a benighted rural people in South Carolina, victims of the curse and aftermath of slavery, but yearning for enlightenment and a better way of life. The history of Claflin is romantic and inspiring, procreated and sparked by the personalities of dynamic and dedicated men, and by the generosity of sensitive and devoted philanthropists.

Claflin University, founded in 1869, had its origin in two schools previously established, "Baker Biblical Institute" at Charleston, South Carolina, and "The Training School" at Camden, South Carolina. An account of the school at Camden is given by Miss Sarah Babcock in a letter to *The Christian Advocate,* March 23, 1869, stating that "the first normal and training school for freedmen in the state is now in successful operation,"[1] and that the Reverend T. Willard Lewis was instrumental in getting the school started.

Regarding Baker Institute, the Freedmen's Aid Society gave the following report in 1869:

Baker Institute, Charleston, S. C. This school has been conducted with great success, and has furnished several classes of promising young men for teachers and ministers. The South Carolina Conference has been greatly strengthened by students educated here, and they have entered upon the service of Christ with the firm belief that they were called of God to this mission, and have spurned tempting offers of wealth, office, and political preferment, that they might consecrate themselves wholly to the work of the ministry.[2]

In the same year, 1869, the Freedmen's Aid Society Report gives the following account of the relocation and uniting of Baker

201

Biblical Institute and the Normal Training School to form Claflin University:

The Training School at Camden and the Baker Biblical Institute at Charleston have been united, and valuable property purchased for five thousand dollars, at Orangeburg, South Carolina, formerly occupied for a female college, which originally cost thirty thousand dollars. The university building is a magnificent one, and contains fifty-six rooms, and offers accommodations for nearly two hundred students. The Bureau has just expended twenty-five hundred dollars in putting the buildings in repair.

Great credit is due to Dr. Webster and Rev. T. W. Lewis for assuming the pecuniary responsibility in the purchase of this property, and for their untiring zeal and labor in its establishment. It has been named in honor of the distinguished Governor of Massachusetts, who, with his venerable father, has contributed so liberally to our enterprise in South Carolina.[3]

In *The Methodist Advocate*, November, 1869, appeared an account of Claflin University:

Claflin University — A correspondent writes of this institution as follows:

We commenced on Wednesday, Oct. 27. Rev. H. J. Moore, A.M., a graduate of Union College, and for a long time Principal of Bakerfield Academy, in Vermont, is now here to take charge of our Normal Department. E. A. Webster who has formerly taught one year in our Biblical Institute, and connected with the Sophomore Class, at Middletown, Conn., will also spend the winter as teacher here. We have also as teacher in Preparatory Department, Miss Mary Magill, of Chelsea, Mass. Our university building is pleasantly located, capacious, and in a fine state of repair. The prospect is excellent for a fine opening and a prosperous term.[4]

There was a close relationship between Claflin University and the South Carolina Conference. The leaders in the founding of the University were also leaders in the Conference. In fact, the University was an essential part of the Annual Conference, under the supervision of the Bishop who presided over the Conference.

The Methodist Advocate early in 1870 referring to the South Carolina Conference and Claflin University indicated that:

This Conference holds its next session at Jacksonville, Florida, January 20th, Bishop Janes, presiding. Bishop Janes will spend the Sabbath following the close of the Conference session, January 30, 1870, at the Claflin University, at Orangeburg, South Carolina, where those elected to orders by the Conference, and not finding it convenient to go from South Carolina to Florida, will be ordained. It is expected that the Bishop will preach on the occasion.[5]

In this same issue of *The Methodist Advocate*, it was reported that:

This University has been incorporated by the South Carolina Legislature. The Trustees of the University will hold their first meeting at the University building January 31st.[6]

In 1871 the "Board of Instructors consisted of the Reverend A. Webster, D.D., President; Reverend I. Marcy, Principal; Mr. W. H. Crogman and Mrs. I. Marcy, teachers."[7]
The Freedmen's Aid Society Report stated also that:

Its Biblical Department is its crown of glory, and its students have placed themselves by their heroic and self-sacrificing labors, and by close application to their studies, in the front rank of their Conference, and are doing valiant service for Christ and their race.[8]

The University had continuous and substantial growth. The Fifth Annual Report of the Freedmen's Aid Society comments on the four departments and the faculty of the University as follows:

There are four departments in the University.
The College Proper. Where the usual four years course of college studies is pursued under able professors, and diplomas awarded to those who complete the course. The usual preparatory studies are required.
Normal Department. Studies and lectures, especially adapted to training teachers of both sexes, and fitting them for their responsible work, is pursued.
Baker Theological Department. The "Baker Theological Institute," removed from Charleston, constitutes this branch of the University. . . .Students are thoroughly drilled in the study of the sciences, theology, and education, by recitation and lectures, under an experienced professor.
Preparatory Department. To which will be admitted a limited

203

number of children of both sexes, and special pains taken in laying the foundation of a thorough education.

Faculty. A. Webster, D.D., President, Rev. George Whitney, Professor in the Theological Department, Howard M. Kinney, A.M., Collegiate Department; Wm. H. Crogman, Normal Department; H. J. Fox, D.D., Lecturer on Elocution; Misses Alice West and Orpha Dennison, Teachers in Music and Preparatory Department.[9]

"The Agricultural College is located here in connection with Claflin University, and it is expected that Dr. Webster through whose instrumentality the location was secured, will remain as President, and develop its resources."

"The State College of Agriculture and Mechanics" Institute was founded in 1869, and by act of the Legislature was approved March 12, 1872 and was located at Orangeburg as a coordinate department of the University.[10] The Agricultural College became known as the "Claflin College," a subsidiary of Claflin University. For a period of twenty years "Claflin College of Agriculture and Mechanics" was under the administration of the President of Claflin University.

Claflin University was, then and for many years afterward, an institution close to the people. It served the agrarian people of a rural state through all the programs it maintained. The Agricultural and Mechanics' Institute was of signal importance. A full account of the work of this unit will be given later.

Claflin University continued to grow. In the Spring of 1873 the attendance was about two hundred students.[11] This was less than the number in the Winter term, according to the Freedmen's Aid Society Report,[12] the students having to work during the late Spring and Summer months for self-support.

The commencement soon came to be a high occasion for the University and the people. At the 1873 exercises:

A large number of visitors, including the trustees of the University and the Agricultural College and Mechanics' Institute, were present; among them, Bishop Haven, of the Methodist Episcopal Church; Rev. Dr. Rust of the Freedmen's Aid Society; Hon. Justus K. Jillson, State Supt. of Education; Sen. H. J. Maxwell of Marlborough; Rev. V. H. Buckley and R. J. Donaldson.[13]

It was mainly through the vigorous efforts of Dr. Webster that the Act was passed by the South Carolina State Legislature in 1872 locating the State Agricultural and Mechanics' Institute at

Orangeburg and affiliating it with Claflin University. The Institute was placed under the administration of Dr. Webster, President of Claflin University. Industrial Education was also begun at the University. Beginning in 1883 the John F. Slater Fund for a number of years made substantial contributions to Claflin University for industrial training. Through this aid Claflin developed one of the best industrial departments in the South and became noted for its work in the area of training. The Agricultural and Industrial Departments were probably the most significant developments during the presidency of Dr. Webster.

Dr. Webster, having served as President for five years, resigned from the Presidency in 1874. He was succeeded by the Reverend Edward Cooke of Massachusetts.

As had been the case with President Webster, the Rev. Cooke faced most difficult problems in trying to carry forward the work of the small and financially deprived institution, located in an unfriendly climate and thwarted by hostile acts of the white community. To add to this, the main building and classrooms of the university were destroyed by fire in 1876. Under the leadership of President Cooke, supported by former President Webster, the Trustees and the South Carolina Conference, the instructional work of the University went forward without serious interruption. The instruction, however, because of the small faculty of five, was of necessity limited. Within about a year after the destruction of the main building, a new building was completed.

Because the University had to borrow funds for the new building, the financial condition of the institution became critical. In 1873 the Reverend Lewis M. Dunton came to Orangeburg, where he became a teacher and where he discovered his life's work among the colored people of the South.[14] The Reverend Dunton was called upon to act as agent to collect money in the North for the University. In accepting this position, Reverend Dunton began a service at Claflin which lasted nearly a half century as Financial Agent, Vice President, and by far the longest service as President.

Despite the financial struggle of the University, substantial progress was made in advancing the academic work. In 1877 the academic program, reported by Dr. R. S. Rust,[15] consisted of (1) instruction in the ordinary branches of an English Education; (2) the classical preparation of those wishing to enter college (the College Preparatory Course); (3) the preparation of teachers, or the Normal Course; and, (4) Biblical Course for young men preparing for the Christian Ministry.

Dr. Rust, on his visit to Claflin, gave high praise to the instructional work, saying: "We listened with great pleasure to

205

recitations of classes in rhetoric, higher mathematics, natural philosophy, *Caesar*, *Virgil*, and *Anabasis*, and these recitations would have been creditable to similar classes in our Northern Seminaries."[15a]

In 1878 the super-script four-year college course was added and in 1883 the first degrees were granted, Bachelor of Arts, to D. W. Harth and Daniel M. Minus.

In 1884, Reverend Dunton was elected President of Claflin University, its third President, to succeed Reverend Edward Cooke.[16] Under President Dunton's leadership Claflin made great strides. In 1891 the following report was made:

> Besides the Collegiate, College Preparatory, Normal and English Courses, twenty distinct industries are taught. The property consists of a campus of one hundred acres adjoining which is the farm of the South Carolina Agricultural College for Colored People. The State of South Carolina makes an annual appropriation for the support of this Agricultural College, the work of which is under the Presidency of President Dunton. Nearly one thousand students attend annually. The Peabody John F. Slater Fund Board, and the South Carolina Conference and the treasury of our own Society, all unite in sustaining this great institution.[17]
>
> * * *
>
> In our opinion there is no missionary operation of the church that yields so prompt, so large and so promising returns as this work of the Freedmen's Aid and Southern Education Society. I confidently believe that if the Church could be made to realize the relative importance of this work as compared with the other Christian enterprises of the Church that the Freedmen's Aid and Southern Education Society would not lack a dollar to aid in vigorously prosecuting the cause of Christian education among the hungry millions of colored and poor white people in the Southern states.[18]

At the end of the seventh year of President Dunton's administration, 1890, Dr. J. C. Hartzell, then Corresponding Secretary of the Freedmen's Aid and Southern Education Society, attended the Claflin commencement. He gave the following report in *The Christian Educator:*

> Commencement-week at Claflin is an event indeed. With Bishop Walden, it was our privilege to be present at the last one. Of Commencement-day the *Charleston News and Courier* says: "The 21st of May, 1890, was the greatest day that ever dawned

for Claflin University. All nature conspired to assist the authorities to make the day agreeable and entertaining in all respects. The crowd, an immense one, was orderly and intelligent. The day passed off pleasantly from beginning to end. Every one was satisfied and happy. The number of graduates yesterday was the largest that has ever assembled on the Claflin rostrum. It was a bright gathering. It showed progress and advancement. It was indicative of good work among the colored people of the State. The plane of scholarship, as shown by the essays, was highly creditable alike to faculty and students.

"Beginning at early dawn, the colored people of the country thronged in procession through the streets of Orangeburg to the grounds. They came in carriages, wagons, or carts, from east, west, north, and south; from Orangeburg, Barnwell, and Richland. The scene on the campus was, indeed, a picturesque one. There was every imaginable conception of serviceable vehicle in the caravan gathered under the pines of Claflin. Some came in 'great style,' with a double team and two passengers; others came on the family plan — a mother, father, and a squad of children in a farm-wagon with a frisky mule. Every colored person in the county who could come, came to the great celebration. Charleston, Aiken, Columbia, Summerville, and other places also sent strong delegations. Hundreds also came on special excursions from Camden and Charleston, and many came from other points along the line. The last excursion arrived at about eleven o'clock, when there were at least five thousand visitors in Orangeburg. This great crowd spent a quiet day, but one full of interest to them."[19]

Relation of Claflin and State

The following editorial comments in *The Christian Educator* in 1890 gives the relationship of Claflin University to the State Agricultural and Mechanics' Institute as it then obtained, and the impending rift that ended this relationship:

The cost of maintaining the university last year was about $26,000. Of this, $10,800 came from the state of South Carolina. The Slater Fund gave $1,800, and the Peabody Fund gave $1,000; the receipts from tuition, room-rent, incidentals, etc., from the students, $3,571.25. The balance of about $9,000 was paid by the Freedmen's Aid and Southern Education Society. The Woman's Home Missionary Society of the Methodist Episcopal Church maintains the Industrial Home for girls.

207

The relation of the State of South Carolina to the school is as follows:

The land-script donated by the United States some years ago to South Carolina for the establishment of an agricultural college was divided equally between the white and colored people, and the annual proceeds of the half belonging to the latter were invested in the establishment and maintenance of a "College of Agriculture and Mechanics' Institute" at Orangeburg, on a farm adjoining the original campus of the school. The State elects and supports three of the professors, who up to this time have been white men and native South Carolinians. The remainder of the State money goes to the support of the agricultural and mechanical department. Last year the State furnished the money for a complete steam laundry outfit. In addition to the income from the Agricultural Fund, which amounts to about $5,000 a year, the Legislature makes an annual appropriation. There was a movement in the last Legislature to defeat this extra appropriation; but after a full discussion of the merits of the school, and the duty of the State to stand by it, the opposition vote numbered only a very few. What the State does is not a secular appropriation to a sectarian school. The State simply plants its School of Agriculture and Mechanics beside our school, furnishes the money to maintain it, and gives the control and administration into the hands of our president. The money thus given by the State is set apart for the education of the colored people and Claflin University is asked to expend it because, in the judgment of the State authorities, more good can be accomplished with the same amount of money than to attempt to establish a separate institution.[20]

Separation of Claflin and State

The intimate and cooperative relationship between Claflin University and the State of South Carolina for more than twenty years came to an abrupt halt and the severing of relationships in 1892. The Spring 1896 issue of *The Christian Educator* gives the following account of the case that led to the break in relationship between the two institutions:

The New Negro College. Claflin College, which has been a state institution under the patronage of South Carolina, has been closely identified with Claflin University for more than a quarter of a century. The State and the Church school both

208

occupied the same campus. Indeed, in the purchase of land, the two properties were so intricately associated that the acres of land ran into a kind of mosaic campus. The State owned about one hundred and twenty acres, and the Claflin University owned less than fifty acres. The principal buildings, however, were on the University land.

The policy of the Methodist Episcopal Church, so frequently expressed, has been to receive no State money for church purposes; and it has been understood that Claflin University and Claflin College were unified only in a *quasi* way, that the two schools were separate in fact, but managed by one administration. The President of Claflin University was duly elected President of Claflin College, and there were professors who were paid by the Church. Nevertheless, the action of the General Conference of 1892 made it necessary for all such relations to cease; and, very happily, the State of South Carolina very soon after, in its Constitutional Convention, authorized the divorcement of the two schools.

In carrying out the instructions of the Constitutional Convention, the General Assembly of the State provided for the transfer of the Claflin College to a Board of Trustees, who were to have the care of the new Negro College, to be known as "The Colored Normal, Industrial, Agricultural, and Mechanical College." A commission was appointed by the Board of Managers of the Freedmen's Aid and Southern Education Society to meet with this Board of Trustees of the new college, and arrange for the separation of the two institutions. The faculty of the new State institution is to be composed of persons of African descent. . . .

Unless the property owned by Claflin University is purchased by the State, which is not very probable, new buildings will have to be erected for recitation halls and dormitories. The State of South Carolina has already authorized an appropriation of $5,000 a year for five years, making a total of $25,000 for buildings.[21]

The Freedmen's Aid and Southern Education Society was desirous of purchasing the state land but the offer was refused. Some of the Claflin University buildings located on state-owned property were given to the state.[22]

The discontinued relationship between Claflin University and the State of South Carolina resulting in the loss of $8,000 or more appropriated annually by the State to the University, created a financial crisis in current operation, and also placed upon the President, Dr. Dunton, the difficult responsibility of raising funds

209

for buildings to replace those given to the State. The following editorial comment appeared in *The Christian Educator:*

> The Rev. Dr. L. M. Dunton is an inspiration to the whole Freedmen's Aid and Southern Education Society. When Claflin University was divorced from the State College of South Carolina, and a plant had to be substituted for the one which fell to the State College to meet the requirements of the students, he set about to put up a new building with a courage that could not be resisted. His wife did not wait until the close of the term, but went to Boston, and solicited $1,500 for a new building. When the school had closed, the Doctor joined his wife, in New England, taking with him the Claflin University Plantation Melody Quintet. All are now at work in securing money to finish and equip the building. The Doctor speaks on "The Twentieth-Century Negro," the quintet stands for the Nineteenth Century Negro, and between them they are getting money to the right of them, to the left of them, and all about them. . .Money that comes by singing ought to be as good as money that comes by shouting; but singing or shouting, let the money come.[23]

Claflin's Progress Continues

Reports indicated that the institution continued to make phenomenal progress, with an enrollment of 550 students and school property valued at $80,000.[24]

In 1898 President Dunton gave the following report on Claflin graduates:

> Our graduates are filling many honorable and lucrative positions — some are preachers, some teachers, some are in business, some are successful farmers, etc.
>
> One of our graduates is receiving a salary of $1,800 as Superintendent of Carpentry in one of the State reformatories in the North. Another, Dr. W. L. Bulkley, our first college graduate, is Vice President of Claflin, and at the head of the Department of Ancient Languages. Another, Professor M. H. Broyles, is in the chair of Mathematics in the Texas Normal School. Another, Professor H. Pearson, has the Ancient Languages in the Georgia State College. Two more of our graduates are in the same school — Charles Hines, in charge of Manual Training, and J. R. Bulkley as Superintendent of Carpentry. The general superintendent of our Manual Training Department here, Professor W. W. Cooke, is also an alumnus of

Claflin. He served with great success in the Georgia State College during three years. One of the most successful men in the Young Men's Christian Association work is a Claflin man, C. C. Dogan, at Norfolk, Va. Quite a number of our graduates are successful as lawyers, as doctors, and as trained nurses. Some have amassed comfortable sums in business as merchants and real estate dealers. On the whole, I think a census of our graduates will show as many reflecting credit upon the institution and their race as any school of its kind has produced.[25]

At the close of the century, Claflin University had enrolled over eight thousand students, and had graduated 322 from the University.

Full Development of Industrial and
Agricultural Work

By the latter part of the century the work in agriculture and in mechanics, or industrial training, had become so well developed as to make Claflin University one of the best institutions in the South where such work was done. President Dunton reported in 1890 that:

The faculty is composed of sixteen members. Twenty superintendents are employed in the Mechanical and Industrial Departments. Nearly one thousand students are in annual attendance. There are three general courses of study; English, five years; College Preparatory and Normal, three years; and College Classical and Scientific, four years.

Twenty trades and industries are taught, some of which are as follows: Carpentry, cabinet making, building, agriculture, steam laundering, printing, painting and graining, brick making and laying, blacksmithing, milling, tailoring, shoemaking, cooking, domestic economy, nurse-training, dress cutting, fitting and making, crocheting, artistic painting, and needle-work. The Trade Departments do the most of the building and all of the repairing. All furniture needed in the dormitories, boarding department, etc., is manufactured by the students.[26]

Dr. Dunton says further:

We are having a good season, and our crops were never looking better at this season of the year. We have fifty acres of corn, knee-high, twenty acres of as handsome cotton as you ever saw, twenty acres of sweet potatoes, and thirty acres of oats, nearly ready for harvest. From last year's crop of corn we have supplied our students with fifteen bushels per week, fed six horses and fourteen cows, and will have several bushels for sale. We raised seventeen hundred bushels of sweet potatoes last year, and have consumed them all in our boarding department. The work on the farm is done mostly by students.[27]

* * *

Experience has taught us that it is practicable to teach trades in connection with literary studies. In order to do this most effectually and efficiently, we have established Thursday of each week as Industrial Day. We thus formally recognize the industrial feature of the university. This plan has many advantages. It enables us to secure the attendance of all of the students. The undivided time and attention of the students is secured. There is time for real progress during each lesson. The influence of the few who do not love work nor need to work is destroyed.

Specialists can be employed in certain departments for one day in the week, and thus improve the superintendence and save money. Over all is the inspiration of the occasion.

The Trade Departments are supported in part by the John F. Slater Fund, and in part by the State of South Carolina.

Students without exception enjoy the relief from study one day in the week, and are eager for the advantages afforded by the Trade schools. A large number have made sufficient progress to enable them to earn a dollar a day where they have been getting only fifty cents.

While the mental and physical effects of the trades and industries have been beneficial, the moral effect has not been less pronounced.[28]

Twenty-two years later, 1912, Claflin was at its peak as indicated in the following report:

Claflin University is carrying forward the largest and most effective system of industrial work, under the care of the Freedmen's Aid Society. The John F. Slater Manual Training Building, 200 x 180, is one of the largest buildings of its kind in any school in the South. It is fully equipped with up-to-date machinery, and is the center of the industrial work carried on at this institution. Twenty-four different trades and industries are taught, prominent which are carpentry, blacksmithing, masonry, wheelwrighting, painting, printing, wagon-making,

212

farming for the boys, and sewing, dressmaking, millinery, cooking, and other lines of domestic economy for girls.

* * *

At the Jamestown Exposition of a few years ago, the gold medal was awarded to Claflin for Excellency in Wagon Building.[29]

The Claflin Method — Threefold

Claflin University is undertaking to demonstrate that the average student is not only able to carry a full course of literary and industrial work at the same time, but that one is the natural complement of the other — the head to think, the hand to execute, and the heart a governor to control and direct all mental and physical processes.[30]

Tingley Hall

Claflin University at Orangeburg, South Carolina, is fortunate in having a most liberal and faithful friend in Mr. S. H. Tingley of Providence, Rhode Island, through whose generosity Tingley Hall was finished at a cost of $52,000. Tingley Memorial Hall was formally dedicated on March 4, 1909. The occasion was made memorable by the presence of Mr. Tingley, Mrs. D. Tingley, Dr. J. M. Buckley, Dr. C. W. Bennett, the school inspector, Dr. M. C. B. Mason, and most of the leading ministers of the South Carolina Conference. The completion of this building gives to Claflin University a fully equipped set of modern up-to-date school buildings, with the single exception of an adequate chapel, which we hope will come in the near future. The interest of Mr. Tingley in this institution and in the new building, which is a memorial to Mrs. Tingley, suggests the hope that similar friends may be secured for all of our institutions.[31]

In 1910 *The Christian Educator* remarked that:

Dr. Dunton and his good wife love their work and the people among whom they labor. No question of race or preferment trouble them. They speak of the people and the students as "our people," not "your people," or "their people." No wonder the South Carolina Conference in which he is the only white member has twice honored him with an election to the General Conference.[32]

Again in 1912 *The Christian Educator* stated that:

Dr. L. M. Dunton, President of Claflin University, is in the midst of his thirty-ninth year of effective educational work in the South. He is, therefore, in point of service dean of our educational work, having served longer than any other teacher. The entire thirty-nine years which he has given to our work has been continual service at Claflin, twenty-nine of which he has been its executive head. The growth of Claflin under his leadership has been most phenomenal. Twenty-nine years ago there were three buildings ill adapted to their purposes, with a real estate valuation of not more than $40,000. Today there are sixteen buildings, five of them up-to-date brick buildings with a student body of nearly seven hundred, forty-three teachers, with lands and real estate valued at $400,000.[33]

Continuing a Tradition

For fourteen years Claflin University has sent out a company of students to assist in raising funds for current expenses, buildings, and equipment, and endowment. The company has been unsalaried, but the students have been allowed their actual school expenses. As a result of this vacation work, five buildings have been sung up, considerable equipment has been added, especially to the Manual Training Department, and about $28,000 has been added to the endowment fund. Indirectly, several students have had the opportunity and experience of travel, and by singing have earned enough money to keep them in school until they graduated.[34]

Fire Destroys Main Building

The main building of Claflin University was completely burned January 9, 1912,[35] destroying offices, teachers' rooms, president's private office, classrooms, dining room, and hospital facilities. Fortunately no life was lost. The building was valued at $75,000.

Immediately after the destruction of this main building President Dunton proceeded with efforts for its replacement. Old bricks were cleaned, timber was cut down and sawed into rough lumber, and stacked up to dry. C. H. McClure, a leading architect of Boston, drew plans and specifications for a new building to accommodate over a hundred girls, and seven classrooms. Dr. Dunton remained on the scene, using men and machinery of the Industrial Department to erect the new building, with the hope of saving up to forty per cent of the cost, supplementing the $50,000

214

received in insurance on the building that was burned.

A Great Team

Dr. and Mrs. Dunton made a great team in their dedicated labors for Claflin University, which is in truth the lengthened shadow of these two great personalities. Through their incessant and untiring labors they endeared themselves in the hearts of the people in South Carolina, whom they served, as few leaders and teachers have done anywhere and at any other time. At the time Dr. Dunton celebrated his twenty-fifth year as President, and ever thereafter, encomiums of love and appreciation were profusely showered upon him and his able companion, Mrs. Dunton. As was pointed out in *The Christian Educator:*

It is important to note that most of the money for the erection of these new buildings was raised by Dr. and Mrs. Dunton, and by contributions from the South Carolina Conference.

The greatest work accomplished by Dr. and Mrs. Dunton at Claflin is not the material enlargement of the institution, but the moral and physical development of thousands of young people that have been committed to their care. South Carolina and adjoining states have been furnished with graduates from this school as their teachers, ministers, Christian physicians, and trained workers in the Church and Sunday schools. The President has not only emphasized industrial education, for which Claflin has become noted, but he has equally emphasized the importance of personal experience in his student body.[36]

Claflin's Forward Movement Campaign

Despite the problems and set-backs incident to the First World War (1914-1918), Claflin continued to make progress. Dr. Dunton always had a vital program with which to challenge the friends and supporters of the University in South Carolina and in the North. In 1916 a program was launched under the caption, "Claflin's Forward Movement Campaign." Reports indicate that this was a successful effort:

For several months past a great campaign has been going on in the South Carolina Conference, which includes our entire colored work in that State, which has had for its object a revival in every local church and $50,000 for the endowment fund of Claflin College, at Orangeburg. Bishop Frederick D. Leete, of

215

the Atlanta Area, and Rev. L. M. Dunton, President of Claflin College, have gone out over the entire state, holding conventions in the leading churches and at such centers as were convenient for the pastors and the people, directing, inspiring, enthusing the district superintendents, pastors and people, arousing the entire Conference to such a pitch of spiritual longing and financial sacrifice as never before in the history of this the greatest of our colored conferences.

* * *

Already the $50,000 goal is reached, the $2,000 necessary to its completion having been placed on the altars of the Lord at the session of the Conference in November.[37]

Dr. Dunton's Crowning Labors

In the period 1917 to 1922 Dr. and Mrs. Dunton laid their hands to the crowning labors of a half century. By their labors, their dedication, and their lives they transmitted to their successors in the cause, and to posterity, a legacy that transcends verbal or written expression.

The Christian Educator in 1924 carried a brief final recognition of the retirement of Dr. and Mrs. Dunton:

Dr. L. M. Dunton and Mrs. Dunton, who have done more than any others to develop Claflin College and place it among the best of the schools of the Board, felt it necessary during the quadrennium to retire from the leadership and responsibility of the institution. Dr. Dunton has served as President forty years. Mrs. Dunton, working by his side as teacher and financial agent, has taught, traveled, written, spoken and prayed thousands of dollars into the plant. Dr. Dunton has been equally industrious in cultivating friends for the institution, whose many gifts now form a part of that great heritage. When, therefore, these people determined to give up the active leadership of the college, there was a time of great mourning among thousands of the people whom they had served. When President Dunton retired he was educating the fourth generation of Negroes in South Carolina.[38]

When Dr. and Mrs. Dunton retired in 1922, the whole May issue (1922) of *The Christian Educator* featured them, with his picture on the cover, and hers following on page one.

216

Dr. J. B. Randolph, President

Following Dr. Dunton in 1922 as President was Dr. J. B.
Randolph, who served Claflin as President from 1922 to 1945, a
period of twenty-three years. He came to Claflin from the
presidency of Samuel Huston College, Austin, Texas, having
previously been Dean of Wiley College, Marshall, Texas, and
President of Haven Institute, Meridian, Mississippi.

Dr. Randolph was the first Negro President in the long history
of Claflin University. He was a scholar and most erudite, having as
a background the classical languages, arts, and music.

Dr. Randolph gave able academic leadership in the development
of Claflin. During his administration the high school work was
discontinued and emphasis was placed on strengthening the work
of the four-year college. The South Carolina Conference continued
its devotion to and support of Claflin. The period of the
"Depression" in the 1930's was most difficult financially. The
conference stood by heroically and by its sacrificial support,
helped Claflin to weather the storm of those lean years.

Though Dr. Randolph was not the builder Dr. Dunton was and
did not have the gift of endearing himself to the people, he moved
the institution forward through a most difficult period.

Dr. John J. Seabrook, President

On the retirement of Dr. Randolph in 1945, Dr. John J.
Seabrook was elected to succeed him. Dr. Seabrook was a native
son of Orangeburg, had grown up under the shadows of Claflin
and had attended there several years. He came to the Presidency
with the spirit and enthusiasm of the Claflin he knew when Dr.
Dunton was President. He came with dreams and ambition for
large accomplishments. He came with an ambition and a slogan for
a "Bigger and Better Claflin." Dr. Seabrook challenged the South
Carolina Conference to give much larger financial support to
Claflin and raised the Conference asking from $10,000 to $50,000
a year. With its historic loyalty, the South Carolina Conference
rallied to the challenge of larger support and set a record of giving
not surpassed nor reached by any of the other Conferences
supporting the historic schools of the Freedmen's Aid Society. In
the ten-year period Dr. Seabrook was President several buildings
were erected — Pearson Music Studio, a gymnasium, the Matthew
S. Davage Power Plant, a science hall, the Bowen Library Building,
and a dormitory to replace the one destroyed by fire.

It was during the Presidency of Dr. Seabrook that the college
received "A" rating by the Southern Association of Colleges and

217

Secondary Schools.

The Rev. Hubert V. Manning Becomes President

In September, 1955, when President Seabrook resigned to accept the Presidency of Huston-Tillotson College in Austin, Texas, an administrative committee consisting of Mr. H. D. Smith (Chairman); Dr. Leonard L. Haynes, Jr., Mr. J. Milton Shuler (Secretary); Mr. Robert Smart, and Mr. P. P. Worthy carried on the work. On March 14, 1956, the Reverend H. V. Manning, Pastor of Wesley Methodist Church, Charleston, South Carolina, and Chairman of the Board of Education of the South Carolina Conference, was elected President and assumed office on June 1, 1956.[39]

During the thirteen years Dr. Manning has been President, Claflin College has moved forward with steady and solid progress. He has been instrumental in improving and expanding the physical plant with the addition of the Mary E. Dunton Hall, a women's dormitory; the Men's Residence Hall; the Fred P. Corson Hall, a student center, housing the dining hall and two floors for women's residence; a new handsome Fine Arts Building; and the new H. V. Manning Library, housing 75,000 volumes. The total physical plant consists of twenty-five acres of campus and seventeen buildings, most of which are modern and in splendid repair.

The high quality of the academic work and the inclusive program of Claflin College is attested by its membership in the Southern Association of Colleges and Schools, attained under the leadership of President Manning.

In 1969 Claflin College celebrated its Centennial. As it entered upon its second century of service under the leadership of Dr. Hubert V. Manning its future is made bright by the sound foundation upon which it was built over a period of one hundred years, by the rich heritage transmitted through the dedicated work and sacrificial lives of so many men and women whose joy it was to labor in this vineyard, and by the challenge to serve this and unnumbered generations of young people who face demands no less exacting for relevant education than those of the century gone by. Dr. Manning seems to be sensitive to the worth of the past and the demands of the future in his words recently penned:

As Claflin University steps into a second century of service, the trustees, faculty, and students are grateful for its past, for its alumni and friends and for its many opportunities. If we can measure our past by the hundreds of courageous leaders among

218

its alumni, then it must foretell its future through the creative students who are among us now and those that will follow.

The ideals of the founders are ever present. Whatever of true worth, tomorrow's world demands those ideals that will persist even in the midst of the educational process. We ask others of various races and faiths to assist us in celebrating the vision of the second century.[40]

REFERENCES AND NOTES

1. Letter by Miss Sarah Babcock to *The Christian Advocate*, April 9, 1868.
2. Freedmen's Aid Society, Third Annual Report, 1869, pp. 9f.
3. *Ibid.*, p. 9.
4. *The Methodist Advocate*, (Atlanta) November 3, 1869, p. 174.
5. *The Methodist Advocate*, (Atlanta) January 12, 1870, p. 6.
6. *Ibid.*
7. Freedmen's Aid Society, Fourth Annual Report, 1871, pp. 9f.
8. *Ibid.*, p. 10.
9. Freedmen's Aid Society, Fifth Annual Report, 1872, p. 17.
10. *The Christian Educator*, July, 1890, p. 143.
11. Freedmen's Aid Society, Sixth Annual Report, 1873, p. 24.
12. *Ibid.*
13. *Ibid.*, p. 25.
14. Stowell, Jay S., *Methodist Adventures in Negro Education*, 1922, p. 154.
15. Freedmen's Aid Society Report, 1877, p. 20.
15a. *Ibid.*
16. Stowell, *Loc. Cit.*
17. Freedmen's Aid Society Report, 1891, p. 187.
18. Freedmen's Aid and Southern Education Society Report, July 1, 1891, p. 188.
19. *The Christian Educator*, July, 1890, pp. 151f.
20. *Ibid.*, pp. 146ff.
21. *The Christian Educator*, April-May, 1896, pp. 65f.
22. *Ibid.*
23. *The Christian Educator*, August-September, 1897, p. 132.
24. *Ibid.*, p. 136.
25. *The Christian Educator*, June-July, 1898, p. 123.
26. *The Christian Educator*, July, 1890, p. 144.
27. *Ibid.*, p. 158.
28. *The Christian Educator*, July, 1890, p. 145f.
29. *The Christian Educator*, February, 1912, pp. 4ff.
30. *Ibid.*, p. 7.
31. *The Christian Educator*, November, 1909, p. 12.
32. *The Christian Educator*, February, 1910, pp. 8f.
33. *The Christian Educator*, February, 1912, p. 1.
34. *Ibid.*, p. 16.
35. *The Christian Educator*, February, 1913, p. 1.

36. *Ibid.*, pp. 2f.
37. *The Christian Educator*, February, 1917, p. 11.
38. *The Christian Educator*, May, 1924, p. 6.
39. The Claflin College Catalog, 1966-1967, p. 21.
40. On The Track, 4th Quarter 1969, p. 4. (*On The Track*, Published Quarterly by the Joseph V. Baker Associates, 1712 Christian Street, Philadelphia, Pa.)

CHAPTER 14

A BRIEF SKETCH OF CLARK COLLEGE

I. EARLY BEGINNINGS

Bishop D. W. Clark Sets the Stage

Dr. Davis Wesgatt Clark was one of the outstanding leaders in Methodism early in the period following the close of the Civil War. It was his interest in the work of the south that led to his being elected the first President of the Freedmen's Aid Society when this society was organized August 8, 1866.

Dr. Clark was elected a bishop in the Methodist Episcopal Church at the General Conference of 1864.[1] During his first quadrennium as bishop, 1864-1868:

He traveled 65,000 miles, presided over forty-two Annual Conferences, visited Oregon and California, organized the Nevada, Holston, Tennessee, Georgia and Alabama Conferences; ordained 746 ministers, and stationed 4,612. This southern work required the utmost prudence and care and most highly did the bishop commend himself to the Church in these delicate duties.[2]

In January, 1866, at Atlanta, Bishop Clark organized a Georgia-Alabama Mission. "On October 10, 1867, Bishop Clark organized in Atlanta the Georgia Mission Conference."[3]

The Georgia Mission Conference was made a regular Annual Conference by action of the General Conference of the Methodist Episcopal Church in 1863.[4]

It was out of this background of efforts to organize and strengthen Methodism in the South that the need arose for training Negro ministers in this section. There was also need for primary schools and teacher training schools. Bishop Clark was profoundly concerned with these educational needs. To implement these concerns, he worked closely with Dr. Richard S. Rust, the corresponding secretary of the Freedmen's Aid Society and other leaders in the establishment of the early school which was the seed of Clark College.

223

Records show that primary school work for colored children was begun in Summer Hill, Atlanta, early in 1868 and possibly in late 1867.[5] The Rev. J. W. Lee reported early in January, 1869, as follows:

We have already accomplished something and by help from the Freedmen's Aid Society of our own Church, established schools at LaGrange, Rome, Oxford, Covington, Griffin, Atlanta, and other parts of the state both among white and colored. . . .

In Atlanta we have a school attached to each charge — a colored school at Clark Chapel and a free school for white children has been established by the successful efforts and untiring energy of Rev. J. Spilman, former pastor of First Charge.[6]

The 1868 report of the Freedmen's Aid Society indicates that "during the year schools have been sustained at the following places. . .Oxford, Covington, Newnan, LaGrange, Griffin, Grantville, Rome, Atlanta, Georgia."[7]

The report of the Rev. J. W. Lee given above and the 1868 report of the Freedmen's Aid Society substantiate the fact that the establishment of schools in Georgia and in Atlanta by the Methodist Church and later supported by the Freedmen's Aid Society had their beginning in 1868 and probably 1867. Dr. Rust had purchased lots in Summer Hill on Jones and Richardson Streets as early as July, 1866.[8] This was before the organization of the Freedmen's Aid Society, August, 1866.

Encouraged by the interest of Bishop Clark and the support of Dr. Rust, several ministers in the Georgia Conference engaged in the establishment of primary schools for Negro children. Most active among these were the Rev. J. W. Lee, Rev. D. W. Hammond, and Rev. J. Spilman.

Early in 1869 the Rev. J. W. Lee took charge of a primary school in Clark Chapel Methodist Chuch in Summer Hill. After a short period of operation of the primary school in Clark Chapel, it proved to be successful and was taken over by the Freedmen's Aid Society. The primary school was carried on in Clark Chapel until a school building was purchased in the same section by the Freedmen's Aid Society at a cost of $4,500,[9] which was a two-story brick building erected by the American Missionary Society and known as the Ayer's schoolhouse.[10] The school then became known as the Summer Hill School. The primary school begun in Clark Chapel and later transferred to the Summer Hill school building was the basic beginning of what came to be known as Clark University.

The Atlanta Public School System had not yet been established. The Atlanta Board of Education was organized in 1869. Tuesday, January 30, 1872, was the day and date set for the opening of the Atlanta Public School System.[11] The school for colored children carried on by the Freedmen's Aid Society and the American Missionary Society antedated the Atlanta Public School System by three or four years.

In November 1871 negotiations began for cooperation between the City of Atlanta and the Freedmen's Aid Society in the operation of the primary school, under the control of the Society. This was a cooperative arrangement whereby the City of Atlanta used the Summer Hill School building rent free and paid the salary of the teachers and other expenses of the school until 1877 when this building was purchased from the Freedmen's Aid Society by the City of Atlanta.[12]

Four Locations

Within its one hundred years of history, Clark has had four different locations in Atlanta. The length of time on each of the four locations was as follows:
1. Summer Hill, five years* — 1867-1872
2. Whitehall and McDaniel Streets, nine years — 1872-1880
3. South Atlanta, sixty years — 1880-1941
4. Westside, or present location, twenty-nine years to date (1970) — 1941-

Presidents and Developments in Each
of the Four Periods

I. Summer Hill
The primary school work initiated in Summer Hill in the school year 1867-68 was supervised by the Reverend J. W. Lee. When this school was taken over by the Freedmen's Aid Society in 1869, the Rev. D. W. Hammond took charge because the ministerial duties of the Rev. Lee became too heavy for him to continue to supervise the school work. The Rev. Hammond served as President during the school year 1869-1870.

Almost simultaneously with the beginning of the supervision of the school at Clark Chapel by the Freedmen's Aid Society, a teacher training program was begun by the Society. The teacher

*Operated two years as elementary school before being taken over in 1869 (date of founding) by the Freedmen's Aid Society.

training class was taught at the Clark Chapel and later, also, in the two-story building purchased by the Freedmen's Aid Society. While a part of this building was being used for the primary school, the teacher training program was carried on in another part of the building or at a different time. On August 4, 1869, Rev. D. W. Hammond, Principal, reported that:

The Atlanta Normal School for Freedmen has been organized for the special training of colored people for teachers and the work of the ministry. There are three departments of instruction in it — Normal, Preparatory and Primary. The course of instruction in the Normal Department embraces Model Schools, Teachers' Institutes, Lectures on the Theory and Drill in Practice of Teaching.[13]

The Methodist Advocate, August 11, 1869, carries a statement by Dr. R. S. Rust, corresponding secretary of the Freedmen's Aid Society, a part of which follows:

Atlanta Training School

The Freedmen's Aid Society has just purchased the commodious brick edifice, called the Ayer School, for forty-six hundred dollars.
It was an imperative necessity, and the Society borrowed the money and purchased the property believing that the friends of the freedom will promptly respond to this appeal for help and furnish funds for its payment.
The Clark Chapel, in which our Normal School has been taught the past year, has been too small for the accommodation of the pupils which came to us for instruction, and we were compelled either to turn away young men and women of Methodist proclivities, desiring to prepare themselves for usefulness, to be educated by those hostile to Methodism, or purchase additional school buildings and educate them under our own auspices.[14]

The educational work of the Freedmen's Aid Society in Atlanta had three main purposes: The first was to provide elementary education for the Negro children; the second was to provide teacher training; and the third was to provide training for ministers. It was intended that the elementary school work would be turned over to the public school system shortly and to concentrate on teacher training and ministerial training.
For a period of about three years, the teacher training program

was carried on in Summer Hill. The developments in Summer Hill were rapid and substantial. The Primary work was made more secure by the cooperative arrangements with the Atlanta Board of Education to pay the salaries of the teachers and bear other expenses incident to the operation of the elementary school. The purchase of the Ayer two-story brick building by the Freedmen's Aid Society provided extended facilities and made possible a larger service to a larger number of pupils. In its wisdom and foresight the Freedmen's Aid Society purchased several parcels of land in the vicinity of Clark Chapel and the Summer Hill school with the idea of expanding into a real university in that section of the city, provided a better site could not be secured.

To inform the church and the public generally, and by way of recruitment, an announcement was made by Rev. D. W. Hammond regarding Clark University in *The Methodist Advocate* (Atlanta), September 1, 1869, as follows:

Clark University

Atlanta Normal School, for freedom, has been organized for the special training of colored people for teachers and the work of the ministry. There are three departments of instruction in it — Normal, Preparatory, and Primary. The course of instruction in the Normal Department embraces Model Schools, Teachers' Institutes, Lectures on the Theory and Drill in Practice of Teaching. . . .

The Fall Term begins September 6th. . . .

Letters of inquiry will be promptly answered when addressed to

D. W. Hammond
Principal.[15]

Clark University
(Name)

Only a few years had passed when it was deemed wise and appropriate to give the school in Summer Hill a name consonant with the dreams and hopes of its founders.

We have, after due consultation, given to our institution the name of Clark University, in honor of our beloved Bishop who has from commencement evidenced the deepest interest in this Southern work. No other man in the Church has done more for this educational work than Bishop Clark. The institution has been purchased and put in good order at an expense of five thousand dollars by the Freedmen's Aid Society, and it is fitting that the institution should be named in honor of its President, and the Bishop who inaugurated and conducted with so much wisdom our mission work in Tennessee, Alabama, Georgia, etc. In a literary point of view, the name is most appropriate. Bishop Clark is an experienced educator, the author of several valuable and popular textbooks, an accomplished writer, and an able divine. The institution, now humble, with only its normal and Biblical Departments in operation, contemplates a full-orbed university, and will be worked up to as rapidly as possible. At some future day it may change its location to a site more in harmony with its name and mission.[16]

Clark University
(Opening)

The program having had a good start and a name given to the institution expressing their hope and affection, the following announcement was made for the school year 1869-70:

The Training School in this city has been put in complete order for the approaching year. It is now open for the instruction of teachers and preachers. Rev. D. W. Hammond, a graduate of one of the best Normal schools in the country, will take charge of the institution, and will be assisted by several first-class educators. Our University flings wide open its doors and welcomes all, without distinction of race or color, to enjoy its advantages.[17]

The Rev. D. W. Hammond served as President of Clark University during the school year 1869-70.[18]

II. Relocation to Whitehall and McDaniel Streets

Presidential Tenures of Mr. Cleary
and Reverend Marcy

In 1870 Mr. Uriah Cleary took charge. His staff consisted of Mrs. Lide E. Lee, wife of Rev. J. W. Lee, and Mrs. Sarah Eichelberger.[19] The report indicates that Mr. Cleary was a graduate of one of our best Normal schools and had devoted special attention to the training of teachers. Mr. Cleary served as President for one year and was followed by the Reverend I. Marcy, a thorough scholar and a successful teacher who served during the school year 1871-72.[20] It was during the administration of

228

Reverend Marcy that valuable property was purchased on Whitehall and McDaniel Streets by the Freedmen's Aid Society,[21] and the theological school was begun on that site.

Prior to locating the theological school on Whitehall Street, some classes had been taught at the Summer Hill site and during the first part of the school year 1871-72 classes in theology were taught in the basement of the Loyd Street Church. The Loyd Street Methodist Church was located on what is now Central Avenue near Hunter Street, where the new section of the Fulton County Courthouse is now located. It was from the Loyd Street Church that the theological classes were moved to Whitehall Street and the formal beginning of the Clark School of Theology was made.

Clark Theological Seminary Opens

The Clark Theological Seminary was opened, with appropriate religious services, in February, 1872. "In this movement we cannot doubt the providence of God," said Dr. Rust.

> He has been preparing the way. Reverend Dr. L. D. Barrows, of New England, residing temporarily in Atlanta to avoid the rigors of a Northern winter, has been selected by the Freedmen's Aid Society, to inaugurate the enterprise. For several weeks he had been instructing a class of thirty ministers, in the Loyd Street Methodist Episcopal Church.[22]

Dr. Barrows was assisted in his duties by Dr. Fuller, Reverend J. D. Knowles, and Reverend J. W. Lee. Professor I. Marcy, of the University, and his wife had oversight of the boarding department, and gave aid in training the students. When the seminary had been in operation only four weeks, twenty-six regular pupils had been enrolled who were busily and enthusiastically at work.[23]

During the latter part of the school year 1871-72 the Preparatory and Normal school work was continued at the Summer Hill site. In the summer of 1872 all work under the name of Clark University was transferred to the new site on Whitehall Street. In the meantime, the Primary work was continued in the Summer Hill school building under the cooperative arrangement with the Atlanta Public School Board of Education. The Summer Hill school building was sold to the City of Atlanta in 1877 for $3,000.[24]

Reverend J. W. Lee Made President

In the summer of 1872 Reverend J. W. Lee, who had assisted

Reverend Barrows the previous year, was made President,[25] assisted by Reverend W. H. Thomas and Mrs. Lida E. Lee. The Reverend Lee served two years as President.

The Sixth Annual Report of the Freedmen's Aid Society indicated that the session 1872-73 was the first full session the Clark University Theological School had operated.[26] During that year seventy-eight students were enrolled as follows: twenty-three in the theological school and fifty-five in the Preparatory and Normal Departments.[27] These students represented three states, Alabama, Florida and Georgia. At the time, there were 300 enrolled in the Primary grades at the Summer Hill school.

Reverend Isaac Lansing, President

In the Fall of 1874 Reverend Isaac J. Lansing, a fine scholar and eloquent preacher, was placed in charge,[28] succeeding Reverend J. W. Lee and wife of the Georgia Conference, and continued two years with the following teachers: Professor Watson, Mrs. Lansing, Mrs. Alice Buck and Miss Martha Smith.[29] The school flourished under his administration. Along with other developments, a wooden structure was added to supplement the brick building of eleven rooms. The two-story wooden structure provided two recitation rooms on the first floor, and dormitory rooms for boys on the second floor. The building was erected at a cost of $1,200.00.[30]

Reverend J. B. Martin, President, 1876; Succeeded
    by Reverend R. E. Bisbee, 1877

The Reverend J. B. Martin succeeded the Reverend Isaac J. Lansing as President in the summer of 1876 and served one year. He was succeeded at the end of that year by the Reverend R. E. Bisbee who remained in the Presidency from 1877 to 1881. His tenure closed the period of the existence of Clark University on the Whitehall-McDaniel Streets site.

During the period 1872 to 1881 significant developments took place. First, the institution was relocated in February, 1872, and the Clark University Theological School had its beginning. A few months after the theological school was begun, the work carried on in Summer Hill by the Freedmen's Aid Society was transferred to the Whitehall site and the University took on a new period of growth.

Beginning with the school year 1872-73, a boarding department was opened with Professor I. Marcy and his wife in charge. As need arose and as land and money became available, the

230

Freedmen's Aid Society purchased additional property. It is difficult to determine accurately just how much property was purchased in the vicinity of Whitehall and McDaniel Streets, but the Fulton County records indicate numerous parcels were purchased, looking forward to the erection of new buildings and full development of the University.

The most important development during the year 1876-77, when Reverend J. B. Martin was President, was the addition of Professor William Henry Crogman to the faculty. Professor Crogman was the first Negro on the faculty. He was a man of unusual ability and maturity. His coming to the University at that time was the beginning of a tenure at this institution of almost a half century as a brilliant scholar and teacher of Greek and Latin, and sometimes teacher of New Testament. Dr. Crogman's coming to Clark marked the beginning of the Classical course. During his tenure he served as Acting President and as President for seven years from 1903 to 1910, and served also as secretary of the Board of Trustees from its organization in 1878 until April 26, 1923, one year after he retired May 10, 1922.[31]

Bishop Gilbert Haven Succeeds
Bishop D. W. Clark

After the death of Bishop Clark, February 24, 1871, Bishop Haven succeeded him in the supervision of the work of the church and education in this section. There were many developments at the University during the time Bishop Haven gave supervision. He worked closely with Dr. Rust, the Corresponding Secretary of the Freedmen's Aid Society, and helped substantially to promote the growth and development of the institution. Bishop Haven passed away January 3, 1880.[32]

Charter Granted

While still on the Whitehall Street site a group of men and women, officers of the Freedmen's Aid Society and others, bound themselves together as a Board of Trustees. Application was made for a Charter March 19, 1877.[33] The Charter was granted bearing the date May 5, 1877.[34] The Charter was broad in character. In addition to the usual administrative functions of a corporate body of this kind, the purpose of the university was made clear: "The advancement of learning and the accomplishment of good." Again, the purpose was to "perpetuate a university and thereby promote learning, afford suitable opportunities for the acquirement of knowledge and to foster piety and virtue as essentials of proper

231

education."[35]

The Charter gives to the University the right and privilege of granting degrees:

> Provided no degree shall be conferred but upon the recommendation of the appropriate faculty, and no instructor in said university, except in the theological department, shall ever be required by the trustees to profess any particular religious opinions as a test of office and no student shall be refused admission to or denied of the privileges, honors or degrees of said university on account of the religious opinion which he may entertain.[36]

The Charter makes no reference to the terms Negro or colored, nor any specific race. It is a broad charter, concerned only with the advancement of learning and the fostering of piety and virtue as essentials of proper education. The Charter, giving the institution the right and privilege of granting degrees, was an important step in the direction of achieving the dream of the institution's becoming a real university.

Board of Trustees Organized

After the Charter was granted, the organization meeting of the Board of Trustees was held February 15, 1878.[37] Bishop Haven was unanimously elected President of the Board. Dr. E. Q. Fuller was elected Vice President, Professor William H. Crogman was elected Secretary and George Standing was elected Treasurer.[38]

Death of Bishop Haven: Bishop Warren
Elected President of the Board

The first Annual Meeting of the Board of Trustees was held January 15, 1880,[39] at the Book Room, 110 Whitehall Street. Bishop Haven, the President of the Board, having passed away January 3, 1880,[40] a special committee was appointed to draw up a resolution on the death of Bishop Haven, and T. S. Eiswald who had also passed away. At this meeting Bishop Henry W. Warren was elected a member of the Board.[41] The following statement was recorded in the minutes:

> In the death of Bishop Gilbert Haven the Society lost a true friend and an eloquent advocate, and the colored people a bold champion of their rights, a fearless denouncer of their wrongs, and a tender sympathizer with their sufferings....On that

232

grand coronation day of Bishop Haven, preparatory to his reception in heaven, he urged his friends to stand by the colored people, and directed his son to pay the balance of his thousand dollar subscription toward the erection of Chrisman Hall, for which enterprise, during the last few years of his life, he had planned and begged and prayed.[42]

End of Location on Whitehall Street

By the end of the period when Clark University was located on Whitehall Street, there had been much growth. The departments had increased, expanding the course offerings and making necessary increases in faculty.

On the Whitehall Street site, work was begun in manual training. The 1881 catalog (p. 15) gives a description of the course in carpentry and architecture. This course was taken in addition to the regular academic work. The bare rudiments of carpentry and architecture were taught and students received a certificate from the instructor at the end of the course.

The school year 1879-1880 brought to an end the period that Clark University was located at 377 Whitehall Street and McDaniel Street. President Bisbee was the administrative head of Clark University one year in South Atlanta, resigning in 1881.

While the institution was making progress on Whitehall Street, it became evident that a better site was needed. In the Tenth Annual Report of the Freedmen's Aid Society, it was reported that four hundred acres of land, beautifully located, overlooking the City of Atlanta, had been secured by the personal solicitation of Bishop Haven, and at an early date a commodious college building would be erected upon these grounds and other buildings would follow as the wants of the students may demand and the donations of funds allow.[43]

The immediate building to be erected upon the newly purchased land in South Atlanta was Chrisman Hall. Construction of Chrisman Hall was begun in 1879. "The stone for the foundation was quarried from its ground and the brick for the super structure burned from its clay."[44]

The cornerstone for Chrisman Hall was laid February 10, 1880. Bishop Matthew Simpson and Dr. Richard S. Rust were invited to lay the cornerstone.[45] Chrisman Hall was dedicated on October 16, 1880.[46] In addition to the officials of the Freedmen's Aid Society, the following dignitaries were present for the dedication: Governor Colquitt; a U. S. Senator, Honorable Joseph E. Brown; two ex-Governors; the School Superintendent; *et al.*[47]

Bishop Haven had labored hard and long for the growth and

development of Clark University. Having passed away January 3, 1880, he did not live to see the first building on the new site dedicated, nor to see the University relocated from Whitehall Street to the new site of more than four hundred acres of land which he helped to secure.

At a meeting of the board June 4, 1880, Bishop Henry W. Warren was elected President of the Board to succeed the late Bishop Gilbert Haven.[48]

III. Relocation of the University to a 450 Acre Site, in South Atlanta

Clark University was relocated from the Whitehall-McDaniel Streets site to the South Atlanta site in late 1880.

Rev. E. O. Thayer, President

Dr. E. O. Thayer was elected President of Clark University at a meeting of the Board of Trustees June 9, 1881.[49] President Thayer's administration extended from 1881 to 1889.[50]

The first building, which was an all-purpose building, was Chrisman Hall. The Clark University Biennial Catalog for 1879-81 gives the following statement regarding Chrisman Hall:

> The magnificent college building, costing over thirty thousand dollars, is named in honor of Mrs. Eliza Chrisman, a highly valued friend of the lamented Bishop Clark, who contributed ten thousand dollars towards its erection, the other twenty thousand being pledged by our beloved Bishop Haven, and by Dr. Rust in behalf of the Freedmen's Aid Society. Bishop Haven, by personal solicitation, secured the money and purchased four hundred and fifty acres of valuable land, the first one hundred of which was purchased and donated to the institution by Dr. Rust, and Chrisman Hall is erected upon its most beautiful elevation overlooking the city.[51]

President Thayer began his administration with enthusiasm and excitement over the expansive area of the new site, the all-purpose building which was new, and the prospect of additional new buildings to come in the near future.

The curriculum carried courses under the following headings: the Grammar School Course, the Normal Course, the College Preparatory Course, and the Full College Course. The College Course led to the degree of Bachelor of Arts. The Industrial Department included four areas of work: Carpentry,

Blacksmithing, Domestic Economy, and Agriculture.[52]

Industrial Home for Young Women

It was out of the interest of President Thayer that the work in Domestic Economy was begun for young women.

> Rev. E. O. Thayer was a very young man in 1875 when he became President of Bennett College in Greensboro, North Carolina — just twenty-three years old, in fact. He had ideas on the education of Negro girls and improvement of home life. . . .When he became President of Clark University in Atlanta, it was natural for him to encourage, even inspire, the teachers in their proposal to building a model home wherein girls could receive training in practical housekeeping.[53]
> A six-room cottage has been completed and will be entirely furnished in readiness for the Fall Term. The young ladies of the highest class will live in the cottage and will learn all the arts of housekeeping under a competent matron. For two years all girls have received thorough instructions in sewing. Every effort will be made to teach the young ladies how to make and keep neat Christian homes.[54]

It is noted that the work in Domestic Economy for the young ladies at Clark University was begun at the beginning of President Thayer's administration. The cottage was first called Fisk Cottage.[55] The industrial work for girls was supported by the women of the church. The first contribution made toward this work on the Clark campus was the gift of a five-dollar gold piece by Mrs. Gilbert Haven, the mother of Bishop Gilbert Haven. Earlier historians credited this mission as being the first work officially recognized by the Women's Home Missionary Society and the worker in charge, Miss Sybil A. Abbott of Maine, was the first missionary. At the beginning of the school year 1883-84, the management of the model home, Fisk Cottage, was assumed by Miss Flora Mitchell,[56] who remained as the supervisor of the home for young ladies at Clark until 1920.

New Developments: Gammon Theological Seminary

For the school year 1883-84, the faculty was increased and new departments were created. One important development was the completion of Gammon Hall in October of 1883 and the employment of Rev. W. P. Thirkield as Dean of the School of Theology, who remained Dean until 1888, at which time the

Gammon School of Theology was completely separated from the University. The name was changed in 1888 to Gammon Theological Seminary and Dean W. P. Thirkield became the seminary's first President.

Another development in the curriculum was the employment of Rev. C. J. Brown as Professor of Natural Sciences and Principal of the Business College.

Warren Hall

Warren Hall was a new dormitory for young ladies and was made possible through a substantial gift from Rev. E. H. Gammon, the remaining cost of building having been secured through the efforts of Bishop Warren, which cost the Rev. Gammon later refunded to Bishop Warren. Warren Hall was completed in 1885 containing forty-five dormitory rooms, a large reading room, large kitchen, laundry, and a dining room capable of seating three hundred.

Industrial Work

The Industrial School at Clark University had tremendous growth and expansion under the administration of President Thayer, 1881-1889. As pointed out in an earlier chapter, manual training was a part of the emphasis of the times upon industrial education. The industrial development in the private institutions for Negro youth was greatly enhanced by the Slater Fund. In 1882, the John F. Slater Fund for Education of the Freedmen was established by John F. Slater of Norwich, Connecticut. The amount of one million dollars was granted by Mr. Slater to establish the Fund for Freedmen.

Dr. Atticus G. Haygood was selected by the Trustees of the John F. Slater Fund as its first Agent to administer the fund for the Negro institutions. Dr. Haygood had shown much interest in the education of Negro youth and believed that industrial education would be one of their greatest assets. He served as General Agent for the Slater Foundation from 1882 to 1890 when he resigned to become one of the Bishops of the Methodist Episcopal Church, South.

Dr. Haygood and President Thayer worked closely together in developing the Industrial Department at Clark University. In a letter by Dr. Thayer regarding Dr. Haygood, dated September 13, 1939, the following comment was made:

When I was President of Clark University in Atlanta, 1880

236

[sic] to 1889, he was Agent of the Slater Fund, and was much interested with me in Industrial Education. Every student — even a candidate for A.B. — was required to learn a trade. We taught housekeeping, dressmaking, and millinery to the young women; farming, painting, wagon and carriage making, carpentry, etc., to the young men. . . .He took a personal interest and frequently visited the school. . . .We became good friends. He made generous appropriations for the work and encouraged us in every way.

The Annual Report of the Freedmen's Aid Society in 1885 gives an account of the work carried on in the Industrial School at Clark University and lists the following areas for training: 1. Carpentry, 2. Wheelwrighting and Carriage Making, 3. Blacksmithing, 4. Painting, 5. Printing, 6. Harness Making, 7. Housekeeping, 8. Sewing and Dressmaking. In the Report of the Freedmen's Aid and Southern Education Society, 1888 (p. 11), it is stated that:

At Clark University, Atlanta, Georgia, an industrial hall and blacksmith shop, costing $5,000, was dedicated last June. Mr. Ballard of Brooklyn, New York, a good Congregationalist friend, donated the money. In this hall the industrial schools of the University will have ample space for continued and successful growth. At the same institution, $500 was expended on an industrial home for girls.

A year later, *The Christian Educator* reported:

At Clark University we have one of the best located, as well as one of the best equipped industrial schools south of Ohio.[57]

Dr. Thayer's Administration Ends

Dr. Thayer's administration as President came to a close May 29, 1889.[58] The University had tremendous growth under his administration. He came just as the institution was relocated from Whitehall Street to the large site of 450 acres in South Atlanta. He had seen erected three major buildings and a model home for the industrial work of young women, which work was begun on a very modest scale under the control and supervision of the Woman's Home Missionary Society. The Woman's Home Missionary Society, through Thayer Home, came to have a major role in the education of the young women of the University. President Thayer had seen the industrial department expanded to the point of providing work in eight different areas as indicated above, and agriculture as one additional area. A course in nurse training had been established with Dr. D. Moury directing the work with one assistant. President Thayer had seen the Clark University School of Theology come of age and separated from the university to become an independent seminary through the generous benefactions of the Rev. Elijah H. Gammon and this separate unit administered by a young President, Dr. Wilbur P. Thirkield, who had served as Dean of the School of Theology from 1883 to 1888. He had seen the faculty greatly increased, for both Clark University and Gammon Theological Seminary. The curriculum was expanded and strengthened. President Thayer had conferred the first Bachelor of Arts degree granted by the University in 1883, which degree was conferred upon Walter H. Nelson,[59] and later, upon a number of other excellent students, all of whom became outstanding alumni of the University.

Dr. Rust Retires; Dr. Hartzell Succeeds Him

In June, 1888, Dr. Richard S. Rust retired from the position of Corresponding Secretary of the Freedmen's Aid Society. He became honorary Corresponding Secretary of the Freedmen's Aid and Southern Education Society by action of the 1888 General Conference.[60] No one contributed more hard work and wisdom than did Dr. Rust in the handling of the property and making possible the early development and continuous progress of Clark University during the twenty years he was Corresponding Secretary of the Freedmen's Aid Society.

Dr. Joseph C. Hartzell had been Assistant Corresponding Secretary of the Freedmen's Aid Society since 1881. It was fitting for him to succeed Dr. Rust as the Corresponding Secretary. He was elected to the position by the 1888 General Conference,[61] which he held until 1896 when he was elected a Bishop for Africa.[62] While serving as Corresponding Secretary, Dr. Hartzell exhibited the same deep interest in Clark University as did Dr. Rust.

The Presidency of Dr. William H. Hickman

Following the resignation of President E. O. Thayer at the meeting of the Clark University Board of Trustees in May, 1889, Rev. William H. Hickman was elected to succeed President Thayer.[63] Rev. Hickman served as President for four years, 1889 to 1893. During his administration he attempted to carry forward the work so ably developed by Dr. Thayer.

238

On April 14, 1892, Chrisman Hall was completely destroyed by fire.[64] The building, however, was soon replaced.

"A new, larger and better equipped Chrisman Hall stands on the campus of Clark University, where the old one went down in smoke and flames a few months ago. The rebuilding of the hall was begun at once and the work was pushed forward to completion at a rapid rate. The dedication occurred November 30, and December 1. The program arranged by President Hickman filled both days."[65]

Outstanding Biologist Appointed to the Faculty

The administration of President Hickman was marked by continuous progress. In the summer of 1892 the science faculty was strengthened by the addition of Mr. C. H. Turner as Professor of Biology. *The Christian Educator*, October, 1892, gives the following account of Professor Turner and his appointment at Clark University:

Professor C. H. Turner, who for two years has been Associate Professor in the Cincinnati University, will take charge of the Department of Natural Sciences in Clark University. His history is quite a remarkable one. He is a member of our Union Chapel in Cincinnati; worked his way through the Woodward High School, and graduated from the Cincinnati University two years ago, and since then has been Associate Professor in the Department of Sciences; his name appearing regularly in the catalogue of this great central institution. He has made a specialty of the study of biology, and has had several articles published in scientific journals, in which original investigations have been made. He has the respect and confidence of the faculty and students of this institution, although he is the only Negro in the faculty or among the students. He goes to give his best service to the development of the Scientific Department of Clark University.[66]

Effort was made to raise the standards of the academic work and to give greater stature to the work done. The catalog for 1891-92 states the requirements for the Bachelor of Arts degree, the Bachelor of Science degree, the Bachelor of Letters degree, and the Bachelor of Mechanics degree. Advanced degrees were also offered.

The degrees A.M. and M.E. will be conferred on the completion of the post graduate course of study prescribed by the faculty. All graduates desiring to take such course are requested to correspond with the President.[67]

The Master of Arts degree was offered as early as 1889.[68]
At the Board Meeting May 11, 1893, President Hickman gave his Annual Report which was received. President Hickman also presented his resignation which was received and ordered by the Board put on record.[69]

Dr. David John Elected President

In the same meeting on May 11, 1893, the Rev. David Clark John was nominated by the Trustees for the Presidency of Clark University.[70] Dr. John served three years as President, his administration ending in the summer of 1896.[71] There was one very significant event in the life of the University near the end of the administration of President John. It was in 1895 that the Atlanta Exposition was held. The excellent work in the School of Industry at Clark University was widely publicized through the exhibition from the Industrial Department. Wagons, carriages, harnesses and numerous other items were on exhibition. It is probable that the industrial work at Clark University reached its peak during the period of 1885 to 1900. It should be pointed out, however, that the development of the industrial department was not made at a sacrifice of other phases of work; but rather the work of the entire University advanced to a higher level.

The Presidency of Dr. John came to an end in the summer of 1896 when he accepted an appointment as District Superintendent of the Milwaukee District, the Wisconsin Conference.[72]

Dr. Thirkield Acting President

Dr. Wilbur P. Thirkield, who was then President of Gammon Theological Seminary, was asked to act as President of Clark University for a few months. It was his expectation that a new President for Clark would be selected shortly and his administration as Acting President would soon terminate.

Instead of serving as Acting President for two or three months as he expected, Dr. Thirkield served in this capacity the entire school year of 1896-97. *The Christian Educator* gives the following account of that service:

The Rev. W. P. Thirkield, D.D., President of Gammon School of Theology, has rendered the Freedmen's Aid and Southern Education Society an incalculable service during the last year.

240

He consented, when Dr. John was removed to be Presiding Elder of the Milwaukee District, to take his place for a little time, without remuneration, as President of Clark University. Notwithstanding, he continued his administration as President of the Theological School; he continued to serve Clark University through the year. The double duty greatly taxed his strength, and at one time threatened his endurance. One of the gratifying results to the Freedmen's Aid Society is the fact that he returned to the Treasury of the Society twenty-five hundred dollars which he had saved.

* * *

...Dr. Thirkield not only saved the Society the twenty-five hundred dollars during the year, but he conducted an admirable school, and greatly increased its numbers.[73]

Dr. Charles M. Melden Becomes President

At the meeting of the Board of Trustees May 19, 1897,[74] Dr. Charles Manly Melden was elected to the Presidency of Clark University, remaining in this position until May 12, 1903.[75]

Dr. Melden was a native of Salem, Massachusetts. He came to the Presidency of Clark University from the ministry in the New England Conference, holding a B.A. degree (1880), a B.D. (1883) and a Ph.D. degree (1892) from Boston University.[76]

Dr. Melden had six successful years of administration as President. A Northern visitor to Clark University early in President Melden's administration made the following comments:

As you know, President and Mrs. Melden are achieving marked success at Clark. If they had been manufactured to order they could not have more exactly fitted into this peculiar place. Not a single mistake, by word or act, has been made. I have heard not a single unfavorable criticism. By his scholarship and acknowledged ability as preacher and teacher and executive officer, he is bringing Clark to occupy the place of large influence for which it is designed by its location and equipment.[77]

In President Melden's last year as President, he made a report on the industrial work at Clark University as follows:

Our plans for the Agricultural Department include scientific instruction in its various branches, as the best methods of tilling the soil, study of plant life, analysis of soils, fertilizers, etc.; the breeding and feeding of stock, including beef and dairy cattle,

241

hogs, etc.
* * *

We have a herd of ten cows on the field, and several head of young stock, some full-blooded Berkshire hogs, and some thoroughbred Plymouth Rock poultry. We desire to show the superiority of pure blood over scrubs. We have mules and horses, and several hundred dollars' worth of modern farm tools. Upon our four hundred acres of land we are going to cultivate field crops and truck garden stuffs, using for the latter hotbeds and coldframes. Of course, this work is only beginning, but our plans are comprehensive, and we shall work toward them.

We also plan to hold an Annual Farmer's Convention in order to reach the farmers. It is a sort of university extension idea.
* * *

We shall also conduct experiments, and publish the results in a series of bulletins.
* * *

In the industries we have under regular instruction: Boys — in agriculture, 20; printing, 6; shoemaking, 7; carpentry, 25; blacksmithing, 13; wheelwrighting, 18. Girls — sewing, 239; cooking, 72; dressmaking, 17; mechanical drawing, 7; total, 424.[78]

Dr. Crogman Succeeds President Melden
As Acting President

President Melden's administration as President came to a close in May, 1903. He tendered his resignation to the Board of Trustees at its meeting May 12, 1903. The Board accepted his resignation and drew up a resolution of commendation and thanks to President Melden for his six years of effective and fruitful administration.[79] Dr. William Henry Crogman, Secretary of the Board of Trustees and Professor of Classical Languages, Greek and Latin, was appointed by the Board as Acting President for the school year 1903-1904.[80]

Dr. Crogman Elected President

At the meeting of the Board, July 1, 1904, Dr. Crogman was elected President of the University.[81] Dr. Crogman served as President until June, 1910.

At the end of the first year that Dr. Crogman was President, it was reported that "Clark University, at Atlanta, Georgia, Dr. W. H.

242

Crogman, President, has enjoyed a year of unusual prosperity."[82]

The agricultural program initiated by President Melden was carried on by the President, Dr. Crogman, with much success.

Mr. P. H. Parks, agricultural instructor, reported the growing of huge crops of vegetables and production of thousands of pounds of pork, thousands of gallons of milk, and hundreds of pounds of butter.

Efforts to reach adult farmers were most successful. Farmers' institutes were conducted reaching scores of farmers and a number of different counties in Georgia. In August 1908 a Round-Up Farmers' Institute lasted six days, registering sixty-five persons from twenty-four counties, including six teachers from five different counties, and fifty-two farmers from twenty-four different counties. Forty-five of the farmers owned their farms. The national Agricultural Department distributed one thousand farmers' bulletins among farmers who knew nothing of its work before and four hundred farmers' bulletins to rural school teachers who did not know how to get hold of agricultural information.[83]

A second Annual Round-Up Farmers' Institute and Summer School was held August 9-14, 1909, when leading farmers of the State of Georgia and agricultural experts from the Department at Washington, D. C., discussed such subjects as follows:

"How to Increase the Yield of Cotton and Corn Crops Per Acre"
"The Plow — Its Care and Adjustment"
"Why the Church Is Interested in Farm Life"
"Butter-Making on the Farm"
"The Housefly and Its Relation to the Health of the Farmer's Family"
"Improvements of the Rural Schools"
"The Negro and the Liquor Traffic," etc.[84]

Professor Parks, who directed the institutes, reported that:

As a result of the Farmer's Congress held at Clark University last year, a large number of new students have entered the institution for scientific instruction in farming, and many farmers who attended the institute ceased to obligate themselves on the credit system beyond their names, and many others have succeeded in paying themselves entirely out of debt.[85]

The agricultural program that was carried on under the direction of Professor P. H. Parks was most fitting for those whom the program served. When it is remembered that at this time, from eighty to ninety per cent of the Negro population was agricultural, it must be concluded that the University exercised great wisdom in its efforts to make the University relevant to the needs of the people it served.

Clark's Fortieth Anniversary and the End
    of Dr. Crogman's Presidency

The year 1910 was celebrated as the fortieth anniversary of the University. Dr. Crogman's administration as President came to an end in June, 1910. Not only did he advance the work in agriculture which was a young department when he became President, but he also did much to raise the standards in all the academic departments.

In May, 1910, Clark University celebrated its Fortieth Anniversary which brought together representatives from all sections of the South. This was not only a celebration for the University, but also a recognition of the services of Dr. Crogman, a great teacher who had "served so faithfully as President or Professor through nearly all the years of the history of the college."[86]

Dr. G. E. Idleman succeeded Dr. Crogman as President of Clark University.

New Administrative Policy

At this time a new policy was adopted by Clark and Gammon whereby one President served the two institutions.

In accordance with instructions, the Secretary conveyed to the Clark Board of Trustees the action of the Board of the Gammon Theological Seminary with reference to the appointment of one man to the Presidency of both schools — Clark University and Gammon Theological Seminary.

After a careful consideration of all the facts by our Board of Managers, the Board of Trustees of Gammon Theological Seminary and the Board of Trustees of Clark University, respectively, the two institutions were placed under one President, the work of each school to remain separate and distinct as heretofore.

Clark and Gammon Under One President

The Rev. S. E. Idleman, D.D., formerly District Superintendent

244

of the Mansfield District of the North Ohio Conference, was elected to the Presidency.[87] Dr. Idleman was a graduate of Ohio Wesleyan and of Drew Theological Seminary, and was thoroughly equipped for this important work. Under the new arrangement, Professor W. H. Crogman, formerly President of Clark University, took the chair of Latin and Greek, which he held before his election to the Presidency, and Dr. J. W. E. Bowen, who was the President of Gammon Theological Seminary, reclaimed the chair of Historical Theology, which he held before and during his term as President of the seminary. Besides providing for unity in the work of these closely associated institutions, it was thought there would be a financial saving in the work of administration.[88]

Dr. Idleman served as President of Clark University and Gammon Theological Seminary two years, 1910-11 and 1911-1912. At the end of the school year 1912 he was relieved of the Presidency at Clark University and was made President of one institution, Gammon Theological Seminary.[89]

Bishop Warren Dies

In 1912 Clark University and the other Freedmen's Aid Society schools sustained a great loss in the death of Bishop Henry W. Warren.[90] Bishop Warren had presided over this section of the church since the death of Bishop Gilbert Haven in 1880. He had served as Chairman of the Board of Trustees of Clark University and had given able leadership and development of this institution. He had given substantial leadership in relocation of the institution from Whitehall and McDaniel Streets to the 450-acre tract in South Atlanta. He had seen the University grow from one building on the new site to several substantial buildings, and the extensive development of the University in its academic program and in the areas of industrial work and agriculture.

Reverend William W. Foster Becomes
   President of Clark

When President Idleman was appointed President of Gammon Theological Seminary exclusively, he was succeeded as President of Clark University by the Rev. William W. Foster, Jr. *The Christian Educator* reported that:

Rev. W. W. Foster, Jr., D.D., who for twelve years was the President of Rust University, at Holly Springs, Mississippi, had

245

returned to the work of the Society as President, and his wife, as Dean, of Clark University. The experience of Dr. Foster warrants the confident expectation that Clark University in all of its departments will rank second to none among all our schools.[92]

The Christian Educator reports further that:

...Here we have eleven teachers, twenty-two practice teachers, and 480 students, with property valued at $256,400, with 450 acres of land, a large amount of which in time will be valuable for city residence property and can be sold, the proceeds to go towards endowment for the institution. At the present time 120 acres of this land is cleared and under cultivation. It is being used as a means of training the young men in agriculture. A dairy and truck garden in connection with the farm are also in operation.[93]

Dr. Foster served as President of the University three years, from 1912 to 1915. There was no new work added nor was there any extension of the work already established. President Foster's administration was concerned with keeping the program at the level established by previous Presidents. This was done with difficulty in view of economic conditions generally resulting from the outbreak of World War I in 1914.

At the close of the school year 1915, Rev. Foster resigned as President of Clark University and returned to the pastorate in his Conference (Troy). Dr. and Mrs. Foster served the Freedmen's Aid Society twelve years at Rust College and three years at Clark University. They desired to close their ministerial work in the pastorate where they began.[94] President Foster was succeeded in the Presidency of Clark University by the Rev. Harry Andrews King.

New President of Clark University

The Rev. Harry Andrews King, D.D., for the previous seven years President of Moores Hill College at Moores Hill, Indiana, was elected President of Clark University.

Dr. King came with fine preparation for this most important post in the Freedmen's Aid Society's system of schools. He was a graduate of Baker University, Baldwin, Kansas, from which he also received the honorary degree of Doctor of Divinity.[95] He also graduated from the Boston School of Theology.[96] He served

246

pastorates in Missouri and New England, and for two years preceding his election as President of Moores Hill College held the post of Educational Secretary of Baker University at Baldwin, Kansas, his Alma Mater. The proposed union of Moores Hill College and DePauw University made it possible for the Freedmen's Aid Society to secure the services of Dr. King.

Clark University was the only institution to hold university grade among the Freedmen's Aid Society's schools. It was intended to concentrate all the university work at this educational center. "With Gammon Theological Seminary on the same grounds, these two institutions ought to prove attractive to the colored youth of the entire South. As rapidly as funds will permit a strong university will be built up at South Atlanta."[97]

Rev. King served as President of Clark University eight years, 1915 to 1923. This was a period unlike any in the previous history of the University and in the history of the work of the Freedmen's Aid Society. Social and economic changes had their effect on Clark University as they affected most institutions at that time. World War I brought many changes with reference to enrollments, finances, faculty, curriculum. There was a lessening of emphasis upon industrial work. Emphasis upon the agricultural work continued for a few years, but soon the agricultural work was also affected by the changing times, particularly the migration of Negroes to the North.

Efforts to Standardize the Academic Work

The course of study listed for 1915-1916 was "provided by the Annual Association of College Presidents of the Freedmen's Aid Schools at the Annual Meeting in Nashville, Tennessee, March, 1910."[98]

The catalog points out that "The credit system is established along with the new curriculum. The Classical College course contains 152 credits, the Preparatory Course contains 190 credits, and the Normal Course contains 200 credits. By 'credit' is meant the number of recitations per week in a single study."[99] These provisions indicate efforts on the part of the University to standardize its work on both the college and high school levels.

Academic Deans Appointed

Isaac Howard Miller was appointed to the Clark University faculty, Summer of 1913, as Principal of the Normal Department.[100] The curriculum of the department was revised, extended, and strengthened. For the school year 1917-1918, a

247

fifth year was added to the Normal Course. Professor Miller directed the Normal Department six years, leaving at the close of school in June, 1919,[101] to take the Principalship of Cookman Institute, Jacksonville, Florida.

In the summer of 1919, John Zedler was made Dean of the College,[102] and Acting Professor of Education. Mr. Zedler served as Dean of the College until 1924[103] and during his five-year tenure in this position he initiated a number of innovations in curriculum organization, specifically, the four-year Junior College; the last two years of the college — Junior and Senior — constituting the Senior College.

In 1920 the Normal Course was extended to six years, including four years on the high school level and two years on the college level.[104]

Affiliation

Affiliation of Cookman Institute with Clark University was approved June 20, 1920. The Board approved the affiliation of Cookman Institute with Clark University and the secretary was instructed to communicate the action to the Board at Cincinnati.[105]

"Endowment Campaigns" Directed by
   Bishop Leete

Referring to a financial campaign conducted for Claflin College, it was reported that:

A similar campaign is being carried through in the Atlanta Conference for Clark University and already over $35,000 has been placed to the credit of the endowment amount, part of the money coming from the Conference, and the balance from the sale of lands belonging to the University. The school has yet some land, which, when conditions are favorable, may be sold, and proceeds added to the endowment, but the good Bishop is not going to wait for this slow process. He is, with leaders of the Atlanta Conference, pushing the endowment campaign up to an even $50,000, and with the experience of his leadership for Claflin, the end of the Quadrennium ought to show this result accomplished.[106]

Naming of Leete Hall

The question of naming the building in the process of erection arose in the Board meeting and was informally discussed. All the speakers, the secretary included, were unanimously in favor of naming it for Bishop Frederick D. Leete.[107]

The Chapel was named in honor of Dr. William Henry Crogman, Professor Emeritus of Greek and Latin, and one time President of the University.

President King Resigns: Rev. J. W.
Simmons Succeeds Him

President King announced to the Board that he had tendered to the Board at Cincinnati his resignation, and that said resignation had been accepted.[108]

Professor J. W. Simmons, for several years Dean of the Christian Education Department of Southwestern College, Winfred, Kansas, was unanimously chosen as successor to Dr. King, and entered upon his work with the new school year.[109]

Dean John Zedler had charge of the school during the interim, and efficiently cared for all of its interests.

It should be made clear that President King's presidency ended in the summer or early fall of 1922, and not in 1923 as some records indicate. As pointed out above, Dean Zedler was the Chief Administrator during the school year 1922-1923, Rev. John W. Simmons taking over the presidency in the summer of 1923.[110]

At the helm of Clark University for the school year 1923-1924 were Dr. John Wesley Simmons, President, and John Zedler, Dean. Rev. Simmons served as President only one year. His administration was too short to advance the University in any significant way. Dean Zedler's tenure at Clark came to an end in the summer of 1924.[111]

Dr. Matthew Simpson Davage Begins
a New Era

In the summer of 1924 a significant change was made and Clark University entered upon a new era. Dr. Matthew Simpson Davage became President of the University as the second Negro President in its long history. Dr. Davage came to the Presidency with an enviable record as an educator and high churchman. He had served as President of four Freedmen's Aid Society schools, coming to Clark directly from the Presidency of the historic Rust College in Holly Springs, Mississippi.[112]

The presidency of Dr. Davage had unusual significance for

249

several reasons. It had been fourteen years since there had been a Negro President of the college. Many social and economic changes had come about as a result of the First World War. There were new demands upon the University in terms of needed changes in education and new approaches in the field of education as a result of social changes that had come about. There was desire and need for drastic changes.

By 1924 all of the work in industrial education had been terminated, except training in Home Economics at Thayer Home. The Preparatory School was still strong and enrolled a substantial number of the total enrollment on the campus.

One of the first significant efforts put forth by Dr. Davage was to strengthen the faculty. During his first year, Dr. Hiram E. Archer served as Dean, succeeding Dean John Zedler. Dean Archer, however, was replaced in 1925 by the appointment of G. Whitte Jordan, who served as Dean for one year, 1925-26. Beginning with the school year 1925-26, the instructional faculty was increased in number and strengthened. This was the beginning of continued efforts to raise the quality of the faculty and to increase substantially the number of faculty members with advanced degrees.

James P. Brawley Made Dean

In the summer of 1926 James P. Brawley was named Dean of the College. After one year on the faculty as a teacher of Religious Education and Education, he assumed the Deanship with a long background of experience as student and teacher in institutions related to the Freedmen's Aid Society. He held a Bachelor of Arts degree from Samuel Huston College, Austin, Texas, had done graduate work at the University of Southern California in Religion, English, and Sociology. After one year of teaching experience at Rust College in Holly Springs, Mississippi, he continued his graduate studies at Northwestern University, received the Master of Arts degree in June, 1925, and immediately joined the faculty at Clark College.

While doing graduate work at Northwestern University, a special study of the Negro colleges, under the auspices of the Board of Education of the Methodist Episcopal Church, was made with special attention being given to the program and provisions for personnel services in the Negro colleges and the emphasis placed upon counseling and guidance. It was out of the background of this kind of experience and preparation that Brawley came to the Deanship at Clark.

Early in this new era at Clark which began with the Davage

250

administration, there were concerns for the raising of academic standards and securing accreditation for the institution. The University had no accreditation. The first step made was to secure accreditation by the State Department of Education for certification of teachers. The efforts extended to securing accreditation by the Georgia Association of Colleges.

Curriculum Changes

A course in "Contemporary Civilization" had been introduced into the curriculum in 1923, which continued several decades as a survey course in the social sciences. Several other innovations beginning in 1928 were important steps toward modernizing the curriculum: (1) a freshman orientation course inaugurated to deal with freshman problems helping to acquire better techniques of study and providing counsel and guidance; (2) a survey course in Bible was introduced to help students develop sound and critical knowledge of the Bible along with their critical studies in Biology, Astronomy, Philosophy and higher criticism. About 1931 a general course in freshman mathematics was introduced, required of all students, and other requirements in mathematics were abolished for students not majoring in mathematics.

By 1931-32 a number of steps had been taken to raise the standards of the academic work and to secure accreditation. The Junior High School had been completely eliminated by 1930 and steps had been taken to eliminate the four-year high school or the preparatory school which was completely abolished by 1934.[113]

With the efforts to modernize the curriculum and standardize the college academic procedures continuing through the years, the University became recognized and was given a courtesy rating by the Southern Association of Colleges and Secondary Schools which at that time did not admit Negro institutions to membership.

Continued Efforts to Reorganize and Modernize
the College Curriculum and the Total
College Program

In 1928 the Office of the Registrar was combined with the Dean's Office and Brawley became Dean-Registrar. One of the first steps taken was to set up a new system of academic record-keeping for the University. Such a system of records was greatly needed to facilitate the establishment of academic policies. Most of the record forms provided in the establishment of the new system of records are still in use. The system of records at Clark College was

251

one of the major contributions made by the Dean-Registrar in the early 1930's.

The economic depression of the 1930's placed a tremendous handicap upon Clark University as it did virtually all other institutions of the nation. This, however, did not discourage efforts to build a strong faculty and to improve the academic program. Faculty salaries at Clark were low and frequently unpaid. The loyalty of the faculty was tested and evidence of dedication came through in the kind of unity sustained and extended efforts by the administration and teachers to keep the University strong and to improve from year to year.

Curriculum Reorganization and New Academic Program

During the school year 1933-34 the faculty, under the leadership of the Dean of the college, began a careful study of the program of the college and started out to reorganize the curriculum and design a new and relevant academic program for the college. The efforts to reorganize, growing out of a study of the total situation, did not limit itself to the academic structure and content alone. The faculty was concerned also with its personnel services to students and made recommendations regarding a plan to improve these services.

Student Personnel Services

As a result of the organization of the curriculum and the statement of the underlying philosophy a new emphasis was placed upon personnel services to students. Facilities for such services were very limited, but the point of view and philosophy of student services came to life. In 1938-39 the University employed its first trained persons in the area of personnel services to students. A man was added to the staff as a counselor for men and a woman was added as a counselor for women.

Careful study was given to the kinds of services that should be provided for students on the new campus, and a basic philosophy regarding student personnel services was formulated.

Cooperation While on the Old Campus

1. Cooperation between Clark and Gammon extended from the time that Gammon became an independent seminary in 1888 well into the period of relocation of Clark in 1941. During the years 1910-1912, the two institutions were under one presidential administration. There was exchange of services between teachers

252

of the two institutions. Particularly was there cooperation in providing courses at Clark University for Gammon students who had not completed their college work and courses for students at Clark University in the areas of Religious Education, Missionary Education and Philosophy. During the period of 1925 to 1941, Gammon students pursued enough work over a period of time to complete requirements for a Bachelor's degree. Clark students pursued enough work at Gammon to meet the requirements of the University in the areas of Religion and Philosophy. Typical of the cooperative arrangements between Clark University and Gammon Theological Seminary may be noted in the following quotation from the Clark University catalog:

Relationship of Clark University and
Gammon Theological Seminary

The administrative organization of Clark University is distinctly separate from that of Gammon Theological Seminary. Yet, the proximity of the two institutions and their general relationship bring about a close academic relationship between the two institutions. By agreement. . .arrangements have been effected whereby students pursuing work at Gammon Theological Seminary may also work in either the high school or the college of Liberal Arts of Clark University, making it possible for theological students who have not done so already, to complete also their high school and college work. Likewise, students registered for their primary work at Clark University may pursue certain courses at Gammon Theological Seminary.[114]

2. Cooperation Between Clark University and
Other Atlanta Institutions Before 1941

Despite the distance between Clark and the other undergraduate campuses, there was a great deal of cooperation between Clark and the other institutions. This cooperation, however, was mainly through the exchange of teachers. For instance: Clark exchanged teachers with Morris Brown College — a teacher in French offering courses at Clark and a teacher at Clark offering courses in Business Administration at Morris Brown. There were exchanges also between Clark and Morehouse.

One specific type of cooperation was of importance and should be mentioned. Clark College began offering courses in Negro History in 1928-29.[115] Importance of teaching Negro History along with other subjects in Negro culture attracted the attention of the General Education Board of New York about 1935.

The Board made salary provisions for Dr. Rayford Logan to be employed by Atlanta University to offer courses in Negro History for all the students in the University Center on their respective campuses by Dr. Logan without charge to the individual institutions.[116] This was an important step in cooperation and was one of the efforts to enrich the curriculum of all the institutions. Dr. Logan remained as a special teacher in Negro History and Culture in the Center for several years.

Developments for Relocation to the West Side

Numerous detailed developments consummated the plan for relocation of Clark College. The Charter was amended in 1940 and the name of the institution was changed from Clark University to Clark College. One further step that had to be taken was the strengthening of the local Board of Trustees of Clark College. Prior to this time, all Clark College property was held either in the name of the Freedmen's Aid Society or the Board of Education of the Methodist Episcopal Church. It was the opinion of philanthropic agencies, agreed by the Board of Education, that the Clark College local Board of Trustees should hold title to all new properties of the college when it consummated its plans for relocation.[117]

The property of Clark University on the old campus continued to be held by the Methodist Board of Education, the money from the sale of which was to go into endowment for Clark College.

Funds had to be raised to relocate Clark to a new site. The General Education Board supplied some of the funds. This Board made a grant of $250,000 to Clark College to build a new academic building on the new site to replace Leete Hall on the old campus. The General Education Board also made a grant of $500,000 for endowment, this amount to be matched from other sources.[118] Dr. Davage and Dr. Holmes were influential in securing a grant of $500,000 from Mr. and Mrs. Pfeiffer to help meet the conditions of the General Education Board for endowment. They also made an additional grant to cover the cost of two dormitories, one for men and one for women which later became known as Pfeiffer Hall for men and Merner Hall for women. (Pfeiffer Hall was named for Mr. Henry Pfeiffer and Merner Hall carried the maiden name of Mrs. Henry Pfeiffer).

The funds made available by the General Education Board, including the cost of the new academic building and the endowment made available, totaled approximately $750,000.

Mr. Henry Pfeiffer died in 1937, but Mrs. Pfeiffer continued her interest in this development and by 1941 she and her late

254

husband had given over $600,000 on this new development of Clark College.

Other funds had to be raised to complete the building needs on the new site. The Julius Rosenwald Fund of Chicago made a grant of $100,000 on the building which was to house the dining hall, the student center, and the Home Economics laboratories, which became known as Thayer Hall.[119] These grants made it possible for Clark College to consummate the plan for relocation to the west side. These plans were completed by summer of 1940 and clearing of the grounds and construction began in August, 1940. Construction was completed in September, 1941, and Clark was relocated to the new site to begin its first year, 1941-42, on its new campus.

Credit and great commendation must be given to Dr. Matthew Simpson Davage who gave leadership in the project assisted by Dr. Merrill J. Holmes, leading to the beginning of construction in 1940.

James P. Brawley, President

In August, 1940, Dr. Davage accepted a position as Associate Secretary of the Board of Education, The Methodist Church. Although he left immediately to assume duties in Nashville, Tennessee, he held the title of President of Clark College until his successor was elected in 1941. In the meantime, James P. Brawley was placed in charge of the College as Administrative Dean during the school year 1940-1941.

On March 19, 1941, James P. Brawley was elected by the Board of Trustees to the Presidency of Clark College which position he held for twenty-four years.[120]

IV. Relocation to Westside, 1941
    Summary — 1941 to 1965

Dean of the College, Dr. A. A. McPheeters

When James P. Brawley was elected President in March, 1941, it became necessary to elect a new Dean. Dr. Alphonso A. McPheeters, who had been on the Clark faculty since 1930, was elected Dean of the college on recommendation of the new President at a meeting of the Board of Trustees, May 22, 1941.[121] Dean McPheeters held this position from his election in 1941 to July, 1962. The strength of the administration on the new campus for a period of more than twenty years was the close association of Brawley and McPheeters. They worked closely together and both

255

having had training in administration in higher education, and both having had a number of years of administrative experience, it was not difficult for them to work most cooperatively in the development of the college on the new site. Because of the knowledge which Dean McPheeters had of Clark College, its academic work and its traditions, and also his knowledge of the Atlanta University Center, his contribution to the cooperative relationship of Clark in the University Center was most valuable.

Dean McPheeters served Clark College with efficiency and a deep sense of dedication until his health became impaired and he had to resign from the Deanship in July, 1962. He retained a professorship in the Department of Education until his death April 23, 1963.

Some Highlights in the Growth and Development
of Clark College, 1941-1965

1. Relocation and beginning of a new cooperative relationship in the Atlanta University Center.

2. At the December, 1941, meeting of the Southern Association of Colleges and Schools, Clark College was accorded for the first time an "A" rating.

3. Inauguration and dedication: The first year on the new site was highlighted with the dedication of the new plant and the inauguration of James P. Brawley as its seventeenth President, April 10 to 12, 1942.

4. The Seventy-fifth Anniversary which was a significant occasion and a high point in the history of the college was celebrated in 1944.

5. Along with the efforts to improve the academic program of the college, much emphasis was placed upon the cultural programs for the enrichment of the education of the students.

6. It was realized that Clark College needed wider recognition and appreciation of the quality of work that it had done across the years and was still doing. To this end a cultivation and public relations program was inaugurated to increase the friends of the college across the nation, but particularly in Atlanta.

7. As the college grew, there was evident need for increasing the buildings on the campus. To add to the original four buildings with which the college started on the new site in 1941, a woman's dormitory was erected in 1949 at a cost of $389,000 which was named Merrill J. Holmes Hall. In 1954 Kresge Hall was erected at a cost of $285,000.00 to serve four purposes: (1) to provide additional rooming facilities for women teachers living on the campus; (2) guest quarters for visitors to the campus; (3) home

256

economics residence facilities for young women majoring in this field; (4) a cultural and recreational center on the ground floor.

Tanner-Turner Hall. This building was a renovation and expansion of a war surplus building secured in 1946. The building was renovated and expanded in 1958 at an expenditure of $108,000 to make provisions for extended laboratories for the Department of Biology, lecture rooms, and the upstairs section for art.

Brawley Hall. To provide for the need of additional dormitory space for men, a dormitory was completed in January, 1959, at a cost of $438,000 to house 122 men with a wing consisting of four 5-room faculty apartments.

Some Other Areas of Progress
(For Figures, See Table I, page 259)

Land. In 1940-1941 Clark College owned 200 acres of land in South Atlanta, the old campus. In 1941 the college moved to a new site of six and one-half acres and still owned the South Atlanta tract. In 1946 the land owned in South Atlanta was sold to the City of Atlanta and Fulton County, the college's land holdings being reduced to the six and one-half acres in the new site. In 1963 the college purchased 5.712 acres, near the new campus, through the City of Atlanta Housing Authority, Slum Clearance. The cost of this land was $40,000 an acre, a total of $228,480.00.

Buildings. In 1940-41 there were four buildings on the campus in South Atlanta. Although the Administration and Classroom building (Leete Hall) was beautiful and imposing, it was not a substantial building, and all other buildings were inadequate and in need of repairs. All four buildings on the new campus were new, completed in 1941. By 1960-61 there were four additional buildings, totaling eight, with a classroom building (9th building) in the planning stages.

Total Plant Value. In 1966 the total plant value was $3,135,839 (Audit, June 30, 1966).

Plant Value. The plant value increased from an estimated $600,000 in 1940-41 to $2,862,482 in 1965-66.

Endowment. In 1940-41 the endowment figure stood at a book value of $550,000. By 1965-66 the book value of the endowment had increased to $1,752,454.

Enrollment. The enrollment of the college increased from 474 in 1940-41 to 901 in 1960-61, and to 911 in 1965-66.

Tuition Fees. The charges for tuition plus fees increased from $63.50 in 1940-41 to $655 in 1965-66, more than a tenfold increase.

Income from Tuition and Fees. The total income from tuition and fees increased from $22,792 in 1940-41 to $259,648 in 1960-61 and $574,752 in 1965-66.

Church Support. In 1940-41 Clark College was receiving less than $10,000 annually from church sources. In 1965-66 the college received $163,700 from church sources for current operation.

Operating Budget. The total budget for current operations in 1940-41 was $74,500. This, however, did not include the dining hall and the women's dormitory which were operated separately by the Woman's Home Missionary Society. The operating budget in 1960-61 was $861,053 and by 1965-66 had increased to $1,601,317.

Student Aid. Figures for student aid are not available for 1940-41. It can be safely concluded that the figure was much lower than the amount of $7,020 provided in 1941-42, the first year of available figures.

Table 1 gives additional information on the areas of progress listed above.

Instructional Salaries. Growth in compensation of the faculty and staff from July 1, 1941, was continuous despite the fact that this was one of the most difficult areas of administrative operation. The following information regarding salaries is indicative of the progress made during the twenty-five-year period, 1941-1966.

In 1940-41 the average instructional salary was $1,450 for nine months, with only 80 per cent of the salary guaranteed. The range of salaries was from $1,100 to $2,000 for nine months. Only one teacher had a salary of $2,000, one had a salary of $1,800, others were clustered between $1,500 and $1,600. A grant from the General Education Board of New York in 1941-1942 made possible the beginning of a trend toward salary raises. In 1947 another grant from the General Education Board helped to increase salaries substantially.

In 1965-1966 salary provisions had increased to the extent that the lowest salary paid a teacher in the instructors rank was four times the average salary of all ranks in 1941-1942, and the highest salary paid a full professor was eight times the average salary of all ranks in 1941-1942.

Cooperative Relationships in the Center

Although Clark's facilities were limited, it was possible to extend the cooperation with the other institutions in the Center

258

TABLE I

SOME OTHER AREAS OF PROGRESS

Areas	1940-1941	1941-1942	1950-1951	1960-1961	1965-1966
1. Land	200 acres	206½ acres	6½ acres	11.62	13.12
2. Buildings	4	4	6	8	8
3. Plant Value	$ 600,000	$ 800,000[1]	$1,513,866	$2,501,764	$2,862,482
4. Endowment	$ 550,000	$ 650,000	$1,007,094	$1,553,443	$1,752,454
5. Enrollment	474	554	837	901	911
6. Tuition and Fees	$ 63.50	$ 98.50	$ 250.00	$ 426.50	$ 655.00
7. Tuition Income	$ 22,792	$ 28,508	$ 154,930	$ 259,648	$ 574,752
8. Church Support	Less than $ 10,000	$ 11,642***	$ 22,632	$ 57,680	$ 163,700
9. UNCF Income	*	*	$ 33,262	$ 42,134	$ 81,335
10. Student Aid	**	$ 7,020***	$ 41,850	$ 57,634	Over $ 200,000
11. Budget	$ 74,500	$ 112,741	$478,111	$ 861,050	$1,601,317

(1) New campus only
* 1945 First Year — $15,571
** Not available
*** 1942 — 1943

259

through the use of classrooms, the auditorium, and instructional facilities. Notably in the cooperative relationship was the fact that for about twenty years all of the physics for the Center was taught at Clark College, special provisions having been made for the teaching of physics when the classroom and administration building was erected in 1941. There was cooperation in the free exchange of students and faculty personnel. In the 24-year period of the Brawley administration, the cooperation reached its highest point in the last two or three years when a University Center Corporation was formed for the purpose of improving the development program of the Center securing funds for the use of all the institutions, and securing funds for buildings to be used in common, and other funds for the extension and enrichment of the academic and cultural program in the Center.

Southern Association Membership

In 1957 when the Southern Association of Colleges and Schools opened its doors for membership of predominantly Negro colleges and schools, there were approximately sixty-five such institutions that sought membership in the Association. Of the 65, the Southern Association admitted to membership in December, 1957, fifteen Senior Colleges and three Junior Colleges. Clark College was among the fifteen admitted to full membership that year.

Ninetieth Anniversary

In 1959 Clark College celebrated its Ninetieth Anniversary. At that time it projected a ten-year program with two main purposes: (1) It improved the quality of the academic program, and (2) It increased the financial resources of the college. This program was begun in 1959 with the initiation of a self-study. The self-study proposed to point out the bases for improving the academic program and the steps necessary to improve the financial resources.

A Period of Administrative Transition

The self-study as well as some of the plans for the ten-year program were seriously affected by some administrative changes. A new business manager was employed. The resignation of Dean McPheeters made it necessary to secure a new Dean. This was done in 1963. The United Negro College Fund Capital Funds Campaign and the impending retirement of President James P. Brawley affected the development program that had been planned. His retirement came August 30, 1965.

New Administration

On January 16, 1965, Dr. Vivian Wilson Henderson was elected President of Clark College[122] by the Board of Trustees, to succeed James P. Brawley, who had spent forty years at the College, as teacher and Dean sixteen years, and as President twenty-four years. Dr. Henderson assumed office September 1, 1965.

REFERENCES AND NOTES

1. General Conference Journal of 1864, p. ?. See also *The Methodist Advocate* (Atlanta), June 21, 1871, p. 97.

2. *The Methodist Advocate* (Atlanta), May 31, 1871, p. 86.

3. General Conference Journal, 1868, p. 311.

4. *Ibid.*

5. May 9, 1867, the Assessor's Report to the Atlanta City Council enumerated four schools for colored children. Among these four, reference was made to a school that had been organized at one of the colored Methodist Episcopal Churches — From Educational Notes, Atlanta and Vicinity, p. 160 (Atlanta City Library).

6. *The Methodist Advocate* (Atlanta), January, 1868, p. 1.

7. Freedmen's Aid Society Report, 1868, p. 15.

8. Fulton County Record of Deeds.

9. Fulton County Record of Deeds, June 3, 1869, Book Q, p. 642. Total expense in securing and renovating the building, $5,000, *The Methodist Advocate*, August 18, 1869, p. 130.

10. *The Methodist Advocate*, July 5, 1871, p. 106.

11. Educational Notes, Atlanta and Vicinity, p. 89. (Atlanta Public Library.)

12. Summer Hill School building was purchased from the Freedmen's Aid Society by the City of Atlanta, October 11, 1877, for the sum of $3,000. (See Fulton County Record of Deeds, Book AA, p. 646. The deed was recorded January 24, 1878.)

13. *The Methodist Advocate*, September 1, 1869, p. 139.

14. *Ibid.*, August 11, 1869, p.

15. *Ibid.*, August 18, 1869, p. 130.

16. *Ibid.*

17. *Ibid.*

18. *Ibid.*

19. Freedmen's Aid Society, Fourth Annual Report, 1871, p. 9.

20. Freedmen's Aid Society, Fifth Annual Report, 1872, p. 18.

21. *Ibid.*, and Freedmen's Aid Society Report, 1872, p. 29.

22. *Ibid.*, p. 20.

23. *Ibid.*

24. Summer Hill School building was purchased from the Freedmen's Aid Society by the City of Atlanta, October 11, 1877, for the sum of $3,000. (See Fulton County Record of Deeds, Book AA, p. 646. The deed was recorded January 24, 1878.)

25. Freedmen's Aid Society, Sixth Annual Report, 1873, p. 28.

26. *Ibid.*, p. 27.

27. *Ibid.*, pp. 27f.

28. Freedmen's Aid Society, Eighth Annual Report, 1875, p. 27.

29. Clark University Biennial Catalog, 1879-81, p. 27.
30. *Ibid.*, pp. 27f.
31. Minutes, Board of Trustees, February, 1878, p. 13.
32. Minutes, Clark University Board of Trustees, February 3, 1880, p. 27.
33. Minutes, Fulton County Court, Book M, p. 545.
34. *Ibid.*, p. 622.
35. *Ibid.*
36. See Minutes of the Clark University Board of Trustees, February, 1878, p. 4.
37. *Ibid.*, p. 13.
38. *Ibid.*
39. Minutes, Clark University Board of Trustees, January 15, 1880, p. 26.
40. *Ibid.*
41. *Ibid.*, June 4, 1880, p. 33.
42. The Freedmen's Aid Society, Thirteenth Annual Report, 1880, p. 5.
43. Tenth Annual Report, Freedmen's Aid Society 1877, p. 23.
44. Freedmen's Aid Society, Twelfth Annual Report, 1879, p. 10.
45. Minutes of Clark University Board of Trustees, January 15, 1880, p. 26.
46. *Ibid.*
47. Report, Freedmen's Aid Society, 1880, p. 13.
48. Minutes, Board of Trustees, June 4, 1880, p. 33.
49. Minutes of Clark University Board of Trustees, June 9, 1881, p. 33.
50. *Ibid.*, June 29, 1889.
51. Clark University Biennial Catalog, 1879-81, p. 21.
52. Clark University Catalog, 1882-83, p. 3.
53. Meeker, Mrs. Ruth Esther, original manuscript, pp. 50f.
54. Clark University Catalog, 1882-83, p. 16.
55. Meeker, *op. cit.*
56. *Ibid.*
57. *The Christian Educator*, October, 1889, p. 58.
58. Minutes, Clark University Board Meeting, May 29, 1889, p. 79.
59. Clark University Catalog, 1883-84, p. 4.
60. *The Christian Educator*, Vol. 1, p. 52.
61. *The Christian Educator*, October, 1889, p. 52.
62. General Conference Journal, 1888, p. ?.
63. See Board Minutes, May 28, 1889, p. 82.
64. *The Christian Educator*, April, 1893, p. 116.
65. *The Christian Educator*, January, 1893, p. 67.

66. *The Christian Educator*, Vol. IV, 1892, pp. 157-58.
67. Clark University Catalog, 1896-97, p. 11.
68. Minutes, Board of Trustees, May 29, 1889, p. 83.
69. Minutes of the Clark University Board of Trustees, May 11, 1893, pp. 104f.
70. *Ibid.*, p. 107.
71. Minutes, Meeting of the Clark University Board of Trustees.
72. *The Christian Educator*, Vol. VIII, February-March, 1897, p. 68.
73. *Ibid.*, June-July, 1897, p. 113.
74. Minutes of the Board of Trustees, May 19, 1897, p. 147.
75. *Ibid.*, May 12, 1903, pp. 209f.
76. *The Christian Educator*, August, 1911, p. 7.
77. *The Christian Educator*, August-September, 1898, p. 149.
78. *The Christian Educator*, February, 1903, p. 10.
79. Minutes, Clark University Board of Trustees, May 12, 1903, pp. 209, 218.
80. *Ibid.*, p. 227.
81. Minutes, Clark University Board of Trustees, July 1, 1904, p. 227.
82. *The Christian Educator*, August, 1905, p. 16.
83. *The Christian Educator*, February, 1909, pp. 9f.
84. *The Christian Educator*, May-August, 1909, p. 5.
85. *Ibid.*
86. *The Christian Educator*, May 1910, p. 10.
87. Minutes, Gammon Board of Trustees, August 25, 1910, p. 237.
88. *The Christian Educator*, August-November, 1910, p. 9.
89. Minutes, Gammon Board of Trustees, June 26, 1912, p. 261.
90. *The Christian Educator*, August, 1912, pp. 5f.*
92. *The Christian Educator*, November, 1912, p. 15.
93. *The Christian Educator*, November 12, 1912, p. 23.
94. *The Christian Educator*, November, 1915, p. 10.
95. *Ibid.*, p. 3.
96. *Ibid.*
97. *Ibid.*
98. The Clark University Catalog, 1915-1916, p. 14.
99. *Ibid.*
100. Stowell, J. S., *Methodist Adventures in Negro Education*, p. 80.
101. The Clark University Catalog, 1918-19 and 1919-20.
102. *The Christian Educator*, August, 1919, p. 2.
103. Clark University Catalogs, 1923-24 and 1924-25.
104. Clark University Catalog, 1921-22, pp. 22, 26ff, and 41f.
    * Footnote 91 has been deleted

105. Minutes, Clark University Board of Trustees, June 20, 1920, p. 371.

106. *The Christian Educator*, May, 1918, pp. 1-2.

107. Minutes, Clark University Board of Trustees, June 2, 1921, p. 380.

108. Clark University Board Meeting, June 10, 1922, p. 395.

109. *The Christian Educator*, August, 1922, p. 1.

110. Minutes, Board of Trustees, May 20, 1922, p. 395.

111. *The Christian Educator*, November, 1922, p. 4.

112. *The Christian Educator*, August, 1924, p. 3.

113. Catalog, Clark University, 1934-35, p.

114. Clark University Catalog, 1931-32, pp. 255.

115. Clark University Catalog, 1928-29, p.

116. Presidential Correspondence, Files, Clark College.

117. *Ibid.*

118. Arnett, Trevor, A Brief Account of the Developments in Cooperation Among the Negroes in Atlanta, Georgia, From Its Inception on April 1, 1939 through June 30, 1941, Winter 1942, p. 9.

119. *Ibid.*

120. Minutes Clark College Board of Trustees, March 19, 1941.

121. Minutes, Clark College Board of Trustees, May 23, 1941.

122. Minutes, Clark College Board of Trustees, January 16, 1965.

CHAPTER 15

A BRIEF HISTORICAL SKETCH OF NEW ORLEANS UNIVERSITY,
LATER, DILLARD UNIVERSITY

I

NEW ORLEANS UNIVERSITY

New Orleans University was an outgrowth of several institutions begun in and near New Orleans several years before the University itself had its beginning. The interest and efforts in providing education for Negroes originated in the Louisiana Annual Conference, founded December 25, 1865, as a part of the Mississippi Mission Conference.[1] The founding members of the Conference were also interested in education to prepare the Negro ministers for pastorates and leadership in the Conference. The first of the several schools begun in and near New Orleans was Thomson Biblical Institute, organized in New Orleans late in 1866.[2] The Reverend J. P. Newman, one of the original members of the Louisiana Conference, took the initiative in providing education for the Negro ministers of the Conference, which efforts led to the beginning of Thomson Biblical Institute. This school was named in honor of Bishop Edward Thomson who presided over the first session of the Louisiana Conference.[3] The Trustees were Rev. J. P. Newman, President; R. K. Diossy, Vice President; H. G. Jackson, Secretary; G. W. Ames, Treasurer.[4] The Institute operated in New Orleans for three years and became known as "Thomson University."

In 1869 Thomson University was relocated to Franklin, Louisiana. The Freedmen's Aid Society Report, 1869, gives account of this move:

This enterprise was started in New Orleans, and has been eminently useful in the preparation of students for the ministry and for teaching. Extensive grounds and buildings, worth thirty thousand dollars, have been donated to this institution, by John Baldwin, Esq., who cherishes the deepest interest in the elevation of the people of Louisiana, and contemplates the

267

endowment of an institution, where all the people, irrespective of color or condition, may enjoy the advantages of a thorough education. We expect the church to rally around this school, and cooperate with our benevolent brother in making it a fountain of moral and intellectual power.[5]

The grounds purchased by Mr. Baldwin consisted of thirty acres.[6] The institution later became known as "Baldwin University," of which Thomson Biblical Institute became a department.[7]

The second of the early schools which later became a part of New Orleans University was the Union Normal School. This school was incorporated July 8, 1869, and opened November 1, 1869.[8] An announcement appeared in *The Methodist Advocate* (Atlanta) regarding the New Orleans Normal School stating that:

> This institution will open its first session on Monday, November, 1, 1869, at their building on the corner of Camp and Race Streets. . . .Students, without distinction on account of sex, complexion or nativity, will be admitted on certificate of scholarship, from public or private schools; or after examination. . . .[9]

The Freedmen's Aid Society reported that:

> The Coliseum in the city of New Orleans has been purchased for a Normal School of high grade. . . .First-class teachers have entered upon their mission, and high anticipations are entertained of its future usefulness. Its commanding position and the great work it contemplates demanded that this institution should be under the supervision of able and experienced educators; and it is the purpose of its friends to make it a first-class Normal School, so that in it model teachers may be educated for the common schools of the State. Our gratitude is extended to Gen. Hatch, of the Bureau, and Dr. Newman, for timely aid in securing this valuable property.[10]

Baldwin, Louisiana, became an important center of educational activity on the part of Methodists. The acquisition of a deal of property in this beautiful location gave promise of great educational development there.

The Freedmen's Aid Society had a major part in the developments at Baldwin.

The Freedmen's Aid Society Report of 1871 gives an account of the Thomson University:

268

This institution is located at Baldwin, Louisiana. John Baldwin, Esq., donated a beautiful site embracing thirty acres on the Bayou Teche, for the University and has opened the Mansion House for a schoolroom, until he can erect a commodious brick edifice, adapted to the wants of the college. A promising class of students is enjoying the advantages of the University under the instruction of the President, Rev. S. L. Beiler, and when the new building shall have been completed, there will be a great increase to the number of its pupils. Mr. Baldwin has laid out a town adjoining the college campus, and proposes to donate the lots for the endowment of the University. . .

The Thomson Biblical Institute has been transferred to the University and the students in theology will enjoy the valuable instructions of Rev. Dr. Wright another year, assisted by the President. Strong hopes are entertained by its friends that a University of commanding influence will be built up here, where scores and hundreds will be educated to teach the young and preach the unsearchable riches of Christ.[11]

Another early institution that was begun before the establishment of New Orleans University was the Orphans' Home. Stowell states that:

It grew out of a movement begun before the close of the Civil War to care for and educate the orphans of colored union officers. General N. P. Banks really initiated the movement in 1863 by providing for the gathering together of these neglected children in the city of New Orleans. Before that time they had often become scattered and lost, and some of them had been found dead by the roadside, famished, while their mothers looked for work. Soon after this work was begun a Frenchman, who chanced to be in New Orleans, visited the Marine Hospital in which the children were established. His heart was touched, and he offered to give ten thousand dollars to purchase a farm home for the orphans on condition that twenty thousand dollars more should be raised to supplement his gift.[12]

The Freedmen's Aid Society reports that:

Dr. Newman raised ten thousand dollars from friends of humanity in the North and West, and obtained the other ten thousand from the Freedmen's Bureau. The trustees purchased a sugar plantation of seventeen hundred acres, which will in a few years render the Home nearly self-supporting.[13]

269

More than one hundred orphans were placed in the Home under the care of Mrs. Roberts, the Matron, a lady of great moral worth and excellent business qualifications.[14]

The land purchased and the orphans' home were located at Baldwin, Louisiana, on the Bayou Teche.[15]

For four years the work of the Thomson Biblical Institute was suspended for lack of funds, and it was removed to the Orphans' Home on the Teche. At the session of the Louisiana Conference held in December, 1871, the institute was ordered to be reopened at New Orleans.[16] A Board of Trustees was appointed, which organized a corps of instructors, namely: Rev. W. M. Daily, Rev. L. C. Matlack, Rev. J. C. Hartzell, Rev. M. C. Cole.[17]

The Institute, when relocated to New Orleans, was operated as a night school with sixteen students meeting from 7:00 to 9:00 P.M. at the Union Normal School Building. Twenty-four lectures were provided.[18]

With this background of several years of educational endeavor, the New Orleans University was established in New Orleans in 1873 on the site where the Union Normal School was located. The following account of the establishment of the New Orleans University is given in the Freedmen's Aid Society Report for 1873:

Previous to January, 1873, the educational work of our Church in Louisiana was carried forward under different names — the Normal School and Thomson Biblical Institute in New Orleans, and Thomson University in Bayou Teche. During 1872, a plan was suggested and, after extended consultation, was fixed upon to merge these institutions into one, to be known as the New Orleans University. The plan was endorsed by the Lousiana Conference, and at the last session of the Legislature an act of incorporation was obtained.

The property of the institution in New Orleans is located on the corner of Camp and Race Streets, in the heart of the city, and fronts on one of its largest and finest public parks. The property, first bought several years ago by a donation from the Freedmen's Bureau, has since been improved, and is worth $15,000. In addition to this, an adjoining property has been bought this year, that will ground ninety by one hundred and fifty feet, with two two-story buildings. The last purchase cost $6,000. The Freedmen's Aid Society assumes one-third of this purchase, and sent a check for $666.66 on the first payment.

* * *

We of Louisiana are indebted to the Freedmen's Aid Society

for almost all the advance made in educational work. Besides assisting to buy the property and to furnish the building, it has employed and paid all the teachers, and has kept continuously from two to six teachers at work in this state.

President I. S. Leavitt, A.M., has entered upon his work in this field the past year with commendable zeal, and has proved himself a most efficient worker. . . .He is a fine scholar and an experienced educator. Associated with him is Professor F. G. Cummings, whose labors have been very successful. He has dedicated himself wholly to this work in the South. Miss Annie E. Leaton, of Carlinville, Illinois, has had charge of the Intermediate Department, and has taught Music. Her class in Grammar excelled in the examination and the good effects of her musical training were evident at the exhibition. Mrs. Dr. A. J. Hammond, Preceptress of the Preparatory Department, has done excellent service. . .

The institution formerly known as "Thomson University," it is expected, will also be a part of the University, with a change of name and academical grade. . . .[19]

The Louisiana Conference at its annual session January 6-13, 1875, made two reports regarding the work and financial status of two of the institutions within its bounds, and assistance from the Freedmen's Aid Society. The first report was as follows:

The Society has furnished and supported four teachers among us during the year, at an expense of about $2,800; also, paid on property for New Orleans University $850, making a total of at least $3,650, as the amount donated by this struggling Society for our educational work.

In addition to this, the Freedmen's Aid Society has loaned our orphan home $5,000, thus saving it from a sheriff's sale.[20]

The second report at the 1875 session of the Louisiana Conference gives a good account of the work of the New Orleans University, but also points out its financial distress:

The New Orleans University represents our unified action in this direction and it is with pleasure that we call attention to its worthy record during the past year.

Three hundred and thirty-seven students have been enrolled and classified.

The following departments have been organized and courses of study prescribed: collegiate, preparatory, normal and Biblical.

271

The following persons have given instruction for all or portions of the year: Rev. I. S. Leavitt, A.M., President; Revs. J. B. Willis, A.B., and R. T. Stevenson, Mr. A. B. Collins, Miss Anna Fisher, Mrs. I. S. Leavitt, Ph.D., Mrs. S. J. Morris, and Miss H. A. Mahoffery.

* * *

The University is greatly embarrassed for the want of finance even to meet current expenses, while the first day of next June a mortgage note of over $30,000 becomes due and the University has not a dollar with which to meet it. . . .

Be it RESOLVED, that we as members of the Louisiana Conference, take a collection in our congregations for New Orleans University, forwarding the same to its Treasurer, Prof. I. S. Leavitt, before the first of June next, said collections to be expended on the indebtedness of the institution.[21]

Dr. O. E. Kriege, the last of the distinguished line of Presidents of New Orleans University, summarizes and clarifies in a few paragraphs the early stages of the enterprise leading to the establishment of New Orleans University. His faculty's account under the caption, "Forerunners of New Orleans University," follows:

As there is little information available concerning the early history of the educational efforts of the Methodist Episcopal Church in Louisiana, the following data, extracted from the Minutes of the Mississippi Mission Annual Conference and the Louisiana Annual Conference will be of particular interest at this time.

. . .The minutes are in very legible and for several years in exceedingly artistic handwriting and bear the certificate of approval of the several General Conferences. The minutes for the first three years are in the handwriting of Rev. J. P. Newman, the last three in that of Rev. J. C. Hartzell, both later elevated to the Episcopacy.

* * *

The minutes have much to say of three institutions, which may be called forerunners of New Orleans University beginning with the first conference, felicitously called the "Second Christmas Conference," in 1865, and continuing down to more recent years.

1. An institution on the Bayou Teche. It was called by various names: Thomson Biblical Institute; Thomson University; La Teche Seminary; Gilbert Academy and

272

Agricultural College. The site was a 1700 acre plantation on the Bayou Teche, 5 miles west of Franklin. Later, a village was platted, called 'La Teche.' This name gave way to that of 'Winsted' and this in turn to that of 'Baldwin,' which is the present name of the little city. Important donors were John M. Baldwin of Berea, Ohio, who gave land and buildings worth $20,000 and W. L. Gilbert of Winsted, Conn., who gave a total of $50,000. The school was opened in 1870 and after vicissitudes of various sorts was merged with New Orleans University in 1919, as the high school department of this school.

2. The Orphan Home. In July, 1863, Gen. N. P. Banks issued an order to Gen. Thomas Conway, Commissioner of the Freedmen's Bureau of the U. S. A., to gather the perishing orphans of colored Union soldiers. Their first home was the mansion of Pierre Soulé; the second the Marine Hospital; the third the plantation on the Teche mentioned above. A school was maintained from the first which was connected in one way or another with the fortunes of the school at the same place and thus with New Orleans University. At present the institution is known as "Sager-Brown Orphanage" and is operated by the Women's Home Missionary Society of the M. E. Church. A noteworthy gift of $10,000 was made by M. de Bossier, of Marseilles, France. Dr. J. P. Newman secured $20,000, of which sum Gen. O. O. Howard contributed $10,000. Dr. W. D. Godman spent two years in the North collecting $6,000 during the years of financial depression in 1874.

3. The Union Normal School. It was incorporated July 8, 1869 and opened Nov. 1, 1869. It occupied, the lower rooms of a two-story building at Camp and Race Streets facing Coliseum Square. This property was a gift from the Freedmen's Bureau, and cost $12,000. . . .The property was deeded to the Ames M. E. Church and later transferred to New Orleans University. The teachers were at first supplied by and paid by the Freedmen's Aid Society of the M. E. Church. The first Principal was Miss R. A. Coit, the next Rev. I. S. Leavitt, who also became the first President of New Orleans University, chartered March 22, 1873, and opened in October 1873. In 1886 the building at 5318 St. Charles Ave., was erected and occupied.[22]

The Reverend J. P. Newman, an original member of the Louisiana Conference and a leader in the movement to provide education, was removed from Louisiana.

"In 1872 the Rev. Isaac S. Leavitt was transferred from the West Wisconsin Conference and made President of the Union

273

Normal School and Thomson Biblical Institute."[2][3]

Meanwhile the Rev. J. C. Hartzell had been transferred from the Illinois Conference and made pastor of Ames M. E. Church. He, like his predecessor, J. P. Newman, at once became active in the educational enterprises of the Conference. Together with President Leavitt, he strove to unify these projects and, Rev. Hartzell leading, they prepared a charter for New Orleans University on broad lines and had it approved by the State Legislature March 22, 1873. Additional property was bought adjoining the Camp Street tract for $6,000. The school under its new title was opened in 1873, and the catalog lists the names of 300 students for the first year. The faculty consisted of: Rev. I. S. Leavitt, A.M., President; Professor J. B. Willis, A.B., and F. G. Cummings and the Misses Anna Fisher, L. S. Morris and L. W. Dawson. Rev. Leavitt served one year as President of New Orleans University and, under the three-year rule of that day, was transferred to the Wisconsin Conference, to enter the pastorate again.[2][4]

This was in 1875.

In the Eighth Annual Report of the Freedmen's Aid Society the following statement was made regarding New Orleans University:

The New Orleans University has a commanding influence among our colored people and a strong hold upon their confidence. . . .We solicit attention to the following statements — a prayerful and earnest attention from a Christian public.

1. There are hundreds (many hundreds) of colored youth, many of them destined soon to graduate into the honors and responsibilities of citizenship, who are not educating themselves. Some have no interest in education, but might become interested through right instrumentalities. Many have not means to go to school, doomed to toil for support. A moderate aid would bring such into the schools.

2. But the New Orleans University, having now 110 students, has not room for more than twenty more. . . .

3. Our building (the school building) is not in good repair, and is not worthy of much expense to put it in repair. The need is a new building.

4. Our location is beautiful, and the grounds are ample, when the old building shall be removed, for the erection of a convenient and commodious University edifice. . . .

5. We have no scientific apparatus whatever. We feel deeply

the need of this. . . .

Our library is very meagre in comparison with what it should be. . . .

6. We have a theological class of eight. Other institutions offer liberal aid to students for the ministry, and already they are reaping manifest advantages from the influence of those whom they send out. If we could command a scholarship fund of two or three thousand dollars annually, it would soon prove to be a most profitable investment for the Church. . . .

The Methodist Episcopal Church has had a grander opportunity than any other Protestant people. She is not now improving it with the zeal and energy required. A few years of this undecided, non-vigorous policy will bring us to great and unavailing regrets.[25]

The Rev. W. D. Godman, in 1875, was called to the leadership of New Orleans University, as its second President. The kind of able and dedicated administration he was prepared to give was greatly needed.

Dr. Godman's call to the presidency of New Orleans University seems to have been fraught with Providence, as the following story attests:

In 1870 Dr. Godman was elected President of Baldwin University, at Berea, Ohio, and after getting settled there, Mrs. Godman found long desired opportunity to study medicine. Dr. Godman's daughter was now of an age to be housekeeper, and Mrs. Godman took her son and baby girl with her to Philadelphia and entered the Woman's Medical College. In two years she accomplished what usually requires three and was home again with her diploma. In 1874 her son was accidentally killed while practicing gymnastics, and her grief threatened to unseat her reason. A change of scene was thought desirable, and Dr. Godman took his wife, mother-in-law and little girl to what was then known as the Orphans' Home, St. Mary's Parish, Louisiana. Here he left them for the winter; but Mrs. Godman became so ill that her life was despaired of, and as soon as she was able to sit up the physician shipped her North again in the care of the little girl, now nine years old, and a colored nurse.

This was in February and although the Northern air revived Mrs. Godman's strength, she was an invalid.

Now came what seems almost a miracle. The little woman laid her pale hands on her husband's and said: "Let us go to Louisiana and teach those poor people." "Why, wife!" said the astonished man, "we are to go to Europe this summer, and I

275

will leave you and Inez there when I return next fall. That will give Inez an early start in the languages and make good change for you."

But one morning as they were on the train going to Cleveland, there came a telegram from the Freedman's Aid Society asking Dr. Godman to take the Presidency of the New Orleans University.

"It looks like God's hand," said Dr. Godman.

"Amen," replied his wife, "I am with you."

He walked away to the end of the car and presently came back.

"Perhaps we had better do the unselfish thing," he said.

"My heart is with yours," was the reply, "God is in it."

So felt Dr. Godman, and he was not the man to resist God. Within six weeks he had resigned the Presidency of Baldwin University, sold his home and started South. It was a foolish thing to do, go back into that Southern climate just as the spring was opening, but they did it, and opened a school in the Orphanage.[26]

In the Spring of 1875 Dr. Godman assumed charge of the Orphan Home at Baldwin, Louisiana. That Fall he became President of New Orleans University. During the two years, 1875-1877, he was President of the University and at the same time presided over the school on the Teche.

The Louisiana Conference was greatly concerned about the development of the New Orleans University and often expressed that concern in conference action. At the 1876 session of the Conference the Rev. J. C. Hartzell presented the following resolution which was passed:

We hereby pledge our hearts and cooperation in the work of building up a University on the corner of Camp and Race Streets in this city. We especially commend the President, Dr. Godman, and his associate teachers, and will do all in our power to unite the interest of our people throughout the church in this state, in securing the attendance of our young men and women upon our University, and in helping to raise money to support it.[27]

With the financial condition of the University growing worse, the Ninth Session of the Louisiana Conference passed a series of resolutions as follows:

The New Orleans University, in this Conference, has been

276

embarrassed by the hardness of the times, so that many students who would otherwise have attended have been kept away. The building needs repairs and it is to be regretted that the ministers of the Conference do not take a more active interest in the school.

Resolved, 1. That the welfare of the Louisiana Conference imperatively demands an institution in which our young men called of God may be prepared to preach the Gospel.

Resolved, 2. That we take a deeper interest in our University, will select promising young men and women to attend it, and do all that we can in every possible way to make the New Orleans University the best institution in the State.

Resolved, 3. That we will not fail to take the collection for this society as the Discipline directs.[28]

The years 1875-1877 were two of the most difficult years in the early history of New Orleans University. The Louisiana Conference never lost faith in New Orleans University as an institution of destiny. They continued to resolve and to keep upon their hearts the responsibility of inspiring and impressing the young men and women with the importance of an education. This is evident in another series of resolutions passed at the 1877 Conference Session, as follows:

Resolved, 1. That we deem it our solemn duty as Christians and as Methodist ministers to sustain our school by sending to it our children, and thus setting an example to our people worthy of their imitation.

Resolved, 2. That we will use our influence constantly to encourage our young men and women to seek a good education, and that we will hold up New Orleans University as in all respects worthy of their confidence, and if it is not so we will not cease to labor until it becomes all that its name implies.

Resolved, 3. That in our judgment the school should be placed more directly under the management of a responsible Board.

Resolved, 4. That in our judgment, as soon as practicable, one or more colored professors should be employed in the school.

Resolved, 5. That we have confidence in the ability and devotion of Dr. Rust, Secretary of the Freedmen's Aid Society; Dr. Godman, President, and the other members of the Faculty, and believe that they should be properly sustained in their work by the Church at large.[29]

Reverend Bean, President

In 1877, the Rev. Jeremy S. Bean became President of New Orleans University and served two years. The institution moved forward. The Freedmen's Aid Society paid the indebtedness upon the property on Camp and Race Streets and provided several thousand dollars a year on salaries.[30]

Because of the deep interest of the Louisiana Conference in Education and in their own institution, New Orleans University, strong support was given the Presidents of the institution. This was true in the case of President Bean, as evidenced in the following action of the 1878 session of the Conference:

Report of Committee on Education.

Your committee on Education beg leave to refer to previous reports in which have been embodied the convictions which lie deep in the great heart of the Methodist Episcopal Church. To this great cause our Church has always been true. If we of today should fail to be true to this high interest of humanity, we should by that failure show ourselves to be unworthy sons of our noble fathers. We offer the following:

Resolved, That we will carry out the spirit of our Church, and preach at least once a year in each of our congregations on the duty of educating the children, both in Common Schools and in the Higher Seminaries of Learning.

Resolved, That we pledge ourselves anew to the support of the New Orleans University by giving our influence in holding it up before the people, and by encouraging our young men to attend it.

Resolved, that we rejoice in the success of the University under its present management, and that we extend to the Acting President, Rev. J. S. Bean, all possible sympathy and effort in his important work, and that we request the Bishop to appoint him to the New Orleans University.[31]

Several Presidents Serve Short Terms

For the year 1879-1880 the Rev. Dr. Godman was called back as Acting President of New Orleans University until a successor to President Bean could be elected.[32]

The fourth President of the University was the Rev. Isaac M. Failor, A.M., who served two years, from 1880 to 1882.[33] The enrollment for 1880-1881 was 369 students, ranging from the primary grades to the college classes.

The fifth president of the University was the Rev. James A. Dean, who held this office from 1882 to 1884. He was described as having "a pure, noble, cultured nature." He died March 30, 1885, one year after leaving the Presidency.

Professor Almon F. Hoyt, A.M., S.T.B., was the sixth president and served two years, 1884 to 1886. During Rev. Hoyt's administration additional property was acquired and plans made for relocation of the University.

A New Location

In 1884 Dr. J. C. Hartzell secured a new site for the University on St. Charles Avenue. The tract was a part of a sugar plantation and the mansion and other buildings were used both for residence and school purposes until a new building was dedicated June 7, 1889.[34] The building cost $50,000, of which sum Dr. Hartzell raised $30,000 and Bishop Mallalieu raised $10,000.[35]

Professor Isaac Lowe, President

In 1886 Professor Isaac Lowe, A.M., Ph.D., was appointed Acting President. In this year construction on the imposing new brick building was begun and the cornerstone was laid with impressive ceremonies.[36] It was on this occasion that the impressive remarks were made by Emperor Williams, a noted Negro preacher of that day. He said in part:

> I wonder if this is the world I was born in! For twenty years I was a slave on these streets. It was a penitentiary offense to educate a Negro. I have seen my fellow-servants whipped for trying to learn; but today here am I, on this great avenue, in this great city, with bishops and elders and the people of the great Methodist Episcopal Church, speaking at the breaking of ground where a building is to be erected for the education of the children of my people. I wonder if this is the world I was born in.[37]

Probably no other remarks or words spoken on that occasion were as impressive and so symbolic as those simple expressions falling from the lips of an ex-slave whose body had been shackled with chains for many years, but whose spirit had always been free.

Medical Department Established

In 1878 a medical department was organized as an experiment, with the intention of making this an established department of New Orleans University, provided sufficient support could be secured. Due to the outbreak of yellow fever, resulting in the death of a faculty member and one student, the work of the medical department was suspended.[38] This work was resumed later.

Title Transferred

At the 1879 session of the Louisiana Annual Conference, in compliance with the desire of Mr. Baldwin, action was taken transferring title of Thomson University to the Freedmen's Aid Society, to be managed by New Orleans University, and electing trustees for this theological school. That action was taken in the adoption of the following resolution:

> Resolved, That the Trustees of the Thomson University are hereby authorized and directed to transfer said property to the Freedmen's Aid Society of the Methodist Episcopal Church, to be held and used for educational purposes in connection with, and under the management educationally, of the New Orleans University, and the representatives of the Freedmen's Aid Society; and to be held and used for the maintenance and support of a Seminary on the Bayou Teche.
> Resolved, That the following are hereby elected Trustees of Thomson University: for three years, Cyrus Bussey, Emperor Williams, J. C. Hartzell; for one year, A. A. Johnson, Stephen Priestley, Josiah Fisk.[39]

Dr. J. C. Hartzell Becomes Editor

The Rev. Dr. J. C. Hartzell joined the Louisiana Conference in 1870. He served a number of pastorates and as Presiding Elder on the South New Orleans District, his time on the district expiring at the end of the Conference year January, 1881. It was requested by several of the brethren that Rev. Hartzell be continued as a District Superintendent even if necessary to transfer him to another District. The Bishop informed the Conference that Rev. Hartzell had by letter earlier requested to be relieved of duties of District Superintendent so as to give his full time to the editorship of the *Southwestern Christian Advocate* to which he had been elected by the General Conference.[40]

The Rev. Hartzell had been a tower of strength in the Louisiana Conference and had given strong support to the educational work of the Conference, particularly to New Orleans University, for which he was instrumental in raising thousands of dollars.

The Rev. Louis G. Adkinson Becomes President

Succeeding Professor Almon F. Hoyt as President and Professor Isaac Lowe as Acting President, the Rev. Louis G. Adkinson served as President of New Orleans University from 1887 to 1901. Up to that time this was the longest presidential tenure of any of the presidents of the University.

Speaking of President Adkinson, the Faculty wrote: "He was a versatile man and left his impress on the school and community. . .He put his hands on capable recent graduates and made them instructors and assistants."[41]

These recent graduates were the first black teachers employed by the University, among whom were: Alexander P. Camphor, who later became a bishop in the M. E. Church; Berry M. Hubbard, minister; Cornelius Johnson, minister; Walter Scott Chinn, minister; Frank B. Smith, later a leading attorney in New Orleans; and M. S. Davage, later a distinguished educator and churchman.

Again quoting the Faculty:

The academic department was made all the stronger and effective. During Dr. Adkinson's administration the experiment was made with industrial departments and courses were offered in printing, tinsmithing, shoemaking, etc. Soon this industrial work was delegated to Gilbert Academy at Baldwin and New Orleans University devoted itself more exclusively to cultural studies. The night school was begun in 1888. The total attendance grew from 228 in 1887 to a high point of 663 in 1891. A Medical College and Nurse Training School were begun in 1889 and many of the present leaders in the profession of medicine received their training at this school.[42]

It was a tribute to New Orleans University and its leadership and to the Louisiana Conference for the Freedmen's Aid and Southern Education Society to report as follows in 1892:

The Louisiana Conference is one of our strongest conferences in the South, and out of their poverty the people in the past few years have paid over ten thousand dollars into this institution, from which are going forth annually scores of Christian leaders and workers.[43]

Dr. Frederic H. Knight, President

The Rev. Dr. Frederic H. Knight succeeded Dr. Adkinson as President in 1901, and remained in office to 1907. He was a native of Saco, Maine, held the A.B. degree from Dartmouth College and the S.T.B. and the Ph.D. degrees from Boston University. His Presidency of New Orleans University effected material improvement in building and equipment, but his most significant and far-reaching service was in the marked advance in the scholastic attainment and standing of the school.

"Its Normal School now received a gratifying recognition by the State educational authorities in that New Orleans University graduates received a certificate to teach without passing an examination. Excepting the State High and Normal School this privilege was granted to no other school."[44]

It was during Dr. Knight's Presidency that Miss Annie J. Parker joined the New Orleans University faculty. She remained twenty-six years as a teacher and was dearly beloved by all.

The Rev. John Wier, President

The Rev. Wier served as President of New Orleans University four years, from 1907 to 1911, succeeding Dr. Knight. Rev. Wier had wide experience as a minister in Nova Scotia, the New York Conference, and in Ohio, and as Chaplain in the British Navy for twelve years. He served as a Professor and President in Japan, President of Sico College in 1897-1898 and President of Virginia Wesleyan University, 1898-1907.[45] Not much has been written about the work of the University under the Rev. Wier's administration, except the following excerpts from a general report by the Freedmen's Aid Society:

The University comprises the following institutions: College of Liberal Arts, Preparatory School, elementary schools, normal school, school of domestic science, manual-training school for boys, school for nurses, school of pharmacy, school of music, medical college, hospital, and orphans' home.[46]

* * *

Besides the departments above described the University comprises the Flint Medical College. Connected with this are the school of pharmacy and the Sara Goodridge Hospital and Nurse Training School. This is the only medical school for colored people within five hundred miles of New Orleans. Within a radius of two hundred miles of the city there are living today more than two millions of colored people.[47]

...Among its graduates are some of the most eminent colored physicians, North or South. The physicians, white and colored, of New Orleans, among whose colored members are many of its graduates, have unquestioned confidence in the school and render their services readily to reinforce the stated faculty.[48]

* * *

The buildings, grounds, and equipment of the University approach in value a quarter million dollars.[49]

The Rev. Dr. Charles Manley Melden, President

Dr. Charles M. Melden was elected President of New Orleans University July 4, 1911, and was inaugurated February 28, 1912.[50] His tenure extended through fourteen fruitful years. He came to the Presidency with years of experience as a pastor in the New England Conference. He had spent six years as the President of Clark University in Atlanta preceding his election to the Presidency of New Orleans University.

President Melden's administration effected a number of changes and improvements at the University. Early in his administration he initiated a program of beautification of the grounds and buildings, removing old fences and planting trees and shrubbery. He began renovation of the main building in 1911, which was not completed until 1922. Some of the buildings were completely changed. A central heating plant, new city water supply, and new sanitary facilities were provided. Peck Home was erected and more adequate facilities for housing young women on the campus were provided during his administration. Progress in the area of academics was noted by the Faculty as follows:

There was a slow but steady growth in College enrollment during the years of the Melden administration, the total number of college registrations increasing from eighteen in 1911 to one hundred fifty-six in 1924-1925. When he became President in 1911, the school was largely a secondary school with the largest enrollment in the grammar grades. Before he left, the character of the student body was reversed, with the largest enrollment in the college department and with the grades having disappeared, except where a few students were taken into the classes of the model school. It was in response to the need for guidance of this larger college personnel that Dr. Melden appointed the first Dean of the college in 1921, Professor Roy L. Heindel, A.B., of Wisconsin.[51]

283

When the Flint Medical College could no longer meet the standards of the American Medical Association it had to close. It was through the efforts of Resident Bishop Wilbur P. Thirkield and President Melden that the resources of the Medical College were retained in New Orleans and transferred to the Flint Goodridge Hospital and a much needed new unit erected for the service of the black community, where no such service was available.

The Last President of New Orleans University

The Rev. Dr. O. E. Kriege was the eleventh and final President of New Orleans University. He was elected to the Presidency in July, 1925, and continued in this office until the merger of New Orleans University and Straight University in 1935.

Dr. Kriege for a number of years had been a minister and a professor. He was a member of the Missouri Annual Conference. For fifteen years he was President of Central Wesleyan College, Warrenton, Missouri. He came from that position to the Presidency of New Orleans University.

Many of the important contributions of Dr. Kriege's administration are set forth in the historical sketch, "Seventy Years of Service," an account of which follows:

The administration of President Kriege has been marked by several well defined developments. First of all, there has been a phenomenal growth in the college enrollment. In 1925 there were one hundred and fifty-six enrolled in college courses; in four years the number had grown to four hundred and twenty-two. While, in part, this increase may be attributed to the general widespread interest in higher education and its attendant growth in college enrollment everywhere, it is equally true that it came in part because of the gains the University had made in program and in faculty personnel. New courses were added to the curriculum and highly trained men and women were secured to conduct this larger course of studies. A wider and more liberal curriculum demanded better facilities and equipment. In response to this demand, new class rooms were created. The science equipment was greatly increased. The library acquired many new volumes and for the first time was properly classified and administered under trained librarians. For the first time also, the teachers in the college and high school departments became distinct. Formerly there had been no separation of the two faculties.

One of the most significant advances was in the character of the college personnel. The minimum requirement for teachers in the college department was a Master of Arts degree. There were increases in the number of teachers in each department. . .

Always seeking higher rating by accrediting agencies, the University affiliated with the ranking association of Negro colleges, the "Association of Colleges for Negro Youth," and won approval of the American Medical Association as an 'A' College.[52]

It is interesting, and probably significant, to note that the eleven presidents of New Orleans University, the acting Presidents, and the Presidents or Principals of the institutions at Baldwin and in New Orleans related to New Orleans University were all ministers, and secondly, during the seventy-year life of the institution there was never a Negro President.

Robert B. Hayes, Dean, was the only black major administrative officer. He came to New Orleans University in 1925 from the Presidency of George R. Smith College in Sedalia, Missouri, when that institution was closed, and was made Dean, which position he held until 1935.

The academic program of New Orleans University in the last few years of the University remained virtually the same. The 1928 Survey by the U. S. Department of the Interior reported that "New Orleans University included a Graduate School, a College of Liberal Arts, Gilbert Academy (a four-year high school), the model grades, the Peck Home, with its department of Home Economics, and the Flint-Goodrich [sic] Hospital, with a nurse training school."[53] With the exception of the graduate school, this was its program when it closed in 1935.

The wide range of work and the enrollment at all levels during the history of New Orleans University may be noted from the following data:

From the founding of the school until recently, New Orleans University offered elementary and academic (high school) work, in addition to regular collegiate courses. Indeed until recently the grade and high school work predominated, and quite naturally so, for the school facilities, for colored children were lamentably meager all through the Southland for several decades after the Civil War. It is a satisfaction to record that the educational opportunities for colored children are now much better in all Southern states.

The following tabulation will indicate the trends in enrollment and the ebb and flow of the numbers in attendance. The figures are taken by decades as nearly as catalogs on file would permit.

285

Year	College	High School	Grades and Depts.	Total	
1873-74	7	126	209	335	
1880-81	11	84	264	369	(1)
1890-91	10	58	454	1200	(2)
1900-01	14	48	461	703	(3)
1913-14	10	166	329	712	(4)
1924-25	156	275	74	505	(5)
1927-28	383	329	163	895	(6)
1934-35	534	138	98	760	

(1) Includes La Teche Seminary, 205. (2) N.O.U. 562; Alexandria Academy, 136; La Harpe St. Academy, 110; Gilbert Academy, 392; (3) N.O.U. 523; Hartzell Academy, 58; Gilbert Academy, 248. (4) Includes Gilbert Academy, 172; Pharmacy, 26. Nurse Training, 11. (5) College enrollment includes 99 in the Teachers' College. Some lower grades were dropped from the elementary school. (6) Includes Summer Quarter and several Extension Schools.[54]

The importance of the educational opportunities offered by New Orleans University from the Primary School through college may be noted in a few statistics from Thomas Jesse Jones' study, 1915-1916 (published 1917). He pointed out that regarding the state of Louisiana, "The 1910 census had reported that the illiteracy of white persons was 14.1 per cent, of Negroes 48.4 per cent. Per capita expenditure in the whole State, for each white child, age 6-14, was $13.73; for each Negro child, $1.31. There were no public high schools for Negroes in the entire State."[55]

The 1928 Survey pointed out that "one of the causes for the limited number attending college is the small percentage preparing themselves for higher learning by attending high schools, 56 out of each 10,000 Negro population."[56] Jones' 1916 study reported only 9.5 per 10,000 attending high school.

The explanation for the few Negro youth attending high school at that time is simple. The public elementary schools for Negro children were woefully inadequate and public high schools for Negro youth were non-existent.

In the late 1920's and early 1930's the public high school movement for Negro youth began to gain momentum. New Orleans University carried its high school department until the

286

University closed in 1935. The high school, Gilbert Academy by name, continued as a private high school, operated by the Methodist Church, on the old New Orleans University site until 1949, when it was discontinued.

Schools Adjunct to New Orleans University

As noted earlier several schools were forerunners of New Orleans University. Some of these were united with the university early in its history. Other schools, located at Baldwin, Bayou on the Teche, Winsted, etc., had quite a career of their own, but were always related to New Orleans University as adjunct schools. An account of these schools is given briefly in the following paragraph from the historical sketch by the New Orleans University Faculty:

Preparatory Schools. In agreement with Section III of the Charter, a number of preparatory schools located in various parts of the State were operated by and affiliated with New Orleans University. Among these were the following: Gilbert Normal and Agriculture College, Baldwin, La., formerly the LaTeche Seminary, Winsted, La.; People's Normal and Industrial School, Lake Charles, La.; Live Oak School, Baton Rouge, La., Mansfield Academy, Donaldsonville, La., La Harpe St. Academy, New Orleans, Corporation Graded School, Thibodaux. All of these were discontinued long ago except the Gilbert Normal and Agricultural College at Baldwin, the most vigorous of the affiliated schools, which in 1919 was merged organically with its endowment fund with New Orleans University and is perpetuated in the official title of the school.[5][7]

When Gilbert Normal and Agricultural College was transferred from Baldwin, Louisiana, in 1919 and was united with New Orleans University, it became the high school or preparatory school of the University. When New Orleans University was closed in 1935 Gilbert Academy continued as a cooperative enterprise of the Methodist Board of Education and the Woman's Home Missionary Society of the Methodist Episcopal Church. About 1935 Mrs. J. W. E. Bowen, Jr., became the efficient principal and Gilbert Academy had a period of some fifteen years of exceptionally good work.

Dr. Horace M. Bond, educator and, at that time, Dean of Dillard University, said: "I am always glad to affirm, everywhere, my conviction that Gilbert Academy is one of the best, if not the

287

best, secondary schools for Negro youth in the country."[58]

Dr. J. W. E. Bowen, Jr., the husband of Mrs. Margaret D. Bowen, was elected to the Episcopacy in 1948, and his residence was changed to Atlanta. Mrs. Bowen resigned from the Principalship in the early Fall of 1948 and moved to Atlanta. Mrs. A. C. Dutton acted as Principal during 1948-1949, at the end of which year Gilbert Academy was permanently closed.

Theological Work

New Orleans University continued its interest in theological training, but the extensive work done in Thomson Theological School was transferred before the turn of the century. In 1888 Gammon Theological Seminary, having become a separate, independent, and chartered Seminary, it was decided by the Freedmen's Aid Society that instead of attempting to operate a number of theological seminaries, Gammon would be the central institution for the training of Negro ministers. At this time New Orleans joined with Gammon in this cooperative plan.

With reference to Gammon Theological Seminary, the Louisiana Annual Conference at its session January 31-February 4, 1889, took the following action:

> We have read with interest the several communications referred to us. We note with much satisfaction the ample foundation for a complete theological institution of the highest order, and the admirable arrangements already made for thorough courses of study, and for the training of our ministry at small expense to them.
>
> * * *
>
> Learning that it is intended to affiliate all the Biblical and theological departments in the South with this Theological Seminary, we offer for adoption the following:
>
> Resolved, That we will heartily concur with the authorities of the Freedmen's Aid Society in such related activities as may be assigned the several institutions. . .[59]

The Flint Medical College, and Flint
Goodridge Hospital

The Medical School, opened in 1889, continued until 1910. When it was closed the medical students were transferred to Meharry Medical College in Nashville. The following account gives

288

some light on the problems and the efforts made to continue a valuable service:

The time came when the standard of the medical colleges of America was raised and Flint was of necessity closed. Later on, when the city was threatened with bubonic plague, the hospital was condemned because of its dilapidated and unsanitary condition.

Face-to-face with this critical situation, the Board of Managers of the Freedmen's Aid Society at Cincinnati voted to transfer all the interests of the Flint Medical College and Sarah Goodridge Hospital to Nashville. Then this million of colored people sat in despair. No hospital within a radius of four hundred or five hundred miles where they could go for treatment under Protestant influences, the only hospital being the charity hospital in the city of New Orleans.[60]

Bishop Thirkfield, resident in New Orleans, saw the urgent need. He got under the load in effort to change the situation. Because of his efforts:

The Freedmen's Aid Society rescinded its action ordering the movement of all interests of Flint and Sarah Goodridge Hospital to Nashville, on the agreement of the bishop, in addition to the society's gift of five thousand dollars, to finance the building and to increase the endowment to fifty thousand dollars, thus assuring the permanency of the enterprise.[61]

Following is a statement in a letter by Bishop Thirkield in March, 1931, regarding the Freedmen's Aid Society action to transfer the interests of Flint to Meharry in Nashville:

As a Trustee for a dozen years or more I was able to enter more intimately into the conservative plans and efficient work of the University. On this Charter Day the story of the preservation of the Flint-Goodridge property on Canal Street, which has rendered such large service as a hospital, is of historical interest. As it had been closed as a Medical School at a meeting of the Board of the Freedmen's Aid and Southern Education Society in Providence, R.I., without conference with me as Resident Bishop of the Area, a committee brought in a request directing that the property be sold, and the proceeds transferred to the Hubbard Hospital at Meharry Medical College. I met this proposal with indignation, and only defeated this plan by agreeing to build the property into a well-equipped hospital and to increase the endowment from $37,000 to $50,000. My first gift was $5,000 from a Presbyterian lady, which gave me courage, and with less than half of the amount in hand I made a contract for building the hospital based on carefully drawn plans. President Melden secured $1,000 and the superintendent some excellent furniture as a gift.

When I think of the service rendered by this institution, I give praise and gratitude to God that this building and equipment were made possible.[62]

On Saturday afternoon, March 11, 1916, the new Flint-Goodridge Hospital was formally dedicated and opened for service by Bishop Wilbur P. Thirkield.

The hospital is a new and modern wing addition, which later on can be added to as necessities and funds will warrant.

* * *

Great credit is due to Bishop Thirkield for his indefatigable interest and untiring energies in raising funds for the Institution. Dr. C. M. Melden, President of New Orleans College, has been a loyal friend, and has assisted at all times in raising funds and aiding by counsel and otherwise in the construction of the building.[63]

Peck Home (and Peck School of Domestic
Science and Art)

The Peck Home and School of Domestic Science and Art was affiliated with New Orleans University, but operated by the Woman's Home Missionary Society of the Methodist Episcopal Church. It had its origin in a mission school for girls opened in 1887 through the influence of Mrs. J. C. Hartzell and named in honor of Bishop Jesse T. Peck. This building stood on Peters Avenue (Jefferson) and St. Patrick (Dannell), on a square of ground consisting of three acres.[64]

Peck Hall. Peck Memorial Home—A loving tribute from Central New York Conference Society of the Woman's Home Missionary Society of the Methodist Episcopal Church to Bishop Jesse T. Peck and his wife, Persis Wing Peck, 1889.

A marble tablet carried this inscription for all to read as they entered the original Peck Industrial Home (in New Orleans, Louisiana). This home, the first Protestant industrial home for Negro girls in Louisiana was built on a lot given by Mrs. Priscilla

290

Lee Bennett of Wilkes-Barre, Pennsylvania. This generous friend, known also as Mrs. Ziba Bennett, was a cheerful giver, especially when gently nudged by Mrs. R. S. Rust.

Fire totally destroyed the building in 1897. While considering the next move, the Society took advantage of the rise in land values and sold the lot in 1899 for $9,000. The purchase price in 1887 was $3,000.

There was another reason, too, for selling the property. Peck Home was affiliated with New Orleans University, but the distance between the two institutions hindered successful cooperation. The Freedmen's Aid Society promptly offered a lot on the campus of the University. Eventually the Society accepted the lot, though some members of the Board of Trustees were reluctant to rebuild Peck Home in New Orleans. The pleas of bureau secretaries ended in study committees. These delaying tactics proved effective for several years.

Meanwhile an enterprising bureau secretary, Mrs. Katherine Falley, reported at the 1903 Annual Meeting that the Peck School of Domestic Science and Art had been established in cooperation with the University. The Society equipped the classrooms and paid the instructors. All girls were required to take the Domestic Science and Art courses (sewing and cooking) in order to graduate. Through this successful venture, hundreds of girls learned to sew and cook.

This was all to the good, but not enough. Home training was lacking. Efforts to rebuild Peck Home continued.

Escalation was the word after Mrs. E. L. Knostman of Manhattan, Kansas, became bureau secretary in 1908. Quiet, persistent, persuasive, she moved toward the goal. Peck Home with a capacity for forty was completed in the spring of 1912 at a cost of $27,000. The continuing School of Domestic Art and Science became the department of Home Economics for the University. And Peck Home girls soon became known for their scholastic ability, winning high honors.

The years brought changes. In 1935, New Orleans University merged with Straight College to form Dillard University and moved to the new campus. This could have ended the days of usefulness for Peck since it was a dormitory for girls attending New Orleans University.

However, a survey revealed the dearth of high schools for Negro youth, both in the city of New Orleans, and the surrounding territory. The Methodist Episcopal Board of Education and the Woman's Home Missionary Society decided to continue cooperative work in supporting a high school in the buildings of the former New Orleans University. Thus, Peck Hall became a boarding home for out-of-town girls attending the school known as Gilbert Academy. This name really perpetuated the work founded many years ago at Baldwin, Louisiana.

Peck Hall and Gilbert Academy became a duo in team work establishing a secure place in the educational life of the region. Though rural education improved in Louisiana and southern Mississippi and high schools were added, yet many girls would have had no opportunity to further their education were it not for this institution. It was an anti-poverty program on its own. In 1940 the Woman's Home Missionary Society presented Peck Hall to the Woman's Division of Christian Service with a sense of pride in the record of the institution and the progress of the girls—worthy girls from the homes of poor families who needed and appreciated the help given to them.[65]

Peck Home had a continued existence from 1912 to its close in 1949.

The Superintendents of Peck School of Domestic Science and Art since the opening of the new building were as follows, the term of office beginning with the year indicated:

    1912—Miss Ida M. Gibson
    1915—Mrs. Emma Wilson Fisher
    1926—Mrs. Emma K. Montgomery
    1927—Miss Elinor F. Neal
    1931—(Spring and Summer) Miss Vevie M. Souders
           Mrs. Florence M. Landon
    1933—Mrs. D. Marie McDonald

The Bureau Secretaries of the Women's Home Missionary Society who have had direct charge of Peck Home during these years were Mrs. E. L. Knostman, 1910-1930, and Mrs. Anna L. Zook, 1930.

II

STRAIGHT UNIVERSITY

Straight University of New Orleans, Louisiana, was founded in 1869 by the American Missionary Association, an official agency of the National Council of the Congregational Church. In the same year, 1869, the Association applied for, and was granted, a charter from the State of Louisiana for Straight University. The charter provided for "Education and Training upon Christian principles for young men and women irrespective of race."[1] The University was named after the Honorable Seymour Straight, an interested local Baptist layman friend and donor.[2]

The first board of trustees was said to have been "nondenominational." The membership was as follows: Seymour Straight, Hudson, Ohio; Rufus K. Howell; John S. Walton; John Turner; Rufus Waples; Charles Heath; W. Van Norden; S. D. Moody; Joseph W. Healey; E. W. Pierce; S. D. Satchell; Edward Heath; A. Aristide Marye; Oscar J. Dunn; and Charles Clinton.[3]

Straight University was founded as a nondenominational institution which was to be free from any denominational emphasis. In contrast, New Orleans University, the first unit of which—Thomson Biblical Institute and the Union Normal School—was founded in 1969 in New Orleans, had for its purpose the training of Methodist ministers and the preparation of teachers.

On March 9, 1870, the original Straight University Charter of 1869 was amended.* Two sections of the amended Charter provided for the establishment of two additional schools, law and medicine. There were two amendments, Sections III and IV, reading as follows:

Section III. Be it further enacted, that the department of law shall consist of four or more persons, who shall be required to give a full course of lectures on international, constitutional, maritime, commercial and municipal or civil law, and instruction in the practice thereof.[4]

*See Charter on File, Dillard University.

Section IV. Be it further enacted, etc., that in the department of medicine there shall never be less than seven professors. This department shall at all times have free access to the Charity Hospital of New Orleans, for the purpose of affording medical students illustrations of the subject taught.[5]

A law department was opened at Straight University with Negro and white students taught by the keenest white lawyers in New Orleans.[6] There was also a medical school in which prominent city physicians taught. The legislative act creating the school provided that instructors might use Charity Hospital of New Orleans as a "laboratory for practical instruction."[7]

The Straight University Medical School was short-lived. Section Seven of the amended charter, 1870, provided an appropriation of $35,000 by the State of Louisiana for the Medical Department to erect a building and to secure illustrations of medical science. The judgment of the lower court of the State was reversed by the higher court of the State which nullified and voided the State appropriation for the medical school.[8] This action ended the early effort to establish a medical department at Straight University.

Brownlee points out that in 1870 there were 1,000 students in all departments at Straight University, three-fourths of whom were Roman Catholics and the majority of the enrollment were Negroes.[9] Later the high school department was added, and later still the college department was added. All departments were retained until 1926, when the schools of law and medicine disappeared.[10]

In January, 1914, and March, 1915, Dr. Thomas Jesse Jones visited Straight University while studying higher education for Negroes in the South.

The following comments are quoted from Brownlee:

Dr. Jones once said of New Orleans, "There are two colleges of liberal arts there, both missionary institutions, their aims are identical. The work in both is hampered by lack of facilities and money with which to pay fair salaries to teachers. It would be well if these two colleges united in forming a single strong college.[11]

Dr. Brownlee said, "I felt the same way when I went to New Orleans for the first time in 1920."[12]

Dr. Jones visited New Orleans University on the same trips to New Orleans when he visited Straight College (the name had been changed from Straight University to Straight College).

The following page (296) shows comparative data on the two institutions. The data indicate similarity of situations and resources, neither giving evidence of being strong. It was easy, from these data, to draw the conclusion that there would be economy and added strength if the two institutions were merged.

The comparative data on page 297 from the Federal Government Survey Report, 1927, show that New Orleans University and Straight College were practically the same as they were in 1915. There was no significant improvement and neither showed a significant difference in strength.

The continued similarity of these two institutions with reference to resources and programs, and the fact that neither one alone was able with its resources to do a creditable quality of academic work, pointed to the inevitability of their merging into one institution.

III

STEPS IN THE DIRECTION OF MERGER

When the 1924 General Conference of the Methodist Episcopal Church merged the former Board of Education for Negroes with the Board of Education of the Church, the Commission on Survey of Negro Schools recommended to the General Conference that "effort be made, perhaps through the General Education Board, to unite New Orleans College and Straight College as one strong well-equipped Protestant College in a different location from that which either now occupies."[17] The Methodist Episcopal Church made the first official proposal for the merger of its educational interest in New Orleans with that of the American Missionary Association. Several years passed before any further official action was taken on either side.

Dr. Brownlee relates an interesting and significant incident that resulted in the larger efforts to consummate the merger of Straight College and New Orleans University:

In 1928 President O'Brien of Straight College sent letters to local citizens asking for help toward raising five hundred dollars for something needed at the college. One of the letters was directed to Edgar B. Stern, a New Orleans cotton broker. He wrote Dr. O'Brien that he was much interested in what Straight College was trying to do and then added, "If all you need is five hundred dollars, I should think the mission board could supply

295

COMPARATIVE DATA, 1914[13]

New Orleans University		Straight University	
1. Founded, 1869		1. Founded, 1869	
2. Founded by Freedmen's Aid Society, Methodist Episcopal Church		2. Founded by, American Missionary Association, Congregational Church	
3. Enrollment:			
Elementary	298		
Secondary	125	3. Enrollment:	
College	9	Elementary	364
		Secondary	203
Total	432 (1)	College	11
		Total	578

Secondary:		Above elementary grades:	
Male	46	Male	70
Female	88	Female	144
Boarders	47	Boarders	53
From N. O.	73	From N. O.	142
From State (La.)	45	From State (La.)	50
Out of State	16	Out of State	22
Enrollment for year	557	Enrollment for year	758
Teachers	18 (2)	Teachers	30

4. Organization: Elementary, High School, College, Industry	4. Organization: 8 Elem. grades, High School, College, Normal, Commercial, Manual Trng.

5. Finances:		5. Finances:	
From Freedmen's Aid Society	$5,400	From American Missionary Association	$9,567
General Donation	1,533	From Slater Fund	1,000
		Donations	144
		Other Sources	1,875

6. Plant Value	$159,000	6. Plant Value	$150,000
Equipment	18,000	Equipment	20,000

(1) Plus 175 at Peck Home
(2) Plus six teachers at Peck Home

COMPARATIVE DATA
(For School Year 1925-1926)

New Orleans University	Straight College
1. Enrollment[14]	1. Enrollment[14]
Men 259	Men 171
Women 444	Women 230
2. Professors[14]	2. Professors[14]
Men 11	Men 7
Women 18	Women 11
3. Finances[15]	3. Finances[15]
Income:	Income:
From Students $17,236	From Students $11,783
From Productive	From Productive
Funds 5,578	Funds —
Total Receipts $17,561	Total Receipts $41,331
(Other than students)	(Other than students)
4. Land Value $250,000	4. Land Value $275,000
5. Equipment $ 20,000	5. Equipment $ 20,500
6. Buildings $150,000	6. Buildings $190,000
7. Productive Funds $105,000	7. Productive Funds —
8. Library Volumes[16] 4,550	8. Library Volumes[16] 5,000

it. Should you ever be interested in bigger things, you will find me interested also."[18]

Within a few weeks Mr. Brownlee received an "intriguing letter" from Mr. Edwin R. Embree, President of the Rosenwald Fund. Mr. Embree asked, "Would you care to attend a meeting in the office of the Chamber of Commerce in New Orleans at which local citizens and representatives of educational foundations will discuss the subject of higher education for Negroes in New Orleans?"[19]

The outcome was a proposal to secure two million dollars

with which to purchase a site and erect the first buildings for a new college provided that New Orleans University and Straight College would agree to merge their interests and programs and that the respective boards would furnish a half-million dollars each toward the capital fund. Meanwhile, the General Education Board of New York was asked for a half-million dollars, the Rosenwald Fund of Chicago for a quarter-million dollars, and the citizens of New Orleans for a quarter-million dollars. The church boards of the two colleges agreed, the local citizens agreed, as did also the General Education Board, and the Rosenwald Fund. The meeting was historic. It meant that what the self-effacing missionary teachers had been doing in isolation for sixty years could now be done in open.[20]

The news broke and the general public of New Orleans became informed of the developing plans to merge New Orleans and Straight Colleges. The following excerpt comes from the February, 1929, issue of the New Orleans University Bulletin:

A Great Negro University in New Orleans. The daily papers have heralded the news that plans are under consideration to merge several of the Colored Colleges in New Orleans and to establish a great University with a strong Liberal Arts College, Graduate Departments and Professional Schools on some new and larger site. . . .The governing boards of New Orleans University and Straight College have taken favorable action on the projected merger and have appointed committees which are to meet in New Orleans February 22. Meanwhile the Association of Commerce of this city has interested itself in the plan and is arranging a joint meeting with the above committees to see wherein the city itself and the Association of Commerce could lend assistance in promoting this enterprise. . . .It will require several years at best to effect a merger and erect the necessary buildings on a new site. Meanwhile both schools in question will carry on with full vigor in their present plants. Should nothing come of the proposed merger New Orleans University will try to conserve the momentum it has gained in the last few years and develop its resources to the fullest extent in order to serve the youth of the land with increasing success.[21]

IV

DILLARD UNIVERSITY

Representatives of the two church boards, and of the two local colleges began immediately to formulate a new charter, a new constitution, operative principles, and a name for the new institution.[22] The charter followed closely the original charters. It provided for an integrated institution in which representatives of different races might teach. It also provided for the new university to be co-educational.[23]

Provision was made for the Board of Trustees to have a membership of seventeen, six to be nominated by each of the two church boards, and five to be nominated by the boards jointly.[24]

A committee was appointed to recommend a name for their new institution. The name of James Hardy Dillard was proposed.[25] Decision on the name was left to the eighteen alumni representatives of the two colleges, present at the meeting. They were both unanimous and enthusiastic about the name of Dillard.[26]

A letter dated November 16, 1929, to Mr. Jackson Davis of the General Education Board, New York, from Dr. M. J. Holmes, Secretary of the Board of Education for Negroes, the Methodist Episcopal Church, Chicago, sets forth the thinking and discussion of the joint committee on merger which met February 21-22, 1929. Several paragraphs of that letter follow:

Mr. dear Mr. Davis:

* * *

I am enclosing a copy of the Minutes of the Merger Conference of February 21 and 22. A reference to the progress of our thinking in the initial stages of this first conference will be of value.

At first the Hospital was not included in the plans for consolidation. The first estimates discussed involved capital fund contributions from the two Church Boards considerably less than $500,000, and annual contribution to the budget considerably less than $35,000 on the part of each Board. At a dinner conference, attended by Mr. Favrot, Mr. Embree, Mr.

Hovey, Mr. Brownlee and Mr. Holmes, it was proposed that the Hospital be included as a first step toward a possible medical school, and that the amount underwritten by each of the two Church Boards should be $500,000, toward a total of $2,000,000 for buildings and grounds, which should include the Hospital unit and an annual contribution of $35,000 from each of the two Boards to the operating budget of the new University.

Coming now to your specific questions: It is proposed that the $2,000,000 investment shall include the cost of the Hospital. It is proposed that the Hospital be a unit of Dillard University, and that the income for Dillard University shall be so handled as to provide for the maintenance of the Hospital. We further propose that each of the two Church Boards shall contribute annually $25,000 toward the budget of Dillard University. The total of $70,000 from the two Church Boards includes the income from certain endowment funds held by the Boards for the use of their institutions in New Orleans.[27]

At a meeting of the Joint Committee on Conference (Re: Dillard University) February 14, 1930, Dr. M. J. Holmes, Secretary of the Board of Education for Negroes, Methodist Episcopal Church, made the following report on action previously taken by the Board of Education:

The matter of the merger in New Orleans was presented to the Board of Education of the Methodist Episcopal Church and received cordial approval, thoroughly in accord with the attitude previously expressed by the Board at its meeting in October. The action now taken is supplementary to that action taken in October. After reviewing the plans as they have been outlined, a resolution was adopted covering four points: The approval of the consolidation, the securing of the charter, the agreement to provide $500,000, and the continuation of the Committee on Conference with power. I quote here the action taken:

* * *

1. That the consolidation of the above mentioned institutions be approved.
2. We recommend that a charter for Dillard University be secured immediately.
3. We agree to provide $500,000 payable to the Board of Trustees of Dillard University in installments as may be agreed upon.
4. That the Committee on Conference be continued with

300

power. To the committee appointed in February, 1929, there should be added the trustees selected by the Board in October, 1929.[2 8]

At the same meeting of the Joint Committee on Conference February 14, 1930, Dr. Frederick L. Brownlee made the following report on action by the Administrative Committee of the American Missionary Association March 12, 1929:

> Voted, that if and when the proposed James. H. Dillard University of New Orleans, Louisiana, is duly incorporated with a Board of Trustees of not fewer than seventeen—six representing the A.M.A., six representing the Methodist Board of Education and five to be chosen at large by these twelve—The American Missionary Association hereby agrees to furnish $500,000.00 toward the purchase of a new site and buildings to cost not less than $2,000,000.00 provided that the Methodist Board furnishes a like amount, and provided further that a total of not less than $1,000,000.00 is secured jointly from the Julius Rosenwald Fund, The General Education Board and the citizens of New Orleans.
>
> The American Missionary Association further agrees to make an annual appropriation of not less than $35,000.00 for the current expenses of the proposed James H. Dillard University if and when said proposed university shall have been duly incorporated and the educational and hospital work now conducted by the New Orleans University, Straight University and the Flint-Goodridge Hospital have been combined and ways and means have been determined for the establishment of a permanent endowment adequate to provide for current expenses.[2 9]

On May 28, 1930, the Acting Chairman of the Board of Trustees of Dillard University sent the following information to the General Education Board:

> Dillard University has now *bona fide* pledges towards this fund of more than $1,500,000, including $500,000 from the Board of Education of the Methodist Episcopal Church: $500,000 from the American Missionary Association; $250,000 from the Julius Rosenwald Fund and over $300,000 in signed pledges from the citizens of New Orleans. It is hoped and expected that the Board of Trustees of Dillard University, at their meeting on June 2nd, will authorize the purchase of the land necessary for the hospital and university campuses, and set

in motion plans for the immediate construction of the hospital, and for the construction of the college buildings as soon as feasible.[30]

Minutes of the Executive Committee of the Board of Education of the Methodist Episcopal Church, June 21, 1930, show that the Charter had been approved and that Dillard University came into legal existence June 6, 1930. The minutes also show the elected members of the Dillard Board of Trustees in accordance with the provisions of the charter; and the minutes show other important items in the report to the Executive Committee.

The following excerpts are taken from the minutes of the Executive Committee meeting June 21, 1930:

The committee appointed by the Board of Education at its meeting on October 28, 1929, with instructions to proceed with the consolidation of the institutions in New Orleans into Dillard University, and pursuant to further action by the Board in February, 1930, presented the following report:

1. The charter of Dillard University, having been approved by the legal adviser of the Board, was duly signed by the trustees—elected and has been formally filed, bringing Dillard University into legal existence on June 6, 1930.

* * *

3. The Board of Trustees of Dillard University consists of the following persons:

Elected by the Board of Education of the
Methodist Episcopal Church

> Lewis N. Gatch, Cincinnati, Ohio
> Thomas F. Holgate, Evanston, Ill.
> Merrill J. Holmes, Chicago, Ill.
> Frank Jensen, Dallas, Texas
> Robert E. Jones, New Orleans, La.
> Thaddeus Taylor, New Orleans, La.

Elected by the American Missionary Association

> Fred L. Brownlee, New York, N. Y.
> C. B. Austin, New York, N. Y.
> Eva H. Eastman, New York, N. Y.
> George E. Haynes, New York, N. Y.
> W. A. Daniel, New York, N. Y.

302

E. J. LaBranch, New Orleans, La.

Elected by the twelve above named

Edgar B. Stern, New Orleans, La.
Alvin P. Howard, New Orleans, La.
Florence Read, Spelman College, Atlanta, Ga.
Monte Lemann, New Orleans, La.
Warren Kearny, New Orleans, La.

The Board of Trustees of Dillard University was formally organized on June 6, 1930, by the election of Edgar B. Stern as President; Robert E. Jones and E. J. LaBranch as Vice Presidents; C. B. Austin as Secretary; Alvin P. Howard as Treasurer; and by the appointment of an executive committee.

4. The trustees of Dillard University report that pledges amounting to more than two million dollars have now been made toward the capital fund for that institution. In addition to pledges previously noted from the church boards and the Foundations, the local campaign in New Orleans produced pledges amounting to more than $300,000. This campaign was formally launched in January as authorized by the Board of Education of the Methodist Episcopal Church in cooperation with a local New Orleans committee acting with the approval of the Community Chest, the receipts to apply on the expense of new grounds and buildings for Flint-Goodridge Hospital. Representatives of the American Missionary Association joined in the campaign in its early progress. The campaign was launched with the understanding that if the merger of the institutions involved should become effective, the campaign would come under the direction of Dillard University, and would be for Flint-Goodridge Hospital as a unit of the consolidated university. The pledges and the cash thus far collected are therefore assets of Dillard University.

5. Action has been taken by the Board of Trustees of Dillard University authorizing the purchase of the new hospital site now held by the Board of Education.[31]

Flint-Goodridge Hospital and
Dillard University

The Flint-Goodridge Hospital that was dedicated March 11, 1916, had, by 1930, become inadequate to serve the needs of the Negro Community of New Orleans. It was pointed out that New Orleans had the highest death rate among the eleven American cities with the largest Negro population, and that unsanitary living

303

conditions were responsible for a large part of the tragic results of deadly diseases. These conditions pointed to the need for "additional opportunities for the training of nurses, studying of diseases, and teaching the gospel of good health."[32]

On the invitation of the local board of Flint-Goodridge Hospital, representatives of the local board of control of Flint-Goodridge Hospital and representatives of the New Orleans Colored Hospital Association met jointly Thursday afternoon, March 20, 1930. The two organizations found themselves in perfect agreement as to the need of larger hospitalization for Negroes in the city of New Orleans and were unanimously willing to heartily cooperate in the promotion of an institution that will more largely and more efficiently serve our group than the institutions that now exist.[33]

The new Flint-Goodridge Hospital was to become a unit of Dillard University and become a part of the campaign for the rebuilding of the hospital and the development of Dillard University.[34]

"The representatives of Flint-Goodridge Hospital and the New Orleans Colored Hospital Association definitely and unanimously agree to merge their interests, pooling into one organization our finances, real estate and assets of any and all kinds."[35]

In this new arrangement the New Orleans Colored Hospital Association was to have one representative on the Board and two representatives if the Board should be as large as eleven or more. The name of the New Orleans Colored Hospital Association was to be preserved by giving its name to a ward or some section of the New Flint-Goodridge Hospital.[36]

In the meeting of the Dillard University Board of Trustees November 24, 25, 1930, it was voted:

That in connection with Flint-Goodridge Hospital there shall be continued a Nurses Training School in which, in addition to training for private and institutional nursing, there shall be developed a program for the adequate preparation of public health nurses.[37]

At the meeting of the Board of Trustees of Dillard University, November 25, 1930, the Chairman brought before the Board the question of the name to be placed upon the cornerstone of the Hospital. It was voted "That there be designated on the building the name 'Flint-Goodridge Hospital of Dillard University.' "[38]

The formal dedication of the new Hospital was held on January

304

31, 1932 and on the following day it was opened to the public for hospital service.[39] The building with furnishings and the lot on which it stands cost $450,000.[40] Mr. Albert W. Dent, a Morehouse College graduate and a young business man in Atlanta, was elected Superintendent of the Hospital and Dr. Rivers Fredericks was elected Chief of Staff.[41] *

Further Developments Relating to the
New Dillard University

At its meeting June 7, 1930, the Dillard University Board of Trustees "turned its attention again to the selection and purchase of a site for Dillard University campus." Action was taken to buy seventy acres of land with a twelve hundred and forty foot frontage on Gentilly Road, at a price of $339,750.

One of the concerns of the Board of Trustees at its meetings November 24 and 25, 1930, was the selection of a President for the University. The Board approved the following recommendation:

That a President of the University be chosen and elected as early as it may be found practicable, who shall be the head of the several schools and divisions of the University.[42]

Dr. Will W. Alexander, who had created the Commission on Interracial Cooperation in Atlanta and was its Director, was invited to become the President of Dillard University. On October 5, 1931, a letter was presented to the Dillard Board from Dr. Alexander dated September 30, 1931, accepting the position of Acting President of Dillard University.[43] It became necessary for the Board to effect arrangements for Dr. Alexander's services as Acting President on a half-time basis.[44] He served as Acting President, giving half-time to the administration of the University and half-time to the Commission on Interracial Cooperation until June, 1936.

Dr. Alexander had before him, beginning late in 1931, the stupendous job of completing the foundation plan and initiating

---

*On the occasion of the dedication of the new Hospital Mr. L. K. Nicholson presented to Mr. Edgar B. Stern the *Times-Picayune* Loving Cup for the most outstanding service rendered by any citizen of New Orleans during the year 1930, in that largely through Mr. Stern's influence the merger of New Orleans and Straight Universities was accomplished. (New Orleans University Bulletin, February, 1932, p. 2.)

305

the program for the new Dillard University. Building the physical plant on the new site of seventy acres was first in order. In addition to the hospital building completed in 1932 and the first unit of the University, the basic buildings had to be erected, including a dormitory for men, a dormitory for women, a refectory, an administration and classroom building, and a science hall. These buildings were completed in 1935 for the beginning of the first year of academic work, 1935-1936.

In preparation for the opening of the University key members of the faculty were selected in 1934. At a meeting of the Board of Trustees May, 1934, President Alexander recommended the following persons for the faculty:[4 5]

1. Horace Mann Bond, Dean of the University and Professor of Education
2. Frederick D. Hall, Associate Professor of Music
3. Countee Cullen, Associate Professor of English
4. Rudolph Moses, Associate Professor of English
5. Byrd Crudup, Assistant Professor, Physical Education

Others were added later. These were outstanding men in their fields and were highly representative of a quality faculty for the new University.

Dr. Alexander did a yeoman's job from October, 1931, to June, 1936, giving leadership in the development of plans for the University. Administering the University on a half-time basis, it was necessary for Dr. Alexander to spend at least half of his time at the Interracial Commission in Atlanta.

Dr. Brownlee says that "Dr. Horace Mann Bond did magnificent work as dean in organizing and administering the new university. He assisted in selecting the first faculty, in formulating the educational aims and methods, and in setting Dillard's quality standards in education."[4 6]

Increasingly Dr. Alexander felt the pressures of two necessities; one was for the University to have a full-time President, and the other was for him to return to the Interracial Commission on Cooperation on a full-time basis.

In the Board meeting April 11, 1935, the Chairman of the Board read the following paragraph from a letter from Dr. Alexander:

For the present, I am willing to continue to carry as best I can the responsibility for the development of Dillard, the understanding being that as soon as it is practical a leader shall be found for the Dillard enterprise. If it is desired by the

306

trustees, I should be willing to go on with Dillard to the first of October under the present arrangement. If absolutely necessary, I should be willing to continue after that date through the first scholastic year, dividing my time between the two tasks, with the understanding that after October 1, 1935, my entire salary shall be paid by the Commission on Interracial Cooperation and that I shall accept only travel expense from October 1935 until June 1936. This suggested financial arrangement would be justified, I am sure, as a part of my work as Director of the Commission and would be very much more acceptable to me personally.[47]

The Board unanimously re-elected Dr. Alexander as Acting President of the University for the fiscal year ending June 30, 1936. It was voted unanimously by secret ballot for a committee of the Board appointed by its Chairman to "make every effort to persuade him to accept the appointment as President of the University."[48]

Dr. Alexander continued as Acting President, part-time, through the first fiscal year of the new University. The Dillard Board on several occasions expressed and recorded their appreciation for the splendid services rendered by Dr. Alexander during the four-year period he served as Acting President.*

Valuable Administrative Assistance

As already indicated Dr. Bond gave valuable service in the administration of the University during the difficult period of its formative years. Another administrator, Mr. Dent, was also of invaluable assistance.

---

*In expressing its appreciation for the services of Dr. Alexander the Executive Committee of the Dillard University Board of Trustees passed, unanimously, the following Resolution:

The Board of Trustees of Dillard University in accepting the resignation of Dr. Will W. Alexander desires to acknowledge its debt to the Commission on Interracial Cooperation for effecting an arrangement between the two organizations which permitted Dr. Alexander during the past four years to share his time between the two groups. Dr. Alexander has served Dillard University faithfully and well, but as Trustees of Dillard University, we feel that the work of Dillard has been in line with the spirit and purpose of the Commission on Interracial Cooperation. One of the fine results of Dr. Alexander's labor at Dillard has been the marked advance of Interracial good will in the deep South.[51]

Mr. Dent became Superintendent of the Flint-Goodridge Hospital, the first unit of the University, in 1932. He took "the lead in initiating various practical services as well as winning for the hospital the highest rating of the American College of Physicians and Surgeons."[49] Effective July 1, 1935, Mr. Dent was elected by the Dillard Board of Trustees to the position of Business Manager of the University.[50] He performed the duties of this new office and at the same time continued as Superintendent of the hospital.

First Full-Time President Elected

At the meeting of the Executive Committee of the Board, authority having been vested in the Executive Committee at a previous meeting of the Board to accept the resignation of Dr. Alexander and to elect a permanent President, the Special Committee to nominate a president presented the name of Dr. William Stuart Nelson. Dr. Nelson was at the time President of Shaw University, Raleigh, North Carolina. The committee reported that "a searching investigation of his record had been made and that he was found to be an able administrator, a good scholar, a man of fine character, who handles his contacts with both races very satisfactorily. . . .The Special Committee felt confident that if Dr. Nelson were elected to the Presidency of Dillard University and he accepted, the University would have an excellent leader."[52] Dr. William Stuart Nelson was unanimously elected President of Dillard University, effective July 1, 1936,[53] later changed to August 1, 1936.

At its annual meeting June 13, 1936, the Full Board "unanimously adopted all acts of the Executive Committee taken since the previous meeting of the Board of Trustees and particularly the election of Dr. Nelson was approved, ratified and confirmed."[54]

Dr. Nelson remained at Dillard, as President, four years. He resigned in 1940 to become Dean of the Graduate School of Religion at Howard University.[55]

Albert W. Dent Becomes President

"Albert W. Dent, who had given excellent account of himself as Superintendent of the Flint-Goodridge Hospital, was advanced to the Presidency."[56]

Dr. Dent had a background of excellent experience that helped to fit him for the administration of the University as President. He had served as branch auditor for the Atlanta Life Insurance

Company and as vice president of a real estate and construction company in Houston, Texas. In 1928 he was employed by his Alma Mater (Morehouse) to organize the Alumni and to direct an endowment campaign for the raising of three hundred thousand dollars to match a like sum offered by the General Education Board. After the successful completion of this assignment he assumed the post of Superintendent at Flint-Goodridge Hospital in 1932.[57]

Doctor Dent served as President twenty-nine years, from July 1, 1940, to July 1, 1969, retiring on the latter date.

Dillard University had remarkable development and growth during the presidency of Dr. Dent. Its physical plant increased by the addition of a modern library building, named for Dr. Will W. Alexander; the building of a beautiful Lawless Chapel, named for father and son; a gymnasium; the expansion of the refectory and the Science Hall; faculty housing and other developments. The Health and Physical Education Building has been appropriately named the Albert W. Dent Hall. The endowment was increased to $3,347,000;[58] the enrollment reached more than a thousand students; the academic and cultural programs became exceptionally strong, unique and significant.

In 1958 Dillard was admitted to membership in the Southern Association of Colleges and Schools.[59] Dillard University is now known as one of the best small institutions of higher education in the Southern Region. The outstanding character of Dillard University can be attributed in a large measure to the excellent administrative leadership of Dr. Dent and the strong faculty he brought to the institution.

But account must be taken also of the strength of the two cooperating denominations giving financial support—the Congregational Church, through the American Missionary Association, and the United Methodist Church, through its General Board of Education. It should be noted also that Dillard University has had from its incorporation to the present an exceptionally strong Board of Trustees, with influence and finance to give the kind of support needed.

Dr. Broadus Butler is the incumbent President of Dillard University, assuming the post July 1, 1969, as successor to Dr. Albert W. Dent. The educational qualification and wide educational experience of Dr. Butler give promise of continued excellence in administrative leadership for Dillard University.

The Dillard University Heritage*

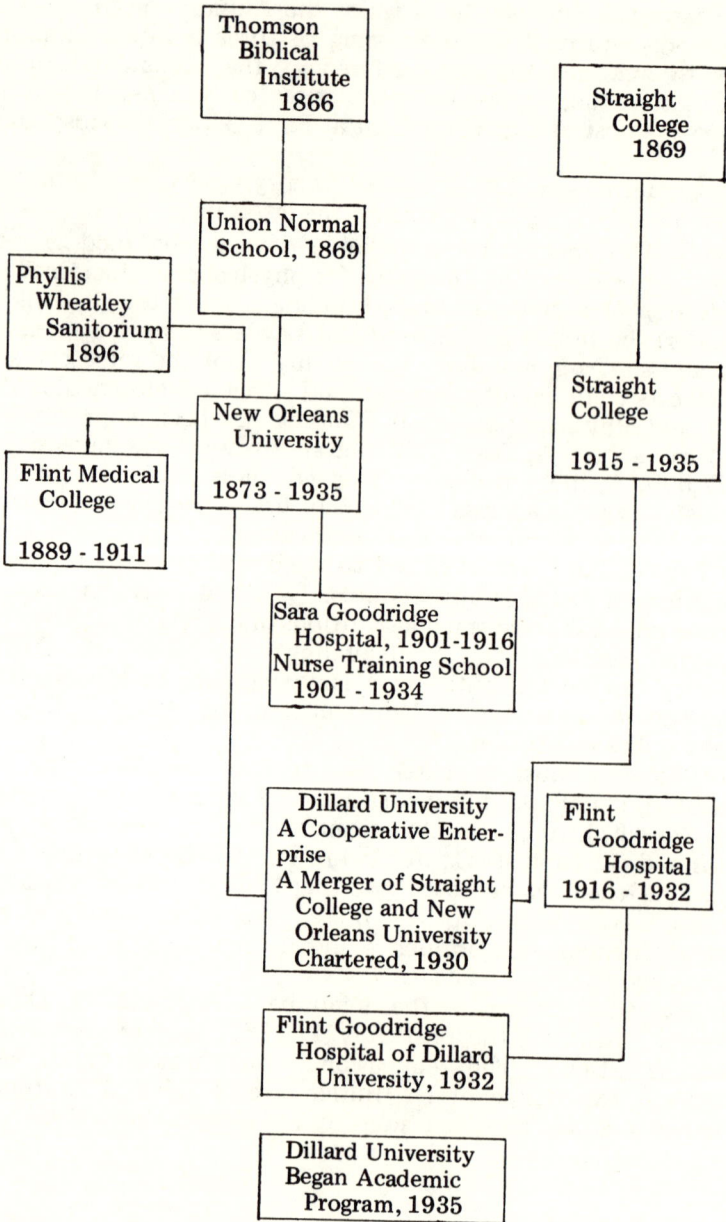

```
                    ┌──────────────┐
                    │   Thomson    │                    ┌──────────────┐
                    │   Biblical   │                    │   Straight   │
                    │  Institute   │                    │   College    │
                    │     1866     │                    │     1869     │
                    └──────────────┘                    └──────────────┘
                    ┌──────────────┐
                    │ Union Normal │
                    │ School, 1869 │
┌──────────────┐    └──────────────┘
│   Phyllis    │
│   Wheatley   │                                        ┌──────────────┐
│  Sanitorium  ├────┐                                   │   Straight   │
│     1896     │    │                                   │   College    │
└──────────────┘    │   ┌──────────────┐                │              │
                    │   │ New Orleans  │                │  1915 - 1935 │
                    │   │  University  │                └──────────────┘
┌──────────────┐    │   │              │
│ Flint Medical│────┘   │ 1873 - 1935  │
│   College    │        └──────────────┘
│              │
│  1889 - 1911 │
└──────────────┘
                    ┌────────────────────────┐
                    │ Sara Goodridge         │
                    │   Hospital, 1901-1916  │
                    │ Nurse Training School  │
                    │     1901 - 1934        │
                    └────────────────────────┘

                    ┌────────────────────────┐  ┌──────────────┐
                    │ Dillard University     │  │    Flint     │
                    │ A Cooperative Enter-   │  │  Goodridge   │
                    │ prise                  │  │   Hospital   │
                    │ A Merger of Straight   │  │  1916 - 1932 │
                    │ College and New        │  └──────────────┘
                    │ Orleans University     │
                    │ Chartered, 1930        │
                    └────────────────────────┘
                    ┌────────────────────────┐
                    │ Flint Goodridge        │
                    │ Hospital of Dillard    │
                    │ University, 1932       │
                    └────────────────────────┘
                    ┌────────────────────────┐
                    │ Dillard University     │
                    │ Began Academic         │
                    │ Program, 1935          │
                    └────────────────────────┘
```

REFERENCES AND NOTES
PART I

1. Barclay, Wade C., *History of Methodist Missions*, Vol. 3, p. 305.
2. *Seventy Years of Service*, by President O. E. Kriege and Faculty, New Orleans University, 1935, p. 8.
3. *Ibid.*
4. *Ibid.*
5. Freedmen's Aid Society, Third Annual Report, 1869, p. 10.
6. *Seventy Years of Service*, p. 9.
7. *Ibid.*
8. *Ibid.*
9. *The Methodist Advocate* (Atlanta), November 3, 1869, p. 175.
10. Freedmen's Aid Society, Third Annual Report, 1869, p. 10.
11. Freedmen's Aid Society, Fourth Annual Report, 1871, p. 11.
12. Stowell, Jay S., *Methodist Adventures in Negro Education*, p. 112.
13. Freedmen's Aid Society, Fourth Annual Report, 1871, p. 12.
14. *Ibid.*
15. *Ibid.*
16. Freedmen's Aid Society, Fifth Annual Report, 1872, p. 22.
17. *Ibid.*
18. *Ibid.*
19. Freedmen's Aid Society, Sixth Annual Report, 1873, pp. 21ff.
20. The Louisiana Annual Conference Journal, January 6-13, 1875, p. 16.
21. Minutes, The Louisiana Annual Conference, January 6-13, 1875, p. 15.
22. The Faculty, *Seventy Years of Service*, New Orleans University, 1935, pp. 7f.
23. New Orleans University Bulletin, November, 1932, p. 4.
24. *Ibid.*
25. Freedmen's Aid Society, Eighth Annual Report, 1875, pp. 32f.
26. *Southwestern Christian Advocate*, January 26, 1905, p. 5.
27. Journal, Louisiana Annual Conference, Eighth Session, January 5-12, 1876, p. 8.
28. Journal, Louisiana Annual Conference, January 10-15, 1877, pp. 27f.
29. *Ibid.*, p. 23.
30. The Faculty, *op. cit.*, p. 27.
31. Journal, Louisiana Annual Conference, 1878, p. 21.
32. The Faculty, *op. cit.*, pp. 5f.
33. *Ibid.*
34. *Ibid.*, p. 5.
35. *Ibid.*

36. The Faculty, *op. cit.*, p. 28.
37. *Ibid.*
38. Journal of the Louisiana Annual Conference, January 29-February 3, 1879, p. 22.
39. *Ibid.*
40. Journal of the Louisiana Annual Conference, January 26-30, 1881, p. 15.
41. The Faculty, *op. cit.*, p. 28.
42. *Ibid.*, p. 29.
43. Freedmen's Aid and Southern Education Society Report, 1892, p. 39.
44. The Faculty, *op. cit.*, pp. 29-30.
45. *Ibid.*, p. 31.
46. *The Christian Educator*, February, 1908, p. 11.
47. *Ibid.*, p. 12.
48. *Ibid.*
49. *Ibid.*
50. The Faculty, *op. cit.*, p. 31.
51. *Ibid.*, p. 32.
52. *Seventy Years of Service*, New Orleans University, pp. 33-34.
53. Klein, Arthur J., *Negro Colleges and Universities*, Bureau of Education, Bulletin, 1928, No. 7, p. 522.
54. Faculty, *op. cit.*, p. 2.
55. Jones, Thomas Jesse, *Negro Education*, U. S. Office of Education, Bulletin, 1916, No. 38, p. ?.
56. Klein, *op. cit.*
57. The Faculty, *op. cit.*, p. 13.
58. From a letter of Dr. Bond to Mrs. Margaret Davis Bowen, Principal of Gilbert Academy in 1937.
59. Journal of the Louisiana Annual Conference, January 31-February 4, 1889, pp. 34 f.
60. *The Christian Educator*, May, 1917, p. 11.
61. *Ibid.*
62. New Orleans University Bulletin, March, 1931, p. 3.
63. *The Christian Educator*, May, 1916, p. 1.
64. The Faculty, *op. cit.*, pp. 19ff.
65. *Ibid.*

PART II

1. Brownlee, Frederick Leslie, *New Day Ascending*, p. 209.
2. *Ibid.*
3. Original Charter of Straight University, June 25, 1869, Dillard University Archives.
4. The Amended Charter of Straight University, March 9, 1870,

Dillard University Archives.
5. *Ibid.*
6. Brownlee, *op. cit.*, p. 209.
7. *Ibid.*
8. 25 La. Ann. 441 (1873); Straight University, *ex. rel.* Graham (See Bond's (H.M.) Unpublished Research Manuscript), Dillard University.
9. Brownlee, *op. cit.*, p. 209.
10. *Ibid.*
11. Brownlee, Frederick L., *Heritage of Freedom*, p. 45.
12. *Ibid.*
13. Jones, Thomas Jesse, *op. cit.*, pp. 300-303.
14. Department of the Interior, Bureau of Education Bulletin, 1927, No. 40, Statistics of Universities, Colleges and Professional Schools, 1925-1926, p. 151.
15. *Ibid.*, p. 86.
16. *Ibid.*

Parts III-IV

17. Journal, General Conference, 1924, p. ?.
18. Brownlee, *op. cit.*, p. 46.
19. *Ibid.*
20. *Ibid.*
21. New Orleans University Bulletin, February, 1929, p. 15.
22. *Ibid.*
23. *Ibid.*
24. *Ibid.*
25. *Ibid.*, p. 47.
26. *Ibid.*
27. Letter, Dr. M. J. Holmes to Mr. Jackson Davis, November 16, 1929. Board of Education Files, Nashville, Tennessee.
28. Minutes, Joint Committee on Conference, re: Dillard University. Dillard University Files.
29. *Ibid.*
30. Minutes, Board of Trustees, Dillard University, June 7, 1930, No. 9.
31. Minutes of the Executive Committee of the Board of Education, June 21, 1930. See also *The Christian Educator*, May-August, 1930, p. 5.
32. *The Christian Educator*, May-August, 1930, p. 7.
33. Minutes, Dillard University Board of Trustees, June 6, 1930, (No. 13).
34. *Ibid.*
35. *Ibid.*

36. *Ibid.*
37. *Ibid.*
38. See Minutes, Dillard University Board of Trustees, November 20, 1930, p. 3.
39. The New Orleans University Bulletin, February, 1932, p. 2.
40. *Ibid.*
41. *Ibid.*
42. Minutes, Dillard University Board of Trustees, November 24, 25, 1930 (No. 7).
43. Minutes, Dillard University Board of Trustees, October 5, 1931.
44. *Ibid.*
45. Minutes, Dillard University Board of Trustees, May 26, 1934.
46. Brownlee, *op. cit.*, pp. 48f.
47. Minutes, Dillard University Board of Trustees, April 11, 1935, p. 6 (No. 7).
48. *Ibid.*
49. Brownlee, Fred L. *New Day Ascending*, p. 213.
50. Board Minutes, April 11, 1935.
51. Minutes, Executive Committee, Dillard University, Board of Trustees, March 17, 1936 (Resolution B).
52. *Ibid.*, p. 3.
53. *Ibid.*, p. 4.
54. Minutes, Dillard University, Board of Trustees, June 13, 1936.
55. Brownlee, *op. cit.*, p. 49.
56. *Ibid.*
57. *Christian Education Magazine*, September-October, 1941, p. 25.
58. Statistical Summary, Methodist General Board of Education, 1968-1969.
59. *Proceedings* of the Sixty-fourth Annual Meeting of the Southern Association of Colleges and Secondary Schools, December, 1959, p. 11.

CHAPTER 16

BRIEF HISTORICAL SKETCH OF GAMMON
THEOLOGICAL SEMINARY

Background

Immediately after the close of the Civil War the Methodist Episcopal Church began rehabilitation of its work in the South. Emphasis was placed upon church extension and the organization of Mission Conferences and Annual Conferences. This work was supported by actions of the General Conferences in 1864 and 1868.

In 1864 the General Conference authorized the Bishops, "when in their judgment they deemed it expedient, within the next four years, to organize a Conference or Conferences in the Southern States and in the Territories."[1]

In their address at the 1868 General Conference the Bishops reported that "under the specific authority" given them four years before, nine Conferences had been organized in that part of "our Southern territory" not previously included in Annual Conferences. . . .The majority of the preachers were freedmen, many of whom as slaves had been licensed Local Preachers. The total number of Traveling Preachers in 1871, according to a computation made by L. C. Matlack, was 630, of whom 260 were white and 370 were Negroes.[2]

The 1868 General Conference repealed the action of 1864 which, in determining that the Conferences formed in the Southern states should be "Mission Conferences," restricted their rights and privileges, and declared the Alabama, Delaware, Georgia, Holston, Mississippi, South Carolina, Tennessee, Texas, Virginia, and North Carolina and Washington Conferences to be Annual Conferences "vested with all the rights, privileges and immunities usual to Annual Conferences." In anticipation of this action these Conferences had elected provisional delegates—twenty-five in number—who on presentation of their credentials were admitted to membership in General Conference. Thus, for the first time in the history of the Church

Negroes were seated as General Conference delegates.[3]

In January, 1866, at Atlanta, Bishop Clark organized a Georgia-Alabama Mission. "On October 10, 1867, Bishop Clark organized in Atlanta the Georgia Mission Conference."[4]

Nine preachers were recognized as charter members, two others as probationers, seven were received on credentials from the Methodist Episcopal Church, South, and twenty-three were received on trial. Of the total of forty-one, ten were colored and thirty-one were white. Of these, twenty-six were southern men. The movement in Georgia, it may be seen, was largely indigenous to the soil.[5]

The Georgia Mission Conference was made a regular Annual Conference by action of the General Conference of the Methodist Episcopal Church in 1868.[6]

It was out of this background of efforts to organize and strengthen Methodism in the South that the need arose for training Negro ministers in this section.

Theological Schools

At the very beginning of the work of the Freedmen's Aid Society in establishing schools, much emphasis was placed upon theological training. The conferences of the Methodist Episcopal Church in the South were organized and some had evolved into separate Negro conferences with increasing churches and memberships. The great need was for trained ministers to pastor the churches of these conferences, and to give religious leadership to the Negro people.

At all of the colleges founded before 1875 there was a theological seminary or a department as follows:

Central Tennessee College—a theological department
Claflin University—Baker Theological Seminary
Clark University—Clark Theological Seminary (later
   Gammon Theological Seminary)
Morgan College (Centenary Biblical Institute)
New Orleans University—Thomson Biblical Institute
Shaw University in Mississippi—theological classes

The Fifth Annual Report of the Freedmen's Aid Society comments on the need for teachers and ministers:

The great want of our work in the South, at the present time, is educated teachers and ministers. Our primary schools

316

prepared the way for graded and normal schools, and these will furnish students for the theological seminary and college. . . .We must provide a few Biblical schools, where these young men can be properly trained and prepared for the ministry. The candidates for our Conferences must have specific and thorough preparation for their work. The interests at stake are too momentous to be entrusted to illiterate and inexperienced youth. The age in which we live, the field we cultivate, the character of the opposition which we encounter, the consequences involved, demand cultivated intellects, pure hearts, and holy enthusiasm. Endow our seminaries, where we may furnish such young men, and the South, blighted by oppression, and scarred by the thunderbolts of war, shall bud and blossom as the rose.[7]

The Fifth Annual Report also describes the preparation the minister should receive in a theological seminary:

Their ministers should be good English scholars, familiar with the elementary branches, able to communicate their thoughts in an intelligible manner; and, though their style may be destitute of rhetorical beauty, it must be characterized by accurate expression and convincing power. The fields of science and literature, if possible, should be investigated. The Natural Sciences should be studied; for these shed light upon the sacred page. With the principles of intellectual and moral science they should be familiar as these affect every fiber of the warp and woof of human life. No study should be neglected, if opportunity affords, that sheds light upon the Bible. All books that treat of its style, its customs and scenery, should be consulted. The Bible is the minister's textbook, and whatever else he may be ignorant of, he must study and understand this. Thorough preparation for the ministry is demanded by the spirit of the age, and the wants of the race, and in view of the fearful responsibility connected with the sacred office, these young men, called of God to preach the Gospel, should enjoy the best facilities for improvement that our seminaries can afford.[8]

EARLY BEGINNINGS OF GAMMON

Bishop D. W. Clark's Interest

It is well known that, during his lifetime, the lamented Bishop Clark was deeply impressed with the necessity of ministerial

317

training in connection with the Methodist Episcopal Church in the South. In accordance with this cherished idea, an institution for elementary and normal instruction was founded, a few years since, by the Freedmen's Aid Society, at Atlanta, Georgia. It was his desire, whenever these elementary departments could be safely transferred to the State, that this institution should then become, in the highest sense, a direct spiritual instrumentality of the Church; that it should be conducted specially in behalf of ministerial education.

His convictions were so profound upon this subject that, in his last will and testament, a noble bequest was left to the institution at Atlanta, for which coming generations will bless his memory.[9]

Clark Theological School

"The Clark Theological Seminary was opened, with appropriate religious services, in February, 1872. In this movement we cannot doubt the providence of God. He has been preparing the way. Rev. Dr. L. D. Barrows, of New England, residing temporarily in Atlanta to avoid the rigor of a Northern Winter, has been selected by the Freedmen's Aid Society, to inaugurate the enterprise. For several weeks he had been instructing a class of thirty ministers, in the Loyd Street Methodist Episcopal Church. Great enthusiasm had been awakened. Almost before we were aware, a theological seminary had been commenced; the hand of God, beckoning onward, was too conspicuous to be disregarded. Impressed with this, and relying upon God and his Church, the representatives of the Freedmen's Aid Society have taken this grand step. Never was there a greater need, never a louder call from God, never such a golden opportunity to consecrate wealth to the high purpose of saving the redeemed millions of the South.[10]

"Dr. Barrows has been assisted in his duties by Dr. Fuller, Rev. J. E. Knowles, and Rev. J. W. Lee. Professor I. Marcy, of the University, and his lady, have the oversight of the boarding department, and aid in training the students. The Seminary has been in operation only four weeks, and twenty-six regular pupils have been enrolled, and are busily and enthusiastically at work. Our accommodations must be increased, as a large number will seek admission another way.[11]

"In entering this new field, the managers of the Freedmen's Aid Society feel that they have assumed grave responsibilities. Already the schools of the South are taxing the Society to its utmost limit. The Church should draw still closer to her throbbing heart this benevolent agency. Its mission is indeed divine among the lowly. The Clark Theological Seminary will be an additional burden.

318

Great is the task undertaken. Insuperable would be the obstacles, were not God enlisted on the side of His cause. The present building must be enlarged, as soon as the funds can be obtained, in order to meet the demand. Indigent students will require assistance. The endowment of the institution must begin forthwith, as the bequest of Bishop Clark is not yet available. There is no time to lose. Hundreds of ministers, thousands of Church members, in the South, will unite with us in our appeal.

"We need $9,000 to meet the required payment on the property. Already a noble brother in Cincinnati, whose name we are not permitted to give, has given his check for $1,000 of that amount. We need furniture immediately for twelve rooms."[1] [2]

Prior to locating the theological school on Whitehall Street, some classes had been taught at the Summer Hill site and during the first part of the school year 1871-1872 classes in theology were taught in the basement of the Loyd Street Methodist Church. It was from the Loyd Street Methodist Church that the theological classes were moved to Whitehall Street and the formal beginning of the Clark Theological Seminary was made.

Clark University Theological School, 1872-1882

During the summer of 1872, all work under the title of Clark University was transferred to the new site on Whitehall Street. Thus, Clark University with its new school of theology had a new beginning. In the summer of 1872, Reverend J. W. Lee who had assisted Reverend Barrows the previous year was made President of the University including the theological school. The Sixth Annual Report of the Freedmen's Aid Society indicated that the session 1872-1873 was the first full year the Clark University Theological School had operated. During that year seventy-eight students were enrolled in the University as follows: Twenty-three in the theological school, and fifty-five in the preparatory and normal departments.[1] [3] These students represented three states—Alabama, Florida, and Georgia.

For a period of ten years the Clark Theological School had normal growth as what was really a department of Clark University. From 1872 to 1881 four different presidents gave administrative leadership to the University: Rev. J. W. Lee, Rev. Isaac Lansing, Rev. J. B. Martin, and Rev. R. E. Bisbee. Bishop Gilbert Haven gave Episcopal leadership.

At the end of this period, 1882, the course offerings in the theological department were as follows:

319

Theological Course[14]

English—All the English studies of the Normal Course.
Scientific—All the sciences of the Normal Course.
Languages—The Greek of the College Preparatory Course and Greek Testament may be substituted for the Sciences of the Normal Course.
Theological—Binney's *Theological Compend;* Hopkins' *Evidences of Christianity;* Raymond's *Systematic Theology;* Lectures on Church Doctrine and Ritual.
Miscellaneous—Church Discipline; Scripture Geography; General Church History; Townsend's *Civil Government;* Kidder's *Homiletics;* Six Written Sermons.

New Leadership and Developments

It was in 1882 under the Presidency of Dr. E. O. Thayer and the Episcopal leadership of Bishop Henry W. Warren that a significant development took place in the theological work. Through the instrumentality and contact of Bishop Warren, the Rev. Elijah H. Gammon became interested in the theological work at Clark University and made the first of a number of gifts in support of the work, leading to its development into a separate and independent theological seminary.

The Rev. Elijah H. Gammon was a native of Maine. Early in his ministry a voice failure interfered with his work in the pulpit. He migrated to Chicago and then to Batavia, Illinois, where he became a manufacturer of harvesting machinery. He amassed a large fortune through this industry.[15]

Out of a basic interest in theological education and "upon a strong presentation of the need of a trained ministry by Bishop Warren, the Rev. Elijah H. Gammon and wife gave $20,000 to endow a chair of Theology in Clark University, and $5,000 toward a new theological hall, Bishop Warren to raise $20,000 more for the hall."

The Clark University Catalog for 1882-1883 indicated that the hall, to be ready in October, 1883, was to be completed at a cost of $25,000, one third donated by Rev. Gammon and the remainder raised by Bishop Warren.[16]

A Partnership

Bishop Warren in his tribute to the late Rev. E. H. Gammon tells interestingly and impressively the story of his early contact with the Reverend Gammon and the initial interest of Reverend

320

Gammon in the theological school at Clark University in Atlanta.

"Having been in partnership with him in his most important business, I wish to put on record some knowledge gained in that intimate relation.

"While I was under a burden of soul and importunateness in prayer for the means of educating the leaders of our half-million Church members in the South, Brother Gammon caused it to be intimated to me by Dr. Fuller that he was interested. I immediately started for Chicago. The result of a long, earnest, and comprehensive conversation was that he would go into partnership to establish a theological school at Atlanta. He was to put in $25,000 and I $20,000. I depended on the Lord's treasure in the hands of his stewards to back me. He needed no backing. Before we got through, we each had put in more than we proposed. When the school was finished, we dissolved the partnership of business, but kept the one of heart, which had grown to be far dearer and more important than the other. To the end of his days we were known to each other as 'my partner.'

"Soon after the school was finished he took out all the money I had put in, and built a hall for Clark University, adjacent, and honored me by calling it by my name. He never knew that the theological seminary was to be called by his name till it was done."[17]

On June 3, 1883, the Rev. Wilbur P. Thirkield, a young pastor in Cincinnati, Ohio, was elected by the Freedmen's Aid Society to serve as dean of the School of Theology at Clark University, recommended by Bishop Warren and Dr. Rust. He assumed duties in October of that year. Under the Presidency of Dr. E. O. Thayer, Dean Thirkield organized the work and began instruction with two students in attendance. A full three-years course was projected and for three full years, Rev. Thirkield alone was left to carry on the school.[18]

"Rev. Wilbur P. Thirkield, B.D., Dean and Professor of Systematic Theology, has been in charge of the school of Theology for the past two years, and his able and enthusiastic labors have been crowned with great success."[19]

In 1885 Dr. J. C. Murray was added to the faculty as Professor of Exegetical Theology.[20] Dr. Edward L. Parks was elected to the faculty in 1886 as Professor of Systematic Theology.[20a]

Seeing the need for residences for the School of Theology, Rev. Gammon gave money for residences for the President and for the two new professors added to the faculty. He later gave money for additional faculty residences and for cottages for married students.[21]

As a School of Theology at Clark University, rapid and

substantial progress was made under the dynamic leadership of Dean Thirkield, and the deep interest of President Thayer and Bishop Warren.

The following account indicates the deepening and growing interest of the Reverend Gammon in this work:

As Mr. Gammon studied the situation, he became convinced that this school, to fulfill its largest usefulness, should be independent in its organization and government, and thus sustain the same relation to each school in the entire system of educational institutions of the Freedmen's Aid and Southern Education Society. His careful study of the field, and his long experience as a trustee of Garrett Biblical Institute, had led him to this view.

The following points are therefore important as outlining his plan. He writes, Feb. 18, 1887:

"They (the Freedmen's Aid Board) will hardly ignore my proposition or put it off indefinitely, as it contemplates securing the school an endowment of not less than two hundred thousand dollars at my death, I reserving the revenue from it during my life. The conditions are:

"First. That it be made an independent school, under the control of the Freedmen's Aid Society.

"Second. That they support the professors, except the senior professor, during my life.

"Third. That they give the school what lands it needs, as Dr. Rust and I can agree upon. I want some land west of Capitol Avenue. I also want to help the school with what means I have to spare in building, etc., during my life."

What noble purpose; what generous confidences are here:

(1887) "I would like to see it the best theological school of the whole South, white or black. I am certain that we are on the right track, and have made no mistake thus far."[2 2]

The proposal by Rev. Gammon to separate the School of Theology from Clark University was approved by the Clark Board of Trustees and by the managers of the Freedmen's Aid Society. Gifts to endow the School of Theology were reported by the Freedmen's Aid Society:[2 3]

In 1883 the endowment fund was started by the donation of $20,000 from the Rev. E. H. Gammon of Batavia, Ill. In February 1888, he increased this amount by another donation of $180,000. The whole amount—$200,000—is held by the trustees of the Methodist Episcopal Church perpetually, to aid in the support of Gammon Theological Seminary, under the control of the Freedmen's Aid and Southern Education Society. The last donation—$180,000—is not available during the lifetime of the donor, and was on that account not included in last year's report.[24]

On establishing the school as an independent School of Theology, Dean Wilbur P. Thirkield, 1888, was elected its first President.

On February 23, 1888, application was filed with the Fulton County (Georgia) Superior Court for a Charter under the name of "Gammon School of Theology."[25] The Charter was granted March 24, 1888.[26] An amendment was filed December 28, 1888, to change the name from Gammon School of Theology to Gammon Theological Seminary. The application for change of name was approved by the Fulton County Superior Court on January 30, 1889.[27]

The Charter for the Seminary having been received, the Board of Trustees of Gammon School of Theology held its organization meeting June 7, 1888. The following officers were elected:

President—Bishop J. M. Walden
Vice President—Dr. J. C. Hartzell
Secretary—Dr. W. H. Crogman
Treasurer—Dr. W. P. Thirkield[28]

Rev. Gammon gave funds for the erection of a new library building in 1888. The building, equipped to hold twenty-thousand volumes, was dedicated May 26, 1889.[29]

In 1889, the Rev. W. H. Crawford was elected Professor of Church History, entering upon his duties in December, 1889. Rev. Gammon provided the funds to build a faculty residence for Professor Crawford.[30]

The two following communications between Dr. J. C. Hartzell, Corresponding Secretary of the Freedmen's Aid Society, and the Rev. Gammon are revealing:

December 21, 1888, was an historic day at Atlanta, Ga. It was Founder's Day and the cornerstone of the new Library Building was laid. We sent the following telegram to Mr. Gammon at his home in Batavia, Illinois: "Please write me without delay how you came to give money for Christian education in the South"; and the following was the reply:

Batavia, Ill., December 14, 1888, [sic]

323

Rev. J. C. Hartzell, Dear Brother: Your telegram of this date is before me. You ask how I came to give money for education in the South. I cannot say how I came to do it, only that I thought I ought. Maybe the Good Spirit led me to it. I wanted to use what means I had to accomplish the largest amount of good. I carefully investigated the matter for some two or three years without mentioning it to anyone—not even my wife—and I became clearly convinced that more good could be accomplished with the same amount of money in educating the colored people of the South than in any other way, and that, first of all, they should have intelligent, Christian leaders; hence, I decided to do what I could to establish a school for the purpose of educating their ministers. I investigated the question of location without revealing my plans, and decided on Atlanta in connection with Clark University. Up to this time I had mentioned the subject to no one. But now I consulted my wife, who approved of my plans heartily and enthusiastically. I afterward laid my scheme before Rev. Hatfield, who also approved it. A few weeks after consulting Dr. Hatfield, I met my old friend, the late Dr. Fuller, of Atlanta. I opened the subject up to him; he spoke very encouragingly, and on his return home to Atlanta he put me in communication with Bishop Warren, who came to see me, and we matured our plans as far as we could; and you know the result thus far.

Very truly yours,
E. H. Gammon.[31]

This letter is characteristic of the man. Devoutly and intelligently he interpreted the influences of God's Spirit, as crystallized in that word "ought." The results are now being manifested, and we earnestly pray that his wife and beneficent plans, yet to be fulfilled for this institution, may be fully realized, to the glory of God and to the honor of a noble, Christian philanthropist. Mrs. Gammon, his wife, heartily cooperated with her distinguished husband in his philanthropic work.   J.C.H.[32]

Death of Rev. Elijah H. Gammon

On July 3, 1891, the Rev. Elijah H. Gammon passed away, leaving behind a rich legacy of good deeds, profound interest in ministerial education, and generous beneficences to Gammon Theological Seminary. He was by far the Seminary's greatest financial benefactor up to that time. Before his death, he had given to Gammon approximately a quarter of a million dollars, two hundred thousand of which was for endowment. His will provided approximately another quarter of a million dollars for the institution that bore his name. His total gifts to Gammon Theological Seminary went well over six hundred thousand dollars.[33]

Following the death of Rev. Gammon, Mrs. Jane C. Gammon, his wife, was elected to the Gammon Board of Trustees. Her interest was just as deep as that of her husband, for they were of one mind in all the benefaction the Seminary received at his hand. On December 22, 1892, Mrs. Gammon followed her husband in death.[34]

For all their interests in and benefactions to this Seminary, the name Gammon is sacred and Gammon Seminary is truly "holy ground."

Dr. John Wesley Edward Bowen Comes to Gammon

In the Spring of 1893, Dr. W. H. Crawford resigned his professorship at Gammon to accept the presidency of Allegheny College, Meadville, Pennsylvania. Dr. John Wesley Edward Bowen, Sr., was elected to the Chair of Historical Theology to succeed Dr. Crawford.[35] This was the beginning of a distinguished relationship to Gammon Theological Seminary by Dr. Bowen for approximately forty years. From 1906 to 1910 he served as President of the Seminary.[36] Dr. Bowen at Gammon was the counterpart of Dr. Crogman at Clark University in administration, instruction, and influence. Each was the first Negro on the faculty of their respective institutions, and each was the first Negro President. Dr. Bowen was not only a distinguished teacher and administrator, but was also a great orator and pulpiteer. He probably influenced more young men to go into the ministry and to attend Gammon than any other man on the faculty from the time he went to Gammon in 1893 to his retirement in 1932, when he became Professor Emeritus.

Theological Work Transferred to Gammon

Immediately following the establishment and chartering of the Gammon School of Theology as an independent Theological Seminary in 1888, the departments of theology at the various Freedmen's Aid Society colleges were transferred to Gammon Theological Seminary, where all of the work was done thereafter in the training of Methodist Negro ministers. The training of ministers, however, was not limited to the Methodists. Other denominations began sending men to Gammon for ministerial

325

training.

The Stewart Missionary Foundation

On January 29, 1894, the Rev. William F. Stewart of the Rock River Conference, Illinois, proposed to establish a Missionary Department in the Seminary to be known as the Stewart Missionary Foundation for Africa.[37] At its meeting May 16, 1894, the Board of Trustees of Gammon Theological Seminary accepted the proposal of the Rev. Stewart.[38] An account of the proposal by Rev. Stewart follows:

Rev. Mr. Stewart has embodied this thought of the Church concerning the American Negro and the redemption of Africa in a Foundation with sufficient endowment to make its work perpetual, and has united it with the greatest Theological Seminary for the colored people to secure the largest results. He has consecrated for the endowment of this Foundation a group of farms of six hundred acres, all tilled and under high cultivation, in Central Illinois, which he proposes to convey in trust, the income to be used to maintain this department. In writing to the faculty, he thus gives his purpose:

"My hope is that it may become a center for the diffusion of missionary intelligence, the development of missionary enthusiasm, the increase of missionary offerings, and through sanctified and trained missionaries hasten obedience to the great commission to 'preach the gospel to every creature.' In addition to the direct work of the recitation-room, I have contemplated other educating means that would reach our schools and missions and the whole membership of the Church. Among the things thought of are:

"1. A system of literary and oratorical missionary prize contests. These might include prize missionary hymns (who knows but we have a Watts or a Charles Wesley among God's ebony images?), prize missionary essays and orations, to be presented in public contests.

"2. I would also arrange correspondence with all our missions in Africa (if not all others,) and invite special reports, the best of which should be awarded prizes.

"3. And I would extend an invitation to the whole membership of the church to write to the department on any feature of missionary work; these papers to be classified, and recognition to be made according to the value of the best.

"4. Added to these might be arranged a monthly course of addresses or sermons by the chief pastor of the denomination.

"5. It might be that from all these an annual souvenir missionary volume might be edited and published that would be interesting and of value."

In the practical carrying out of the plans of the Foundation, Mr. Stewart expects to be guided by the providential indications of the needs of the work. He writes:

I shall make the Foundation permanent, and with what light may come to us from the Master, through his honored servants having the "great commission" on their hearts, and through the providential teachings that the practical working of our initial plan shall bring, I think we may confidently hope to attain wisdom in our plans and successes in our work.'[3] [9]

The work of the Foundation began in 1894 and became a great institution, supplementary to and a part of a greater institution Gammon Theological Seminary.

The spiritual concern and the philanthropic motivation of the Rev. W. F. Stewart were quite similar to those of the Rev. E. H. Gammon. The Christian lives of the two men gave a spiritual heritage to Gammon Theological Seminary quite as significant as their philanthropies. The impact of the Stewart Missionary Foundation over a period of a half century resulted in scores of young men and women dedicating their lives for service in the Mission Field, particularly Africa.

Among the secretaries of the Stewart Missionary Foundation for Africa were the Rev. G. W. Arnold, the Rev. W. W. Lucas, Dr. D. D. Martin, and the Rev. Roger S. Guptil.[40] The longest term of the secretaries of the Foundation was by far that of Dr. Martin, who was secretary from 1911 to about 1933.[41]

Department of Missions

A Department of Missions[42] shall be maintained in Gammon Theological Seminary, subject to the rules of the Seminary and related to the faculty of the Seminary the same as other departments of study. The professor in charge of this department shall be nominated by the Trustees of the Stewart Missionary Foundation and elected as provided in the Charter for the election of members of the faculty. He shall be paid from the funds of Stewart Missionary Foundation; but in other respects his relation to the Seminary shall be the same as other members of the faculty, unless the Trustees of the Stewart Missionary Foundation shall make other provisions, he shall superintend all the work of the Stewart Missionary Foundation as set forth in the deed of trust executed by William F. Stewart and wife to the trustees of the Stewart Foundation.[43]

The salary of the Professor of Missions, and of any other person in their employ shall be fixed by the trustees of the Stewart Missionary Foundation, and paid through the Treasurer of Gammon Theological Seminary.[44]

* * *

Mr. Stewart nominated D. D. Martin, D.D., and Mr. I. Garland Penn as the two members to serve with the President, *ex-officio*, as the committee of three provided for in the By-Laws for the administration of the Stewart Missionary Foundation for Africa, and the nominations were confirmed.

Mr. Stewart also presented, for the trustees of the Stewart Foundation for Africa, the nomination of Rev. D. D. Martin as Professor of Missions. The nomination was confirmed.[45]

Clark and Gammon—Continued Relationship

The Clark University Theological School continued as a unit of Clark University until 1888.[46] Dr. Wilbur P. Thirkield assumed the deanship of the Theological School in 1883 and continued on the faculty of the University until 1888.[47] Bishop H. W. Warren made contact with the Rev. E. H. Gammon in 1882 and secured gifts for the strengthening of the Theological School at the University. One of the earliest gifts of the Rev. Gammon was $5,000 to be applied on a hall for the Theological School. The hall, which later became known as Gammon Hall, was erected on land owned by the University.[48] Although Dean Thirkield had complete charge of the instruction in the Theological School, he had to draw upon the faculty of the University for some of the courses.[49] Dr. W. H. Crogman had been a teacher of New Testament prior to the coming of Dean Thirkield and continued to teach New Testament Exegesis until the Theological School was separated from the University.[50]

As indicated elsewhere in this document, the Clark University Theological School was completely separated from the University in 1888 and became an independent institution, being chartered in March, 1888, under the name Gammon Theological School and later in the year, by amendment to the charter, the name was changed to Gammon Theological Seminary.[51] Nineteen acres of land were purchased adjoining the Clark University campus[52] on which Gammon Theological Seminary's future development was to take place. The campus of Gammon Theological Seminary adjoined the campus of Clark University. The close proximity of

328

the two institutions made cooperation easy and also the continuation of the historically close relationship of Gammon and Clark University.

From 1883 to 1888, Dean Thirkield and President O. E. Thayer worked closely together in the interest of both the University and the Theological School. Bishop Warren was a member of the team. He had established residency in Atlanta in 1882 as the Episcopal leader.[53] He, Dr. Thayer, and Dr. Thirkield worked closely together in seeking funds for the two institutions. Until 1888, Clark and the Theological School were administered by the same Board of Trustees. After Gammon became an independent and chartered institution, its own Board of Trustees was established under its Charter.[54] Gammon and Clark, however, continued under the same general control and management, the Freedmen's Aid Society. Bishop Warren gave Episcopal leadership from 1882 to 1912[55] and gave evidence of profound interest in both Clark and Gammon.

In the Fall of 1896 Dr. D. C. John resigned from the Presidency of Clark College and Dr. Thirkield, President of Gammon Theological Seminary, assumed responsibility of Acting President of Clark for the remaining part of the school year.[56] He was so profoundly interested in Clark University that in addition to his Gammon Presidency, he served as Acting President for Clark University almost a full year and returned the compensation for his services back to the Freedmen's Aid Society.

President Thirkield Resigns

Dr. Thirkield served Gammon administratively a total of seventeen years, six years as dean and eleven years as President of the Seminary. In the Fall of 1899 he resigned the Presidency of Gammon Theological Seminary to take the position of General Secretary of the Epworth League of the Methodist Episcopal Church.[58] The Gammon Board in session January 4, 1900, accepted the resignation of President Thirkield with appropriate expressions of appreciation of his many years of valuable service and leadership at Gammon.[59]

The Board did not elect a President to succeed Dr. Thirkield but at this meeting placed the administration of the Seminary in the hands of the faculty, each of the professors in the order of seniority to serve as Chairman of the faculty, each to serve one-third of the time to the close of the Seminary year.[60]

329

Rev. L. G. Adkinson, D.D., Becomes President

To succeed Dr. Wilbur P. Thirkield, Dr. L. G. Adkinson was elected President of the seminary on May 30, 1901.[61]

On May 30, 1901, the Board of Trustees elected Rev. L. G. Adkinson, D.D., President of the Seminary. As soon as he could close his work as President of New Orleans University, he entered upon the duties of his new position. By his customary complete devotion to his work, careful attention to details, large sympathy with students and kindly consideration of the members of the faculty, he laid the foundations for a prosperous administration.[62]

Dr. Adkinson served the Seminary well, advancing its development in a number of ways. His administration, however, was cut short; after a little over four years of service, he died in office January 19, 1906.

Dr. Adkinson's services as President of Gammon Theological Seminary mark the culmination of his long years of work. He threw himself into his work with his well-known painstaking care and far-reaching experience. He commanded the respect and confidence of the Board of Trustees, Faculty, Students and friends of the Seminary. In his relationship with the young men of the Institution, he was wise in council, fatherly in spirit, sound in doctrine, and brotherly in his dealings. He succeeded in winning the love as well as the respect of all the students. From year to year the Seminary has steadily grown from its inception to the present and at no time did that growth exceed the growth of the years of the late President. He leaves the Seminary in good condition as to finance, number and strength of students and social and spiritual life. By his will power and a conviction to a sense of duty he was able to keep at his post of duty to within two weeks of his death.[63]

Dr. John Wesley Edward Bowen Becomes President

At the meeting June 12, 1906, the Gammon Board of Trustees selected six names for nomination to the Board of Managers of the Freedmen's Aid Society for election of one to the Presidency of Gammon Theological Seminary.[64] Among the six nominees was the name of Dr. J. W. E. Bowen. Dr. Bowen had been on the Gammon faculty since 1893 as Professor of Historical Theology. On October 18, 1906, the Board of Managers of the

Freedmen's Aid Society elected Dr. Bowen as President of the Seminary.[65] He began his duties immediately. Dr. Bowen served as President from October, 1906, to June, 1910.[66]

Action Providing Single Administration for Clark University and Gammon Theological Seminary

At this time, it was thought wise to provide a single administration for the administration of Clark University and Gammon Theological Seminary under one President.

Resolution from the Gammon Board:

Resolved, That we declare it the judgment of this Board that the same person should be chosen President of this institution and of Clark University.[67]

"The Board of Clark University here voted it is to be their judgment that the interests of the two schools would be best conserved under one head."[68]

"The Board voted to refer to the Board at Cincinnati the nomination of the new President for the two schools."[69]

The single administration of the two institutions continued for two years 1910-1911 and 1911-1912 under the Presidency of Dr. S. E. Idleman. Before the end of the two-year period, the trustees of Gammon passed the following resolution:

Resolved: That the administrative question relating to the joint administration of Gammon Theological Seminary and Clark University shall be open for review and final consideration at the close of the present school year.[70]

By the end of the second year of the single administration, the Boards of Trustees of Gammon and Clark had definitely decided to change the policy of having one president administer the two institutions.

At its Spring meeting in 1912, the Gammon Board took the following action:

"On motion, Dr. S. E. Idleman nominated President of Gammon Theological Seminary, and the Board at Cincinnati was requested to provide a president for Clark University as soon as possible."[71]

Dr. Idleman was elected President of Gammon Theological Seminary to serve that institution alone.[72] Dr. William W. Foster was elected president of Clark University.[73]

The Death of Bishop Henry W. Warren

The death of Bishop Warren, July 23, 1912,[74] brought to an end a most significant era in the history of Gammon Theological Seminary. From the time that Bishop Warren took up residence in Atlanta, he, President Thayer, Dr. Thirkield and the Rev. Elijah H. Gammon formed a powerful team that gave Gammon a brilliant period of development. Bishop Warren and Rev. Gammon in 1882 formed a partnership that lasted to the death of Rev. Gammon in 1891. Bishop Warren continued his commitment in the partnership after the death of Rev. Gammon and persevered to his own death in 1912. He gave brilliant leadership and Rev. Gammon gave his wealth and the two working as partners helped to make Gammon Theological Seminary an outstanding institution, and up to that time, it experienced its greatest growth and expansion during the time Bishop Warren served as Episcopal leader.

New Administration

After dissolving the policy of a single administration for the two institutions, Clark and Gammon, President Idleman served as President of Gammon alone for two years, 1912-13 and 1913-14. At the board meeting March 11, 1914, President Idleman tendered his resignation and Dr. Philip M. Watters who was then serving as pastor of the Washington Square Methodist Episcopal Church, New York City, was nominated for the Presidency to succeed Dr. Idleman.[75] The election was unanimous by standing vote. Dr. J. W. E. Bowen who had served as President of Gammon from 1906 to 1910 was made Vice President of Gammon[76] to serve with the new President, Dr. Watters.

At this meeting the board passed a resolution commending President Idleman for his effective administration of the Seminary.[77]

The Refectory

May 14, 1914, a committee was appointed to select an architect and landscape engineer and report the location of the proposed refectory to the executive committee with the entire cost not to exceed $15,000. After approval of the executive committee and the Cincinnati Board, construction on the refectory was to go forward.[78]

At the meeting of the Board, May 12, 1915, it was reported that the proposed refectory had been completed.[79]

The date for the dedication of the refectory and the

inauguration of the President was referred to the executive committee and an appropriation of $500.00 was made for expenses.[80]

On January 6, 1916 President Philip M. Watters was inaugurated and the refectory dedicated.[81]

The new refectory was named the J. W. E. Bowen Hall.[82]

Plans for New Administration Building

At the meeting of the board, June 12, 1921, a committee was appointed on location and plans for a new administration building.[83]

Committee on Appreciation of Dr. Crogman

The board appointed Bishop R. E. Jones, Dr. J. P. Wragg, and Dr. I. G. Penn to draft a resolution in appreciation of the 33 years of service of Dr. W. H. Crogman as secretary of the Board of Trustees of Gammon Theological Seminary.[84]

Dr. Watters Resigns as President

At the meeting of the Board of Trustees, May 14, 1924, President Philip M. Watters who had served the institution since 1914 tendered his resignation to become effective at the end of the school year 1925.[85]

Dr. George H. Trevor

Dr. George H. Trevor who served as acting President the school year 1925-26, was elected President of the seminary at the meeting of the Board April 30, 1926.[86] Dr. Trevor served as President two years. He tendered his resignation to the Board at its meeting, April 20, 1927, to become effective at the end of the school year 1928.

Dr. Franklin Halsted Clapp Becomes President

At the meeting of the Board, May 11, 1928, Dr. Franklin Halsted Clapp was confirmed as President of the Seminary.[87] At this meeting recognition was given to the long tenure of service of Dr. Trevor as professor and President of the Seminary.[88] By action of the Board, retirement allowance was provided for Dr. Trevor.

Board of Trustees Meeting, May 22, 1929

At the meeting of the Gammon Board of Trustees, May 22, 1929, the following actions were taken:[89]

1. Election of professors for the Department:
(1) Professors for Department of Practical Theology
(2) Professor for Department of Religious Education
2. A policy of sabbatical leave was established.
3. Professor Willis J. King was given sabbatical leave to study at Oxford University, England.
4. Action of compliance with the General Conference action of high school training was ministerial requirement for admission to an Annual Conference.
5. Bible training school was discontinued.
6. The development of an interdenominational summer school.
7. Gammon's relation to the west side affiliation to the executive committee.

Committee on Resolution

At its meeting, May 22, 1930, the board appointed a committee to draw up an appropriate resolution on the death of Rev. H. W. B. Wilson who had served as secretary of the board since May 14, 1924.

President Clapp Resigns

At the meeting of the Gammon Board, June 9, 1932, President Clapp presented his resignation to become effective immediately. Professor John R. Van Pelt was named as acting president.

Dr. Willis J. King Becomes President

In the summer of 1932 Dr. Willis J. King was elected President of Gammon Theological Seminary.[90] Previously he had had a long tenure at the Seminary as professor of Old Testament, ending 1929. Dr. King was a recognized scholar in his field and an inspiring teacher. On return in 1930 from a sabbatical leave, studying at Oxford University, England, he became President of Samuel Huston College, Austin, Texas. He was elected to the Presidency of Gammon from Samuel Huston College. Dr. King served as President of the Seminary from 1932 to 1944, when he was elected to the episcopacy. During the administration of Dr. King, Gammon made significant advancement in program development and the raising of standards for ministerial training.

President J. W. Haywood

In the meeting of the Board, July 25, 1944, Dr. J. W. Haywood was elected President of Gammon Theological Seminary, coming from the Presidency of Morristown Junior College, Morristown, Tennessee.[91] Dr. Haywood was an eminent educator and a most eloquent preacher. He had served as a general officer in the church in connection with the Centenary Movement beginning 1918, and for a number of years was Dean at Morgan College, Baltimore, Md., before going to Morristown College as President. Dr. Haywood served as President until 1948. These were four years in which Gammon was trying to determine its future, whether to remain on its then historic location in South Atlanta, or to relocate to the west side of the city near the Atlanta University Center.

Crusade for Christ Gift

In 1944 the Methodist Church made a gift of $500,000 to Gammon Theological Seminary from its Quadrennial Emphasis Fund known as the Crusade for Christ.[92] This grant was made to Gammon to help formulate and consummate a program for its future. From the time that Clark College changed its location in 1941 there had been a question and much discussion as to whether Gammon should remain on its then present site or relocate to the west side of Atlanta. The Crusade for Christ Gift was conditioned upon a satisfactory plan for Gammon's future.[93]

Discussions, Plans and Proposals for
Gammon's Relocation

In a special meeting of the Gammon Board of Trustees January 2, 1947, "A document was read containing an exhaustive study of the advantages coming to the seminary by moving close enough to become a part of the Atlanta University Center and a recommendation that appropriate steps be taken looking toward relocation to the University Center was made.

After general, thorough and somewhat lengthy discussion, the Board of Trustees went on record favoring the recommendation.[94] At this meeting, January 2, 1947, a special committee was appointed consisting of the executive committee of the Board of Trustees with Bishop R. N. Brooks (taking the place of Bishop L. H. King), Dr. M. J. Holmes and Dr. H. W.

335

McPherson. This was to be a general committee working through appropriate sub-committees to take needed preliminary steps toward moving to the University Center.[9 5]

A sub-committee of the general committee was appointed consisting of Dr. M. S. Davage, Dean H. B. Trimble, President J. W. Haywood and Dr. D. H. Stanton to study the proposed relationship of Gammon Theological Seminary with schools making up the University Center; to explore thoroughly and report to the Board at a subsequent meeting. A sub-committee on finance was appointed to raise funds for Gammon. The committee consisted of Bishop A. J. Moore, Dr. M. S. Davage, President J. W. Haywood, Bishop R. E. Jones and Dr. D. H. Stanton.[9 6]

At a meeting of the Board in November, 1947, a committee was appointed to talk with President Rufus E. Clement regarding land for relocation of Gammon Theological Seminary in the University Center. The proposed site was discussed and left in the hands of the newly appointed committee.[9 7]

Dr. Harry V. Richardson Elected President

At the meeting of the Board, June 11, 1948, Dr. Harry V. Richardson was elected President of Gammon Theological Seminary to succeed Dr. John W. Haywood who resigned to take another position. Dr. Richardson, a member of the A.M.E. Church, was elected to the Presidency of Gammon from the Chaplaincy at Tuskegee Institute, Alabama.[9 8] Shortly thereafter, he joined the Methodist Church with membership in the Central Alabama Annual Conference. Dr. Richardson gave leadership to Gammon Theological Seminary through the period of its being relocated and also, statesmanlike leadership in the formation of the Interdenominational Theological Center of which Gammon, with its historical background, its services and its extensive resources, was the principal unit.

The Gammon Board held an important meeting on September 19, 1951. The purpose of this meeting was stated by the Chairman of the Board:

1. To consider the details involved in the proposed relocation of Gammon Theological Seminary;
2. To discuss the terms under which the seminary would move to the University Center.[9 9]

Extended discussions ensued upon the land to be acquired for the relocation of Gammon and the condition that Gammon should move as Gammon and not as a part of a federated institution. "In other words, if Gammon should move to the University Center, its present status as a separate autonomous school is not to be changed." And "that should Gammon move to the University Center, it will be prepared to undertake the leadership in providing graduate instruction in religion for all interested students in the University Center."[100]

More Meetings and Discussions

The meetings and discussions by the Gammon Board of Trustees continued, dealing with the difficult problems of Gammon's future. At the meeting of the Board March 5, 1953, the following recommendation was approved:

> Motion offered by Mr. Everett, and seconded by Bishop Brooks, authorized and directed the chairman to appoint a committee of five (in and out of Atlanta) to formulate a policy with reference to moving Gammon Theological Seminary and report to the Executive Committee by October 1, 1953, such statement of policy to be in line with recommendations suggested by the members of the Board at this meeting and previous meetings.[101]

At this same meeting the President, Dr. H. V. Richardson presented "some recommendations," on the future of Gammon.[102] Essentially and in summary, the recommendations proposed that an affiliated group of denominational schools center around Gammon as the graduate unit, similar to the Atlanta University Center with the undergraduate colleges affiliated with Atlanta University. A general faculty, as well as a faculty for each school or denomination was recommended, members of the denominational faculties to help make up the general faculty. The plan was basically what was later worked out as the Interdenominational Theological Center.

Accommodations for Married Students

At the Board meeting, June 23, 1953, a new building for married students was proposed. Several of the cottages for married students had been condemned by the city. The President was authorized to proceed with the erection of a dormitory for married students. The sum of $35,000 was set aside for the building and $5,000 for furnishings. These monies were to be taken from capital funds from the United Negro College Fund.[103] At this same meeting $5,000 was approved for land for the new

337

Bethlehem Center.[104] At the Board meeting, March 4, 1954, transfer of land to the Woman's Division of Christian Service for the Bethlehem Center was approved.[105] This land, known as the Thayer Hall site, had been conveyed to Gammon Theological Seminary by Clark College. The price of the land paid by the Woman's Division of Christian Service was $5,000.

Report on Action by the Board of Education
 of the Methodist Church

"This action was carefully read by Dr. John O. Gross which follows:
1. That a committee be appointed from the Gammon Board of Trustees to work with the committee appointed by the Board of Education to work out plans for the advance program of Gammon Theological Seminary looking towards the relocation of the seminary at the Atlanta University Center.
2. That this plan be presented to the General Education Board, by this joint Committee at its April meeting this year.
3. That contact be made with the Sealantic Fund to ascertain what that organization may be willing to do, and
4. That this joint committee be asked to prepare, in detail, a report and bring it to this Board, and that the Chairman be authorized to call a special meeting of the Board to receive such report.
After a brief discussion a motion was made by Bishop Willis J. King and seconded by Col. Willis M. Everett, Jr., that this action which was a request of the Board of Education be granted and that the committee asked for be appointed. Motion carried.
On motion the Chairman was asked to appoint such committee. The following named persons were appointed: Mr. L. D. Milton, Col. Willis M. Everett, Jr., Dean Ernest C. Colwell, Bishop M. W. Clair, and Bishop J. W. E. Bowen. Pres. Harry V. Richardson is to be ex-officio member."[106]

The above named committee held a meeting at 2:30 in the afternoon, March 1, 1956, at which it outlined some of the requirements and conditions for the establishment of a cooperative theological center.
"Following the discussion, it was voted that a committee be appointed to contact the General Education Board and the Sealantic Fund to explore possibilities for financial aid for a cooperative Theological Center in Atlanta. The committee: J. W. E. Bowen, James P. Brawley, Ernest C. Colwell, Gerald O.

338

McCulloh and Harry V. Richardson."[107]

As separate action from the general committee a letter to Mr. Dana Creel, President of the Sealantic Fund, New York, was formulated and signed by Benjamin E. Mays, Morehouse College; John H. Lewis, Morris Brown College; Harry V. Richardson, Gammon Theological Seminary, setting forth their desire and plan to cooperate in the relocation of Gammon Theological Seminary and the development of the theological center. This letter was written March 21, 1956.[108]

Action by the Board of Education
   The Methodist Church

It was in 1944 that the Methodist Church granted one-half million dollars from the Crusade for Christ Fund for Gammon to use in its future development. The money, however, would not be released to Gammon until its plans for the future were definitely and satisfactorily formulated. Twelve years after the grant had been made, the Board of Education of the Methodist Church took the following action:

Dr. Gross reported the following action taken by the Division of Educational Institutions concerning Gammon Theological Seminary:
Resolved, That the Board of Education of the Methodist Church notify the Board of Trustees of Gammon Theological Seminary that the $600,000 of Crusade for Christ funds now held by the Board of Education be held until June 1, 1957, pending Gammon's completing plans to move to the Atlanta University Center, and should such plans not be completed by June 1, 1957, the Board of Education will distribute these funds immediately after that date; and further
Resolved, That a committee of five from the Board of Education and the University Senate be elected to work with the Gammon Board of Trustees.[109]

Note: The committee appointed by Bishop Garber was as follows: Drs. Donald H. Tippett, Gerald O. McCulloh, Fred G. Holloway, Goodrich C. White, Merrill J. Holmes.

Special Board Meeting on Relocation of
   Gammon Theological Seminary

On May 28, 1957, the Gammon Board of Trustees held a special meeting on the relocation of Gammon Theological

339

Seminary. After a committee report presented by Dr. Ernest C. Colwell and due discussion thereof, the following action was taken:[110]

After discussion, the following motion was made by Dr. Gerald O. McCulloh and seconded by Dr. C. W. Loughlin:

1. Resolved, That the Gammon Theological Seminary Board of Trustees approve in principle the plan of cooperation in an Interdenominational Theological Center in accordance with the report of agreements of the Planning Committee.

The following motion was made by Mr. L. D. Milton and seconded by Dr. C. W. Loughlin:

2. Resolved, That all rules and regulations regarding the conditions of membership and participation in the Interdenominational Theological Center which shall be adopted by the Board of Trustees of the Center, including title to land, location of denominational buildings, and financial obligation of the participating institutions shall be referred to the Board of Trustees of the several participating institutions for ratification before becoming effective. Motion passed.

The following motion was made by Col. Willis M. Everett, Jr., and seconded by Dr. Gerald O. McCulloh:

3. Resolved, That in order to advance the organization of the proposed Interdenominational Center, the Gammon Theological Seminary Board of Trustees elect six persons to serve as its representatives on the new Board of Trustees. Motion passed.

The following persons were elected:

Bishop J. W. E. Bowen, Dr. Ernest C. Colwell, Col. Willis M. Everett, Jr., Dr. Gerald O. McCulloh, Mr. L. D. Milton and Dr. James S. Thomas.

The following motion was made by Col. Willis M. Everett and seconded by Dr. Gerald O. McCulloh:

4. Resolved, That Gammon Theological Seminary Board of Trustees recommend the employment of legal counsel to serve in drawing up a form of title to land in the proposed new Center that will be mutually satisfactory to Gammon Theological Seminary, to Atlanta University, and to the other participating institutions. Motion passed.[111]

Study Grant From the General Education Board and
a Plan for Relocation of Gammon and Formation
of the Interdenominational Theological Center

In 1956 the General Education Board made a grant of $15,000 to Gammon Theological Seminary to finance the necessary studies and primary planning for the future. A committee was appointed for the study which made its report in November, 1957. The study was presented by the committee on the basis of several grants to consummate the relocation plan and the formulation of the Interdenominational Theological Center. President Richardson reports that:

On June 6, 1958, word came that the Sealantic Fund of New York City, a Rockefeller family foundation, had appropriated $1,750,000 for the establishment of an interdenominational center in Atlanta. This amount, along with the $500,000.00 that had previously been appropriated by the General Education Board, also a Rockefeller agency, brought into being the grandest achievement in interdenominational cooperation that had ever been undertaken by Negroes in America. It marked a new day in Negro religious history.[112]

Gammon Theological Seminary in a
New Relationship

As a result of several years of study and planning and through the resources and leadership of Gammon a new institution emerged—the Interdenominational Theological Center. This new institution consists of four cooperating institutions and their respective denominations. Participating in this cooperative enterprise are: (1) Gammon Theological Seminary, the United Methodist Church; (2) Morehouse (College) School of Religion, Baptist; (3) Phillips School of Theology, Christian Methodist Episcopal; and (4) Turner Theological Seminary, African Methodist Episcopal.

Each of the participating units of the Interdenominational Theological Center has a director operating under the administrative direction and leadership of the President of the Center. Gammon, however, not only has a Director as do the other units, but the Gammon Director is also known as the President of Gammon Theological Seminary. Because Gammon retained its original corporate status, it had to have a President to comply with the legal requirements of its Corporate Charter. Dr. M. J. Wynn was elected President-Director of Gammon. He was succeeded in 1967 by Dr. M. J. Jones in this office.

The historical background, its services for more than three-quarters of a century, and its affluence in resources put Gammon in a different category from the other cooperating units. Dr. Harry V. Richardson, former President of Gammon and first President of the Interdenominational Theological Center, speaks of Gammon's role and leadership and status:

> We have spoken as if Gammon were only a participant in the proposal for a cooperative theological center, but as a matter of fact, Gammon is the leader. It was largely through Gammon that the effective proposal was advanced. It is Gammon's academic standing and greater resources that do much to make the project possible. In recognition of Gammon's prior position, it was readily agreed that the head of Gammon should be head of the new Center.[113]

The Old Gammon Property

Gammon Theological Seminary removed to the new Center in 1960, leaving the old campus where it had been located since its first building (Gammon Hall) was erected in 1883, and its becoming an independent institution in 1888. The campus consisted of some thirty acres. As indicated elsewhere in this document, five acres were purchased from Gammon by the Woman's Division of Christian Service for a new Bethlehem Center. Approximately five or six acres were sold to the City of Atlanta for public school buildings. Six faculty residences and two apartment buildings for married students occupy approximately ten acres. These residences and apartment buildings are to be sold. Thirkield Hall, the administration and classroom building, Gammon Hall, dormitory, the library building, and Bowen Refectory are to be torn down and on these grounds is to be built a new structure to be used as a Home for Senior Citizens, known as Asbury Hills, under the sponsorship of the United Methodist Church.[114]

REFERENCES AND NOTES

1. General Conference Journal, 1864, pp. 216, 225.
2. *Ibid.*, p. 304.
3. *Ibid.*, p. 309.
4. General Conference Journal, 1868, p. 311.
5. Barclay, Wade C., *History of Methodist Missions*, Vol. III, p. 307.
6. General Conference Journal, 1868, p. 311.
7. Fifth Annual Report of the Freedmen's Aid Society, 1872, pp. 7f.
8. Fifth Annual Report of the Freedmen's Aid Society, 1872, p. 8.
9. *Ibid.*, p. 20.
10. *Ibid.*
11. *Ibid.*
12. *Ibid.*
13. Freedmen's Aid Society, Sixth Annual Report, 1873, pp. 27f.
14. See Clark University Catalog, 1879, p. 15.
15. *The Christian Educator*, April, 1893, p. 115.
16. Clark University Catalog, 1882-1883, p. 15.
17. *The Christian Educator*, January, 1892, p. 325.
18. Gammon Quarterly Bulletin (Memorial Edition), p. 11.
19. Eighteenth Annual Report, Freedmen's Aid Society, 1885, p. 8.
20. Freedmen's Aid Society Report, 1885, pp. 8f.
20a.Faculty List, Catalog, Gammon School of Theology, 1885-86.
21. Freedmen's Aid Society Report, 1887, p. 10.
22. Gammon Quarterly Bulletin (Memorial Edition), February, 1892, pp. 13-14.
23. Catalog, Gammon School of Theology, 1888, p. 6; and Freedmen's Aid Society Report, 1887, p. 9.
24. *The Christian Educator*, October, 1889, p. 45.
25. Minutes, Gammon Board of Trustees, 1888, pp. 2—6.
26. *Ibid.*, pp. 6—7.
27. *Ibid.*, pp. 8—9.
28. *Ibid.*
29. *The Christian Educator*, October, 1889, p. 16.
30. Quarterly Bulletin, Gammon Theological Seminary, April, 1890, p. 5.

31. *The Christian Educator*, April, 1890, pp. 95-96.
32. *Ibid.*, pp. 95-96f.
33. *The Christian Educator*, July, 1891, p. 258.
34. Minutes, Gammon Board of Trustees, February 25, 1892, p. 29.
35. *The Christian Educator*, April, 1893, p. 115.
36. Minutes, Gammon Board of Trustees, May 16, 1894, p. 45.
37. *The Foundation*, January-March, 1948, p. 7.
38. Board Minutes, May 16, 1894, p. 47.
39. *The Christian Educator*, June-July, 1895, p. 61.
40. Gammon Board of Trustees, Minutes, May 8, 1902, p. 141; June 13, 1905, p. 159; February 15, 1911, p. 240.
41. Gammon Trustee Minutes, February 15, 1911, Dr. Martin first elected Secretary; Retired 1933—Gammon Catalog 1932-1933, p. 9 and 1933-34, p. 5. Dr. J. W. E. Bowen was elected first Secretary of the Stewart Missionary Foundation for Africa (*The Foundation*, January-March, 1948, p. 7).
42. Gammon Trustee Minutes, May 16, 1911, pp. 243f.
43. *Ibid.*, p. 243.
44. *Ibid.*, p. 244.
45. *Ibid.*, p. 245
46. Gammon Trustee Minutes, February 23, March 24, December 28, 1888, pp. 2—8.
47. *Ibid.*
48. The School of Theology was still a part of the University; separation came in 1888. *Ibid.*
49. *Ibid.*
50. *Ibid.*
51. Minutes, Gammon Board of Trustees, December 27, 1888, p. 14.
52. *Quarterly Bulletin*, Gammon Theological Seminary, June, 1898, p. 9.
53. Freedmen's Aid Society Report, 1882, p. 8.
54. Catalog, Gammon School of Theology, 1888, p. 6.
55. Freedmen's Aid Society Report, 1882, p. 8, and *The Christian Educator*, August, 1912, p. 5.
56. *The Christian Educator*, June-July, 1897, p. 113.
57. *Ibid.*
58. Minutes, Gammon Board of Trustees, January 3, 1900, p. 114.
59. Minutes, Board of Trustees Gammon Theological Seminary, January 4, 1900, p. 120.
60. *Ibid.*, pp. 118-119.
61. Minutes, Board of Trustees, Gammon Theological Seminary, May 30, 1901, p. 135.
62. Gammon Theological Seminary Bulletin, Memorial Edition,

February, 1906, p. 5.
63. *Ibid.*, p. 8.
64. Minutes, Gammon Board of Trustees, June 12, 1906, p. 166.
65. Minutes, Gammon Board of Trustees, June 12, 1906, p. 166, and August 8, 1910, p. 237.
66. *Ibid.*
67. Board Minutes of Clark University, June 28, 1910, p. 293.
68. *Ibid.*
69. *Ibid.*
70. Gammon Trustee Minutes, May 16, 1911, p. 245.
71. Gammon Trustee Minutes, June 26, 1912, p. 261.
72. *Ibid.*
73. Minutes, Clark University Board of Trustees, May 1912; and *The Christian Educator*, November, 1912, p. 15.
74. General Conference Journal, Methodist Episcopal Church, 1916, p. 855.
75. Minutes, Gammon Board of Trustees, March 11, 1914, p. 290.
76. *Ibid.*, p. 293.
77. *Ibid.*, p. 294.
78. Minutes, Gammon Board of Trustees, March 14, 1914, p. 300.
79. Minutes, Gammon Board of Trustees, May 12, 1915, p. 325.
80. *Ibid.*, p. 306
81. Minutes, Gammon Board of Trustees, June 16, 1916, p. ?.
82. Minutes, Gammon Board of Trustees, April 25, 1923, pp. 357f.
83. Minutes, Gammon Board of Trustees, June 12, 1921, p. 342.
84. *Ibid.*, p. 345.
85. Minutes, Gammon Board of Trustees, May 14, 1924, p. 364.
86. Minutes, Gammon Board of Trustees, March 30, 1926. p. ?.
87. Minutes, Gammon Board of Trustees, May 11, 1928, p. 403.
88. *Ibid.*, p. 407.
89. Minutes, Gammon Board of Trustees, May 22, 1929, pp. 409ff.
90. Minutes, Gammon Board of Trustees, May 2, 1933. p. ?.
91. Minutes, Gammon Board of Trustees, July 25, 1944, p. 456.
92. See Minutes Gammon Board of Trustees, January 2, 1947, p. 463; November 4, 1947 (attached to) p. 467; September 10, 1951, p. 476 (p. 4 of attached report of sub-committee); March 1, 1956, p. 486, sub page 2. Yearbook, 1956, Annual Report and Proceedings, p. 240.
93. *Ibid.*
94. Minutes, Special Meeting of the Gammon Board of Trustees, January 2, 1947, p. 462.
95. *Ibid.*, p. 463.
96. *Ibid.*

97. Minutes, Gammon Board of Trustees, November 4, 1947, p. 467.

98. Minutes, Gammon Board of Trustees, June 11, 1948, p. 470.

99. Minutes, Gammon Board of Trustees, September 19, 1951, pp. 476ff, sub pp 1ff.

100. Minutes, Gammon Board of Trustees, September 19, 1951, p. 476, sub pp. 1—3.

101. Minutes, Gammon Board of Trustees, March 5, 1953, p. 480, sub. p. 3.

102. Minutes, Gammon Board of Trustees, March 5, 1953, p. 480, sub pp. 1—5 of "Some Recommendations on the Future of Gammon."

103. Minutes, Gammon Board of Trustees, June 23, 1953, p. 481, sub p. 2.

104. *Ibid.*

105. Minutes, Gammon Board of Trustees, March 4, 1954, p. 482, sub p. 2.

106. Minutes, Gammon Board of Trustees, March 1, 1956, p. 486, sub p. 2.

107. Minutes, Meeting of the Joint Committee on the Future Development of Gammon, March 1, 1956, p. 487, sub p. 2.

108. Minutes, Gammon Board of Trustees, p. 489.

109. Minutes, Gammon Board of Trustees, p. 490.

110. Minutes, Gammon Board of Trustees, Special Meeting, May 28, 1957, p. 492, sub pp. 3—4.

111. *Ibid.*

112. Richardson, Harry V., *The Interdenominational Theological Center: Gammon Today and Tomorrow*, 1958, p. 2.

113. *Ibid.*, p. 1.

114. *Ibid.*, p. 8.

CHAPTER 17

HISTORICAL SKETCH OF THE FOUNDING AND DEVELOPMENT OF SAMUEL HUSTON COLLEGE: SUBSEQUENTLY HUSTON-TILLOTSON COLLEGE

In the First Session of the West Texas Annual Conference, January 22-26, 1874, there was expressed a deep interest in education and a desire to provide the benefits of education for its members through an educational institution.

With faith in the Freedmen's Aid Society the Conference, at this First Session, passed the following Resolution, presented by the "Committee on Freedmen's Aid Society":

> Your Committee beg leave to report that we believe this institution to be an honor as well as a blessing to the church, and with our cooperation it will always result in glory to God and good to his Church. Therefore, we resolve to contribute not less than ten cents for each member and as much more as we can get.

> 1. *Resolved*, That in view of the urgent necessities of our work in the West Texas Conference, we earnestly request the Freedmen's Aid Society to establish a school for the colored people within the bounds of the Conference.
> 2. *Resolved*, That a Committee of five (5) be appointed to canvass, with a view to the selection of a proper location of the said school, the Bishop presiding to appoint said committee.[1]

This action in the First Session of the West Texas Conference was the beginning of long and unrelenting efforts to establish a permanent conference educational institution. During a period of twenty-six years there continued to be expressed this deep and increasing interest in education and a conference school.

In the Third Session of the Conference in January, 1876, the following statement on education was approved:

> We value an educated ministry, and declare it to be our purpose to raise the standard of ministerial qualifications as fast

as we can, and we trust providence will soon open the way for the establishment of a Conference Seminary.[2]

At the Fourth Session of the Annual Conference in November, 1876, the following action was taken:

William Brush, L. H. Carhart, and T. C. Read were made a committee to look after and secure proper site and endowment for an Educational Institution to be located at Austin.[3]

In the fall of 1875 the Reverend George W. Richardson of Minnesota went to Dallas, Texas, for the improvement of his health. He had served as a Chaplain of the "Colored Regiment, the Seventh United States Artillery, 1864-1866, in the Civil War."[4] Seeing the conditions and great need he leased the St. Paul's Methodist Episcopal Church for a period of five years, and on February 22, 1876, opened a school with six scholars.[5]
On Saturday morning, April 22, the church-schoolhouse was destroyed by fire. Arson was evident.

It was a pitiful sight to see the despair written on the faces of that faithful colored pastor, Reverend J. G. Webster, and the members of his flock as they stood around the smoking brands.
They had worked hard and had sacrificed much to build their church and had hoped that this school would be the beginning of a permanent institution for their children's education, and now everything seemed lost.[6]

Through heroic efforts and continuous work by the members and two carpenters a temporary building was erected within twenty-four hours. On Sunday morning the Sunday School and Preaching Service went on as usual and on Monday the school opened as though nothing had happened.[7]
On November 7, 1876, the following action was taken by the Quarterly Conference of the St. Paul's Methodist Episcopal Church:

Whereas, The Reverend G. W. Richardson and his son, Reverend George O. Richardson, have leased from the trustees of this church property for school purposes for five years, and have met with such success that the list of registered scholars is about two hundred; and
Whereas, We are thoroughly identified with the school by the losses we suffered in common with these brethren, and by the benefit we receive from their school and their help in the Sunday School; and

348

Whereas, We have the utmost confidence in the ability of these brethren to build up and conduct a first class institution of learning; therefore,

Resolved, That we request the West Texas Conference to adopt the above described school as a Conference school, to be known as Andrews Normal College.

Resolved, That we request the appointment of Reverend George O. Richardson as President, and Reverend A. J. Burris as Local Agent of said College.[8]

William Brush, P. E.
George O. Richardson, Secretary

Pursuant to the action of the St. Paul's Quarterly Conference November 7, the following statement and request were presented to the West Texas Annual Conference Session November 25, 1876.

To the Bishop and Members of the West Texas Conference
Dear Fathers and Brethren:

We, the undersigned, being intensely interested in the education of the Freedmen, have opened a school and have undertaken to build up a permanent institution of learning at Dallas, one of the largest commercial centres within the bounds of the West Texas Conference.

The school received the encouragement of Bishop Andrews and a promise of some financial aid when he was in Texas last winter.

The school was opened in the St. Paul's Methodist Episcopal Church February 22 and during the first term of four months enrolled 225 scholars.

For the winter term nearly two hundred names are already registered.

The design is to educate teachers and preachers for the Freedmen. We desire to be identified as thoroughly as possible with the West Texas Conference; and therefore ask that the school be adopted as a Conference school, and that a President and Trustees and Financial Agent and Visiting Committee should be appointed.

We would respectfully suggest the names of the following as a Board of Trustees: Reverend L. H. Carhart, Reverend Melvin Wade, Reverend William Brush, Reverend J. G. Webster, Reverend G. W. Richardson, Reverend A. J. Burris, Reverend George Mickle, Reverend Alonzo Jones and Brother E. Stare.

We would further suggest that the institution should derive its name from Bishop Andrews, who has done more than any

349

one else, aside from the teachers, to give it an existence.[9]

George W. Richardson,
George O. Richardson,
Miss L. L. Webb
Teachers in Andrews Normal School
Dallas, November 25, 1876

The Conference Committee on Education in consideration of the action of the St. Paul's Quarterly Conference recommended the following action by the Annual Conference:

Resolved, That the Andrews Normal School at Dallas be accepted and adopted as a Conference school.

Second. That its name be changed to Andrews Normal College.

Third. That Reverend L. H. Carhart, Reverend Melvin Wade, Reverend George Mickle, Reverend William Brush, Reverend J. G. Webster, E. Stare, Reverend G. W. Richardson, Reverend A. J. Burris, and Alonzo Jones be appointed Trustees of Andrews Normal College.

Fourth. That Reverend George O. Richardson be appointed President, and Reverend A. J. Burris, Local Agent of said College.

Fifth. That we will welcome to our congregations the Financial Agent of Andrews Normal College, and will encourage our people to contribute towards the erection of suitable buildings for said college.

L. H. Carhart, Chairman of Committee[9a]

Subsequent to the presentation of the above report of the Committee on Education to the Conference the following action was taken by the Conference:

College at Austin, "Supplemental"

Whereas, There is a large tide of immigration pouring into this State from the various Northern and Western States, and many of these are Methodists or of Methodist proclivities; and

Whereas, No provision has yet been made by the Methodists of this State for the education of her white membership; therefore

Resolved, That a special committee of three be appointed to consider the question of locating a college or university somewhere within the bounds of this Conference.

Resolved, That said committee be invested with plenary power to take temporary charge of any funds or donations that may be secured for this purpose, to turn them over to a Board of Trustees that shall hereafter be appointed by this Conference, and that this subject in all its bearings be committed to the judgment and oversight of this committee with instructions to report at the next session of this Conference.

Professor T. C. Reade, Reverend William Brush, and Reverend L. H. Carhart were constituted a Conference Board, with power to act.[9][b]

George O. Richardson gives the following account of the action of the West Texas Conference regarding the Andrews Normal School:

Your Committee would report their conviction that the hand of God is in the enterprise, and that the Messrs. Richardson, who have in the face of so much difficulty, inaugurated the enterprise, deserve our gratitude and cordial support, We, therefore, recommend the following action:

Resolved, *First.* That the Andrews Normal School at Dallas be accepted and adopted as a Conference School.

Second. That its name be changed to Andrews Normal College.

Third. That Reverend L. H. Carhart, Reverend Melvin Wade, George Mickle, Reverend William Brush, Reverend J. G. Webster, E. Stare, Alonzo Jones, Reverend G. W. Richardson, Reverend A. J. Burris, be appointed Trustees of Andrews Normal College.

Fourth. That Reverend George O. Richardson be appointed President and Reverend A. J. Burris Local Agent of said College.

Fifth. That we will welcome to our congregations the Financial Agent of Andrews Normal College and will encourage our people to contribute toward the erection of suitable buildings for said College.

L. H. Carhart
Chairman of Committee

The Report of the Committee on Education was adopted by the Conference, and Andrews Normal College became a Conference Institution at the afternoon session of the fourth day of the West Texas Conference, December 2, 1876.[10]

It became evident that Dallas was not the best location for the Conference School and action was taken to relocate Andrews Normal College to Austin, Texas. Richardson gives the following report:

I here copy part of the Report of the Committee on Education which was adopted unanimously November 26, 1877:

351

We report that the Andrews Normal College which was adopted as Conference School has continued its work through the year.

It has become apparent to the teachers and to many members of the Conference that our Conference School should be more centrally located.

We, therefore, recommend the following action:

Resolved, 1st. That our Conference School be relocated and placed at Austin, Texas.

2nd. That Samuel Gates, Charles L. Madison, and A. M. Gregory be a committee to select and purchase property for such school, provided the Conference furnish funds.

3rd. That we will do our utmost to collect on our several charges an average of fifty cents per member for the purpose of buying property for Andrews Normal School.

4th. That A. R. Norris be appointed Financial Agent of the Conference School to travel at large through the Conference and solicit funds.

B. F. Smith

C. Young

Committee on Education

We opened our school in Austin, Texas, the first Monday in September, 1878, in the Wesley Chapel Methodist Episcopal Church which we had rented. At the end of October we had about fifty pupils, and my wife, Clara A. Richardson, came to my assistance as a teacher.[10a]

* * *

At the sixth session of the West Texas Conference which met at Columbus in December, 1878, with Bishop Gilbert Haven presiding, the following report of the committee on Education was adopted:

We are glad to report that the West Texas Conference School is a fixed fact, that an acre and a half of ground has been purchased in Austin for the school at a cost of $1,350. A payment of $400.00 has been made thereon, the remainder to be paid in a year.

The school has been opened in Wesley Chapel in Austin and the teachers are at their post ready to receive the students.

We, therefore, recommend the following action:

Resolved, 1. That Mack Henson be appointed the Financial Agent of the school.

2. That we will at all times welcome the Financial Agent to our congregations and will encourage our people to contribute liberally toward the erection of suitable buildings for the school.

352

3. It is the wish of this Conference that the property purchased for this school should be deeded to the Freedmen's Aid Society of the Methodist Episcopal Church.

4. That we respectfully request Bishop Haven to bestow a name upon this young child of the Conference and to use his influence, as far as possible, to secure funds from the Freedmen's Aid Society and other sources to build up this much needed institution.

> James Henderson
> Granville Norman
> J. Humphries
> Committee on Education

On December 2, 1878, this Conference changed the name of the school to West Texas Conference School and turned over the property purchased and the institution to the Freedmen's Aid Society of the Methodist Episcopal Church for adoption as one of its educational institutions, and for financial support.[11]

In September, 1878, the work of the Andrews Normal College was transferred to Austin, Texas. The name was changed to the "West Texas Conference Seminary." For a period of time the instructional work of the college was carried on in the Wesley Chapel Church.

The Conference Committee on Education reported December 3, 1879, that:

We are thoroughly convinced that our usefulness and happiness depends on our intelligence and piety. We are not qualified to take our place among the evangelistic forces and do our full part in the conversion of the world without education. Our people will be 'driven about by every wind of doctrine,' and there can be but little stability in our work, till they have acquired the ability to read the Holy Bible and understand the doctrines of our church.

Being thoroughly roused to feel our wants in this direction, we have established a conference school at Austin, which is now in successful operation with four competent teachers, and have contributed, and collected from our people, over $500, which has been used for the purchase of lots for the school buildings. The six lots were purchased at a cost of $1,350, of which amount a little more than $200 remains unpaid.[12]

At the Eighth Session of the West Texas Conference, December, 1880, the following action was taken:

353

Report on Education

A Conference Seminary or College—well established, well sustained and well manned with teachers, will be a center of educational influence which would quicken and strengthen all these educational forces. Therefore,

1st Resolved, That James Henderson be appointed Financial Agent of the West Texas Conference Seminary to solicit funds to purchase property and put up buildings for said school.

2nd Resolved, That C. L. Madison, M. Henson, G. W. Richardson, S. Gates and J. W. Robinson be appointed a committee to arrange with Financial Agents to meet his traveling and other expenses while in the Agency, and to employ an Assistant Agent for two months, if they deem it necessary; and to do such other business relating to the Conference School as may come before them.

3rd Resolved, That M. Henson be appointed Treasurer to receive all the funds raised to purchase property for the Conference School, and to disburse the same according to the direction of the Conference School Committee.

4th Resolved, That S. Gates, M. Henson, J. W. Robinson, A. R. Norris, C. L. Madison, R. S. Rust, D. D., Richard Dukes, Batties Lott, and Henry Chambers be appointed Trustees to hold all property belonging to the West Texas Conference, and to dispose of the same according to the direction of said Conference.

5th Resolved, That the Trustees of West Texas Conference Seminary be authorized to sell our present school property, and to purchase other property; provided they can obtain buildings ready for use by such exchange.

* * *

9th Resolved, That we, as a Conference, declare our approval of the teachers of West Texas Conference Seminary, by tendering to them our most profound gratitude for the work they are doing; and we pray that the financial embarrassment now surrounding this much needed enterprise may soon pass away, and we hereby pledge ourselves to do what we can to accomplish the end in view.

Committee
J. W. Robinson
M. Henson
Merit Anderson
C. C. Robinson
James Henderson
W. J. Mitchell[13]

In 1882 the Freedmen's Aid Society reported:

At Austin, the Capital of Texas, we have purchased an elevated site of five acres and a half of ground, overlooking the city, within three-fourths of a mile of the Statehouse, upon which we propose to erect a commodious school edifice at the earliest moment that funds can be obtained for this purpose. We cannot accomplish much here until our building is erected, and we invite any person of means to give a name to this institution and a school building for its accommodation. The West Texas Conference has pledged several thousand dollars towards this enterprise, and it is expected that the new building will be erected and be ready for occupancy by the commencement of another year.[14]

Several years later, encouraged and helped by a substantial gift from Mr. Samuel Huston of Marengo, Iowa, the building for which the Conference had hoped, prayed and labored, was begun and the name of the West Texas Conference Seminary was changed to "Samuel Huston College." The Committee on Education at the Annual Conference December 7—12, 1887, reported as follows:

We, your Committee on Education, after due consideration of our needs, pledge the faith of the West Texas Conference to continue our efforts to raise money to complete the college building now in course of erection. Up-to-date we have expended two thousand five hundred and twenty dollars ($2,520) which amount includes the twenty-two hundred ($2,200) which was in the hands of the managers of the Freedmen's Aid Society, at interest of 6 per cent per annum; the above amount has been used in the erection of the basement story of the Sam Huston College. The $2,520 thus expended is only 80 per cent of the cost of the basement story, leaving a balance due of $630, due contractor and builder, Mr. J. W. Alexander, of Austin. We further rejoice at and highly appreciate the successful efforts made by Dr. R. S. Rust, Corresponding Secretary of the Freedmen's Aid Society, for aiding the West Texas Conference in procuring a $10,000 donation from Mr. Sam Huston. This institution takes his name, and it will be known in the future as the Sam Huston College. We feel deeply impressed with the idea and sense of our need for these new facilities, and deem it wise to let no opportunity pass unimproved, we labor under the conviction that our future success depends largely upon our moral intellectual and religious development as a race; and we believe that as ministers

355

we stand identified with the general and practical educational work, and do rise up to the dignity and importance of the hour by engaging to labor more earnestly for our own improvement in these directions, the better to enable us to lift up our down-trodden race.[15]

Also, the Freedmen's Aid Society reported that:

In accordance with the recommendation of the Board of Managers one year ago, the building of the Samuel Huston College at Austin, Texas, has been carried forward to completion so far as to finish the walls and roof, and put in the rough floors and studding for the partitions. The foundation and first story having been built, the contract for the remainder of the work was for $7,075. The Society was indebted to the Building Fund $4,741.62. If the West Texas Conference pays over what monies have been subscribed and collected within its bounds, there will be no debt. When this is done, there will be an effort made to complete the building.[16]

As reported by the Freedmen's Aid and Southern Education Society the college, for want of funds, was not in operation during the school year 1888-1889:

This institution was not opened the past year for lack of money. The foundation of a new building is in and stands waiting for the super structure. The West Texas Conference is working heroically to raise money. At least $5,000 more is needed to put up and finish the building. Our grounds are located in the city and are valuable.[17]

This setback was a great and grievous shock to the Conference as shown in the report on education to the Annual Conference in 1889:

We have been much discouraged by the discontinuance of our school at Austin, and parted with Professor T. M. Dart with regret for want of means to continue the school or to erect or complete the well-planned building, whose basement story was completed one year ago the 29th of last October (1888). This basement was built by the advice of Dr. R. S. Rust, D. D., the then Corresponding Secretary of the Freedmen's Aid Society. We were led to believe that he would follow up our action, in spending the twenty-two hundred dollars we had in our easury; but in this we were sorrowfully disappointed.

356

...Resolved, That we use our influence to have our people everywhere to cooperate with us to make Samuel Huston College a reality.

* * *

...Resolved, That we hold ourselves in readiness to sanction, and carry into execution, any plans Dr. Hartzell may lay before us, which may lead to victory by completing our building. We hear the voice of eight thousand members within our own territory crying to earth and heaven, for means to finish this building.

We tender our most sincere thanks to dear Brother Samuel Huston, of Marengo, Iowa, for his generous gift of Ten Thousand Dollars, to help us in our great struggles to supply the much needed educational facilities. May Heaven's choicest benedictions rest upon him...[18]

Despite discouragement because of lack of funds, the West Texas Conference continued to labor with the hope of making Samuel Huston College a reality, as indicated by the report of 1890:

We are not doing all we ought to do for this noble cause for want of the spirit of enterprise. We pledge ourselves and our constituency to keep up a living identification and helpful relation with the great work of education, and rise to the dignity and importance of the hour by engaging to labor more earnestly. . . .

* * *

Resolved, That we use all of our influence to have our people everywhere to put forth greater effort by cooperating with those well-aimed influences to help make Samuel Huston College a success and a reality.
Resolved, That we hold ourselves in readiness to sanction and carry into execution any plans the President of the Board of Freedmen's Aid and Southern Education Society may lay before us.[19]

* * *

The leaders of the West Texas Conference believed deeply and unreservedly in education, demonstrated by the ardent efforts, continued interest, and sacrificial struggle for more than a quarter of a century to make Samuel Huston College a reality. Their interest and efforts extended beyond education. They saw a college in their midst as an essential means of attracting members and strengthening Methodism in the West Texas Conference and the Southwest. The college was conceived as an intricate part of

357

the work of the Conference. An entrenched educational philosophy was developed.

We, as a Conference, are enabled to see that education is an art of developing the faculties, the training of the human mind, or human beings, for the function for which they are destined.
We are convinced of the soundness of the principles of education, and in order to the perfection of it, it must be founded upon a corresponding science; and of nothing is this more true than education.

* * *

We, therefore, recommend that all our ministers enforce moral habits among our people as much as possible; they need it to increase their love for truth and obedience. Also, to better enable them to exercise self-control. In whatever community this has been done, faithful and impartially, our people are better in every way.
The above work of training and imparting instruction is incumbent upon the ministers and teachers, and without the completion of Samuel Huston College, how are we to have them?

* * *

We have, according to the Minutes of the last Annual Conference, 9,486 full members and probationers in our territory, with possibly a following of 18,000 or 20,000; entirely too many for any other denomination to provide means for their education and religious and moral training.

* * *

We need an educated ministry, and must have it, for we cannot succeed much longer without it.
Methodist schools and Methodist preachers are necessary to the production of Methodist Preachers. Give us the school, the teachers, and the preachers, and the people are ours.
We would also recommend in this report that this conference renew its pledges and energies to complete the Samuel Huston College, and hereby ask the Society to allow us with the means we have in mind, and what may be gathered here at this Conference, and subsequently to resume the work of constructing the walls of the building.[20]

It was reported at the Annual Conference of 1891 that the delay in completing the building, which was to cost $18,000, and in reopening the school had become an expensive delay. The unfinished building, standing for several years, was deteriorating and being defaced and destroyed by intruders. Also, the property

358

consisting of six acres of land situated between East 11th and East 12th Streets was being heavily taxed by the City to help pay a large bond issue and could in no way be exempt until occupied as school property.[2][1]

Twenty-Four Year's Efforts Crowned:
R. S. Lovinggood, President

Almost another decade passed before any success was achieved in completing the building started in 1887, and before the school was reopened in 1900.

Over a period of twenty-four years, 1876 to 1900, an institution was being born through the hopes, yearnings, labors, prayers, sacrifices, patience, and faith of the people of the West Texas Conference. There were dark days of discouragement, and bright days of encouragement and new hope. There was never a thought of giving up. The struggle of the leaders and people of the Conference for so many years to establish an educational institution the Conference could call its own helped to make this one of the great Conferences of Methodism. This Conference, saturated with love, sacrifice and enthusiasm for education, became the soil prepared through sweat, blood, and tears in which Samuel Huston College was planted and, from 1900 on, grew to be more than a high place of learning; it became a temple of the spirit, embodying the spirit of great men, all the magnanimous souls that labored for a quarter of a century to bring it into reality, and embodying the life and spirit of a great man, Reuben Shannon Lovinggood, who came as a Moses to give it the leadership it sorely needed.

The good news was reported by the Freedmen's Aid Society in *The Christian Educator:*

The Samuel Huston College at Austin, Texas, has just been opened. The school has had an eventful history. The first donation for this property was made by Mr. Samuel Huston, of Iowa, over fifteen years ago. Nearly twelve years ago the foundation was laid; but the money gave out and the work was suspended. In the meantime, the people on the grounds raised money to supplement what might be done by the central office; but the financial panic of 1893 made it impossible to further proceed with the work. Two years ago, the Board of Managers, by urgent request of the local Board of Trustees, contracted for the completion of a portion of the building at a cost of $8,000. The first and second floors are completed and the school has begun. There is a small debt; but enough property has been deeded to the Society by the local Board, and several other parties, to more than cover this indebtedness.

Professor R. S. Lovinggood, one of our own graduates, who for four years held the chair of Latin and Greek in Wiley University, has been elected Principal. Professor Lovinggood is one of the best and truest products our work in the South has given us, and begins his labors at Austin with marked enthusiasm. Under his trained leadership, and with the aid and cooperation of the West Texas Conference, much good will be accomplished.[22]

The remarkable ability, enthusiasm, and dedicated leadership qualities of Dr. Lovinggood were pointed out in the following statement by the Freedmen's Aid Society in the Summer Issue of *The Christian Educator*, 1901:

...Reuben S. Lovinggood, A.M., now President of Samuel Huston College, Austin, Texas. With an appropriation of five hundred dollars, this brave and cultural son of the Church opened a school last October in an unfurnished building, without a stick of furniture. This is our first school in all Southern Texas. The members of our Conference had given for the building until they were discouraged. And now, only five hundred dollars available for the work! What could be done with such a sum? But we had found a man; and every institution is but the lengthened shadow of a man. At our request, he was willing to go, with his brave wife, and lay the foundation of a new school, hoping for a larger appropriation next year. Little was expected. Results simply amazing have been achieved. The finished part of the building has been furnished for school purposes. Over two hundred students have already been enrolled. Three teachers and two assistants have responded to his call for heroic service on small pay. . .

The West Texas Conference nobly responded with generous gifts. At the Conference session, out of their poverty, they laid down one hundred and thirty-nine dollars cash on the table. Resolved not to go into debt, and yet pressed for furniture by the unexpected number of students, President Lovinggood organized a "Chair Social" and then a "Dish Social," and finally, as cold weather was on him, a "Bed-clothing Social"; thus, getting from the generous people furnishings for his school. Of course, he has closed this year without a debt.

The story of this achievement came through our good friend, Dr. Thayer, to Mr. E. T. Burrowes, of Portland, Maine. Correspondence was opened with the office. The large opportunities of this field were presented to him, and a strong plea for the finishing of the building was made. The opportunity strongly appealed to this generous-hearted layman. Soon the promise came of $5,000 for the finishing of the building, conditioned on the $2,500 additional necessary, being raised. This is but a single example of the way in which God is working for us.

* * *

. . .If the church could realize all this work means for the church and for the saving of the Nation, what a response they would make to our appeals.[2 3]

Getting a faculty for the first year was no easy task. Dr. Lovinggood, however, assembled an excellent group of loyal men and women who dedicated themselves to the work at Samuel Huston and remained there many years. Special mention must be made of Professor J. W. Frazier, Dr. Lovinggood's right hand man, who came to the institution with Dr. Lovinggood, labored with him during the sixteen years he was President, was at his bedside when he passed away, and after the passing of Dr. Lovinggood in December, 1916, carried the college forward until a new President took over in the summer of 1917. Professor Frazier was a real "corner stone" of the college during the first quarter of a century of its life. The list below indicates the faculty for the first year, 1900-1901:

R. S. Lovinggood, A.M., President, Mental and Moral Sciences
J. W. Frazier, A.B., Mathematics
C. L. Eason, Greek and Latin and Modern Languages
_____, Natural Sciences (to be filled)
Miss Bertha Hamilton, Department of Pedagogy
Miss Mamie E. Starnes, History and English
Mrs. R. S. Lovinggood, Preceptress and Domestic Economy
Mrs. M. E. Fairchild, Primary Department
Mrs. Laura Frazier, English Grades
Miss Clara Jackson, Department of Music
Miss M. D. Brown, Miss Lemuel Morrow, R. T. Brown, Assistants
Miss Malinda E. Webb, Department of Sewing
J. W. Frazier, A.B., Librarian
Miss M. E. Starnes, Secretary of Faculty
C. L. Eason, Shorthand
Miss Clora Madison, Typewriting[2 4]

At the beginning of the first year of the work of Samuel

Huston College, Dr. Lovinggood had the strength and help of a loyal and devoted Board of Trustees, listed below:

Almost all of these members of the Board had been a part of the long struggle to bring the college into existence; consequently, they were a part of the college and it was a part of them, and their labors for it were real "labors of love."

Mr. Burrowes' interest in Samuel Huston College grew. When he visited the institution which he helped to make possible, he was greatly impressed. The following statement is a part of a report May, 1902:

> . . .Mr. E. T. Burrowes of Portland, Maine, through whose gift of $5,000 the completion of our building for Samuel Huston College was made possible. We know of no investment of money that has brought larger immediate returns. President Lovinggood promised to pack the building with students the first year. What a tribute to his energy and ability is found in a building over-crowded, and three cottages on the borders of the campus filled with boys! Mr. Burrowes will accompany Secretary Thirkield to Austin, and be present at the feast of dedication on May 21st. He also made a generous gift for the liquidation of our debt. Mr. Burrowes is head of the E. T. Burrowes Screen Company, the largest of the kind in the world, now having offices in all the large cities of America.[26]

Dr. Lovinggood was an eloquent speaker. The impressiveness of his eloquence was to be found in his sincerity and in his obvious dedication to the work for which he always displayed a deep sense of mission. When he spoke to the people, whether in large crowds or small groups, out of his experience of struggle and dedication, and out of his love for the cause, with tears in his eyes he drew tears from the eyes of his audience, and he always sold Samuel Huston College to his listeners as an institution that was living, vital and with a purpose so compelling that they were irresistibly moved to respond to help this noble cause. The following report regarding the Freedmen's Aid Society Anniversary gives proof of the eloquence of Dr. Lovinggood:

The anniversary on Monday night was very largely attended. Bishop W. F. McDowell and President R. S. Lovinggood of Sam Huston College, one of our graduates, spoke. His address was unique. It was the story of his struggles for an education, his conversion, and his present work as President of Sam Huston College at Austin, Texas. And what a story it was! Eloquent, thrilling, pathetic, soul-stirring—it was all that and more. The people cheered and laughed and cried.[27]

Another illustration of the ability of Dr. Lovinggood to reach the hearts of people is given in the following statement:

"Took the Audience, Bag, and Baggage"
At several of the Fall Conferences where the Secretaries could not well be present, the anniversary address was made by President R. S. Lovinggood, of Sam Huston College. An indication of the effectiveness of his story, which represents in general the experiences of hundreds who have gone through our schools, is found in the following account of his visit to the Detroit Conference, by the editor of the Michigan *Christian Advocate*:
"The story was so simply, so artlessly told, so interspersed with humorous turns, so articulated with pictures of ludicrous situations, put in such a genial way that he just took the audience bag and baggage. It was effective in a very high degree. People were won. They saw things. They got a view of Southern life and work. The good sense and Christian spirit permeating the whole speech made it a rarely fine one. We wish all our Conferences might hear it. The collection looked as if it took in all the money the preachers had left at that time."[28]

The story of the life and works of Dr. Lovinggood is a thrilling and inspiring story; which he himself tells under the caption: "Fruits of Emancipation" in *The Christian Educator*, February, 1904 (pp. 13-19). The story is too long to be related here, but should be read for the deep insights it gives into the life and character of this great man. Much of this story to which reference

363

is made describes his labors and leadership at Samuel Huston College during the first four years of its life.

By 1904 Samuel Huston College was well on the way to becoming an exceptionally good institution in the Southwest. The Minutes of the General Conference of 1904 record the following report:

The main college building at Samuel Huston College, Austin, Tex., begun more than a dozen years ago, has been completed during this quadrennium at a cost of $8,500. The balance was raised by the West Texas Conference through President Lovinggood. This building is used for a girls' dormitory and for general school purposes. Plans have also been inaugurated for a boys' dormitory to cost $10,000, of which $2,000 has already been raised by the West Texas Conference and is now in our treasury for that purpose.[29]

In November 1905, with reference to the progress of the college, it was reported that:

At Samuel Huston College, Austin, Texas, contracts have been let for a new building which, with equipment, will cost $15,500—of this amount, our generous benefactor, Mr. E. T. Burrowes, of Portland, Maine, has given $6,000. The building is now in process of construction, and will accommodate the sixty or eighty boys who now have to be inadequately housed in neighboring cottages.[30]

Through the untiring labors and leadership of President Lovinggood, the continued generosity of Mr. Burrowes, and the sacrificial support of the West Texas Annual Conference, Samuel Huston College continued to make phenomenal progress. In the Summer of 1908 reports showed that:

At Sam Huston College, Austin, Tex., a boys' dormitory has been completed at a cost of $15,000—$5,000 of which was given by Mr. E. T. Burrowes, of Portland, Maine, who is a strong friend of the institution, and has given liberally to its work. The remaining $10,000 was raised principally by the West Texas Conference, by the secretary in charge and by President Lovinggood, with an appropriation of $1,200 from our Board. This is of brick, three stories high, and will accommodate 100 students.[31]

364

The work of the first ten years of Samuel Huston College was summarized in *The Christian Educator*, February, 1911, as follows:

I had heard of "making bricks without straw," but had never seen it done until I visited Samuel Huston College a few weeks ago. There I found the operation in actual process. "Can a man make something out of nothing?" Six weeks ago I would have answered with an emphatic "No"; today I must admit that it appears possible. President Lovinggood has done it.

Ten years ago the Freedmen's Aid Society of the Methodist Episcopal Church sent him to Austin to open a school for colored youth of Texas. The sole assets of the new institution consisted of six acres of ground and one partly finished building. It had no faculty, no students, and no money. At the end of a decade, Samuel Huston College had nineteen teachers, five hundred and seventeen students, seventy-one graduates, five buildings, and $87,000 worth of property. If there is a school anywhere, white or black, which has a better record, the writer does not know where to find it.

All this has been achieved in the face of the most discouraging conditions. When President Lovinggood arrived in Austin he found only an unfinished and unfurnished building awaiting him. From these meager beginnings Samuel Huston College has grown in ten years to one of the largest and best schools of our church for colored youth in the South. Today Samuel Huston College is regarded as one of the valuable assets in Austin. The leading citizens regard it with favor and are numbered among its benefactors. President Lovinggood possesses the confidence of the City and is considered one of its most useful and influential citizens.[32]

Further:

The College should have increased dormitory facilities at once. It also needs a new industrial building for the teaching or the practical trades. President Lovinggood has already raised $6,000 toward such a building, but he needs $10,000 additional to complete his plans.[33]

The property holdings of the college were increased in 1911 by the addition of an eight-and-a-half acre farm, to make agriculture a part of the training offered by the college. The farm, located within a mile of the campus, was purchased for $2,300, and was also to be used for an athletic field.[34]

In keeping with the general emphasis at the time on industrial education, Samuel Huston incorporated industrial training into its program. Provision for this phase of the program was completed in 1912:

> Through the generosity of Mr. E. T. Burrowes, of Portland, Maine, a new industrial building, costing $7,500, has been erected at Sam Huston College, Austin, Tex. In addition to the $3,000 given by Mr. Burrowes, $2,000 has been contributed by the citizens of Austin, $2,000 from the funds of the Society, and the balance from the West Texas Conference.[35]

In 1912 additional property was acquired near the campus consisting of a house and three lots, costing $4,500. The West Texas Annual Conference raised the money for this additional property.[36]

Academic Work Development

Amazing progress was made during the first twelve years (1900-1912) of the life of Samuel Huston College in securing funds and developing the physical facilities. Progress in the academic area was equally amazing. For the first year of operation, 1900-1901, a faculty and staff of fifteen, including the President who taught Mental and Moral Science, was assembled to offer instruction.[37] The incredibly wide range of the curriculum included the Primary Department, the English Grades, Latin and Greek and the Modern Languages, English, History, Mathematics, Natural Science, Pedagogy, Music, Domestic Economy, and Shorthand and Typing.[38]

Obviously, not all of the students who enrolled the first year were beginners. Some came from other schools in Austin, and elsewhere with advance grade standing; some were ready for high school, and some were seeking preparation for teaching.

The levels of the curriculum were the primary grades, the English or grammar school grades, the high school grades, and the normal or teacher training course. The high school included four years above the eighth grade, and the Normal course first included only two years above the eighth grade and was later extended to include four years above the eighth grade, the first two years being the same in content as the high school course and the last two years gave special courses in pedagogy or teacher training.

The annual catalog for 1901-1902 gives an outline for a

366

four-year college Preparatory Course.[38a] The enrollment in the Preparatory Course for 1901-1902 follows: First year, 7; Second year, 3; Third year, 7; Fourth year, none.[38b] The first two years of the high school were the same in the normal course and the preparatory course. At the beginning of the third year in high school those students intending to teach took the normal course subjects for two additional years, and those intending to go on to college continued in the preparatory course for two additional years. In 1909 the college course leading to the Bachelor of Arts degree was initiated, and in 1913 the first college class was graduated with the Bachelor of Arts degree. With the graduation of this class the college was well on its way academically and continued to gain through additions to the curriculum and to the faculty.

Supplementary to the academic curriculum was industrial work, including carpentry and cabinet-making, blacksmithing and wheelwrighting, printing, and some practical aspects of farming. From the beginning, work was offered in domestic economy for young women. Samuel Huston College soon became known and renowned through the fine young men and women it graduated and sent out over Texas and the Southwest as teachers, preachers, and workers in other professions.

Eliza Dee Home

Eliza Dee Home, under the auspices of the Women's Home Missionary Society of the Methodist Episcopal Church, was a significant part of the history of Samuel Huston College. In fact, this home was an institution in its own right and service.

A moving spirit in the founding and development of Eliza Dee Home was Mrs. Elizabeth S. Spriggs, later (1910), Mrs. E. Spriggs Ratliff, of the West Texas Conference. Mrs. Spriggs, as Conference Corresponding Secretary, obtained permission in 1895 to raise the first $500.00 for a home for the training of girls of the West Texas Conference. The money was raised over a five-year period from poverty giving.[39] As a next step, Miss Melinda Webb, a graduate of the King Home Dressmaking Department at Wiley College, Marshall, Texas, was sent in 1901 to take charge of the industrial department of Samuel Huston College.[40] Just at this time an undesignated bequest of $3,000 came into the treasury of the Women's Home Mission Society Bureau from the Estate of Mrs. Eliza M. Dee of Burlington, Iowa. Mrs. Lavenda Murphy, Bureau Secretary, petitioned to use the bequest to purchase property in Austin, Texas. The petition was granted.[41]

Eliza Dee Home opened on the first Monday in October, 1904. Miss Clara I. King was transferred from King Home at Wiley College to become the first superintendent of Eliza Dee Home.

For the next twenty-four years, Clara King and Eliza Dee Home were inseparably linked.[4 2]

To know Miss C. I. King was to know a true friend to all young people who had high ideals and strong aspirations to achieve worthy goals.

In 1916 construction was begun on a beautiful white-pillared building to replace the little cottage in which the Home was begun, and was always overcrowded. When finished in 1918, it accommodated fifty girls and stood on a high hill overlooking the city, a thing of beauty and a monument to Mrs. E. Spriggs Ratliff, other women on the West Texas Conference, and the Woman's Home Missionary Society, whose sustained interest and untiring labors made this new Home possible.

There was great demand by young women for a place in Eliza Dee Home from its beginning until the mid-twenties. Crop failures, lack of scholarship funds, and deletion of the high school classes at Samuel Huston resulted in sharply reduced attendance. Decreased enrollment was also due to discontinuance of work in Home Economics. In 1931, under the administration of President Willis J. King, Eliza Dee Home became the official residence for freshmen and sophomore young women. The Society again assumed responsibility for the home economics department, which became one of the academic departments, offering a major in home economics.[4 3]

Had it not been for the fine contribution made by Eliza Dee Home, the story of Samuel Huston College would be quite different, and the West Texas Conference and the Southwest would be deprived of a rich heritage.

The End of an Epoch

For sixteen years Samuel Huston College grew, prospered, and yielded abundant fruit under the magnificent leadership of President R. S. Lovinggood, who endeared himself in the hearts of his students, the faculty, the West Texas Annual Conference, the Methodist Episcopal Church generally, and thousands of people of Texas and the Nation. The college, from 1876 to 1916, had seen many dark and discouraging days and had suffered many blighting setbacks; but none so tragic as the death of its beloved President, Dr. Reuben Shannon Lovinggood. On Sunday evening, December

368

17, 1916, the campus was silenced and hearts stricken with unassuageable grief when word came that President Lovinggood had died. The only thought or expression that gave any comfort at that time was the parting words that fell from his dying lips: "I have fought a good fight, I have finished my course, I have kept the faith."

It is appropriate to include here the following statement that appeared in *The Christian Educator* shortly after President Lovinggood's death:[44]

FEBRUARY, 1917

President Lovinggood Is Dead

Reuben Shannon Lovinggood was an indomitable spirit. Born of a different race and with a slight change of circumstances, he would have been recognized as one of the world's great men. He was nevertheless great; great in his courage, great in overcoming obstacles, great in his faith in humanity and in God, and great in achievement. While the list of his achievements may not bulk large as compared with the achievements of some other men and women of the world, yet Professor Lovinggood is to be reckoned as one of the constructive leaders of our present time.

He was born in the depths of poverty, shut off from the lure of educational life, when by accident he heard of Clark University in a log church. Once hearing the call and failing not to follow the lead, he arrived at Clark University with only a few dollars in his pocket to purchase its equivalent in education. He soon found that his ideal was too low. Undismayed, he faced the journey through the college course with a self-denial and heroism that are a sacred heritage to his children and an inspiration to all who will read of his unselfish life.

On leaving college he threw himself at once into the uplift work for his people. He was a teacher by choice as well as by training and disposition. His pupils loved him and he loved them. He loved his work and gave himself to it without reservation.

Samuel Huston College stood an unopened school for years. Our Bishop Thirkield, then corresponding secretary of the Freedmen's Aid Society, proposed to Reuben Shannon Lovinggood the opening of this institution with an appropriation of $500 for all purposes. Lovinggood gave up a comfortable professorship in Wiley University and immediately

369

undertook the task. Those who have heard him tell the story of the first month's experience in the uncompleted building of Samuel Huston College were always impressed with the heroism of the man and the indomitable spirit that possessed him. A weaker man would never have undertaken the task; a man less consecrated to the uplift of his people would have shrunk from the job. He had both consecration and determination, and above all he had faith in the ultimate outcome.

But Reuben Shannon Lovinggood made friends, when he went to Samuel Huston College his friends saw him under this great task, they came to his relief. An old professor, Dr. E. O. Thayer, interested Mr. E. T. Burrowes. Mr. Burrowes and Dr. Lovinggood became partners, and they, jointly with the other friends who came to the rescue of Samuel Huston College, have built up in the course of sixteen years one of the outstanding institutions of all Texas and of our Freedmen's Aid System.

Dr. Lovinggood had been in poor health for some time, but he was none the least valiant. Only recently was he confined to his bed, and his friends were shocked when word was received that he had passed quietly and peacefully into rest on Sunday evening, December 17.

Reuben S. Lovinggood was born in 1863, at Wahalla, S. C. Graduated from Clark University with the degree of A. B. in 1890, and was subsequently granted the master's degree by his Alma Mater. New Orleans University accorded him the degree of Ph.D. He did some post work in the University of Chicago. For two years immediately on leaving college he was editor of the Atlanta Times; three years principal of the city school in Birmingham, Ala.; 1896-1899, professor of Greek and Latin in Wiley University. In 1900 he opened Samuel Huston College. He was president of the Texas Teachers' Association, a member of the Southern Sociological Congress, and a member of five General Conferences of the Methodist Episcopal Church.

The story of Professor Lovinggood's life is so varied, so thrilling, so inspiring, that it cannot be told in a single chapter. We shall be a long time telling our youth of the virtues and the heroism of this good man.—Southwestern Christian Advocate.

New Administration

In the summer of 1917 President Matthew Simpson Davage, a bright young star in educational leadership in the Methodist Episcopal Church was selected for the Presidency of Samuel Huston College to succeed Dr. Lovinggood. Dr. Davage being known as an outstanding young churchman and an educational leader of great promise, gave new hope for bright days for the college. *The Southwestern Christian Advocate* gave the following account of Dr. Davage's election to this important position:

The loss of the late President R. S. Lovinggood as an educational leader in the West Texas Conference was a very great one. The whole church, our society and our colored leaders and followers in West Texas wondered where there was an available man to fill the vacant presidency of Samuel Huston College. The choice of Matthew S. Davage, M.A., for the vacant post has its genesis among the colored leaders and constituents of the West Texas Conference, who so loyally have supported the former President and made possible the glorious results which have been accomplished. The choice of President Davage for this important post also met the unanimous approval of our Board of Managers.

He combines ripe scholarship needed, a character untarnished, a churchwide reputation which his predecessor had in so marked degree, a spiritual fervor essentially necessary for fruitful leadership of young people, and administrative ability that has been tested in several important positions he has held in the church.

President Davage is in his thirty-eighth year. He is the son of a Methodist preacher and hence of sturdy Methodist ancestry. He was graduated from the Classical Department of New Orleans College and filled the chair of Mathematics for several years in his alma mater.

From 1905 to 1915 he was Business Manager of the *Southwestern Christian Advocate*. In 1915-16 he was elected President of George R. Smith College, at Sedalia, Missouri, and was transferred to the Principalship of Haven Institute, Meridian, Mississippi, for the scholastic year 1916-17. In the rapid promotion of President Davage from one of our institutions to another for three times in three years it has proven not only to have been wise, but providential, that we had in him the very man to take up unfinished tasks of greatest magnitude like that of Samuel Huston College. *The Southwestern Christian Advocate*, which had for so many years President Davage's help, very aptly says that "he is fittingly chosen to succeed the late Dr. R. S. Lovinggood. In his new field of increased responsibilities and larger opportunities, all of Professor Davage's friends predict for him a brilliant career."[44a]

For three years President Davage gave able administrative leadership to Samuel Huston College and won the hearts and high respect of the students, faculty, and the West Texas Conference. It was hoped that he would for many years give leadership to this institution, but his administration was all too short, as he was transferred in 1920 to the Presidency of Rust College, Holly Springs, Mississippi.

During three and a half decades, from 1917 to 1952, Samuel Huston had a series of eight presidencies of relatively short lengths. The Presidents during this period of thirty-five years and their tenure follow.

1917—1920: President M. S. Davage. An account of his administration is given above.

1920—1922: President J. B. Randolph, who came to Samuel Huston from the Presidency of Haven Institute, Meridian, Mississippi. President Randolph was a scholar and was most erudite. His tenure as President here came to an end in 1922 when he was transferred to the Presidency of Claflin College, Orangeburg, South Carolina.

1922—1926: President R. N. Brooks. Although all of President Brooks' predecessors were high churchmen, he was the first minister since 1900 to serve as President. President Brooks came to this position at Samuel Huston from the Presidency of Central Alabama College at Birmingham, Alabama. In 1926 President Brooks resigned the Presidency of Samuel Huston to become Professor of Church History at Gammon Theological Seminary.

1926—1930: President Thomas R. Davis, who came from the Presidency of Walden College, Nashville, was a layman. His four-year tenure came to an end in 1930. At this time he resigned to return to Tennessee for Public School work.

1930—1932: Dr. Willis J. King. He and the next three Presidents to 1952, were ministers. The two-year tenure of Dr. King ended in 1932 when he was elected to the Presidency of Gammon Theological Seminary, where he for a long period previously had served as a Professor.

1932—1943: President Stanley E. Grannum. The Reverend Grannum's tenure of eleven years was the longest since that of Dr. Lovinggood. The college advanced under his leadership. He resigned in 1943 to pursue study for the doctorate, and later joined the faculty of Gammon Theological Seminary.

1943—1948: Reverend Karl E. Downs served as President four and a half years. He was the first graduate of Samuel Huston to be elected to the Presidency. He was a product of the West Texas

Conference. His hard work, noble spirit, and great enthusiasm in a very large measure typified the work and spirit of the late President Lovinggood. Like President Lovinggood, he died in office. Something of his work as President and the high esteem in which he was held are reflected in the following excerpts from his Obituary:

In recognition of his unusual leadership he was called in September, 1943, to the Presidency of Samuel Huston College whose doors were about to close. To this institution of which he was an alumnus, the future of which the Peabody Report of 1943 had declared uncertain, Karl Everett Downs brought not only superior intellectual preparation and training, but a deep and abiding faith in the inherent possibilities of Samuel Huston to help meet the need for the Christian training of our youth.

* * *

The spiritual life of the students was one of his major concerns. Once a month the entire college family including faculty, students and alumni attend church in the community as a group with one of the ministers of the college delivering the message and the college choir rendering the music. The 'Power Hour' weekly voluntary prayer services held in the college chapel; the Religious Extension Service instituted through a grant from the Board of Home Missions and Church Extensions; the Community Vespers, jointly sponsored by Wesley Methodist Church and the college; and the Religious Emphasis Week provide additional means through which the spiritual life of the students and faculty is enriched. President Downs emphasized constantly the need of building character on Samuel Huston's campus. He declared that this college was founded on the major premise "that the important thing at the end of a college career is not knowledge of facts, but devotion to duty in the light of life's highest truth."

* * *

Karl Everett Downs recaptured what had been almost completely lost, the faith of the people in Samuel Huston College.

1948—1952: Reverend Robert F. Harrington, President. Reverend Harrington came to the Presidency of Samuel Huston from a successful pastorate in the South Carolina Conference. His tenure as President was the final five years in the history of Samuel Huston College as such. In 1952 a new relationship with Tillotson College began a new history for the two institutions under new Presidential administration.

373

Changes and Developments

During the period 1917 to 1952 many changes took place, some of which helped to strengthen the college. The institution was affected by two world wars and a ten-year period of economic depression. With very great struggle it survived the difficulties of this period and made substantial progress.

Some of the developments were: (1) all high school classes were discontinued, concentrating on the four-year college work; (2) more land was acquired, making possible additional classroom and laboratory facilities, and added equipment; (3) curriculum changes and development were adapted to modern requirements; (4) major and minor fields of concentration were established; (5) the faculty was increased and improved, with earned higher degrees; (6) Dean of the college appointed with training to give academic leadership to the faculty; (7) office of the registrar was established and a good system of records instituted; (8) the college enrollment greatly increased through a better recruitment program; (9) personnel services to students were initiated; and (10) library facilities provided, with substantial increase in library volumes.

These developments, by 1952, placed Samuel Huston in position to offer a sound educational program, despite its financial limitations and struggles.

In 1950 Samuel Huston College celebrated its Fiftieth Anniversary. Talks had become serious regarding a closer relationship and possible merger of Samuel Huston and Tillotson Colleges, the two institutions having been located in Austin, less than a mile apart, for a half century. Following is a brief historical sketch of Tillotson College:

Tillotson College

In 1875 under the sponsorship of the Reverend George Jeffrey Tillotson, Tillotson College was founded in Austin, Texas. It was chartered in 1877 and opened to students on January 17, 1881. The school was sustained by the American Missionary Association and was opened as the Tillotson Collegiate and Normal Institute under the administration of the Reverend William E. Brooks. In 1894 the school was re-named Tillotson College. The College was organized as a private liberal arts educational corporation under the laws of Texas on June 2, 1909. In 1925 the school was recognized by the State Department of Education as a junior college. In 1926 the College became a woman's college; in 1931 the State of Texas Department of Education approved Tillotson College as a senior

374

college; in 1935 it returned to co-educational status; and in 1943 Tillotson College received an "A" classification by the Southern Association of Colleges and Secondary Schools.[46]

Because of the pressure of financial need of both institutions and the danger of neither being able to continue, a closer relationship demanded more serious consideration.

The Merging of Samuel Huston and
    Tillotson Colleges

Earlier Discussions and Actions

Discussions regarding a closer relationship between Samuel Huston College and Tillotson College were begun as early as January, 1924. On file in the Gammon Archives[47] are letters exchanged between Dr. Fred L. Brownlee, Corresponding Secretary of the American Missionary Association, and Dr. I. Garland Penn, Corresponding Secretary of the Department of Education for Negroes of the Methodist Episcopal Church, regarding a possible relationship, affiliation or merger, between their respective institutions in Austin, Texas. The series of letters exchanged between January 17 and June 9, 1924, indicate that the communications extended beyond the two Corresponding Secretaries. There were joint meetings of representatives and the Executive Committees of the American Missionary Association and the Department of Education for Negroes to consider this new relationship of the institutions in Austin. Some efforts were made to secure financial assistance from a foundation to study the situation as a basis for the new relationship. With some hope and expectation that a cooperative plan would develop, the following announcement was made by a representative of Samuel Huston College:

There is now in prospect a co-ordination and unification of the two schools for Negroes located in Austin, known as Tillotson College, under the auspices of the American Missionary Association, and Samuel Huston College, so that the two schools shall be operated as one under the probable name of Samuel Huston-Tillotson College. The expenses incident to operating the combined institutions under one management will be borne by two Boards owning the property. In the combination, State requirements with reference to standards will be met, as well as increased efficiency, and avoidance of overlapping and wastage of funds.[48]

For reasons not yet discovered, the new relationship did not materialize at that time. The talks, however, were renewed occasionally and there were intermittent efforts toward cooperation by the two colleges. The Samuel Huston College Bulletin for 1930-1931 gives the following statement:

> Tillotson and Samuel Huston are the Negro Colleges. While the relations between the two schools have always been friendly, an unusual spirit of cooperation has characterized the relations of the two schools this year.
> The first evidence of this new era is the joint summer school conducted by the two colleges, during the summer of 1931. This cooperation will be carried further during the regular session 1931-1932, when two professors from each of the colleges will give courses in the sister college.[49]

The Cooperative Summer School and exchange of instruction in the regular school year were short-lived, and there was little or no effort to bring the two institutions closer together for another decade.

The Huston-Tillotson College Bulletin gives an account of the final and successful efforts to merge the two colleges:

> Eventually, certain concrete and tangible steps were taken, for in 1944 a number of meetings of special committees were convened in Austin to discuss definite plans for accomplishing this merger. These committees were made up of the administrators of the colleges, church officials, prominent members of the staff of the University of Texas, and representative citizens of the state. On October 27, 1944, the Tillotson College trustees voted: 'That an Exploration Committee from the Board of Trustees continue investigations as to the possible merger of Samuel Huston and Tillotson Colleges and that the trustees be asked to appoint a similar committee to work jointly with the Tillotson Committee.' And, on May 18, 1945, the Tillotson trustees voted: "That, after careful consideration, the entire suggested merger herein presented is approved as the next step towards cooperation with Samuel Huston College, and that the present committee of the trustees be empowered to move toward fulfillment of the proposed plan."

Then, on July 27, 1945, the following action was taken by the American Missionary Association Division Committee:

376

VOTED: That the A.M.A. Division express its approval of the proposed merger of Tillotson and Samuel Huston Colleges in Austin, Texas, and adopt in its general outline the memorandum already unanimously accepted by the Trustees of both colleges.

In 1947, the Methodist Board of Education took the following action:

WHEREAS representatives of the Boards of Trustees of Samuel Huston College, of our Church, and Tillotson College, of the Congregational Church, have reaffirmed the following position—representing the wisdom of the two Boards of Trustees:
WE REAFFIRM the wisdom which has been expressed through various scientific studies made of higher educational opportunities for Negroes in Texas, namely: that the two colleges in Austin should seek ways and means for the uniting of their forces in one strong and substantially supported college.
WE COMMEND the administrations of the colleges, the Trustee Boards, and parent bodies of these two institutions for the efforts which have already been made in the direction of unity.
WE HIGHLY ENDORSE the conviction that the present and potential resources of these two institutions should be pooled in a united effort to do better what each is now doing inadequately and with a sense of insecurity, provided this can be done in such a way as to best conserve the financial support and loyalties of all of the constituent supporters of the individual institutions.
We, the Standing Committee on Educational Institution for Negroes, RECOMMEND that a committee consisting of Bishops R. N. Brooks, Charles C. Selecman, Drs. M. S. Davage, J. N. Score, and Edmund Heinsohn be empowered to work with a similar committee from the American Missionary Association in the perfecting and completion of arrangements.
WE FURTHER RECOMMEND that the plan of merger be prepared for presentation in the 1948 session of the General Board of Education of the Methodist Church; or, in case of urgency demanding earlier action that the Executive Committee be authorized to consummate the merger with full power.
VOTE: To recommend to the Executive Committee to concur in the action already taken by the Trustees of Tillotson College and the above stated action of the Board of Education of the Methodist Church, and ask Dr. Samuel C. Kincheloe of Chicago, Mrs. Elbert Read of Iowa, Mr. John Moore and Mr. Fred E.

377

Brooks of Houston and Austin, Texas, and Mr. Fred Brownlee of New York, to serve as their special committee to work with the committee of the Methodist Board in perfecting plans to be recommended for adoption by the trustees of each college and by the directors of each church board.

Transition from Idea to Reality: On the afternoon of January 26, 1952, the Boards of Trustees of Samuel Huston College and Tillotson College met in Austin, agreed to the proposal to merge, and formulate plans to accomplish it at once. Then, on April 16, 1952, emphasized and dignified by two large mass meetings in Austin and by nationwide radio and newspaper publicity, the new Huston-Tillotson College became a reality.

The Plan of Union: (a) the pooling of the present and potential tangible assets of the two colleges in a united effort to do better what each has been doing inadequately and with a sense of insecurity; (b) the creation of a joint and thoroughly representative board of trustees, which shall be responsible for the maintenance and operation of the new college; (c) the formation of a new charter; (d) a building program which will involve a minimum cost of $1,500,000 and the ultimate location of the institution on one campus, and an approach to philanthropic foundations for special aid towards building and endowment; (e) preservation of the supporting constituencies of both denominations. It is the wish of both the Congregational and Methodist Boards to conserve this interest and also to increase it. It is believed that this can be done by preserving Congregational and Methodist connections through the name of the new college and in forms of promotion within both church bodies. Congregationalists are, however, centered primarily in the New England, North Central, and Pacific Coast States, but there are approximately 600,000 Methodists in Texas, of whom, approximately 36,000 are Negroes. Of the latter, almost 17,000 belong to the same conference area in which the new Huston-Tillotson College is located.[50]

Merger Consummated

The merging of Samuel Huston and Tillotson Colleges having been decided, Dr. Matthew S. Davage—the old mentor, sage and elder statesman—was called upon to consummate the merger in fact.

Dr. Davage had not only served previously for a period of three years as President of Samuel Huston College, but had subsequently served for four years as President of Rust College, seventeen years as President of Clark College, and twelve years as Associate

378

Secretary of the Board of Education, the Methodist Church. He retired from the latter position in 1952 and was chosen for his experience and wisdom to unite the two colleges in educational matrimony and to serve as the first President of the new college.

During the three years, 1952-1955, Dr. Davage was President, Samuel Huston College was relocated from its site on East Avenue between 11th and 12th Streets to the Tillotson College Campus, which had a larger acreage. The facilities were combined, and the Presidents of the former institutions respectively, became Vice Presidents of the new Huston-Tillotson College.

To succeed Dr. Davage in 1955, Dr. John J. Seabrook was elected President. Dr. Seabrook came to Huston-Tillotson from the Presidency of Claflin College, Orangeburg, South Carolina, where he had been President for ten years. During the ten years Dr. Seabrook was President of Huston-Tillotson, the college made good progress and moved to the stage of development that proved the success and wisdom of the merger.

When Dr. Seabrook retired from the Presidency in 1965, Dr. John T. King, an alumnus of Samuel Huston College, was elected President and is the present incumbent. Under his able administration and leadership, the constituencies and the two church bodies that give support can look to the future with great hope and confidence that Huston-Tillotson College will realize in abundance the dreams of the Founders and the long line of predecessors of Dr. King, and that the college will be recognized, even more than now, as one of the best small colleges in American higher education. In the few years Dr. King has been President, he has moved the college forward in pursuit of this objective.

REFERENCES AND NOTES

1. Minutes of the West Texas Annual Conference, January 22-26, 1874, pp. 26-27.
2. Minutes of the West Texas Annual Conference, January 20, 1876, p. 24.
3. Minutes of the West Texas Annual Conference, November 20, 1876, p. 11.
4. Manuscript by George O. Richardson, son of Reverend George W. Richardson, p. 1 (Original Document filed in the Library, Huston-Tillotson College).
5. *Ibid.*, p. 2.
6. *Ibid.*, pp. 3-4.
7. *Ibid.*, p. 5.
8. Minutes, West Texas Annual Conference, November 22, 1876, p. 19.
9. Minutes, West Texas Conference, November, 1876.
9a. Journal and Minutes, West Texas Annual Conference, November 29, 1876, pp. 20f.
9b. *Ibid.*, p. 21.
10. George O. Richardson, *op. cit.*, pp. 10-11.
10a. *Ibid.*, p. 16.
11. *Ibid.*, pp. 14-19.
12. Minutes, West Texas Conference, December 3, 1879.
13. Journal and Minutes, the Eighth Session, West Texas Conference, December 1-6, 1880, pp. 18f.
14. Freedmen's Aid Society, Fifteenth Annual Report, 1882, p. 6.
15. Minutes, West Texas Annual Conference, December 7-12, 1887, p. 16.
16. *The Christian Educator*, December-January, 1888-1889, p. 39.
17. Twenty-Second Annual Report, Freedman's Aid and Southern Education Society, July 1, 1889, p. 39.
18. Journal and Minutes, West Texas Annual Conference, February 7-8, 1889, pp. 19-20.
19. Minutes, West Texas Annual Conference, February 6-10, 1890, pp. 25-26.
20. Minutes, West Texas Annual Conference, December 16-21, 1891, pp. 49-50.
21. Minutes, West Texas Annual Conference, December 16-21,

1891, pp. 44ff: and Freedmen's Aid Society Report, July 1, 1891, p. 230.

22. *The Christian Educator*, December-January, 1900-1901, p. 30.

23. *The Christian Educator*, June-July, 1901, p. 70.

24. Catalog, Samuel Huston College, 1900-1901, p. 6.

25. Catalog, Samuel Huston College, 1901-1902, p. 7.

26. *The Christian Educator*, May, 1902, p. 3.

27. *The Christian Educator*, November, 1904, p. 5.

28. *The Christian Educator*, February, 1905, p. 9.

29. The Journal, General Conference, 1904, p. 865.

30. *The Christian Educator*, November, 1905, pp. 19ff.

31. *The Christian Educator*, May-August, 1908, p. 21.

32. *The Christian Educator*, February, 1911, p. 8.

33. *Ibid.*, p. 9.

34. *The Christian Educator*, May, 1912, p. 12.

35. *Ibid.*

36. *Ibid.*, p. 13f.

37. Samuel Huston College Catalog, 1900-1901.

38. *Ibid.*

38a. Annual Catalog, Samuel Huston College, 1901-1902, p. 20.

38b. *Ibid.*, p. 39.

39. Research Manuscript, by Mrs. C. A. Meeker, Section on Texas, p. 3.

40. *Ibid.*

41. *Ibid.*

42. *Ibid.*

43. *Ibid.*

44. *The Christian Educator*, February, 1917, p. 1.

44a. *The Christian Educator*, August, 1917, pp. 4-5.

45. Obituary of Karl Everett Downs, College Files.

46. Huston-Tillotson Bulletin, 1969-1970, p. 17.

47. Gammon Archives, Interdenominational Theological Center Library, Atlanta, Georgia.

48. *The Christian Educator*, May, 1924, p. 7.

49. Bulletin Catalog Edition, 1930-1931, p. 17.

50. Huston-Tillotson College Bulletin, 1952-1954, pp. 9-11.

CHAPTER 18

A BRIEF HISTORICAL SKETCH OF
MEHARRY MEDICAL COLLEGE

"Beside that muddy road there in the wilds of Kentucky was born Meharry Medical College. . . .Meharry's history. . . .did not begin in brick and mortar. Meharry's history, like the story of every other human achievement, began in that vague realm of mind, began in thought."[1]

These words by the second President of Meharry Medical College, Dr. John J. Mullowney, were inspired by a thrilling event out of which sprang the story of interest and philanthropy that not only gave Meharry Medical College its beginning and its name, but also, its life and a most significant part of its history.

Samuel Meharry was one of seven sons of Alexander and Jane Meharry. When Samuel grew to manhood he started a home of his own in Adams County, Ohio.

"One day he was hauling grist from a mill in Kentucky to his farm. He was miles from a town, and the road which he was traveling was rough and muddy. The wagon slipped over the edge of the road and was mired and, while he was trying to extricate the wagon, an old colored man came along and helped him. Night came on, and the colored man's cabin being near at hand, he invited Samuel Meharry to share his humble home. In the morning the two succeeded in getting the load out of the mire.

"This response or sympathy of the colored man so touched Samuel Meharry's heart that he resolved, if ever he were able, he would do something worthwhile to help the Negroes. On parting with his Negro friend he said: "I have no money to pay you now, but when I can I shall do something for your race."[2]

It was beside this muddy road where a little favor had found its way to a big heart, that an institution, Meharry Medical College, was born.

In 1875 a number of students of Central Tennessee College went to Dr. John Braden, President of the College, and asked him if he could not devise some plan by which the students could study medicine. Dr. Braden, not knowing of the incident on the Kentucky road, went to Reverend Samuel Meharry who was then living in Shawnee Mound, Indiana, and succeeded in interesting Reverend Meharry in the project for a medical course, and secured from him $500 with which to purchase the equipment which at that time was deemed necessary for a medical school.[3]

In 1876 Dr. R. S. Rust, secretary of the Freedmen's Aid Society, authorized Dr. Braden to employ Dr. George W. Hubbard to organize this rudimentary medical school as a department of Central Tennessee College.[4] Dr. Hubbard had spent a few years in Nashville during which time he had taught colored children and had taken medicine at Nashville University, later Vanderbilt University Medical School. He opened the Medical School at Central Tennessee College in 1876 with nine students.[5]

Dr. Hubbard stated that "In the latter part of 1875 while I was completing my medical course. . .Dr. Braden consulted me regarding the establishment of a medical department for Central Tennessee College, and after careful deliberation it was finally decided that I should organize and supervise the work. I secured the services of Dr. W. J. Sneed, who had served for four years as Surgeon General in the Confederate Army. He gave the preliminary instruction in dissecting in the basement of Old Tennessee Hall. . . .

"The first regular session was opened in October, 1876, and the entire faculty consisted of Dr. Sneed and myself. Eleven students were enrolled during the session."[6]

This was the beginning of a historic institution to provide training for Negroes in the field of medicine, and the initiation of the services of Dr. G. W. Hubbard, a former Union soldier, who for forty-five years served this institution, as dean for thirty-nine years, and as President for six years.

More About the Meharrys

Alexander and Jane Meharry migrated to the United States from the North of Ireland in the latter part of the 18th century. They landed at New York and after living there and in Pennsylvania a short time, floated down the Ohio River, landing at Lancaster, Adams County, Ohio. They located eight miles northwest of Lancaster in the midst of a dense forest where they lived a pioneer life, clearing the forest for farm land. While returning from a camp meeting Alexander was killed by a falling tree, leaving his wife with eight children, one girl and seven boys.[7]

In early manhood the boys went to Indiana and Illinois, where they bought land at low cost, and soon had comfortable homes of their own. By industry and economy they amassed what was in those days a small fortune. They were liberal in their contributions to religious and other worthy causes.[8]

384

After the first gift of $500 by Samuel Meharry for the Medical School, Dr. Braden approached other brothers of the Meharry family in the interest of this enterprise. The continued interest of Reverend Samuel Meharry stimulated responses on the part of four other brothers, Alexander, Hugh, David, and Jesse, who together contributed ultimately a little over $30,000.[9]

The Reverend Samuel Meharry visited Nashville a short time before his demise, along with other brothers, and saw a beautiful knoll near the Central Tennessee College campus. He called the attention of the secretary of the F.A.S. to this appropriate site and expressed his desire for its purchase, and gave $1,000 toward it. Mrs. Meharry, his wife, increased the gift to $1,700.[10] A new building was erected on the site. Samuel Meharry gave $2,000; David donated a large tract of land; Jesse also contributed; and Hugh, the oldest brother, endowed a professorship in the literary department of the College, by a gift of a farm valued at $10,000.[11]

Because of the interest and generosity of the Meharry Family the medical school was named The Meharry Medical School in honor of five brothers: Hugh, Jesse, David, Alexander, and Samuel.[12]

This medical school made rapid progress. In the brief period of some eight or nine years it had furnished one half of the regularly educated physicians then practicing in the South.[13] Dr. George W. Hubbard, Dean of Meharry Medical College, 1896, prepared a list, with dates of founding, of other Medical Schools in the South preparing Negro doctors, giving data on graduates by schools and the locations of the respective school graduates by states:

SUMMARY IN SOUTHERN STATES

	Alabama	Arkansas	Florida	Georgia	Kentucky	Louisiana	Mississippi	Missouri	North Carolina	South Carolina	Tennessee	Texas	Virginia	West Virginia	Total
Meharry Medical College .	5	17	7	19	16	8	8	17	2	5	51	55	...	...	210
Howard University	3		1	9	9	2	...	2	2	11	1	2	12	...	54
Leonard Medical School .	1	2	2	7	...	...	...	...	19	9	...	...	9	2	51
New Orleans University ..	...	...	...	...	...	13	...	...	...	...	...	6	...	...	19
Louisville National	...	...	...	...	20	...	1	...	...	...	2	1	...	...	24
Other Colleges	4	3	1	4	8	2	...	...	...	1	1	1	2	...	27
Total	13	22	11	39	53	25	9	19	23	26	55	65	23	2	385

"The Medical Department of Howard University, Washington, D.C., was established in 1868, and it has had 211 white and 229 colored graduates.

"Meharry Medical College is the Medical Department of Central Tennessee College, Nashville, Tennessee. It was opened in 1876, and has had 263 graduates. It is under the care of the Freedmen's Aid and Southern Education Society of the Methodist Episcopal Church.

"Leonard Medical School, of Shaw University, Raleigh, North Carolina, was established in 1882, and has had 63 graduates. It is supported by the American Baptist Home Mission Society.

"The Louisville National Medical College was opened in 1888. It has 36 graduates.

"The Medical Department of New Orleans University was organized in 1889. Eighteen young men have received diplomas from this department. It is under the care of the same Society as the Meharry Medical College.

"The Medical Department of Knoxville College was opened in November, 1895.

"The total number of colored physicians who have graduated from the above mentioned institutions is 609.
According to the census of 1890 these fourteen states contained a colored population of 6,578,537, which comprises eighty-eight per cent of all the colored people in the United States.

"The above summary shows the great work accomplished by our own Meharry Medical College. Out of the 385 Negro physicians in the midst of 6,578,537 colored people in these fourteen states named, 210 have graduated from Meharry."[14]

In testimony of the quality of work done by the College, it was reported that:

"The Meharry Medical College has graduated a Negro physician, who passed the white State Board of Examination in Alabama, with nearly one hundred white candidates, and his certificate giving him the right to practice in the State was granted on the basis of the same examination the others were compelled to pass. He was credited with having passed the best examination of all."[15]

This was a demonstration of the determination expressed by Dean Hubbard in 1879, that "no one shall receive a diploma of graduation without the attainments and ability essential to reflect honor upon the degree and the college that confers it."

386

Schools of Dentistry and Pharmacy

In October, 1886, the School of Dentistry was organized. Dr. W. H. Morgan, M.D. and D.D.S., dean of the Dental Department of Vanderbilt University, gave valuable counsel and assistance, and hearty sympathy in the work of establishing and operating this department.[16]

A school of pharmacy was opened in October, 1889, with five young men pursuing the course.[17]

On October 20, 1889 the Meharry Dental and Pharmaceutical building was dedicated. The cost of the building was about $6,500, nearly all of the cost being contributed by the Meharry family and friends.[18] Dr. R. S. Rust and Reverend J. C. Hartzell of the Freedmen's Aid and Southern Education Society, and Dr. A. G. Haygood, General Agent of the John F. Slater Fund were most cooperative and helpful in these developments.[19]

The growth of Meharry Medical School, with its departments of dentistry and pharmacy, becomes more important when it is noted that this was the first medical school established in the deep South for the education of Negro physicians, and that the doors of many northern medical colleges were closed to Negro students. Fifteen years after its opening, Meharry had graduated more than one-half of the educated Negro physicians in the Southern and Southwestern states.[20]

In recognition of the need for trained nurses, a nurse-training school was organized during the school year 1900-1901, with an enrollment of eight. Two courses of study were set up for nurses; one, a non-professional course of two years; and the second, a three-year professional course.[21]

Mercy Hospital was erected during the school year 1901-1902, under the management of the faculty.[22]

In 1900 the name of Central Tennessee College was changed to Walden University. Meharry Medical School continued as one of the federated schools of the University. In this same year the University sustained a great loss in the death of President John Braden. The medical school continued to move forward under the supervision of Dean George W. Hubbard.

In 1904 the Meharry Auditorium was built with a seating capacity of 1,000 persons. The building, a brick structure with stone foundation, containing laboratories in the basement, classrooms on the third floor, and auditorium on the second floor, was built largely by Negro skill and labor, and was valued at $1,500.[23]

With the steady growth of Meharry Medical School, Mercy Hospital became inadequate and had to be replaced. A new

387

hospital, which was named the George W. Hubbard Hospital, erection of which was begun in 1911-1912, was not completed until 1916, with rooms to accommodate seventy-five patients. The cost of the hospital was $43,000. Andrew Carnegie gave the last $10,000 on the cost of the hospital.[24]

New Charter: Meharry Medical College

From its beginning in 1876 to 1915 Meharry had been one of the federated schools of Central Tennessee College and (after 1900) Walden University, operating under the charter of the University. Because of the declining operating finances of the medical school and the increasing pressure of standardization requirements by the American Medical Association, changes had to be made. The Carnegie and Rockefeller Foundations indicated interest in making grants to build up the endowment of the Medical School. Recalling the experience of the Methodist Episcopal Church, South, there in Nashville, with the same two Foundations in the case of the Vanderbilt University, and the loss of the University to the church, the Board of Managers of the Freedmen's Aid Society was reluctant to accept the terms of the proposed new charter for Meharry Medical College. The contention of a number of the members of the Board of Managers was that Meharry Medical College was a Methodist institution and in no wise should they lose control "for the sake of a few thousand, or many thousand dollars."[25]

Bishop McConnell shaped the action of the Board of Managers by favoring the grants by the Foundations on the ground that a medical school was of a special technical character involving no ethical or religious principle that would be jeopardized by the transfer under a new charter. He stated further that in the interest of this special technical school which the church could not support as it should be supported, and whose expenses would pile up with each succeeding year, he saw no other way than to adapt the charter to the requirements of the Foundations.[26]

The Board of Managers of the Freedmen's Aid Society came to agreement on the new charter, and on the date of September 30, 1915, application was filed with the clerk of the county court, Davidson County, State of Tennessee, for a separate charter of incorporation in the name of Meharry Medical College. The new charter was granted October 13, 1915.[27] The incorporation of Meharry Medical College, under a new and separate charter was intended to make the college more secure financially and to provide for improvement of the quality of its programs and services and the expansion of its physical facilities.

The Carnegie and Rockefeller Foundations in the interest of building up the endowment offered grants of $150,000 each, on condition that the Freedmen's Aid Society, the Board of Trustees of Meharry Medical College, and friends of the college would raise $200,000 additional for endowment.[28]

Dr. George W. Hubbard, President

For thirty-nine years, to 1915, with genius, devotion, dedication, and leadership acumen, the founder of the Meharry Medical College, Dr. George W. Hubbard, as Dean, had guided it through difficult years to phenomenal development and high professional standing. Through investment of his life for nearly forty years, he had already reared in Meharry Medical College a lasting monument to himself. It would have been incredible to think of anyone else at that time for the first President of Meharry.

On October 19, 1916, educators and other dignitaries from far and near assembled in the Meharry Auditorium to witness the inauguration of Dr. George Whipple Hubbard as President of Meharry Medical College.

On this occasion it was said: "Think of a man being made President of an institution after having served as Dean for forty years. It is significant that after all these years Dr. Hubbard should be asked to serve the institution as its first President. It is an honor to Meharry for him, at this time, to accept the position."[29]

On the occasion of his inauguration Dr. Hubbard gave a review of the history of Meharry Medical College from its founding October, 1876, referring to Dr. W. J. Sneed who joined him as the first two faculty members of the Medical School, and to the philanthropy of the five Meharry brothers. He pointed to the more than five hundred students then enrolled in medicine, dentistry, pharmacy, and nurse training, and to Meharry's two thousand graduates practicing medicine all over the United States, and some having gone as missionaries to "dark Africa."[30] The alumni of Meharry presented $10,000 to be expended for an anatomical hall.[31] The inaugural occasion marked a great day for Meharry, with prospect of a bright future.

Half Million Dollar Campaign

Immediate efforts were begun to consummate the raising of a half million dollars as endowment for Meharry Medical College. To meet the conditional grants of $150,000 each from the Carnegie and Rockefeller Foundations, an additional $200,000 had to be raised by the Freedmen's Aid Society to make a total of $500,000 endowment for Meharry.

The conditional grants from the Carnegie and Rockefeller Foundations were claimed. The $200,000 contributed by the Board of Education for Negroes (formerly the Freedmen's Aid Society) was made possible because of increased income of that Board and the million dollars that came to the Board through the Centenary Movement.[32] The successful achievement of more than a half million dollars for endowment for Meharry Medical College was the crowning accomplishment of President Hubbard in his long career at this institution.

President Hubbard Retires

On February 1, 1921, Doctor Hubbard, at his own request, was retired from the active Presidency, and was made President Emeritus of the College by the Board of Trustees.[33] At a meeting held in Cincinnati, Ohio, April 26, 1921, the officers and members of the Board of Education for Negroes, of the Methodist Episcopal Church with great enthusiasm unanimously adopted resolutions expressing their appreciation of the life and distinguished services of George Whipple Hubbard, who for forty-five years was Dean and President of Meharry Medical College. In part they said:

"Dr. Hubbard is a devout Christian, and a firm believer in God and in His plans for the redemption of mankind. He has no race prejudice. After emancipation he saw the appalling need of the American Negro for racial leadership in every profession, and consecrated his life to his chosen field. No financial embarrassment, or criticism or intrigues incident to racial prejudice, or the burdens and problems of a complicated administration, could dim his vision or lessen his faith. As a financier he never went beyond his income. He commanded the confidence and support of this Board and of the whole church, and also of the great educational organizations interested in the training of the Negro. He saw Meharry Medical College, to which he had given nearly a half century of his life, develop until it had property worth $250,000, and a permanent endowment of $560,000.[34]

"The Negro race is the debtor, and the South acknowledges his work, and the nation has been blessed by his full measure of service.

"He began his work in ignominy and ostracism, and sometimes suspicion, in a field untried and with an equipment of an irreducible minimum, but lived to see his work recognized

390

as a national asset.

The name of George Whipple Hubbard will be enrolled among the great benefactors of his fellow men, and will be an inspiration to future generations."[3][5]

The alumni raised the money for the building of a beautiful modern home in which Doctor Hubbard and his beloved wife could spend their closing days. The Carnegie Foundation for the Advancement of Teaching granted him a life pension with an annual allowance of $1,600.[3][6]

Meharry's New President: Dr. John J. Mullowney

To succeed the venerable Dr. Hubbard, Dr. John J. Mullowney was elected second president of Meharry Medical College. Dr. Mullowney, aged forty-two and a native of England, came to the Presidency of Meharry from Girard College where he had been Head of the Department of Science and Professor of Chemistry and Biology.

Dr. Mullowney graduated from Phillips Exeter Academy and pursued the medical course at the Medical Department of the University of Pennsylvania. While pursuing his medical course he became interested in Christian Missions, and after graduating, went to China, served three and a half years in the Hopkins Memorial Hospital in Peking, and taught in the North China Union Medical College. For his work in helping to stay the ravages of an outbreak of bubonic plague and for other services with the Red Cross, the Chinese Republic awarded him appropriate certificates and medals.[3][7]

Returning to America, Dr. Mullowney took special training in Public Health and Preventive Medicine. He held important positions in the health departments of Philadelphia and the State of Pennsylvania from which he assumed a professorship at Girard College. Dr. Mullowney was considered to be especially well equipped for administrative leadership at Meharry Medical College.

Dr. Mullowney took hold of Meharry with administrative vigor. He began immediately to further improve the quality of medical education to meet standards required for full and continued recognition. Early in his administration there were several significant developments. Meharry was classified as an "A" institution by the Council on Medical Education and Hospitals of the American Medical Association.[3][8]

This came about through support by The Board of Education for Negroes, the General Education Board, and the Carnegie Corporation. The endowment was brought up to $590,050.[3][9]

391

Five-year appropriation commitments were made by the Board of Education for Negroes and the General Education Board, to bring the total annual income to $50,000, exclusive of student fees.[40] The five-year commitments were made pending the securing of another half-million dollars for endowment.

Of the second half million dollars for endowment the Alumni had subscribed $200,000. The General Education Board had made a grant of $89,000 for the enlargement of Hubbard Hospital. A fourth floor was added to the hospital increasing the capacity from seventy-five to 150 beds, and to an emergency service of 175.[41]

In 1922, in order to relieve the great pressure of need by Meharry Medical College for additional buildings and campus, the Board of Managers, after purchasing a new site for Walden College, transferred in fee simple the old Walden College property to Meharry Medical College.[42] This transaction represented a $100,000 gift to Meharry. The total contribution of the Board of Education for Negroes to Meharry for endowment and expansion totaled $375,000.[43]

Semi-Centennial of Meharry Medical College

The year 1926 marked a half-century milestone in the history of Meharry Medical College. The three men, Dr. John Braden, Dr. George W. Hubbard, and Dr. W. J. Sneed, who were the founders of Meharry, had passed on from labor to their reward and eternal rest. There was gratifying evidence that their labors had prospered and had borne abundant fruit. This half-century enterprise had grown to Meharry Medical College with 700 students; physical plant and equipment valued at a quarter of a million dollars, endowment of three quarters of a million dollars; and over four thousand graduates—doctors, dentists, pharmacists, and trained nurses.

The semi-centennial was observed with a program of five days—October 20-24, 1926—with the principal and closing address being delivered by Bishop Thomas Nicholson, a member of the Board of Trustees of the College, Sunday morning, October 24. The celebration was a part of a campaign to raise a quarter of a million dollars for the endowment of the College. The campaign money was to have been raised primarily from the Alumni. Nearly $100,000 had been contributed by the Alumni by the close of the five-days celebration.[44] In addition, one graduate, Dr. Anderson of Dallas, Texas, gave $12,000 for the erection of a building, and contributed liberally toward the endowment.[45]

The most gratifying characterization of the College at the time

392

of this celebration was the thousands of graduates serving human needs primarily in the south, but also in all sections of the nation.

During the 1920's Meharry's continued expansion and growth, coupled with the obsolescence of its early plant and facilities, made it necessary that a new plant be built on a more advantageous site.[46] The present site was acquired, and in 1932 Meharry was relocated,[47] in close proximity to Fisk University, cooperation between the two institutions being anticipated. This move was made possible through grants totaling $2,000,000, mainly from the General Education Board, but also from the Harkness, the Julius Rosenwald, and the Eastman Foundations.[48]

Development of Meharry Medical College on the new site was well on the way when Doctor Mullowney retired from the Presidency[49] in 1938. He had given seventeen years of fruitful administrative leadership to this institution.

Dr. Edward L. Turner Elected President

To succeed Dr. Mullowney, Dr. Edward L. Turner was elected President of Meharry Medical College in 1938.[50] He came to the Presidency from the Deanship of Meharry, in which position he had given academic guidance and development for a number of years. For a period of six years Dr. Turner served as President and made notable contributions to the progress of Meharry. His Presidency ended in 1944.[51]

Dr. M. Don Clawson, President

In 1944 Dr. M. Don Clawson was elected President of Meharry, to succeed Dr. Turner.[52] He, like Dr. Turner, served six years as President, his administration ending in 1950.

Dr. Harold D. West

During two periods, 1950-1952 and 1966-1968, Meharry had no President.[53] In 1952 Dr. Harold D. West was elected President and served in this capacity of administrative leadership fourteen years, his tenure as President ending in 1966.[54]

Dr. West entered upon a teaching tenure at Meharry in 1927. As a teacher for twenty-five years in the field of biochemistry holding the B.S., M.S. and Ph.D. degrees from the University of Illinois, his performance was brilliant. As a teacher and President, for thirty-nine years Dr. West was connected with Meharry and contributed in a very large measure to this institution during this period of almost four decades of significant growth and development on the present site. His continued activity, after retirement, as research chemist, adds much to the distinction of this outstanding scholar and to Meharry Medical College which he served so long and so well.

A Period of Exceptional Growth

From the time of the relocation of Meharry Medical College to its present site in 1932 to 1970, this institution has experienced phenomenal growth.[55] In 1932 there were 94 faculty members; in 1970 there were 338. The plant value in 1932 was $2,000,000; in 1970 it was $9,200,000. The endowment in 1932 was $750,000; in 1970 it was $7,200,000. In programs and extended services the growth has been even greater than the growth in the physical aspects of the institution.

Dr. Lloyd Charles Elam, President

In 1968 Dr. Lloyd C. Elam was elected President of Meharry Medical College. He not only is the successor to Dr. Harold D. West, but he follows in the train of a long succession of distinguished Presidents of Meharry. His is a goodly and great heritage. The confidence that he will add significantly to that heritage has already been confirmed by the quality of his administration during the short time he has been in office.

The hope for Meharry in the years immediately ahead is expressed in the following statement about Dr. Elam and the task to which he has chosen to dedicate his talents:

Doors swing open to wider vistas of greatness with the inauguration of Dr. Lloyd Charles Elam as president of Meharry Medical College, and with his announcement of an extensive college expansion program that will cost more than $50 million. . . .

Dr. Elam comes to his new post from within the administration, where he has been interim Dean of the School of Medicine since 1966. He came to Meharry to develop the Department of Psychiatry, which he organized in 1961. Since its inception, the department has grown to meet the challenges of modern psychiatry.

Dr. Elam is known and respected nationally as a brilliant psychiatrist. Thirty-nine years old and a native of Arkansas, Dr. Elam received his Bachelor of Science degree from Roosevelt University in Chicago in 1950. And in 1957 he was granted his

394

Doctor of Medicine degree from the University of Washington in Seattle.

The new President comes to Meharry in a time of great social change. It is a period of change that touches not only economic and academic circles, but also affects the hearts and minds of the peoples of the world. He comes strong in faith and with the determination to develop Meharry into a greater institution of learning, to strengthen and maintain Meharry's position as the nation's leader in the field of innovative community medicine, and to expand its sphere of influence. He comes with vision and an understanding of human behavior equaled by few men.[56]

REFERENCES AND NOTES

1. *The Christian Educator*, February, 1931, p. 4.
2. *Ibid.*
3. *Ibid.*, November, 1926, p. 3.
4. *Ibid.*, February, 1931, p. 5.
5. *Ibid.*
6. *Ibid.*, November, 1926, p. 4.
7. *Ibid.*
8. *Ibid.*, p. 5.
9. *Ibid.*, February, 1931, p. 5.
10. Report, FAS, 1879, p. 9.
11. *Ibid.*
12. *The Christian Educator*, November, 1926, p. 4.
13. Report, FAS, 1885, p. 8
14. *The Christian Educator*, Feb., Mar., 1896, p. 36.
15. *Ibid.*, April, 1894, p. 118.
16. *Ibid.*, April, 1890, p. 110.
17. *Ibid.*, p. 111.
18. *Ibid.*, January, 1890, p. 42
19. *Ibid.*, April, 1890, p. 112.
20. *Ibid*, p. 107.
21. Central Tennessee College Catalog, p. 115.
22. *Ibid.*, 1901—1902.
23. Walden University Catalog, 1905, p. 23.
24. *Ibid.*, 1911—12, p. 25; and *The Christian Educator*, Nov., 1916, p. 4.
25. *The Christian Educator*, Nov., 1914, p. 5.
26. *Ibid.*
27. Corporation Record Book O. 7, page 248, State of Tennessee at the Department in the City of Nashville.
28. *The Christian Educator*, May, 1919, p. 1.
29. *Ibid.*, November, 1916, p. 3.
30. *Ibid.*, p. 4.
31. *Ibid.*
32. *Ibid.*, February, 1921, p. 1.
33. *Ibid.*, August, 1921, p. 7.
34. *Ibid.*
35. *Ibid.*
36. *Ibid.*
36a. *Ibid.*
37. *Ibid.*, February, 1921, p. 2.
38. *Ibid.*, May, 1924, p. 4.
39. *Ibid.*

40. *Ibid.*
41. *Ibid.*
42. *Ibid.*, pp. 4f.
43. *Ibid.*, p. 5.
44. *Ibid.*, November, 1926, p. 3.
45. *Ibid.*
46. Information supplied by Dr. Harold D. West, former teacher, President (1952-1966), and currently engaged in research at the College.
47. *Ibid.*
48. *Ibid.*
49. *Ibid.*
50. *Ibid.*
51. *Ibid.*
52. *Ibid.*
53. *Ibid.*
54. *Ibid.*
55. *Ibid.*
56. *Opening New Doors to Greatness with Meharry Medical College*, 1969.

CHAPTER 19

A BRIEF HISTORICAL SKETCH OF
MORRISTOWN NORMAL AND INDUSTRIAL COLLEGE

Morristown (Tennessee) Junior College was founded and chartered in 1881. The name the school carried for the longest period of time was "Morristown Normal and Industrial College." The name under which it was founded was "Morristown Seminary."

At the request of Bishop Henry W. Warren and W. C. Graves, Dr. Judson S. Hill organized this school for the education of colored youth, with a promise on the part of the Bishop of $500 to pay his own salary and that of any other helpers he might need.[1]

The building in which Morristown Seminary was opened was an old Baptist Church, a frame building erected in 1830. The building was converted into a slave market before the Civil War, and during the War was used as a hospital by Bragg and Longstreet of the Confederate Forces, and afterwards by Burnside of the Federal Forces.[2]

One of the first to enter was a boy named Andrew Fulton who, with his mother, had been sold for $1,400. After graduation, in 1887, Andrew was employed as a teacher.[3] He was a teacher at this institution more than a quarter of a century. Another early student at the seminary was a boy who was sold as a slave, from this slave market, along with a calf. He graduated and became a Presiding Elder.[4]

The Freedmen's Aid and Southern Education Society reported that Morristown Seminary was situated in a population of 250,000, and there was only one other school of the same grade within a radius of 300 miles.[5]

In 1891, ten years after the school had its beginning, there was an enrollment of 306 students, with eight teachers. The school was greatly overcrowded. In one room, thirty by forty feet, five, and often six, classes were reciting at one and the same time, and every desk was occupied by three students.[6] Despite the overcrowded situation and the dilapidated condition of the building, the students received good

399

preparation. In 1886 it was made one of the normal schools for Tennessee so that its graduates could teach in any public school of the State without any further examination.[7]

Morristown Seminary was located within the bounds of the East Tennessee Annual Conference, with which it was closely related from its founding. In its session of 1884 the Conference resolved to thank Bishop Warren, the Presiding Bishop, and Rev. R. S. Rust, for the great interest in the welfare of Morristown Seminary. This year (1884) a class was begun and conducted by the Seminary for the study of the books in the course of study for traveling preachers of the East Tennessee and other conferences.[8]

In 1888 the name was changed to Morristown Normal Academy. In 1889 additional land was purchased and plans made for the erection of a new three-story brick dormitory, to cost $20,000.[9] Rev. J. C. Hartzell pledged $5,000.[10] In this same year the Woman's Home Missionary Society laid plans for the erection of an industrial Home for Girls, to be ready for occupancy early in 1890.[11]

As early as 1896 some cooperative arrangements were worked out between Morristown Academy and the City of Morristown. An arrangement was made for the school to have one thousand gallons of water daily, for which the Freedmen's Aid Society deeded to the City the spring on the school property.[12]

From the beginning President Hill, with tremendous sacrifice and hard work, gave great leadership to this institution.

At the end of the century Dr. Buckley, editor of *The Christian Advocate*, visited Morristown. In ascertaining how the school kept going on the meager allowance of $2,500 appropriated by the Freedmen's Aid and Southern Education Society, he said:

"I learned that the teachers are paid from $160 to $300 each, exclusive of the salary of Dr. Hill, which is small; and what is paid over and above this $2,500 for new buildings, land, etc., has been and must be raised by the President. At the present time, all told, there is a debt of only $6,000 on the property; $1,300 of this is in the salaries of teachers."[13]

In 1900, Crary Hall, the foundation having stood ten years, 1890 to 1900, was completed at a cost of $21,750.[14] This building was made possible through a bequest of $15,000 from Mrs. B. F. Crary, of Binghamton, N. Y. Ten thousand two hundred and fifty dollars had been given by herself and husband before her death, making a total of $25,250.[15] Mr. Crary, an invalid for some time, passed away. He was soon followed by his devoted and consecrated widow who by will bequeathed $15,000 for the completion and furnishing of the "handsome and stately dormitory building of one hundred rooms, bearing the honored name Crary."[16]

Morristown Normal Academy was another one of the Freedmen's Aid institutions where the Woman's Home Missionary Society developed a cooperating interest. In 1888, through the influence of the President, Mrs. General Fisk, and other friends in New Jersey, members of the Woman's Home Missionary Society, became interested, and soon the New Jersey Industrial Home for Girls was built, at a cost of $8,000 for building and furniture.[17] The work in domestic science, begun in Crary Hall in 1903, was transferred to the new home.

Through the incessant and fruitful efforts of President Hill and his ingenious ability to plan and convince people of the worthwhileness of his cause, the institution prospered and grew through the gifts of many friends and agencies. About the same time Crary Hall was completed, a large residence was being built near the campus by a gentleman in Ohio. This property value totaled $17,000, but because of difficulty in financing, it was purchased by Morristown Normal Academy for $4,000.[18]

In 1911 funds were secured for a much needed administration and classroom building. A generous friend gave $10,000 to match the same amount given by Mr. Andrew Carnegie on condition that his gift be matched.[19] The clay for the brick and rock for the lime, with a large quantity of the wood for burning, was taken from the grounds belonging to the school.[20] At this time the value of the grounds and buildings amounted to more than $100,000.[21]

In 1912 it was pointed out that "in the early years of the school much prejudice existed in the community against the school, and the workers were compelled to endure ostracism; but this has gradually but surely given way, so that today no other school in the entire South stands higher in the good esteem of the white people than does this school."[22]

For the school year 1911-1912 the enrollment was 326, and the faculty numbered twenty-two. At that time and for many years thereafter Morristown Normal and Industrial School did the public school work for the colored people of the City of Morristown, the City paying a stipulated sum for this service.[23] This is another instance of the good relationship of Morristown Normal and Industrial School with the City and the community, and the high respect for President Hill.

President Hill was deeply interested in the development of

the physical plant, but he was even more interested in the students. Through his generosity many students were given assistance, although he had no appropriation for such relief. The following account of a poor student graphically illustrates a condition that might have been found among many students, and the deep concern of President Hill:

About two months ago there came a young man to our school, asking admittance. He had rented a very poor cabin just outside of our gate, for which he paid five dollars in advance; then he bought books, for which he paid seven dollars; then he must fit up some kind of a place for sleeping, and furnish a skillet for cooking; wood for the old fireplace was also called for, and last, but surely not least, the boy must have something for food, and for this necessity, he provided himself with some corn-meal and one-half of a pig's jaw, or jowl, I think it is called.

At the end of two months he came to Mr. Hill, saying, "I don't know what in the world to do; I have no money and fear I must leave school unless you can help me out."

"How much will you need?" asked Mr. Hill.

"Well, sir, I think four dollars will take me through three months," was the reply.

And then, by asking questions, Mr. Hill found that he had sixteen dollars when he came here, and that during the sixty days of his stay he had nothing to eat but the meal and the jowl and cold water.

Once he came to the matron for a little oil, for his lamp had failed him at midnight, and he must study his lessons "tonight" for tomorrow, adding, "I can't buy just now."

You can well understand that Mr. Hill's large heart would not let such a boy go.[24]

The total cost for a full year was only fifteen dollars,[25] including room, board, tuition and fees, but many students were unable to take advantage of an education even at such a reasonable cost. Most of the students at Morristown, and many who were never fortunate enough to reach the campus, yearned for an education and were willing to make unbelievable sacrifices for the opportunity of being in school, as the following two cases indicate:

Among the pathetic stories that Dr. Hill tells of his historic students is that of one who walked eighty-nine miles from

402

Nashville, [sic]* and had ten dollars with which to go through school. He rented a room in an old hovel, and lived in a simple way, making his own bedstead, table, and chairs. He lived on $3.50 from December 1st to March 12th. He made no complaint. Only by questioning him did Dr. Hill find out that he had been living on hog's jowl, Irish potatoes and corn-meal. He stood among the first in his class, and now is an earnest worker among his people. Another boy made a journey of two hundred and forty miles on foot in order to get to this Christian school, which, under the inspiring leadership of Dr. Hill, has gained a wide reputation throughout the South.[26]

With the strengthening of the faculty and the academic program, and also the industrial work, late in the 1890's the name of the school was changed to the Morristown Normal and Industrial College.

New developments took place in 1917 which gave considerable advancement to the college.

After long and arduous work the Department of Agriculture has been opened. Through the generosity of Mr. Frank B. Wallace a farm of three hundred acres has been purchased near Morristown. Here will be taught to the students everything connected with intensive and scientific farming. The students are being taught how to judge the soil, exactly what will best grow on particular soil, and how to make the soil yield a maximum crop. This phase of education of the Negro is meeting with great approval, as it is the intention of the college to make this a model farm, and plans are under way to hold farmers' meetings. It will be a help not only to the student body, but the whole community, both white and colored.[27]

The other department started this year is home and school gardening. . .Not only will they learn how to beautify their surroundings in a pleasing, uplifting way, but will learn the secrets of successful truck-gardening. In fact, they are being taught how to utilize the smallest plot of ground so that it will bring material results.[28]

In 1923 the main building at Morristown Normal and Industrial College was destroyed by fire. The buildings erected after the fire disaster provided a much better plant, as reported in 1924.

During the quadrennium plans, specifications, and contracts

*Probably Asheville

403

were let for three new buildings at Morristown Normal and Industrial College, at Morristown, Tenn., to take the place of the main building destroyed by fire. This main building contained dormitories, classrooms, with dining-room and kitchen. A dormitory for boys, Wallace Hall, and a dormitory for girls, Crary Hall, with the dining-room and kitchen, Kenwood Hall, located between these two buildings, far enough apart so that a fire originating in one may not necessarily destroy the other, and yet connected together by covered passageways, are about finished and will be used during the current school year. This whole outfit, including furnishings cost $175,000, $125,000 of which is provided by the Board, $25,000 from the fire insurance, and the balance collected by Dr. Hill from friends of the institution. The City of Morristown contributes $10,000 toward these buildings, in view of the fact that the institution does the school work for the Negro children of that city. With these new buildings finished and occupied, this school has one of the most complete and up-to-date plants anywhere in the South.[29]

Great credit is due Dr. Judson S. Hill who was and is the first President of the institution, now closing more than forty-three years of service as President.[30]

By 1927 the buildings, equipment, and land at Morristown Normal and Industrial College had reached a value of $265,000.[31]

The year 1924 was Dr. Hill's forty-third year at the helm of Morristown Normal and Industrial College. By this time he was beginning to feel the weight of the stupendous load he was carrying, and had carried for more than four decades.

John Zedler was transferred from the deanship at Clark University, Atlanta, Ga., to the deanship of Morristown Normal and Industrial College. Dr. Hill felt the need of a man capable of taking the entire burden of the local administration from his shoulders. Dean Zedler he found to be the man.[32] Dean Zedler, a very able educator, was a tower of strength as the academic administrator and assistant to Dr. Hill. Unfortunately Dean Zedler's administrative tenure was cut short by his death April 3, 1927.[33]

In the Fall of 1928, Dr. Hill, approaching his 74th birthday, entered upon his 47th year as President of Morristown Normal and Industrial College. His accomplishments were little less than miraculous. Eight well-constructed buildings dotted the campus. Three hundred acres of land were the institution's holdings, and a plant valued at $500,000.[34]

Professor Miller W. Boyd, a graduate of Morristown Normal and Industrial College and a protégé and great admirer, said this of Dr. Hill in appreciation of this great personality:

Although President Hill is approaching his seventy-fourth birthday he lets neither age, weather nor his own misfortunes deter him from the labor he feels necessary for the promotion of the interests of the school. His greatest joy seems to be in pointing out the successful men and women who have been able to succeed in life's by-ways because they found here in his school the opportunity to be started upon the right road. This without doubt is his greatest achievement—namely, affording Negro boys and girls the opportunity to discover their resident powers. The grandeur of the physical plant wanes in significance when compared to the unfettering of minds and the elevation of souls. Thus the sacrifices of President Hill can never be measured in dollars and cents but only in terms of humanity.[35]

In 1931 Dr. Judson S. Hill passed away. He spent a half century in the East Tennessee Conference giving leadership and at Morristown Normal and Industrial College laboring to build an institution which indeed became the lengthened shadow of this great man.

At the Annual Session of the East Tennessee Conference September 29 to October 4, 1931, the Rev. L. N. Hamilton, speaking for the Conference paid tribute to the late Dr. Hill in a eulogy, excerpts from which follow:

I would not close this address on the part of the Conference, without referring to the fact that this is the first official meeting of our entire Conference, when we have been without the presence and guiding spirit of Dr. Hill. He was the accepted leader of this body. No great or important decisions were ever made by us without first consulting him. . . .He came among us as a brother of his own volition; once having chosen us, we were never cast aside.

* * *

. . . .in speaking words of praise in his memory, we pay a tribute to ourselves. How poor some of us would have been without him.

Dr. Hill came into the Southland in the midst of the reconstruction era,. . .when the country needed men of pride, of principle and courage, no man with a spaghetti backbone could have carried on as he did. . . .Dr. Hill stood firm; he was a

405

man of superb courage; he was one that reduced passion to common sense; who tempered judgment with mercy, who mastered impulse with patience, and one who relied upon God for guidance and comfort. Beneath his mild manners was a determination that could not be shaken.

Behind his personal restraint lay a reserve of will-power and courage that has seldom if ever been equalled. . . .Dr. Hill was not an individual in the sense that we usually speak; he was an institution; he was a versatile man, an artist. . . .His boundless sympathy extended to all created things, his interests went to the root of every human problem. It was as much his nature to befriend everyone as it was to sponsor every righteous cause.

* * *

. . .He came. . .simple in speech, plain in manner, straightforward in action, tender as a child, fearless as a hero, humble and lowly, he came to speak and to act. The hero never feels like one; greatness is unconscious, so is goodness. I do not believe that Dr. Hill spent five minutes of his whole life feeling like a great man.

. . .In what spirit did he meet the troubles and trials of everyday life? He never complained; you never knew what burdens were on his heart; he was sympathetic, easily approached, people were instinctively drawn to him, his mind was always open to their aspirations, his hand outstretched to their aid, his voice outspoken for their rights. . . .

Dr. Hill died a poor man so far as money and property was concerned. . . .But in honor, integrity and brains he was a millionaire.[36]

Reverend E. C. Paustian, President

After the passing of Dr. Hill in 1931, Dean Ralph D. Minard was placed in charge of the college until a new President could be elected. In 1932 the Rev. E. C. Paustian was made President as successor to Dr. Hill. Rev. Paustian served as President four years. This was in the midst of the great depression of the 1930's. It was most difficult to even keep the college open under the trying financial pressures. Efforts were made to use the farm land to relieve the financial pressure. Help came from dairy products and other produce such as corn, greens, potatoes, etc. The farm gave opportunity for a number of students to earn their expenses at the college.

406

Dr. John W. Haywood, President

In 1936 Dr. John W. Haywood became the third President of Morristown Normal and Industrial College. He had the distinction of being the first Negro to serve the college as President. Dr. Haywood was eminently prepared to give leadership as President. A graduate of Lincoln University (Pa.) with the B.A. degree, he also held the A.M., S.T.B., and S.T.D. degrees from the same institution, and the D.D. degree from Gammon Theological Seminary. He had been a pastor and was an eloquent preacher and speaker. Dr. Haywood had served as Professor of Greek and Dean of the College at Wiley College, Marshall, Texas, and Dean of the College at Morgan College, Baltimore, Maryland. The college took on new life when Dr. Haywood became its President. The pall of the depression, however, still hung over the college and made it difficult to achieve any significant advancement. Dr. Haywood's tenure at Morristown College came to an end in 1944, when he was elected President of Gammon Theological Seminary.

Dr. Miller W. Boyd, President

Following the resignation of Dr. John W. Haywood, Dr. Miller W. Boyd was elected President of Morristown Normal and Industrial College. Dr. Boyd was a graduate of the college and embodied the spirit and life of the college with which he became imbued under the influence of Dr. Hill. He was also a graduate of Lincoln University (Pa.). Dr. Boyd was a good public relations man. He was well-known and highly respected in the City of Morristown. He made a magnificent contribution in strengthening the relationship of the college with the business interests of the city and the community at large. Dr. Boyd was a strong layman in The Methodist Church and continued the good relations within the church at which Dr. Haywood had labored, and which had been the primary historic source of the college's financial success, directly and indirectly. For a period of eight years Dr. Boyd gave good leadership to the college, his administration coming to an end at his death in 1952. Mrs. Miller W. Boyd, whose experience had been enriched as a long time Registrar at the college and as wife of the President for eight years, was made acting President until a successor to Dr. Boyd could be found.

Change of Name

During the 1940's requirements in the preparation of teachers continued to be raised, so that a two-year Normal Course was no longer adequate for teacher certification. Toward the end of the decade Morristown Normal and Industrial College had shifted to the Junior College emphasis, which meant terminal education for some of its students, and for others, entering a four-year college. In 1960 the name was changed from "Morristown Normal and Industrial College" to "Morristown Junior College"[36 a] and as such received approval by the University Senate of The Methodist Church, and by the Southern Association of Colleges and Secondary Schools.

Dr. Henry L. Dickason, President

In 1953 Dr. Henry L. Dickason was made President. Dr. Dickason came to the Presidency of Morristown with a long career in the field of education. He had served for a number of years as President of Bluefield State College, Bluefield, West Virginia. Upon his retirement from Bluefield, Dr. Dickason was invited to the Presidency of Morristown Junior College. Dr. Dickason remained as President until his death in 1957, when again Mrs. Miller W. Boyd was called upon to serve as Acting President.

The East Tennessee Annual Conference in session in 1957 recorded the following statement in its minutes:

The College has gone through a crisis in the last decade. It has lost two outstanding Presidents in the person of Dr. Miller W. Boyd, and Dr. H. L. Dickason, both were vitally interested in the college and the work of the East Tennessee Conference. Each time following the deaths of these Presidents Mrs. M. W. Boyd has carried on the work very courageously.[37]

Dr. L. L. Haynes, Jr., President

Dr. Leonard L. Haynes, Jr., was elected President of Morristown Junior College in 1957 as successor to Dr. Dickason. Dr. Haynes held a B.A. degree from Samuel Huston College, a B.D. degree from Gammon Theological Seminary and a Th.D. degree from Boston University. Dr. Haynes, a minister, had had experience primarily as a pastor, a college Dean, and some teaching experience at the college level. He was President two years; thus his administration was too short to advance the college in any significant manner.

Rev. Elmer P. Gibson, President

From 1959 to 1969, the Rev. Elmer P. Gibson was President of Morristown Junior College. Rev. Gibson, a retired Army chaplain, gave good administrative leadership to the college. Perhaps the most significant development during his administration was the admission of the college to membership in the Southern Association of Colleges and Schools. This bespeaks the quality of the academic program, the physical facilities and equipment to support the program, and the faculty to execute the program.

In November, 1967 President Gibson gave the value of the plant as $966,816; the endowment as $136,152; the enrollment as 298 students, and the faculty and staff as fifty-five.

In 1969 President Gibson resigned, and was succeeded by the Reverend J. Otis Erwin, the present incumbent.

Morristown Junior College is approaching the end of nine decades of service in the eastern section of the State of Tennessee. Its service, however, has not been limited to that section nor to the State of Tennessee. Students have been drawn from other states, and many other sections of the country, some from Africa. The Methodist Church has felt the impact of the significant work this institution has accomplished.

REFERENCES AND NOTES

1. *The Christian Educator*, May, 1913, p. 15.
2. *Ibid.*
3. *Ibid., p. 16.*
4. Report, Freedmen's Aid and Southern Education Society, 1891, p. 255.
5. *Ibid.*
6. *Ibid.*
7. *Ibid.*, p. 255.
8. Minutes, East Tennessee Conference, Oct. 23-27, 1884, p. 21.
9. Minutes, East Tennessee Conference, 1889, p. 27.
10. *Ibid.*
11. *Ibid.*, p. 28.
12. Minutes, East Tennessee Conference, Oct. 8-11, 1896, p. 39.
13. Report, Freedmen's Aid and Southern Education Society, 1899, p. 147.
14. *The Christian Educator*, Dec.- Jan. 1900-1901, p. 26.
15. *Ibid.*
16. *The Christian Educator*, May, 1912, p. 2.
17. *Ibid.*
18. *Ibid.*
19. *Ibid.*, p. 3.
20. *Ibid.*, p. 4.
21. *Ibid.*
22. *Ibid.*
23. *The Christian Educator*, November, 1911, p. 21.
24. *The Christian Educator*, July, 1890, p. 160.
25. Annual Catalog, 1894-1895.
26. *The Christian Educator*, May, 1902, p. 19.
27. *The Christian Educator*, August, 1917, p. 10.
28. *Ibid.*
29. *The Christian Educator*, May, 1924, p. 13.
30. *Ibid.*
31. *The Christian Educator*, February, 1927, p. 6.
32. *The Christian Educator*, May, 1927, p. 8.
33. *Ibid.*
34. *The Christian Educator*, August, 1928, p. 5.
35. *Ibid.*
36. Minutes, East Tennessee Annual Conference, September 29 to October 4, 1931.
36a. College Catalog, 1960, p. 8.
37. Minutes, East Tennessee Annual Conference, 1957, p. 61.

CHAPTER 20

A BRIEF HISTORICAL SKETCH OF PAINE COLLEGE

Augusta, Georgia

The history of Paine College emerges from the relationship of the Colored (now Christian) Methodist Episcopal Church and the Methodist Episcopal Church, South. Developments within the decade following the Emancipation in 1865 resulted in the establishment of the Colored Methodist Episcopal Church in America, composed of Negro membership which to that time was based in the Methodist Episcopal Church, South. The Journal of the 1866 General Conference of the Methodist Episcopal Church, South records the following statement regarding the impending separation of the Negro membership:

The interest of the colored population should engage your serious attention. Heretofore the colored people within our bounds have deserved and received a large share of our labors. We have expended our means and strength liberally and patiently for many years for their salvation and improvement, and if anywise our conduct has not been appreciated by some on earth, nevertheless, our witness is with God, and our record on high. It is grateful to our own feelings to know that if the colored people do not remain under our pastoral care, their departure reflects no discredit upon our labors in their behalf, and is necessitated by no indifference on our part to their welfare. Many of them will probably unite with the African M. E. Church, some of them with the Northern Methodist Church, while others, notwithstanding extraneous influences and unkind misrepresentations of our Church, will remain with us.

Let us be content to leave to Providence to vindicate in due time our scriptural relation to the interest of the colored people. For those who remain with us the Church should provide generously everything important to their religious culture. Convinced that your body takes the deepest interest in

411

this subject, and will give it your special attention, we deem it only needful to speak of it in this general and suggestive form; and especially as the Bishops in their Pastoral Address last August brought the subject prominently to the notice of our people.[1]

At the same General Conference specific questions were raised and answers presented by the Committee on the Religious Interests of the Colored people, chaired by J. E. Evans, and submitted April 13 for adoption by the Conference. The report of the Committee follows:

The Committee on Religious Interests of Colored People present Report No. 2.

ON COLORED MEMBERS.

Question. What shall be done to promote the Religious Interests of the Colored People?

Answer 1. Let our colored members be organized as separate pastoral charges, wherever they prefer it, and their numbers may justify it.

2. Let each pastoral charge of colored members have its own Quarterly Conference, composed of official members, as provided for in the Discipline.

3. Let colored persons be licensed to preach, and ordained deacons and elders, according to the Discipline, when, in the judgment of the Conference having jurisdiction in the case, they are deemed suitable persons for said office and order in the ministry.

4. The Bishop may form a District of colored charges, and appoint to it a colored Presiding Elder, when in his judgment the religious interests of the colored people require it.

5. When it is judged advisable by the College of Bishops, Annual Conferences of colored preachers may be organized, to be presided over by our Bishops.

6. When two or more Annual Conferences shall be formed, let our Bishops advise and assist them in organizing a separate General Conference jurisdiction for themselves, if they so desire, and the Bishops deem it expedient, in accordance with the Doctrines and Disciplines of our Church, and bearing the same relations to the General Conference as the Annual Conferences bear to each other.

7. Let special attention be given to Sunday-schools among the colored people.

The above chapter is recommended by the Committee on the Religious Interests of the Colored People to the General Conference for its adoption.[2]

By 1870 plans had developed for the consummation of the establishment of a separate and independent body, to become an all Negro body stemming from the Methodist Episcopal Church, South. On May 5, 1870, a committee consisting of Bishops J. O. Andrews, R. Paine, G. F. Pierce, H. H. Kavanaugh, W. M. Wightman, E. M. Marvin, D. S. Doggett, and H. N. McTyeire, gave their report to the General Conference assembled at Memphis, Tennessee. In part, the report follows:

Conformably to the wish of the last General Conference, we have organized and presided over five Annual Conferences, composed exclusively of colored members; have formed forty-five Districts, with circuits and stations, in all of which, with a few exceptions, in which white preachers have volunteered to act as supplies, our colored brethren are performing the duties of Presiding Elders and pastors. The principal field of these operations extends through portions of Georgia, Tennessee, Kentucky, Mississippi, Arkansas, Louisiana, Alabama, South Carolina, and Florida; and is widening by applications for the organization of new Conferences. The colored preachers have conducted themselves, both in their Annual Conferences and in the exercise of their pastoral duties, so as to win the confidence and cooperation of those of their white brethren who have become best acquainted with their deportment. It is our purpose, unless otherwise advised by your body, to call a General Conference, to be holden next winter, for the purpose of organizing them into an entirely separate Church, and thus enabling them to become their own guides and governors.[3]

The College of Bishops presented to the General Conference of May 1874, their report on the religious interests of the colored people. In part, the report follows:

Report of the College of Bishops on
The Religious Condition of the Colored People

We respectfully submit to the General Conference the following report:

The General Conference of 1866 directed that if our colored membership should desire it, and whenever, in our godly judgment, it was expedient, we should organize them into an

413

independent ecclesiastical body. We formed several Annual Conferences composed of colored preachers belonging to our Communion, but had gone no farther in this direction, when the General Conference of 1870, approving what had been done, renewed the authority upon the former terms for a separate General Conference jurisdiction of the colored Churches.

* * *

The experiment, so far as made, proving satisfactory, and a very general and earnest desire having been expressed by our colored preachers and members for the consummation of their Church-order and independence, we called for them a General Conference to meet in Jackson, Tenn., Dec. 16, 1870. Eight Annual Conferences sent delegates, elected on the basis of our Discipline. Two of our Bishops were present and presided, by whom, on the 21st December, and according to our form, two Superintendents, elected by the body, were ordained. A Discipline was established, agreeing in creed and polity with our Discipline, and but slightly changed in its statutory provisions so as to suit their case. Exercising the right belonging to them, and expressly recognized by the enabling act, they chose for their name and title, "The Colored Methodist Episcopal Church in America". Their proceedings were in excellent order and spirit throughout.

Thus organized, and with our best advice and blessing, the Colored M. E. Church in America was started upon its career.[4]

At the General Conference of 1874 "J. E. Evans, Chairman of the Committee on the Organization of the Colored Methodist Episcopal Church in America, presented the report of said committee, which was read and adopted."[5] It is as follows:

Report of The Committee on The Organization of the
Colored Methodist Episcopal Church in America

The committee to whom was referred the report of the Bishops on the organization of the colored people of the Methodist Episcopal Church, South, into a distinct ecclesiastical Connection, have had the same under consideration, and respectfully submit the following resolutions, for the adoption of the Conference:

Resolved, That the report of the Bishops, setting forth the organization of the colored people of the Methodist Episcopal Church, South, in conformity with the action of the General Conferences of 1866 and 1870, into a distinct ecclesiastical

414

Connection, under the name and style of "The Colored Methodist Episcopal Church in America," meets the entire approval of this Conference.

Resolved, That it is with great pleasure, and devout gratitude to the Great Head of the Church, that we receive the intelligence the report conveys of the peace, harmony, prosperity, and encouraging prospects for the future, of this new organization; thus fully justifying the wisdom of the policy of the Church touching our colored members.

Resolved, That in providing a distinct organization for the colored members of the Church, and committing to their hands the ecclesiastical oversight and spiritual interests of the colored people among us, we have given them additional proof of parental love and good will; and we do hereby commend the "Colored Methodist Episcopal Church in America" to the confidence and Christian affection of the Methodist Episcopal Church, South, and to all Christians of every name.

Resolved, That the efforts making to establish an institution of learning for the education of their ministry is worthy of all praise, and we commend this cause to the friends of the colored people everywhere. They need material aid; let it be given.

Resolved, That the report of the Bishops be recorded in the Journal of this Conference as an important part of the history of this question.

Respectfully submitted,
J. E. Evans, Chairman[6]

To the General Conference of 1878 a report was made by a committee, W. P. Harrison, Chairman, to whom had been referred "a paper relating to the education of the colored people." The committee indicated that they recognized the education of the colored people to be a great religious duty and reported that considerable progress had been made in the provision of education. Referring to the withdrawal of the Negro membership and the establishment of the C.M.E. Church, the committee report stated that "The changes of the past have wrought no change in the heart of the church; it is still ready to work for the salvation of this people to the full measure of its ability and opportunity." The following resolutions were submitted:

Resolved, That the education of the colored people of the South is demanded alike by Christian duty and enlightened benevolence.

Resolved, That in all efforts that may be made by the Colored Methodist Episcopal Church in America to establish

415

educational institutions for the moral and religious training of the colored race, we bespeak the cordial sympathy and practical aid of our people.[7]

The General Conference of the Methodist Episcopal Church, South, assembled in Nashville, Tennessee, May, 1882, passed several resolutions pertaining to the establishment of a school for the benefit of the colored Methodist Episcopal Church in America:

Resolved, That our Bishops be also authorized and requested to appoint, in consultation with the Bishops of the Colored Methodist Episcopal Church in America, a preacher or layman of our Church, properly qualified for the work, who shall be a Commissioner of Education in aid of the Colored Methodist Episcopal Church in America, whose duty it shall be to solicit subscriptions, contributions, donations, and bequests from whatever source he may find accessible, for the purpose of creating an Educational Fund for the benefit of said Colored Methodist Episcopal Church in America.
2. That our Bishops be also authorized and requested to appoint three members of our Church, who, together with the Commissioner of Education and three members of the Colored Methodist Episcopal Church in America, to be appointed by their Bishops, shall constitute a Board of Trustees for the custody and control of this Educational Fund when it shall have been raised.
3. That the Commissioner of Education herein provided for be appointed a committee of one to see that the said Board of Trustees be completed in legal form by securing proper acts of incorporation.
All of which is respectfully submitted.
W. R. Harrison, Chairman.[8]

The General Conference of The Methodist Episcopal Church, South, in 1886, heard a report stating that "The action of the last General Conference provided for a School Agency and a Trusteeship for creating a foundation for educating colored teachers and ministers. . . .A school has been opened at Augusta, Ga., mainly through the liberality of our people during the last round of Conferences, at which some $15,000 were contributed, and the donation by Rev. Moses U. Payne of $25,000 for an endowment fund."[9]
On November 1, 1882, an historic meeting was held in the lecture room of St. John's Church. Bishop George F. Pierce

explained the object of the meeting and indicated that the following persons had been appointed as Trustees of Paine College from the Methodist Episcopal Church, South:

W. P. Patillo, of Atlanta, Ga., W. B. Hill, of Macon, Ga., W. A. Candler, Sparta, Ga., and Rev. J. E. Evans, D.D., had been appointed Educational Commissioner.[10]

Bishop L. H. Holsey of the Colored Methodist Episcopal Church in America reported names of the following persons as Trustees from that body:

J. S. Harper, Augusta, Ga., R. A. Maxey, Barnesville, Ga., L. H. Holsey, Augusta, Ga.[11]

Upon acceptance of the resignation of W. B. Hill of the Methodist Episcopal Church, South, Rev. W. H. LaPrade was elected trustee to fill the vacancy.[12]

A committee of three was appointed to prepare a set of By-Laws membership consisting of W. P. Hill, L. H. Holsey, and W. A. Candler.[13]

A committee was appointed to select a temporary location for a school, and also a permanent location, the committee to act in consultation with the Commissioner of Education.

Officers of the Board of Trustees were elected by ballot, as follows:

President, James E. Evans; Treasurer, W. H. LaPrade; and Secretary, J. S. Harper.[14]

The Board took action to call the proposed institution Paine Institute of the Colored Methodist Episcopal Church in America in honor of Bishop Robert Paine of the Methodist Episcopal Church, South, lately deceased.[15]

First President

At a meeting of the Board of Trustees December 1, 1882, the Rev. Morgan Calloway, D.D., was elected first President of Paine Institute.[16] In a letter by Dr. A. G. Haygood, December 8, 1882, to Bishop E. R. Hendrix, Dr. Haygood says: "I have become personally responsible for $2,000 to put the President through the first year. He is my dear friend and right arm here, Dr. Morgan Calloway. He has resigned and takes charge of the new work January 1st. It has made a tremendous impression in Georgia and it is a big thing. Dr. Calloway comes of a long line of aristocratic slave-holders, was a colonel of artillery in the Confederate Army and a man of high character in every way."[17]

Money to help start Paine Institute came in small amounts from the C. M. E. Church, but the Negro people were proud to have a share in the initiation of this important work. At the meeting of

417

the Board of Trustees December 12, 1882, Bishop Holsey stated that he wished to present to the Trustees of Paine Institute the first money; he accordingly presented $7.15 from the Virginia Conference and $8.85 from the South Georgia Conference.[18]

Paine Institute was incorporated June 1883.[19] Classwork began in rented quarters on Broad Street, January, 1884.[20]

Reverend George Williams Walker, President

On December 28, 1884, the Rev. George Williams Walker was elected President of Paine Institute to fill the vacancy occasioned by the resignation of Rev. Morgan Calloway. Rev. Walker, being present, indicated his acceptance of the position. Rev. Walker had been serving as a teacher at the Institute before being elected President.[21]

New Developments

In 1886 a permanent site on Fifteenth Street was purchased, where the institution has had remarkable development over a period of eighty-four years.

The year 1888 was an important one for Paine Institute. The following resolutions were offered by W. A. Candler and were unanimously adopted by the Board of Trustees:

Resolved, That President George W. Walker be authorized and directed, if the needs of the Institute in his judgment requires another teacher, to employ John Wesley Gilbert, a recent graduate of Paine Institute and now recently graduated from Brown University.[22]

Mr. Gilbert was employed. He was the first Negro teacher employed by Paine.

In the same year (1888) Paine Institute received the largest gift in its history, made by the Rev. Moses U. Payne, a Missouri local preacher, in the amount of $25,000 for endowment.[23]

From the incipient efforts in the embryonic stages of raising an institution of learning and training for the black children of cultural darkness, across several decades the engagement of the Methodist Episcopal Church, South in this all-important cause for many became indeed an ardent mission and a work of romantic adventure. The Bishops of the parent church regularly included in the Episcopal Address to the General Conference a section on the relation and responsibility of the Methodist Episcopal Church, South to the Colored Methodist Episcopal Church in America. In

418

1890 the Bishop's Address said:

> The General Conference of 1882 committed the church (we may say wisely) to the support of the educational undertakings of the Colored Methodist Episcopal Church in America. This movement is of grave importance in the present aspect of special affairs and to the future of our country. It represents our attitude upon the question of the relations between ourselves and the colored people. We cannot disregard their claim upon us. We cannot refuse to aid, as far as in us lies, in providing a safe and sound ministry for, and in educating and elevating them, and by all Christian means preparing them for a higher life in this world and for the fellowship of the Kingdom of God.[24]

This General Conference took action endorsing the section of the Bishops' address relating to the support of the educational work of the Christian Methodist Episcopal Church in America. The Conference passed the following resolution:

> That the College of Bishops be requested to appoint a Commissioner of Education for the Colored people, who shall be kept actively in the field soliciting aid for this enterprise, and who shall report annually to the Board of Trustees of the Paine Institute.[25]

At the general Conference of 1894 the Bishops expressed the same concern regarding support to Paine and Lane Colleges, and expressed hope that the General Conference would devise some plan for more efficient aid to these institutions.[26] At the same General Conference a General Board of Education was established and the management of the colored educational work was placed in the charge of this new board. During the following quadrennium $22,363.66 was raised by Annual Conferences.[27]

Despite the sense of mission and continued interest evidenced in General Conference resolutions and actions, the monetary support for the development of Paine Institute fell far short of the need and expectation. In 1895, less than one year before he died, Bishop Atticus G. Haygood wrote an article, published in *The Methodist Review*, under the caption: "Loaf and Bottle to Hagar," in which he sharply chided his church for its failure to give to Paine Institute and others the support needed and expected. "What help we have given them," he said, "has been incidental and sporadic. . . .The Southern white churches have recognized and set forth, in wise and earnestly worded declarations, their duty to the emancipated people. The trouble is, they have seemed to content themselves with words. . . .We pass resolutions every Conference and make a pitiful assessment, collecting annually only a part of it."[28]

In 1898 plans were completed for the erection of a new hall for Paine Institute, to be known as Haygood Memorial Hall. At that time the sum of $10,398.85 in cash had been received by the Board of Trustees, and enough in good subscriptions to raise the sum to $20,000.00.[29] Haygood Hall was completed in 1899.[30]

Paine Institute Rechartered as Paine College

At the meeting of the Board of Trustees, June 5, 1901, Bishop Holsey moved that the charter be amended by striking out the word "Institute" and inserting the word "College." The motion prevailed.[31] Rechartering of the institution as Paine College was consummated in 1903.[32]

Death of President Walker

Dr. George W. Walker, elected as second president in 1884, served in this capacity for twenty-six years. He gave effective leadership to the institution during this quarter of a century of its formative history. His death came in 1910. Dr. N. L. Campbell served as Acting President during the year 1910-1911.[33]

Third President Elected

At the meeting of the Paine College Board of Trustees June, 1911, attention was given to the matter of filling the vacancy occasioned by the death of President George W. Walker. The name of the Rev. John D. Hammond was placed in nomination and he was unanimously elected to fill the vacancy as the third President of Paine College.[34] The Rev. Hammond served as President four years. At the meeting of the Board, June 4, 1915, Rev. Hammond tendered his resignation, action on which was deferred.[35] At a meeting of the Board, September 15, 1915, the Rev. D. E. Atkins was elected President of the College.[36]

At a meeting of the Board of Trustees in July, 1915, a change was made in policy regarding the employment of faculty. Up to that time the Board of Trustees had been selecting the faculty. By vote of the Board at this meeting the President of the college was given the authority to select his own faculty; the selections, however, had to be confirmed by the Executive Committee of the Board.[37]

The administration of Rev. Atkins was short. His resignation was tendered January 5, 1917,[38] less than two years after his election. The action on the resignation of Rev. Atkins was deferred until the next meeting. On April 17, 1917, the Board of Trustees gave expressions of thanks and appreciation for President Atkins' services, and elected another President on recommendation of a Selection Committee.

Rev. Albert Deems Betts Elected President, Succeeded by Rev. Ray S. Tomlin

Reverend Albert Deems Betts was elected President in 1917. He held the position five years. His term of office closed in 1922. The Rev. Ray S. Tomlin served as Acting President during the school year 1922-1923.[39] At the end of the year as Acting President, Rev. Tomlin in 1923 was elected to the Presidency.[40] He served as President six years. During his administration two buildings were added to the campus: (1) "Epworth Hall, a gift of Epworth Leaguers of the Methodist Episcopal Church, South, erected 1925; and (2) Mary Helm Hall, a gift of the Woman's Home Missionary Council of the Methodist Episcopal Church, South, erected 1926."[41]

The Rev. Tomlin's administration ended in 1929.

Dr. E. C. Peters Elected President

The Rev. Tomlin was succeeded in the Presidency of Paine College by Mr. Edmund Clarke Peters in 1929. Mr. Peters, a native of Burrville, Tennessee, held a B.A. degree and a B.S.A. degree from the University of Tennessee, and an A.M. degree from the University of Chicago. He had been a Principal of several high schools, Director of Louisiana State Normal College, and Director of Educational Work and Y.M.C.A. work in Siberia. Serving as a missionary in China he was Principal of the second Middle School of Soochow University, China.[42]

Dr. Peters served as President of Paine College for twenty-seven years. During his administration the college had substantial development. The physical plant was expanded and the academic program improved. Some of the accomplishments of the college were, (1) accreditation as a "B" class institution in 1931 by the Southern Association of Colleges and Secondary Schools;[43] (2) acceptance as a member of the Association of American Colleges, December, 1932; (3) accreditation by the Southern Association of Colleges and Secondary Schools, Class "A", March, 1945; (4) completion of the Warren A. Candler Memorial Library Building,

421

and dedication, September 5, 1947; (5) completion of the Randall A. Carter Physical Education Building, and formal opening October 31, 1952.[44] The George Williams Walker Science Building, which was dedicated October 30, 1956,[45] was completed in the final months of Dr. Peters' administration.

The Journal of the General Conference of the Colored Methodist Episcopal Church, May, 1938, states that "Paine College has had phenomenal growth in many instances, during the quadrennium. President Peters reports a reduction of the bonded debt from $35,000.00 to $10,000.00 together with interest payments of nearly $7,000.00."[46]

The financial aid to Paine College during the Quadrennium ended 1938 was a substantial increase over previous quadrennia, the largest amount by far, $174,999.92,[47] having been given by the Methodist Episcopal Church, South. The General Board of Education of the Colored Methodist Episcopal Church gave during that quadrennium $5,781.32.[48] This amount was increased during the next quadrennium to $7,912.94 by the C.M.E. Church Board.

During the presidency of Dr. Peters there emerged an emphasis on the larger role of Paine College in race relations. Dr. Peters gave time and effort in pointing out and strengthening the relationship between the Methodist Episcopal Church, South, and the Colored Methodist Episcopal Church. Speaking in 1939 of the origin and duration of this relationship, Dr. Peters said, "For a period of fifty-five years now the church [M. E. Church, South] has continued its interest in this institution, giving it some of its best men and women in its leadership and providing almost all of the funds necessary for its maintenance. It was the only institution then—it is the only institution now—in which the trustees and faculty are made up of Southern white and Southern colored people. It has had a large part in the formation of centers of good will between the two races in the South."[49]

New Relations—Unification

The new emphasis on the historic relation, from a race relations point of view, between the Colored Methodist Episcopal Church and the Methodist Episcopal Church, South, gained importance with the reunion of the three branches of Methodism in 1939. The renewed relationship between the Methodist Episcopal Church and the Methodist Episcopal Church, South, gave Paine College a new and wider relationship with the Methodist Church nationally, and not just the former Southern branch of Methodism. It was within this wider framework that Dr. Peters had the privilege of working for more than half of his administration. In 1934 the Woman's

422

Home Missionary Council of the Methodist Episcopal Church, South, was merged with the Woman's Home Missionary Society of the Methodist Episcopal Church to form a new national organization, the Woman's Division of Christian Service. It was through the Board of Missions of the Woman's Division of Christian Service that the base of support of Paine College was broadened through Methodist unification in 1939.

In 1956 Dr. Peters retired from the Presidency of Paine College. The Presidency of Dr. George W. Walker, twenty-six years, was the only previous administration to approach in length that of President Peters. Through the leadership and devoted labors of Dr. and Mrs. Peters for twenty-seven years, 1929 to 1956, Paine College had growth and advancement such that it had not experienced in any previous period.

The Rev. E. Clayton Calhoun, President

Following the retirement of President E. C. Peters in 1956, Dr. E. Clayton Calhoun was elected President of Paine College.[50]

Dr. Clayton Calhoun, the eighth President of Paine College assumed office with the heritage of devotion, hard work, and sincerity transmitted to him from his seven predecessors in this office. What Paine was in 1956 was the fruition of the labors of seven Presidents, faculties and trustees for almost three quarters of a century. President Calhoun had not only a grave responsibility, but also a great challenge. He spent fourteen years as President, expending all of his energy, supported by Mrs. Calhoun, in meeting the challenge of probably the most difficult period of administration in the history of Paine College. If any other period was more difficult it was in the early years when the institution had only a few stalwart founders and concerned friends, one or two poor cabins for buildings, and a racial climate that would have destroyed the efforts of men of lesser determination and faith.

Following closely upon his assumption of office in 1956 was the beginning of a number of significant developments[51] which continued across the fourteen years of Dr. Calhoun's Presidency.

The Seventy-Fifth Anniversary of the college was celebrated February 22-24, 1958, giving added confidence of a historical background of successful achievement, and the hope of a brighter future.

In 1959 Paine College was approved by the University Senate of The Methodist Church. This put the college in the ranks of other Methodist Colleges approved by this agency of the church and made it eligible without question for certain funds appropriated by the Board of Education. This, President Calhoun had worked hard to accomplish.

Paine College, in December, 1961, was admitted to full membership in the Southern Association of Colleges and Schools. This accomplishment not only gave evidence of the quality of instruction, the quality of the faculty, and the adequacy of the physical plant and facilities, but also opened the way for membership in the United Negro College Fund and more favorable consideration by foundations and corporations for supporting grants. Paine College in 1966 was admitted to membership in College Entrance Examination Board.

Additions to the physical plant formed a part of the significant developments. The Emma C. W. Gray House, a dormitory for women, was completed and formally opened in January, 1962. Also, Belle Bennett House, a dormitory for women, was completed and opened in September, 1962. Hollis House, a dormitory for women, was completed and formally opened in September, 1967. At the same time, September, 1967, Ervin House, a dormitory for men was completed and formally opened. Gilbert-Lambuth Memorial Chapel and Music Building was completed and dedicated in January, 1968, and Edmund and Ethel Peters Campus Center was completed in March, 1969.

The following section under the heading of buildings gives a complete listing and description of the complex of campus facilities and physical plant.

Buildings

HOLSEY HALL, a frame structure, is the oldest building on the campus. The ground floor houses various offices. The Academic Skills Clinic and Upward Bound occupy the second floor.

MARY HELM HALL, a reinforced brick and concrete building, contains some administrative offices and serves as a general purpose classroom building.

THE WARREN A. CANDLER MEMORIAL LIBRARY, completed in 1947, provides library facilities at the college. It is a two-story building of steel, brick and reinforced concrete. The two large reading rooms provide space for approximately 250 people. There is stack room space available for approximately 75,000 volumes. The building also contains offices for the librarians and two committee rooms.

RANDALL A. CARTER GYMNASIUM is a building carefully planned and unusually well constructed. It is constructed of reinforced concrete, steel and brick for protection from fire hazard. As an auditorium it has a seating capacity of 1500 to

1800; as a gymnasium from 1000 to 1200.

GEORGE WILLIAMS WALKER SCIENCE BUILDING, dedicated October 30, 1956, is a modern fireproof structure of architectural style in keeping with other campus buildings. It houses the classrooms and laboratories for Biology, Physics and Chemistry. It bears the name of the second president of the college who served in that capacity for twenty seven years—1884-1911.

THE GILBERT-LAMBUTH MEMORIAL CHAPEL, completed in 1968, was dedicated January 30, 1968. The basic structure is that of a cross and the interior provides space to seat 1200 persons in air-conditioned comfort. The rear of this building contains classrooms, sound-proof practice rooms, a music library, several studios, robing rooms for both men and woman, and an auditorium which will seat 200 persons. The music program of the college is housed here.

HARPER HOUSE is occupied by freshmen and sophomore men students.

EPWORTH HOUSE, a student dormitory, has been reconditioned for use by women students. It represents the interest of the young people of the former Methodist Episcopal Church, South, who composed the membership of the Epworth League of this church, in the educational development of Negro youth. It was through gifts of the Epworth Leaguers that this building was made possible. It is a modern, three-story brick structure, convenient in every way. It provides accommodations for approximately 115 students.

BELLE BENNETT HOUSE was occupied in September, 1962. The dormitory faces Emma C. W. Gray Hall, and is almost identical to the other building. It houses fifty women students, and contains a faculty apartment. The dormitory was furnished through aid of the Women's Division of Christian Service of The Methodist Church. The name Belle Bennett originally was applied to Harper Hall, which was once a dormitory for women. Miss Bennett was a leader of the Women's work of the Southern Methodist Church, and was instrumental in starting a department for girls at what was then Paine Institute.

THE EMMA C. W. GRAY HOUSE, a dormitory for upperclass women is of very modern construction and formally opened, January 1962. Most of the money for the construction of the Emma C. W. Gray Hall was contributed by the women of the Southeastern Jurisdiction of the Methodist Church. This women's dormitory is named after a devoted servant of the Church, who served Paine College for more than 30 years as teacher in the high school division, acting principal of the high school, teacher of

425

English in the College Division, and Dean of Women. The dormitory will accommodate fifty students in double rooms, and contains one faculty apartment.

HOLLIS HOUSE was occupied in September, 1967. It is an air-conditioned building of modern construction and built to house fifty women in the upper college division. It is named for Mrs. Rossie Thompson Hollis, an alumnus of the college who also served on the Board of Trustees.

ERVIN HOUSE was occupied in September, 1967. It is an air-conditioned building of modern construction and built to house fifty men. It is named for the late W. C. Ervin, business manager of the college from 1929 until his death in 1964.

EDMUND AND ETHEL PETERS CAMPUS CENTER, recently completed, houses the dining facilities of the college; the offices of the Dean of Student Affairs and his staff; offices of various student activities; and areas for recreation and relaxation.

PAINE HOUSE, completed in December 1968, houses the President and his family.[52]

The main campus of the college consists of twenty acres, on which most of the buildings are located. In addition, there is an adjoining plot of twenty acres (total forty acres) where the athletic field is located, and located on this plot also are the Randall A. Carter Auditorium-Gymnasium, and the Gilbert-Lambuth Memorial Chapel.[53]

The future will long recognize the years of Dr. Calhoun's administration as one of the fine and illustrious periods in the history of Paine College, and generations will remember with deepest appreciation the sterling qualities of this man who made such a remarkable contribution to the development of Paine College, giving good leadership to the faculty and service to the constituency, and who gave so much inspiration to thousands of students whose good fortune it was to be at this institution while he was President.

In 1970 Dr. Calhoun resigned from the Presidency of Paine College to accept a fund-raising position as Director of the Negro College Advance, the United Methodist Church.

The End of An Era

The year 1970, for Paine College, marked the end of an era. It was in many instances an era of difficulties and discouragements; but never was any night of gloom so dark that those involved failed to see the light of morning stars that presaged the dawn of a new day of hope.

426

Regarding this era of nearly nine decades, a few brief summary statements are apropos.

The Colored Methodist Episcopal Church In America, now the Christian Methodist Episcopal Church, established in 1870, grew out of the Methodist Episcopal Church, South. Certain common interests kept the two bodies in close and friendly relations. The Bishops and leaders of the C. M. E. Church, an all black denomination, were at once interested in educational opportunities and sought help from the M. E. Church, South, in this enterprise. The main leader for the C. M. E. group was Bishop L. H. Holsey who requested the establishment of a school as early as 1870.

"Paine grew out of the organizational structure of two branches of Methodism in the South in the 1880's. When Methodism in the South tried to meet the needs of education for Negro leaders, especially preachers and teachers, Paine Institute resulted."[54]

As an indication of the difficulty of the venture of establishing Paine Institute, Dr. Clary states further: "On January 2, 1884, a chastened leadership finally opened the doors of the school to a handful of pupils. Before the end of 1884, President Calloway resigned and gave up the task which he had taken up so enthusiastically two years before."[55]

Where President Calloway felt compelled to remove himself from the Presidency Dr. George Williams Walker, a stalwart leader in the Methodist Episcopal Church, South, who succeeded him, felt compelled to take up this administrative responsibility, which he pursued with vigor, courage, and determination for twenty-six years.

This early venture had the support and aid of such strong men in the M. E. Church, South, as the Reverends W. A. Candler, W. B. Hill, W. P. Patillo, J. E. Evans, W. H. LaPrade, Morgan Calloway, and many others. Especially, mention must be made of the Reverend Atticus G. Haygood, who as an educator and administrator, and before becoming bishop in the M. E. Church, South, as Director of the John F. Slater Fund, gave more help to the Presidents in strengthening Paine Institute than any other single man.

During this long era of development of Paine College, there were two major characteristic elements which are believed to justify its claim to uniqueness. First, its emphasis, in an unusual setting, upon Christian education for Negro youth. This element, though claimed as an objective in other institutions was reinforced at Paine by the practical aspects of relations sustained. Secondly, Paine College, over this period of years, claimed uniqueness in the fact that the college was a mecca, indigenous to the South, for

427

racial contacts and the development of interracial understanding and goodwill. The two churches and the institution itself conceived this to be a unique campus situation where Southern Negroes and Southern white people were engaged in an important cooperative interracial venture.

The late Dr. William L. Graham in his unpublished Doctoral Dissertation points out that "In 1934, of one hundred and nine colleges for Negroes, Paine College was the one institution controlled jointly by Southern Negro and white people."[56] Dr. Graham found in his research on the relationship of the two groups over the years that "There was no recognizable influence of contemporary concepts of innate difference in the mentality of the Negro. . . .Execution of the common task seemed to have been the primary concern of the interracial group."[57]

If Dr. Graham's observation was in reality the true characteristic attitude of the two groups working together, it was indeed unusual, for the dominant philosophy, conscious and subconscious, of the white South during slavery and all the Southern history from 1865 to the present was, and still is, a history of structured social caste and class, emphasizing white supremacy—superiority of the white man and inferiority of the black man. In view of the long policy and unbroken practice of white administration, from 1882 to 1970, the question inevitably arises, should not the probability of subtle or unintended white paternalism be more closely examined? Whatever the answer to this question might be, it must be granted that the claim to uniqueness of Paine College in its race relations emphasis is valid; for as Dr. Graham states: "Evidence tends to support the major hypothesis that mutual involvement is one of the better approaches to the improvement of inter-group relations."[58]

Some Fruits of The Years

Much of the fruitful work of Paine College has been revealed and implied in the foregoing paragraphs of this document. The fruits of the relationships can never be put into words; nor can the effects of this institution upon the lives of thousands of young men and women ever be measured. In speaking of the fruits this college has borne in terms of its graduates, thousands of whom have been servants of humanity, but have not made the headlines, one's efforts become noticeably feeble. The best that this writer can do is to list six or eight distinguished graduates whose attainments justify the labor, anxiety, dedication, and devotion of men and women across the years to make Paine College what it is.

John Wesley Gilbert was the first student and the first graduate

428

of Paine College, having graduated in 1886. Because of his brilliance and promise he was the first Negro employed on the Paine faculty, serving as a teacher at his alma mater twenty-six years, from 1886 to 1912.

Randall A. Carter graduating in 1892, became a distinguished minister in the Colored Methodist Episcopal Church in America, and later elected a bishop in this church.

Channing H. Tobias graduated in the class of 1902. For nine years, 1902-1911, he taught theology at his alma mater. Later he entered Y.M.C.A. work and became nationally and internationally known for his leadership in the Y.M.C.A.

Frank Yerby graduated in 1937 and has distinguished himself as a novelist.

William L. Graham, a 1929 graduate, joined the Paine College faculty and distinguished himself as a teacher of English and a community leader in Augusta until his death in 1963.

Emma C. Gray was a teacher of English and Dean of Women at her alma mater for a period of thirty years, ended by untimely death, and for whom a women's dormitory on the campus is named.

Lucius H. Pitts was a 1941 graduate of Paine College. He is a nationally known civic leader and educator, a college president, and is the new president of Paine College.

Beginning of a New Era

Paine College was without a President during the school year 1970-1971. The affairs of the college were administered by an *Interim* Committee.

As successor to Dr. E. Clayton Calhoun in the office of President, Dr. Lucius H. Pitts, President of Miles Memorial College in Birmingham, Alabama, was elected. Dr. Pitts has the distinction of being the first alumnus to become President, and the first Black man to be elected to this position. His election to the Presidency begins a new era in the history of this eighty-eight-year-old institution.

REFERENCES AND NOTES

1. Journal of the General Conference, Methodist Episcopal Church, South, April, 1866, p. 18.
2. *Ibid.*, pp. 58f.
3. Journal, General Conference, Methodist Episcopal Church, South, May, 1870, p. 168.
4. Journal, General Conference, Methodist Episcopal Church, South, May, 1874, p. 458.
5. Journal, General Conference, Methodist Episcopal Church, South, May 1874, p. 528.
6. *Ibid.*
7. Journal, General Conference, Methodist Episcopal Church, May, 1878, pp. 203f.
8. *Ibid.*, May, 1882, p. 101.
9. Journal, General Conference, Methodist Episcopal Church, 1886, p. 18.
10. Minutes, Paine College Board of Trustees, November 1, 1882.
11. *Ibid.*
12. *Ibid.*
13. *Ibid.*
14. *Ibid.*
15. *Ibid.*
16. Minutes, Paine Institute, Board of Trustees, December 1, 1882, p. 35.
17. Dempsey, Elain Franklin, *Atticus G. Haygood*, p. 335.
18. Minutes, Paine Institute Board of Trustees, December 12, 1882, p. 37.
19. Board Minutes June 4, 1902, p. 153 and Paine College Catalog (Current), p. 8.
20. Paine College Catalog, 1959-1970, p. 8.
21. Minutes, Paine Board of Trustees, December 28, 1884, p. 63.
22. Minutes, Paine Board of Trustees, May 4, 1888, p. 89.
23. Catalog, Paine College, 1969-1970; and Dempsey, Elain Franklin, *op. cit.*, p. 653.
24. Minutes, General Conference Journal, Methodist Episcopal Church, South, May, 1890, p. 39.
25. *Ibid.*, p. 183.
26. Journal, Methodist Episcopal Church, South, General Conference, 1894.
27. Southern Methodist Handbook, 1906, p. 119.
28. Dempsey, Elain Franklin, *op. cit.*, pp. 652 and 654.
29. Journal, Methodist Episcopal Church, South, General Conference, p. 23.
30. Paine College Catalog, 1969-70, p. 8.

31. Minutes, Paine Institute, Board Meeting, June 5, 1901, p. 150.
32. Catalog, Paine College, 1969-1970, p. 8.
33. Minutes, Board of Trustees, June 7, 1911, p. 179.
34. *Ibid.*, p. 181.
35. Minutes, Paine College Board of Trustees, June 4, 1915, p. 202.
36. Minutes, Paine College Board of Trustees, September 15, 1915.
37. Minutes, Paine College Board of Trustees, July 20, 1915, p. 210.
38. *Ibid.*, January 5, 1917.
39. Minutes, Paine College Board of Trustees, 1922, p. 268.
40. Paine College Catalog, 1967-70., p. 8.
41. *Ibid.*
42. Biolgraphical data taken from *Leaders In Education*, Biographical Directory, The Science Press, New York, 1932, p. 731.
43. Paine College Catalog, 1969-70, p. 8.
44. *Ibid.*
45. *Ibid.*, p. 9.
46. Journal, General Conference, the Colored Methodist Episcopal Church, May, 1938.
47. *Ibid.*, p. 156.
48. *Ibid.*
49. *The Missionary Yearbook*, Methodist Episcopal Church, South, 1939, p. 341.
50. Paine College Catalog, 1969-70, p. 9.
51. See Paine College Catalog, 1969-70, p. 9.
52. Paine College Catalog, 1969-70, pp. 13, 14, and 16. Note: Unfortunately, Haygood Hall, the administration building, was destroyed by fire in 1969.
53. *Ibid.*, p. 13.
54. Clary, George Esmond, Jr., "The Founding of Paine College—A Unique Venture in Inter-racial Cooperation in the South 1882-1903." Doctor of Education Dissertation, University of Georgia, 1965 (Summary-Order No. 65-10, 276, p. 2575).
55. *Ibid.*
56. Graham, William L. "Pattern of Intergroup Relations. . ." A Dissertation for the Ph.D. degree, New York University, 1955 (Publication No. 12, 215), p. 1275.
57. *Ibid.*, p. 1276.
58. *Ibid.*

CHAPTER 21

HISTORICAL SKETCH OF PHILANDER SMITH COLLEGE

On November 7, 1877, Walden Seminary, Little Rock, Ark., later taking the name Philander Smith College, was founded.[1] It was the second institution founded west of the Mississippi River by the Freedmen's Aid Society to provide education for the Freedmen.

"The school was opened in Wesley Chapel, an open dilapidated church, entirely unfit for a schoolroom. . .Here it remained until January 1, 1879, when it was removed to a suite of rooms on the second floor of a building. . .a store."[2] This location was inconvenient, but was an improvement over the church building.

From the beginning Walden Seminary was closely related to the Little Rock Annual Conference of the Methodist Episcopal Church. The Conference in session February 21, 1879, expressed appreciation to the Freedmen's Aid Society for the establishment of a "Conference School where our young men may be educated for the ministry and our people may have the benefit of a first-class seminary education."[3]

The Conference approved the following resolutions:

"Resolved, That we recognize in the Freedmen's Aid Society as one of our greatest benefactors.

"Resolved, That we pledge ourselves to do all we can for this Society, and take up a collection for it in each of our charges."[4]

Miss H. M. Perkins was the first Principal of Walden Seminary.[5] The Little Rock Annual Conference February 21, 1880, expressed satisfaction with Miss Perkins as Principal and recommended that she be continued.

Rev. Thomas Mason, Principal

At the 1882 session of the Little Rock Conference it was written into the Minutes:

"We note with great pleasure the marked degree of prosperity that has attended Walden Seminary during the past term, under the efficient superintendence of our Brother T. Mason. Without a suitable place in which to hold school,

Brother Mason came and assumed charge under the appointment of Dr. Rust, and opened in Wesley on the 14th of November, last, with 22 students. . . .At the close of the first three months there was an enrollment of 59 students. . . .future success and permanency depends upon the erection at once of a suitable building, provided with modern appliances. . . ."[6]

The Conference resolved to take steps for raising a subscription to erect the building, and to petition Reverend Dr. Rust to furnish an additional male teacher.

Trustees of Walden Seminary

The Little Rock Conference in session in 1883 elected the following men as the first trustees of the seminary:[7]

Bishop I. W. Wiley, D.D., Reverend R. S. Rust, D.D., Reverend T. Mason, Reverend L. W. Elkins, Reverend S. Johnson, Reverend Frank Garland, Reverend I. G. Pollard, Reverend G. W. Sams, Reverend W. O. Emory, Mr. William LaPort and Mr. A. L. Richardson.

In the same year, 1883, the name was changed from Walden Seminary to Philander Smith College and was chartered in this name and began offering for the first time instruction leading to a baccalaureate degree, the first degree being conferred in 1888.[8]

The first and main building for Philander Smith College was erected in 1883, a gift for this purpose having been made by Mrs. Adeline M. Smith of Oak Park, Illinois, who carried out the wishes of her late husband, in whose memory the college was named.[9]

In 1883 Mrs. Adeline Smith made an initial gift of $1,000 toward an industrial home for girls. The building was begun in 1883 and was dedicated February 25, 1884, bearing the name "Adeline M. Smith Industrial Home."[10] The home and its work were initiated through the interest of the Woman's Home Missionary Society. The Adeline Smith Home was located on the Philander Smith College campus, the work of each complementing that of the other. Both the college and the home were made possible by the Philander Smith family, who contributed to this enterprise seventeen thousand dollars.[11]

With these developments Philander Smith College, within the six years after its founding in 1877, was well established and on its way to becoming a highly respected institution.

There was great affection for Philander Smith College on the part of the Little Rock Annual Conference, to which the Conference frequently referred in its minutes as "one of the grandest schools in the country."[12] At the Conference session of

434

1890 it was "Resolved, to place someone in the field to work in the interest of Philander Smith College, to raise means for the institution and to organize college aid societies."[13]

In 1891, under the presidency of Rev. Thomas Mason, the estimated property value of the college was $30,000.[14] The total student enrollment was 364, elementary, secondary, and college levels.

Mr. Budlong of Illinois made a subscription of two thousand dollars to the college for a new building for school and dormitory purposes, on condition that the colored people themselves raise a like amount.[15] This, they set themselves to the task of accomplishing.

By 1891 industrial work had become an important part of the program. President Mason wrote May 4, 1891:

> "We have reached the point in our history at Philander Smith College when we no longer regard the manual training system as an experiment. In our Department of Carpentry we have 114 students, nearly all of whom are anxious to acquire a knowledge of the trade and the use of tools....Among our numerous visitors, and by all the friends of the college, our manual-training department is universally commended."[16]

At the same time the Woman's Home Missionary Society maintained an excellent industrial home for young women on the opposite corner of the campus.[17]

Rev. James M. Cox, President

The Rev. Thomas Mason gave administrative leadership to Philander Smith College for fifteen years, 1882 to 1897. He was succeeded by Professor J. M. Cox as Acting President,[18] who became President the following year.[19] Professor Cox joined the Philander Smith College Faculty in 1886 as teacher of Greek and Latin, having received the B.A. degree from Clark University, Atlanta, in 1884, and the B.D. degree in 1886 from Gammon School of Theology. The Rev. Cox was the first man to receive a degree from Gammon.[20]

The election of the Rev. Cox as the first Negro President of Philander Smith College was considered as an experiment. Most of the faculty members were white. After one or two years, the appointment was no longer considered an experiment, the affairs of the college having been so well administered by the new President. In 1900 the students numbered 465, the faculty fourteen, and the property was valued at $30,000.00[21] By 1904 the enrollment had grown to 521 and the faculty to seventeen. The property remained the same.[22] By 1908 the enrollment of the college in all departments numbered 659, the faculty numbered thirty-four and the property value had increased to $47,100.[23] The Report of the General Conference of 1912 indicates that the enrollment had dropped to 473 and the faculty had been decreased to twenty-two. The property value had increased to $56,785.00.[24]

A new dormitory for women, Webb Hall, was completed and occupied in 1916. The building was named in memory of Mr. J. B. Webb, formerly of Oak Park, Illinois, who organized the first school for Negroes in Little Rock in 1868, and through whose efforts Mrs. Philander Smith was induced to give the money for the establishment of the college.[25]

On March 29, 1920, President Cox sent a telegram to Dr. P. J. Maveety, one of the Corresponding Secretaries of the Freedmen's Aid Society, informing him that the two-story frame structure known as the Industrial Building had been completely destroyed by fire. The insurance allowed on the building was $3,200.00. The industrial work for men was never completely restored. The value of the plant at the end of the school year 1924 was $67,000.00.[26]

The year 1924 was one of climax for President Cox, bringing his career as President to a close. He had a vision of what Philander Smith College should become and laid the foundation for its expansion. A new site of forty-two acres, costing $42,000.00, had been purchased. The land was purchased with money made available by the Board of Education from proceeds of the Centenary.[27] The site overlooked a part of the city, two and one half miles from the business section. The old property was to have been sold and new buildings erected on the new site. The Arkansas State Board of Education had given Philander Smith College "A" rating as the leading institution in the State for the education of the Negro.[28] The new site with buildings, equipment and faculty was to provide a future for the college surpassing any in the State.[29]

Dr. James M. Cox was President of Philander Smith College twenty-seven years, guiding its destiny to a highly recognized institution. He gave his whole life to that one institution, having taught there eleven years before becoming President and having given it a total of thirty-eight years of service. The cause of Negro education in the Methodist Episcopal Church was greatly enhanced by his life of humility and dedication. He made a remarkable impression on the Negro youth of Arkansas and adjoining States, having helped to educate and train more than one-half of the Negro public teachers in the State of Arkansas.[30]

Dr. Cox retired in June, 1924, highly respected and greatly beloved by all who had known him or had come under his tutelage.

Dean George C. Taylor, President

To succeed President Emeritus James M. Cox, Dean George C. Taylor was elected President of Philander Smith College in June, 1924. President Taylor, a native of Mississippi, assumed the Presidency at the age of forty-one. He received his early education in the public schools of Arkansas, and completed his college education, with the A.B. degree, at Philander Smith College where he worked his way doing chores for President Cox.[31]

President Taylor came to this new office with many years of educational experience as Principal of the high school, Van Buren, Ark.; teacher of English, Ft. Smith High School, Ft. Smith, Ark.; Superintendent of the Normal Department, New Orleans University, New Orleans, La.; Principal of Peabody High School, Helena, Ark.; Chairman of the Department of Mathematics, Philander Smith College; and Dean of the College, Philander Smith College. He was highly regarded as a leader in the field of education.[32]

President Taylor, inaugurated at the May Commencement, 1925, assumed the Presidency of Philander Smith College with high hope for immediate growth and expansion. The new site of forty-two acres had just been purchased and the building of a new campus was anticipated. The relocation of the college, however, never materialized. A number of problems arose. The needed funds from the Board of Education and the Centenary were not forthcoming. There was not sufficient demand, in fact no demand, for the property of the site where the college was located to raise any hopes of getting enough money to even begin the new project of relocation. All the disadvantages of relocating the college had to be considered. Long delay ensued. The depression of the late 1920's and 1930's came and resulted in further delay. In the meantime, very little could be done toward improving the old property, for lack of money, and until a final decision was reached regarding relocation.

President Taylor, with the assistance of Professor H. H. Sutton who became Dean of the college in 1928, made heroic efforts to advance the college during the period of uncertainty regarding its location, and a period of financial difficulties and instability.

President Taylor's administration came to a close in June 1936. The developments for which he had hoped had to wait passing of another dozen years and the leadership of another president.

Dr. Marquis LaFayette Harris, President

Dr. Marquis L. Harris, a young man and strong physically, was called to the Presidency of Philander Smith College to succeed President George C. Taylor. He was elected to this post while serving as teacher and Dean of the College at Samuel Huston College, Austin, Texas, and assumed duties in September, 1936.

Dr. Harris came to the Presidency of Philander Smith College with an excellent background of academic preparation. He was a graduate of Clark University (Clark College), Atlanta, Georgia, with a Bachelor of Science degree; he held a Bachelor of Divinity degree from Gammon Theological Seminary, he held a Master of Sacred Theology degree from Boston University; and he had earned the degree Doctor of Philosophy from Ohio State University. He had, unmistakably, the qualities for intellectual and academic leadership, with which he immediately went to work with great devotion.

When President Harris assumed office the college still owned the forty-two acres of land purchased back in 1924. It was still located on the old site of approximately three acres. There were five buildings, greatly in need of heavy repairs or replacement. The college had only $200.00 of endowment, and the total value of the property and all assets of the college was $159,700.[33] The general economic depression of the 1930's, and diminishing appropriations from the Board of Education gave no hope for the funds needed for immediate improvement of the college. President Harris set himself to the task of creating and building new resources from which to draw support. The manner in which this was done over a period of years was phenomenal.

Though Philander Smith for years had been recognized by the Arkansas State Department of Education, the college needed regional accreditation. Being located in the territory of the North Central Association of colleges and secondary schools, it had to gain its accreditation from that association, and could not receive the courtesy rating of the Southern Association of Colleges and Secondary Schools granted to some other Negro colleges in the Southern Region. Accreditation was one of the difficult problems that had to be solved.

In addition to finding additional financial support for the college, President Harris worked to build up the enrollment. He and the faculty revised the whole program and he appealed to the church for recognition of the place and importance of Philander Smith College in that section. In making his appeal, he said:

438

I wish to make the following observations: Philander Smith College is the only standard four-year college operated by any church for Negroes in the large territory north of Texas and west of the Mississippi River. It is the only standard private college of any kind in this vast territory. It is the only standard church college for Negroes in the dual educational societies of Arkansas, Missouri, and Oklahoma.

Philander Smith is the only college operated for Negroes by our church within the bounds of the North Central Territory and certainly should be made a high-class institution to serve the Mississippi Valley Region where Methodism is on the march and Methodist constituency rapidly growing.[34]

Philander Smith College was one of the first twenty-seven members of the United Negro College Fund, Inc. Because it had no rating by its regional accrediting association, a problem arose regarding its membership in the United Negro College Fund and the share of money to be distributed to it. This placed a tremendous hardship upon the college; but fortunately, the Fund agreed to hold in escrow Philander Smith College's share of the funds and to give a reasonable time for the college to become accredited.

In 1948 the labors of President Harris began to come to fruition. The following information was reported:

"Philander Smith College. . . .increased the value of its physical plant by approximately $600,000 during the summer, according to President M. LaFayette Harris. The additions include a student union building, a gymnasium, a special building for music and drama, a science building, and a general academic administration building of more than 40,000 square feet of floor space. The student union building was erected outright. The other buildings, all recent brick structures, adjoin the Philander Smith College campus and have been used by the Little Rock Junior College."[35]

In a later report President Harris stated that, "Because of the fine relationships which the college has enjoyed over the years and its unusual reputation for effective service, the School Board made the properties available for $222,350. The purchase was made on a cash basis, with only $40,000 advanced by the Board of Education of The Methodist Church still outstanding. . . .in the campaign to raise funds for this purchase, the four Negro Annual Conferences of the St. Louis Area which support the institution, raised $44,000 in a 90-day period through a simple letter campaign, letters from the office of President Harris."[3][6]

From these reports it is evident that Philander Smith College was highly regarded by the Board of Education and the people of Little Rock as an important educational instrument in the community, that was worthy of their help. Also, the institution was still alive in the Negro Conferences that have supported it from the beginning of the institution in 1877. According to President Harris, these new developments mean, first, relief from an overcrowded situation in which it was impossible to do effective work; second, it assured the future of the institution, the outlook for which had been critical because of the inadequacy of the plant; and third, it meant earlier accreditation by the North Central Association of Colleges and Secondary Schools.[3][7]

Philander Smith College earned accreditation by the North Central Association, which was granted in 1949. This gave the college an entirely new standing in the educational world. It was restored to full membership status in the United Negro College Fund, and its share of funds held in escrow was turned over to the college. President Harris, working over a period of some thirteen years, had led Philander Smith College to a new level of efficiency and service, and much closer to the goal of his dream for the college.

In his Inaugural Address, October 26, 1937, President Harris stated what he conceived to be a fundamental philosophy regarding an educational institution and its educational task. He said: "Institutions, like persons, live their own lives and periods of usefulness. They must possess their own personalities."[3][8] He further stated the "Science of Human Relations and the Art of Creative Living: to be the two concepts constituting the "First Principle of the new Educational Pattern at Philander Smith College."[3][9]

This was probably the first time in the Presidential leadership of the college there emerged a stated creative philosophy of personal and personality influence in the educative process at the college, indicating that "Life is regarded as a ceaseless process and the major concern with human beings is that of creative adjustment."[4][0]

It was within the framework of this philosophy that President Harris labored for twenty-four years to make Philander Smith College an exceptional institution in physical plant, academic excellence, and the quality of its graduates.

At the end of the school year 1959-1960 a new dormitory center and a fine arts building were in the process of being erected; the enrollment had reached approximately 1,000, including

440

summer school; the annual operating budget was approximately $750,000; and the plant value, including thirty acres of land, was about $3,000,000.

In 1960 President Harris was elected to the Episcopacy in The Methodist Church. His untiring labors, his productive work, and his magnanimous service to Philander Smith College and the cause of Christian higher education, recognized by all, contributed more than any other factor to his elevation to the highest office in The Methodist Church.

Dr. Roosevelt David Crockett, President

In March, 1961, Dr. Roosevelt D. Crockett was elected President of Philander Smith College to succeed President Harris D. Crockett, assuming office June 1, 1961; he brought to this position excellent educational preparation and promise of continuation of the splendid progress of the college made during the administration of his predecessor. He held the B.A. degree from Philander Smith College, B.D. degree from Drew University, and the Ph.D. degree from Boston University. He had broad experience in the ministry, teaching, and college administration.

During the three years of Dr. Crockett's administration notable improvements were made in the physical plant and the academic program was strengthened. Construction was completed on the M. L. Harris Library and Fine Arts Center and it was placed in use in January, 1963. Six city blocks of Urban Renewal Property adjacent to the main campus were acquired, and in 1963 a $3,000,000 housing project and shopping center were opened.

Dr. Crockett resigned from the Presidency in August, 1964.

Dr. Ernest Thomas Dixon, President

To succeed Dr. Crockett, Dr. Ernest T. Dixon was elected President of Philander Smith College in October, 1964, and took office January 1, 1965. Dr. Dixon, a graduate of Samuel Huston College, holding a B.D. degree from Drew Theological Seminary and a D.D. degree from Huston-Tillotson College, came to the Presidency of Philander Smith from a staff position at the Board of Education, The Methodist Church.

During Dr. Dixon's administration final payment was made to the Little Rock Housing Authority for four and one-half blocks of land adjacent to the main campus, bringing the campus to more than ten city blocks of land.

Dr. Dixon's resignation became effective March 1, 1969, after four years of presidency.

Dr. Walter Raphael Hazzard, Incumbent

Succeeding Dr. Dixon, Dr. Walter R. Hazzard took office as Philander Smith's seventh President on July 1, 1969. Under his administration "already significant improvements have been made in the academic program, the physical plant, strengthening of the faculty, and the establishment of closer administration-faculty-student-trustee relationships."[41]

Philander Smith College during its history of ninety-five years has established a rich Christian heritage. "Across the years, it has earned the designation as a 'college of service and distinction.' "[42]

REFERENCES AND NOTES

1. Report, Freedmen's Aid Society, 1879, p. 50.
2. *Ibid.*, p. 51.
3. Minutes, Little Rock Annual Conference, February 21, 1879, p. 12.
4. *Ibid.*
5. Report, Freedmen's Aid Society, 1879, p. 50.
6. Minutes, The Little Rock Annual Conference, February 9-13, 1882, p. 22.
7. *Ibid.*, February 8—11, 1883, p. 15.
8. American Universities and Colleges, 10th Edition, 1968, p. 131, and General Conference Journal, 1936, p. 1048.
9. *The Christian Educator*, January, 1891, pp. 69f.
10. Meeker, Mrs. Ruth Ester, *op. cit.*, pp. 124f.
11. *The Christian Educator*, January, 1891, p. 70.
12. Journal, Little Rock Annual Conference, February 13-17, 1890, p. 31.
13. *Ibid.*, p. 32.
14. *The Christian Educator*, July, 1891, p. 209.
15. *Ibid.*, p. 210.
16. Report, the Freedmen's Aid and Southern Education Society, 1891, p. 211.
17. *Ibid.*, p. 210.
18. *The Christian Educator*, April-May, 1898, p. 97.
19. *The Christian Educator*, December-January 1898-99, p. 37, and *The Christian Educator*, April-May, 1899, p. 99.
20. Stowell, Jay S., *Methodist Adventure in Negro Education*, p. 146.
21. Report, Freedmen's Aid and Southern Education Society, 1901, p. 131.
22. General Conference Journal, 1904, p. 855.
23. *Ibid.*, 1908, p. 1296.
24. *Ibid.*, 1912, p. 1278.
25. General Conference Journal, 1916, p. 1403.
26. *The Christian Educator*, November, 1924 (Back Cover).
27. *Ibid.*, November, 1922, p. 1, and May, 1924, p. 10.
28. *Ibid.*
29. *Ibid.*
30. *Ibid.*, November, 1924, p. 3.
31. *Ibid.*, August, 1924, p. 8.
32. *Ibid.*
33. General Conference Journal, 1936, p. 1048.
34. Manuscript: "A General Statement on the Case of Philander

Smith College"—President M. L. Harris, 1943.

35. *The Christian Education Magazine*, Nov.-Dec., 1948, p. 30.
36. *Ibid.*, January-February, 1949, p. 7.
37. *Ibid.*, pp. 7f.
38. Harris, M. LaFayette, *The Voice in the Wilderness*, p. 45.
39. *Ibid.*, p. 46.
40. *Ibid.*, p. IX.
41. Philander Smith College Bulletin, 1970-1971, p. 7.
42. *Ibid.*

CHAPTER 22

A BRIEF HISTORICAL SKETCH OF RUST COLLEGE
(FOUNDED AS SHAW UNIVERSITY, LATER BECAME
RUST UNIVERSITY AND THEN RUST COLLEGE)

The founding and development of Rust College was entwined with the inception and growth of the Mississippi Annual Conference of the Methodist Episcopal Church. On December 25, 1865, the Mississippi Mission Conference was organized by Bishop Edward Thomson, at New Orleans, La.,[1] covering the States of Louisiana and Mississippi, with one district in Texas. By action of the 1868 General Conference, the Mississippi Mission Conference became a full Annual Conference and its boundaries embraced only the State of Mississippi.

While yet a Mission Conference, the Reverend Albert C. McDonald became a member and at the session of the Mississippi Conference in December, 1867, when a district was created at Jackson and one at Holly Springs, he was made Presiding Elder of the Holly Springs District.[2] The Rev. McDonald in late 1866 had begun classes in the Asbury Church for Negro children. This was the beginning of the institution which was later to become Shaw University. The Asbury Methodist Church had been organized in 1866 by Rev. McDonald and Rev. Moses Adams, an ex-slave.[3]

In its Third Annual Report the Freedmen's Aid Society states:

"We have purchased a valuable property embracing a commanding site in this healthful locality, and the Bureau has appropriated five thousand dollars for the erection of our Normal School, which will soon be ready for occupancy.

"The colored people take a lively interest in the institution, and have subscribed two thousand dollars toward its erection. Great credit is due to Rev. A. C. McDonald for untiring efforts and the responsibility assumed in behalf of this enterprise. This University is full of promise, and the eyes of anxious students are turned toward it from the whole Mississippi Valley, and it promises to become a powerful instrumentality in the elevation of this race."[4]

The "Bureau" referred to in the Freedmen's Aid Society Report was the Bureau of the Federal Government, and the "valuable property" was the site of the former Slave Auction Grounds of Holly Springs, as well as the campground of General Ulysses S. Grant's Army.[5]

When the Freedmen's Aid Society took full charge of the school in 1868, the Rev. McDonald was placed in charge of the enterprise and became its first President. The first building erected on the newly purchased site was called the McDonald Hall. The Reverend S. P. Shaw made a gift of $10,000 for the erection of the first building and the institution was named Shaw University in his honor.[6]

A State Normal School was operated on the Shaw University site until 1872, when the State School was removed and the University opened its own Normal Department.[7]

The reactions to the opening of Shaw University were varied. The following quotations illustrate some of those reactions:

"When the first building. . .went up. . .a bell was installed in connection with it, and when it sounded for the first time an old colored woman shouted aloud with joy. In all her life up to that time the only bell she had heard had been the plantation bell calling the slaves to work. Now to have a real bell calling black boys and girls to school was an experience so profound and epoch-making as to be well worth shouting about."[8]

Among the more enlightened portion of the white community as well there was support for the College, as evidenced in the annual report for 1875:

"However hostile to the education of the Freedmen the whites may be elsewhere in the South, here both teachers and pupils are respected and encouraged by the most influential of them. One of the first men of this place, an ex-slave holder, has voluntarily taken it upon himself to raise means for us among his people."[9]

Most of the white community, however, regarded the College and its faculty with suspicion and hostility as being, like the other activities of white Northerners in Holly Springs, a threat to Southern white supremacy.

In 1870 the little school begun in 1866 in Asbury Methodist Church was incorporated by the State Legislature of Mississippi in the name of Shaw University. The Charter of incorporation was granted to the following twenty-one incorporators as Trustees: J.

446

L. Alcorn, R. S. Rust, William M. Compton, James Lynch, B. B. Emery, Moses Adams, W. L. Jones, A. C. McDonald, S. H. Scott, A. M. West, J. Garret Johnson, C. W. Fitzhugh, Albert Johnson, W. G. Millsaps, R. W. Flournoy, Alex Phillips, J. W. Deshazo, G. C. Sullivan, J. Aaron Moore, Merriman Howard, and S. P. Shaw, dated May 26, 1870.[10]

The Charter is a broad and liberal document indicating that the University is forever to be conducted on the most liberal principles; accessible to all, irrespective of their religious tenets, and designated for the benefit of our citizens in general.[11] The broad and liberal powers granted in the charter made it possible then and now for Rust College to admit students without regard to racial or religious distinction. This was in keeping with the policies of the Freedmen's Aid Society and the Methodist Episcopal Church, and meets the demands of modern social changes.

Speaking of Shaw University, the Freedmen's Aid Society in 1871 stated:

"This is located at Holly Springs, Mississippi, on the brow of a hill overlooking the city. We have secured, in connection with it, a tract of land, containing eighty-five acres, which will be cultivated in the interests of the University. The University building is brick, and was erected at an expense of nearly ten thousand dollars. The State has made an appropriation of four thousand dollars for the Normal Department, and by arrangement with the Trustees will support, for the present year, the teachers of this department. Professor Gorman, the Principal of the Normal Department, is a graduate of the Illinois Normal School, an excellent scholar and a successful educator. Pupils from all parts of the State are resorting to this school. The Biblical Department is under the care of the President, who will be aided by competent assistants.

"*Board of Instruction.* Reverend A. C. McDonald, President; Professor A. H. Gorman, Principal; Miss Lue A. Henly, Mr. J. D. Backentose, Miss M. A. Wilder, teachers."[12]

The following year, 1872, the support given the Normal Department by the State was discontinued.

The Reverend President McDonald was, in 1871, one of the six effective elders of the Mississippi Conference and as a member of the Conference, his conference appointment each year was to the Presidency of Shaw University. He was active in the conference and kept the University in the hearts of the ministers and close to the people. He served as Secretary of the Conference.[13] At the

447

December, 1871, session, the Mississippi Conference passed the following Resolution:

"Resolved, That we recognize, in Shaw University an institution which promises a rich harvest, and which is well worthy of our patronage; and that we will use our influence in its support, by collecting funds for it, and by inducing the young people of the church to enter it as students, especially young men who are called of God to the Ministry.

"Resolved, That we request the Bishop to appoint the Rev. A. C. McDonald, A.M., President of Shaw University, with the understanding that he devote his time and attention to the duties of this institution."[14]

President McDonald gave full attention to the development of the institution and it made strides of progress under his administration and leadership. In 1870 a Biblical Department was established to prepare ministers, especially for the Mississippi Conference. A report from the University in 1872 showed an enrollment of 260 students not including the grades. In the preparatory department the enrollment was 158; in the Theological Department, 27; and in the Normal Department, 75.[15] The grades carried a heavy enrollment.

Instruction went beyond the academic subjects. The school was deeply interested in the spiritual life of the students and the teachers helped to perform a "wonderful work of grace."

In 1875 the instructional staff at Shaw consisted of the Rev. A. C. McDonald, D.D., President, who also taught; Rev. W. W. Hooper, A.M., Principal and teacher; C. A. Weaver, A.M., Professor of Mathematics; Mrs. M. A. Weaver, teacher; and Mrs. W. W. Hooper, teacher.[16]

The Freedmen's Aid Society's Eighth Annual Report further indicates that:

"We have enrolled during the year upward to two hundred students, who have averaged an attendance of six months each. More than one hundred of this number have taught at least three months the year, having an average attendance of above fifty pupils each, making more than five thousand pupils that have been directly or indirectly under the influence of our University during the year. The great majority of these have not only received mental but spiritual instruction. And who shall estimate the vastness of the harvest that the future will reap from the seed thus sown?"[17]

In view of the apparent superficial training given for the teaching referred to above President McDonald sets forth the standards and true aims of Shaw University in the following statement:

"It is our aim to do no hot-house work, seeking to hurry students through a college curriculum, as do many mushroom schools in the South, sending them into the battle of life only to disgrace themselves and bring reproach upon the cause of education at large, but take the by far more difficult and tedious plan of trying to lay well a foundation for a broad, thorough, and practical education, such as shall fit our pupils for long lives of usefulness to themselves, their race, and the church."[18]

President McDonald imbued the whole school with high standards and the spirit of excellence, holding that "all labor is honorable if well done." During the years he was President of Shaw University, the Reverend McDonald wrought well and laid a solid foundation on which to build an excellent institution in the future. He resigned in 1876[19] and died in 1877. The Rev. W. W. Hooper was elected President to succeed President McDonald.

The Reverend W. W. Hooper became the second President of Shaw University in 1877, succeeding President A. C. McDonald. He had joined the Shaw faculty under President McDonald two years earlier. For a period of eight years (1877-1885) President Hooper advanced the work of Shaw University in all of its phases. It was during his administration, in 1878, that the Shaw University conferred its first two college degrees. In 1879 the total enrollment was 225, distributed as follows: Theology, 17; college classes, 45; preparatory, 60; and under-preparatory, 103.[20] It is probable that the enrollment was larger than the total given inasmuch as no figure is given for the enrollment in the Normal Department, which was always one of the larger departments.

The Mississippi Conference continued its interest in and concern for Shaw University under the administration of President Hooper. The Conference, in its 1878 session, passed the following resolution:

"We rejoice in the good that has already been done by our institution, the Shaw University, in its training of young ministers and its sending teachers all over the State, who are now engaged in public schools as teachers."[21]

In another resolution, the Conference gave its approval of President Hooper's work in his first year as President:

"Resolved, that we most heartily approve of the manner in which our worthy President, W. W. Hooper, has conducted business at the University the past year. . ."[22]

This approval was supported by a third resolution of commitment to give financial aid:

"Resolved, that we will renew our efforts, and pledge ourselves to raise at least $5,000 during the coming year to meet the pressing wants of the University."[23]

In every session of the Mississippi Conference from year to year the interest and loyalty of the Conference gave assurance that the Conference was with the college in every step it took to achieve progress. In the 1880 session the Conference set the last Sunday in November for a special collection to be reported at the next Annual Session.[24] The Conference requested the presiding Bishop to re-appoint the Rev. Hooper as President, and pledged themselves to raise $5,000 during the coming four years to aid in the erection of a new building at Shaw University.[25]

Regarding the students: Several human interest stories were told by the presidents regarding the ability of the students at Shaw and their desire for education. President Hooper told the following story:

"We graduated our first class, two young men, in 1878. . . .One of them, a boy sixteen, has thoroughly mastered mathematics through trigonometry, has read Latin through Horace and is equally good in Greek. After reading through the first book of the Odes, we gave him as a test, the first Ode of the third book; after one hour's study he was able to translate, analyze, and parse the entire Ode.

"Most of our students are enduring great hardships to obtain an education. One young man, last Fall, walked more than one hundred miles to reach school, and is working morning and evening for his board. He is a zealous Christian minister, thoroughly in earnest in his efforts to fit himself for the responsible duties of this office."[26]

Later, President Libby told the following story of three young men with a determination to get an education:

"Three bright young colored men walked three hundred miles at the beginning of a school year at Rust University, to be at school for the first day. Someone had told them that they would get their education at Rust University free. When they reached their destination they had hardly clothes enough to cover their nakedness, and were without a cent of money.

"The President. . .fixed them up with clothing, gave them a little work to do, and they started into school. They were cheerful and happy through all the year, and the three of them lived on less than $20 each for the seven months. They frequently came to school in the morning without having had any breakfast. . .They walked back to their home at the close of the school, and wrote the President a cheerful letter when reaching there."[2 7]

The abilities and talents of the students found at Shaw University from its earliest years to the present day students of Rust College have been remarkable. Especially is this true of their singing talents, which expressed as individual singers and in choral groups have established a rich and valuable tradition noted and appreciated across a whole century, down to the talented artist, Ruby Elzy, whom death claimed much too soon in her young life, and to the excellent choral groups of the last two or three decades under the direction and inspiration of Natlie Doxie, who herself is a symbol of this tradition and heritage.

The record of this tradition and heritage began, probably, with the following account given by a visitor to the Shaw campus in 1873:

"The school sings. How it does sing! The fragments of Jubilee and Hampton Singers that visit the North are discordant silence to the mellifluous thunders of these choruses. There is a male voice at Holly Springs sweeter than I have heard anywhere else. It is a tenor, so mellow and strong that, as you hear it, you can but think of those golden bells of poor poetic marriage-bells, whose sacred sweetness he touched alone in song, not life. As one hears their exquisite untrained music utterances, he wonders how the Creator could have ever hidden such a harp in such a throat."[2 8]

President Hooper's administration, which was a successful one in advancing Shaw University, came to an end in 1885. He was succeeded by the Reverend Charles E. Libby. President Libby gave able leadership to the University from 1886 to 1906.

In 1888 a great calamity befell the institution in the burning of

Rust Hall, the magnificent structure and principal building on the campus.[29] This loss was a tremendous setback and posed very difficult problems. With determination and heroic courage President Libby kept the institution on its academic course and raised the funds for the erection of a building to replace the one that was burned. This building was more complete than the former and stood as the main building on the campus for a half century. Included in this building were administrative offices, classrooms, laboratories, library, chapel, dining room, and four stories of dormitories for men on the west side and for women on the east side.

By 1891 Shaw University had reached phenomenal academic strength, covering all levels. The fields of academic work included philosophy, theological courses, mathematics, natural science, ancient languages (classical), English literature, French, history, the Normal Department, music, commerce, and nurse training.[30]

The University had also developed a strong industrial department, including carpentry, printing, agriculture, shoe-making, needlework, millinery, dress-making, and painting.[31]

On petition of the Trustees, the Legislature of the State of Mississippi amended the charter of the institution, changing the name from "Shaw University" to "Rust University."[32] in honor of Dr. Richard S. Rust, Corresponding Secretary of the Freedmen's Aid and Education Society, and who had labored so many years in behalf of the Freedmen's Aid Society and Shaw University.

President Libby resigned from the Presidency in 1896 because of ill health. He died in October 1897. The following account was a fitting tribute to the Reverend Libby and his years of dedicated service to Rust University:

"The Rev. Charles E. Libby, D.D., President of Rust University, died October 24th, after a long and painful illness. He had resigned the Presidency of the University about a year before his death, and gone to the home of his friends in Boston, with whom he resided most of the time during the illness which excited so great sympathy with him and his family. Dr. Libby was dearly beloved by the school, of which he had been President for years. No man in the Southern work was more thoughtful for the future of his school and more devoted to liberal things. He bore heavy burdens. It was during his administration that the large building which is really the best edifice connected with the schools of the Society, was erected. His burden-bearing may have had much to do in breaking him down. He was highly esteemed by the preachers and teachers of

Mississippi, and was popular with the citizens of Holly Springs. While in other sections of the South, much was heard and said of ostracism, it must be said to the credit of the good people of Holly Springs that they were very kind and courteous to Dr. Libby. They appreciated his services, and many kind letters were written to his family by the citizens, who expressed their sincere sympathy with them in their great loss. He was a brave man; none of the discouragements moved him; neither counted he his life dear unto himself, so that he might finish his course with joy, and the ministry which he had received of the Lord Jesus."[33]

At the resignation of President Libby in 1896, followed by his death in 1897, the Reverend D. H. Sayer served as Acting President for approximately one year.

In 1897 Dr. William W. Foster became President of Rust University and had a tenure of twelve fruitful years.

A prominent educator visiting Rust University stated:

"You have shown great wisdom in the selection of Dr. Foster. He is not only a man of first-class ability, but he shows admirable adaptability to the work. He and his accomplished wife are showing rare tact, and their consecrated ability and contagious enthusiasm are working a transformation at Rust University. They have won the hearts of the preachers and the large number of students who are flocking to Rust are all singing their praises."[33a]

When Dr. Foster became President he was heir to a fine heritage of growth and progress.

By 1898, Rust University had made a considerable contribution. From the establishment of the school in 1866 to the closing years of the century, many Negro students had received an education. The total of graduates numbered 195, and were classified as follows: Post-graduate, 1; college course, 32; academic, 59; normal, 59; nurse-training, 40; and music, 4. Two university presidents were listed among its graduates, namely, E. Robert Fulkerson, Nagasaki, Japan, and Matthew W. Dogan, of Wiley University, the latter a school of the Freedmen's Aid Society. One graduate, the Reverend John L. Wilson, had been appointed as Principal of the Meridian Academy. Eight graduates in 1898 were teaching in various departments in the Negro universities of the South. Others were listed as successful principals in city schools, and a few of the graduates of the school were serving their people as physicians, nurses, merchants, government clerks, ministers, and common-school teachers.[34]

The University had justified and continued to exemplify the

motto of the school given by the first President, Dr. A. C. McDonald: "By their fruits ye shall know them."

In 1909 Dr. Foster resigned from the Presidency of Rust University to accept a call to the Presidency of Beaver College at Beaver, Pennsylvania.[35]

The following statement summarizes Dr. Foster's administration at Rust and pays fitting tribute to his services as President:

"For twelve years Dr. Foster gave us most efficient and faithful service as President of Rust University, and was ably assisted by his devoted wife. During this time the attendance was more than doubled, $50,000 in buildings and equipment added to the institution, the industrial department greatly enlarged and systematized, and the whole institution developed and strengthened. Notwithstanding the large amount of improvement made, Dr. Foster leaves the institution without a dollar of indebtedness and in most excellent condition."[36]

In addition to the physical progress of Rust under the administration of Dr. Foster, he made an even more valuable contribution, that of inspiration to the students and the indelible impression upon their lives for good.

Through the medium of the annual conference, and countless other ways, Rust University reached the people all over Mississippi and not only kept alive in them, but also kept them alive to the need of an education, inspired young men and young women to put forth every effort to secure an education and always found a way to help them when their limited resources were inadequate. The help of the University extended beyond the limited economic resources of the students to help them find greater resources within themselves, and to commit themselves to the will of God. This was as much a part of education as the development of intellectual powers. One of the distinguished graduates of Rust University, Dr. M. W. Dogan bears testimony to the influence of the University upon the spiritual life of the student:

"I was converted while a student in Rust University. . .but for this institution, with its saving influence, I fear what little strength I might have possessed would have been used against rather than for the development of my people, for there were thrown before me so many temptations to go astray. The good teachers of this institution were such practical Christians, and took their religion so fully into their everyday affairs, that my conversion and that of scores of my mates followed as a matter of course."[37]

Between the presidencies of Dr. Foster and his successor, Professor E. H. McKissack served as Acting President, 1909. Professor McKissack was an instructor in Natural Science, having graduated in 1890, and the only graduate to have served at that

454

time in such a high position at Rust University.

In 1909 the Reverend James T. Docking acceeded to the Presidency of Rust University. Rev. Docking served as President of Rust for six years, 1909-1915.

Rev. Docking was a graduate of Albion College and was also a graduate of the Boston School of Theology. After several years of successful pastorates he was, in 1905, elected President of Cookman Institute, Jacksonville, Florida, where he remained five years before coming to the presidency of Rust University.[38]

Two years after Reverend Docking came to the Presidency of Rust, according to a Freedmen's Aid Society Report, the institution had buildings and grounds worth $111,200, nine teachers, and 438 students. The Upper Mississippi Conference had just begun an effort to raise $25,000 for endowment, $900 of which had been paid. A new industrial building had just been completed.[39]

With some assistance from the John F. Slater Fund, the Industrial Department at Rust had grown considerably, and the work in this department was flourishing as may be noted from the following report:

"At Rust University, Holly Springs, Miss., basket weaving and 'mission furniture' are specialties. The drawing room of the new Presbyterian college for white girls in Holly Springs is fitted out with this furniture made at our neighboring industrial shops.

"A new industrial building has just been finished and equipped with engine, woodworking machinery, forge and blacksmith outfit, and other tools.

"Here also farming, vegetable gardening, care of stock and poultry raising are taught. The institution raises most of its own milk, butter, eggs, and vegetables."[40]

President Docking did not spare himself in his efforts to advance the work of Rust University in all of its phases. Both the Faculty and the academic work were strengthened during his administration.

The personal influence of Dr. Docking on the lives of his students is attested by the following statement by Baker:

"Webster B. Baker, a Rust graduate, in his *History of Rust College*, pays high tribute to Dr. Docking. He says, 'During my stay in Rust, one of the most prominent men under whom I was guided was Rev. James T. Docking, who was President of Rust. . .I am safe in saying, that I have learned as much from him as I have from all the books that I have studied. His idea of Principles and his expression of high sentiments gave a wonderful greatness to his masterful sermons and speeches."[41]

In 1915, Dr. Docking was compelled to retire from the

Presidency of Rust University on account of ill health.[42] On March 24, 1916, Dr. Docking died,[43] having made, during his Presidency an appreciable contribution to the life of Rust University.

The presidency of Dr. Docking came to an end in the last year of the first fifty years of the history of Rust University. He had helped with his own labors to bring to fruition the labors of the Reverends McDonald, Hooper, Libby, Foster, and hundreds of other ministers and laymen of the Mississippi Conference. The humble beginning of classes by Rev. McDonald in a modest little church, Asbury, in Holly Springs almost a half century past, had grown to be a stalwart tree, bearing fruits of the intellect and the spirit of thousands of black boys and girls who came from poor and humble homes hungering and seeking for the best that Rust could offer them.

After almost fifty years Rust University could offer a good physical plant where the students could live, work, and achieve. It offered them a sound academic program and competent teachers. Industrial training was in the offering to prepare them to make a living and meet the practical demands of the times, to go back into their communities and demonstrate to the hundreds of thousands of black people the value of an education. Rust offered the students the opportunity to develop pride in themselves.

At this point of history in the life of Rust University, it could offer inspiration by pointing to a large number of graduates who were destined to become outstanding and nationally known figures in Church and State, among whom just a few examples are given: Matthew W. Dogan, who became a College President and an outstanding educator; Perry Howard, who became outstanding in law, and several years as Assistant to the U. S. Attorney General; Sidney Redmond, a noted physician; J. B. Redmond, an outstanding minister in the Methodist Episcopal Church; J. Beverly Shaw, a minister, educator, and president of two Freedmen's Aid Society schools; Alexander P. Shaw, a great preacher, and became a Bishop in The Methodist Church; and Lee Marcus McCoy who became an outstanding teacher of mathematics, an educator, and President of his alma mater thirty-three years.

These were but a few of the graduates of Rust University during its first half century, along with hundreds of other unsung greats, to whom the institution could point and say: "By Their Fruits Ye Shall Know Them."

In 1915 the Reverend George Evans was elected President of Rust University to succeed Dr. James T. Docking. President Evans

456

had a tenure of five years; his first year being the last year of the first fifty years of the institution, and the other four leading into the second half century. The tenure of President Evans was notable also because he was the last of the white ministers from the North to come and serve as President of Rust.

Rev. Evans came to Rust from the Presidency of George R. Smith College,[44] Sedalia, Missouri, where he had served two years. He came to the Presidency of Rust at a difficult time, the first World War being in progress and affecting all educational institutions of America as it affected the national economy. To his credit the work of the college continued to go forward and suffered no serious setback. The administration of President Evans came to an end in June 1920. This was also the end of an era in the history of Rust University.

A New Era

In the Spring of 1920 Dr. Matthew Simpson Davage was elected President of Rust University. Dr. Davage was the first Negro to be elected to the Presidency of this historic institution. His election marked the beginning of a new era. Dr. Davage came to Rust from Samuel Huston College, Austin, Texas. His election to head this historic institution of the Freedmen's Aid Society, one of the first two to be founded in 1866, was an advancement for him in his brilliant educational career in the making.

During his administration, Dr. Davage directed his efforts toward improving the quality of education at Rust. Letters in the files of institutional archives of the Library at I. T. C. reveal Dr. Davage's concern with the improvement of the teaching staff, improvement of the library, acquisition of equipment for the science laboratories, renovation of several buildings, and a new science hall. The enrollment grew as a result of strengthened bonds with the two Annual Conferences of the State, and a different and closer relationship to the Negro people of Mississippi. He also established a wider relationship of Rust to the general church.

The administration of Dr. Davage ended in 1924 when he was elected to the Presidency of Clark University, Atlanta, Georgia.

To succeed Dr. Davage, Dr. Lee Marcus McCoy was elected President of Rust. Dr. McCoy was the second Negro, and the first alumnus (Rust B.A., 1905) to become President of Rust University. He came to the Presidency with a rich educational background as a teacher of Mathematics, two years at Rust, as a high school principal, and as a college dean. He was Dean at Morgan College, Baltimore, Maryland, when he was chosen for the Presidency of Rust.

457

Dr. and Mrs. McCoy came to Rust as a team in 1924, and they worked closely together throughout his administration, as many of the previous Presidents and their wives had done. For a number of years Mrs. McCoy served as Librarian and Dean of Women.

Dr. McCoy was a remarkable man with singular optimism and a great faith. He moved the college forward and into new areas of work amidst great financial difficulties. Men of lesser faith and optimism would have become discouraged and would have given up, but not Lee Marcus McCoy. His success resided, in a large measure, in the truth of the statement: "His characteristic method was the ingenious use of limited means."[4][5]

President McCoy began early in his administration to raise the academic standards of the college. Progress was slow because of the ever present and pressing needs of the college, arising out of the fact that the financial resources were so limited and the clientele was poor. The situation was aggravated by disasters and the general economic depression. By 1931, however, Rust had become a member of the Association of Colleges For Negro Youth, and was fully accredited by the Mississippi State Department of Education, and the American Medical Association.[4][6]

Curriculum Re-Organization

As efforts were continued to raise standards, the "Normal School" was abolished and replaced by two- and four-year college courses in Education, leading to the B.A. or B.S. degree in Education. Other two-year courses were initiated, leading to certificates in business, pre-medicine, pre-nursing, and a general Junior College course. The B.S. degree in Home Economics was provided. All of the new innovations were in addition to the regular four-year college course leading to a B.A. degree.[4][7]

The flood disaster of 1927 in Mississippi struck hard the families of students attending Rust. President McCoy, who was appointed by the Secretary of the Interior, Herbert Hoover, as Chairman of the Flood Relief Committee, appealed for scolarships for his students affected by the flood to keep them in school.[4][8]

The flood disaster was followed, beginning in the early 1930's by the great Depression. Rust and all colleges were affected and being able to keep the doors open was greatly threatened. Austerity programs were initiated. Hard sacrifices were inescapable.

"Faculty members were asked to pledge part of their salaries to the college. The response was heartening. In 1931 President

458

McCoy reported $321.99 had been pledged monthly out of a payroll of $2,417.00 or better than 13% of total earnings. Dr. McCoy commented, 'this is really a sacrifice on the part of the teachers, but they did so gladly and without compulsion; for when I explained to them the situation, they rose up to meet it cheerfully.' . . .by 1941-2 the total annual payroll for a faculty of 18 full-time members was down to $8,032, out of a budget of $37,487.39."[48a]

This story tells graphically what Rust College had to face and the burden placed upon the President. Dr. McCoy, however, with characteristic optimism and faith never faltered. In a miraculous kind of way, he sought and found solutions.

During the depression he employed the self-help philosophy and applied it to both students and the college. With the use of the farm, he gave help to many students and raised produce for the college dining hall. He also used this opportunity to teach students how they could take the knowledge gained on the college farm under expert instruction and direction back to their communities that so much needed their help.

The Rust College Singers became a great asset in raising funds for the college. They traveled extensively over the States of Iowa, the Dakotas, and Minnesota, covering the Annual Conferences assigned the college for cultivation. "The direct financial contribution of the singers to Rust was considerable, amounting in at least one year (1941), to almost 10 per cent of the budget."[49]

Additional support was forthcoming from these conferences from Race Relations Sunday Offerings. The results were much greater than the monetary gains, in terms of inter-racial understanding and appreciation.

Another misfortune befell Rust College just when hopes were being raised for a better day.

"Rust received a severe blow when, on January 8, 1940, Rust Hall was swept by a devastating fire which destroyed the chapel, library, classrooms, offices, and dormitories in one blow. There was temptation to despair, and closing the college completely was considered, but a spirit of faith and courage sustained Rust in the hour of crisis; when President McCoy, who was absent at the time of the fire, received word by telephone that "the college has burned down," he is said to have replied, "No—the building has burned, the college still stands!"

"Makeshift facilities were improvised with such speed that classes were resumed the day after the fire, and friends of the college, Negro and white, South and North, rallied to its support. By 1947 the college had not only survived, but expanded, and had, with the extensive assistance of the Church, replaced Rust

Hall with an equally imposing edifice, the present McCoy administration building."[50]

There were many educational needs faced by the people of Mississippi. President McCoy had the interest and the genius to see the needs and to devise a plan to help meet them. This is evident in the following paragraph on at least one of the needs:

"Even in the face of the grave obstacles which confronted the college during this period, it never ceased to seek new ways to serve the community, and indeed, the McCoy administration saw Rust more involved in off-campus and part-time adult education than in any previous period. One such activity of major importance was the extension program, which derived, like Rust's internal reforms, from rising standards in Negro education. Many teachers lacked college or even high school training, and, as they were unable to financially become full-time students, both they and their pupils suffered. With the encouragement of local education officials, Rust undertook to provide in-service training for these teachers, and the first experimental center was set up in Memphis in 1924. By 1935 there was an extensive program under the direction of Dr. J. R. Reynolds, Dean of Extension Courses, under which some 476 students received instruction at 20 centers throughout the State of Mississippi."[51]

World War II brought a number of advantages to Rust College. One advantage was the large number of returning soldiers seeking to continue their education under the G. I. Bill.

"This in turn gave President McCoy an opportunity to continue his mission of improving Rust by increasing both the size and quality of the faculty. The result of this was that the College progressed from a faculty of 21 members, in which only 40% had earned Master's degrees and 15% had no degrees at all, (1945), to a faculty of 28 members, of whom 65% had Master's degrees and 14% held Doctorates (1956). In recognition of this progress, Rust was accredited as a class 'A' college by the Southern Association of Colleges and Secondary Schools in 1949. In 1954 it was decided that improvements in public education justified the discontinuing of the high school, and Rust became at last fully and exclusively a liberal arts college."[52]

Out of President McCoy's long years of educational experience in Mississippi and his profound interest in the people, a philosophy of the educational needs of the Negro people emerged. In a letter to Dr. S. D. Redmond of Jackson, he set forth, in part, that philosophy of educational need, a part of which letter follows:

The Negro, like all other groups, must have a professional group trained to meet all the requirements:. . .physicians,

460

dentists, attorneys, ministers, teachers prepared to meet the highest standards, business men; these are some of the necessary leaders that the entire educational system of any state should make (it possible to train). . .for the benefit of society. . .The million Negroes in Mississippi are not adequately supplied with these guardians of health and well-being for all the people of the community or state.

Mississippi, therefore, needs schools and colleges capable of training a certain per cent of (the) citizenry for these professions. The undergraduate college should, therefore, so build its curriculum offerings, so choose its student personnel, as not to defeat the real aim of producing men and women who are not only capable, but fit from every standpoint to give the needed service required to maintain the health of the entire community or state along these lines.

. . .We need to do something now about the physical condition of the 1,000,000 Negroes in Mississippi. We cannot wait until they are educated, for these needs are so real that the attack must be made now by our would-be dentists, physicians, nurses, (and) social workers, or the very foundation of what is required to produce the next generation won't be there when the time comes. . . .

We need good colleges in Mississippi for Negroes. . .We need not only good colleges, but we need colleges to meet our various needs; e.g., Junior Colleges. . .Of the 115,000 Negro children of high school age, a large per cent should attempt not more than a Junior College education before entering some gainful occupation, thereby gaining a respectful livelihood, creating respectable homes, and rearing healthy children as good citizens.

The Mississippi Negro needs schools where he may be trained in the several skilled vocations, schools of technology where many of high school age may be. . .trained as mechanical engineers, electrical engineers, agricultural engineers, civil engineers, chemical engineers, architectural engineers, aeronautical engineers. . .Mississippi, in its development of its depleted forest, of its new building materials, of soil conservation, of its electrical power, of its mechanized farm program, will need men and women skilled in the work of the engineer. Negroes should have the opportunity to learn the skills. Some one of our colleges of the state should make possible the needed training center or centers.

Mississippi being an agricultural State, many of the 115,000 Negro children of high school age should be trained and versed in agriculture in all its phases. . .under the modern scientific methods.

And, too, Mississippi is becoming an industrialized state as well as an already agricultural state;. . .all these things must be considered in the educational program of the State.

I have not said all that I would like to say on the subject, but I've tried to say what I consider most important as an all-out program of higher education for Negroes in Mississippi in particular, in general for any other state, for Mississippi has peculiar problems of its own—transient in nature—that will disappear with more and better educational facilities, etc.[53]

President McCoy retired in 1957 after an administrative tenure of thirty-three years, the longest in the college's history. Despite the difficulties, pressures, and limited resources, he literally kept Rust College alive, and its door open to the youth of Mississippi. His work was creative and his accomplishments great. Although he fell far short of what he would like to have done for Rust and his people of the state, he must be given the approbation, well done! For, he accomplished so much with so little.

To succeed Dr. McCoy when he retired in 1957, the Reverend Ernest A. Smith was elected President of Rust College. Reverend Smith was the third Negro and the second alumnus to be elected President of Rust. He came to the Presidency from the pastorate of St. Paul Methodist Church in San Antonio, Texas. His ten-year tenure covered the last decade of the one hundred years of the life of the institution born in Asbury Church, about a mile away from the hill and auction grounds to which it was shortly moved, and where glorious history has been made for more than a century.

Reverend Smith came to the Presidency of Rust College knowing full well that it was a difficult task, but the true loyalty of a devoted son challenged him to take hold of the work without hesitancy and with faith and enthusiasm.

In 1957 the Southern Association of Colleges and Schools removed the bars of discrimination and opened its doors to the historic predominantly Negro institutions. Although Rust had enjoyed an "A" rating by the association, this did not qualify the institution for membership. Being an unaccredited college was an added obstacle which faced the new President. Accreditation was a hope of President Smith during his ten years at Rust, which hope he was unable to realize.

Limited financial resources and limited sources from which to secure finances compounded the problems of administration. The interest and loyalty of the Northern Conferences cultivated with the singing groups and by President Smith, who was an excellent speaker, and the continued support, though meager, from the

Mississippi and Upper Mississippi Conferences, with the Central Alabama Conference added, kept a small stream of financial assistance flowing to the college. Securing and maintaining a competent faculty and staff was an understandable problem. Student aid was limited, and the fact that the college was not accredited made it difficult to keep the enrollment up to a normal level. These were some of the kinds of problems with which President Smith was confronted.

The Annual Conferences in Mississippi in which Rust had its birth, almost simultaneously with the birth of the original Mississippi Conference itself, sustained a close and supportive relation, as evidenced in the following statement by the Upper Mississippi Conference:

> For almost a century, Rust College has survived and projected the light of Christian influence beyond the border of our human knowledge. The place which this institution has filled and the role which she has played in the Christian educational field across the years have won a distinctive position in the hearts and minds of our people throughout the country. For her our prayers ascend, and we shall bestir ourselves to the point of giving our best in moral, financial, and spiritual support to keep the pendulum vibrating in the right direction to meet the needs of our young folk now and in the years ahead.
>
> Dr. E. A. Smith, President, and his efficient staff must be commended for their undaunted faith and spirit in these turbulent days. For, they walk by faith and not by sight.[54]

The decade of President Smith's administration was another one of those "rocky" periods for the college in which it seemed to have been his mission to save the institution and give it strength to finish its first century of service.

Under the administration of President Smith the physical plant was improved and extended. The new Shaw Dining Hall was added to the facilities and a new residence for the President was built. In the centennial year, three new buildings were erected and dedicated—the McDonald Science Hall, the John O. Gross Hall for men, and the Emma G. Wiff Residence Hall for women.

"The Presidency of Dr. Smith was one of planning and implementing the initial phase of a long-range development effort to substantially improve the educational program of Rust and bring it into the mainstream of present-day American higher education."[55]

The dedication of the above named buildings, in May, 1966,

463

was a fitting climax to the centennial celebration, and to the close of President Smith's administration. Dr. Smith resigned from the presidency of Rust College in November, 1966, to accept a position as Associate Secretary on the General Board of Christian Social Concerns, The Methodist Church, Washington, D. C.

Dr. William A. McMillan Becomes President

During the interim of several months between the resignation of Dr. Smith and the election of his successor, an Administrative Committee, chaired by Dr. Robert E. Hunt, Trustee, was in charge of the administrative affairs of the college, with key members of the Board giving assistance when needed.

On March 7, 1967, Dr. William A. McMillan, Dean of Faculty and Instruction at Bethune-Cookman College, Daytona Beach, Florida, was elected President of Rust College and took office April 1, 1967.[56] He came to the position holding the Ph.D. degree from Michigan University, and with a long and rich background of teaching and administrative experience in higher education at several institutions, including Bethune-Cookman and Wiley Colleges. He had served as Visiting Dean at Rust for two years, 1964-1966, and was well acquainted with Rust and its instructional program, which he helped to formulate.

One of the first problems which the new President tackled immediately was to improve and strengthen the faculty. Notable progress has been made in this area. A second problem was to rectify financial records and establish better accounting and budgetary procedures. These have been much improved. Increasing and stabilizing the income have moved the college forward. Revision of the curriculum as a whole, and adjusting the freshman program and instruction particularly, are in process.

Accreditation by the Southern Association of Colleges and Schools was a goal of Rust College for a number of years. This goal has been achieved and this college now holds full membership in this association.

One of the most important phases of the Rust College program at present is its Development Program, under the title: "The Upward Thrust Toward Excellence." The grounds have been improved, with hard surface roads. Three new buildings are being added to the physical plant this school year—a men's dormitory to house sixty students has been completed and is being occupied; a beautiful and commodious two-story library building has just been completed and will be dedicated December 14, 1969, and named for the internationally known vocal artist, Leontyne Price; and a women's dormitory to house 160 students will be finished by

Spring, 1970.

A good Board of Trustees gives active support to the Presidency with every confidence in him, and looks to the future with great hope, in these initial years of the second century of service by Rust College.

Elizabeth L. Rust Home

The story and work of the Elizabeth L. Rust Home constitutes an important part of the history of Rust College. This Home is "a symbol of the close-working relationships between the Women's Home Missionary Society and the Freedmen's Aid Society in the early years. Rust College was named for Dr. R. S. Rust, Corresponding Secretary of that society. The industrial home was opened October 1, 1884, and was dedicated March 30, 1885, as Elizabeth L. Rust Industrial Home in honor of his wife, Mrs. R. S. Rust, Corresponding Secretary of the Women's Home Missionary Society."[57]

The basic program of the E. L. Rust Industrial Home began with training in housekeeping, cooking, plain sewing, dressmaking, and millinery. Two other courses were added; namely, printing and bee culture.

Mrs. Meeker writes:

"The sharing spirit developed in all the industrial homes found a distinct outlet in the E. L. Rust Home. Many poor aged people, former slaves, lived in Holly Springs, too old and feeble to work. From proceeds of an entertainment, the Rust girls furnished rooms in an old building on the grounds for an old Sister's Home. . . .It exerted a good influence over the girls who gladly aided in caring for the half dozen old women."[58]

The preparation and experiences of the Rust Home girls carried over into community life as they became teachers and homemakers.

Miss Sophia Johnston was the first Superintendent of the E. L. Rust Home. She remained as Superintendent thirteen years, retiring in 1897.[59] Three superintendents had brief tenures between 1897 and 1903. Miss Ella Becker, who was Assistant Superintendent beginning in 1901, became Superintendent in 1903. Miss Rebecca Barbour became Assistant Superintendent in 1905. This was the beginning of a partnership between Misses Becker and Barbour which continued until their retirement in 1927.[60]

Between 1927 and 1932 there were four brief tenures as Superintendent. In 1932 Miss Elfreda Myser assumed the Superintendency, remaining Superintendent until Rust Home became a regular college dormitory in 1940.

The E. L. Rust Home, like similar homes under the supervision of the Women's Home Missionary Society, had a tremendous influence on young women in the Home, and rendered a far-reaching service in preparing them for homemaking, and church and community service.

In 1940 there were two changes that re-directed the course of the E. L. Rust Home. First, the fire that destroyed the main building at Rust College, including the main women's dormitory, made it necessary for the Rust Home to become a general women's dormitory for the college.

Second, the Methodist unification in 1939 brought about a reorganization of the women's work of The Methodist Church. The Woman's Home Missionary Society was replaced by the Women's Division of Christian Service, and much of the work of the former program (W.H.M.S.) was changed.

The E. L. Rust Home continued to be a vital factor in the program of Rust College. The work formerly offered and supervised by the W. H. M. S. was upgraded and made a part of the Rust College curriculum, with a major in Home Economics. The work became more academic and Rust Home became more of a dormitory for a large number of young women, rather than a small home for the training of a smaller number.

In recent years the E. L. Rust Home has been exclusively a dormitory for women of the college. With the changes beginning in 1940, the Woman's Division of Christian Service continued its interest and some financial support.

The E. L. Rust Hall is soon to be razed, with the completion of the new women's dormitory now in process of erection. So far as physical structure is concerned, the razing of the E. L. Rust Hall will end an era begun in 1884; but the remarkable tradition and heritage of this work of the women of the church will remain to enrich the history of the combined services of Rust College and Rust Home.

REFERENCES AND NOTES

1. Barclay, Wade C., *History of Methodist Missions*, p. 305.
2. *The Methodist Advocate* (Atlanta), January 20, 1869, p. 1.
3. Morrow, Ralph E. *Northern Methodism and Reconstruction* East Lansing, 1956, p. 167; *History of Holly Springs*, Published by Garden Club, 1936—Article by E. Cottrell on "Churches".
4. Freedmen's Aid Society, Third Annual Report, 1869, p. 10.
5. Houghton, Frederick, Goodspeed's *Memoirs of Mississippi*, Chicago, 1891, p. 11.
6. *Ibid.*
7. Mayes, Edward, *History of Education in Mississippi*, Washington, 1899, p. 267.
8. Stowell, Jay S., *Methodist Adventures in Negro Education*, p. 125.
9. Freedmen's Aid Society, 1875, p. 25.
10. Original Charter, May 26, 1870, p. 1.
11. *Ibid.*
12. Freedmen's Aid Society Fourth Report, 1871, p. 10.
13. Journal of the Mississippi Annual Conference, p. 4.
14. *Ibid.*, p. 13.
15. Freedmen's Aid Society Report, 1872, p. 15.
16. Freedmen's Aid Society Eighth Report, 1875, p. 23.
17. *Ibid.*
18. Freedmen's Aid Society Report, 1875, p. 25.
19. Simpson, Bishop Matthew, *Cyclopedia of Methodism*, p. 795.
20. Freedmen's Aid Society Report, 1879, p. 30.
21. The Mississippi Conference Journal, January 17, 1879, p. 9.
22. *Ibid.*
23. *Ibid.*
24. Mississippi Conference Journal, January 14-19, 1880, p. 29.
25. *Ibid.*, p. 30.
26. Freedmen's Aid Society Twelfth Annual Report, 1879, p. 30.
27. *The Christian Educator*, April-May, 1895, p. 35.
28. The Freedmen's Aid Society Report, 1873, pp. 19f.
29. Freedmen's Aid Society Report, 1891, p. 182.
30. The Freedmen's Aid and Southern Education Society Report, July 1, 1891, pp. 182ff.
31. *Ibid.*
32. See Charter Amendment February 19, 1890.
33. *The Christian Educator*, February-March, 1898, p. 74.
33a. *The Christian Educator*, August-September, 1898, p. 141.
34. *The Christian Educator*, August-September, 1898, p. 139.
35. *The Christian Educator*, May-August, 1909, p. 4.

36. *Ibid.*, pp. 4f.
37. *The Christian Educator*, May, 1911, p. 12.
38. *The Christian Educator*, November, 1915, p. 5.
39. *The Christian Educator*, February, 1911, p. 19.
40. *Ibid.*, May, 1910, p. 4.
41. Baker, Webster B., *A History of Rust College*, p. 34.
42. *The Christian Educator*, August, 1915, p. 15.
43. *Ibid.*, May, 1916, p. 4.
44. *The Christian Educator*, August, 1915, p. 15.
45. Manuscript, by F. Houghton, *op. cit.*, p. 27.
46. Rust College Catalog, 1931.
47. *Ibid.*
48. *Ibid.*, p. 31.
48a. Letter of President to Mr. McCoy, July 20, 1944.
49. Houghton, F., *op. cit.*, p. 34.
50. Houghton, F., *op. cit.*, p. 35.
51. *Ibid.*, p. 36.
52. *Ibid.*, p. 38.
53. Letter by Dr. McCoy to Dr. A. S. Redmond, Jackson, Miss., 1945.
54. Journal of the Upper Mississippi Confenrece, May 10-13, 1962, p. 33.
55. Dr. W. Astor Kirk, Chairman of the Board of Trustees, "The Rust College Story," November, 1967, p. 10.
56. Minutes, Rust College Board of Trustees, March 7, 1967.
57. Meeker, Mrs. C. A., Research Manuscript, 1967, on Women's Home Missionary Society Work in Mississippi.
58. Meeker, *op. cit.*
59. *Ibid.*
60. *Ibid.*

CHAPTER 23

A BRIEF HISTORICAL SKETCH OF WILEY UNIVERSITY
NOW WILEY COLLEGE

Wiley University, established by the Freedmen's Aid Society, was the first school to be located west of the Mississippi River by the Society. The school was named in honor of Bishop Isaac W. Wiley, a native of Lewistown, Pennsylvania, and a charter member of the Freedmen's Aid Society. He was elected a Bishop in the Methodist Episcopal Church in 1864. After the death of Bishop D. W. Clark in 1871, Bishop Wiley succeeded him as President of the Freedmen's Aid Society.[1]

"He visited every school, not only to inspect the work, but to encourage the teachers and the students with his wise counsel and instructive addresses."[2]

Wiley University was first opened March 17, 1873. The Rev. F. C. Moore was the first President.[3]

Dr. R. S. Rust, Corresponding Secretary of the Freedmen's Aid Society, in the Sixth Annual Report of the society,[4] states that the property consists of a two-story frame house and two hundred acres of good land, which was located some distance from the town of Marshall, Texas. President Moore and his wife immediately suffered great embarrassment because of the limited facilities, a hundred students having entered the first term. The school was situated in a farm area heavily populated by Negro people whose needs were great, but wanted an education. The strong desire to learn is typified in a story told by President Moore of two young ladies, ages fourteen and sixteen, and several young men who walked nine miles a day to and from school during the first session, and part of the time with blistering feet through heat and frequent rain.[5]

The property was estimated to have a value of at least $13,000, eighty acres having been reserved for school purposes, and the balance divided into wide avenues, and two hundred and seventy-six building lots, for sale to families at a low price.[6] Plans were made for the erection of a frame building with the hope that it would be the forerunner of a larger and more substantial building.

469

Reverend Moore served as President from 1873 to 1876. He was succeeded by the Reverend W. H. Davis, who remained in the office nine years—1876 to 1885.

It was early in the Presidency of Reverend Davis that Wiley was relocated to a site in Marshall. In 1897 the Freedmen's Aid Society report account of the relocation is given:

"The Presiding Elder of Marshall District, intrusted with authority by the officers of the Freedmen's Aid Society, unfortunately purchased a farm for the Wiley University in a poor location, remote from town, and difficult of access. After a trial of a few years it was found impossible to build up a first-class institution in that place, and the location was exchanged for a fine elevation in the town, healthful, with pleasant surroundings, commanding a charming view of the country. We have erected on this beautiful site, in a grove of thirty trees, two plain brick edifices, as wings of the main university building, to be erected when some benevolent friend of this enterprise shall furnish the funds.[7]

"These wings cost about seven thousand dollars in addition to the materials taken from the old buildings."[8]

The wisdom, as well as the thinking, of the Freedmen's Aid Society in locating Wiley University at Marshall, in the Northeastern section of Texas may be understood and justified from the following information in the Society's Twelfth Annual Report:

This school is located in Marshall, Harrison County, Texas, a thriving city and of great commercial importance. . . .It is in the midst of a dense colored population, and is central to the extensive territory included in North Texas, Northwestern Louisiana and Southern Arkansas, being no other school of high grade for the colored people in all this region. . . .From the last reports of the Commissioner of Education there is shown to be in the states of Texas, Louisiana, and Arkansas schools located at New Orleans, at Marshall, Texas, and a Normal School at Pine Bluff, Arkansas, for the benefit of colored people. There are besides these, however, schools now located at Austin, Texas, and Little Rock, Arkansas. But these are all struggling for life and for victory. It is evident to all that the only hope of a true evangelization of these multitudes in this great extent of territory is in the help afforded by the churches of the North. . . .

. . .Multitudes of young men and women, if properly encouraged, would avail themselves of the opportunities for study here offered. . . .

Our relations with the white people of the city are the most friendly. There is evidently a growing sentiment in favor of our work. Constant tokens of this are being given. The development manifest in our students is calling forth commendations and increasing interest from the people. . . .[10]

One great source of encouragement to us in all this work is the earnestness and devotion characterizing those who have come under our influence. . . .These people are worthy of the fullest sympathy and active help of the church and Nation.[11]

President Davis was succeeded in 1885 by the Reverend N. D. Clifford as President of Wiley. Reverend Clifford served as President a brief period of two years, having passed away in the school year 1886-1887. The Texas Annual Conference in session December 14-19, 1887, referred to Wiley University as follows:

The deaths of President N. D. Clifford and Professor N. Coleman during the past year threw for a season gloom and uncertainty over the prospects of our university at Marshall, Texas. But with the opening of the new school year the appointment of an entirely new faculty of carefully selected instructors, all of whom are college graduates, and one of them an accomplished gentleman of our own race, gives peculiar life to the new year's work, and special promise that in due season, our most sanguine hopes for its efficiency and prosperity will be realized.[12]

The Reverend George Whitaker became President of Wiley University in 1887, succeeding President Clifford.[13]

The Texas Annual Conference in session December, 1887, passed the following resolution:

Resolved, That we heartily indorse the appointment of so noble a man as Professor George Whitaker to the Presidency of Wiley University.[14]

Reverend Whitaker's tenure as President extended from 1887 to 1891.[15] At the end of President Whitaker's administration, it was reported that the University had fifty acres of land (and 100 acres some distance away) and eight buildings.[16] Also, the Woman's Home Missionary Society had just completed a beautiful industrial home for girls, where several industries were taught.[17] This home known as the "King Home for Girls" was a very important addition to the program of the university, to complement the industrial work for boys. Although Wiley never developed a strong industrial department, comparable to the departments at Central Tennessee, Claflin, and Clark Universities,

471

it had a strong engineering course and a good practical industrial program. In the school year 1891-1892, there were raised on the farm 450 bushels of sweet potatoes, 125 bushels of corn, and a large amount of vegetables.[18]

From 1891 to 1893 the Reverend P. A. Pool served as President of Wiley University.[19] At the end of his first year, July 1, 1892, President Pool reported property valued at $25,000; expenditures for the year, $12,444.12; paid on improvement of real estate, including a girl's dormitory, $1,445.04; amount paid by students, 337 enrolled, $4,291.03.[20]

President Pool laid stress on the need of a central building, which need had been emphasized by all of the Presidents preceding him. As evidence of the loyalty and continued support of the Texas Conference, $3,000 was apportioned to the districts, at the December 1892 session, to be raised for Wiley University.[21]

The Texas Conference covers the eastern half of Texas and is one of the largest conferences among colored people of the South. Wiley, the only institution located in that Conference, located at Marshall, Texas, is in the midst of a colored population of at least a half million, so the Freedmen's Aid Society reported.[22]

The close of President Pool's administration in 1893, also closed an era in the history of Wiley University. He was the fifth President, and the first five Presidents were white. After the first era of Wiley's history which covered a period of twenty years, there has not since that time been a white President of the institution.

By 1893, Wiley University was well established. It had been relocated from its first site, some distance south of Marshall, to a beautiful site in the town of Marshall, in the midst of a colored population of more than a half million. On this site eight buildings had been erected, though it still did not have a central building. The University owned 150 acres of land and its property value had reached more than $25,000. The curriculum included the academic courses, the preparatory course, and the collegiate course.

"In the year 1888 the first graduation was held. In the college of Liberal Arts, one student, H. B. Pemberton, received the Bachelor of Arts degree, and three from the Normal or Teacher Training Department received diplomas."[23]

In 1893 the first Negro President of Wiley University, the Reverend Isaiah B. Scott, was elected by the Freedmen's Aid Society. Dr. Scott was a most unusual man. He, the youngest of fourteen children, was born near Midway, Woodford County, Kentucky, in 1854,[24] eleven years before Emancipation. He was taught at home to read and spell. He and his youngest sister

472

attended a private school until the death of their father, when they were compelled to return home. The widowed mother, with several of the children, joined five other children who had been taken to Texas before the War. Austin, Texas, was made the permanent family home.

On visiting Georgia with his mother in 1873, young Scott entered Clark Seminary. After completing the Preparatory Course there, he entered Central Tennessee College in 1876, from which he graduated in 1880 with the A.B. Degree.[25]

After graduation Scott entered the Theological Department of Central Tennessee College where he spent one year. After marrying in 1881, he returned to Texas, taught one year at the State Normal School, and then entered the pastorate full-time.

Reverend Scott held several important pastoral appointments in the Texas Conference and several as Presiding Elder of the Marshall and Houston Districts. In 1883 Central Tennessee College conferred on him the degree Master of Arts, and in 1889 New Orleans University conferred on him the D.D. degree.[26] He was a member of three General Conferences up to this time, and was Presiding Elder of the Houston District when he was elected to the Presidency of Wiley University.[27]

Dr. Scott served three years as President of Wiley University. At the end of his second year as President, he reported that the condition of the University when he assumed the Presidency was most critical. The school was burdened with a heavy debt.[28] A large number of students had been alienated, and many of its patrons were lukewarm or in actual rebellion against it.[29] In the three years of President Scott's administration most of the wounds were healed and the friends re-united in support of the University. The internal workings were healthful, and the "school was probably never in better condition for solid growth."[30] The urgency and plea was still for a large central building with classrooms and a chapel.

In 1896 President Scott was elected by the General Conference to the Editorship of the *Southwestern Christian Advocate*.[31] At that time *The Christian Educator* said:

His rare personal magnetism, giving him an influence over men which he invariably uses for good, cannot but bring to him success in his new field of labor. The deserved honor which the church and people have paid him, together with the wholesome example of his upright life, served as an inspiration to the youth who came under his tuition as President of Wiley University, and will be of value to him in his present enlarged sphere of service.[32]

473

The Rev. Matthew W. Dogan Becomes President of
Wiley University

When Rev. Scott went to the editorship of the *Southwestern Christian Advocate, The Christian Educator* remarked that he had left no easy task to the man who must come after him in Wiley University, but expressed confidence that the man would be found to take up the work where President Scott had laid it down.

The man was found in the Reverend Matthew W. Dogan, who was elected in 1896 as the seventh President, second Negro, of Wiley University. It is probable that no one, not even young Dogan himself, had any idea that he was entering upon such a monumental administrative career that would span a period of forty-six years at this one institution. From 1896 to the present, Wiley University, now Wiley College, has been but the lengthened shadow of a great man—Matthew W. Dogan.

Reverend Dogan was a distinguished graduate of Rust University, having taken there the B. A. degree in 1886. He was an outstanding student in Mathematics. Because of his scholarship, after graduation he was invited to join the faculty of his alma mater to teach Mathematics. Having completed three years on the Rust faculty, young Dogan was invited to Central Tennessee College as Professor of Mathematics. While at Central Tennessee College he was observed by Secretaries of the Freedmen's Aid Society, Dr. John W. Hamilton and Dr. J. C. Hartzell. He was noticed by these Secretaries and by Dr. John Braden, President of the College, for his intellectual acumen, his poise and common sense. When the need arose for a new President at Wiley University, it was the conviction of the powers that be that Matthew W. Dogan was the man. To this task he and his wife went with enthusiasm and dedication. Through the years they worked together for the building of Wiley University, until her passing away in 1929, and then he, without a helpmate, until his retirement, supported by a fine family of four daughters and a son.

One of the great needs of Wiley University from the beginning, that all of Dr. Dogan's predecessors sensed and pleaded for was a central building. In 1892 the Texas Conference apportioned $3,000 for Wiley.[33] In 1896 the colored people of Marshall and vicinity began to raise money for the building.[34]

"Former students and graduates joined in, and out of their poverty some $3,000 was raised for a new central building."[35]

By 1900 sufficient funds had been raised for the Finance Committee of the Freedmen's Aid and Southern Education Society to give permission for work on the central building to be begun, provided no debt was incurred.[36] The remaining amount needed to finish the building with four floors, twelve large classrooms, a chapel to seat 500, and dormitory space to accommodate 200, was $5,000.[37]

The Texas Annual Conference in December 1902, took note of several rooms of the central building having been completed. In 1904 it was reported to the Conference that the new central building at Wiley University had been completed and that it was the best building in the Freedmen's Aid system.[38] This project had been kept before the Conference for more than twenty years. The Conference then pledged $2,000 a year for Wiley.[39]

From this time on, President Dogan devoted himself even more assiduously to the task of building Wiley University, its physical plant and its program.

In 1908 *The Christian Educator* reported that:

At Wiley University, an industrial building has been completed at a cost of $4,000; home for the President at a cost of $3,500, and a library, costing $15,000, the gift of Mr. Andrew Carnegie.[40]

For the school year 1910-1911, it was reported that Wiley University had thirty teachers, and an enrollment of 602 students. It owned fifty acres of land, had fourteen buildings, including the machine shop, carpentry shop, printing office, hospital, and King Home, owned by the Woman's Home Missionary Society.[41]

The Christian Educator for May, 1911, was devoted in its entirety to featuring Dr. Dogan, and Wiley University. This was fifteen years after Dr. Dogan had become President of the institution. The first building erected by Dr. Dogan was the central building at a cost of $32,000, of which $21,000 was raised by the people on the ground and $11,000 by Secretary M. C. B. Mason.[42] The total value of the plant in 1911 was estimated to be $260,000, as against $25,000 in 1896.[43] This special issue of *The Christian Educator* gave an impressive list of Wiley graduates, in several major professional fields: School Principals, 8; Heads of College Departments, 4; Ministers, 8; Physicians, 9; Business, 7; and others.[44] It is understood that the largest number by far was in the teaching profession in Public School Systems.

Wiley University attempted to make education relevant through what was described as "the Wiley Method." This method attempted to combine higher education and industrial training. This method was illustrated by a young man, who graduated with highest honors from the college department, took at the same time the highest honors in the department of electrical engineering, and

475

became the Superintendent of the Electrical Light and Power Company of Boley, Oklahoma.[45] This was a town in Oklahoma with an all black population of about 3,000, administered entirely by Blacks. In the summer of 1910 three students of the Wiley Engineering Department, under the direction of their teacher, Professor J. R. Reynolds, set up and put in good running order an electrical plant in Boley, Oklahoma. One of the students, George Palmer, having graduated, was placed in charge of the system as Superintendent, the first colored man in such a position in the United States.[46]

The Mayor of the town, the Honorable Haynes, praised Professor Reynolds and the three young men, and went on to say, "We are proud of our system, and appreciate the fact that we represent the only Negro town in the world which is lighted by a commercial electric system owned, installed, and operated by colored men."[47]

Wiley University, under the leadership of President Dogan, fired the interest and enthusiasm of the local Negro people and the whole Texas Conference. No task in support of their institution was too stupendous. The special issue of *The Christian Educator* gives an account of the Conference's voting to raise $100,000 for the endowment of the institution.

"Indeed, it would seem as if it were a huge joke to see these men, ministers, whose average salary is less than $300, with a lay membership behind them composed largely of laborers on the cotton farms of Texas, enthusiastically voting to raise $100,000 for the endowment of this institution. When, however, it is remembered that during the last ten or fifteen years this conference has raised in special collections for Wiley University more than $50,000, we are not without hope that the whole amount in due time will be raised,"[48] so said *The Christian Educator.*

The next major building to be erected on the Wiley campus was Coe Hall, designed to accommodate 350 men. Mr. H. G. Coe, of Clarence, Iowa, contributed $5,000 towards the erection of Coe Memorial Hall, as a memorial to his sainted daughter.* Miss Coe was one of the most earnest and faithful teachers Wiley has ever had, and the erection of this hall is a fitting tribute to her sincere and devoted work.[49] The final cost of the building is not known. At May, 1911, the sum of $20,000 had been spent on the building, all of which, with the exception of the $5,000 given by Mr. Coe, had been raised by the colored people themselves.[50]

From the story in the May, 1911 issue of *The Christian*

*Miss Isabell Coe

476

Educator featuring Wiley University, it is clear that this institution at this time was enjoying great respect and popularity, and was rendering a remarkable service.

At its Annual Session December, 1914, the Texas Annual Conference recognized the need for strengthening Wiley financially, its financial condition being its greatest drawback. It expressed a hope that the University might soon meet the requirement of the University Senate of the Methodist Episcopal Church: "That all institutions listed in the grade of colleges, shall have endowment of at least $100,000." The conference identified itself with a movement to acquire the endowment needed.

In 1916 Thomas Jesse Jones, for the office of Education, U.S. Dept. of the Interior, visited Wiley College including it among the Negro schools evaluated in his far-reaching survey and recommendations. He reported an attendance of 384, distributed as follows: elementary, 176; secondary, 170; college, 38. The all-black faculty consisted of 26 teachers. Dr. Jones commended the college on having a good library structure. The new Carnegie Library costing $15,000 was said by Dr. Jones to have been "one of the best libraries in colored schools."[51]

Dr. Jones recommended that the college classes at Wiley be restricted to Junior College grade until the secondary course was on a sound basis.[52]

This recommendation was not followed, and Wiley continued its four-year degree-granting course. Efforts were made, however, to improve the curriculum at all points of criticism.

On the evening of February 22, 1918, a great calamity befell Wiley College when the main building was completely destroyed by fire.[53] Only the furnishings and other contents were saved. The insurance covering the building was insufficient to replace it. Bishop Wilbur P. Thirkield, Dr. I. Garland Penn, Corresponding Secretary of the Freedmen's Aid Society, with the assistance of the trustees and district superintendents of the Texas Conference, began immediately to raise funds to supplement the insurance and replace the building that had been lost. They set themselves to this undertaking with confidence that the money would be raised to put up a modern structure that would better meet the demands of an up-to-date college.[54]

Dr. Dogan was an outstanding churchman. His leadership as an educator and minister placed him in the top echelon of the Methodist Episcopal Church. For a number of quadrennia he was a delegate to the General Conference, elected by the Texas Annual Conference. The General Conference of 1920 was of unusual interest and significance to Black leadership of the church. The question of a Black bishop had been discussed since 1872, and the

477

opinion was widespread that a Black bishop would be elected in 1920. Dr. Dogan's outstanding leadership as an educator and a minister eminently qualified him for consideration. Dr. Dogan, however, had no such ambition. In a letter to Dr. I. Garland Penn, Corresponding Secretary of the Freedmen's Aid Society, April 4, 1920, he said: "I am wanting nothing within the gift of the General Conference. I will devote the rest of my active life to building up this institution, if you care to have me in your employ."[55] This he did with abandon.

In the development of Wiley College, Dr. Dogan went from one achievement to another with a great joy in each. In another letter to Dr. Penn April 11, 1920, he reported, "We have just entered our new refectory, which must be the best in our entire work."[56]

Dr. Dogan's vigilance kept the cause of Wiley College continuously before the Texas Conference. In 1925 this Conference approved an endowment and expansion fund campaign for the college and committed itself to a five-year campaign to raise $150,000 for endowment, assessing one dollar per member per year for the five-year period.[57]

In 1928 the General Education Board of New York City made a challenge grant of $300,000 to Wiley College for endowment, provided that the college would raise a like amount.[58]

Regarding this challenge grant *The Christian Educator* answers the question Why?: "Why did the General Education Board subscribe $300,000 to the campaign for $600,000 for endowment of the liberal arts work at Wiley College. . . .The answer is to be found in the fact that with quiet efficiency and uncompromising standards Wiley College has achieved results of high quality in the field of college education."[59]

In 1928 the United States Bureau of Education made another survey of Negro colleges. It is gratifying to note the progress made by Wiley College in eleven years, and the difference between the evaluation of the college in this survey, compared with the Thomas Jesse Jones' evaluation in 1916. *The Christian Educator* in 1928 reports the following:

"The 1928 U. S. Bureau Educational Survey of Negro Colleges stated in their findings:

"Wiley College is strategically located and is rendering a high character of public service in preparation for achievement and leadership. The institution has, during recent years, concentrated on the development of a college of standard rank, meeting the requirements set up by recognized accrediting agencies. In a large measure this objective has been accomplished. The survey committee was impressed with the efficiency of the organization and the concentrated effort being made to provide an educational service of a superior type.

"No finer vote of confidence is possible than that expressed by the Federal Bureau of Education and the General Education Board. Wiley College is thus recognized, not only by our Board of Education, but by other agencies, as a proper institution to receive endowment funds."[60]

Raising the $300,000 to qualify for the $300,000 conditional grant by the General Education Board was no easy task, and required a number of years of hard work. When the sum of $150,000 had been raised by Wiley College, a like amount was turned over to the college by the General Education Board. In 1937 an appeal was made to the Texas Conference to help bring the endowment campaign to a successful finish and claim the remaining $150,000 from the General Education Board.[61] The finish of this campaign was one of the crowning successes of Dr. Dogan's long and fruitful administration.

Forty-Six Years of Brilliant Leadership

Dr. Matthew W. Dogan retired from the Presidency of Wiley after forty-six years at the helm of this institution, giving dedicated service and brilliant and fruitful leadership. He came to the Presidency of this little school in 1896 when it was unknown, unimpressive, and its greatest asset being its potential, waiting for development by the church and such an able leader as the young Rev. Dogan.

Dr. Dogan built a great institution. There were many reasons why he was able to build Wiley, among them being:

1. His devotion to the cause drew others to it and caused them to see its value. This is illustrated in the manner in which the Texas Conference rallied to Wiley, and always out of a profound interest set for the Conference tasks bigger than they could accomplish but never failed to challenge themselves to get under the staggering financial load and try with all their might to carry it for the sake of their needy institution. Again, Dr. Dogan never lost the confidence of the Freedmen's Aid Society and the church which responded as fully as possible to his calls for help.

2. Dr. Dogan never lost courage. Within a period of twelve or fifteen years, five buildings were destroyed by fire—the main building, Central Hall, being one to be destroyed by fire in 1918. Despite these losses Dr. Dogan continued to rebuild and to add other needed buildings. When he retired in 1942, there were eight buildings on the campus, which were built during his administration, three others destroyed by fire were not rebuilt. To his credit the college had a good physical plant.

479

3. Dr. Dogan built a strong faculty for which Wiley was well known. Outstanding men such as R. S. Lovinggood, J. R. Reynolds, J. W. Haywood, and J. B. Randolph served on the Wiley Faculty and, later, all became Presidents of Freedmen's Aid Society institutions.

A list of some of the most outstanding teachers at Wiley consists of thirty-four names made available, exclusive of the four given above. The teaching fields are quite varied. Beginning as early as 1904 there were twenty-one of the thirty-four most outstanding teachers whose tenure ranges from twelve to fifty-seven years. Ten of the group taught at Wiley from twelve to twenty-five years with an average of 18.5 years. Seven taught from twenty-five to thirty-five years with an average of 30.5 years. One taught thirty-six years, one taught forty-three years, one taught forty-eight years, and one taught fifty-seven years.

All of these twenty-one teachers were employed by Dr. Dogan and worked with him through these years to build a good college. Many others helped whose tenures were less than twelve years. Also, many helped who had exceptionally long tenures, but were not on the instructional faculty, such as librarians, personnel workers, building engineers, and others.

With a faculty of such high quality and such stability, Wiley, under Dr. Dogan's leadership, moved forward in establishing and maintaining higher academic standards. It was among the first Negro colleges (1933) to be given "A" rating by the Southern Association of colleges and Secondary Schools. Since 1962 it has held membership in the Southern Association of Colleges and Schools.

For many years, Wiley's prowess in athletics was little short of miraculous for a small college. Particularly was this true in football under the tutelage of the inimitable mentor, Coach Fred T. "Pops" Long. During the thirty-five years of his reign as Coach at Wiley his Southwest Athletic Conference Championships (12) and his National Championships (3)[62] were the envy of colleges across the Nation of much greater size and affluence.

For most of the period of Dr. Dogan's administration his fame was widespread; the faculty and the academic program ranked high; and the student life was inviting. The college was so popularized that it drew students from the Northeast, Midwest, Far West, and from all over the South, rural areas, small towns, and large cities. A number of students from various sections of Africa attended Wiley. It can be said that this institution has, indeed, extended its influence and services to all parts of the United States and to lands across the seas.

Hundreds of outstanding men and women make up the roster

of distinguished alumni of Wiley College. Illustrative of its fine alumni the following ten persons are taken from a list of forty made available:

1. Henry B. Pemberton, '88, first distinguished graduate of Wiley College, A.B. degree; first Principal of Central High School in Marshall in whose honor the school was named.
2. Willis J. King, '10, B.A., Ph.D., Theologian, Methodist Bishop.
3. Penkie D. Johnson Williams, '19, A.B., Teacher, Church-woman, Wiley College Trustee.
4. Maggie Brown Daniel, '26, A.B., Ph.D., Wiley Faculty.
5. Thomas W. Cole, Sr., '34, A.B., Ed. D., President, Wiley College.
6. Melvin B. Tolson, '41, A.B., Ph.D., Professor, University of Oklahoma.
7. Nolan H. Anderson, '31, B.S., M.D., Teacher, Practicing Physician, Wiley College Trustee.
8. Joseph T. Johnson, '26, A.B., Business Executive, Wiley Trustee.
9. Aaron Baker, '20, A.B., Science Teacher; Bequeathed $91,000 toward Wiley Science Building, named in his memory.
10. Henry J. Mason, '07, A.B., Teacher, Fund Raiser, Business Manager, Wiley College.

Many more alumni, equally distinguished as these, could be listed.

In 1942 Dr. Dogan retired from the Presidency of Wiley College, having served as President for forty-six years. His retirement came twenty-two years after he said to Dr. I. Garland Penn in 1920, "I am wanting nothing within the gift of the General Conference. I will devote the rest of my active life to building up this institution, if you care to have me in your employ."

At Wiley he remained and established one of the longest records of administrative service made among all of the institutions founded by the Freedmen's Aid Society, exceeded only by Dr. Judson S. Hill, at Morristown, who served there half a century; the nearest to it and with a great deal of similarity was the record of Dr. L. M. Dunton, who was President of Claflin College for forty years.

Dr. Dogan's daughter, Mrs. Lucille Dogan Teycer, taught at Wiley fifty-seven years. The two of them jointly gave 103 years in service to this one institution—a most extraordinary and inspiring record!

In 1947 Dr. Matthew W. Dogan passed away, having certainly

481

earned the approbation: "Well done, thou good and faithful servant. . . .Enter thou into the joy of thy Lord."

Changes in Administration

It is usually difficult for a person to succeed a long administrative tenure, especially if the successor has not been a part of or related to the long tenure. It was no exception for the Rev. Egbert C. McLeod who succeeded Dr. Dogan after almost a half century in the presidency. Long imbedded administrative practices, whether they are strong or weak, are difficult for a new man to cope with in working with faculty and students. The Rev. McLeod became President of Wiley in 1942 and remained in the office six years, resigning in 1948. During his tenure President McLeod attempted to move the college forward. Under his administration two buildings were erected, McLeod Hall, a dormitory for women, and the Alumni Gymnasium was begun.[6][3]

Rev. McLeod was succeeded in 1948 by the Rev. Julius S. Scott, Sr., as President.

"Under the prudent guidance of Dr. J. S. Scott who became the ninth President in 1948, the college continued to move forward physically, intellectually, and spiritually."[6][4]

The long experience of Dr. Scott as a pastor, his calm nature, and his wise judgment were valuable assets in his administration. During the ten years he was President, 1948 to 1958, he did much to get Wiley back on the track and running smoothly. The gymnasium was finished, additional land acquired, and Smith-Nooks Music Hall erected during the Scott administration.

President Scott, having long been a member of the Texas Conference, helped to keep the bond strong between the Conference and the College while he was President.

When Dr. Scott retired in 1958, Dr. Thomas W. Cole, Sr., succeeded him as President of Wiley College. There were two innovations related to Dr. Cole's election. He was the first layman to serve as President of Wiley, and the first alumnus of the college to serve as President.

During President Cole's administration the physical plant was much improved and expanded. Thirkield Hall, a classroom building, was remodeled and renovated, and new equipment added. The old library building was remodeled and converted into an administration hall, named "The Willis King Administration Building," in honor of Bishop Willis J. King, a distinguished alumnus of the College. The Aaron Baker Science Building was erected and named in memory of this distinguished alumnus (deceased). The Fred T. Long Student Union Building was erected,

482

the Thomas W. Cole, Sr., Library Building was erected, named in honor of the incumbent President of the college at the time, and the President's Residence was remodeled.

Dr. Cole gave Presidential leadership to Wiley College for a period of thirteen years. He resigned from the Presidency in May, 1971.

As successor to Dr. Cole, the Reverend Robert E. Hays, Sr., was elected President and acceded to the office in June, 1971.

King Home At Wiley College

Central Ohio Conference "constantly provoked to good works by the missionary zeal of sister conferences"[1] in turn aroused a concern among its membership which led to liberal gifts. One member, Mrs. Jane King of Delaware, Ohio, left a legacy of $2300 to the work.

This bequest supplemented by gifts from the Conference enabled the Society to build a much needed industrial home in connection with Wiley University in Marshall, Texas. King Industrial Home with just the first and second stories completed opened in the fall of 1891, at the beginning of the college year. When the third story was finished in 1899, King Home ranked as one of the largest industrial homes enrolling an average of sixty girls in its peak years.

Being a King Home girl was a status symbol in Marshall. This was due to the religious emphasis, character-building activities, and training in domestic science, plain sewing and dressmaking, and millinery. This pattern of excellence was set during the ten-year tenure of the superintendent, Miss E. O. Elliott and her assistant, Miss Clara King of Fairfield, Iowa.

Fire swept through the tired, worn building on January 9, 1919, burning it to the ground and consuming most of the belongings of the staff and students. Miss Luella Johnson, the intrepid Superintendent, secured a cottage to house the girls and arranged for classrooms in Wiley University. Work went on with twenty-seven girls remaining in the improvised home until the end of the year.

A rebuilding program was adopted in the spring of 1920. That fall the first unit was ready for occupancy. Though it was small, thirty girls were enrolled during the year with successful class work at the college.

The new King Home burned November 11, 1921. Domestic Science classes were carried on throughout the school year. The Home was discontinued by vote of the Board of Trustees on January 19, 1922. The property was deeded to the Board of Negro

Education for expansion of Wiley College. And, on August 18, 1931, the Trustees of the Women's Home Missionary Society voted to apply the funds received from insurance on King Home to the debt on Browning Home, Camden, South Carolina.

The King Home and its influence on the Wiley campus was one of the strong assets in the history of the college.

REFERENCES AND NOTES

1. *The Christian Educator*, 1891, p. 119.
2. *Ibid.*
3. Freedmen's Aid Society, Sixth Annual Report, 1873, p. 26.
4. *Ibid.*
5. *Ibid.*
6. *Ibid.*
7. Freedmen's Aid Society, Twelfth Annual Report, 1879, p. 8.
8. *Ibid.*
10. Freedmen's Aid Society Report, 1879, pp 33f.
11. *Ibid.*, pp. 36f.
12. Journal, Texas Annual Conference, December 14-19, 1887, p. 32.
13. Freedmen's Aid Society Report, July 1, 1891, p. 206.
14. Journal, Texas Annual Conference, December 14-19, 1887, p. 35.
15. Freedmen's Aid Society Report, July 1, 1891, p. 206.
16. Freedmen's Aid Society Report, July 1, 1892, p. 43.
17. *Ibid.*
18. *Ibid.*
19. *Ibid.*
20. *Ibid.*, p. 44.
21. Journal, Texas Annual Conference, December 1, 1892, p. 39.
22. *The Christian Educator*, July, 1891, p. 207.
23. Gibbs, Warmoth T., *President Matthew W. Dogan of Wiley College*, p. 17.
24. *The Christian Educator*, February - March, 1897, p. 58.
25. *Ibid.*
26. *Ibid.*
27. *Ibid.*
28. *The Christian Educator*, April - May, 1896, p. 71.
29. *Ibid.*
30. *Ibid.*
31. *The Christian Educator*, February-March, 1897, p. 54.
32. *The Christian Educator*, February-March, 1897, p. 59.
33. Minutes, Texas Annual Conference, Dec. 1, 1882, p. 39.
34. *The Christian Educator*, August-September, 1901, p. 98.
35. *Ibid.*
36. *Ibid.*, p. 98.
37. *Ibid.*, p. 98.
38. Minutes, Texas Annual Conference, 1904, p. 41.
39. *Ibid.*
40. *The Christian Educator*, May-August, 1920, p. 20.

41. *The Christian Educator*, May, 1911, Front Page.
42. *The Christian Educator*, May, 1911, p. 2.
43. *Ibid.*
44. *Ibid.*, p. 6.
45. *Ibid.*, p. 8.
46. *Ibid.*, p. 10.
47. *Ibid.*
48. *Ibid.*, pp. 11-12.
49. *Ibid.*, p. 13.
50. *Ibid.*
51. Jones, Thomas Jesse, *op. cit.*
52. *Ibid.*, p. 583.
53. *The Christian Educator*, May, 1918, p. 3.
54. *Ibid.*, p. 4.
55. Wiley College Correspondence, I. T. C. Library.
56. *Ibid.*
57. Journal of the Texas Annual Conference, October 21-25, 1925, p. ?.
58. *The Christian Educator*, August, 1928, p. 3.
59. *The Christian Educator*, November, 1928, p. 4.
60. *Ibid.*
61. Minutes, Texas Annual Conference, 1928, p. 28.
62. Record in College's Files.
63. Record in College's Files.
64. *Ibid.*

CHAPTER 24

INSTITUTIONS UNDER OTHER AUSPICES,
AND INSTITUTIONS DISCONTINUED

A. INSTITUTIONS UNDER OTHER AUSPICES

Morgan College (Baltimore, Maryland)

Morgan College was founded December 25, 1866, at Baltimore, Maryland, in the name of Centenary Biblical Institute, and was organized under the supervision of Bishops Levi Scott and Edward R. Ames. At this time the church was celebrating the centennial of Methodism in America, thus the name "Centenary" Biblical Institute was given.

The following Trustees were appointed by Bishops Scott and Ames: Thomas Kelso, William Harden, William Daniel, William B. Hill, John Lanahan, Henry W. Drakley, Hugh L. Bond, James H. Brown, Charles A. Reid, Isaac P. Cook, Francis A. Cook, Robert Turner, and Samuel Hindes.[1] The sum of $5,000 from an appropriation by the Missionary Society of the Methodist Episcopal Church, for the education of colored preachers, was paid into the treasury.[2] The Institute was chartered by the Superior Court of Baltimore November 27, 1867,[3] with provisions similar to those of Drew Theological Seminary.

Classes were conducted by various members of the Board of Trustees. It was not until 1872 that the school was formally organized under the administration of a President. On October 19, 1868, Rev. J. H. Brown, D.D., and Rev. William Harden were elected Professors. Under their direction, two sessions of the Institute were held—the first, in the Fall and Winter of 1868-69, and the second in 1869-70.[4]

In May, 1872, under the earnest appeal of Dr. R. S. Rust, Corresponding Secretary of the Freedmen's Aid Society, and the hearty endorsement of the Baltimore Conference at its previous session, a building was purchased at 44 Saratoga Street in Baltimore.[5]

First President

On September 6, 1872, the Rev. J. Emory Round was elected

President of the Institute.[6] On October 9, 1872, the Institute was formally opened with nine students.[7] The Freedmen's Aid Society was expected to pay the faculty salaries, and the Baltimore, Delaware, and Washington Conferences were depended upon for financial support. Drew Theological Seminary and Garrett Biblical Institute were the patterns the institute were to follow with the hope, eventually, of offering equally as good education as the patterns being emulated.

In 1877 President Round reported that the previous year seventy-three students were in theology, and thirty-nine were in the Normal Course. Three graduated and were teaching. He reported further that thirty-four former students were on probation in Annual Conferences and nearly forty were local preachers.

President Round reported in 1879 that the building occupied was entirely inadequate, and that Rev. J. F. Goucher had purchased a lot on the corner of Fulton and Edmondson Avenues, one of the best building sites in the City, which site was offered the President, in fee simple, and also $5,000 in cash for a suitable building on the site provided the President would raise $6,500 more for the same purpose. The Trustees voted to accept the proposition, with the expectation of raising the funds and completing the building for occupancy by the beginning of the ninth academic year, September, 1880.[8]

In 1880 Centenary Biblical Institute was moved to the new site presented by Dr. Goucher and wife. It was expanded and in 1890 the name was changed to Morgan College, in honor of Rev. Littleton F. Morgan, D.D., a native of Virginia and a prominent member of the Baltimore Conference.[9]

President Round suffered physical exhaustion, and the Trustees appointed the Rev. Maslin Frysinger, A.M., D.D., as the second President July 3, 1882.[10] Dr. Round remained on the faculty as Professor of Historical and Exegetical Theology until his death in 1892.[11] The Normal Department was added, and women were admitted in 1874.[12] In 1882 the enrollment was 136 students, of whom thirty-six were women, and thirty-one were in Theology. In 1886 the Delaware Conference Academy was established at Princess Anne, Maryland, as a branch of the institution in Baltimore.[12a]

President Frysinger resigned in 1888, and was succeeded by the Rev. Francis J. Wagner, as the third President.[13] President Wagner, the Rev. Littleton F. Morgan, Chairman of the Board of Trustees, and Dr. John F. Goucher, Vice Chairman, formed a strong trio of leadership for Morgan College. In 1890, on recommendation of the President, the Chairman of the Board, and the Vice Chairman, the Board approved unanimously (1) the appointment of a committee to seek from the School Commissioner of Baltimore, equal rights and privileges for the Morgan graduates, with other ladies and gentlemen holding certificates from the City's examiners; (2) to amend the charter, changing the name to Morgan College, with authority to grant degrees and increase the number of trustees from thirteen to twenty-four; (3) to establish an academy at Lynchburg, Virginia, in the name of Virginia Collegiate and Industrial Institute, to be a branch of Morgan College; and (4) to enter agreement with the Board of Regents of the Maryland Agricultural College in order for Princess Anne Academy to receive land grant funds from the Federal Government to maintain Agricultural and Industrial schools.[14] The Delaware Conference Academy, established in 1886, was changed in 1890 to Princess Anne Academy.[15] In 1892 Virginia Collegiate and Industrial Institute was established on a site of twelve acres at Lynchburg, Virginia. It was also a branch of Morgan College.[16]

Dr. John O. Spencer, President

In September, 1902, Dr. John Oakley Spencer was elected as the fourth President of Morgan College.[17] The college, with its two branches at Princess Anne, Maryland, and Lynchburg, Virginia, was supported and directed by the Baltimore, Wilmington, Delaware, and Washington Conferences. The total property values reported in 1912 was $84,000.[18]

In 1907 Dr. Spencer initiated a campaign for funds and secured from Andrew Carnegie a gift of $50,000 for a building, on condition that another $50,000 be raised for endowment. The campaign was to include funds for a new site for the college. After ten years, the site on Hillen Road was purchased in 1917. In the Fall of 1918 Morgan College moved from its site in the residential section of the City to the new site on an eighty-acre tract on Hillen Road.[19] The Virginia Collegiate and Industrial Institute had already moved to the same site after destruction of its main building by fire.

Mr. Carnegie doubled his original gift and in 1919 Carnegie Hall, an administration and classroom building, was erected. The new site with its buildings represented a plant worth $378,000. With the endowment of $60,000 added, the total valuation was placed at $438,000,[20] not including Princess Anne Academy with 117 acres. In 1920 the total assets were listed at $453,610.[21]

The College made good progress and in 1925 was accredited by the Middle States Association of Colleges and Secondary Schools.

In 1925 the General Education Board made a conditional grant of $50,000 to Morgan College, provided that the college pay all debts and raise an additional $50,000. It was reported in November, 1929, that a total of $484,818 had been raised in addition to the General Education Board's gift, the college was free of debt, and a new men's dormitory opened November 23, 1929, and $125,000 drawn from the State.[22] The Delaware and Washington Conferences played an important part in these developments, assuming in 1927 and 1928, respectively, responsibility for "a sufficient amount of any deficit—June 1, 1928, to make certain the gifts from the General Education Board and the State of Maryland, totaling $175,000."[23]

Dr. Dwight Oliver Holmes Becomes President

Dr. Spencer retired in 1937 and was succeeded in the Presidency by Dr. Dwight O. Holmes. Dr. Holmes, the fifth President, came to the office from Howard University, where he was Dean of the Graduate School, and gave administrative leadership to Morgan College for eleven years.

Early in the administration of President Holmes one of the most significant developments in the history of the college took place. A State Commission on Higher Education recommended that the State of Maryland secure Morgan College from its Board of Trustees, to become a state institution predominantly for Negroes. This recommendation was consummated in 1939 by Act of the Maryland General Assembly.[24] The name was changed to Morgan State College, thus ending almost three quarters of a century of relationship of this institution to the Methodist Episcopal Church, under whose auspices it was founded in 1867. The interest of the church, particularly the Delaware and Washington Conferences, was continued in Morgan Christian Center, which was established on the campus when Morgan became a State College.

Dr. Holmes Retires, Dr. Jenkins Becomes President

Dr. Holmes retired from the Presidency of Morgan State College in 1948,[25] and was succeeded by Dr. Martin D. Jenkins as the sixth President. Dr. Jenkins, like Dr. Holmes, came to the Presidency of Morgan from the faculty of Howard University, a scholar with the prerequisites for distinguished academic leadership.

Since becoming a state institution in 1939 Morgan State College has had phenomenal growth, in physical plant, in student enrollment, and in faculty.

490

One Hundred Years of Service

In 1967 Morgan College celebrated its centennial. The Methodist Church, the State of Maryland, and a long procession of dedicated men of vision, wisdom, and courage can be thanked for this institution, its contributions of the past and its promise for the future.

Princess Anne Academy
   (Princess Anne, Maryland)

Princess Anne Academy was established in 1886 as the Delaware Conference Academy.[1] It was begun to meet the needs of the Delaware Conference. The name was changed in 1890 to Princess Anne Academy.[2] The Academy was established as a branch of Morgan College. All of the teachers for several years were graduates of Morgan. The school had sixty-two students the first year, all enrolled in the English Course, and all took at least one trade such as agriculture, blacksmith, carpentry, tailoring, shoemaking, sewing, cooking, millinery, etc.

In 1890 the Trustees of Morgan College entered into an agreement with the Board of Regents of the Maryland Agricultural College which made it possible for Princess Anne Academy to receive land grant funds from the Federal Government to maintain agricultural and industrial schools.[3]

The Academy continued as a branch of Morgan College until 1936 when its name was changed to Princess Anne College and it became an independent institution. In 1947 another change was made, and Princess Anne College became Maryland State College.

During the half century it was an academy, 1886-1936, some prominent men of the Methodist Church served as Principal; to name a few: B. O. Bird, Rev. Frank Trigg, Rev. Pezavia O'Connell, and Rev. Thomas Kiah.

B. INSTITUTIONS DISCONTINUED

Central Alabama College

Central Alabama College was organized by the Freedmen's Aid Society in late 1866 under the name of Rust Institute. George W. Pepper in a letter dated April 14, 1864, gives an account of the initial work of this institution prior to the beginning by the Freedmen's Aid Society. He states:

The contrabands are collecting here by the hundreds. . . .A detachment of the Fifteenth Tennessee Colored Infantry is here. They are a splendid set of fellows, and their soldierly qualities win the admiration of all. There is a large school for colored people in Huntsville; almost five hundred are in daily attendance. They are anxious for instruction in the elements of education and very apt in the acquisition of knowledge. . . .The chaplains of the different regiments employ the weekdays in the teaching of these schools.[1]

The first teachers of the school in Huntsville were sent out by the Pittsburgh Aid Society in 1865. The following year they withdrew from the field and the Freedmen's Aid Society of the Methodist Episcopal Church assumed responsibility for the school.[2]

In 1866 a site was purchased for the school by Dr. R. S. Rust with funds from the Freedmen's Aid Society and the Freedmen's Bureau. A school building was erected and equipped at an estimated cost of $8,000 and without any indebtedness. The instructional work in the first year of the school under the Freedmen's Aid Society was conducted by the Misses Hindman and Lakin.[3] Miss Lakin was the daughter of the Reverend A. S. Lakin, who had been engaged in the organizational work of the Methodist Episcopal Church in Alabama.

This school over the years was known by several different names: Rust Institute; Rust Normal Institute; Rust Biblical and Normal Institute; Central Alabama Academy; and Central Alabama College. The purpose of this school was two-fold; first to furnish education for the training of ministers and second to give special attention to the training of teachers.

In 1871 the Freedmen's Aid Society made plans to establish a Biblical Department at Rust Institute for the preparation of ministers, which plans were completed in 1873. At this time the name of the institution was changed to the Rust Normal and Biblical Institute.

In 1879 it was stated that "this school has done more for the elevation of our race than any other in the state. The best teachers in the county and North Alabama come from its rooms—every teacher in this and many other counties in the state is indebted directly or indirectly to Rust Institute for what education he possesses."[4] By 1890 the school was listed as Central Alabama Academy and carried the following courses: college preparatory course; a normal course; English course; the theological course; music, carpentry; domestic economy; and bookkeeping. This was the only academy in Alabama to serve the needs of the growing conference and the vast Negro population. The Central Alabama Conference consisted of 79 traveling preachers, 12 ministerial

492

supplies and 10,233 church members.

In 1904 the college was removed to Birmingham. Not being well located, it was not easily accessible. This was a grave handicap to its growth. Although it became known as Central Alabama College, it was in reality an academy.

In the summer of 1923 the main building was completely destroyed by fire caused by an electrical storm and the school had to close. It was never re-opened. When it closed its doors in 1923, it had provided education for more than 2,000 Negro students, many of whom became ministers and a larger number became teachers.

During this period of more than a half century of existence of Central Alabama College, it was given administrative leadership by a number of outstanding ministers and educators, among whom were: Dr. J. B. F. Shaw, an outstanding scholar; the Rev. Alexander P. Camphor, later a Bishop to Africa; and the Rev. Robert N. Brooks, later President of Samuel Huston College, a Professor at Gammon Theological Seminary, the Editor of the *Central Christian Advocate*, and elected to the Episcopacy in The Methodist Church.

George R. Smith College
    Sedalia, Missouri

The founding of George R. Smith College was somewhat different from the founding of any other Freedmen's Aid Society college. The spirit and intention were no different, but the circumstance was unique.

"On March 27, 1888 Mesdames Smith and Cotton, two philanthropic Christian ladies, and daughters of General George R. Smith, a distinguished union man in Missouri during the war, donated a very valuable tract of land within the corporate limits of Sedalia, for the establishment of an institution of learning for the education of colored people.[1]

"General Smith was a Virginian by birth, grew to manhood in Kentucky, and in 1833 settled with his family in Pettis County, Missouri. He was the son of a Baptist clergyman; but in later years, both he and his family became active and influential members of the Christian church. He was a man of large intellectuality, tremendous energy, intense conviction, and practical benevolence. He filled with success several important offices under the United States and State Governments, and had a large influence in the railway and industrial development of Missouri. He located and planned the growing city of Sedalia in 1856[2] . . . .

"General Smith was a slaveholder by inheritance, but never believed in the institution. Rev. Dr. Shumate, of the Missouri Conference of the Methodist Episcopal Church, preached the first sermon in the Village of Sedalia. The General welcomed him to his home and said: 'Your church does not believe in slavery; but slavery will go, and your church will be strong and powerful in Missouri.' He opened with all his energy the scheme to colonize Kansas by friends of slavery, so as to vote it into the Union a slave state."[3]

* * *

"He died an old man in his home in the midst of the beautiful city he had founded, respected and honored by all."[4]

"General Smith's plans for the freedmen were philanthropic and practical. He felt that, first of all, they should have homes of their own. He sold them many lots on easy terms, so that 'Lincolnville' grew to be a part of Sedalia. Next, they must have education and so, besides the public school, he proposed to devote several lots to a school of higher grade; but he died before the scheme was consummated."[5]

Two daughters, Mesdames Smith and Cotton, inherited their father's estate and gave their lives and fortune to philanthropic work.

"They. . .donated twenty-five acres of land, valued at $25,000, in Sedalia, for the founding of a college for the education especially of colored people. The donation was made March 27, 1888, on condition that a $25,000 building should be built by January 1, 1892.

. . .After the donation was finally determined upon, a season of prayer was had. John*, representing the slave of yesterday and the rising freedom of today, was invited in. The writer** led, and, in blessed unison of spirit and faith, the founding of George R. Smith College was inaugurated."[6]

The conditions stipulated in the granting of the land were met. In July, 1894, *The Christian Educator* reported that the Freedmen's Aid and Southern Education Society had erected the building costing $25,000, it was complete and partially furnished. It reported also that "a three-months school was held in it last year." P. A. Cool served as the first President of the college.[7]

Sunday and Monday, March 25th and 26th, were dedication days.[8] Following are excerpts from the report:

"The dedicatory services proper occupied Monday afternoon

*John, a Negro boy and a former slave was considered a member of the family. **"The writer" was Dr. J. C. Hartzell, Corresponding Secretary of the Freedmen's Aid and Southern Education Society.

494

and evening, and were preceded by a ceremony full of interest and enthusiasm, the raising of a large American flag over the building. Hundreds of people shared in the exultation and patriotic ardor of the occasion. Principal Page, of the Lincoln Institute, the State institution for the training of the colored normal students, made a rousing address, and Bishop Bowman paid a glowing tribute to the stars and stripes. The donors of the ground, Mrs. Smith and Mrs. Cotton, assisted by Mrs. President Cool and Mrs. Dr. Hartzell, pulled the rope by which the banner was raised. At the sight of the unfurling flag, the crowd cheered with exuberant gladness."[9]

The following letter from Mrs. Smith and Mrs. Cotton fitly closed the report:

Friends, Fellow-citizens, Brethren, and Sisters, we are most humbly grateful to the great Creator and Sustainer of all things in heaven, and in earth, to have it in our power to offer this tract of land to our Christian brothers of the Methodist Episcopal Church, to be used for the soul purpose of lifting up morally and educating in all things that make for righteousness our colored people. This enterprise for our colored friends we have long cherished in our heart of hearts, and we believe on the completion and operation of this college there will come a new era, an era of good faith, good feeling, and good conduct, that will be felt through every avenue of life in this town.[10]

The feelings and sentiments regarding this enterprise, from its inception to the consummation of the plans for the college were best expressed in editorials by the local newspaper; the *Sedalia Democrat* said:

It means for the country a pouring in of light; it means the refinement and elevation of a class of citizens whose future in the social economy of the country is one of the gravest problems that confronts the statesman and the philosopher. . . . Sedalia and her citizens are proud today that she is soon to have an institution for the bettering of her colored population.[11]

The *Sedalia Gazette* said editorially:

It is the acceptance of the new and broader Christianity. Christianity in its spirit and essence is larger than any church that ever yet stood for it; and that which the church of old Missouri would not accept nor believe possible, it is now compelled to accept by the spirit of the new era, so that now even the secular press is commending the course of education for the colored people, and is urging the communities of the

Southern States to stand by the rights and open the door of privileges and opportunity to the Negro race.[1 2]

Never was there a finer spirit or greater enthusiasm engulfing the founding and development of a Freedmen's Aid Society college than that at George R. Smith College, which got off to a good start under the leadership of President Cool.

It is probable that President Cool was head of the college only two years—1894 to 1896. *The Christian Educator* for October-November, 1896, refers to the Rev. E. A. Robertson as President.[1 3]

Reverend Robertson continued as President six years, 1896 to 1902. During this period the facilities of the college were limited to one building. *The Christian Educator* gives the following information for the school year 1899—1900: "One building, 62 rooms, containing a chapel seating 400, rooms for teachers and seventy-five students; enrollment the past year, 180."[1 4]

Reverend E. A. Robertson is listed as President.

Reverend I. L. Lowe, President

In 1902 the Reverend I. L. Lowe was made President of George R. Smith College.[1 5] He served as President six years, from 1902 to 1908. During this period the general situation remained the same with reference to plant, students, and teachers.

Professor A. C. Maclin, Acting President

In 1908 Professor A. C. Maclin was made Acting President, which position he held three years, 1908 to 1911.[1 6] Report on the college in 1910 gave teachers, 14; students, 192; total real estate and equipment, $54,175.

Reverend J. C. Sherrill, President

In the summer of 1911 the Reverend J. C. Sherrill was elected President of the college.[1 7] He was the first black man to serve as President of this institution. The Reverend Sherrill came to the Presidency after extensive experience as a missionary in Africa. There was one building, as described above, an unfinished industrial building, the total property value being $54,175. There were ten teachers and 148 students.[1 8] In 1912 an Agricultural Department was organized, but never reached any significant development. Reverend Sherrill was President two years, 1911 to 1913.

496

Reverend George Evans, President

In August, 1913, Reverend George Evans became the new President of George R. Smith College.[19] Reverend Evans was a native of South Ireland. He came to the Presidency after eight years of pastorate in Texas, and six years as Professor at Claflin College, Orangeburg, South Carolina. He succeeded President Sherrill who had accepted a position as Field Agent for the Foreign Missionary Society.[20] Reverend Evans held the Presidency two years, 1913 to 1915.

Professor M. S. Davage, President

Professor Davage became the new President of George R. Smith College in September, 1915,[21] succeeding President George Evans. President Davage, the second black President of the college, was a graduate of New Orleans University. He had been for five years a teacher of Mathematics at his Alma Mater immediately after graduation, and for ten years had been Business Manager of the *Southwestern Christian Advocate.* He served as President one year, and in 1916 transferred to the Presidency of Haven Institute, Meridian, Mississippi.[22]

Robert B. Hayes, President

Professor Robert E. Hayes succeeded M. S. Davage as President of George R. Smith College in August, 1916.[23] He came to this position as a graduate of Baker University and after thirteen years in charge of Natural Science at Philander Smith College, Little Rock, Arkansas. For nine years he served as President.

In 1923 it was reported that "George R. Smith College at Sedalia, Missouri, has but one building. At present the teachers and all the non-resident students live in this building. It also contains chapel, offices, and classrooms. Everybody and everything cramped."[24]

In 1924 the entire plant was renovated and new equipment installed at a cost of $16,618.02.[25]

For the school year 1924-25 there were thirteen teachers and 106 students. The total plant value including furniture and equipment was $67,000.[26]

On April 26, 1925, tragedy struck George R. Smith College. The main and only building was completely destroyed by fire. The college was just thirty years old, started with a gift of land from the daughters of George R. Smith, only one of whom, Mrs. Cotton, was living at the time the building burned. She still lived at Sedalia, advanced in age and honored by the whole community.

The building, including contents, was covered with insurance in the amount of $45,000, which was insufficient for replacement.

It was stated that "the future of the school is now up for most serious and careful consideration by the Board of Education."[27] A special committee was appointed May 13, to visit the school. Dean Thomas A. Holgate of Northwestern University was Chairman of the committee. The decision was not to open the school for 1925-1926.[28]

The citizens of Sedalia, colored and white, were very anxious for the school to be rebuilt, but the college never reopened. President Hayes, who was President nine years, was transferred to New Orleans University as Dean of Instruction.

Haven Normal School (Waynesboro, Georgia)

The Haven Normal School was established in 1868 at Waynesboro, Georgia, in a very large Negro population.[1] For a long time it was the only school in the whole region.[2] A large majority of the students were enrolled in the elementary department. By 1879 three courses were offered: the English Course, the Normal Course, and Theology.[3] In 1891 the College Preparatory Course was added, with three students enrolled. The English Course enrolled 178, making a total enrollment of 181. This was one of the adjunct schools serving as a feeder to Clark University during most of its history.

Some of the principals who gave direction to this school were: Rev. J. R. Goodier, Rev. C. W. M. Mahen, Rev. C. P. Wellman, Miss Carrie Fairchild, Professor E. T. Barksdale, Professor W. M. Gordon.[4]

Haven Normal School was closed about 1915.[5]

Haven Institute (Meridian, Mississippi)

Haven Institute was founded in 1879 as Meridian Academy,[1] at Meridian, Mississippi. It had its origin in the mind of a black man, Moses Adams, an ex-slave, and a preacher before the Civil War. He urged the Negro people of Meridian to establish an educational institution. Robert Adams, son of Moses Adams, had control of and taught in the school until 1888.[2] This was one of the few schools supported by the Freedmen's Aid Society that always had black leadership.

The Freedmen's Aid Society gave aid for the first time in 1888.[3] In that year, J. H. Brooks became Principal,[4] with C.

E. Mabry in Music as First Assistant, and A. G. Brooks, as Second Assistant. The enrollment was 164, of which five were in the college preparatory course, eighteen were in the normal course, and 141 were in the English course.

In 1908 Dr. J. B. F. Shaw became Principal[5], and served until 1912. The property value was listed in November, 1911, at $15,920. At that time there were seven teachers and 337 students.[6] When Haven Normal School, at Waynesboro, Georgia, was closed in 1915, the name "Haven" was transferred to Meridian Academy and it became Haven Academy.

A large transaction was consummated in 1920. The white school, Meridian College and Conservatory, was purchased by the Freedmen's Aid Society, at a cost of $151,250, including equipment.[7] The Trustees of the College and Conservatory took the Haven property at $20,000. The purpose of the Society in purchasing the new property was to develop a college and a great Conservatory of Music. The Rev. R. N. Brooks, then President of Haven Institute, was transferred to Central Alabama College and Dr. J. B. F. Shaw was brought back to Haven to give leadership in the development of a college and conservatory at Meridian.

The property value of Haven College and Conservatory was listed in 1924 at $170,000, plus equipment, $40,000.[8]

The new location for Haven College and Conservatory was purchased with funds from the Centenary. The necessary money for carrying out the projects was not forthcoming, and the new development was almost completely arrested. In 1926 this institution was listed as Haven Teachers College.

For the lack of finances, and with the rising competition of the Public School System in Mississippi, the question was raised and had to be answered as to whether the church could afford to maintain two Methodist institutions for Negro youth in Mississippi. In 1928 Haven Teachers College was closed.

Key West Academy

Key West Academy was begun in 1889. The Rev. S. A. Huger interceded for a school to give "Christian Industrial Education" among the blacks of that section.[1] Nothing was done until 1895. Mrs. S. A. Daley, secured by Rev. Huger, opened a school in the basement of the Methodist Episcopal Church at Key West, with forty students. A fee of ten cents a week was charged each student. The school was discontinued about 1900.

LaGrange Seminary
(LaGrange, Georgia)

LaGrange Seminary was established by the Corresponding Secretary of the Freedmen's Aid Society in 1870, in a rough unplastered church in LaGrange, Georgia.[1] The efforts of the colored people of this community, out of their poverty, to provide educational facilities for their children, make a moving story. The most notable contributions for a school building were made by Negroes themselves, mostly by women earning only $4.00 a month.[2]

LaGrange Seminary gained the status of an academy in 1890.[3] The value in 1900 was $8,000. The Rev. Henry M. White was Principal, with an enrollment of 170.

In 1908 Professor S. R. Singer became Principal. LaGrange Academy was one of the adjunct schools, serving as a feeder to Clark University. About 1915 LaGrange Academy was discontinued and its resources turned over to Clark University.

Richmond Normal School
(Richmond, Virginia)

The Richmond Normal School was established in 1867 for the purpose of training teachers.[1] In 1872 a handsome building was erected at a cost of $25,000.[2]

In 1872 the Superintendent of Public Schools of Virginia advised his County Superintendent to visit the Richmond Normal School "to observe the methods of the Methodists in their operation of the Institution," and said that "such a visit will wholly relieve any curable case of skepticism in regard to the capacity of the Negro to receive a good education."[3]

The Richmond Normal School was discontinued in 1875.

Rome Normal School
(Rome, Georgia)

The Rome Normal School was an outgrowth of an elementary school established in 1866 by the Freedmen's Aid Society.[1] Its purpose was to train teachers and ministers. About 1869, the Rev. T. B. Gurney, the church pastor, and Miss M. M. Harrington, teacher, stated that "with our present accommodations, we cannot draw students from abroad, or do justice to the advanced pupils at Rome."[2] The school was discontinued in 1870 and the interests centered on Clark University.[3]

Virginia Collegiate and Industrial Institute
(Lynchburg, Virginia)

The Virginia Collegiate and Industrial Institute was established in 1892 as a branch of Morgan College.[1] It remained in Lynchburg as a branch until about 1917. The Institute was moved to the Morgan College site in Baltimore when its main building was destroyed by fire.[2]

Walden College
(Formerly Central Tennessee College, Nashville, Tennessee)

The founding and development of Central Tennessee College (later Walden University) from 1865 to 1900 is one of the most romantic and moving stories in the history of American education. The life of the institution and the lives, dedication, and service of several men were so intertwined, and the results were so compelling that there can be no doubt that the will and hand of God were in this work, and all such work carried forward by the Freedmen's Aid Society in behalf of the Freedmen.

In 1865 the Methodist Episcopal Church began its denominational work in Nashville. A school was organized under the direction of Bishop Clark, by Reverend A. A. Gee. The building used was a church formerly belonging to the Methodist Episcopal Church, South and known as Andrew Chapel. The church was purchased by the Methodist Episcopal Church and became known as Clark Memorial Chapel. In 1866 Reverend John Seys was appointed pastor of Clark Chapel and principal of the missionary school. Reverend Seys had been for many years a missionary in Africa. Associated also with the early beginning of this school are the names of O. O. Knight, Mrs. Mary Murphy, Mrs. Julia North, Miss O. D. Barber, Miss Julia Evans, Mrs. S. L. Larned, Misses Nettie and Mary Mann, and Miss Emily E. Preston. A large brick building known as the "gun factory" was made available for the use of this school.

In 1866 the Freedmen's Aid Society took the school under its care. A Board of Trustees was organized and application for a charter was made. On July 9th the Board of Trustees met, accepted the charter and otherwise organized as a body corporate.[1]

At the first session of the Tennessee Conference of the Methodist Episcopal Church in the fall of 1866, Reverend W. B. Crichlow was appointed pastor of Clark Chapel and principal of the school.[2] On July 14, 1866, the sum of $11,500 was granted to

501

the trustees by the Missionary Society of the Methodist Episcopal Church to purchase a site and erect buildings thereon for the college.[3] In the same year Reverend John Braden was appointed pastor of Clark Chapel and principal of this college school.[4]

In 1866 Central Tennessee College, which began its existence in the basement of Clark Memorial Methodist Episcopal Church, was moved to the Gun Factory secured by Bishop J. M. Walden for the opening of a colored school. Bishop Walden had appointed Reverend John Braden of the Cincinnati, Ohio Conference, who came to Nashville and with his wife and little daughter made his home in the Gun Factory and took charge of the school.

In 1867 the Federal government saw fit to return the Gun Factory property back to the citizens. Another location was secured for this school but because of opposition to a Negro school the sale of the property was annulled by a chancery court and the money refunded. In the 1868 Annual Report of the Freedmen's Aid Society it was stated:

We have been compelled to give up the Gun Factory at Nashville where we held our Normal School for the past two years. But, the Trustees of Central Tennessee College have purchased valuable property, worth fifteen thousand dollars for the school, and the Bureau has made us an appropriation of ten thousand dollars for the erection of appropriate buildings.[5]

The Bureau referred to in this quote was the Federal Government's Freedmen's Bureau.

Another location toward the south city limits was secured. The school was housed here in a two-story brick building for one year and was given the name Central Tennessee College. The Reverend G. H. Hartupee of Ohio was placed in charge of the school. Reverend John Braden remained at the Gun Factory one year as the principal of a city public school for colored children, but was appointed to succeed Reverend Hartupee who resigned at the end of the first school year.[6]

Dr. Braden had a long and illustrious presidency at Central Tennessee College. His labors and dedication brought to Walden its greatest era of success. His wife labored by his side. Mrs. Braden "with her own needle, made sheets, pillow cases, pillow ticks, bed ticks for straw filling, tied or quilted comforts, besides helping arrange furniture in teachers' living rooms; and this, in addition to the care of her home and family."[7]

Dr. Braden and Mrs. Braden were an inspiration to their daughter, Mary E. Braden, who gave most of her life also in faithful service at the same institution and later spent her

502

concluding years at Morristown College, Morristown, Tennessee. In 1869 the Freedmen's Aid Society reported:

One hundred students are now enjoying the advantages of thorough training under the care of the most successful educator, Rev. John Braden, and his accomplished assistants . . .halls are crowded with earnest students preparing to teach school, practice law or medicine, or preach the glorious gospel.[8]

In 1871 the Freedmen's Aid Society "reported three commodious and imposing brick edifices, the college chapel, dormitory, and boarding-house, ample for hundreds of pupils."[9] The Board of Instruction consisted of Reverend John Braden, President; Miss Maggie Hebert, Miss Mary C. Owens, Miss Helen M. Perkins, and Miss Mary Hebert, teachers.[10] The college property was reported to be worth $50,000. There were three departments, normal, preparatory, and theological.

Four years later, in 1875, the college showed much progress. The number of buildings had increased to four, valued at $70,000. In addition to the President the instructional faculty consisted of six persons, and facilities had been increased to accommodate more than three hundred students. The first college class was begun in 1875. In speaking of the work of the college the Secretary of the Freedmen's Aid Society indicated that:

. . .demands for teachers and preachers are so urgent that they are taken from the school with very limited qualifications; yet, such are the necessities of the colored people. They are feeling more and more the necessity for higher qualifications for the school room and the pulpit, as well as professional life.[11]

He further indicates that:

. . .work already performed by the Freedmen's Aid Society is telling with wonderful results on the interests of the colored people. They have learned something of equality, the value of money, the duties of husband and wife, the relation of labor to independence and the duties to the country and to God which their freedom enjoins upon them.[12]

By 1889 Central Tennessee College had made remarkable progress. Its land and buildings were valued at $100,000. The enrollment had reached 545 students. On the faculty there were 45 teachers and six special lecturers. Instructional work was offered in the following areas or departments: collegiate and academic, theological, medical, dental, legal, and industrial. At this time the college was in a period of most rapid development. The areas of work were not only being increased, but offered such extensive and thorough training as to point toward the university which it, within a few years, became.

During the period 1891 to 1900 Central Tennessee College became outstanding in many areas of its work. The four-year collegiate work leading to the Bachelor of Arts degree was well-established. The medical school which was dedicated in 1880 as Meharry Medical School was doing very outstanding work. The dental department which was established in 1886 had graduated its first class in 1887. A pharmaceutical department had been added and the pharmaceutical hall dedicated in 1889. The John F. Slater Industrial Department was opened in 1884 and offered a strong industrial program. More will be said about Meharry Medical College under separate treatment. A further statement should be made here regarding the industrial programs.

By 1892 the industrial department, which was named the John F. Slater School in 1884, had grown to large proportions. In the industrial buildings the offerings included carpentry, blacksmithing, printing, iron-work machinery, electrotyping, etc. In this department, the school of mechanical arts was reported to be one of the finest of its kind in the country, and the only one of its kind open to colored youth in this country. The machinery was reported to be worth $20,000 and consisted of a thirty-five horsepower engine, thirty-three pieces of machinery ranging from the large Garvin Number 3 Universal Milling machine down to the minute gear-cutters with lathes, planers, sharpers, tiers, forges, spinning tools, sand-blasts and other varieties of tools. The comment was made that "we are indebted for the magnificent outfit in machinery to Professor Sedwick, who consecrates it all, with his own splendid genius in mechanic art, to the work of Christian education."[1][3]

The Presidency of Dr. John Braden came to an end at his death on June 10, 1900. *The Christian Educator* had this to say about Dr. Braden:

At the time of his death he had been in the work of the Society longer than any of his associates, for in June, 1867, he was appointed President of a school that afterward became Central Tennessee College, which was then conducted in a building known as a gun factory. From this time to his death the history of this remarkable man was the history of this institution, and *vice versa.* It was indeed his child as truly as his

504

sainted daughter who with the spirit of her father continued his work, where for so many years they toiled lovingly together. . . .Central Tennessee College was his crowning work. From the crude beginning in the gun factory, where fathers and mothers and children met in one grade, this institution has grown to a well-organized university with its departments of literature, pedagogy, medicine, dentistry, pharmacy, law, theology, music, industry, business and normal. Hundreds of souls have been converted at her altars. More than 6,000 students have come under her influences, and of this number 3,000 have gone forth as Christian teachers to bless and uplift the race.[14]

The Board of Managers of the Freedmen's Aid and Southern Education Society in 1897 in recognition of the service of Bishop John M. Walden, who was for two years Corresponding Secretary and for many years President of the Society, recommended that the several schools of Central Tennessee College be federated and the name changed to Walden University.[15] The recommendation was not carried out until 1900 when on October 18th the Board of Trustees, by unanimous vote, adopted a resolution changing the name from Central Tennessee College to Walden University. In 1866, in accordance with a request from Dr. Walden, then the Corresponding Secretary of the Freedmen's Aid Society, General Clinton B. Fisk gave a two-story brick building, known as the Gun Factory for the use of the school for Freedmen. The school which was begun in such humble surroundings and circumstances had grown to be a great institution appropriately bearing the name of its founder.

At his death in 1900, President Braden had served as President of Central Tennessee College thirty-three years. Dr. G. W. Hubbard served as Acting President one year, 1900-1901; Dr. J. Benson Hamilton of New York was elected President in 1901 and served three years. Dr. Hamilton was succeeded by the Reverend Dr. John A. Kumler of Ohio who held the Presidency with distinction for eight years. President Kumler's statement in 1911 gave the first indication of the declining state of Walden University. He pointed to the university as the oldest institution of the Freedmen's Aid Society and stated that: "The buildings are mostly old and worn out, and ought every one of them to be replaced with new ones. The girls' dormitory, which was burned a few years ago, it is hoped may be replaced in a short time."[16]

A series of unfortunate circumstances and misfortunes during the next few years beset the institution. Dr. Jay S. Stowell spoke of these incidents as follows:

505

In recent years, however, a series of circumstances and accidents has tended to limit the work of the school. In 1900 President Braden died and the school was deprived of his capable leadership. Three years later, near midnight of December 18, 1903, a disastrous fire broke out in one of the buildings and twelve lives were lost. . . .Suits were instituted to the amount of one hundred and twenty thousand dollars. For years, while these suits were pending, it was deemed inadvisable to rebuild or to purchase new equipment. The school inevitably suffered and it has never regained the prestige and standing of its early days.[17]

After serving as President eight years, Dr. Kumler was succeeded by Dr. George F. Durgin of New England who served as President three years, 1912-1915. He was succeeded by Mr. Elam A. White of the Lexington Conference who served as President two years, 1915-1917. Mr. White was the first Negro President of the University.

During the year 1918-1919 Walden University was turned over to the Federal Government for use as an Instruction Camp for the Students' Army Training Corps. During this year, it was under the supervision of a Board of Managers.

On August 6, 1919, the college was reopened and the Reverend J. H. Lovell was elected President, who served three years.

In 1920 there were discussions on discontinuing Walden. The reasons for this discussion are set forth in *The Christian Educator:*

Nashville, Tennessee, is a school center for both races. Four or five colleges compete in that territory for the patronage of the Negroes who are desirous of obtaining a higher education. The modern tendency is to distribute these institutions so that their constituency may be enlarged and the results of their work spread over a greater extent of territory. In the interest of this movement for a reduction in the number of competing institutions in the same city, the question of the discontinuance of Walden College has been before the Board for many years.

Meharry Medical College, located on adjoining lots, needs all the space and buildings, if provision is to be made for its future growth. In view of these circumstances, and the further fact that the local patronage of Walden College had been declining in later years, the Board decided to discontinue the school and turn over so much of its buildings and grounds as belongs to the Freedmen's Aid Society to Meharry Medical College. This Medical College is the largest institution for the education of

506

Negro physicians anywhere on the earth.

The General Education Board and the Carnegie Foundation seemed willing to cooperate with the Freedmen's Aid Society and the Board of Trustees in providing for endowment, buildings, and equipment, sufficient to put the College into the very forefront of the medical schools of the country. If this is to be accomplished, the school needs all of the space and buildings formerly occupied by Walden College. In harmony with the program of the Board for the future usefulness of the entire system of schools, this plan is being carried out. Provision will be made, if desired, to take care of the Alumni and the constituency of Walden College, either at Rust College, Holly Springs, Mississippi; Clark University, Atlanta, Georgia; or, Morristown Normal and Industrial College, Morristown, Tennessee.[18]

At this time the matter of discontinuing the college did not get beyond the discussion stage.

In 1922 Mr. T. R. Davis was elected President. In this same year, the Board of Education for Negroes of the Methodist Episcopal Church, formerly the Freedmen's Aid Society, renewed its supervision and support of the college. A new site was purchased at a cost of $155,000. The old site was turned over to Meharry Medical College. When the college was re-located in 1922 it became a two-year junior college, instead of a four-year senior college. In 1926 President Davis was transferred to the Presidency of Samuel Huston College, and Dean H. H. Sutton was placed in charge of Walden. In 1928 the college became a college preparatory school and Mr. W. M. Brown was selected as Principal.

In 1935 the Walden College preparatory school was permanently closed. The work of this institution, begun in 1865, had spanned a period of seventy years. No one is wise enough to estimate the measure of influence this institution had during those seven decades, or when and where the influence will end.

On May 22, 1935, at a special meeting of the Trustees of Walden College, formal action was taken by which the interests of Walden College were combined with Clark University, with the request that Clark University recognize the alumni of Walden College. The Trustees Board of Clark University, at its Annual Meeting on June 4, 1935, took appropriate action accepting the interests of Walden College and recognizing its alumni. The Board of Education of the Methodist Episcopal Church approved the action of the two Boards of Trustees.[19]

507

West Tennessee Seminary

West Tennessee Seminary was established at Mason City, Tennessee, by the Freedmen's Aid Society in 1876.[1] Its primary work was at the elementary school level. In 1888, with Rev. Charles Alexander in charge, assisted by Miss Amanda Davis, the school had 166 students in attendance, eighty-six in the primary department and the rest in the academy. This school was discontinued in 1889.

REFERENCES AND NOTES
MORGAN COLLEGE

1. Eight Annual Report, Freedmen's Aid Society, 1875, p. 29.
2. *Ibid.*
3. *Ibid.*
4. *Ibid.*
5. *Ibid.*
6. *Ibid.*, p. 30.
7. *Ibid.*
8. Report, Freedmen's Aid Society, p. 52.
9. *The Christian Educator*, August, 1914, p. 8.
10.Wilson, Edward, Unpublished Manuscript, Morgan State College, "A Century of Purpose in Action, 1867-1967", November 27, 1967, p. 10.
11. *Ibid.*
12. *Ibid.*
12a. *The Christian Educator*, August, 1914, p. 8.
13. Wilson, Edward, *op. cit.*, p. 11.
14. *Ibid.*
15. Report, Freedmen's Aid and Southern Education Society, 1891, p. 229.
16. *The Christian Educator*, August, 1914, p. 8.
17. Wilson, Edward, *op. cit.*, p. 14.
18. *The Christian Educator*, November, 1912, p. 24.
19. *The Christian Educator*, May, 1920, pp. 11f.
20. *Ibid.*
21. *The Christian Educator*, November, 1920, p. 3.
22. *The Christian Educator*, November, 1929, p. 3.
23. The Washington Conference Journal, March 21-26, 1928, p. 283.
24. Agreement, State of Maryland and Board of Trustees of Morgan College, September 25, 1939, pursuant to Senate Bill No. 377.
25. Wilson, Edward, *op. cit.*, p. 15.

REFERENCES AND NOTES
PRINCESS ANNE ACADEMY

1. Report, Freedmen's Aid Society, 1891, p. 229.
2. *Ibid.*
3. Report, Freedmen's Aid and Southern Education Society, 1891, p. 229.

CENTRAL ALABAMA COLLEGE

1. *The Christian Advocate and Journal*, April 14, 1864, p. 1.
2. Tenth Annual Report of the Freedmen's Aid Society, 1878, p. 30.
3. Third Annual Report of the Freedmen's Aid Society, 1869, p. 9.
4. Eleventh Annual Report of the Freedmen's Aid Society, 1879, p. 48.

GEORGE R. SMITH COLLEGE

1. Report, Freedmen's Aid and Southern Education Society, July 1, 1888, p. 47.
2. *The Christian Educator*, April, 1891, p. 94.
3. *Ibid.*
4. *Ibid.*, p. 95.
5. *Ibid.*
6. *Ibid.*, p. 96.
7. *The Christian Educator*, July, 1894, p. 158.
8. *Ibid.*
9. *Ibid.*, p. 159.
10. *Ibid.*, p. 163.
11. *The Christian Educator*, July, 1893, p. 158.
12. *Ibid.*
13. *The Christian Educator*, October-November, 1896, p. 160.
14. *The Christian Educator*, December-January, 1899-1900, p. 13.
15. *The Christian Educator*, November, 1902, p. 19.
16. *The Christian Educator*, November, 1908, p. 14; and August, 1911, p. 1.
17. *The Christian Educator*, August, 1911, p. 1.
18. *Ibid.*
19. *The Christian Educator*, August, 1913, p. 5.
20. *The Christian Educator*, August, 1913, pp. 5 and 6.
21. *The Christian Educator*, November, 1915, p. 2.
22. *The Christian Educator*, August, 1916, p. 6.
23. *The Christian Educator*, August, 1916, pp. 8f.
24. *The Christian Educator*, November, 1923, p. 10.
25. *The Christian Educator*, May, 1924, p. 9.
26. *The Christian Educator*, February, 1925 (Opposite Front Cover)
27. *The Christian Educator*, May, 1925, p. 9.
28. *Ibid.*

HAVEN NORMAL SCHOOL

1. Report, Freedmen's Aid Society, 1873, p. 33.
2. *Ibid.*
3. Report, Freedmen's Aid Society, 1879, p. 42.
4. Reports, Freedmen's Aid Society, 1868-1912.
5. *The Christian Advocate*, 1917, p. 21.

HAVEN INSTITUTE

1. Report, Freedmen's Aid Society, 1891, p. 223.
2. *Ibid.*
3. *Ibid.*
4. *The Christian Educator*, 1908, p. 14.
5. *The Christian Educator*, November, 1911, p. 21.
6. *The Christian Educator*, November, 1921, p. 2.
7. *The Christian Educator*, August, 1924, p. 4.
8. *The Christian Educator*, May, 1928, p. 5.

KEY WEST ACADEMY

1. Report, Freedmen's Aid and Southern Education Society, December-January, 1897-1898, pp. 4-5.

LAGRANGE SEMINARY

1. Report, Freedmen's Aid Society, 1879, p. 44.
2. *Ibid.*, p. 45.
3. Report, *The Christian Educator*, pp. 229 and 461.

RICHMOND NORMAL SCHOOL

1. Report, Freedmen's Aid Society, 1872, p. 25.
2. *Ibid.*
3. *Ibid.*

ROME NORMAL SCHOOL

1. Report, Freedmen's Aid Society, 1873, p. 33.
2. *Ibid.*
3. *Ibid.*

VIRGINIA COLLEGIATE AND INDUSTRIAL INST.

1. *The Christian Educator*, August, 1914, p. 8.
2. *The Christian Educator*, May, 1920, p. 11.

REFERENCES AND NOTES
WALDEN COLLEGE

1. Central Tennessee College Catalogue, 1909-1910, p. 16.
2. *Ibid.*
3. *Ibid.*
4. *Ibid.*
5. Second Annual Report of the Freedmen's Aid Society, 1868, p. 16.
6. The Walden Catalogue, XXVI, 5, p. 7.
7. Braden, Mary E., *John Braden - A Pioneer in Negro Education* (Morristown, Tennessee, 1936), p. 16.
8. Third Annual Report of the Freedmen's Aid Society, 1869, p. 8.
9. Fourth Annual Report of the Freedmen's Aid Society, 1871, p. 8.
10. *Ibid.*
11. Eighth Annual Report of the Freedmen's Aid Society, 1875, pp. 16f.
12. *Ibid.*, pp. 17f.
13. Twenty-Sixth Annual Report of the Freedmen's Aid Society, 1892.
14. *The Christian Educator*, June-July, 1900, p. 121f.
15. The Freedmen's Aid and Southern Education Report, 1897, p. 37f.
16. *The Christian Educator*, November 11, 1911, p. 20.
17. Stowell, Jay S., *Methodist Adventures in Negro Education* (New York: Cincinnati, The Methodist Book Concern, 1922), p. 171.
18. *The Christian Educator*, May, 1920, pp. 5-6.
19. Proceedings of the Board of Education of the Methodist Episcopal Church, January 29-30, 1936, p. 74.

WEST TENNESSEE SEMINARY

1. Report, Freedmen's Aid Society, 1885, p. ?.

512

PART V.
FINANCIAL SUPPORT, HISTORICAL PERSPECTIVE; A CENTURY OF SERVICE; STATUS

CHAPTER 25

FINANCIAL SUPPORT, HISTORICAL PERSPECTIVE

Immediately following the organization of the Freedmen's Aid Society in August, 1866, the Bishops of the church issued an appeal to the membership for support of this worthy new venture.[1] This was the initiation of a continuous effort to gain support for this cause. In 1872, after official approval was given to the Freedmen's Aid Society by the General Conference, it was officially listed as an agency of the Church that might seek Annual Conference financial support.[2] The first apportionment to Annual Conferences was made in 1872.[3] The Corresponding Secretaries of the Freedmen's Aid Society and certain key Bishops made constant efforts to justify to the whole church the importance of providing schools for the Freedmen and made strong appeals to the church at large and to individuals for their financial support.

During its first year, 1866-1867, the Freedmen's Aid Society disbursed to the schools $37,139.89.[4] Annual Conference collections were first reported in 1872. In that year the receipts totaled $45,024.00, of which the Annual Conferences reported $12,048.00.[5] In the period of the first six years of the Society, the highest receipts were, 1868-69, $92,190.77, and 1869-70, $82,617.00.[6]

In the 25th year of the Freedmen's Aid Society, 1890-91, receipts reached $322,656.44, and the total receipts for the first twenty-five years was $2,776,243.18.[7] During the quadrennium 1883-87, Conference collections totaled $293,285.00, and for the quadrennium 1887-91, the Conference collections totaled $381,433.00, an increase of $88,148.00.[8] From all sources, the total for 1883-87 was $624,000.26 and for 1897-91, the total from all sources was $981,197.18, an increase of $357,196.92.[9] During the quadrennium 1891-95 there was a net increase of $63,718.57 in receipts from Conferences and a net increase of $259,363.14 from all sources.[10]

Receipts and Disbursements First Half Century
  (Or 49 Years)

There was, with few exceptions, continuous growth in Annual

515

Conference receipts for the Freedmen's Aid Society Schools from 1872 to 1915, inclusive. In 1872 the Annual Conference receipts for this purpose were $12,048. In 1915 these receipts had increased to $178,689.[11] These receipts were in support of twenty-three professional and collegiate institutions, academies and lower schools. Total receipts from all sources rose from $37,139.00 in 1866-67 to $528,970.83 in 1914-15. The grand total receipts for the forty-eight years' period ended 1914, was $8,796,562.44, and disbursements for the same period, $9,261,267.47.[12]

Jubilee Celebration

At the 1912 General Conference of the Methodist Episcopal Church a report from the Freedmen's Aid Society requested that the General Conference make the year 1913 a jubilee year for the Society, in commemoration of the semi-centennial celebration of the emancipation of the colored people. The report was adopted as follows:

> We endorse the recommendations of the Board of Managers of the General Committee and the Board of Bishops that the year 1913 be observed as the Semi-Centennial Jubilee of the glorious Act of Emancipation—and that special offerings be made in connection with this anniversary celebration, for the support, endowment, and more perfect equipment of the Freedmen's Aid Schools.[13]

The year 1913 was designated as a great year, in which a half million dollars was to have been raised for the Negro schools. The Negroes themselves assumed the responsibility of one dollar per member, or a total of $350,000.[14] It was expected, however, that the Negro people would raise $100,000, and the remaining $400,000 would be given by the church at large.[15] Many obstacles were encountered in seeking a favorable response from the general church in support of this effort, even the giving of merely twenty cents per member. As of October 1913, contributions from conferences for the Jubilee totaled $32,283.99, and of this amount $25,551.54 came from colored conferences.[16] In May, 1914, Secretary I. G. Penn wrote:

> It is well known that the colored people are to give $100,000 of the Jubilee Fund. They have covered their part with subscriptions amounting to $133,000, of which $50,000 is in cash to date, and the remainder constantly coming in. If the

whole church had given in the same proportion, the entire $500,000 and more would be now covered by subscriptions and quite half of the same paid in cash.

. . .Many have apparently not taken seriously to the Jubilee at all.[17]

At the end of the first fifty years the conference collections for the Freedmen's Aid Society institutions had increased considerably over the collections of the year 1872, but it should be noted that the conferences provided only 33 per cent of the receipts in 1914-1915, while the remaining receipts came from sources other than conference support. This fact, along with the flat failure of the Jubilee effort, authorized by the 1912 General Conference, does not indicate any great enthusiasm on the part of the general church at that time to give anything like adequate financial support to the Freedmen's Aid Society institutions. As it will be pointed up later, individual and foundation philanthropies have been the largest sources of financial aid to most of these institutions.

The Centenary

The Centenary Movement was initiated in 1918 by the general church in an effort to raise funds in celebration of the centenary of Methodist missions and in support of all the boards of the church related to the missionary enterprise. The General Conference, May 10, 1916, approved a resolution by C. M. Boswell proposing that the Board of Home Missions and Church Extension join with the Board of Foreign Missions in celebrating in 1918 and 1919 the One Hundredth Anniversary of the beginning of American Missions in the Methodist Episcopal Church, and authorized to enter into such plans that would make the anniversary "inspiring, informing, and profitable."[17a]

A total of $115,003,375[17b] was subscribed over a period of five years.[18] The Freedmen's Aid Society was listed for one million dollars from the Centenary for the support of Negro institutions.[19] These funds and much more were needed for long overdue repairs to buildings, the erection of new buildings, and the upgrading of equipment, facilities, and instructional standards in line with new demands for improvements in these areas. All of the institutions were without debt and all centenary funds were to be used "in the development of the great work of Christian education."[20] To the end of such development, the following guarantees were restated:

1st. The Board of Education for Negroes is to receive its regular apportionment of $350,000 per annum.

2d. The Board is to receive the amounts raised by the Negro Conferences annually as special gifts for the institutions within their territory, amounting to $75,000 a year, the same being for buildings, improvements, and endowment. This was over and above the regular apportionment.

3d. The Board is to receive one million dollars, or $200,000 per year out of Centenary Funds of the whole church, if the same amounts to sixty million dollars. This amount is to be used exclusively for new buildings and endowment.[21]

The total receipts from the Centenary for Negro schools was $2,375,762.71.[22] The results of the Centenary over a period of five years, the share received by the Board of Education for Negroes, enabled the Board to expend more than two million dollars on the Negro institutions for instructional improvements, new property, new buildings and endowment.[23] Most of the expenditures were for new buildings and new property.

Following the Centenary

In 1930 the Board of Education authorized "a campaign for Better Schools for Negroes" to raise approximately two million dollars in order to insure gifts totaling three million dollars from the General Education Board and the Julius Rosenwald Fund.[24]

It was unfortunate that upon the heels of the Centenary came the depression of the late 1920's and the economic crash of the 1930's, the results of which were almost disastrous to most of these institutions, and for all, there was at least a decade of arrested progress.

Special Day Observances

1. Children's Day

The second Sunday in June was designated as Children's Day by action of the 1872 General Conference, and inserted into the Book of Discipline.[25] The purpose of this special day was to encourage and aid "the youth and children of our Sunday schools in all parts of the land to attain a more advanced education."[26]

Children's Day was initiated and promoted by the Board of Education of the Methodist Episcopal Church in the interest of all the youth and children. This was not a special emphasis by the Freedmen's Aid Society, except in a cooperative manner. Negro children and youth, however, were greatly benefited through encouragement on this special day to get an education, and through the general loan fund established by the Board of Education with collections taken on Children's Day.

With unification in 1939, and reorganization in 1940, "Children's Day" was changed to "Methodist Student Day," still observed the Second Sunday in June.[26a]

2. Lincoln Day

The taking of a collection for the support of Negro education had its first Disciplinary authorization in 1876. The Discipline for the 1876 General Conference states:

> It shall be the duty of each preacher in charge to present this subject (the support of the Freedmen's Aid Society and its educational institutions for Negroes) to his congregation, or cause it to be presented, once each year in sermon or address to aid the diffusion of intelligence in regard to the work of the Society and the wants of the Freedmen, and to use due diligence to collect the amount apportioned to his charge. He shall report to the Annual Conference the sum collected and the collections shall be published in a column in the general minutes and in the Minutes of the Annual Conference.[27]

The observance of Lincoln Day had its origin in 1896, under the name "Freedmen's Aid and Southern Education Day." In 1898 the Freedmen's Aid and Southern Education Society reported:

> The appeal which was made to the churches two years ago to take a special collection for the society on the Sunday immediately following Lincoln's birthday (February 12) resulted in receipts amounting to several thousand dollars. It is now recommended that the appeal be renewed and that the Lincoln birthday Sunday be set apart as Freedmen's Aid and Southern Education Day.[28]

In 1899 the Society made the following statement and recommendation:

> The adoption of the Sunday immediately following the birthday of Abraham Lincoln (February 12) as the Freedmen's Aid Day was received with great favor and doubtless the offering taken on that day would have been a great collection

519

but for the weather. Other denominations have followed the example and are observing the day in the same manner. It is recommended that the appeal be renewed and that the Lincoln birthday Sunday again be observed as the Freedmen's Aid and Southern Education Day.[29]

In 1903 the February issue of *The Christian Educator* was made the "Lincoln Day Number," with emphasis upon the celebration of Lincoln's birthday, but more specifically paying tribute to Lincoln himself. Effort was made to stress the work of education for Negroes and make appeals for its support, by stressing the virtues of Lincoln, the great Liberator. Again, the February 1904, issue of *The Christian Educator* was made the Lincoln Day Number. This practice became well established by continued repetition in February of the succeeding years.

In 1904 Bishop John M. Walden, President of the Freedmen's Aid and Southern Education Society, speaking to the General Conference said:

Lincoln Birthday Sunday has taken its place throughout the Church as Freedmen's Aid and Southern Education Day, and is now more widely observed than ever before. . . .We believe that the increase in conference collections is largely due to this presentation of our work on its merits, and we earnestly hope that no action will be taken by your body that would limit the opportunities of this Society to fully present its work before the Church.[30]

The Lincoln Day observance gained momentum. The February, 1905, issue of *The Christian Educator*, "Lincoln Birthday Number," carried a series of articles and statements on Lincoln Day observance and the education of Negroes. Ten of the statements were by Methodist Bishops, including Bishop Warren A. Candler of the Methodist Episcopal Church, South. Other prominent authors of statements were Governor John L. Bates of Massachusetts, Andrew Carnegie, Henry W. Gady, and Charles Parkhurst, Editor of *Zion's Herald*.[31]

Along with the articles and statements regarding Lincoln, literature was prepared for programs to facilitate the observance of this Special Day. In 1905 over 3,000 pastors requested programs of songs and literature prepared for Lincoln Day observance.[32] For the February 9, 1908, observance 35,000 pieces of literature were distributed among the churches.[33] Beginning in 1916 the Sunday nearest Lincoln's birthday was observed as "Lincoln Day."

Lincoln Day was used for intensive cultivation throughout the

Methodist Episcopal Church. The financial results were included in Conference collections to apply on apportionments. The financial success of Lincoln Day was probably overshadowed by the Jubilee and Centenary emphases from 1913 to 1923. Despite the great emphasis placed upon the special programs such as the Jubilee and Lincoln Day Observances for support of Negro education, the results fell short of goals and hopes. The Centenary was the most productive of all; but it will have to be remembered that the Centenary was successful in a large measure because it was a total church fund-raising effort for missions and not just for Negro education.

Lincoln Day was observed in the Methodist Episcopal Church until unification, 1939. In 1940 another new program was initiated in The Methodist Church for the financial support of the institutions historically serving Negro students.

3. Race Relations Sunday

Race Relations Sunday, observed the second Sunday in February, was an outgrowth of Lincoln Day observance. The transition came at the time of unification reorganization in 1940. Previous special day observances were based in the Methodist Episcopal Church. Unification brought together in one body three branches of Methodism, two of which did not have Negroes in their membership. It was necessary to have a program of cultivation to facilitate racial adjustment within the new church, and at the same time to provide a new orientation and broader base of financial support of the institutions for Negro education within the church.

By way of clarification of Race Relations Day, the following resolution was recorded in the Proceedings of the Board of Education in 1940:

It is recognized that this day is essentially a Board of Education Day to be observed in the interest of the schools and colleges for Negroes developed or controlled by the church. The list of institutions to be formally presented will be the schools developed under the Board of Education of the Methodist Episcopal Church and Paine College developed by the Methodist Episcopal Church, South. The list will not include the institutions sponsored solely by the Woman's Home Missionary Society nor the schools of the Colored Methodist Episcopal Church to which grants are now being made by the Board of Missions at Nashville.[34]

The 1944 Discipline states:

As a means of educating the church in regard to better race relations and the needs of Negro schools, Race Relations Sunday (second Sunday in February) shall be observed in all the congregations as the date when the interest of Christian education for Negro youth shall be presented.[35]

Race Relations Sunday, having been officially established by Disciplinary provision for observance throughout The Methodist Church a procedure was fixed similar to Lincoln Day observance. Several different Annual Conferences were assigned to the respective colleges for cultivation and visitation. In addition to cultivation by specific colleges, the Board of Education assumed responsibility for general promotion and cultivation in effort to achieve greatest possible financial returns on Race Relations Sunday. As indicated elsewhere in this volume, Race Relations Sunday has not been favored a hundred per cent by the whole church. Many members, particularly since 1954, have not favored black colleges, claiming that they perpetuate segregation.

This is not the place to advance arguments pro or con regarding objections to black colleges. The purpose at this point is to indicate that Race Relations Sunday observance has met opposition by many who hold liberal views regarding race relations and argue that there should be no separate black colleges and consequently no support by the church for them. Every quadrennium brings fuller realization of the growing necessity of being unmistakably clear and certain of the need for black colleges and for their support by the church.

In some instances Race Relations Sunday has not gained support because of a lack of interest in the institutions and a lack of interest in race relations. In other instances this cause suffers because other appeals have a much higher priority. Despite all the variables that cause ambivalence, Race Relations Sunday has had three decades of year-by-year growth, with few exceptions.

In the last five years of Lincoln Day observance the results were as follows:

1934-35	Receipts	$ 13,586.35
1935-36	Receipts	15,024.70
1936-37	Receipts	14,727.02
1937-38	Receipts	10,032.64
1938-39	Receipts	7,684.12[36]

The growth in Race Relations offerings may be noted from the following figures for the period 1940-41 to 1962-63, inclusive.[37]

Year	Amount	Increase	Decrease
1940-41	27,363	10,000	
1941-42	37,656	10,000	
1942-43	56,936	19,000	
1943-44	73,707	17,000	
1944-45	80,306	7,000	
1945-46	125,916	45,000	
1946-47	166,348	41,000	
1947-48	190,527	24,000	
1948-49	208,843	18,000	
1949-50	195,157		13,000
1950-51	213,873	18,000	
1951-52	239,726	26,000	
1952-53	251,611	12,000	
1953-54	269,313	18,000	
1954-55	292,517	23,000	
1955-56	289,802		3,000
1956-57	345,524	56,000	
1957-58	355,452	10,000	
1958-59	401,538	46,000	
1959-60	396,542		5,000
1960-61	420,775	24,000	
1961-62	426,046	6,000	
1962-63	493,643	67,000	

By 1967-68 the Race Relations Day offerings had reached a gross total of $519,485.44,[38] an increase of $492,122.44 over 1941.

523

In addition, many conferences have written certain institutions into the Annual Conference budgets. The grants from these sources are not reflected in the table given above. Again, special capital funds from the Annual Conferences and from World Service Funds are not reflected in Race Relations giving.

In view of the encouraging growth in Race Relations giving and Annual Conference budget support, it must be recognized that in the period from 1941 to 1968 the support of Negro colleges was much more substantial than the two decades prior to 1941. In addition to Race Relations Sunday offerings, there was growth in the regular annual appropriations to the colleges by the Board of Education, from World Service Funds.

During the past three quadrennia a goal of $1,000,000 annually has been set for Race Relations Sunday offerings for the black colleges of the Methodist Church. Just over half this goal has been achieved in any one year. While the goal is far from being adequate, it does indicate that there is a realization of the need for the support to be increased. It should also be pointed out that during the past two quadrennia approximately $2,000,000 has been made available to the black colleges from World Service Funds for capital outlay.

Growth in Church support during the past three decades is significant, without which the black institutions of the Church would have suffered financially even more than they have. As welcome and as much appreciated as the increased support has been, it must be viewed critically.

First, the financial support given should be viewed in the light of the full potential, or what could have been given. The total membership of The Methodist Church is over 10,000,000 (since 1968 the United Methodist Church, over 11,000,000). The highest amount raised, $519,485.14 (1968), represents approximately five cents per member for the black colleges, while at the same time more than one dollar per member was raised in a large number if not most of the conferences for higher education generally within the church. The goal of one million to be raised on Race Relations Sunday for the black colleges was in no way fantastic and the failure to raise this amount by fifty per cent is most revealing.

In the second place, the growth in support during the past three decades must be measured in terms of adequacy based on need. The inadequacy of the support becomes immediately evident from the number of institutions, thirteen, (at present; a larger number earlier) sharing the money raised. If all of the money raised could have been given to any one of the institutions, this would not have been adequate support with probably one exception.

The Black colleges from the beginning in 1866 to the present have never come within a reasonable expectation of adequate support. As recently as 1968 only two of the institutions in this group had over $3,000,000 in endowment: Meharry Medical College had $6,262,462, and Dillard University had $3,547,185.[39] All the rest of the institutions had less than $2,000,000, in endowment; six had less than $1,000,000, one had $576,615, and four had less than $500,000 in endowment.[40] Tuition charges have always been low and an inadequate source of income because of the poor economic background, generally, from which the majority of the students come.

Fortunately, nine of the ten four-year colleges and Gammon Theological Seminary hold membership in the United Negro College Fund, the tenth four-year college having been admitted within the past few months. In 1970 the Fund raised the highest amount in its history, $7,000,000, to be divided among thirty-six colleges. For four or five of these institutions, this would have been an astronomical figure, but for thirty-six, it is obvious that, as helpful as this income surely was, it was far from meeting the needs.

The adequacy of the growth in income from church sources must be determined against the basic needs of the institutions and the adequacy of income from other sources, such as those indicated above. Also, the adequacy of church support must be determined in the light of operation costs and continued increase in such costs. The story of inadequacy of support for Black colleges is a story a century old—an eternal and painful financial struggle, never enough money for any purpose, always operating at sub-minimal level, always "making brick without straw."

Some Reasons for Inadequate Support

Among the reasons, historically, for inadequate financial support to the Negro institutions, the following may be listed:

1. It was thought, when the schools were first established, that the need for them would not be continuing. The thinking was that:

(a) The need for church support would diminish as the Freedmen become literate and acquired the rudiments of education.

(b) It was expected that the state would establish public schools and take over the job of providing education for the children of Freedmen.

2. The intensity of prejudice and the negative local climate was not anticipated or foreseen, resulting in the long delay in developing public educational facilities for Negro children.

525

3. Opposition to public education generally by the South was not expected.

4. The development of a dual public school system with all of its prejudices and inequities and implications was not generally understood.

5. The church expected to "turn these institutions over to the freedmen" and free itself of the responsibility of supporting them.

6. There has been a continuing hope that there would be no necessity for continued support by the church. There has always been an anticipation of a divorce, even if indeed there is a question as to whether there had ever been a real marriage.

7. There seems to be a belief among many white people that Negro schools do not need as much money as white schools.

8. There seems to be a notion that Negro administrators and educators cannot use or administer large sums of money. These two (7 and 8) are reflected in amounts raised or given by the church, in grants by foundations and frequently by individual philanthropists for Negro education.

9. In its support to Negro institutions the Church has been slow to lift its sights above the level of missionary giving to real educational support.

10. The Black colleges have never been brought into the mainstream of higher education in the thinking, use, and support within the larger membership of Methodism.

Philanthropic Salvation

Historically, in the life and existence of all of the Black colleges and schools founded by the Freedmen's Aid Society, at the crucial hour it was the philanthropy of an individual or family or of a foundation that saved the institution or set it on a new course of financial survival. Only some typical examples need to be cited.

Bennett College: In its early beginning it was the gift of $10,000 by Lyman Bennett of Troy, New York, that got the seminary going. Later the Carnegie Fund gave assistance. Within the period of about thirty years, 1926 to 1956, the Pfeiffer family gifts of more than $2,000,000 made Bennett the outstanding woman's college it is. These generous beneficences supplemented by grants from foundations such as the General Education Board, the Ford Foundation and others have added the needed strength to the support given by the Woman's Home Missionary Society, the Woman's Division of Christian Service and the Board of Education.

Claflin College: The philanthropy of the distinguished Governor Claflin of Massachusetts and his father, and the

526

benefactions of the S. H. Tingley family of Rhode Island, established Claflin University as a remarkable institution. Grants from the Slater Fund helped to advance it to a college renowned for a long time for its industrial program.

Clark College: The benefactions to Clark College came in the early years from Miss Eliza Chrisman, Mrs. Augusta Clark Cole, Mr. Ballard of Evanston, Illinois, and the Slater Fund. In later years its benefactors were the General Education Board, and Mrs. Henry Pfeiffer (and later the Pfeiffer family), the Rosenwald Fund, and the Ford Foundation.

Dillard University: The generosity of Mr. John Baldwin in the early years of New Orleans University gave this institution a good start. Dillard University was made possible through the philanthropy of the General Education Board, the Rosenwald Fund, the Stern Family, the T. K. Lawless gifts, and others, representing a philanthropic investment of an estimated $15,000,000.

Gammon Theological Seminary: Gammon became an independent School of Theology and developed as a strong institution because of the benefactions of the Rev. E. H. Gammon, and the Rev. William F. Stewart. In large measure the new Interdenominational Theological Center, of which Gammon is the core came into existence through grants from the General Education Board and the Sealantic Fund.

Meharry Medical College: The story of Meharry Medical College is a story of the generous philanthropies of the five Meharry brothers. Beginning in 1916 the grants of the Carnegie Fund and the General Education Board made the difference between death and the life of a medical school whose services can hardly be matched in the training of Negro doctors. From 1916 to 1960 the General Education Board granted to Meharry $8,673,706, exclusive of fellowships.[41]

Huston-Tillotson: It was the initial gift of $10,000 from Mr. Samuel Huston of Marengo, Iowa, that at last got the school on its way. Mr. E. T. Burrowes of Portland, Maine, was probably its most substantial single donor. When the merger was made in 1952 resulting in Huston-Tillotson College the philanthropy of foundations made the union possible.

Some Dimensions Beyond Money

It is deplorable that the institutions treated in this volume have for more than a century been so destitute of money for operation and development. There have been and still are many people all over America who have degraded, and still do degrade, these

527

institutions for at least two reasons. One, they are so-called "Negro" institutions and are thought to be inferior, just as Negroes are still thought to be inferior. Two, these institutions have been and are still short of the necessary financial resources to meet their needs.

In judging the quality of the Negro college and its effectiveness in the past, and present, there are certain dimensions that have been overlooked by the critics and by those even of very recent years who say that the Negro colleges have been and are inferior. It will suffice just to mention a few of those dimensions that gave Negro institutions quality and educational respectability even though nothing like sufficient money was available. These dimensions were beyond money.

(1) *Preparedness:* From the beginning some of the best prepared white men and women educated in the best educational institutions of the North came into the South as teachers and administrators and gave the best they had intellectually and culturally to the cause of educating Black people.

(2) *Dedication:* Those people who taught, and administered the schools were dedicated beyond measure; they gave themselves, which was beyond money.

(3) *Sacrifice:* The teachers and administrators sacrificed time, money, labor, and life for this cause. Some salaries were unbelievably small; some worked without salaries.

(4) *Love:* It was love of the profession, love of the cause, and love of people who needed this love and their help.

(5) *A Sense of Mission:* They came and they worked with a sense of mission. No money could buy this; no money could pay for it. This sense of mission was inherent in life meaning and life work.

(6) *Identification:* There was a sense of identification with a great cause that gave meaning to their lives and satisfaction in their labors.

(7) *Leadership:* They had the ability to give leadership and to inspire leadership. They produced leadership through personal examples of leadership.

(8) *Personality Impact:* The impact of personality upon personality is the heart of education. The Negro people needed inspiration and they were inspired by teachers and leaders both white and black. There was created within the student the desire for an education, the desire to learn, the desire to be somebody, the desire to do something, the desire to *use his life.* Negro teachers, white teachers, administrators—all—exerted great influence through the force of their personalities and set the process of education to work. The Negro colleges have never had

528

much money but they have always had great personalities around to make education meaningful and to inspire students to overcome whatever limitations they may have had and through hard work to achieve.

These schools with able faculties and able administration have been magicians in the use of small money and in stretching dollars; they have been artists in preparing young people for more than a century for leadership in a world that requires ability and in competition, successful competition, with graduates of the most prestigious institutions of America. What more could be asked in fruits and rewards; who can degrade any institutions characterized by these dimensions of greatness, so much needed but so greatly lacking in so many institutions of our time, even in those where money is much more abundant?

REFERENCES AND NOTES

1. Report, Freedmen's Aid Society, 1867, p. 4.
2. Report, Freedmen's Aid Society, 1873, pp. 36f.
3. *Ibid.*, pp. 38f.
4. Report, Freedmen's Aid Society, 1886, p. 49.
5. Historical Memorandum, Freedmen's Aid Society Report, 1892, p. 73.
6. *Ibid.*
7. *Ibid.*
8. Freedmen's Aid Society Report, May, 1892, p. 7.
9. *Ibid.*
10. *The Christian Educator*, October-November, 1895.
11. *The Christian Educator*, November, 1915, p. 24.
12. *Ibid.*
13. *The Christian Educator*, August, 1912, p. 1.
14. *Ibid.*
15. *The Christian Educator*, November, 1913, p. 14.
16. *Ibid.*, p. 15.
17. *The Christian Educator*, May, 1914, p. 1.
17a. Journal, General Conference, May, 1916, pp. 321f and 341.
17b. Journal, General Conference, 1920, p. 424.
18. *The Christian Educator*, August, 1919, p. 1.
19. *Ibid.*, November, 1918, p. 1.
20. *The Christian Educator*, November, 1920, p. 2.
21. *Ibid.*, pp. 2f.
22. *The Christian Educator*, May, 1924, p. 24.
23. *The Christian Educator*, November, 1922, Editorial Page.
24. *The Christian Educator*, February, 1931, p. 14.
25. Report, Board of Education, Methodist Episcopal Church, 1882, p. 9.
26. *Ibid.*, p. 10.
26a. Discipline of The Methodist Church, 1944, Par. 197, p. 66.
27. The Discipline, Methodist Episcopal Church, 1876, Par. 304.
28. Report, Freedmen's Aid and Southern Education Society, 1898.
29. *Ibid.*, 1889, p. ?.
30. The Journal, General Conference, 1904, p. 869.
31. *The Christian Educator*, February, 1905, pp. 1ff.
32. *The Christian Educator*, November, 1905, p. 21.
33. *The Christian Educator*, May-August, 1908, p. ?.
34. Report of Proceedings of the Board of Education, The Methodist Church, January 31-February 1, 1940, p. 274.
35. Discipline of The Methodist Church, 1944, Par. 198, p. 66.

36. Report of Associate Secretary, Department of Educational Institutions for Negroes, Board of Education.
37. *Ibid.*
38. *Ibid.*, June 1969.
39. President's Bulletin Board, Statistical Summary, Division of Higher Education, Board of Education, United Methodist Church, May, 1970.
40. *Ibid.*
41. General Education Board, *Review and Final Report*, 1964, p. 37.

CHAPTER 26

SOME LEADING PERSONALITIES, GROUPS AND INDIVIDUALS, RELATED TO THE MOVEMENT

"We are indebted to the pioneers who went forth in their day weeping, sacrificing, toiling, and bearing precious seed. We are indebted to the churches which sent them. We, their inheritors, now have the privilege of reaping the abundant harvest which they planted."

So spoke the venerable Dr. Matthew Simpson Davage at the joint meeting of the Board of Education and the Executive Secretaries of the Annual Conference Boards of Education, The Methodist Church, at Atlantic City, New Jersey, January 10, 1963. Indeed the pioneers did plant precious seed which, watered by their tears and nurtured by their assiduous toil, sprang to fruition and produced abundant harvest. Tribute must be paid not only to the early pioneers, but also to a long line of successors who followed in their train.

As pointed out elsewhere (Chapter 25), the most significant factors in the successful work of these Black institutions of the Church have not been financial resources, not minimizing the importance of finances, but the most important factors have been human resources—Freedmen's Aid leadership, bishops, corresponding secretaries, trustees, presidents, teachers, and the human interests of philanthropists.

It would be impossible to list all of the persons, numbering into thousands, who made significant contributions to the Methodist Movement providing education for Negro youth. Listed below in the several categories are some of the men and women who by their office and or long years of tenure and services are chosen to represent all who labored for and gave to this cause, under the leadership of the Freedmen's Aid Society, and its successor, the Board of Education for Negroes.

Founders—Freedmen's Aid Society

All of the Founders of the Freedmen's Aid Society (*see* Chapter 4) sustained a continuing relation to and maintained a profound interest in the Society. Some of the Founders were more closely related to the movement and gave valuable leadership.

Bishop Davis W. Clark. Bishop Clark was elected first President of the Society at the organization meeting, August, 1866. Bishop Clark was elected to the Episcopacy in 1864,[1] and during the following quadrennium gave himself to the establishments of Annual and Mission Conferences in the Southern and Western regions, and to the establishment of schools by the Freedmen's Aid Society of which he was president. He was desirous to furnish this neglected people not only material aid, but schools, churches, teachers, missionaries, books, and papers to instruct them how to use their liberty and to act as worthy citizens and subjects of a great republic.[2] In his honor Clark University, Atlanta, Georgia, was named in 1869.

The Executive Committee of the Freedmen's Aid Society in a meeting July 24, 1871, adopted the following resolutions:

1. *Resolved,* that in the death of our beloved President, Bishop D. W. Clark, the Freedmen's Aid Society of the Methodist Episcopal Church has lost an early and true friend, a wise counselor, a liberal supporter, and an able advocate.

2. *Resolved,* that we place this memorial of his valuable services in behalf of this long-neglected race on our Journal, while we cherish in our hearts and endeavor to imitate his noble life and Christian character.[3]

The Reverend John M. Walden was probably the first man of prominence in the Methodist Episcopal Church to become identified with the education of Freedmen.[4] He was a prominent figure in the undenominational work which began in 1862. He was the first to see the importance of the Methodist Episcopal Church's organizing its own Society. He wrote the call for the meeting at which the Freedmen's Aid Society was organized. On the strength of his paper presented to the convention, August, 1866, the Freedmen's Aid Society was organized and direction given to its future course. Rev. Walden was the first Corresponding Secretary of the Society, serving in this office two years, 1866 to 1868. He afterwards served as Recording Secretary, and as Treasurer, and was President, succeeding Bishop Wiley, when he was elected as Bishop in 1886. In October, 1900, the name of Central Tennessee College, by action of the Board of Trustees, was changed to Walden University in honor of Bishop Walden.

The Reverend Isaac W. Wiley, D.D.: Dr. Wiley, one of the Vice Presidents elected August 8, 1866, presided over the Society until

1872, when he was elected as the second President of the Society, filling the vacancy left by the death of Bishop D. W. Clark. For two years Dr. Wiley gave presidential leadership to the Society. He was elected to the bishopric in 1872,[5] and manifested deep interest in the work of the Freedmen's Aid Society in the conferences over which he presided. Wiley University in Marshall, Texas, was named in his honor. Bishop Wiley was succeeded as President of the Society in 1874 by Bishop R. S. Foster,[6] who served as President until 1876. In 1876, Bishop Wiley again became President of the Freedmen's Aid Society and held the office until his death in 1884. He was succeeded in this office in 1884 by Bishop J. M. Walden.[7]

The Board of Managers

In addition to the General Officers of the Freedmen's Aid Society, the Constitution provided for a Board of Managers consisting of the Bishops of the Methodist Episcopal Church, two persons—one minister and one layman—named by any Annual Conference organizing an Auxiliary Society, together with the persons hereinafter named, their successors and such other persons as may be elected at any Quarterly or Annual Meeting of the Society.[8] The membership of the first Board of Managers of the Freedmen's Aid Society consisted of the following named persons:

Adam Poe	J. M. Reid
I. W. Wiley	William Nast
R. S. Rust	J. M. Walden
J. C. Harrison	T. M. Eddy
L. Hitchock	R. M. Hatfield
C. H. Fowler	H. Crews
B. F. Crary	A. C. George
B. St. J. Fry	Robert Allyn
F. C. Holiday	Grant Goodrich
Clinton B. Fisk	John Pfaff
Harvey DeCamp	J. F. Larkin
M. B. Hagans	John Dubois
T. F. Shaw	A. R. Scranton
Daniel Gross	George F. Foster
R. F. Queal	A. S. W. Goodwin
S. Rich	David McDonald
B. R. Bonner	Michael Ihle[9]
J. H. Ross	

535

The Board of Managers established policies that related to all of the schools, especially in the areas of general operations, establishment of schools, fund-raising and financial administration, selection of principals and presidents and often instructional personnel, reporting to the General Conference, and promotion of the interest of the Society throughout the church. The Board of Managers functioned for all of the schools in much the same way as a modern board of trustees functions for a single institution. The individual members of the Board of Managers and the group as a whole functioned always with great dedication, giving strength and effectiveness to the work of the Freedmen's Aid Society.

Treasurers

At the organization meeting of the Freedmen's Aid Society, August 8, 1866, Rev. Adam Poe, D.D., was elected treasurer. He was succeeded in this office by the Rev. Luke Hitchcock, D.D., who held the office from 1867 or 1868 until 1880. The Rev. J. M. Walden held the office of treasurer, succeeding Dr. Hitchcock, from 1880 until his election as Bishop in 1884.[10] In 1884, the Rev. Earl Crauston became treasurer and held this office until 1896.

These were men of very great influence in the church, which influence they used to strengthen the financial support of the cause of education for Negroes.

Other founders who might be listed for their influence and labors are: R. S. Rust, R. M. Hatfield, Clinton B. Fisk, J. F. Larkin, George F. Foster, and many more.

Methodist Bishops and the Work of
the Freedmen's Aid Society

The Freedmen's Aid Society was strongly abetted by the influence, support, and leadership of the Bishops of the Methodist Episcopal Church. Immediately following the organization of the Society the Board of Bishops issued a strong appeal to the whole church for its financial support. Among the key bishops, in addition to Bishops Clark, Walden, and Wiley, interested in the Negro problem, and who gave support and leadership to the Freedmen's Aid Movement were the following:

Bishop Edwin S. Janes, in 1838, was elected Secretary of the American Bible Society[11] and traveled extensively in the South. He was a favorite of the delegation of the Southern Section when he was elected to the Episcopacy at the historic General Conference of 1844.[12] Bishop Janes was a liberal and a staunch

536

supporter of the cause of education for the Freedmen. His voice was heard in many places in the United States, and as far away as Birmingham, England, where in 1865 he closed a thrilling speech by saying, "Never, in the history of our race, has there been an appeal so pathetic, so forcibly to the philanthropy of a civilized people as made by the Freedmen at this crisis."[13]

Bishop Matthew Simpson, D.D., Ll.D., was a scholar and possessed "natural, if not supernatural, eloquence."[14] He studied and practiced medicine; in 1839 was elected President of Asbury College (now DePauw University); in 1848 was elected Editor of the *Western Christian Advocate;* in 1852 was elected a Bishop; and in 1859 was elected President of Garrett Biblical Institute.[15] He strongly supported the Union Army, and was urged by the Secretary of War to undertake the organization of the Freedmen at the establishment of the Freedmen's Bureau.[16]

Because of the relation of the Methodist Episcopal Church to the Federal Government, Bishop Simpson with his great leadership ability had much influence on developments in behalf of the Freedmen until his death in 1884.

Bishop Edward Thomson, elected to the Episcopacy in 1864,[17] was recognized everywhere for his high scholarship, broad sympathy, eloquence, and devotion.[18] He presided over the organization of the Louisiana Conference as a part of the Mississippi Mission Conference, December 25, 1865.[19] It was his interest, efforts and leadership in providing educational opportunities for Negro ministers in the Conference that led to the founding of Thomson Theological School, named in his honor, later a part of New Orleans University. The labors of Bishop Thomson in the cause of Negro education continued to his death, March 22, 1870.[20]

Bishop Randolph S. Foster, elected to the Episcopacy in 1872,[21] became a leader in the Freedmen's Aid Society, having served as President of Northwestern University and Drew Theological Seminary[22] before becoming a Bishop. He was President of the Freedmen's Aid Society from 1874 to 1876.

Bishop Gilbert Haven, "A brilliant conversationalist, a radical reformer, and a versatile writer, he devoted all his powers to the help of the lowliest."[23] The Rev. Haven was the first commissioned chaplain of the 8th Regiment when the war began in 1861.[24] In 1867 he became editor of *Zion's Herald.* He was elected to the Episcopacy in 1872.[25] From 1872 until his death in 1880[26] his labors and generosity helped to make Clark University in Atlanta, Georgia, one of the strongest and most promising institutions under the auspices of the Freedmen's Aid Society.

Bishop Haven's services extended beyond Georgia where he was resident Bishop. He traveled through Mississippi and other states of the South and purchased most valuable property for both church and school sites. In his honor many churches and schools bore his name.

Bishop Henry White Warren was born in Massachusetts, January 4, 1831. He graduated from Wesleyan University in 1853. He was elected to the Episcopacy in 1880.[27] Within thirty days of his consecration he took office as resident Bishop in Atlanta, succeeding Bishop Gilbert Haven. Within a year he founded Morristown Seminary, Morristown, Tennessee.

It was the partnership Bishop Warren formed with the Rev. Elijah H. Gammon that resulted in the latter's large investment in the institution that bears his name, Gammon Theological Seminary. This partnership with Rev. Gammon and other labors by Bishop Warren from 1880 to 1912 brought large money and laid the foundation for Clark's becoming the University of the Freedmen's Aid System of Schools.

Death claimed Bishop Warren July 23, 1912.[28] In tribute to him it was said: "He was constant and loyal in his friendship and help of Christian education of the Negro. Few men put their impressions so indelibly upon men and agencies in church and state as did Bishop Warren. He was greatly beloved."[29]

Bishop John P. Newman, having been sent to New Orleans, Louisiana, in 1864, was a pioneer in the efforts to establish the Methodist Episcopal Church in Louisiana and to provide education for the Freedmen. He was one of the original members of the Louisiana Annual Conference, and took the lead in providing education for Negro ministers. His efforts led to the establishment of Thomson Biblical Institute, which later became New Orleans University. He accomplished much in five years, before being appointed in 1869 to the Metropolitan M. E. Church in Washington, D. C. The Rev. Newman was elevated to the Episcopacy at the General Conference of 1888.[30]

Bishop Joseph C. Hartzell was one of the great stalwarts in the movement to build and strengthen Methodism in the South and to provide education for the Freedmen. Transferring from Illinois in 1870, he pastored the Ames Methodist Episcopal Church for three years, served as Presiding Elder of the New Orleans District for four years.[31] He established and became editor of the *Southwestern Christian Advocate* in 1873.[32] Dr. Hartzell was editor of this paper until 1881, when he became assistant corresponding secretary of the Freedmen's Aid Society. In May, 1888, the General Conference elected him corresponding secretary of the Freedmen's Aid and Southern Education Society.[33] The General Conference of 1896 elevated Dr. Hartzell to the

Episcopacy,[34] and he went as a Missionary Bishop to Africa,[35] where he served until retirement in 1916. His death on September 6, 1928, "marked the passing of a great and beloved pioneer in the field of Christian education among Negro youth. His was a truly unselfish life, the impress of which has been felt the world around."[36]

Bishop Wilbur P. Thirkield, for almost four decades, was an arduous worker and a fearless leader in the cause of Negro education. Coming into the work at an early age in 1883 as Dean of the Clark University Theological School he remained Dean of the School until 1888, and became the first President of Gammon Theological School, later Gammon Theological Seminary, when it became separate and independent. For eleven years he gave leadership as President of Gammon Theological Seminary, resigning in the fall of 1899 to become Secretary of the Epworth League of the Methodist Episcopal Church. At the General Conference in 1900, the Rev. Thirkield was elected a Corresponding Secretary for the Freedmen's Aid and Southern Education Society, in which position he served two quadrennia. In 1908 Dr. Thirkield saw a larger service in the cause of Negro education and accepted the Presidency of Howard University, where he remained until 1912, when he was elected to the Episcopacy.[37]

In all of Dr. Thirkield's positions and in all of his relationships, the cause of the Negro always had first place in his thinking and in his heart. He never faltered and never relinquished the fight in behalf of this cause. His grasp of the Negro problem and his views regarding the solutions, especially in the field of education, gave him stature and a unique position of leadership in the Methodist Episcopal Church and in the nation.

Bishop Frederick D. Leete, was elected to the Episcopacy in 1912[38] and was assigned to Georgia to succeed Bishop Henry W. Warren who at the time of his death had given thirty-two years of episcopal leadership to this area. Bishop Leete with great devotion administered the work of this area for two quadrennia, ending his administration in May, 1920.

Bishop Atticus G. Haygood, although a Bishop in the Methodist Episcopal Church, South, must be listed along with the episcopal leadership of the Methodist Episcopal Church. No man during the period 1880 to 1896 was more helpful to the educational cause of the Freedmen and had more influence upon the Methodist Church, North and South, than did Bishop Haygood.

To his brethren and friends of the South, his remarkable book, *Our Brother In Black* written in 1881, was radical, and repugnant, but epochal. This book brought persecution and

539

ostracism. In 1882 the John F. Slater Fund of $1,000,000 was established as an endowment to be administered in the interest of Negro education, and Dr. Haygood accepted the responsibility as the first agent of the Fund.[39] From 1882 to 1884 Dr. Haygood served as agent of the Slater Fund in addition to his duties as President of Emory College, Oxford, Georgia. He was elected to the Episcopacy in the Methodist Episcopal Church, South in 1882, but declined consecration in order to continue in the educational work.[40] In December 1884, Dr. Haygood resigned the Presidency of Emory College in order to devote all of his time to the Slater Fund.[41]

Through the interest and help of Dr. Haygood, strong departments of industrial education were built up at a number of the Freedmen's Aid Society schools, and at other Negro institutions in the South.

The best testimony to the effectiveness of Dr. Haygood's life and work and the high esteem in which he was held is the fact that after his declination of the bishopric in 1882 to continue work in education, all of which after 1884 was in the field of education for Negroes, he again in 1890 was overwhelmingly elected to the Episcopacy in the Methodist Episcopal Church, South.[42]

Here was truly a great man, who, until his death in 1896, with conviction and courage led the way to a better southland where his "Brother In Black" might have in a larger measure justice, freedom, and better educational opportunities.

Bishop Isaiah B. Scott falls into this category in a somewhat different but no less important role. Early in the history of the Freedmen's Aid Society schools emphasis was begun on the inseparable relationship of the Negro in America and his kinsmen in Africa. Equal importance was attached to the Christian redemption of the "dark" continent of Africa and the "uplift" and education of the Black man in America. Even before the Freedmen's Aid Society was organized in 1866, two Negro Bishops to Africa had been elected in the Methodist Episcopal Church, Bishops Francis Burns in 1858, and J. W. Roberts in 1866. A succession of white bishops to Africa had been elected by 1904 when Bishop I. B. Scott was elected. The aim was to relate the mission to the Freedmen and the mission to the people of Africa and to prepare missionaries for Africa to fulfill the mission of the church, evangelistic and educational, to the people of color there. The missionary emphasis in all of the Freedmen's Aid Society schools was definitely related to the missionary work in Africa.

Other bishops related to the work of the Freedmen's Aid Society that should be listed are Bishops Edward R. Ames,

Thomas Bowman, Earl Cranston, William L. Harris, Isaac W. Joyce, Willard F. Mallalieu, and Jesse T. Peck.

Corresponding Secretaries of the Freedmen's Aid
   Society 1866 to 1920, and Secretaries of
      Successor Organizations

The success of the Freedmen's Aid Society and its successor organizations was accomplished through the devoted labors and the excellent leadership of the able corresponding secretaries elected to the position from the beginning across the years. Volumes could be written on all of the men individually who have given leadership in this office. It is with apology to them and their noble work that only the following brief statements are recorded.

Dr. John M. Walden

Dr. John M. Walden was a founder and the first corresponding secretary of the Freedmen's Aid Society 1866-1868. Full account of his official relationship and services is given above.

Dr. Richard Sutton Rust

Dr. Richard S. Rust, one of the founders of the Freedmen's Aid Society, was officially associated with the Society from 1866 to 1888. He was Field Secretary of the Society two years, 1866-1868, and then succeeded Dr. J. M. Walden in 1868 as Corresponding Secretary, which position he held for twenty years, retiring in 1888.

Soon after Dr. Rust's retirement, Dr. J. C. Hartzell, then Corresponding Secretary, wrote: "More than to any other one man, under God, the Methodist Episcopal Church is indebted to the Rev. Richard Sutton Rust, D.D., Ll.D., for the development of the educational work of the Methodist Episcopal Church in the South."[43]

Early in life Dr. Rust identified himself with the anti-slavery movement. As a student at Wesleyan University he was an agent of the Connecticut Anti-Slavery Society. Later, he was for four years President of Wilberforce University, then under the auspices of the Methodist Episcopal Church. After the war he was active in the non-denominational movement for the relief and education of the Freedmen. All of these activities and experiences helped to prepare Dr. Rust for the long and valuable services rendered as Corresponding Secretary of the Freedmen's Aid Society.

It is but little short of miraculous how extensively Dr. Rust

541

traveled all over the South at a time when there was not even good train transportation, establishing and visiting schools, visiting annual conferences, raising funds; and how he accomplished such monumental work in so many different places. Dr. Hartzell indicates that Dr. Rust's excellent judgment as a businessman was exercised in the purchase of nearly every piece of property owned by the Society in the South.[44] Again, Dr. Hartzell says of Dr. Rust: ". . .it is not too much to say that, in all the history of the church, no one man has given twenty-two years' service to the church in a more responsible and difficult position and accomplished more and made fewer mistakes."[45]

Reverend J. C. Hartzell

In 1882 the Rev. Hartzell became assistant corresponding secretary of the Freedmen's Aid Society,[46] which at that time had supervision of both white and Negro schools in the South. At the 1888 General Conference Dr. Hartzell was elected Corresponding Secretary to succeed Dr. Richard S. Rust,[47] which office he held until 1896, when he was elected Missionary Bishop of Africa.[48]

Dr. J. W. Hamilton

In 1892 the number was changed from one to two Corresponding Secretaries of the Freedmen's Aid and Southern Education Society. Dr. J. W. Hamilton was elected[49] by the General Conference as the second Corresponding Secretary along with Dr. Hartzell. Dr. Hamilton held this office two quadrennia, being elected to the Episcopacy in 1900.[50]

Reverend M. C. B. Mason

The Reverend M. C. B. Mason was elected a Corresponding Secretary for the Freedmen's Aid and Southern Education Society in 1896[51] to succeed the Rev. J. C. Hartzell who was elected to the Episcopacy. Dr. Mason and Dr. Hamilton served together as Corresponding Secretaries during the quadrennium 1896-1900. During the two quadrennia 1900-1908 Dr. Mason and Dr. Thirkield gave leadership as Corresponding Secretaries of the Freedmen's Aid and Southern Education Society. Dr. Mason continued in office until 1912.[52] Over a period of sixteen years in this office he served with Secretaries Hartzell, Hamilton, Thirkield and Maveety.

Dr. Mason was the first Black man to serve as Corresponding Secretary of the Freedmen's Aid Society.

When he was elected Senior Corresponding Secretary this interesting comment was made about him:

Doesn't it seem strange that only a generation ago the lad who drove an old cow fastened with a rope harness to an old wagon, on which was loaded a little bit of wood, to the market place, and was so surprised on seeing a church spire, never having seen one before, that he allowed his cow to get away from him, that that boy, who could hardly count the money that he received for his wood which he sold in the market place, is today the honored custodian of great interests such as are represented in the Freedmen's Aid and Southern Education Society?[53]

A great orator and preacher, Dr. Mason gave distinguished leadership as Corresponding Secretary, until his death in 1912.

Dr. Wilbur P. Thirkield

Dr. Thirkield was elected a Corresponding Secretary of the Freedmen's Aid and Southern Education in 1900.[54] He served two quadrennia in this position, and in 1908 resigned to take the Presidency of Howard University.

Dr. P. J. Maveety

Elected in 1908[55] to succeed Dr. Thirkield, Dr. Maveety remained a Corresponding Secretary of the Freedmen's Aid Society until 1920, and of the Department of Educational Institutions for Negroes, Board of Education,* until 1924. From 1924 to 1928 Dr. Maveety was "Head of the Department and Director of Property Equipment."

Dr. I. Garland Penn

Dr. I. Garland Penn, the second Black man to be elected to this position succeeding Dr. M. C. B. Mason, served as Corresponding Secretary from his election in 1912,[56] until 1920, and Secretary, Department of Educational Institutions for Negroes, until 1924, at which time he became "Secretary of Endowment and Field

*The name of the Freedmen's Aid Society was changed in 1920 to the Board of Educational Institutions for Negroes. Dr. Penn and Dr. Maveety continued as Secretaries of this Board until 1924, and then were given special assignments until 1928.

543

Promotion for the Negro schools."[5][7] This position he held until the time of his death July 22, 1930. Dr. Penn had the unusual distinction of being a delegate to ten successive General Conferences, 1892 to 1928, inclusive.

Secretaries for the Board of Educational Institutions for Negroes

Holmes, M. J., with the restructuring of the Board of Education in 1928, Dr. M. J. Holmes became the new Secretary for the Board of Educational Institutions for Negroes. He continued in this position until the reorganization of the church in 1940, following unification in 1939.

Davage, M. S. In 1940 the Board of Education reorganized and made provisions for a General Secretary of the Board, and several Associate Secretaries in charge of various divisions. Dr. M. S. Davage was elected as one of the Associate Secretaries of the Board of Education to supervise, and promote the interests of the Negro institutions under the auspices of the Board. With his wealth of educational experience, he gave statesmanlike leadership in this position from 1940 to his retirement, 1952.

Thomas, James S. As successor to Dr. Davage, the Reverend Dr. James S. Thomas assumed the position of Associate Secretary in 1952 and gave able and invaluable leadership until his election to the Episcopacy in 1964. As Associate Secretary Dr. Thomas broadened the scope of the office and gave to the whole church a new perspective of the Black colleges.

Wynn, Daniel W. In 1964 Dr. Daniel W. Wynn succeeded Dr. James S. Thomas, and is the present Associate Secretary of the Board of Education, relating his work primarily to the Black college of the church.

A Line of Distinguished Presidents

The institutions founded by the Freedmen's Aid Society for the education of Negro youth had a long succession of able and distinguished presidents. With very few exceptions all would warrant being listed in this category. Because of the length of the full list, all who gave presidential leadership to these institutions cannot be listed. It is in order, however, to pay tribute to all who with great interest and a sense of dedication gave their best, whether the period of leadership was long or short. An account of the administration is given in the historical sketch of each institution.

Because of the peculiar circumstances, or the uniqueness of the

544

situation, or the long term of service, the following accounts are given, listing names, institutions, and length of services.

Braden, John, President of Central Tennessee College, (later Walden University) 1868-1900, first President of the institution.

McDonald, A. C., President of Rust College (founded as Shaw University), Holly Springs, Mississippi, 1868-1876. Reverend McDonald started this school in Asbury Church in 1866 and had charge until the Freedmen's Aid Society took over in 1868 and elected him the first President.

Darnell, S. B., President of Cookman Institute, Jacksonville, Florida, 1873-1892. First President of the Institute, serving nineteen years.

Thayer, E. O., First President of Bennett College, Greensboro, North Carolina, 1874-1881; President of Clark University, Atlanta, Georgia, 1881-1889. Served fifteen years as President of the two institutions.

Hill, Judson S., President of Morristown Normal and Industrial College, 1881-1931, a half century of Presidential administration at this one institution.

Dunton, L. M., President of Claflin University (Claflin College) 1884-1922. He was a teacher and Special Financial Agent at Claflin 1873-1883; Vice President, 1883-1884; elected President 1884. He was President thirty-eight years, and connected with the institution a total of forty-nine years.

Walker, George, President of Paine College, Augusta, Georgia, 1884-1910, a period of twenty-six years.

Adkinson, Louis G., President of New Orleans University, New Orleans, Louisiana, 1887-1901; President of Gammon Theological Seminary, Atlanta, Georgia, 1901-1906, a total of nineteen years as President.

Thirkield, Wilbur P., President of Gammon Theological Seminary, Atlanta, Georgia, 1888-1899; Dean of the Seminary 1883-1888. Dr. Thirkield served the Seminary sixteen years, five as the first Dean, and eleven as the first President.

Grandison, C. N., President of Bennett College, Greensboro, North Carolina, 1889-1892. First Negro President of Bennett and first Negro President of a Freedmen's Aid Society school.

Chavis, J. D., President of Bennett College, Greensboro, North Carolina, 1892-1905. He was the second Black President of Bennett and second Black President of a Freedmen's Aid Society School.

Scott, Isaiah B., President of Wiley College, Marshall, Texas, 1893-1896. First Black President of Wiley and third Black President of a Freedmen's Aid Society school.

Dogan, M. W., President of Wiley College, Marshall, Texas, 1896-1942, a Presidential tenure of forty-six years at this one institution. His Presidency at Wiley was the second longest in the history of the institutions founded by the Freedmen's Aid Society.

Melden, C. M., President of Clark University, Atlanta, Georgia, 1897-1903; President New Orleans University, New Orleans, Louisiana, 1911-1925. As President of the two institutions he served twenty years.

Cox, James M., President of Philander Smith College, Little Rock, Arkansas, 1898-1924. As teacher and President he gave a total of thirty-eight years of service to Philander Smith College. He was the first Black man to be elected President of the College.

Lovinggood, R. S., President of Samuel Huston College, Austin, Texas, 1900-1916. First President of the institution and died in office.

Spencer, John O., President of Morgan College, Baltimore, Maryland, 1902-1937. Dr. Spencer was the last President of Morgan College while it was related to the Board of Education of the Methodist Episcopal Church, negotiations for the change to a State College having been initiated, in 1937, the same year he retired. His Presidency of Morgan College extended over a period of thirty-five years.

Bowen, J. W. E., Sr., first Black President of Gammon Theological Seminary, Atlanta, Georgia, 1906-1910. Dr. Bowen assumed a professorship at Gammon in 1893 as professor of Historical Theology. On his retirement in 1936, he had spent forty years in the service of Gammon Theological Seminary.

Watters, Philip M., President of Gammon Theological Seminary 1914-1925, a tenure of eleven years.

Davage, M. S., President of George R. Smith College, Sedalia, Missouri, 1915-1916; President of Haven Institute, Meridian, Mississippi, 1916-1917; President, Samuel Huston College, Austin, Texas, 1917-1920; President, Rust College, Holly Springs, Mississippi, 1920-1924; President, Clark University, Atlanta, Georgia, 1924-1941; President, Huston-Tillotson College, Austin, Texas, 1952-1955—a total of twenty-nine years of service as President of six different institutions.

Hubbard, George W., President of Meharry Medical College, Nashville, Tennessee, 1916-1921. Prior to becoming President he was Dean of the Medical School thirty-nine years. As the first Dean and first President of Meharry Medical College his services covered forty-five years.

Randolph, J. B., President of Haven Institute, Meridian, Mississippi, 1917-1920; President of Samuel Huston College,

1920-1922; President of Claflin College 1922-1945. Dr. Randolph's Presidential tenures covered twenty-eight years, twenty-three of which were at Claflin College.

Mullowney, John, second President of Meharry Medical College, Nashville, Tennessee, 1921-1938, a total of seventeen years.

Bethune, Mrs. Mary McLeod, President of Daytona Normal and Industrial Institute for Negro Girls, Daytona, Florida, 1904-1923; after merging with Cookman Institute of Jacksonville, Florida, in 1923, Mrs. Bethune was President of Bethune-Cookman College from 1923 to 1942, the time of her retirement. She served a total of thirty-eight years as President of the two institutions.

McCoy, L. M., President of Rust College 1924-1957, a rigorous administrative tenure of thirty-three years.

Jones, David D., first President of Bennett College for Women, Greensboro, North Carolina, 1926-1955, and President Emeritus until his death January 24, 1956. His active presidency extended over a period of twenty-nine years.

King, Willis J., President of Samuel Huston College, Austin, Texas, 1928-1932; President of Gammon Theological Seminary 1932-1944, from which position he was elected to the Episcopacy. His relation to Gammon began in 1918 as Professor of Old Testament, and he became recognized as a scholar in this field having taught until 1928 when he took leave to study at Oxford University, England.

Peters, E. C., President of Paine College, Augusta, Georgia, 1929-1956, a total of twenty-seven years.

Harris, Marquis L., President of Philander Smith College, Little Rock, Arkansas, 1936-1964. His Presidency of twenty-eight years ended with his election to the Episcopacy, 1964.

Seabrook, John J., President of Claflin College, 1945-1955; President of Huston-Tillotson College, 1955-1965. Dr. Seabrook gave twenty years of presidential leadership to the two institutions.

Moore, Richard V., President of Bethune-Cookman College, Daytona Beach, Florida. Assuming the Presidency in 1947, President Moore still is giving excellent presidential leadership to Bethune-Cookman College, having been President twenty-four years to this date.

Richardson, Harry V., President of Gammon Theological Seminary, Atlanta, Georgia, 1948-1958; President of the Interdenominational Theological Seminary (including Gammon), 1958-1968. Last President of Gammon Theological Seminary as a separate institution on the South Atlanta campus. His Presidential tenure was a total of twenty years.

West, Harold D., Served as President of Meharry Medical College, Nashville, Tennessee, 1952-1965, and as a teacher, 1927-1952. He continued teaching and has engaged in research since retirement from the Presidency in 1965.

Calhoun, E. Clayton, President of Paine College, Augusta, Georgia, 1956-1970, a total of fourteen years. Dr. Calhoun was the eighth and last white President before the election in 1970 of Dr. L. H. Pitts, the first Black President of Paine College.

REFERENCES AND NOTES

1. Journal, General Conference, 1864, p. 180.
2. Fifth Annual Report, Freedmen's Aid Society, 1871, p. 3.
3. *Ibid.*, p. 4.
4. *The Christian Educator*, Vol. II, p. 43.
5. Journal, General Conference, 1872, p. 305.
6. Report, Freedmen's Aid Society, 1874, p. 2.
7. *The Christian Educator*, Vol. 1, p. 50.
8. Report, Freedmen's Aid Society Organizational Meeting, 1866, p. 12.
9. *Ibid.*
10. *Ibid.*
11. Buckley, James M., *History of Methodism*, p. 131.
12. *Ibid.*
13. Report, Freedmen's Aid Society, 1869, p. 20.
14. Hurst, John Fletcher, *The History of Methodism*, p. 1205.
15. Simpson, *op. cit.*, p. 801.
16. *Ibid.*
17. Journal, General Conference, 1864, p. 180.
18. Baker, J. D., *History of Ohio Methodism*, p. 253.
19. Barclay, *loc. cit.*
20. Simpson, *op. cit.*, p. 860.
21. Journal, General Conference, 1872, p. 300.
22. Simpson, Bishop Matthew, *Cyclopedia of Methodism*, pp. 371f.
23. Simpson, *op. cit.*, pp. 434f.
24. *Ibid.*
25. *Ibid.*
26. *Ibid.*
27. Journal, General Conference, 1880, p. 201.
28. Journal, General Conference, 1916, p. 855.
29. *The Christian Educator*, August, 1912, pp. 5f.
30. Journal, General Conference, 1888, p. 350.
31. Simpson, *op. cit.*, Supra, p. 433.
32. *Ibid.*
33. *The Christian Educator*, Vol I, p. 52.
34. Journal, General Conference, 1896, p. 286.
35. *The Christian Educator*, November, 1928, p. 3.
36. *Ibid.*, p. 4.
37. Journal, General Conference, 1912, p. 928.
38. *Ibid.*
39. Dempsey, Elam Franklin, *Atticus G. Haygood*, p. 14.
40. *Ibid.*

41. *Ibid.*
42. Dempsey, *op. cit.*, p. 269.
43. *The Christian Educator*, Vol. II, October, 1890, p. 45.
44. *Ibid.*
45. *Ibid.*
46. *The Christian Educator*, November, 1928, p. 3.
47. Journal, General Conference, 1888, p. ?.
48. Journal, General Conference, 1896, p. ?.
49. Journal, General Conference, 1892, p. 315.
50. Journal, General Conference, 1900, p. 312.
51. *The Christian Educator*, April-May, 1900, p. 104.
52. *The Christian Educator*, August, 1915, p. 6.
53. *The Christian Educator*, April-May, 1900, p. 104.
54. Journal, General Conference, 1900, p. 305 and 500.
55. Journal, General Conference, 1908, pp. 415 and 775.
56. Journal, General Conference, 1912, p. 476.
57. *The Christian Educator*, May-August, 1930, p. 4.

CHAPTER 27

SUMMARY OF CONTRIBUTIONS—1866-1966; AND
CURRENT STATUS OF INSTITUTIONS

Contributions

Across the span of a hundred years the contributions of the
institutions founded by the Freedmen's Aid Society have been
numerous, varied, valuable, and enduring. The demonstrations of
great courage, heroism, dedication and perseverance by so many
people over so long a period are in themselves significant
contributions.

In summary, the major contributions of the educational
movement initiated by the Freedmen's Aid Society, and of the
institutions established may be noted as follows:

1. The establishment of schools, elementary, grammar,
academic, and preparatory schools, and schools of higher
grade—colleges, and universities—was the first contribution. These
schools were literally planted over the South when not only were
there no public schools for Negroes, but there was opposition to
the establishment of schools for their education. The major
burden of providing learning opportunities for Negro children and
youth was carried by private schools for more than a half century.

2. The educability of the Negro had to be proven. Slavery
arguments and post-emancipation propaganda attempted to
disprove the capacity of the Negro to learn and to become
educated. Evidence had to be provided giving proof of Negro
talent and potential for intellectual development. Incredible
results were achieved in an amazingly short time through the
mastery of Greek, Latin, logic, and higher forms of mathematics.

3. A valuable contribution was made in giving practical training
that helped to provide for the economic growth of the individual
Negro and the Negro community, the primary training for this
purpose being industrial and agricultural.

4. The cultural level of individual Negroes and of the Negro
community was lifted. This was essential for a people
predominantly agrarian and just emerging from slavery and its
direful aftermath. It was also necessary to help Negro people begin
to develop a culture of their own for the world to which they were

551

confined.

5. In the early years of freedom the Negro had need of being recognized as a man and to be accorded the dignity of a man. This need was in part met, theoretically at least, when the Methodist Episcopal Church as early as 1864 adopted a non-discriminatory practice in conference membership, and in 1884 the General Conference adopted clear and emphatic policies of non-discrimination with reference to all institutions of the Church and the Church itself.

Charters granted to the Freedmen's Aid Society institutions in this early period, through the wisdom and foresight of the officials of the Society, provided that there should be no discrimination regarding admission of students and employment of teachers, on the basis of race or color.

These wise policies gave the Negro and his institution a high level of dignity and freedom of operation that stands them in good stead even today.

6. Every community in which a Freedmen's Aid Society school was located became a different community. The Negro community was influenced culturally and economically, and the white community, as well, felt the impact of the institution.

7. All over the South for a century after Emancipation, interracial communication was a problem. The general patterns and practices of segregation prohibited any normal interracial communication and intercourse in a community, except on the campus of the Negro private school. These institutions for a hundred years were contributors to interracial contacts and understanding, for there was no other place for white and Black contacts and meetings for discussion of problems of mutual interest, and the cultivation of interracial goodwill.

8. The claim cannot be honestly made that the institutions founded by the Freedmen's Aid Society furnished most of the professionals providing services to Negroes in the South and other sections of the country. It can be said, however, that the contribution of professionally trained persons has been among the largest and best. It is generally admitted that a great majority of the trained Negro ministry of the South, and other sections included, was trained at Gammon Theological Seminary. Over half of the Negro doctors and dentists of the country, from the founding of Meharry in 1876 to date, have been trained at Meharry Medical College, and also a high percentage of the nurses have been trained there. Thousands upon thousands of public and private school teachers received their professional training in the institutions founded by the Freedmen's Aid Society.

9. The contribution of inspired and inspiring leadership to the

growth and development of a people was most significant. For their own faculties and for other faculties these institutions prepared outstanding and dedicated teachers who poured their lives and highest ideals and aspirations into the lives of their students. They made their own Presidents, the first as early as 1889, less than a quarter of a century after the founding of the first of these institutions in 1866. Since the election of the first Black President, C. N. Grandison to Bennett College in 1889, some fifty-one graduates of these colleges have become their Presidents and their combined administrations total well over five hundred years of service.*

The churches of the Negro annual conferences of the Methodist Church, and churches outside of these conferences, have looked to the Negro colleges of the church for trained leadership to fill their pulpits.

From these colleges have come four corresponding and associate secretaries of the Freedmen's Aid Society and its successor, namely, M. C. B. Mason, I. Garland Penn, Matthew Simpson Davage, and James Samuel Thomas.

All but one of the twenty Negro bishops elected to the Episcopacy in the Methodist Church have been graduates of these colleges or attended one or more of the institutions—Bishops I. B. Scott, Alexander P. Camphor; since 1920, Bishops Robert E. Jones, Matthew W. Clair, Sr., Alexander P. Shaw, Lorenzo H. King, W. A. C. Hughes, Willis Jefferson King, Robert N. Brooks, Edward W. Kelly, John Wesley Edward Bowen, II, Mathew W. Clair, Jr., Edgar A. Love, Prince Albert Taylor, Jr., Noah W. Moore, Jr., Charles F. Golden, Marquis L. Harris, James S. Thomas, L. Scott Allen. Several graduates became bishops in other denominations.

The lay leadership from Negro churches and conferences has reflected a high level of representation at the local church level, as delegates to General and Jurisdictional Conferences, and in membership on general boards and agencies. They have also held high offices in the Church.

This leadership has not been confined to the American scene. Scores of graduates of these institutions have gone to Africa as missionaries, and many Africans have come to these colleges for their education and returned to give leadership and service in their native land.

The work of these Negro institutions and the kind of leadership produced have made valuable contributions through the tremendous impact at the local, national, and international levels.

*1966

10. The Negro colleges have not been mere recipients of charity. They have been catalysts, contributing to the opportunity for Methodism to involve itself in the solution of the "great American Problem." If this had not been true the Methodist Church would not have been in the past, and would not be today, a church of social reform. Though it has much still to do and faces challenges equally as great in race relations as those of the past, it at least has this historical record of social concern. The Methodist Church has struggled with itself in the matter of race relations. The struggle must continue. The involvement of the Black colleges in the search for solution may be one of their most valuable contributions of the future.

Current Status

The number on the current list of institutions under the auspices of the Board of Education of the United Methodist Church stands at thirteen. Of this number ten are four-year senior colleges of liberal arts and sciences, one is a medical college, one is a theological seminary, and one is a two-year junior college. All of these institutions are fully accredited holding membership in their respective regional and national accrediting associations.

The accompanying Table of Statistical Data, page 512, indicates the strength and/or weakness of each institution in several areas, especially the areas relating to finances.

For the year 1970-71 the thirteen institutions had 793 faculty members serving 8,587 students. Library resources included 677,572 volumes. The combined plant value total was $63,551,255, and the combined endowment totaled $21,666,572. During that year expenditures for current operations totaled $47,100,463. While recognition must be given to the development and current status of these institutions, the evident inequities and inadequacies of the resources must be noted.

TABLE OF STATISTICAL DATA*

Institution	Faculty	Enrollment	Library Volumes	Value of Physical Plant	Endowment	Expenditures, Current Operation
Bennett College	74	597	62,601	6,102,005	2,038,533	2,360,341
Bethune-Cookman College	70	1,147	60,000	4,553,375	1,298,938	2,760,832
Claflin College	48	749	55,479	4,298,958	636,333	1,766,162
Clark College	84	1,038	42,675	5,501,644	1,603,029	4,036,380
Dillard University	102	961	97,366	10,475,654	3,600,077	3,545,124
Huston-Tillotson College	45	754	50,688	3,959,161	350,359	2,495,276
Paine College	52	715	48,138	5,284,564	409,112	2,465,065
Philander Smith College	37	695	62,700	3,491,570	613,080	1,555,659
Rust College	43	660	62,016	4,358,284	579,658	2,081,218
Wiley College	44	493	31,060	4,337,491	356,170	1,588,228
Morristown Junior College	13	188	20,000	1,392,019	253,691	617,994
Gammon Theological Seminary	14	59	60,000	1,287,111	1,128,894	253,843
Meharry Medical College	167	531	24,849	8,509,419	8,798,698	21,574,341
	793	8,587	677,572	63,551,255	21,666,572	47,100,463

*Statistical summary for educational institutions related to the Methodist Church, 1970-71.

PART VI.

THE CHURCH AND THE HISTORICALLY NEGRO COLLEGE
IN A NEW ERA OF CHANGE

CHAPTER 28

THE NEED FOR THESE BLACK INSTITUTIONS AFTER
A HUNDRED YEARS: ANOTHER LOOK

In the course of a hundred years since the Freedmen's Aid Society in 1866 established its first schools for Negroes, much has happened and much progress has been made. Many of the first elementary purposes for which the schools were established have long since become irrelevant. The battle for public school education in the South was won over a half century ago. The Negro children, however, to put it mildly, have always been on the short end of the provisions. More than four decades ago the private and church related colleges withdrew from secondary education to concentrate exclusively on college instruction.

Between 1900 and 1964 public institutions at the college level for Negroes were established and expanded rapidly, especially has the expansion been rapid since 1945. McGrath in his study[1] published in 1965, shows in addition to private colleges, thirty-six state, twelve county, and three city institutions extant for Negroes. Since the battle began in 1936 for admission of Black students to the all-white institutions, and particularly since the Supreme Court Decision of 1954, many changes have come about and the doors of all-white and predominantly white institutions have opened to Negro students. It might be pointed out also that most, if not all, of the private all-white colleges in the South are now open to Negro students.

With the developments indicated above and with the adamant refusal, with few exceptions, of white students to enter all-Black colleges, the question inevitably arises with reference to the future of the Black colleges. Is there a need for them, and if so, what should be their function? What are these Negro colleges doing that cannot be done by any other institution, perhaps at less cost?

Discussion of these questions will be confined, for the most part, to the Black institutions of the United Methodist Church included in this volume. Other denominations may have different functions and approaches for their Black institutions, and the Black independent and state institutions should be treated in a different context from the church related colleges in as much as the basic problem of existence is different with them.

Rationalization for Black Colleges Today in the United Methodist Church

Rationalization for Black colleges today in the United Methodist Church, for the most part, is the same for Black colleges generally. There are, however, some unique arguments for the Black colleges in the United Methodist Church that have importance because of the connection of the institution with this particular church and because of some of the historic purposes that have increased in significance adhering in the urgency of local problems and the mission, concern, and program of the church. The Black colleges and the mission of the church will be given attention in the following chapter.

There is no defensible rationale for a Black college to remain exclusively so on a discriminatory basis just for the sake of being Black. Black colleges founded by the Freedmen's Aid Society have not been and are not now discriminating institutions to the exclusion of other racial groups. They are Black colleges because of discrimination against them. They have been Black colleges historically not by choice but by rejection. They have been and are Black colleges because of prejudice and rejection, just as there has been prejudice against and rejection of Black people. By charter provisions and long established racial policies these Black colleges have been open to all without regard to race, color, or creed. At this point in efforts to advance good race relations in the church, and in the American society generally, it would be a tragic step backward to maintain Black colleges for Blacks only. This would be a reversal of the discriminatory practices inflicted upon Black people and their institutions for more than a century. This, however, is not to say that there should be no Black colleges. There are many good reasons why there should be Black colleges, some of which I shall enumerate with brief comments.

1. The Black colleges listed among the institutions of higher education of the United Methodist Church are good colleges. All hold membership in their respective accrediting associations. Most of them have excellent physical plants. The existence, or continued existence of any college, should be determined by the criteria of the excellence of the quality of its educational performance, the relevance of its program, and the importance of the services rendered.

There is a subtle, fallacious, and vicious idea of long standing but more recently emphasized that all Black colleges are inferior institutions; they should go out of existence and all Negro students who want to attend college should transfer to or enter white institutions controlled and administered by white people.

This is racist propaganda based on the ideology of white superiority, white supremacy, and white domination. This propaganda is being related to the Black institutions in the same way it has been applied to Negro people for more than a hundred years—superiority of the white man and inferiority of the Black man. Black colleges are needed, if for no other reason than to resist and refute this kind of effort at brainwashing.

In 1965, Earl J. McGrath reported on a carefully made study of *The Nation's 123 Predominantly Negro Colleges and Universities.* McGrath's report asserts that "except at the topmost level of excellence represented by a few celebrated institutions, the Negro institutions run the entire gamut of quality within American higher education. Some educators as well as laymen unfamiliar with the Negro colleges seem not to realize this fact."[2] He further states, "when compared with the predominantly white colleges they can be matched institution by institution."[3]

Admittedly, there are some poor Black colleges. By the same token there are some poor white colleges. Regarding the Black colleges, McGrath's view is sound:

Contrary to the proposal for disestablishment, a deliberate weighing of the evidence of this study leads to the conclusion that most of the predominantly Negro institutions ought to be preserved and strengthened.[4]

This conclusion is applicable to most, if not all, of the Black institutions of the United Methodist Church.

2. The increasing college enrollments generally, among Black students particularly, indicate a need for all good colleges. Figures in the 1970 U. S. Census indicate that in the decade 1960-1970 Black college students more than doubled,[5] up to 492,000. Of this number more than a third were enrolled in predominantly Black colleges. Black undergraduate enrollment is expected to increase 50 per cent in the decade of the 1970's.

The Carnegie Commission believes that colleges founded for Negroes share responsibility to "provide higher education for 1,100,000 Black Americans by 1980 and for 2,000,000 Black Americans by the year 2000."[6] These estimates are based on previous growth in college entrances and on estimated population growth. It should be noted, as pointed out by Sowell, that:

The overwhelming bulk of black youth do not go on to college, and while the *proportion* of these youth who are educationally well prepared for college is very low, in *absolute numbers* there are literally tens of thousands of them who are, by all the usual indices—far too many for the top universities to be *forced* to have as many inadequately prepared Black students as they do.[7]

Here is another potential for an increase in college enrollments.

3. All good colleges are needed and will be needed for many years ahead. As the number of Black students graduating from high school each year increases and the college enrollments mount there will be need for the good colleges.

Educational opportunities ought always be open to Black students, many of whom would not be accepted in white colleges because of excessive enrollments, and many would be rejected for other reasons. There are many Black students who prefer to go to predominantly Black colleges. They should have this choice. Accessibility of the desired kind of education within the best setting and climate can become a crucial problem for the Black student.

4. The Black colleges can best deal with the problems of educational and cultural deficiencies of Black students. Over a long period of years the Black colleges have had the problem of working with Black students with limited or deficient educational and cultural backgrounds and have worked out techniques and programs for doing so.

They have also worked with the exceptionally bright students. There was a period when preparatory schools were attached to the colleges and when the student entered college from the preparatory school he was ready to do college work. With the passing of the preparatory school, the Black colleges had to develop instructional programs and techniques in the freshman and sophomore years for dealing with deficient students. The selective process did not solve the problem, for even the best high school graduates, with few exceptions, had deficiencies, because of deficient high school training and limited cultural background. The high percentage of graduates from Black colleges who have gone to the best graduate schools all over America and the success achieved in terms of graduate degrees, including the Ph.D. degree, attest the quality of the instruction and special academic work at these institutions. Moreover, the graduates of these institutions, many of whom would never have had a chance to enter the all-white colleges have been outstanding in many fields other than academics, and have been good competitors with graduates from the best colleges of the nations. The Black colleges have done an unusually good job in taking Black students with all their deficiencies and preparing them for the rigors of competitive life. The Black colleges offer a unique experience in education which

562

will be needed for many years to come.

There is need to remedy the educational and cultural deficiencies of Black students without over-emphasis on the deficiencies and creating a feeling of inferiority. The Negro college can create a climate conducive to strengthening "Black Pride," "Black ego," "Black *me*," without too much conceit. The psychological aspects of the Negro student educational situation is important. There needs to be developed a deeper consciousness and appreciation of Black achievements, Black culture, and Black creative ability, much of which has been emphasized in Black colleges in the past, and must be continued with greater emphasis.

5. Black identity is important. In the process of the historical development since 1865, the Negro had to have institutions to which he could relate himself—churches, fraternal organizations, business enterprises, schools, etc. He had to have a sense of ownership and possession. He had to relate himself to something that would give him a sense of identity, a sense of belonging, a sense of becoming, and a sense of dignity. This identity was essential as the Negro built his "world"—a world within a world. This was a part of the ingredient of his ambition, his desire to achieve, his striving to be a man—a man of recognition and worth.

The Negro still has to live in two worlds in America—a Black world and a white world. Though he moves with a great deal more freedom in the white world at present than ever before, it is still true that he must live in a Black world. He must still have ownership of institutions of all types to which he can relate himself with a true sense of identity. If there should happen to be no Black colleges for such identity, the light of pride, achievement, and progress would go out.

6. Group importance and group respect have come to be crucial issues for the Negro in the United Methodist Church.

The historically Negro college is the only organic or structural unit remaining around which the Black people of the church may rally or claim ownership as a group. The central jurisdiction is gone, and rightly so. The Negro annual conference is gone; ideally this is good, but the practical good is at present in question. So important a group as the Negro in the United Methodist Church whose membership dates back to the first society, 1766, before the Methodist Episcopal Church was organized, must have some instrumentality of identity, signifying his contribution to the church and to society. The Black colleges of the church administered by Black educators are such instrumentalities; further, they are resources for continued contributions to the life of the whole church, and to society in general.

7. The continued development of Black leadership is an

important part of the rationale for the Black colleges of the United Methodist Church. The leadership training function of the institutions founded by the Freedmen's Aid Society, described in Chapter 26, has been well performed. There is no less need now and in the future for such able leadership. This leadership is needed among the Negro people, within the church, and in the American society.

In the Black colleges of Methodism, leadership training has always had high priority. This leadership has not been limited to bishops. presidents, ministers, and missionaries; but has included varied types of community leadership.

The Black colleges have a unique opportunity and a special obligation to train a kind of community leadership for a time when the problems of Black people are becoming more numerous and more difficult. To meet this obligation the administration must seek and stimulate Black teachers (not to the exclusion of teachers of other ethnic groups) with a sense of mission to Black youth. The college must be a place where a growing sense of mission among Black professors might have expression and support in church-related Black colleges, where the meaning and mission of life are emphasized and where they can help students to discover themselves in a climate of Christian humanism, and give some direction toward self-realization. Traditionally and historically this has been one of the most significant things the Negro church-related college has done.

Again, in the words of "A Special Task Force Report":

The traditionally Negro universities and colleges are in strategic positions to assume leadership in meeting some of the more pressing problems of higher education and of society as a whole.[8]

8. Black colleges are the best resources and instruments for the creation, development, and preservation of Black culture. The connotation of Black culture employed here is not limited to Black studies or a Black curriculum. Black culture is a far broader, deeper, and more inclusive philosophical and spiritual concept. It is a philosophical concept that is pragmatic, idealistic, intellectual, and artistic.

Black culture has come and continues to come out of the life experience of Black people. The life experiences of Black people consist not merely of their contacts with other people in another world, but what they themselves are as a people—their physical make-up, which some of late have discovered to be beautiful

564

(many for generations have known this to be true); their abilities; their talents; their intellect; their inner depth; and their potential, endowed with many gifts known and unknown. Life experiences of Black people include their long-sufferings, their hopes, their ambitions, their dreams, their faith, their ability to forgive, and their ability to love, to love even those who persecute them. Black experience gives added dimensions to other cultures the Negro acquires. Black culture is valid and valuable not for Black people only, but, also, for all America through the enrichment of the total culture.

Illustrative of Black culture, the following twelve areas might be examined for notable Black cultural contributions to American life: (1) art; (2) athletics and sports; (3) business; (4) communications—news media, writings, books, etc.; (5) education; (6) entertainment; (7) law; (8) medicine; (9) music; (10) politics; (11) religion; and (12) science.

It might also be observed that the current Black revolution in America demonstrates in spirit the essence of Black culture; it is the spirit and struggle of the new Negro striving to enhance, strengthen, and establish more firmly the identity and worth of Black people, who have helped to make America, and whom America cannot continue to ignore lest it invalidates its total claim to democracy.

It is a fact that for generations to come Black people in America will constitute a distinct and distinctive segment of the American society. The Negro is not going to be absorbed into the general society. There are movements to indicate that he doesn't want to be absorbed. There is also abundant evidence that he wouldn't be absorbed if he wanted to be. The Negro has a cultural heritage which he has developed. He should continue this development for purposes of creative expression, self-realization, Black identity, enrichment of the total American culture, and for posterity.

There is no need for racial conflict, ideological or otherwise, because Black people work to develop a distinctive culture of their own. This might become a means of communication, racial understanding, and interracial cohesiveness and unity.

There should no longer be two mutually exclusive racial worlds in America. When Negro and white worlds cease to be mutually exclusive, then mutual understanding, communication, and goodwill will result. Black culture might lead to, certainly make possible, a process of acculturation, moving away from segregation, separatism, and absorption. The process of acculturation, or any other solution of the problems of race relations, must engage the thinking and efforts of the institutions of higher education, both Black and white.

9. The functions of the Black church-related colleges have, over a period of a century, become more valuable assets, have broadened their functions in the changed and changing American society. In the very nature of their reason for being and their church relatedness, these institutions have taken on an increasingly great importance and relevance in relation to the social and spiritual functions of the church, and in relation to the problem of race, with which the church must deal responsibly.

At this time, as in all the past, the Black colleges of the United Methodist Church are needed, not alone for the sake of Black students, but also for the sake of the Church, to help bring about a new church in spirit and social vision. Here are potentials for new dimensions in human relations and church life.

REFERENCES AND NOTES

1. McGrath, Earl J., *The Predominantly Negro Colleges and Universities in Transition*, p. 20.
2. *Ibid.*, p. 5.
3. *Ibid.*
4. *Ibid.*
5. U. S. Census Report, 1970, p. ?.
6. From Isolation to Mainstream: A Report and Recommendations by the Carnegie Commission on Higher Education, February, 1971, p. 17.
7. Sowell, Thomas, "The Available University," *The University of Chicago Magazine*, November-December, 1970, p. 5.
8. Institute for Higher Educational Opportunity: Southern Regional Education Board: Task Force on Financing Negro Higher Education, Report 1969, p. 3.

CHAPTER 29

THE CHURCH (U.M.C.) AND ITS BLACK COLLEGES, THE SECOND CENTURY

At this early stage of the second century in the history of Methodist concern regarding education and relations of Black people of the Church, it is important to note the nature of the current social and racial situation in America and the problems confronting Black people in general, with specific reference to Black people of the United Methodist Church and with implications for the Church.

In the course of a hundred years since 1865, it must be granted that in America much progress has been made with reference to Black and white race relations. Particularly has there been significant progress within the past two decades.

Negroes have made substantial progress. This progress must be taken into account on the one hand, but on the other hand the slowness, and in some instances or areas almost complete lack of progress must be pointed out. The difficulty of making progress in race relations in America is appalling. When the complexity of the race problem and racial barriers for more than a century are noted, the slowness and lack of progress might be understood, and the phenomenal progress that has been made by Negroes despite the barriers encountered may be recognized with appreciation.

The problems that the Black people of America encounter are not isolated, detached, and single problems met one by one at different times. The problems are numerous, interrelated, difficult, and complex, and are experienced daily. These problems form a great network that blankets this country from Gulf to Lakes and from ocean to ocean like a strong web of steel. Some parts are stronger and more difficult in some regions, particularly in the Southern Region, but the network in most respects covers every state of the Union. Certain practices by white America regarding the Negro have become so institutionalized that they form a pathological socio-racial system* of practices and behavior. This "system" has been structured over a period of more than a

*Hereafter referred to as "the system."

century and maintained through:

1. Structured class—segregation
2. Enslavement (in some sections)
3. Stigmatization—(association of "identical twins," black and inferiority)
4. Prejudice
5. Customs, mores, laws, ordinances
6. Exploitation
7. Cheating by devious methods
8. Intrigue
9. Injustice
10. Institutionalization of inequality
11. Deprivation
12. Degradation (destruction of personality)
13. Humiliation and destruction of dignity
14. Brutality and violence
15. Terror and fear
16. Murder
17. Depredation
18. Racism (conscious and unconscious)
19. Circumscription
20. Circumvention
21. Maneuvering
22. Unemployment
23. Occupational immobility
24. Discrimination
25. Oppression

Black people find themselves hopelessly trapped in the maze of conflicts and barriers of this horrendous "system." A little ray of hope may come through when the Negro is able to stick one hand or one foot out of an opening in the webbing; but instantly he comes to realize that he is still trapped in the netting of "the system."

In efforts to extricate himself from the entangling, strangling, defeating, and annihilating effects of the cross-currents of this pathological socio-racial system in America, the Negro has struggled all the years since his emancipation. His involvement and his inescapable capture in the grinding wheels of "the system" gave birth to the National Association for the Advancement of Colored People, to the National Urban League, and to the Marcus Garvey Movement in the first two decades of the current century. In protest against "the system" for many years the voices of W. E. B. DuBois, Charles Houston, Walter White, all deceased, and many others were heard. In more recent protests, Black people of America in varying groups have involved themselves in movements under the leadership of A. Philip Randolph; Roy Wilkins; Thurgood Marshall; the late Martin Luther King, Jr.; the late Malcolm X; Stokely Carmichael; Eldridge Cleaver; Rap Brown; James L. Farmer, and the late Whitney M. Young, Jr. Along with the movements led by adults in recent years, the student movement of the 1960's was just as revolutionary, and secured more immediately some of the results for which Black people have struggled since 1865. To begin the second century in the struggle for freedom, Black people and the white people of America are caught in this emasculating "system," the existence of which, it seems, white America is unaware or is too insensitive or too paralytic to do what needs to be done to eradicate "the system."

In brief and in part, this is the problem faced at the beginning of the second century of the Methodist Church's endeavors in education involving Black people. The schools were established in 1866 and later to help solve the social problems of that time. Equally important is the joint involvement of the Black colleges and the United Methodist Church in efforts to resolve the social and racial problems of this day, the magnitude of which is equally as great as ever before.

Because of its long historical duration, its depth, its effects upon the Black people of America and upon all America, and because of its international implications, the race problem, "the system," is now the number one moral issue in the United States. To come to this conclusion one needs only to examine and reflect upon the destructive effects of "the system" that includes the twenty five forces listed above (page 571).

"The System," in America, has been and remains a blockade to democracy and a counter religion to Christianity. This "system" has been built and maintained, particularly in the Southern Region, through what the late W. J. Cash, in his classic and monumental book of three decades ago, describes as "The Mind of the South." It should be recognized that for decades the "South" has not been merely a geographical region, but a state of mind characteristic, to some degree, of all sections of the United States.

The Purpose and Function of The
    Church-Related Colleges

The fact of a college's being church related places upon it a distinctive responsibility. The basic relationship is not merely an organic or structural relationship, but is one rooted in the oneness of the fundamental purposes of the two institutions. The two institutions have kinship in the task they work together to perform within the individual, within the church, within the community, and within society at large. The relationship of the church and its colleges is not just an institutional relationship. It is a relationship that grows out of the oneness of purpose of religion and education. The church and the church-related college, therefore, have unique relationships, and reciprocal responsibilities one to the other.

The church-related college must have deep concern about being truly Christian. Its role is to emphasize and teach moral values and provide a climate for spiritual growth. The Christian college is obligated to create and maintain educational situations that evidence high moral standards and wholesome living. The Christian college cannot abdicate its moral responsibility; nor can it condone moral laxity, as so many are doing today. The approach must be positive and the position on moral values must be essentially the philosophy of the whole college, including trustees, administration, faculty, and students. Moral growth through the exercise of will and choice is essential, leading to a growing sense of responsibility. A sense of responsibility is essentially the proper attitude or attitudes toward others, toward duty, toward the purposes of life, and toward God. In the development of these attitudes, religion and education are one in purpose, and the Church and the church-related college are one in responsibility.

The role of the Christian college is to commit itself to a search for truth. The search for truth is a search for meaning. The search for truth is a search for answers to the great questions: (1) What is life? (2) What is the meaning of life? (3) What is the purpose of life? (4) What is man and what is his destiny? (5) What is the nature of God? (6) What is the relation of man to God? and (7) How does God relate Himself to the creative universe in which man attempts creatively to discover himself and to achieve his destiny?

The Christian college should maintain an atmosphere of freedom in which teachers and students may be stimulated and inspired to search for answers to the great questions of life. Within the framework of this approach the science laboratory takes on new meaning and scientific research (and all research) becomes a partner with faith in a challenging and inspiring adventure in the search for truth. Truth discovered through the intellectual processes should lead to deeper spiritual growth.

Intellectual growth may involve the mastery of mathematical equations and an understanding of principles and laws of physics and chemistry; but unless the mastery of mathematics and the understanding of the principles and laws of physics and chemistry are undergirded by a deeper understanding and appreciation of the original source of all principles and laws, leading to a spiritual basis of life and a Christian outlook on life, then this knowledge will lead only to a paganism that is dangerous, and annihilating.

Following the line of thinking of the eminent Charles H. Malik, current education should be an unshackled search for truth. The college should create the climate of freedom and thought to nurture the minds of young people toward maturity. Malik maintains that:

> The soul of the learned these days is quite empty—empty to the bare bones. The students will rebel, not knowing why they are rebelling or what they are rebelling against, although they think they do. For they have come to the great banquet of being, seeking food and fullness, and are turned away empty.[1]

The following declaration by Malik reinforces my statement a paragraph or two above: "Learning is wonderful; science is wonderful; knowledge is wonderful, but life, responsibility, depth, maturity, personal existence, and the grace of the spirit, are infinitely more wonderful."[2]

The following and final quote from Malik is the epitome of challenge to the Christian college: "Until the fear of God and the dimension of the spirit are fully affirmed at the heart and being of the university [college], we shall see many more casualties among the faculty and the students."[3]

All colleges related to the United Methodist Church, Black and white, have the responsibility of being Christian and of providing Christian education within the Christian frame of reference. It is only in this Christian context that the church-related college, Black and white, working to deepen spiritual growth in the individual and change within society, can justify the claim of being church related.

The Black Constituency and Black Colleges
of the United Methodist Church

The Negro is an important part of the membership of the United Methodist Church, dating back to the inception of American Methodism in 1766. During all of the two centuries of being a part of Methodism, under varying conditions and levels of status, he has been appreciatively aware of the benefits derived, and has hopefully aspired for better conditions. Time has brought us to the present situation. There is regret that our responsibilities have not been so discharged and our opportunities as a great

573

church have not been grasped to realize the oneness of the total constituency of the church and the importance of the Black membership as an *integral part of the whole church.* As we move into a new century there is need to approach the problem of our relationship, in and outside the church, with contrite hearts in search of reconciliation. This is of first importance. Then we may be able to covenant together and work with a new understanding of ourselves and problems, and with a new concept of our relationships.

We, therefore, should think not of what the church can do *for* the Black membership—but, rather, what all of us can and must *do together* to discover our "Oneness" in the church and our "Oneness" in Christian fellowship with one another. If this can be done, then we will bring the Black constituency and the Black colleges into the mainstream of thought and action for use by all and for the furtherance of understanding of our common needs and our common fulfillment of those needs.

The Black constituency of the United Methodist Church should not be unaware of its charge to renew its covenant, and its accountability for its share of any default or failure in giving itself to the fulfillment of this prophetic call. As stated by Will D. Campbell:

> God has called and is yet calling the Negro churches to be the source of renewal for the whole church of Christ. Upon their understanding of the struggle for racial justice hangs the possibility of the church seizing or missing the opportunity God holds out to it in this generation.[4]

Involvement of the Black Colleges

The Black colleges of the United Methodist Church afford unique opportunities as instruments which the church might employ in a new approach to a solution to racial barriers within and outside the church.

The germ of most of the revolutionary thinking and action in the 1960's was begun on Black campuses by Black students, and the struggle as it goes on is in a large measure a search for values that have relevant and personal meaning for Black students in a multi-racial nation and a pluralistic society. More than in any other group the mind of the college student in the future will be the mind that will give shape, form, and substance to the destinies of the communities of our society and of the world. This fact alone should say much to the church regarding the nature of its commitment to the college campus and its message to the college student, especially the Black student.

The commitment of the United Methodist Church to its Black colleges stems from the importance of having able and intelligent Black leadership and representation at all levels of the church structure. The Black institutions are a significant source for some of the leadership and representation needed, growing out of the black experience captured only in Black institutions—the college, church, and other Black institutions.

The current revolution engaging the young Black people of college and high school ages is a social one, but equally it is a religious revolution where there is rejection, mainly, of the forms and institutions of religion and a search for more relevant expressions, and new ideas. This ferment is in the young people where resides the greater hope of the church of the future. The only way this revolution and the generation gap can be dealt with is through dialogue and communication, with the young people doing much of the talking. Here is a remarkable opportunity for the church to experience a new birth in its work with young people. This suggests again something of the nature of the United Methodist Church's commitment to its Black colleges.

We are now at the vertex of danger in the relationship of Black and white people in the United Methodist Church, and in the American society generally. The responsibility is on both Black and white in the church to come to grips, in sincerity and in depth, with the problem of race relations, exploring, and utilizing every good means to create a new church and a new and better society. Where can we find a more fertile and more appropriate place to begin than on the campuses of Black (and white) colleges where the disillusioned and disturbed young people are, and where revolution is in ferment.

If the church does not make an effort to understand youth, Black and white together, and support them in their adventure and search for the values which the long experience of the church has found to be good, then young people will identify themselves with other forces, destructive of *all* values, destructive of society and themselves. Then, the church will have failed in one of its most important missions and will have placed its future in great jeopardy.

A Critical Look

The United Methodist Church should continue its support to its Black colleges with eyes ever open to the possibilities of improvement of the total educational program through cooperation, merging, relocation, and other such strategic moves

575

to strengthen the educational cause and contribute to the objectives of quality education and more excellent opportunities for Black youth, whether these Black colleges remain so or become different in racial or ethnic composition as a result of changes mentioned above or other radical changes.

After more than a hundred years there has been no venture toward structural integration or cooperation of any of the church's institutions. There should be exploration of what meaningful relations might be worked out between Black and white colleges of the United Methodist Church. For example, there are in Georgia twelve unrelated institutions of the United Methodist Church—one university, two theological schools, four senior colleges, four junior colleges and one high school. Experiments in cooperation, exchange, consortia, and even merger might prove feasible.

Significant Church Support

For church support to be significant, it ought to be adequate, certainly more adequate than it now is. The adequacy and significance of church support should be determined by the significance of the church's program in higher education involving the Black and white constituencies. There has never been a more critical time than now for the church to have a vital and relevant program relating to Black and white people. Historically the educational support of the church has been a missionary effort, and support of Black schools has been a peripheral enterprise, and has never been adequate. The problems of our time demand that the Black colleges be brought into the mainstream and be supported adequately as a basic part of the essential program of church renewal. This program should be concerned with the social and religious problems affecting (1) the Black minority and other minorities; (2) the United Methodist Church, especially the young people of high school and college ages; and (3) race relations in the church and in our society in general. These should be programs for confrontations in the areas indicated and a search for solutions. This is the challenge to the church in this day when race relations is one of the most important and most critical problems in the church and in the nation.

Significant church support must be thought of in terms (a) of what the individual institutions, and the institutions as a group, need in order to become and remain institutions of higher quality, contributing significantly to the program in higher education sponsored by the church; (b) the support ought to be adequate enough to make the Black colleges so good that white students

576

would be just as eager to attend them as they are to attend good white colleges; (c) the number of institutions the church can afford to support; and (d) the actual contribution the institution can and will make toward the achievement of the goals set by both the church and the college. The church has no obligation to give financial support to an institution that gives no evidence of being identified with the church and the church's program; nor does the institution under these circumstances have any right to expect financial support from the church.

In the light of the limited economic ability of Black students to pay high tuition charges, the competition the Black colleges must meet, and the difficulty the Black private colleges face in raising money from the usual sources that support higher education, it is not unreasonable to expect that the church (United Methodist) would provide from ten to fifteen per cent of the annual operating budgets of the colleges, and in addition, a substantial amount annually for capital expenditures.

Basic Assumptions

Statements and suggestions in the two final chapters have been predicated upon certain basic assumptions, such as follows:

1. That private and church-related institutions will continue to be an integral part of American higher education.

2. That the United Methodist Church will continue to maintain institutions of higher education as important instruments of a vital educational program within the interests and operation of the church.

3. That the college population will continue to grow, and there will be increasing need for all good colleges.

4. That in view of their magnificent contributions over a period of more than a century the Black colleges of the United Methodist Church will be recognized for their worth and value now and in the years ahead.

5. That it will be recognized that the continuation of Black colleges will be for purposes quite different from purposes that brought them into existence a hundred years ago; that their *raison d'être* now is determined on different levels of problems, needs, and services.

6. That the United Methodist Church will continue its work in the area of social concerns as a basic part of the mission of the church.

7. That there is and will continue to be a willingness and determination on the part of the United Methodist Church to involve itself in confrontation with issues and problems of race.

577

8. That the Black colleges are considered to be important and vital factors in creating better race relations and working toward a solution of the race problems.

9. That these colleges will be involved in a meaningful and in-depth solution to the continuing human relations problems.

10. That there is still, and will continue to be, a basic concern of the church regarding the problem of race in America and the removal of the barriers to its solution.

Concluding Statement

Out of a century of educational experience in the church and the struggle of a people to secure the rights in a democracy and to contribute to its meaning and growth; and from the currents of social change and the voice of the present generation of students comes at this time a three dimensional message: (1) a message of the past; (2) a message to the present; and (3) a message for the future.

Message of the Past

The message of the past is one of gratitude for the conviction of the church expressed in John Wesley, Francis Asbury, Thomas Coke, and scores of others who fought for the Negro's freedom from physical bondage; and gratitude for their faith in the freedmen and their vision, courage and labors to set them free educationally.

The message of the past speaks to the historic inhumanity of man to those of lesser position because of the indignities of slavery, the stigma of servitude, and the shame of human exploitation. It speaks to the awesomeness of brutalities and assassinations in a sick society; the unfairness of building a nation economically on the labors of a people who are not given equal opportunity to share in the fruits of their own labor and being robbed of their birthright of freedom and justice.

The message of the past speaks to the United Methodist Church and to all America, calling for atonement for the sins and injustices of the past through continued repentance and penance; not penance in terms of dollars, though billions of dollars will have to be spent, but penance in terms of a tolerant will and a contrite heart in a new relationship of man to man.

A Message That Speaks to the Present

The swift currents of social change provide the dynamics for

578

the action and reaction of people. Human behavior is affected by social dynamics and that behavior is either positive or negative, good or bad. The whole current of social changes and social dynamics is moving in the direction that would demand and accord to everyone in a democracy the inherent rights of democracy without regard to artificial barriers that would preclude such rights. The struggle of the Negro for a whole century has been in the course of securing those rights and guarantees which American Democracy stipulates in terms of its basic principles. The Negro's claims and actions are based on these basic social dynamics and assumptions.

The process of education in free institutions such as those founded by the Freedmen's Aid Society of the Methodist Episcopal Church has liberated the minds of Negro students and has taught them the true meaning of democracy and liberal education. In this day when the minds and spirits of young Negroes are being liberated there can no longer be a denial of privileges, rights and basic needs that should come through normal democratic processes. They can no longer be forced into ghettoes and blighted communities, deprived of the basic necessities of life and then expected to be happy. They cannot be told to be patient, when they have waited a hundred years and still are told to wait. The Negro's impatience grows out of decades of unkept promises, thwarted endeavors, and blasted hopes.

The Negro marches and demonstrations are pleas for full justice; for just laws and justice before the law; for protection of the law; for freedom from violence; for full rights of citizenship; for full employment and equal opportunity to be employed and paid by the same standards of merit and efficiency applied to all; for equal educational opportunities and for the quality of education equal to that of his white counterpart.

The Negro can no longer be told that these things will come if he will be patient. He insists that they must come now. There will be more demonstrations, marches, unrest, civil disobedience, and threats of violence, as would be with any other group under the same circumstances, unless the causes are removed. Discovery and discussion of causes are of little or no help unless the causes are completely removed.

College students in the current scene are susceptible to all the dynamic forces of our society. It should here and now be stated emphatically that while students have every right to pursue through proper channels all the rights, privileges and guarantees of American Democracy, there is nothing to be gained and much to be lost by violence, destruction of property, looting, vagrancy, and the like. These types of behavior only obstruct the achievement of worthy goals and complicate and aggravate the problems of human relations. Let there be light and clear vision for the present, recognizing and pursuing constructive and creative means of securing desired ends.

A Message for the Future

The movement begun in 1866 by the Methodist Episcopal Church to provide education for Negro youth has just entered upon its second century. Both the progenitors of the movement and the beneficiaries alike can look back on the first century with justifiable pride.

Despite the passing of a century and the progress and remarkable achievements, the problem of race which involves the major problems of the Negro is still one with deep roots and amazing complexities. The United Methodist Church has not finished its work. The problem has grown to one of greater proportions and the task is equally as difficult as in 1866.

The challenge is ours. It is a challenge that calls for greater efforts in the solution of the problem, or greater effort will be required for the church itself to survive, threatened by the ravages of disintegrating race relations.

The challenge is one of discovering new dimensions in educational thinking and educational results. The new dimensions must be found in human relations, in the fields of education and religion, and must be programmed with expected results far more significant than mere courses, subject matter, and intellectual development. There must be discovery of new spiritual dimensions.

The church must gain a new perspective in financial support of its Black institutions and must lift its sights more nearly to the level of the needs, which are tremendous.

The hope and the promise of the future rest with and within this cause. This is a spiritual adventure where together we "climb Jacob's Ladder," engaged in the creative endeavor of achieving the full destiny of every man and all people, looking hopefully to the day when the "kingdoms of this earth shall become the Kingdom of our Lord and of His Christ."

REFERENCES AND NOTES

1. Malik, Charles H., "Education in Upheaval: The Christian's Responsibility." *Foundation For Christian Living*, Vol. 21, No. 18, Sept., 1970, p. 5.
2. *Ibid.*, pp. 8f.
3. *Ibid.*, p. 11.
4. Campbell, Will D., *Race and Renewal of the Church*, p. 72.

APPENDIX A

FREEDMEN'S AID AND SOUTHERN EDUCATION SOCIETY OF THE METHODIST EPISCOPAL CHURCH

DECREE CHANGING NAME
COURT OF COMMON PLEAS OF HAMILTON COUNTY
Term of July, A. D., 1888

81,248
In the matter of the Freedmen's Aid Society
of the Methodist Episcopal Church. *Ex-parte.*

The Petitioners herein, by M.B. Hagans, their attorney, now come and produce the publication required by law, duly sworn to; and the Court having examined the same, and finding that thirty days' notice has been given of the object and prayer of the Petition according to the statute, the said publication and notice are hereby approved and confirmed, and the same ordered to be filed and made part of the record in this cause.

And thereupon this cause came on to be heard upon the petition and notice, and upon good cause shown it is ordered that the name of the said The Freedmen's Aid Society of the Methodist Episcopal Church be, and the same is hereby changed to "The Freedmen's Aid and Southern Education Society of the Methodist Episcopal Church," according to law and the prayer of the Petition, and the Petitioners are ordered to file a copy of this order with the recorder of Hamilton County, Ohio, and to publish a copy hereof in some newspaper of general circulation in said county, as required by law, and to pay the costs of this proceeding taxed at _____ dollars.

The State of Ohio, Hamilton, County. ss.

I, Daniel J. Dalton, Clerk of the Court of Common Pleas within and for Hamilton County, do hereby certify that the foregoing is a true and correct copy of an order made by the said court on the 27th day of July, 1888, Min. 106.

Witness my hand and seal of said Court at Cincinnati this 1st day of August, A. D., 1888.

Daniel J. Dalton, Clerk

Court Seal.

by Louis R. Prenot, Deputy

Received and recorded September 3, 1888, in Book No. 6., page 261, Hamilton County, Ohio, Records.

John Hagerty, Recorder

CHARTER
of
Clark University

The petition of Gilbert Haven, Richard S. Rust, Mary J. Clark, Eliphalet Remington, Joseph H. Chadwick, Washington C. DePauw, Henry K. List, Eliza Chrisman, Robert T. Kent, Charles O. Fisher, John C. Kimball, Josiah Sherman, Theodore G. Eiswald, William H. Crogman, James Mitchell, Henry R. Parmenter, George Standing, James V. Martin, Seaborn C. Upshaw and E. Q. Fuller, shows that they are the Trustees of Clark University, in the city of Atlanta, in said county, and that they desire that they and their associates shall become a body corporate and politic, by the name of

"The Trustees of Clark University,"

and that they, and such persons as shall be duly elected members of said corporation, shall be and remain a body corporate by said name for twenty years, with the privilege of renewal at the end of that term.

The said corporation not being for profit, and no stock, dividends or other pecuniary gain accruing to the corporators, but being simply intended for the advancement of learning, and the accomplishment of good, they have no capital stock, and only such property as has accrued from the benefactions of the charitable and philanthropic; and for further acquisitions, and to effect the objects of incorporations, must look to the income from present possessions (which are valued at Forty Thousand Dollars, and consist of the buildings and grounds now occupied by said University, furniture and apparatus, land in Fulton County, and Atlanta City bonds,) and to bequests and donations and prudent management.

That the location of said University and the place of business of said corporation is in said county.

That the object and business of said corporation are to establish and perpetuate a University, and thereby promote learning, afford suitable opportunities for the acquirement of knowledge, and to foster piety and virtue as essentials of proper education; and for the orderly conducting of the business of said corporation, petitioners desire:

1. That said corporation shall have power and authority from time to time, as occasion may require, to elect a President, Vice-President, Secretary and Treasurer, and such other officers as

584

may be found necessary, and to declare the duties and tenures of their respective offices, with the power of removal, and the right to fill vacancies in the way and manner, for the causes, specified in the By-Laws of the corporation; and also to elect new members of said corporation, provided the number of members shall never be less than ten nor greater than thirty, and at least ten shall be necessary to constitute a quorum when any change is made in the By-Laws, a Trustee removed, or a vacancy in the Board filled.

2. That the said corporation shall have full power and authority to determine at which times and places their meetings shall be held, and the manner of notifying the Trustees to convene at such meetings; to establish Boards of Instruction in all departments of science, literature and the arts, and to determine and regulate the course of instruction; to elect a President of said University, and such professors, tutors, instructors and other University officers as they shall judge for the interests thereof, and to determine the duties, salaries, emoluments, responsibilities and tenures of their respective offices, to confer degrees; and generally to make and ordain such rules, orders, regulations and By-Laws as shall not be repugnant to the Constitution and the laws of Georgia or the United States; provided no degree shall be conferred but upon the recommendation of the appropriate faculty, and no instructor in said University, except in the Theological Department, shall ever be required by the Trustees to profess any particular religious opinions as a test of office, and no student, except in the Theological Department, shall be refused admission to or denied any of the privileges, honors or degrees of said University on account of the religious opinions which he may entertain.

3. That said corporation may have and use a common seal, which they may alter and renew at pleasure; and may sue and be sued, plead and be impleaded, by said corporate name.

4. That they, their associates and successors, as Trustees, under said corporate name, shall have the right and power to receive by donation, gift or will any property, real or personal, and to rent, lease, purchase and hold such real or personal property as may be necessary to effect and promote the objects of incorporation, and to dispose of the same at pleasure, being fully empowered to do all such acts as may be necessary for the legitimate forwarding and execution of the objects of incorporation; provided that the clear rents and profits of all property, real and personal, of which said corporation shall be seized and possessed shall be appropriated to the maintenance and endowment of said University in such a manner as shall most effectually promote virtue and piety, and learning in such of the languages and of the liberal and useful arts and sciences as shall be recommended from time to time by the

585

said corporation, they conforming to the will of any donor or donors in the application of any charter which may be given, devised or bequeathed for any particular object connected with the University.

Petitioners further pray that this their application may be entered for record on the Minutes of Fulton Superior Court, that it be published in "The Methodist Advocate," of Atlanta, and that, after due record and publication, an order be passed granting the incorporation as desired.

CANDLER & THOMPSON,
Petitioners' Attorneys.

A true extract from the Minutes of Fulton Superior Court.
March 19, 1876.

James D. Collins, C. S. C.

STATE OF GEORGIA
Fulton County.

To the Superior Court
of said County:

The petition of John M. Walden, Wm. H. Crogman, R. S. Eggleston, Charles M. Melden, Seaborn C. Upshaw, W. H. Formosa, John P. Wragg, Wm. I. Haven, Willis M. Everett, Geo. Standing, John T. King, John W. Price, John Watts, Fannie Clark Davis, Aaron P. Melton, Geo. W. Arnold, William Deering, Matthew M. Alston, Henry W. Warren, John W. Hamilton, Jos. C. Hartzell, Daniel A. Goodsell, Richard S. Rust, Silas A. Peeler, Madison C. B. Mason, James Mitchell, and Wilbur P. Thirkield respectfully shows:

1: They are the duly constituted Trustees of Clark University of Atlanta, Ga.

2: That the "Trustees of Clark University" is an educational corporation and was duly incorporated by the Superior Court of Fulton County, on the 7th day of May, 1877, as will fully appear by reference to the records found in Minute Book "M," pages 545 and 622.

3: Your petitioners pray that the aforesaid corporation be revived for a term of twenty years and that they and their successors in office be clothed with all powers and possessed of all the rights and privileges conferred by said charter upon said original corporation and be subject to all the debts, liabilities and burthens of the old corporation which shall be hereby revived.

Willis M. Everett
Atty. for petitioners.

Filed in office June 26, 1900.
G. H. Tanner, Clerk.

Upon hearing the foregoing petition and it appearing that said petition has been published as required by law, it is ordered and adjudged by the Court that said corporation be and the same is hereby revived for a term of twenty years, unless sooner revoked by law, and that the said

"Trustees of Clark University"

be clothed with all the powers and possessed of all the rights and privileges conferred heretofore by this Court upon said original corporation and that it be subject to all the debts, liabilities and burdens of the old corporation which is hereby revived in it.

Judgment signed this 6th day of Sept., 1900.

J. H. Lumpkin, Judge S. C. F. C.

STATE OF GEORGIA,
County of Fulton.

I, G. H. Tanner, Clerk of the Superior Court of said County, do hereby certify that the foregoing is a true copy from the files and records of said court, of the Petition to Revive the Charter of

"Trustees of Clark University"

and the order of said Court granting said petition.

Said Charter and order have been recorded in Charter Book 3, page 675, of Fulton County Records.

Witness my hand and seal of said Court, this the 7th day of Sept., 1900.

G. H. Tanner,
Clerk Superior Court,
Fulton County, Ga.

Charter taken from: Clark University Bulletin, 1904, pp. 5-8.

REFERENCES

The Methodist Advocate (Atlanta), 1869-1873.

American Universities and Colleges, 10th Edition, 1968.

Arnett, Trevor, *A Brief Account of the Developments in Cooperation among the Negro Colleges in Atlanta From Its Inception on April 1, 1929 through June 30, 1941*. Winter, 1942, An unpublished Manuscript.

Baker, J. D., *History of Ohio Methodism*.

Baker, Webster B., *History of Rust College*. Greensboro, North Carolina, 1924.

Barclay, Wade Crawford, *History of Methodist Missions*. New York, Board of Missions and Church Extension of The Methodist Church, 1949.

Bardolph, Richard, *The Negro Vanguard*. Rinehart & Co., Inc., New York, 1959.

Beard, Charles A., and Mary R., *The Rise of American Civilization*, Vol. I Edition. The Macmillan Co., New York, 1930.

Bond, Horace Mann, Unpublished Manuscript on Dillard University.

Braden, Mary E., *John Braden—A Pioneer in Negro Education*. Morristown, Tennessee, 1936.

Brown, Ina Corrine, *The Story of the American Negro*. Friendship Press, New York, 1936.

Brownlee, Frederick L., *Heritage of Freedom*. United Church Press, Philadelphia - Boston, 1936.

Brownlee, Fred. L., *New Day Ascending*. The Pilgrim Press, Boston, 1946.

Buckley, James M., *A History of Methodism in the United States*. New York, The Christian Literature Co., 1896.

Bulletin, New Orleans University, November, 1932; March 1, 1931; February, 1929.

Butts, R. Freeman, and Lawrence A. Cremin, *A History of Education in American Culture*. Henry Holt and Company, 1953. Cameron, Richard M., *Methodism and Society In Historical Perspective, Methodism and Society,* Vol. 1, Abingdon Press, Nashville, Tennessee, 1961.
(*Edited by the Board of Social and Economic Relations.)

Campbell, Will D., *Race and Renewal of The Church*. Philadelphia, Westminister Press, 1962.

Carnegie Foundation, *From Isolation to Main Stream*, A Report and Recommendations by the Carnegie Commission on Higher Education, February, 1971.

Carter, Hodding, *The Angry Scar, the Story of Reconstruction*. Garden City, New York: Doubleday and Co., 1959.

Charter, Shaw University (Later Rust University), May 26, 1870. Amended Charter, 1890.

Charter, Straight University, June 25, 1869. Archives of Dillard University, New Orleans, La. Amended Charter, March 9, 1870.

Clary, George Esmond, Jr., *The Founding of Paine College*, A Unique Venture in Inter-racial Cooperation in the South, 1882-1903. A Doctor of Education Dissertation, University of Georgia, 1965.

Corporation Record Book O, No. 7; State of Tennessee, Department in Nashville, Tennessee.

Cubberley, Ellwood P., *The History of Education*. Houghton Miflin Company, Riverside Press, Cambridge, 1948.

Culver, Dwight W., *Negro Segregation in the Methodist Church*. Yale University Press, 1953.

Cummings, A. W., *The Early Schools of Methodism*. Phillips & Hunt, Cincinnati, 1886. Part IV, pp. 396-423, Three Negro Schools: Central Tennessee College, Clark University, Baker Institute and Claflin University.

Dempsey, Elam Franklin, *Atticus Green Haygood*. Parthenon Press, Methodist Publishing House, Nashville, Tennessee, 1940.

Department of the Interior, Bureau of Education Bulletin, 1916, No. 38, Vol. I.

Department of the Interior, Bureau of Education Bulletin, 1927, No. 40. *Statistics of Universities, Colleges, and Professional Schools, 1925-1926.*

The Discipline, Methodist Episcopal Church, 1876.

The Discipline, The Methodist Church, 1944.

DuBois, W. E. B., *Black Reconstruction: an Essay toward a History of the part which the Black Folk played in the Attempt to Reconstruct Demoncrary in America - 1860-1880*. New York, 1935.

DuBois, W. E. B., *The Souls of Black Folk*. Avon Books, Hearst Magazine Division, New York, N. Y., 1953, 1961.

Durmond, Dwight Lowell, *Anti-Slavery Origins of the Civil War in The United States*. The University of Michigan Press, Ann Arbor, Michigan, 1959.

Farish, Hunter O., *The Circuit Rider Dismounts: A Social History of Southern Methodism, 1865-1900*. Richmond, Va. The Dietz Press, 1939.

Foundation for Christian Living. Pawling, N. Y.

(*Freedmen's Aid Society of the Methodist Episcopal Church, Annual Reports, Cincinnati and Chicago.)
    1867-1888: Freedmen's Aid Society of the M. E. Church
    1888-1908: Freedmen's Aid and Southern Education Society of the M. E. Church

1908-1920: Freedmen's Aid Society of the M. E. Church
1920-1924: Board of Education for Negroes of the M. E. Church
1924-1931: Board of Education of the M. E. Church

Fulton County Record of Deeds. County Courthouse, Atlanta, Georgia.

Garber, Paul N., *The Methodist Are One People.* Cokesbury Press, Nashville, Tennessee, 1939.

General Conference Journals, The Methodist Episcopal Church, Quadrennial editions, 1848 to 1936. The Methodist Church, Quadrennial editions, 1940 to 1968.

Quarterly Bulletin, Gammon Theological Seminary, April, 1890; June, 1898., Gammon Quarterly Bulletin (Memorial Edition, 1901).

General Education Board, *Review and Final Report,* 1902-1964. New York, N. Y., 1964.

Gibbs, Warmoth, *President Matthew W. Dogan of Wiley College.*

Graham, William L., "Pattern of Intergroup Relations—" A Dissertation for the Ph.D. degree, New York University, 1955.

Harris, M. LaFayette, *A General Statement on the Case of Philander Smith College* (Unpublished Manuscript), 1943.

Harris, Marquis LaFayette, "The Voice In The Wilderness." The Christopher Publishing House, 1941, Boston.

Hartzell, J. C., "Methodism and the Negro in the United States," The Journal of Negro History, Vol. VIII, No. 3, July, 1923, pp. 301-15.

Haygood, Atticus G., *Our Brother in Black: His Freedom and His Future.* Nashville, Tennessee, Southern Methodist Publishing House, N. Y., Phillips and Hunt, 1881.

Heller, Colia S., *Structured Social Inequality* (A Reader in Comparative Social Stratification). The Macmillan Company, New York, 1969.

Houghton, Frederick, *History of Rust College.* Unpublished Manuscript, Rust College Library.

Hurst, John Fletcher, *The History of Methodism.* New York, Eaton & Mains, 1902.

Johnson, Oliver, *William Lloyd Garrison and His Times.*

Jones, Thomas J., Negro Education, *A Study of the Private and Higher Schools for Colored People in the United States.* U. S. Bureau of Education Bulletin, 1916, Nos. 38 and 39. Washington, 1917.

The Journal of Negro Education, Vol. XXIX, 1960, No. 3. The Yearbook, Number XXIX, The Negro Private Church-Related College.

Journal, Texas Annual Conference, 1887, 1892, 1904, 1925, 1928.

Journal, Upper Mississippi Annual Conference, May, 1962.

Journals of the Mississippi Annual Conference.

Kirk, W. Astor, *The Rust College Story,* Rust College, 1967.

Klein, Arthur J., *Survey of Negro Colleges and Universities.* Bureau of Education, Bulletin (1928), No. 7, 522.

Kriege, O. E., and Faculty of New Orleans University, *Seventy Years of Service.* New Orleans University, 1935. New Orleans, La.

(*Also referred to as *The Faculty.*)

Leaders In Education, Biographical Directory. The Science Press, New York, N. Y., 1932.

Leavell, Ullin W., *Philanthropy in Negro Education.* Nashville, George Peabody College for Teachers, 1930.

Louisiana Conference Journal. January, 1875; January 1876; January 1877; January, 1878; February, 1879; January, 1881; and January, 1889.

Malik, Charles H., "Education In Upheaval: The Christian's Responsibility," *Foundation For Christian Living,* Vol. 21, No. 18. September, 1970, Pawling, N. Y.

Matlack, Lucius C., *The Anti-Slavery Struggle and Triumph in the Methodist Episcopal Church.* Phillip and Hunt, New York, 1881.

Matthew, Donald G., *Slavery and Methodism, A Chapter in American Morality 1780-1845.* Princeton University Press, Princeton, N. J., 1965.

Mayes, Edward, *History of Education in Mississippi.* Washington, 1899.

Meeker, Ruth Esther, *Six Decades of Service: A History of the Woman's Home Missionary Society, the Methodist Episcopal Church, 1880-1940.* Published by the Continuing Corporation of the Woman's Home Missionary Society, The Methodist Episcopal Church, 1969.

Merriam, Charles Edward, *A History of American Political Theories.* New York, The Macmillan Company, 1936.

Methodist Quarterly Review, No. 47 (1865).

Minutes, Clark College Board of Trustees, Atlanta, Georgia.

Minutes, Board of Trustees, Clark University, Atlanta, Georgia.

Minutes, Board of Trustees, Dillard University, New Orleans, Louisiana.

Minutes, Board of Trustees, Gammon Theological Seminary.

Minutes, Board of Trustees, Paine College. November, 1882; December, 1882; December, 1884; May, 1885; June, 1901; June, 1902; June, 1911; June, 1915; July, 1915; September,

1915; January, 1917, 1922.

Minutes, Executive Committee, Board of Education, The Methodist Episcopal Church, June 21, 1930. (See *The Christian Educator*, May-August, 1930).

Minutes, East Tennessee Annual Conference, 1884, 1889, 1896, 1931, 1957.

Minutes, Florida Annual Conference, 1878, 1882, 1883, 1885, 1886, 1889, 1890, 1892, 1898.

Minutes, Little Rock Annual Conference, 1879, 1882, 1883, 1890.

Minutes, North Carolina Annual Conference, 1882, 1888, 1886, 1889, 1892, 1912, 1929, 1930.

Minutes, Rust College Board of Trustees, March, 1967.

Minutes, West Texas Annual Conference, 1874, 1876, 1879, 1880, 1887, 1889, 1890, 1891.

The Missionary Yearbook, Methodist Episcopal Church, South, 1939.

Morrow, Ralph E., *Northern Methodism and Reconstruction*. East Lansing, Michigan, 1956.

McGrath, Earl J., *The Predominantly Negro Colleges and Universities in Transition*. Bureau of Publications, Teachers College, Columbia University, New York, N. Y., 1965.

McTyeire, *Holland N., *A History of Methodism*. Nashville, Tennessee, Southern Methodist Publishing House, 1884. (*One of the Bishops of the Methodist Episcopal Church, South.)

New Orleans University, New Orleans University Bulletin, 1925-1935, Will W. Alexander Library, Dillard University, New Orleans, La.

Peare, Catherine Owens, *Mary McLeod Bethune*. The Vanguard Press, Inc., New York, 1951.

Perry, Jennings, "Dillard University Today," Article in *The Christian Educator*, May, January, February, 1952, pp. 14-16.

Proceedings, of the Board of Education, The Methodist Episcopal Church, January, 1936.

Proceedings of the Sixty-Fourth Annual Meeting of the Southern Association of Colleges and Secondary Schools, December, 1959.

Richardson, George O., Unpublished Manuscript. Archives, Huston-Tillotson College, Austin, Texas.

Richardson, Harry V., *The Interdenominational Theological Center: Gammon Today and Tomorrow.*, 1958.

Richardson, James D., ed. Messages and Papers of the Presidents (10 Volumes). Washington, D.C., 1896-99, VI.

Simkins, Francis B., *A History of The South*. New York, Alfred Knopf, 1953.

Simmons, Virginia, *Bennett History* (Unpublished Manuscript) June, 1939, Addendum, 1958., Bennett College Library, Greensboro, N. C.

*Simpson, Matthew, ed. *Cyclopaedia of Methodism*. Philadelphia, 1878.

Smith, T. V., *The American Philosophy of Equality*. The University of Chicago Press, 1927, Chicago, Illinois.

Southern Methodist Handbook, 1906.

Sowell, Thomas, "The Available University," *The University of Chicago Magazine*, November-December, 1970.

Statistical Summary, Methodist General Board of Education, 1968-1969; 1969-1970; 1970-1971.

Stowell, Jay S., *Methodist Venture in Negro Education*. The Methodist Book Concern, New York - Cincinnati, 1922.

A Task Force Report: "Special Needs of Traditionally Negro Colleges." Institute for Higher Education Opportunity, Southern Regional Education Board, 1969, 136 Sixth Street N. W., Atlanta, Georgia 30313.

Taylor, Prince Albert, Jr., Gammon Theological Seminary, A History of, 1948. Thesis for Ed. D. degree, New York University. *On the Track*, 4th Quarterly, 1969, Published Quarterly by Joseph V. Baker, Philadelphia, Pa.

Wesley, John, *Thoughts on Slavery*. 2nd ed. London, Printed by R. Hawes, 1774, p. 28.

*West Texas Conference, *Minutes*, 1876.

Wilson, Edward N., *Morgan State College, A Century of Purpose in Action,1867-1967*. Unpublished Manuscript, 1967.

INDEX

Corson, Bishop Fred P.—218
Cox, Rev. James M.—435-437, 546
Crockett, Roosevelt David—441
Crogman, William Henry—203, 204, 231, 232, 242-243, 244, 245, 249, 328
Daniel, Dr. Maggie Brown—481
Darnell, Rev. Samuel B.—129, 177-179, 181, 182, 183, 184, 546
Davage, Dr. Matthew S.—78, 249, 250, 254, 255, 281, 336, 370-372, 377, 378, 379, 457, 497, 544, 546, 553
Davis, Jackson—299
Davis, Thomas R.—372, 507
Davis, Rev. W. H.—470, 471
Daytona Normal and Industrial Institute—184, 186, 188, 189, 190, 191
Declaration of Independence—22, 23, 24, 27, 33
Dee, Mrs. Eliza M.—133, 367
Eliza Dee Home—133, 367, 368
Dent, Albert W.—305, 307-309
Dew, F. R.—32
Dickason, Henry L.—408
Diderot, Denis—22
Dillard, James Hardy—299, 301
Dixon, Ernest Thomas—441
Docking, Rev. James T.—182, 183, 455-456
Dogan, Rev. Matthew W.—456, 474-481, 546
Downs, Rev. Karl Everett—372-373
Doxie, Natlie—451
DuBois, W. E. B.—41$_f$, 44, 49, 120
Dumond, Dwight L.—42
Dunton, Rev. Lewis, M.—129, 205, 206, 209-211, 213-217, 481, 545
Durbin, John P.—30$_f$
Durgin, George F.—506
Dutton, Mrs. A. C.—288
Eichelberger, Mrs. Sarah—228
Elam, Lloyd C.—394
Elzy, Ruby—451
Emancipation Proclamation—42, 43
Embree, Edwin R.—297, 299
Endowment—87, 554-555
Enrollments—86
Erwin, Rev. J. Otis—409
Evans, Rev. George—456$_f$, 496$_f$
Evans, J. E.—412, 414, 415, 417

597

Everett, Willis M., Sr.—584, 586
Everett, Willis M., Jr.—337, 338, 340
Failor, Rev. Isaac M.—278
Fairchild, Miss Carrie—181
Farmer, James L.—571
Favrot, Leo M.—299
Federal Government—49
Fisher, Rev. C. O.—71,
Fisk, Clinton B.—60, 505, 536
Flint Goodridge Hospital—284, 288, 289, 301, 303, 304, 308, 310
Flint Medical College—282, 284, 288, 289, 290, 310
Ford Foundation—167, 526
Foster, Rev. William W.—245-246, 331-, 453-454
Frazier, J. W.—361
Freedmen's Aid Society, Managers of—535$_f$
Freedman's Bureau—49
Frysinger, Rev. Maslin—488
Fuller, Rev. E. Q.—229, 232, 318, 321, 324
Gamble, James N.—185, 187, 188
Gammon, Rev. Elijah H.—236, 238, 320-324, 327
Gammon-Clark Relation—244, 253, 328
Gammon, Mrs. Jane C.—324, 325
Garrettson, Freeborn—33
Garrison, William Lloyd—32-35
Garrisonian Abolitionists—34
Gee, A. A.—501
General Education Board—167, 254, 258, 301, 340, 341, 392, 526, 527
George R. Smith College—493-498
Gibson, Elmer P.—409
Gilbert, Academy—135-136, 272, 285, 286, 288, 292
Gilbert, John Wesley—418, 425, 428
Godman, Rev. W. D.—275, 276, 277, 278
Goode, Mrs. W. H. C.—164, 165, 166
Goucher, Rev. J. F.—488
Graham, William L.—428, 429
Grandison, Charles N.—157$_f$, 545
Grannum, Rev. Stanley E.—372
Gray, Emma C.—424, 425, 429
Gross, Dr. John O.—338, 339
Gross, Hall; John O.—463
Gun Factory—501, 502
Guptil, Rev. Roger S.—327
Hamilton, Alexander—31

Hamilton, Dr. J. W.—542
Hammett, R. W.—67
Hammond, Rev. D. W.—224, 225, 226, 227, 228
Hammond, John D.—420
Harrington, Rev. Robert F.—373
Harris, Bishop Marquis LaFayette—438-441, 547
Harrison, W. P.—415, 416
Hartzell, Rev. Joseph C.—94$_f$, 206, 238, 270, 272, 274, 276, 279, 280, 323, 324, 357, 400, 474, 495, 538, 542
Hartzell, Mrs. J. C.—124-125, 128, 134
Haven, Bishop Gilbert—204, 231, 232, 233, 234, 235, 353, 537
Haven, Mrs. Gilbert—235
Haven Home—134
Haven Institute—498
Haven Normal School—498
Hayes, Robert B.—285, 497-498
Haygood, Rev. Atticus G.—118, 236, 387, 417, 419, 420, 539
Haynes, L. L., Jr.—408
Hays, Rev. Robert E., Sr.—483
Hays, Mrs. Rutherford B.—125, 126
Haywood, Rev. John W.—335, 336, 407, 480
Hazzard, Rev. Walter Raphael—442
Henderson, Vivian Wilson—261
Hickman, Rev. William H.—238-240
Hill, Judson S.—399, 400, 401-406, 407, 545
Hooper, Rev. W. W.—449-451
Holgate, Thomas F.—164, 498
Holmes, Dwight Oliver—490
Holmes, Rev. Merrill J.—254, 255, 299, 300, 302, 544
Holsey, Bishop L. H.—417, 418, 420, 424, 427
Houston, Charles—570
Howard, Oliver O.—49, 273
Hoyt, Almon F.—279, 281
Hubbard, George W.—384, 385, 386, 387, 389, 390, 391, 392, 505, 546
Hubbard, George W., Hospital—388
Huger, Rev. S. A.—181, 499
Huston, Samuel—355, 357, 359
Idleman, Rev. S. E.—244-245, 331, 332
Industrial Education—99, 116, 118, 119, 120
Interdenominational Theological Center—340, 341
Janes, Bishop Edwin S.—203, 536

Jay, John—31
Jefferson, Thomas—22-23
Jenkins, Martin D.—490
John, Rev. David Clark—420, 329
Johnson, Joseph T.—481
Johnson, Miss Luella—133, 483
Johnson, Mrs. Penkie D.—481
Johnson, Miss Sophia—465
Jones, David D.—165, 168, 169, 170, 171, 547
Jones, Rev. Major J.—341
Jones, Bishop Robert E.—156, 165, 166, 302, 333, 336
Jones, Mrs. Susie Williams—165
Jones, Thomas Jesse—139, 142, 183, 286, 294, 477
Jordan, G. Whitte—250
Jubilee Celebration—516
Kemerer, Rev. S. W.—181-182
Kent Home—132, 162
Key West Academy—499
Kiah, Thomas—491
King, Miss Clara I.—133, 368, 483
King, Rev. Harry Andrews—246-247, 249
King Industrial Home—133, 483
King, Mrs. Jane—133, 483
King, John Q. Taylor—379
King, Martin Luther, Jr.—571
King, Bishop Willis J.—334, 338, 368, 372, 481, 547
Knight, Rev. Frederic H.—282
Kriege, Rev. O. E.—272, 284
Kumler, John A.—505, 506
LaGrange Seminary—500
Lane Seminary—32
Lansing, Rev. Isaac—230, 319
Leavitt, I. S.—271, 272, 273, 274
Lee, Rev. J. W.—224, 225, 228, 229-230, 318, 319
Leete, Bishop Frederick D.—215, 248, 249, 539
Lewis, Rev. T. Willard—201, 202
Libby, Charles E.—450, 451-453
Liberator—32, 33
Lincoln, Abraham—33, 42
Lincoln Day—529, ff
Lloyd Street Methodist Church (Atlanta)—229, 319

Methodist Review—419
Milton, L. D.—388-440
Mitchell, Miss Flora—130, 235
Miller, Isaac H., Sr.—161, 183, 184, 247$_f$
Miller, Isaac H., Jr.—172
Moore, Rev. F. C.—469
Moore, Rev. H. J.—202

Moore, Richard V.—195-197, 547
Morgan College—457, 487-491
Morgan State College—490
Morgan, Rev. Littleton F.—488
Morgan, W. H.—387
Moury, Rev. D.—238
Mullowney, John J.—383, 391, 393, 547
Myser, Miss Elfreda—131, 465
McConnell, Bishop Francis—388
McCoy, Lee Marcus—457-462, 547
McCullough, Gerald O.—338, 339, 340
McDonald, Rev. Albert C.—445, 446, 447, 448, 449, 545
McGrath, Earl J.—571
McIntire, O. E.—72
McLeod, Egbert C.—482
McMillan, William A.—464
McPheeters, Alphonso A.—255-256
National Commission—56
Negro Conferences—93
Negro Membership—36$_f$
New Jersey Home—133, 401
Nelson, William Stuart—308
Newman, Rev. J. P.—267, 268, 269, 273, 538
New Negro College—208$_f$
New Orleans University—267-292
Normal School—268, 274
O'Brien, Rev. James P.—295
O'Connell, Pezavia—491
Orphan Home—273
Osborn, W. B.—177
Paine Institute—417, 418, 419, 420
Paine, Bishop R.—417
Palmer, George—476
Parks, P. H.—243

Rome Normal School—500
Roosevelt, F. D.—194, 195
Rosenwald Fund, Julius—140, 167, 297, 298, 301
Round, Rev. J. Emory—487-488
Rousseau, Jean Jacques—22
Rust, Mrs. Elizabeth (Mrs. R. S.)—123-124, 127, 131, 465
Rust, Elizabeth L., Home—131, 465-466
Rust Biblical and Normal Institute—492
Rust Normal Institute—491
Rust, Richard S.—55, 57, 60, 123-124, 127, 131, 177, 204, 205, 223, 224, 226, 229, 233, 234, 238, 277, 321, 354, 355, 356, 383, 387, 434, 447, 452, 465, 469, 487, 492, 536, 541-542, 584, 586
Rust, University—452, 453, 454, 456
Sager-Brown Home—135
Samuel Huston College—347-374
Sayer, Rev. D. H.—453
Schism, Methodist—35
Scott, Rev. Isaiah B.—472-473, 474, 540, 545
Scott, Rev. Julius S., Sr.—482
Scott, Bishop Levi—487
Scott, Rev. Orange—33, 34, 35
Seabrook, Rev. John J.—217, 379, 547
Sealantic Fund—338, 339, 341
Seys, Rev. John—501
Shaw, Bishop Alexander Preston—456
Shaw, Rev. J. Beverly F.—456, 493, 499
Shaw University—446, 447, 448, 449, 451, 452
Sherrill, Rev. J. C.—496
Simmons, Rev. J. W.—249
Simpson Home—130
Simpson, Bishop Matthew—233, 537
Slater, John F.—236
Slater, John F. Fund—167, 180, 205-206, 212, 236
Smith, Adeline M.—434
    Industrial Home—131, 434
Smith, Rev. Ernest A.—462-464
Smith, General George R.—493
Sneed, W. J.—384, 389, 392
Speedwell Home—134
Spencer, John Oakley—489, 490, 546
Spilman, Rev. J.—224

604

Southern Association of Colleges and Schools—146, 171, 256, 260
Stampp, Kenneth—11
Stanton, Rev. Daniel H.—336
Stern, Edgar B.—295, 303, 305
Stewart, Rev. William F.—326-328
Stone, Rev. G. Barts—183-184
Storrs, George—33, 34, 35
Straight University—293-295
Summer Hill—224, 225, 227, 229, 230
Sunderland, LeRoy—33, 34, 35
Sutton, H. H.—437, 507
Talbot, M. J.—69
Tarbell, Dr. Ida M.—194
Taylor, George C.—437
Teycer, Mrs. Lucille Dogan—481
Thayer, Rev. E. O.—130, 155, 156, 234, 235-236, 237-238, 320, 321, 370, 546
Thayer Home—130, 235
Theological Schools—316
Theological Work Transferred to Gammon—325
Thirkield, Mrs. Mary Haven—128f
Thirkield, Wilbur P., Bishop—235, 236, 238, 240, 284, 289-290, 321, 323, 328, 329, 330, 332, 539, 543, 545
Thomas, Bishop James S.—14, 78, 544
Thomas, R. S. W.—182
Thompson, Mrs. Eloise Troutman—196
Thomson, Bishop Edward—267, 537
Thomson Biblical Institute—267, 269, 270
Thomson University—267, 268, 270, 271, 280
Tillotson College—374, 375
Tillotson, Rev. George Jeffrey—374
Tingley, S. H.—213
Tobias, Channing H.—429
Tomlin, Rev. Ray S.—421
Trevor, Rev. George H.—333
Trigg, Frank—160-161, 163
Trinity Methodist Church—57, 125
Turner, C. H.—239
Turner, Edward L.—393
Unification, 1939—144, 422, 521
Union Normal School—268, 270, 273